Student Teaching:

EARLY CHILDHOOD **PRACTICUM GUIDE**

Student Teaching:

EARLY CHILDHOOD PRACTICUM GUIDE

6TH EDITION

JEANNE M. MACHADO, EMERITA
San Jose City College

HELEN MEYER-BOTNARESCUE, PH.D., EMERITA
California State University—East Bay

DELMAR
CENGAGE Learning·

Australia • Brazil • Japan • Korea • Mexico • Singapore • Spain • United Kingdom • United States

DELMAR
CENGAGE Learning™

Student Teaching: Early Childhood Practicum Guide, Sixth Edition
Jeanne M. Machado, Emerita,
Helen Meyer-Botnarescue, Ph.D., Emerita

Vice President, Career Education SBU: Dawn Gerrain

Director of Learning Solutions: John Fedor

Managing Editor: Robert L. Serenka, Jr.

Senior Acquisitions Editor: Erin O'Connor

Product Manager: Philip Mandl

Editorial Assistant: Alison Archambault

Director of Production: Wendy A. Troeger

Production Manager: Mark Bernard

Production Assistant: Jeff Varecka

Director of Marketing: Wendy E. Mapstone

Channel Manager: Kristin McNary

Marketing Coordinator: Scott A. Chrysler

Cover Design: David Arsenault

Composition: GEX Publishing Services

Interior Design: Judi Orozco

NOTICE TO THE READER

Library of Congress Control Number: 2007009860

ISBN-13: 978-1-4180-6648-2

ISBN-10: 1-4180-6648-6

Delmar
10 Davis Drive
Belmont, CA 94002-3098
USA

Cengage Learning is a leading provider of customized learning solutions with office locations around the globe, including Singapore, the United Kingdom, Australia, Mexico, Brazil, and Japan. Locate your local office at: **www.cengage.com/global**

Cengage Learning products are represented in Canada by Nelson Education, Ltd.

To learn more about Delmar, visit **www.cengage.com/delmar**

Purchase any of our products at your local college store or at our preferred online store **www.ichapters.com**

Printed in the United States of America
2 3 4 5 6 7 11 10 09 08

Contents

1 ORIENTATION TO STUDENT TEACHING

2 PROGRAMMING

3 WORKING WITH CHILDREN

4 COMMUNICATION

5 INTERACTIONS

6 PROFESSIONAL CONCERNS

INFANT/TODDLER PLACEMENTS

Preface

Student Teaching: Early Childhood Practicum Guide, 6th edition is designed for students who are assuming teaching responsibilities under guided supervision. Student teaching is a memorable, individual struggle to put theory into practice. It is a synthesizing experience from which each student emerges with a unique professional style. This text attempts to help each student teacher reach that goal.

It is our wish that this text guide student teachers in their studies and in the practical application of the knowledge acquired. *Student Teaching: Early Childhood Practicum Guide , 6th edition* will serve as a useful reference tool for teaching tips and problem-solving techniques as the student enters the professional world.

Many aspects of teaching that affect the student teacher, both now as a student and later as a professional, are discussed. The topics are diverse and include teaching the child with special needs; teaching infants and toddlers; working with families; principles of classroom management, including discipline; interpersonal communication skills; observation and assessment, of both children and student teachers; values identification; trends and issues affecting children and families; early childhood education; and the education career field. Text is accompanied with case study examples, which are related to current and classic theories of child development and education.

As we watched student teachers struggle with wondering what to do during the initial days of student teaching—wanting ideas about classroom management and discipline strategies, seeking to understand atypical children in their classrooms, questioning assessment, and wondering how to build partnerships with families—we were inspired to write this book. As it has gone through six revisions, we hope that each one has been better able to meet the needs of student teachers, their instructors, and the children and families they serve.

ORGANIZATION OF THE TEXT

All chapters offer learning objectives, chapter summaries, suggested activities, review questions, Web sites to search, and lists of references. Comments of former student teachers begin the chapters. These personal revelations may provide insight and reading enjoyment. A short case scenario at the end of each chapter presents a narrative that focuses readers' attention on chapter content. Each case scenario deals with issues, problems, and dilemmas others have encountered.

Questions following each scenario promote contemplative and reflective thought, and can be used for class discussion.

Chapter 1, Introduction to Student Teaching Practicum, includes training guidelines, initial feelings, key participants, the currently employed student teacher, useful forms, professionalism, an orientation to first working days, and an introduction to the National Association for the Education of Young Children's (NAEYC) *Code of Ethical Conduct* and *Standards for Programs*. Differences between student teaching at the prekindergarten and elementary school level are included, as are suggestions related to the student's supportive relationships and health. Descriptions of the variation that may exist in cooperating teachers' supervision styles and in placement classrooms offer students insight into how quickly they might assume full teaching responsibilities and duties. Maintaining records, writing in a journal, and collecting items for a professional portfolio are explained. Meeting with administrators and identifying student teacher goals help prepare the student for what is to happen, and what is expected.

Chapter 2, A Student Teacher's Values and Developing Teaching Style, introduces student teachers to the subject of how their values impact their teaching style. We firmly believe that teaching style evolves from each teacher's individual values. Thus, student teachers are presented with exercises designed to help them define their values and see how these translate into classroom activities. The acquisition of values is mentioned, as is the development of teaching style. Professional ethics are discussed in greater detail than in previous editions. An example, using sections of NAEYC's *Code of Ethical Conduct*, illustrates how the code may guide the student teacher in relating to differences in values between one culture and another. Examples of authoritative and authoritarian styles are given, along with precautions related to stereotyping and the need for flexibility.

Chapter 3, Being Observed: Discovering Your Competencies, includes the goals and methods of observation, and provides several examples of observation forms college supervisors or cooperating teachers might use, along with a self-rating sheet that student teachers can employ to assist them in identifying strengths and weaknesses. Competency-based training, critical thinking, and reflective behaviors are discussed as we believe that self-analysis is critical to becoming an effective teacher. Standards for associate and initial licensure levels are introduced and display the recommended skills and abilities successful candidates accomplish before graduation.

Chapter 4, Review of Child Development and Learning Theory, has been updated to include recent discoveries related to memory, critical thinking, and multiple intelligences. Also included is research on brain development and emotional intelligence.

Chapter 5, Instructional Planning, encourages student teachers to look at child interests and needs and the ways that early childhood curriculum is planned and delivered. Accepted standards are discussed and authentic assessment is introduced. Activity resources and other curriculum approaches are mentioned, along with the implications of the federal *No Child Left Behind* legislation. How play affects learning and the need to be an adept conversational partner are emphasized. Written activity plans for prekindergartens and lesson plans for elementary school settings are presented in detail. Sample plans and forms a student teacher might use are also included. Theme and project approaches to teaching are explained, to alert the student teacher to instructional advantages and possible drawbacks of each. Topics such as promoting cognitive skills, using community resources, and additional teaching strategies are also included.

Chapter 6, Classroom Management: Beyond Discipline, includes information on conflict resolution and looks at the five areas of classroom management: physical arrangement of the classroom, curriculum choices, time management, managing classroom routines, and the guidance or disciplinary function. New research on guidance as social development is discussed and several management techniques are suggested. The role of the family is also introduced.

Chapter 7, Using Case Studies to Understand Behavior, highlights information related to Erikson, Maslow, and other developmental theorists. The relationship between Erikson's psychosocial theory and the professional development of student teachers has been clarified. The chapter includes several observation forms, together with their applications, when looking at specific children. The forms are then analyzed to demonstrate how theories help in understanding behavior.

Chapter 8, Working with Children with Special Needs, introduces the student to federal laws that mandate special education and related services to all identified children with special needs. Ideas for how a student teacher might be involved in a preliminary diagnosis and strategies for working with children having specific disabilities have been expanded. Team efforts and the role of the family have been emphasized.

Chapter 9, Common Problems of Student Teachers, starts with a focus on the relationship between stress and classroom conditions. Causes and effects of stress on student teachers are discussed, as are ideas about how to reduce stress. Conferencing, time management, when to seek help, authenticity, *I* messages, active listening, interpersonal communication, preparing *one-day wonders*, and conflict resolution all receive attention, along with problem-solving techniques.

Chapter 10, Student Teachers and Families, begins with the importance of school-home collaboration and the school's family-relations philosophy and goals. We cover how student teachers may interact with families, daily exchanges at opening and pick up times, oral and written communications, planning and conducting conferences, home visits, and parenting education meetings. Other topics included in this chapter are other adults in the classroom, home cultures, and pitfalls and precautions for new teachers.

Chapter 11, Quality Programs in Early Childhood Settings, discusses programs and whether they meet children's needs, are balanced, and meet other standards of quality. The relationship between different types of accreditation and quality are discussed, along with findings of several studies that have looked at quality in preschool and elementary school programs.

Chapter 12, Professional Commitment and Growth, discusses professionalism and looks at a teacher's growth as a professional. Behavior and commitment, advocacy, individual learning cycles, the NAEYC's professional development position statement, and diverse professional growth opportunities are given attention.

Chapter 13, Trends and Issues, first cites facts and figures affecting American children and families. Child abuse, family characteristics, immigrant families, Latino families, school attendance and child care arrangements are discussed. A section on trends and issues pertinent to the career field of education and early education is also included. Educators searching for employment are provided with recommendations, tips, and suggestions to aid their search.

Chapter 14, Student Teaching with Infants and Toddlers, includes updated material on quality indicators and studies related to quality. Special issues such as separation from parents, infant/toddler child care and identity formation, infants born to teenage parents, toilet learning, and biting are discussed. Signing is described, as a technique to enhance infant communication, and several activities for encouraging early learning are included.

FEATURES OF THE SIXTH EDITION

The sixth edition has been streamlined and updated to reflect changes in the field, and we have removed some of the previous review material that may have been encountered in previous courses. Chapters have been combined and condensed where possible but essential information has been retained. Professionalism, advocacy, and leadership are given added attention, and a section dealing with employment is new, in Chapter 13. Web sites for students' further study and research are still included, as are case scenarios and their discussion questions.

The authors and Delmar Learning have made every effort to ensure that all Internet resources are accurate at the time of printing, however, due to the fluid, time-sensitive nature of the Internet, we cannot guarantee that all Web site addresses will remain current for the duration of this edition.

Photographs have been updated, new figures appear, and current research has been cited. Activities that promote in-class discussion and the sharing of individual student teacher discoveries, insights, and happenings are a continued feature. Retained from the fifth edition are text areas that many educators have found valuable. These include:

- quotes from former student teachers.
- reading objectives stated at each chapter's beginning.
- chapter summaries.
- a suggested activities section.
- chapter review questions, to allow feedback on the students' grasp of content.

The text also continues to encourage journaling and gives advice for the development of a professional portfolio.

ANCILLARIES

The following ancillaries are available to accompany the sixth edition of *Student Teaching: Early Childhood Practicum Guide*.

Instructor's E-Resource CD

Many helpful resources are included on this CD, including:

Electronic Instructor's Manual. This manual provides general instructional activities for student teachers, suggested instructional activities by chapter, answers to chapter review questions, and teaching resources.

Computerized Test Bank (CTB). This test bank comprises true/false, multiple-choice, short answer, and completion questions for each chapter. Instructors can use the CTB software to create sample quizzes for students. Refer to the CTB User's Guide for more information on how to create and post quizzes to your school's Intranet.

PowerPoint Lecture Outlines. Notes for each chapter are included.

Online Companion

The Online Companion that accompanies this sixth edition is your link to early childhood education on the Internet. The Online Companion provides evaluation forms from the text that students can download and use in their student teaching experiences. Forms that appear in the Online Companion are identified by an Online Companion icon in the text. New forms are also presented and identified by chapter.

We have added readings and activities that supplement text chapters, and can be used for extra credit, class discussion, or independent study. A number of activities involve job search and employment-seeking skills including cover letter and resume development.

 The Online Companion can be found at http://www.earlychilded.delmar.com.

USING THE TEXT

Instructors are urged to select those chapters most relevant to the needs of their students. We recognize that many associate degree programs have required courses in child development, home, school, and community. Instructors may choose to omit chapters they feel are unnecessary for their students.

Instructors in both associate and baccalaureate degree programs may want to pick and choose the trends and issues presented in Chapter 13. Some may be relevant only in certain situations but the new employment section will be valuable to both educational levels. Instructors may find the comprehensive test questions of value and are urged to select those that they feel are most appropriate.

 # Authors

Jeanne M. Machado and Helen Meyer-Botnarescue are actively involved in child study and teacher-training programs. Jeanne received her MA degree from San Jose State University and a vocational life credential from the University of California, Berkeley. She has experience as an early childhood education instructor and department chairperson at San Jose City College and Evergreen Valley College. As a past president of two professional associations—Northern California Association for the Education of Young Children (Peninsula Chapter) and California Community College Early Childhood Educators—Jeanne is deeply involved in early childhood teaching issues.

Her book *Early Childhood Experiences in the Language Arts* is currently in its eighth edition. In 2006, she authored *Employment Opportunities in Education: How to Secure Your Career,* also published by Delmar Learning.

Helen Meyer-Botnarescue received her Ph.D. from the University of Alabama. She also received a life credential in psychology. Currently, Helen is a professor of education emerita from the Department of Teacher Education at California State University, East Bay. In addition, she has served as graduate coordinator of the Early Childhood Education master's program. She has been an advisor to the campus Early Childhood Center. Helen is an active member of four professional organizations: California Association of Early Childhood Teacher Educators, an affiliate group of the National Association of Early Childhood Teacher Educators; the California Association for the Education of Young Children, a branch of the National Association for the Education of Young Children; the World Organization for Preschool Education; and the Association for Childhood Education International (ACEI), and its state and local affiliates. She has served on the governing board of both the National Association of Early Childhood Teacher Educators and its California affiliate. Helen has been an active member of l'Organisation Modiale pour l'Éducation Préscolaire (OMEP) and has presented at its international congresses. She is a former president of the California Association for Childhood Education and has written extensively for the ACEI journal, *Childhood Education*, and has authored columns for the newsletters *The Activist* and *The Retirees' Review*.

Acknowledgments

The authors wish to express their appreciation to the following individuals and institutions for their contributions to this text.

Reviewers

Linda Aulgur, Ph.D.
Westminster College
Fulton, Missouri

Audrey Beard, Ed.D.
Albany State University
Albany, Georgia

Alice Beyrent, M.Ed.
Associate Professor
Hesser College
Manchester, New Hampshire

Joan Campbell, Ed.S.
Santa Fe Community College
Gainesville, Florida

Amy Huffman, B.S., M.A.,
Professor
Guilford Technical Community College
Jamestown, North Carolina

Judith Piskun, M.Ed.
Associate Professor
Villa Maria College
Buffalo, New York

Jean C. Murphy, Ed.D.
Illinois State University
Chicago, Illinois

Lynda Venhuizen, B.S., M.S.
South Dakota State University
Brookings, South Dakota

Illustrations and Photos

Mary Stieglitz, Ph.D.
Jody Boyd
The parents of photographed children

Individual Assistance

The directors and staff of the San Jose City College and Evergreen Valley College Child Development Centers, and enrolled student teachers.

Barbara Kraybill, Director, Afterschool Programs, Livermore, California

Preschools, Centers, and Elementary Schools

San Jose City College Child Development Center

Evergreen Valley College Child Development Center

Young Families Program, San Jose, California

California State University Associated Students' Child Care Center

Pexioto Children's Center, Hayward, California

Parent-Child Education Center, Hayward, California

Festival Children's Center, Hayward, California

Jackson Avenue School, Livermore, California

Harder School, Hayward, California

St. Elizabeth's Day Home, San Jose, California

Donnelly Head Start, Donnelly, Idaho

Cascade Elementary School, Cascade, Idaho

Redeemer Lutheran Church Child Development Center, Redwood City, California

We also wish to express our appreciation to We Care Day Treatment Center, Concord, California, for permission to photograph attending children.

Students, Instructors, and Professors

San Jose City College

Evergreen Valley College

California State University, East Bay

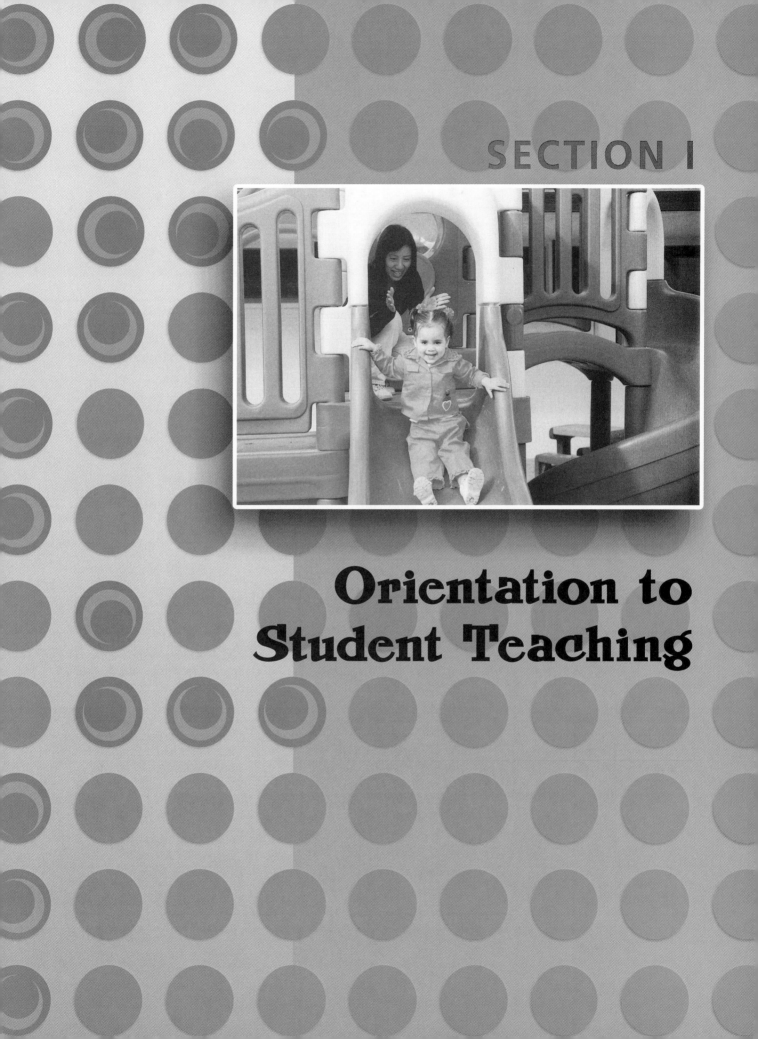

Orientation to Student Teaching

CHAPTER 1

Introduction to Student Teaching Practicum

OBJECTIVES After reading this chapter, you should be able to:

1.... Identify some important goals of a student teaching experience.
2.... Describe the relationships and responsibilities of student teacher, cooperating teacher, and supervisor.
3.... List three professional conduct considerations for student teachers.
4.... Describe activities that take place before student teachers enter their assigned classrooms.
5.... Name two characteristics of professional educators.
6.... Name three important skills for a participant in a staff meeting.

Comments of student teachers after their first week in the classroom:

On the first day of student teaching I was very excited. I felt nervous and tried my best to fit in as though I had been there many times. I memorized all the children's names before the day was over.

May Valentino

I worked hard to get into this final class in the training program. I did it part-time, going evenings after a full day of work with young children. My college supervisor insisted I student teach at a center away from my job. I resented it but found I was able to grow, gain new skills, and observe quality I'd never experienced.

Janice Washington

On my first day of student teaching I was scared and nervous . . . shaking in my boots. Not knowing where things were made me feel unsure. It was a good thing that I had a compassionate cooperating teacher; she put me at ease and directed me so I could begin to find my own way.

Felicia Martinez

Student teaching—also called *practicum teaching*, *field experience*, or *internship*—is both a beginning and an end. It begins a training experience that offers the student a supervised laboratory in which to learn. New skills will develop, and the student will polish professional skills already acquired.

Practicum teaching is usually the final step in a formal training program offering a certificate, degree, license, or credential. It completes a phase during which exposure to theory and practical applications has occurred. It requires reflecting upon and synthesizing previous coursework, training, workshops, and background experience. Congratulations! You have satisfied all the prerequisites for practicum teaching. Now you will assume the duties and responsibilities of a teacher and become a member of a professional teaching team.

One of the culminating phases of your professional preparation for teaching, your practicum experience, provides opportunities to "try your wings" if you are not presently employed. If employed, the experience will sharpen and expand already acquired competencies. Hollingsworth (1998) reports that former student teachers judge student teaching to be the most valuable experience in their training.

TRAINING GUIDELINES

In consultation with other professional groups, the **National Association for the Education of Young Children (NAEYC)** has taken the lead in advocating training guidelines for higher education programs in early childhood education, which includes all institutions that award associate of arts degrees, four- and five-year baccalaureate degrees, and advanced degrees. NAEYC's revised and updated standards were published in 2003. They complement and support other professional standards, such as those developed by the Council for Exceptional Children (CEC), Division for Early Childhood (DEC), the **National Council for Accreditation of Teacher Education (NCATE)**, and the National Board for Professional Teaching Standards (NBPTS).

The importance of supervised, practice teaching has not been overlooked or ignored by other organizations. The **Child Development Associate (CDA)** program demands that 50 percent or more of a trainee's total training time be spent in supervised fieldwork, and NAEYC's guidelines propose a minimum number of practicum hours, to be spent in each of two settings. Many states have developed their own training guidelines, which dictate a specific number of student teaching hours and cite-approved, or suggested, placement settings. Each graduating student of a college, or university, or other type of early childhood teacher training program is expected to have successfully completed a supervised, practicum experience, or alternative equivalent, during which the student assumes major responsibility for a full range of teaching duties for a group of young children. Skills, knowledge, and attitudes gained prepare the student to demonstrate the knowledge and competencies required to meet state licensing requirements or to acquire permits, certificates, or credentials.

National Association for the Education of Young Children (NAEYC)—largest American early childhood professional organization, which deals with issues of children from birth to age eight and those who work with young children.

National Council for Accreditation of Teacher Education (NCATE)—an organization that accredits colleges, schools, or departments of education in higher education programs at the baccalaureate and advanced degree levels in the United States. It is a coalition of 35 specialty, professional associations.

Child Development Associate (CDA)—an early childhood teacher who has been assessed and successfully judged to be competent through the use of the national CDA credentialing program.

INITIAL FEELINGS

Many students approach student teaching with mixed feelings of trepidation and exhilaration. The challenge presents risks and unknowns, as well as opportunities for growth, insight, and increased self-awareness. Student teaching will be memorable. You will cherish and share with others this growth stage in your development as a person and teacher.

THE MECHANICS OF STUDENT TEACHING

Student teaching in an early childhood program involves three key people: the student teacher, a cooperating teacher who is responsible for a group of young children, and a supervisor who is a college instructor or teacher trainer. The cooperating teacher models teaching techniques and practices, and the supervisor observes and analyzes the development of the student teacher's skills. Both also serve as collaborators, mentors, consultants, and advisors. These three key people are more fully described as follows:

Student Teacher: A student experiencing a period of guided teaching, during which the student takes increasing responsibility for the work with a given group of learners over a period of consecutive weeks. Other terms used include *practicum student*, *apprentice*, and *intern*.

Cooperating Teacher: An experienced early childhood professional who works with children and serves as a mentor who collaborates, guides, and counsels. A cooperating teacher also interfaces and collaborates with an early childhood teacher-educator, employed by an institution of higher education, or an early childhood, not-for-credit, teacher-training program. Other terms used include *mentoring teacher*, *supervising teacher*, *laboratory school teacher*, *critic teacher*, *master teacher*, *directing teacher*, and *resident teacher*.

College/University Supervisor: An early childhood educator in an institution of higher learning, or an educator conducting not-for-credit training, who instructs, guides, consults, collaborates, and supervises early childhood practicum students. This educator assesses student progress in attaining professional practice and standards. Other terms used include *early childhood adult educator*, *off-campus supervisor*, *resident supervisor*, *clinical teacher*, *teacher trainer*. In some college training programs, two or more educators are responsible for a student teacher group.

KEY PARTICIPANTS PLAY A ROLE IN STUDENT TEACHER DEVELOPMENT

Personality, settings, child groupings, the commitment and professionalism of individuals, and many other factors contribute and influence the quality and variety of training opportunities. Key participants (student teacher, cooperating teacher, and supervisor) each play a role in student teacher development.

Each student teacher is responsible for serious effort. We have all met people who have a desire and knack for getting everything possible from a given situation. Their "antennae" are actively searching, receiving, and evaluating. As a student teacher, you will guide much of your own growth.

Your cooperating teacher and supervisor will support and reinforce your commitment to learn but your increasing skill will depend, in part, on you.

As their first duty, cooperating teachers must fulfill the requirements of their positions; child instruction is paramount. Student teacher collaboration and guidance are additional tasks, for which a cooperating teacher may or may not be compensated. Even in laboratory school settings, educating and caring for children supersedes the training of student teachers, which is seen as an auxiliary function.

Cooperating teachers differ. One might place mentor teachers on a degree-of-control continuum, ranging between *highly directive* (high structure) to *collaborative* (unstructured) styles. Cooperating teachers falling nearer the unstructured end believe student teachers should be given considerable latitude, as emerging professionals learning to make decisions on their own. These would promote collaboration and student ownership of problem solving. Directive-style cooperating teachers may choose to adopt a more unstructured mode as their student teacher becomes more competent in handling classroom responsibilities, or this may not happen at all, depending on the mentor teacher's dedication to a directive style.

Justen and McJunkin (1999) describe effective cooperating teachers as monitors who urge student teachers to suggest alternative solutions to classroom problems. Cooperating teachers, who explain teaching strategies and techniques, and what was done and why, aid student teacher growth. A student teacher who observes closely and takes part in discussions about classroom practice gains increased insight (Schriver, 1999). During the early weeks of the practicum, most cooperating teachers try to identify the student teacher's strengths, particular needs, concerns, and what the student is uniquely equipped to offer and share with children, such as piano playing or cultural insight.

The supervisor's role includes being encouraging, understanding, sensitive, supportive, and responsive to the student's concerns, as well as being serious and rigorous in promoting each student teacher's attention to high, professional standards of performance and timely completion of responsibilities. Supervisors also plan, schedule, and conduct meeting times when practicum students can voice evolving ideas, discoveries, and insights; they may also serve as a mentor to a cooperating teacher, meeting with them periodically as well, to give supportive assistance and suggestions. End of term evaluations of student teachers, recommendation letters to school districts and other employers, final reviews of portfolios, sending recommendations to state certification agencies, and providing career counseling can be additional responsibilities and tasks. Most supervising educators are aware that although they are instrumental contributors to their student teacher's professional development, the student's mentor teachers may be more influential.

BEFORE PLACEMENTS

College and university departments, and individual college instructors (supervisors), develop guidelines for selecting placement sites long before the practicum begins. Decisions may be influenced by college, university, or state standards, or by the NAEYC, the National Association of Early Childhood Teacher Educators (NAECTE), or the American Associate Degree Early Childhood Teacher's (ACCESS) joint position statement, *Code of*

Ethical Conduct: Supplement for Early Childhood Adult Educators (2004). (See the Appendix for a section of text from this document.) Some colleges and universities endeavor to canvass their community preschools, elementary schools, or child care centers, to identify those meeting their training standards and designate these as certified, practicum placement sites. Others exclusively select NAEYC-accredited child development programs. Decisions involve selection of the best training sites for students, considering the constraints involved in each situation. Selection criteria may depend on location, staff experience and training, licensing and accreditation of the placement site, state laws and guidelines, the willingness and ability of the site administrators and staff to carry out procedures and responsibilities, as well as other factors.

A number of group and individual consultations take place as supervising college and university instructors set the scene for student teacher experiences, activities, assignments, and their evaluation. Informational written material, including a student teacher and cooperating teacher handbook, may have been designed and produced. The handbooks attempt to cover all facets of training and need to be read carefully and kept handy.

The student teacher should recognize that decisions concerning the number of placements per semester, quarter, or training period have already been established. In some communities, a wide variety of child classrooms are available and possible. In other areas, placement classrooms are few or limited.

Colleges and universities may offer early childhood education training programs that include preparation for diverse teaching specialties. School-age and infant/toddler teaching are two areas provided within traditional, early childhood or child development training programs. Some colleges and universities make student teacher placements in both private and public kindergartens and elementary school classrooms, where students assume assistant teacher or aide duties, in AA degree training programs or student teacher positions in BA degree training programs.

Student teaching classes are offered at baccalaureate degree-granting colleges and universities, both private and public. Students enrolled in these classes are completing coursework to fulfill state credentialing requirements or to acquire an advanced degree, such as a Master of Arts, which includes teaching certification. Student teachers at a primary grade level usually function as practicing teachers, with full responsibility for their assigned classrooms while under the supervision of their assigned cooperating teachers. Rarely do student teachers at the preschool or primary school level immediately assume full teaching responsibilities. More commonly, they gradually perform an increasing number of duties, program planning, and instruction, working their way up to taking on all teacher responsibilities while still under their mentor teacher's supervision.

The Currently Employed Student Teacher

In some instances, currently employed student teachers may be required to student teach in one or two different child facilities or classrooms. For the currently employed student teacher, the logistics of putting in unpaid hours at another center may seem an undue hardship, yet many will welcome the opportunity to gain insight into another teacher's competencies and will benefit from the professional consultation that occurs. In some training programs, one may have to become a day student instead of a night student, to enroll in a student teaching class. College and university supervisors are sometimes able to work out placements that allow a student to do their practicum at their place of employment, by placing a special, student teacher mentor in the cooperating teacher's classroom. This arrangement does not deprive the student of the chance to work and view a quality early childhood model, for the mentor is felt to provide and model excellent practice. Increasingly, students entering early childhood work start classes after employment.

Health Concerns

Since you will need all the strength and endurance you can muster during your practicum, take care to monitor your health. Make getting enough sleep a priority. Many colleges offer health and psychological services to their students. Eating properly, exercising, and having time for fun (even if you are wholeheartedly enjoying your classroom experience) is important. It is wise to take care of minor health problems and schedule medical, dental, and eye examinations so they will not interrupt your practicum assignment.

Careful attention to hand washing while student teaching can help eliminate some of the germs encountered while working with children, but it is not unusual to be exposed to common childhood illnesses and become sick while student teaching. Taking time out during the day to relax may help you maintain balance. Some universities may provide informal meetings with other student teachers, to share thoughts and voice concerns regarding the student teaching experience. Close friends, family, and peers usually offer the opportunity to clarify thoughts and voice concerns. They may provide moral support, function as a cheering section, and often can be therapeutic sounding boards.

Learning and Growth

As unique individuals, each student teacher has developed a unique learning style. Life and school experiences mold how you see yourself, and how you proceed toward knowing and accomplishing new knowledge or skill. Hopefully, your student teaching class will offer diverse ways to learn and will also give structured aid in the form of clear guidelines, directions, and suggestions, by both your instructor and your mentor teacher.

A portion of your time will be spent pondering what you have read and experienced. You will closely observe other adults in child classrooms, to gauge the outcomes of their behaviors, but you will also need to become an avid watcher of yourself, and of the reactions of others to you. Professional teaching requires continuous analysis, adjustment, reflection, and refocusing. Growth will build and proceed on what you already know as you take tentative and then firm steps in new directions.

Part of the joy of teaching is experimenting, innovating, and inventing new approaches. These new ways will always be offered after judging whether they mesh with your basic conclusions, considering what is safe and developmentally appropriate for young children.

Most cooperating teachers and college supervisors were student teachers at the beginning of their own careers. Their feelings tend to be empathetic and supportive, while at the same time they expect a serious student attempt to develop competence.

The whole student teaching experience can be viewed as a miniature world, a slice of life, or a human laboratory that will be full of memorable events including the ups and downs all student teachers experience. Ideally, every student comes to a clarification of self in relation to people and environments that are designed to provide quality care for young children. New insights concerning values, goals, cultures, self-realization, and other important life issues are examined.

Figure 1-1
Consulting with your cooperating teacher happens frequently in student teaching.

Student Teacher Progress. If the student completes student teaching duties and responsibilities successfully, the student receives recognition of teaching competency. Observation and analysis of the student's performance, followed by consultation with the teaching team, is an integral part of student teaching (see Figure 1–1).

How should student teachers view their progress and learning in a student teaching class? An early childhood or primary school classroom may be seen as a growing place for everyone, not only for the student teacher. Everyone who enters the classroom can grow from each experience. It is presumed that all adults—even the mentor teacher and supervisor—are unfinished products. Each participant is viewed as a combination of strengths and talents, with the possibility of expanding.

ORIENTATION

Orientation meetings may take place before your first working day, and may include meeting staff, taking a facility tour, reviewing oral and written school guidelines, and completing various forms. Not all schools provide a formal orientation. Making a conscious effort to remember people's names and taking notes is advisable. Remember, first impressions are important; be aware that your body language will send messages to others.

Introductions and tours enable the student teacher to become familiar with people and settings and help reduce anxieties (see Figure 1–2). Anxieties may also increase when responsibilities and requirements are described. Supervisors and mentor teachers can require the completion of various assignments; keeping each in order may be accomplished by color coding or using different folders or binders. A date book or daily appointment calendar is also recommended because many important meetings, appointments, and deadlines will occur. As always, the newness, details, and the amount of information to read and remember may temporarily produce stress.

Notice the center's surroundings; look for uniqueness, and observe special features of the neighborhood and community. Observe the diversity of the placement classroom's attending children and families.

Forms, Forms, Forms

You will encounter various written forms and guides during orientations. Possible supervisor guides and forms follow:

- Practicum class guide sheet
- Listing of student teacher responsibilities (see Figure 1–3)
- Suggested tips (see Figure 1–4)
- Forms used for assessment
- Instructions for cooperating teachers (see Figure 1–5)

Figure 1-2
The school receptionist/secretary is an important staff member.

1. Be prompt and prepared.
2. If you are ill on your assigned days, call your supervisor and cooperating teacher as close to 8 A.M. as possible.
3. If you must be absent, phone ahead and let your school know you are unable to be there that day. Preferably, let the school know ahead of time if there will be an unavoidable absence during your student teaching assignment.
4. Remember, the cooperating teacher depends on your services as a fellow teacher.
5. Sign in and out if required.
6. Consult with your supervisor on lesson planning when help is needed.
7. Make an appointment with your supervisor to discuss class-related questions or problems.
8. Remember to avoid conversations that label children or deal with confidential information.
9. Sign in the lesson plan book at least one week in advance if your cooperating teacher or supervisor requests it.
10. Complete assignments.
11. Complete your student teacher file, and take it to the director's office as soon as possible. (Included in this file are TB clearance, personal data sheet, rating sheets, return envelope.)
12. Be sure to have your fingerprint card and background check completed prior to beginning your first observation and/or student teaching assignment.
13. Please see and do what needs to be done without direction. Ask questions. Assume as much teaching responsibility as you can handle.

Figure 1-3
Sample of student teacher responsibilities.

1. Get your TB and criminal background clearances to your center's director as soon as possible. (Note: This is not required in some states.)
2. Leave your belongings in the place provided.
3. Sign in.
4. Enter the children's room quietly, wearing your name tag.
5. Look for emergency room evacuation plans (posted on wall).
6. Consider child safety. Watch and listen for rules and expectations.
7. Actively involve yourself helping staff and children. See what needs to be done. Ask only what is necessary of staff after saying hello or introducing yourself. (Do not interrupt an activity. Wait until the cooperating teacher is free.)
8. Let the staff handle child behaviors that are puzzling on the first days.
9. Write down any questions concerning children, programs, and routines that baffle you, and discuss them with your supervisor.
10. If you are sick on your scheduled day, call both your supervisor and your cooperating teacher.
11. Keep a brief diary of your activities, feelings, perceptions, and the like. You may want to buy a pocket-sized notebook.

● **Figure 1-4**
Sample of trainer's tips for student teacher's first days.

1. Let your student take as much responsibility as possible.
2. Give feedback on progress if possible.
3. Written tips, hints, and suggestions on lesson plans are helpful.
4. Let your student teacher work out the "tight" spots when possible. You may want to set up a signal to indicate when the student wishes you to step in and remedy the situation.
5. Gauge your student's ability. (Some student teachers may be able to handle a full morning's program from the beginning.) Each student needs the experience of handling the group.
6. Discuss the student teacher's performance in confidence after the activity. Some suggestions while an activity is occurring may be necessary for child or equipment safety.
7. Your student teacher may ask you for a letter of reference.
8. Peer evaluations have been assigned. This means perhaps that another student teacher may observe and rate the student assigned to you. This may happen twice during the semester.
9. Please call the student's supervisor if a difficulty or question arises.
10. Rate the student on the last week of participation. A rating sheet is part of your student teacher's folder. The student will remind you a week in advance.
11. The student teacher has been instructed to consult with you on lesson plan activities. If you want the activities to deal with particular curriculum areas or themes, this is your choice. The student has been told to abide by your wishes.
12. Your student's personal data sheet has information concerning special interests, background, and so on.
13. The student's supervisor will visit periodically to give the student feedback on competencies and possible growth areas.
14. Frequent conferences help the student obtain a clear picture of skill progress.
15. Near the end of the student teacher's assignment, the college/university will schedule a three-way conference with you, your student teacher, and the supervisor for the closing student teacher evaluation.

Thank you for taking on the extra work involved in having a student in your classroom.

● **Figure 1-5**
Sample of supervisor's written instructions to cooperating teachers.

Placement center forms and written materials may include parent guides, policy statements, newsletters, center handbooks, and visitor and observer rules. Cooperating teachers may provide you with a student teacher assignment sheet, a responsibilities sheet, a daily schedule, a listing of children's names (with pronunciation guides if necessary), classroom rules, assessment and observation forms, staff meeting dates and times, and suggestions for guiding child behavior(see Figure 1–6).

Suggestions for guiding behavior:
1. Redirect behavior in a positive way whenever possible (e.g., feet belong on the floor).
2. Do not give a choice when one does not exist.
3. Give help only when it is needed.
4. Do not be afraid to limit or channel destructive behavior.
5. Help the children understand by explaining.
6. Encourage children to use their words during peer disagreements.
7. Inform the children a few minutes ahead of the next activity to come. ("It's three minutes until cleanup/snack.")
8. Watch for situations that may be explosive, and step in. Try to let the children settle problems themselves. If they cannot, redirect them.
9. Remember, an ounce of prevention is worth a pound of cure.

Inside:
1. Modeling dough stays in the creative activities room.
2. Parents have been asked not to send their children with toys, except on sharing days.
3. Running is for outside; walking is for inside.
4. Encourage children to pour their own drinks from the pitchers provided. This will probably mean frequent spills so sponges should be available on all tables. Have children pass things to each other.

Outside:
1. Adults need to distribute themselves throughout the center and the playground rather than grouping together. Your attention should be on the children, observing them so you can be ready to step in when guidance is needed.
2. Children are to climb up the ladder and slide down on their bottoms when using the slide.
3. All sand play and sand toys must be in the designated area.
4. Remind the children that water from the fountain is for drinking. Sand and cornmeal should be kept away from the water fountain to avoid clogging.
5. Help children park wheeled toys along the fence before going in. Please keep the gate area clear.
6. All wheeled toys have a specific use and should be used properly.

Figure 1-6
Sample of one center's guidelines for guiding child behavior.

Many forms must be on file before the student's first working day; the following forms are common to student teaching:

- Student teacher sign-in sheets, to keep track of arrivals, departures, and volunteer and assigned work hours
- Tuberculin (TB) clearance, which is mandatory in many states
- Staff information form and personnel record
- Personal background form
- Physical examination form or physician's report
- Criminal background clearance
- Immunization records

Criminal History and Background Check

An increasing number of states require a criminal history and background inquiry prior to field placement. All paid and volunteer staff members may be required to comply and receive clearance, which is then placed in the school's personnel files.

PROFESSIONALISM

Continuous learning is the mark of a professional in any occupational field (Machado & Reynolds, 2006). VanderVen (1988) defines an educator's professionalism as the ability to knowledgeably and competently make a sustained difference, to diagnose and analyze situations, to select the most appropriate interventions, to apply them skillfully, and to describe why they were selected. Another definition by the NAEYC (Hyson, 2003) reads

> Candidates identify and conduct themselves as members of the early childhood profession. They know and use ethical guidelines and other professional standards related to early childhood practice. They are continuous, collaborative learners who demonstrate knowledgeable, reflective, and critical perspectives on their work, making informed decisions that integrate knowledge from a variety of sources. They are informed advocates for sound educational policies.

You learned the term *transition* during your training. A planned transition intends to move children smoothly from one activity to another. You will move from being a professional student to being a professional educator. During student teaching you are in a transforming phase of your career. NAEYC has provided help to smooth your transition with two important published guides, *The Code of Ethical Standards and Statement of Commitment* (Feeney & Freeman, 2005), and *Preparing Early Childhood Professionals: NAEYC's Standards for Programs* (Hyson, 2003) which identifies standards for the following levels of training:

- associate degree standards
- initial licensure standards, usually baccalaureate
- advanced master's and doctoral program standards
- the early childhood special education standards per the CEC/DEC (Council for Exceptional Children/Division for Early Childhood)
- the Early Childhood/Generalist Standards per the NBPTS (National Board for Professional Teaching Standards)

The first book presents professional parameters for responsible and ethical educator behavior. (See a sample section of the code of conduct in Figure 1-7.) Professionals regard this as a necessary guide for professional conduct and **professional ethics** invaluable to all in the career field. If you can count on but one thing during your practicum experience, it will be to face unexpected decisions, dilemmas, and situations daily, which will test your professional resolve to do the right thing. You will encounter many types of diversity and a wide variety of behaviors and conditions.

The second book is the product of NAEYC's accreditation efforts, and contains clear descriptions of what teacher training programs in institutions of higher learning attempt to accomplish with their early childhood graduates. Teacher standards and competencies are listed. In some sections, characteristics and behaviors indicating whether a candidate has not yet met expectations, has met them, or has exceeded them is included. NAEYC's five standards for associate degree programs include a supporting explanation for each standard, a listing of key standard elements, opportunities for student learning, and identifiers of evidence of student growth.

In addition, we suggest you obtain a copy of your state's standards for early childhood teacher licensing and/or certification and study them. The three volumes listed above can serve as reference books in your developing professional library—must-have career and guidance manuals.

You may become a different type of professional educator than your classmates. Your diversity, gifts, talents, career accomplishments, and training program will have produced a professional educator of a unique sort. Although standards are designed to promote quality and excellence in graduating teacher candidates, they are not used to create cookie-cutter teachers—just the outstanding ones that children deserve. Extra attention

professional ethics— beliefs regarding appropriate occupational behavior and conduct as defined and accepted by recognized professionals in that occupation.

SECTION I ETHICAL RESPONSIBILITIES TO CHILDREN

Ideals

I-1.1—To be familiar with the knowledge base of early childhood care and education and to stay informed through continuing education and training.

I-1.2—To base program practices upon current knowledge and research in the field of early childhood education, child development, and related disciplines, as well as on particular knowledge of each child.

I-1.3—To recognize and respect the unique qualities, abilities, and potential of each child.

I-1.4—To appreciate the vulnerability of children and their dependence on adults.

I-1.5—To create and maintain safe and healthy settings that foster children's social, emotional, cognitive, and physical development and that respect their dignity and their contributions.

Figure 1-7
Sample section, Ethical Responsibilities to Children from NAEYC's Code of Ethical Conduct, Revised April 2005. Source: Copyright © The National Association for the Education of Young Children, Washington, DC.

practitioner—person engaged in the practice of a profession or occupation, in this case, early childhood education. Other terms used: educator, teacher, assistant teacher, aide, student teacher.

confidentiality—requirement that results in evaluations and assessments be shared with only the parents and appropriate school personnel.

to teacher or **practioner** conduct is required, because of the impressionable vulnerability of young children, and the influence a teacher may have with parents. Katz and Ward (1978) point out:

> In any profession, the more powerless the client is in relation to the practitioner, the more important the practitioner's ethics become. Power necessitates internal restraints against abusing that power, especially in work with children.
>
> Early childhood practitioners have great power over young children in early care centers. Practitioners' superior physical power is obvious. In addition, they have virtually total power over the psychological goods and resources valued by the young in their care.

When you reach the level of student teaching, others presume you have a certain amount of educational background and some degree of professional skill. Some families may feel you are an expert in child-rearing and may try to seek your opinion on a wide variety of developmental issues. You will need to direct these people to your cooperating teacher, who may refer them to the director or other staff, who in turn may refer them to professionally trained individuals or community resources.

Confidentiality protects children and families, and should be maintained at all times. Staff meetings and individual conferences are conducted in a spirit of mutual interest and concern for the welfare of everyone involved, as well as for the center's high standards. At such conferences, student teachers are privy to personal information that should not be discussed elsewhere. This point needs to be stressed. Student teachers can become so involved with classroom happenings and individual children that they inadvertently discuss privileged information with a fellow student teacher or friend, or in earshot of a parent or another individual. One can easily see how this might happen—and cause irreparable damage. Classes of student teachers are frequently reminded by their instructors that actual child and family names cannot be used in class discussions.

The student teacher's appearance, clothing, and grooming contribute to a professional image. Take your cues from observing what other staff at your placement site are wearing. Fortunately, comfortable and functional clothing that allows a student teacher to perform duties without worry or hindrance is relatively inexpensive (see Figure 1–8). Many supervisors suggest a pocketed smock or apron and a change of shoes.

Chapter 12, Professional Commitment and Growth, expands this discussion further. It contains an in-depth description of professionalism and advocacy.

Responsibilities

A clear picture of the responsibilities of the student teacher, cooperating teacher, and supervisor will help students make decisions about handling specific incidences as professionals. As a general rule, it is better to ask for help than to proceed in any questionable situation that goes beyond your responsibilities and duties (barring emergency situations that call for immediate action).

 **Figure 1-8**
A smock can be both colorful and protective.

Your main responsibilities at the beginning of your practicum experience are:

- prompt arrival
- reliable attendance
- active participation
- completion of assigned duties
- decision making based on knowledge of best practices
- research
- working with minimal direction, but consulting when in doubt
- working as a supportive and caring team member

Exposure to Bloodborne Pathogens

You will be instructed at your placement site about exposure to potentially infectious materials and substances, such as children's blood, skin, eye, and mucous membrane secretions, and will be provided with protective gloves and equipment. Should a classroom situation occur, mentor teachers will prefer to handle the incident. Discuss this with your cooperating teacher. Privacy laws protect parents who do not wish to disclose child conditions; therefore, it is wise to follow exposure guidelines strictly. The Occupational Safety and Health Administration, by means of the Occupational Safety and Health Acts of 1970 and 1992, mandated the need for child care worker training and protection. Each center by law (with few exceptions), must develop a written exposure control plan, provide protective clothing and equipment, give employees information and training, and provide vaccine and medical help to exposed employees. Centers are to instruct student teachers concerning who gives first aid.

It is suggested that each student teacher consult their private physician regarding the advisability of hepatitis B vaccination.

Kindergarten and Primary Grade Student Teaching When assigned to student teach in a kindergarten or primary grade classroom, your first days will involve many of the same activities assigned to you while student teaching in a prekindergarten. You will, no doubt, notice an increase in efforts to teach children reading, mathematics, and science skills as a result of No Child Left Behind legislation.

Most elementary schools have staff handbooks. You will be given a copy and be expected to read it. A handbook will contain vital information, such as the school calendar and personnel policies. The names of the school principal, secretary, nurse, librarian, head maintenance person, community liaison, and so forth, will be listed. School rules and regulations will be presented. After reading the handbook, you will have a firm idea of what rules and regulations you will be expected to follow during your student teaching period.

Different colleges and universities have different ways in which student teaching is arranged. In some states that have certification for nursery/kindergarten/primary (NKP) teaching, you may have three different placements: one at a preschool, another at the kindergarten level, and a third in a primary grade. Other states require only two experiences: one at a preschool and one at either a kindergarten or primary level. In some certification programs, all theory and method classes precede a one-semester, 12-week, all-day student teaching experience. Other programs integrate some of the theory and method courses with short observation assignments, lasting approximately four weeks. Again, these precede a major student teaching assignment that most typically covers one academic semester. In California, early childhood education is an *emphasis*, appended to the multiple-subject (elementary) credential. Colleges and universities, with similar state-approved programs, must provide student experiences at both primary and intermediate grade levels in addition to an experience in a preschool. Assignments, then, often involve a short practicum observation in a preschool, often only in the mornings (sometimes paid experience may be substituted), another assignment in the intermediate grades (usually grade four), and a final, longer assignment of approximately 12 to 15 weeks, all day, in a kindergarten or primary grade.

In student teaching assignments that cover only one semester, you probably will have only one college or university supervisor. Most supervisors are chosen for their expertise and are former primary grade teachers themselves. In colleges and universities with programs that include short practica or observation periods prior to student teaching, you may well have more than one supervisor. Some of these short observation periods may not be directly supervised; the college may rely on the cooperating teacher or principal for any supervision that is needed. Having different supervisors can provide you with the benefit of exposure to more than one supervision style or technique. One supervisor may stress the need to see lesson plans as you are teaching. Another, schooled in clinical supervision techniques, may focus on the communication and questioning strategies you use. A third may watch your interactions with your pupils.

Student teaching assignments are usually made very carefully. Mentor teachers are chosen for their expertise as well as for their willingness to help train a student teacher. Many states require mentor teachers to have at least three years of experience prior to being considered and most principals choose their most competent teachers for this role.

Distance Learning

A few colleges offer a student teaching practicum using satellite locations and electronically monitored classroom placements. Packaged course content may be provided and accessed through the Internet, by interactive television, audiocassettes, or some other technological vehicle. Students may conference with their college supervisors by phone lines, e-mail, periodic face-to-face meetings, or by other means and arrangements. Some distance learning classes have evolved with unique features that attempt to promote a quality student teaching experience in rural settings. Distance learning often makes study available at any hour of the day or night and at nontraditional campus locations. It is becoming commonplace to keep in touch with one's college supervisor by computer, or through video conferencing.

STUDENT TEACHING GOALS

The most important goal of student teaching is to gain professional teaching competence. The acquisition of skills allows the completion of training and new or continued employment. Specific objectives vary, but they generally are concerned with understanding children, planning and providing quality programs for children and families, acquiring technical teaching skills, and personal and professional development. Individual

goals reflect each student teacher's idea of professional conduct and skill, and how each feels about the kind of teacher and person she would like to become.

You will probably begin by working to establish a collaborative and cordial relationship with your cooperating teacher and your supervisor. You will meet and exchange ideas and concerns; accept the suggestions, advice, and the supportive assistance each provides to aid your professional growth.

Becoming a reflective educator is another objective. Understanding family circumstances and discovering what parents want for their children's education are others. The prime concern of many student teachers is their personal goal of developing confidence in their teaching abilities.

goals—overall, general overviews of what student teachers expect to gain from the practicum experience.

Student Teacher Observational Record-Keeping

Before your student teaching class, you completed coursework covering methods, techniques, and observational strategies. It is time to review that material now because you will be watching and listening to children closely. You will be focusing on how your behavior and actions affect individual children or the total child group. Remember that children's nonverbal messages are as important as their verbal ones; you will be constantly alert to new and repeated behaviors as well as puzzling ones.

Busy cooperating teachers are usually quite interested in daily observations and accounts of child incidents and happenings written by student teachers. It gives cooperating teachers an outside opinion of what's going on in the classroom. This may be the first perception shared by another concerning child behavior the cooperating teacher is trying to trace or evaluate. You may want to do some note taking and record keeping concerning child behaviors. The cooperating teacher may assign more lengthy observation exercises. Any notes are confidential and should be guarded closely as one can easily understand the danger of student notes lying around. Anecdotes are jotted down quickly, with the date and time, unlike records of accidents, injuries, or illnesses noted during the day, which are detailed in a specific format for school record-keeping. Each site has its own specific form to use.

Student Journals (Logs)

Many training programs require the student teacher to begin a **journal** or log of experiences and feelings. This is sometimes called a *reflective journal* (Hillman, 2006).

Supervisors periodically monitor journal entries or student audio or video tape recordings to keep on top of student growth, work actions, concerns, feelings, questions, and needs. It is suggested that student teachers make at least one, five-minute daily entry, written or typed, on participation days, while impressions are still fresh. Some college supervisors provide suggestions for recorded topics including:

- personal views, insights, and expressions
- classroom dilemmas
- feelings about all aspects of the classroom
- insights concerning the philosophy of the cooperating teacher

journal—a written, pictorial, or audio record of experiences, occurrences, observations, feelings, questions, work actions, reflective thoughts, and other happenings during student teaching.

- relationships with particular children
- perceptions of student teacher skills
- what is going well; what is not
- staff relationships
- areas a student pinpoints for self-growth
- ways the student has overcome a problem
- new ideas to improve instruction and how they worked
- why it would be great (or not) to be a child in this classroom
- special children's needs
- children's interests
- planned activities
- unscheduled activities
- favorite spots in the classroom
- difficult times of day

Other supervisors may assign journal questions that require analyzing and reflecting that need to be answered during the practicum period (Hillman, 2006).

In journaling students jot down reflections, perceptions, and opinions that are based on their current and evolving knowledge. One purpose of journaling is to have student teachers focus on themselves as learners. Student teachers can wonder, question, celebrate insights, describe setbacks, generate ideas, and keep track of their growth as teachers. Supervisors may suggest that students write in their journals on the right two-thirds of the page, so supervisor or cooperating teachers can dialogue with them in the left-hand space. Journal entries can use a variety of formats; some are dated in left hand margins, some are word-processed or electronic.

Reading assignment reactions may also be recorded in journals, if supervisors so request. Time required either to write or react to journal entries may be built into training class seminars.

When college supervisors comment in their student's journals and give supportive assistance or encouragement, a journal becomes a communication device and promotes shared understandings and intimacy. Log entries are sometimes included when student teachers develop professional career portfolios which will be mentioned later in this chapter.

PREPARING FOR YOUR FIRST DAY

Before your first day of student teaching, you have been given your cooperating teacher's name and the school's address, and you may have attended orientation meetings for student teaching. Your first working day is near. You have either an on-campus or off-campus child center or school assignment. If your soon-to-be students live off-campus, a stroll through the neighborhood will help you discover something about them. Observe the community, its businesses, its recreation, its uniqueness, and do not overlook the opportunity to observe resources for planning child activities. Perhaps a construction site is an interesting possibility for a field trip, or an orchard or park holds treasures to be discovered.

With an on-campus laboratory school placement, you may have previously participated in the children's program and perhaps completed observation assignments. The center and its staff and children may be familiar. Take a new look at the campus and the resources of the campus community.

If you have been asked to meet with the director or principal at an off-campus school, call to make an appointment. Plan to have the meeting at least fifteen minutes to a half hour before you are scheduled to be in the classroom. Ask about available staff parking. Remember to avoid parent parking spots or drop-off areas.

It is time to dust off the resource idea files and books you have collected during your training, because you may be using them to plan activities. Choose a short activity to offer on your first day, even if one has not been assigned. Brush up on finger plays, or short songs that may be used as fill-ins, or *transitions*. If you do not have them memorized, put them on cards that slip into your pocket. It is important for you to be prepared to step in with an activity if you are asked to do so (see Figure 1–9).

Some good ideas for first-day activities that have worked well for other student teachers include:

- a name tag–making activity
- puppet who tells a short story about his name, introduces the student teacher's name, and wants to know the children's names
- favorite book or short audio recording to discuss
- an art or craft activity that uses children's names
- a collage or chart that shows interesting things about a student teacher's life

● Figure 1-9
A movement activity created by a student teacher can capture child interest, and lead to spur-of-the moment fun.

- a flannelboard activity
- a game made by the student teacher that involves children's names and places in their community
- a beanbag activity that uses children's names
- a new song or movement activity
- a storytelling experience
- a tape recording of school or neighborhood sounds to guess and discuss

Last-Minute Preparations

Activities that can be easily carried and set up quickly work best. Get the necessary materials together the night before your class. If you received a set of classroom rules and a schedule of routines and planned activities, study it beforehand.

Think about clothing. Make sure you wear something comfortable and appropriate. A smock, shirt, or apron with a pocket will hold a small notebook, pen, tissues, and other small necessities. You should wear shoes that will protect your toes and help you maintain balance and speed on the playground.

MEETING WITH THE ADMINISTRATOR

It may be customary to meet individually with the administrator before going to the classroom. At that time, the student teacher's records may be needed for the personnel file. The file usually includes a TB clearance, a physical examination form, an emergency form, a personal background form, criminal clearance, information on how to contact your supervisor, and rating sheets from the supervisor. A personnel file may also be maintained at your college or university by your supervisor.

Some topics you might discuss with the director or principal are the procedures for storing your personal items, sign-in and sign-out requirements, and miscellaneous items, such as parking permits. Additional possible subjects for this first meeting with the administrator might include queries about the school's history of operation, its enrollment, parent participation, family diversity, and community involvement. Ask questions you want answered, not ones that fill conversational silences.

Address administrators in a formal manner, as you will other adults on your teaching team (Mr. Silva or Miss Brown). If they wish to be called otherwise, they will tell you. This is the right time to state your intent to follow suggestions and directions, and mention your appreciation for any help and guidance. You should do this also in your first discussions with your cooperating teacher. And you will add that you desire to help where most needed in the classroom, and want to know if there are any classroom materials, equipment, or furnishings that are off-limits to student teachers.

Most center and school handbooks describe operational policies, and include a mission statement, an educational philosophy, program goals and curriculum, and personnel policies. (See Figure 1-10 for other items you may want to inquire about if they are not covered in the handbook.)

- Organizational chart
- Job titles and description of duties and responsibilities
- Salary schedule
- Benefits
- Yearly calendar including events, meetings, holidays, and in-service dates
- **Code of ethics** or code of conduct
- Dress code
- Professional growth and development, **career lattice particulars**
- Job performance procedures and assessment criteria
- Absences and substitute policy
- Grievance procedure
- Resignation, termination procedures
- Licensing or other state or local regulation information
- Parent involvement or other parent procedures
- Child and staff health policies
- Center or employee record forms

code of ethics—agreed-upon professional standards that guide behavior and facilitate decision making in working situations.

career lattice particulars—recognizes that the early childhood profession is made up of individuals with varied backgrounds; a lattice allows for both horizontal and vertical movement among positions, with accompanying levels of education, experience, responsibility, and pay. Sometimes called a *ladder*.

Figure 1-10
Common personnel handbook topics.

Student teachers usually make a good impression with administrators and staff when they look them in the eye, speak clearly and with confidence, and smile.

 # YOUR CLASSROOM

There probably will be time for a smile and a few quick words with your cooperating teacher your first day. Your introduction to the children can wait until a planned group time. Introduce yourself briefly to other classroom adults when you are in close proximity. Your cooperating teacher may ask that you observe instead of participate. This will give you time to scan the classroom environment and play areas and become familiar with classroom rules and schedules, which are usually posted in young children's classrooms. Next, focus on child behaviors and planned child instruction. Otherwise, actively participate in supervising and interacting with the children. Pitch in with any teaching or assistant tasks. Wear a provided or self-made name tag.

Ask questions only when necessary; jot down others on a note pad that you carry with you. Judge where you are the most needed. Do not worry about assuming too much responsibility; your cooperating teacher will let you know if you are overstepping your duties. New student teachers tend to hold back and wait to be directed. Put yourself in the teacher's place. Where would the teacher direct you to supervise or assist children when she is busy with other work? Periodically scan the room to determine where you can be the most useful.

Class Computers

Many classrooms have multiple computers and software programs available. Usually, computers in child areas have rules and require adult supervision. Prepare yourself by learning operational procedures. Preview child programs before or after class sessions, after first consulting with your cooperating teacher.

Ask your cooperating teacher for a school password if you are asked to enter student data. Some classrooms require student teachers to do digital record keeping.

Supplies

Familiarize yourself with storage areas to minimize the need to ask questions about the location of equipment and supplies. Make your inspection when you are free from room supervision (see Figure 1–11). Become familiar with yard storage also. During team meetings, inquire about your use of supplies for planned activities.

Child Records

Some early childhood centers will allow student teachers access to child and family records; others will not. Knowing as much as possible about each child increases the quality of your interaction. Confidentiality is

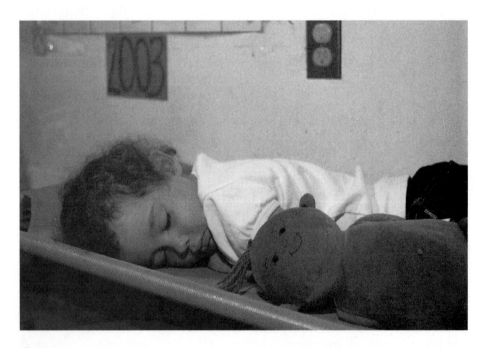

● **Figure 1-11**
Do you know where sleeping cots are stored after naptime?

expected. If a review takes place, you may wish to make note of any child **allergies**, specific interests, or special needs.

Emergency information, children's health histories, attendance data, court orders, Individual Education Program (IEP) records, observation records, assessments, test results, conference notes, and other information may be included in children's files.

More commonly, cooperating teachers or directors will informally alert you to the special needs or circumstances, prohibitions, health-related conditions, and the individual particulars of attending children: in other words, everything you need to know.

allergies—physiological reactions to environmental or food substances that can affect or alter behavior.

Emergency Procedures

Acquaint yourself with the location and use of first aid supplies. For emergencies such as fire and earthquake, familiarize yourself with procedures and evacuation plans showing exit routes and evacuation areas. Most states require that plans be posted. Enforce all classroom health and safety rules. If you have any questions regarding health and safety, be sure to note them for discussion.

Opening

Be aware of how children and parents are greeted on arrival. What room activities or choices are available for child exploration at arrival time? A keen observer will notice which children separate and make the transition from parent to center with ease, and which classroom adults contribute to the classroom's welcoming atmosphere or tone.

Dismissal Procedures

Be aware that each center or school has a policy regarding adults who can remove a child from the classroom at a session's close or at any other time. You should not release children to arriving adults. This is your cooperating teacher's responsibility. In most schools, adults coming to pick up children are directed to talk with the child's teacher before exiting. Because of security concerns, people authorized to pick up children may have to have special badges or security cards.

In today's society, some families may consist of a variety of related or unrelated individuals and children. Because of problems that exist between single or divorced parents or other family factors, court-issued restraining orders can affect who is authorized to pick up a child.

Knowing the Program Well

Cooperating teachers overwhelmingly state that they appreciate student teachers who are watchful and learn room and program particulars quickly. This is difficult for new student teachers unless they consciously endeavor to discover the lay of the land. Figure 1–12 attempts to help you focus on aspects of the classroom, program, procedures, and interactions with children.

Facilities

Where are materials and supplies stored?

Are storage areas organized?

Where are exits? How do windows open, lights work, temperature controls operate?

How do doors open?

What is the classroom layout? Traffic patterns?

What school area or rooms have specific functions? House particular staff?

What is the play yard's appearance, equipment, built-ins?

Where are the safety controls, fire extinguisher, alarm, etc.?

Is any safety hazard apparent?

Are there special building features for individuals with special needs?

Where are emergency health supplies? Who is authorized to administer first aid?

Children

What individual physical characteristics are apparent?

What is the multicultural composition of the group?

What activities are popular?

Can all children in the room be viewed from one spot in the room?

Do all children seem to lose themselves in play?

What kinds of play exist? Solitary? Cooperative? Other?

What languages are spoken?

Does any child seem uncomfortable with adults?

What seems to be the group's general interest, general behavior?

Are there any children who need an abundance of teacher attention?

Are there any children with special needs?

Teaching Behaviors and Interactions

Are children "with" teachers?

How is guidance of child behavior undertaken?

Are all children supervised?

What style of teaching seems apparent?

Are feelings of warmth and acceptance of individuality shown?

If you were a child in this room, how might you feel?

Do teachers show enthusiasm?

Program

Does an atmosphere exist where children and teachers share decision-making and show respect for individual differences?

Are children exploring with teachers more often than being directed by them?

What are the planned activities?

Is there small group or large group instruction?

Is it a developmentally appropriate program?

How do activities begin and end?

Is the program based on child interest?

Does lots of dialogue exist among children? Among children and adults?

Are the children "tuned in" or "out"?

How are children moved from one activity to the next?

Overall First Impressions

What immediate questions would you like answered about the classroom?

What emotions have occurred as you observed?

What were your first impressions of the classroom?

● **Figure 1-12**
Knowing your classroom.

Pitfalls

During the first days of work, it is not unusual for the student teacher to acquire some bad habits unconsciously. It helps to be aware of these pitfalls in advance. During class time, avoid having extended social conversations or small talk with other adults. This can happen when a student teacher seeks the company of other adults as a source of support. Use your breaks for this purpose if necessary.

Refrain from talking about children to other adults in the child's presence. Avoid the tendency to label children; keep your judgments and evaluations to yourself and save questions for staff meetings.

THE EARLY DAYS

Your first few days are going to be both exciting and exhausting. Many factors contribute to this. The comments that follow, although dated, are still relevant today:

> The induction of the student into actual teaching is a delicate and critical process. Unfortunately, no procedure exists that would guarantee universal success because many uncontrollable factors must be considered. The attitude of the student, the classroom climate, the inclination of the cooperating teacher, and the time of year are but a few of the many factors. (Kraft & Casey, 1967.)

First impressions are important. Show initiative, be alert to the total classroom, listen closely, and try to be self-directed, and if the situation calls for it, take action. Your natural enthusiasm and life-is-an-adventure attitude will be catching. Display your caring nature and positive attitude toward child accomplishment. Smile and make eye contact with children frequently.

After-Session Conferencing

At team meetings, after the critical issues have been discussed, the cooperating teacher and other staff will be interested in the questions and impressions you have gathered. Be prepared to rely on your notes or journal; they are useful in refreshing your memory. Think of team conferences as debriefings, where participants compare ideas, hypothesize, reflect, and make assumptions calling for the cognitive processing of information.

This meeting is also an appropriate time to clarify your cooperating teacher's expectations during your next few workdays. If a class calendar and weekly activity sheet are available these will aid your activity planning. (Samples of these are found in the Appendix.) Most schools have their own system for planning activities. You may be asked to schedule your own activities at least a week in advance, on a written plan. The cooperating teacher may want you to stay within the planned subject areas or may give you a wide choice.

BECOMING A TEAM MEMBER

You will become aware of each staff member's function and contribution to the operation of your assigned classroom. Support staff efforts may be connected to the realization of the center's goals (see Figure 1–13).

Do the following staff members exist at your placement center?

	Yes	No	Names
1. Clerical staff	_____	_____	_____
			_____
2. Food service personnel	_____	_____	_____
			_____
3. Maintenance staff	_____	_____	_____
			_____
4. Bus drivers	_____	_____	_____
			_____
5. Community liaisons	_____	_____	_____
			_____
6. Health or nutrition staff	_____	_____	_____
			_____
7. Consultants or specialists	_____	_____	_____
			_____
8. Classroom aides	_____	_____	_____
			_____
9. Volunteers	_____	_____	_____
			_____
10. Others	_____	_____	_____
			_____

In what capacity? _____

● **Figure 1-13**
Checklist of non-teaching support staff.

In addition to your own growth and development, one of your major goals as a team member is to add to the quality of young children's experiences. This involves teamwork. Teamwork takes understanding, dedication, and skill. Your status and acceptance as a member of the team will be gained through your own efforts.

For purposes of this field of study, **team teaching** involves and includes those people employed or connected to the daily operation of an early childhood center who work to achieve the goals of that center. They include paid and volunteer staff and parents. Understanding the duties and responsibilities of each team member will help you function in your role.

GOALS OF THE TEAM AND PROGRAM

Joint planning with your cooperating teacher is crucial to your success and competency growth. The team spirit is enhanced when your efforts reinforce or strengthen the efforts of other members.

Inadvertently, and unfortunately, some student teachers may tend to emphasize what they feel is the superiority of their college's training and its laboratory center. Teaching methods, materials, furnishings, supplies, staffing patterns, and just about every school feature may differ from what was experienced in the college's training program. It may take a while for the student to realize that community programs have fewer resources, tighter budgets, and perhaps less expertise. Sensitivity is necessary, along with an open mind. It is commendable to be enthusiastic and idealistic, but also to appreciate the cleverness and ingenuity many developmentally appropriate centers display while operating on limited funding and resources.

Team Meetings

Team meetings often include only the staff members associated with child instruction. Because staff meetings are new to student teachers, they are full of learning opportunities. Attend staff meetings if your student teaching schedule permits; the extra time involved will be well spent.

To make these meetings as successful as possible, and to make them work for you, there are several things you can do before, during, and after the meeting. Before a meeting, mark your calendar and obtain an agenda, if it exists. Study it and jot down any questions or notes, and try to identify the meeting's purpose. Arrive on time for meetings and stay for the whole thing if possible. Bring writing materials. During the meeting, record comments concerning your classroom work. At first, participate as a listener until you discern if contributing is appropriate. Watch and learn from staff interactions. Notice that team members help others reach their individual objectives. Take note if another expresses an individual preference in teaching tasks.

After the meeting, mark your calendar with future meeting dates, including times and places. Complete any tasks assigned, and be prepared to discuss these if asked.

The more understanding you possess concerning individual and group dynamics, the better prepared you will be to function as an effective team member. As you become a part of the group, it is highly likely that your initial thoughts and feelings will change.

Ask yourself the following questions:

- Do common bonds exist?
- Was satisfaction of individual needs apparent?
- Is there shared responsibility in achieving group goals?

team teaching—an approach that involves co-teaching, in which status and responsibility are equal rather than having a pyramid structure of authority, with one person in charge and others subordinate.

- Was group problem solving working?
- Are members open and trusting?
- Are individual roles clear?
- Did you notice cooperation?
- Do members know each others' strengths?
- Was the meeting dominated by one or a few?

Staff Behaviors

A number of behaviors may be exhibited during staff interactions. Some of these can be evaluated as positive team behaviors, because they move a team toward the completion of tasks and the handling of responsibilities. The following is a summary of supportive and positive staff behaviors:

- giving or seeking information; asking for or providing factual or substantiated data
- contributing new ideas, solutions, or alternatives
- seeking or offering opinions to solve the task or problem
- piggybacking, elaborating, or stretching another's idea or suggestion; combining ideas
- coordinating activities
- emphasizing or reminding the group of the task at hand
- evaluating by using professional standards
- motivating staff to reach decisions
- bringing meeting to a close and reviewing goals; making sure everyone understands the expected outcome
- recording group ideas and progress

During staff meetings, individual staff members sometimes exhibit attitudes and sensitivities that soothe and mediate opposing points of view. Some examples follow:

- encouraging, praising, respecting, and accepting diverse ideas or viewpoints
- reconciling disagreements and offering a light touch of humor to help relieve tension
- compromising
- establishing open lines of communication
- drawing input from silent members
- monitoring dominance of discussions

Student teachers increasingly find that teaching teams contain differing cultural viewpoints. In situations where communicating across cultures takes place, Delpit (1995) suggests careful listening to alternative viewpoints.

> To do so requires a very special kind of listening, listening that requires not only open eyes and ears, but open hearts and minds. We really do not see through our eyes or hear through our ears, but through our beliefs. To put our beliefs on hold is to cease to exist as ourselves for a moment— and that is not easy, but it is the only way to learn what it might feel like to be someone else and the only way to start the dialogue.

As a student teacher, you may have a clearer picture of the student teacher/cooperating teacher relationship than you do of your professional relationship with the assistant teacher, aide, or parent. Usually, student teachers, aides, and volunteers work under the direction of a cooperating teacher who makes the ultimate decisions regarding the workings of the classroom. Moving from assistant to fellow teacher, a student teacher assumes greater responsibility as time passes. Because of the changing role and increasing responsibilities, clear communication is a necessity. When one becomes an employed teacher, one becomes legally responsible for the direction of other adults in the classroom. This is a form of protection for enrolled children.

Continuing to Observe

You will observe the unique characteristics of enrolled children, constantly monitor their behaviors, and conjecture causes for behaviors and their underlying needs (see Figure 1–14). Unconsciously or consciously, you will begin to sort children into loose groupings that may change daily, in an almost unlimited number of ways. More noticeable characteristics will be the first to be recognized, but as you gain additional experience, subtle differences and similarities will also appear.

You will experience differing emotions with each child as you observe and interact with children in the class. Many of the children will become memorable, as children in your first class, the ones who taught you something about all children, or something about yourself.

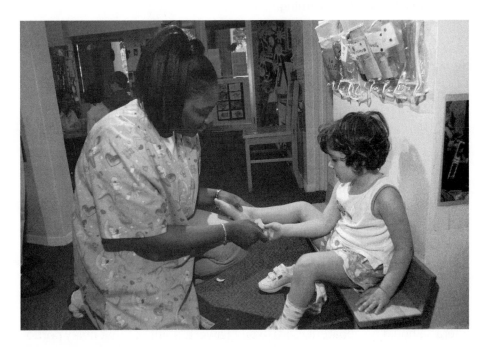

◉ **Figure 1-14**
You will come to know each child as an individual.

Family Contacts

Upon first meeting parents and family members, they may wonder who you are or immediately accept you as another adult classroom worker. Read their faces and introduce yourself if they seem interested. Be friendly and open rather than talkative. Mention your student teacher status and your training program. Remember, in this meeting as in all others you are representing the early childhood teaching profession.

Every classroom has a *feeling tone*; that is, it projects a certain atmosphere that creates feelings and perceptions in the minds and hearts of those who enter. Your classroom, no doubt, was designed and furnished with children in mind, but possibly includes a parent corner, or an area making parents also feel welcome.

In today's busy world, some families will look rushed and anxious to get their child out the door. Others you observe will take time to touch base with their child and teachers before leaving. All parents will appreciate your knowing the location of their child's belongings and what needs to be taken home, and also your aid in promoting the child's transition back into parental care. Activities planned for parent pick-up times should allow children to easily stop and finish.

Professional Portfolio Development

professional portfolio—
a representative collection of your student teacher accomplishments.

You may be required to put together a representative collection of your training accomplishments, called a **professional portfolio**. Wolf and Dietz (1998) define a teaching portfolio as follows:

> A teaching portfolio is a structured collection of teacher and student work created across diverse contexts over time, framed by reflection and collaboration that has as its ultimate aim the advancement of teacher and student learning.

A student teacher portfolio is not a miscellaneous collection but rather selected items, records, and documentation of student teacher growth, progress toward goals, and attainment of professional standards. It represents a student teacher's accomplishments and teaching effectiveness. Wade and Yarbrough (1996) note that training programs hope developing a portfolio will help student teachers become more reflective and therefore will improve their classroom practice. Other advantages can be the recognition of a student teacher's past performance compared to present skills and identified future growth areas. Input and interactions with college supervisors and cooperating teachers are sometimes included in a portfolio.

The portfolio represents who you are, what skills and competencies you possess, and what experiences occurred during your training. The majority of teacher training programs require students to develop a portfolio before graduation.

Caruso and Fawcett (1999) advise that an examination of portfolio materials should enable a supervisor, staff member, or peer to raise questions and draw inferences about the portfolio's owner. The owner's assumptions of how young children learn, what the educator values, how children should spend their time, and the ways in which the educator and children should interact should be apparent. Caruso and Fawcett point out that bulky portfolios can be too time consuming if the reader tries to evaluate their contents, so select and organize material to emphasize quality, not quantity.

A portfolio may also include before and after features, or may display specialized student talents and abilities. It can include a vast number of diverse visual, audio, electronic, and written materials such as:

- a statement of educational philosophy or mission.
- supervisory comments, observations, evaluations, or ratings.
- letters of recommendation from supervisors, instructors, mentors, fellow staff members, parents, and others.
- thematic units of study, projects, or activities.
- examples of child work and case studies.
- photographs of such things as developed room centers, and so on.
- sample lesson plans and outcomes.
- examples of developing specializations.
- certificates for CPR or first aid, awards, and other commendations.
- examples of individualized instruction and individual learning plans.
- conference attendance documentation or other professional activities.
- accreditation activities.
- examples of self-created classroom instructional materials.
- college transcripts and certification test results.
- any items that display teaching ability or competency.

The formatting of portfolios differs from one institution to another, but written materials usually include *articulation of learning outcomes*, *reflections* or related experience, and *documentation*.

The state of New Mexico, like many other states, has developed portfolio guidelines for certificate, associate, and bachelor's degree programs. Guidelines specify elements to be included and completed. These elements are reviewed by peers, faculty, and community representatives at the time of the student's exit from a training program (Turner, 2002). This type of portfolio may differ from the one your area or supervisor requires. (To review characteristics of a sample portfolio according to New Mexico's guidelines, see the Appendix.) Note that training instructors can attempt to evaluate the efficacy of instruction in offered courses, and the training program as a whole, using New Mexico's student portfolio elements. You may be able to compare your state's portfolio requirements to other states by logging on to your state education department's Web site.

The purpose for having a student teacher create a portfolio can be manifold, as in the case of New Mexico's portfolios. Some training programs review portfolios at college exit interviews, and also suggest their student graduates use them when appropriate during job interviews. Most often a portfolio is used to facilitate, highlight, and chart student teaching competency, ongoing growth, and a student's ability to use accepted, current, and professional learning theories and actually apply them in daily practice. Jones and Shelton (2006) cite another purpose they call *showcasing*. A showcase portfolio is displayed in exhibits and presentations to a professional community, including prospective employers. Jones and Shelton explain, as follows:

> We use this type of portfolio in the child development degree
> completion option at our university. At their exhibition celebration,
> program graduates display their showcase portfolios, which highlight

their learning and accomplishments as evidenced by specific work products. They share these accomplishments and products with their peers, instructors, families, and with the larger early care and education community.

Some training programs require student teachers to document how they have accomplished the five NAEYC performance standards. Documentation can include artifacts, visuals, writings or other evidence. Often finalized student portfolios are reviewed by a panel of educators who judge a student's acceptability, grade, and determine the panel's recommendation or rejection. Electronic portfolios require technological expertise and have advantages not found in print portfolios. Jones and Shelton mention the following:

> On the opportunity side, e-portfolios are compact, easy to store and distribute, and inexpensive to duplicate. The hyperlink feature common to e-portfolios makes navigating through them quite easy and efficient.
>
> [And] their nonlinear structure means support documentation can be virtually attached where appropriate, without comprising the overall continuity and flow of the document.

Getting Organized

Suggestions for managing the multiple tasks and projects assigned in student teaching follow:

- Plan one week in advance.
- Color-code project folders.
- Decide what is (1) important and urgent, (2) important but not urgent, (3) not important but necessary, and (4) not important and not urgent.
- Work on only one thing at a time.
- Narrow focus by working on parts of a task.
- Gather resources and bring tasks to closure.

● SUMMARY

The practicum teaching experience is a culminating step in a training sequence for early childhood teachers. Three key participants—the student teacher, the cooperating teacher, and the supervisor—form a team, enabling the student teacher to gain new skills and sharpen previously acquired teaching techniques.

Student teaching involves the integration of all former training and experience. The cooperating teacher and supervisor guide, model, mentor, observe, collaborate, and analyze the student teacher's progress in an assigned classroom as the student teacher assumes greater responsibilities with children. Initial orientation meetings, and written requirements and guidelines, acquaint the

student teacher with expectations and requirements. The student teaching experience is unique to each training institution, yet placement in a classroom for a supervisor's analysis of professional competency is common to all.

A caring, supportive atmosphere helps each student teacher attain professional educator skills, based on accepted ethics and standards, and helps develop the student teacher's personal style and philosophy.

It is a good idea to get an understanding of the children's environment by acquainting yourself with their home neighborhood and community.

Active classroom interaction, as well as asking questions, should typify your first days. You can obtain necessary information concerning your work from the cooperating teacher when you both have no supervision responsibilities.

In time, you will develop smooth working relationships and earn team status and acceptance with other staff members. Meetings are important vehicles for learning, and they will be a part of your future employment. You will study to understand how each staff or team member contributes to the goals of your assigned classroom through observation and interaction.

HELPFUL WEB SITES

http://www.childrensfoundation.net
The Children's Foundation. This site offers publications, including the *2001 Child Care Licensing Study.*

http://nccic.org
National Child Care Information Center. This resource provides links to other sites, and information promoting high-quality care is available.

http://www.nncc.org
National Network for Child Care. Search for items of interest.

http://ericeece.org
ERIC Clearinghouse on Elementary and Early Childhood Education. This site is best known for its information, research, and publications.

http://www.aft.org
American Federation of Teachers. A national teacher's union web site that gives voice to professional concerns.

http://nbcdi.org
National Black Child Development Institute. A critical web site resource for information that improves the quality of life for African American children.

http://www.nea.org
National Education Association. A special membership category exists for college students.

 Additional resources for this chapter can be found by visiting the Online Companion at www.earlychilded.delmar.com.

SUGGESTED ACTIVITIES

A. Read the following early childhood center's philosophy statement. Which ideas or phrases do you feel are important? Discuss with the class how this description relates to centers or schools where you have observed or have been employed.

Philosophy for a Children's Center or Classroom

An early childhood center is an environment where professional trust exists, and adults and children grow emotionally, intellectually, socially and physically as they interact and participate. All people involved in center operations and functions are viewed and treated as possible learners who may have diverse learning styles.

It is believed that what the young child encounters and experiences promotes their learning. An early childhood center is a place where both children and adults become aware of themselves through their relationship with others in the classroom environment. It is also a place full of human feelings that are accepted and valued. A center should provide opportunities to wonder, question, explore, succeed, celebrate life, and ponder meanings and discoveries. It recognizes ethnic, cultural, economic, and social similarities and differences, and believes each individual possesses talents, gifts, and abilities. It promotes the sharing of self.

In a supportive environment each person is accorded worth, and is respected. Individuals learn and know their rights and accept the rights of others without causing harm to self or others. It is believed that growth occurs at an individual pace as individuals follow their own destiny and design.

B. If you were to describe yourself using a self-designed logo or a popular song title, what would it be? As you enter this student teaching experience, try to describe briefly who you are, what you do, and any individual unique teaching perspectives or life experiences you might hold. Share with a classmate.

C. Use Figure 1–15 as the basis for an early portfolio or journal entry, or create a guide to daily teaching responsibilities similar to Figure 1–16. If you choose the first task, give it a heading such as "First Practicum Week Observations."

D. Obtain a copy of your placement school's disaster plan. Bring it to class to discuss.

1. Make a rough map of your classroom and yard.
2. Briefly describe the child group. Identify children about whom you would like additional information.
3. List names of staff members.
4. Describe your relationship with your cooperating teacher during your first days.
5. Describe available materials and equipment. Do you feel they are adequate and satisfactory in all aspects?
6. What are some memorable experiences of your first days?

Figure 1-15
Placement observation form.

THREE-YEAR-OLDS—MORNING PROGRAM

8:00–8:30   Check to see that room is in order and materials are on proper shelves. Check snack supplies. Check day's curriculum. Know what materials are needed.

8:30–8:45   **Arrival of Children**
- Greet each child and parent.
- Help children locate their lockers.
- Help children with name tags.
- Help children initiate an activity.

8:30–9:20   **Free-play Time Inside**—Art, block play, dramatic play, manipulative materials, science, math, housekeeping area, language arts.
- Supervise assigned area. Proceed to another area if there is no child in your area.
- Interact with children if you can. Be careful not to interfere in their play.
- Encourage children to clean up after they finish playing with materials.
- Manipulative materials, including modeling dough and scissors, stay on the table.
- Be on the child's level. Sit on the floor or on a chair, or kneel.
- Children wear smocks when using paint or chalk. Print children's names on their art work in upper left corner.
- Give five-minute warning before clean-up time.   continues

Figure 1-16
Guide to daily teaching responsibilities.

9:20–9:30 **Transition Time**—Clean up, wash hands, use bathrooms. Help with clean-up. Guide children to bathroom before coming to group. All children should use the bathroom to wash hands and be encouraged to use the toilet.

- Place soiled clothes/underpants in plastic baggies and place them in children's cubbies.
- Children flush the toilet.
- Let them wash hands, using soap.
- Bathroom accidents should be treated matter-of-factly.
- Use word "toilet."
- Help children with their clothes but remember to encourage self-help skills.

9:30–9:45 **Large Group**—Assist restless children. Leave to set up snack if it is your responsibility. Put cups and napkins around table. Make sure there are sufficient chairs and snack places.

- Teacher of the week leads group time.
- Show enthusiasm in participating with the activities.

9:45–10:00 **Snack**

- There should be one teacher at each table.
- Engage in conversation.
- Encourage self-help skills. Provide assistance if needed.
- Encourage children to taste food.
- Demonstrate good manners such as saying please and thank you.
- Help children observe table manners.
- Children should throw napkins in trash can.
- If spills occur, offer a sponge. Help only if necessary.
- Quickly sponge down tables.

10:00–10:45 **Outside Play**—Check children and cubbies to make sure children are wearing outside clothing if the weather is cold. If a child does not have sufficient clothing, check the school supply of extra clothing.

Outside Activities—Tricycles, sand toys, climbing equipment, balls, and so on.

- Supervise all areas. Spread out.
- Help children share toys and take care of the equipment.
- Always be alert to the physical safety of the children.
- When necessary, remind them that sand is to be kept in the sandbox.
- Water faucet is operated only by adults or when there is adult supervision.
- Children may remove shoes during warm weather only.
- If raining, children stay under shelter.
- Teachers should refrain from having long conversations with each other. Attention should be on the children all the time.
- Bring tissue outside to wipe noses if needed.
- Give five-minute warning to clean up and go inside.
- Children must help return toys to the storage room.   *continues*

● **Figure 1-16** (continued)

10:45–11:00	**Clean up, Use Bathroom, Prepare for Small Group**
	• Children go to assigned small groups.
	• Each child sits on a carpet square.
11:00–11:20	**Small Group**—Transitional activities include flannelboard stories, discussion with visual aids, games, filmstrip if applicable, songs, and fingerplays. Teacher puts children's rest mats out.
11:20–11:30	**Rest Time**
	• Children lie on mats.
	• Quiet music is played.
	• Children do not bother other children. Whisper to restless children and tell them it is a quiet time.
	• Children fold blankets, rugs, or mats and put them in their cubbies.
11:30	**Departure**
	• Get children's artwork to take home and put in their cubbies.
	• Help children with coats, shoes, etc.
	• See children off.
11:30–12:00	**End-of-Morning Session**—Help with clean-up. Double check that all areas are clean and all materials are in their correct places. Share any observations with teachers, and solicit their observations and feelings during your team meeting.

NOTE: This daily guide is typical of guides used in a morning prekindergarten laboratory school placement for student teachers. A similar guide can be developed for any placement site by a student teacher once room schedules are known.

● **Figure 1-16** (continued)

○REVIEW

A. Select the answer that best completes each statement.

1. Student teaching practices and procedures are:
   a. very similar when one compares different teacher training programs.
   b. as different as pebbles in a pile.
   c. uniform and dictated by state law.
   d. different at training institutions and agencies but always involve five key individuals.

2. The individual who is supposed to gain the most new skills through student teaching is:
   a. the student teacher, but the cooperating teacher's and supervisor's new skills may surpass the student's skills.
   b. the child.
   c. the supervisor, who has learned each student teacher's unique way of performing duties.
   d. the reader of this text.
   e. impossible to determine.

3. Being observed and analyzed during student teaching means:
   a. being watched and criticized.
   b. self-evaluation and evaluation of others will take place.
   c. others will try to pinpoint the areas where the student teacher needs to sharpen skills.
   d. parents, directors, and all members of the adult team will evaluate student competency.
   e. children's behavior will determine ratings of student teacher competency.

4. In most states, the record that must be completed before the student teacher works with children is the student teacher's:
   a. health history.
   b. personal history.
   c. bonding agreement.
   d. insurance clearance.
   e. TB clearance.
5. Professional conduct can mean:
   a. insisting that a child say "please" and "thank you."
   b. dressing appropriately with attention to personal hygiene.
   c. speaking candidly to a parent about the limitations of a cooperating teacher's method.
   d. none of these.

B. List four considerations in preparing for your first day as a student teacher.

C. Describe two activities you might plan for your first day as a student teacher. List two reasons you selected these activities.

D. Read "Getting the Most out of Student Teaching" (Figure 1–17). Write a one-minute summary of the items that you feel will be the most difficult, and also the easiest, to follow.

1. Examine your attitude and decide you are going to expend every effort to learn new skills. Risk trying new ways and making mistakes. Communicate your desire to be given added and more challenging responsibilities. Welcome and encourage feedback from those supervising you.

2. When in doubt, ask questions. Select the time and place most convenient for your supervisors or write questions down for them if conferencing is immediately impossible. Be willing to come early or stay late if necessary.

3. Being professional involves a timely arrival and telephone calls when you need to be late or absent. Inform your college supervisor of field trips, testing, or special events when her observation of your work would not be possible. Your dress, personal appearance, and manner represent your professional image.

4. Make decisions using your best judgment. Seek clarification if you are uncertain of rules or expectations.

5. Realize the cooperating teacher's first priority is the needs, safety, and welfare of children. You are an added responsibility. Be aware there are times when the cooperating teacher cannot focus on you or your concerns.

6. See what needs to be done and do it without waiting for directions. Observe and study the children, program, and environment. Familiarize yourself with all aspects of the situation. Know where equipment and materials are stored. Be alert to daily schedules and routines.

7. See yourself as a needed assistant being increasingly responsible and alert to where you are most necessary.

8. Be friendly, learn names, and fit into classroom life quickly by being helpful and sensitive to school staff members.

9. Watch teacher skills, techniques, and behaviors with children and parents. Try to identify the goals of instruction behind words and actions.

10. Avoid socializing with other adults during work periods and instead be watchful, observant, and ready to learn from children and classroom situations. Scan the area, develop "eyes in the back of your head." When sitting, choose positions that allow the best classroom views.

11. Remain nonjudgmental when site politics are present. Try to inwardly evaluate staff conflicts. Discuss with your college supervisor your position as a "fence sitter" who avoids taking sides if a difficult situation or power struggles between adults arise.

12. When viewing new techniques or methods, remain open-minded and reflective. If ethics are involved, ask for a college supervisor consultation quickly.

13. Receive input from supervisors with the belief that both compliments and suggestions for growth will enable you to become a more skilled and valuable early childhood educator.

Figure 1-17
Getting the most out of your student teaching.

CASE SCENARIO

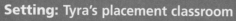

Setting: Tyra's placement classroom

Tyra's worst fears faced her on the first day in her student teacher placement classroom. Talk about feeling like an outsider—there wasn't one child who spoke English well. The children were friendly enough, and only a few children stared at the color of her skin. Tyra understood about half of what the children said to her. A few children seemed really out of control and ignored what she said to guide them. The cooperating teacher was welcoming but so busy she had little time to interact with Tyra. Things improved slightly as the school day progressed because Mrs. Solorozano, the teacher's aide, interpreted what the children said and explained classroom routines and procedures when Tyra had a question. Tyra felt this classroom would be a great learning opportunity, even if she felt uncomfortable at times.

She planned an activity for later in the month that involved making a large collage of families after she shared some large photographs of her own family, the family of her cooperating teacher, and Mrs. Solorozano's family. Of course, she would have to obtain their permission. She wanted a variety of ethnic representations, so she planned to obtain pages torn from magazines, with photographs and pictures for the children to cut out. She would urge children to bring photographs or make drawings of their own families to add to the collage. She felt a class discussion of the finished collage could highlight diversity and similarities, and decided to discuss her plan with her cooperating teacher.

Questions for Discussion:

1. According to the chapter, something evidently did not take place or did not prepare Tyra for her first day. What could have helped prepare her?

2. Should Tyra consult her college supervisor quickly or perhaps wait and see if things improve?

3. Could seeking her college supervisor's help make the supervisor suspect Tyra was not ready for student teaching?

REFERENCES

Caruso, J. J., & Fawcett, M. T. (1999). *Supervision in early education: A developmental perspective.* New York: Teachers College Press.

Delpit, L. (1995). *Other people's children: Cultural conflict in the classroom.* New York: The New Press.

Feeney, S., & Freeman, N. (2005). *Ethics and the early childhood educator: Using the NAEYC code.* Washington, DC: National Association for the Education of Young Children.

Freeman, N. K. (2004, November). Exploring the ethical dimensions of the early childhood profession. *Young Children, 59*(6),10–11.

Hillman, C. B. (2006). *Mentoring early childhood educators: A handbook for supervisors, administrators and teachers.* Portsmouth, NH: Heinemann.

Hollingsworth, S. (1998, Fall). Making field-based programs work: A three-level approach to reading education. *Journal of Teacher Education,* 39, 46-57.

Hyson, M. (Ed.). (2003). *Preparing early childhood professionals: NAEYC's standards for programs.* Washington, DC: National Association for the Education of Young Children.

Hyson, M. (2005, November). Enthusiastic and engaged: Strengthening young children's positive approaches to learning. *Young Children, 60*(6),68–70.

Jones, M., and Shelton, M. (2006). *Developing your portfolio: Enhancing your learning and showing your stuff.* New York: Routledge.

Justen, J. E., and McJunkin, M. (1999). Supervisory beliefs of cooperating teachers. In M.Scherer (Ed.). *A better beginning: Supporting and mentoring new teachers* (173–180). Alexandria, VA: Association for Supervision and Curriculum.

Katz, L., & Ward, E. (1978). *Ethical behavior in early childhood education* Washington, DC: National Association for the Education of Young Children.

Kraft, L., & Casey, J. R. (1967). *Roles in off-campus student teaching.* Champaign, IL: Stipes.

Machado, J. M., & Reynolds, R. E. (2006). *Employment opportunities in education: How to secure your career.* Clifton Park, NY: Delmar Learning.

National Association for the Education of Young Children, National Association of Early Childhood Teacher Educators, and The American Associate Degree Early Childhood Teacher Educators (2004). *Code of ethical conduct: Supplement for early childhood adult educators.* A joint position statement, retrieved February 6, 2005, from http://www.naeyc.org.

Schriver, A. K. (1999). I am so excited! Mentoring the student teacher. In M. Scherer (Ed.). *A better beginning: Supporting and mentoring new teachers* (77–84). Alexandria, VA: Association for Supervision and Curriculum.

Turner, P. (Ed.). (2002). *La ristra: New Mexico's comprehensive professional development system in early care, education and family support.* Santa Fe, NM: Office of Child Development, Youth and Families Department.

VanderVen, K. (1988). Pathways to professionalism, In B. Spodek, O. Saracho, & D. Peters (Eds.). *Professionalism and the early childhood educator* (37–160). New York: Columbia University Press.

Wade, R., & Yarbrough, D. (1996, Spring). Portfolios: A tool for reflective thinking in teacher education. *Teaching and Teacher Education, 12,* 72–88.

Whitmire, R. (2000, May). Survey: New teachers love jobs, feel unprepared. *Idaho Statesman,* 10A.

Wolf, K., & Dietz, M. (1998, Winter). Teaching portfolios: Purpose and possibilities. *Teachers Education Quarterly, 25*(1).

CHAPTER 2

A Student Teacher's Values and Developing Teaching Style

OBJECTIVES **After reading this chapter, you should be able to:**

1.... Define the role of personal values in teaching.
2.... Describe how values influence what happens in the classroom.
3.... Describe how activities you enjoy reflect personal values.
4.... List at least five values that guide a student teacher's lessons and activities.
5.... Identify at least two different teaching styles.
6.... Define and describe your own teaching style.
7.... Discuss the relationship between a philosophy of education and a teaching style.

Comments of student teachers:

> *I've learned that I am a rather biased person rather than the enlightened minority group member I thought I was. Understanding and accepting this was my first step toward change. I've had to analyze the origins of my attitudes.*

Felecia Arii

> *My cooperating teacher had very definite attitudes concerning the celebration of Halloween. When she explained how she felt, I had a new view. Now I'm feeling it's good to question if some traditional celebrations add to the quality of children's lives.*

Mannington Lee

> *I like a well-organized, tidy classroom. My cooperating teacher likes the three-ring circus approach to classroom activity, which offers plenty of child choices. I suspect my supervisor chose to place me here to broaden my horizons, to "loosen me up" so to speak, and it's happening. I can tolerate clutter and minor confusion better.*

Bobbette Ryan

> *I was intimidated watching my cooperating teacher. She was so professional. After a while I realized I had teaching strengths she admired and appreciated. We made a great team. She "zigged," I "zagged," but we pulled together. Our different approaches to the same goals made the classroom livelier. Oh what discussions we had!*

Maeve Critchfield

40

KNOWING YOURSELF AND YOUR VALUES

We will begin this chapter with an exercise. On a separate sheet of folded paper, number the spaces from 1 to 20. Then list, as quickly as possible, your favorite activities. Do this spontaneously; do not pause to think.
Now go back and code your listed activities as follows:

- Mark those activities you do alone with an *A*.
- Mark those activities that involve at least one more person with a *P*.
- Mark with an *R* those activities that may involve risk.
- Mark those in which you are actively doing something with a *D*.
- Mark with an *S* those activities in which you are a spectator.
- Mark activities that cost money with an *M*.
- Mark activities that are free with an *F*.
- Mark with a *Y* any activity you have not done for one year.

Now that you have coded your activities, what have you learned about yourself? Are you more a spectator than a doer? Do you seldom take risks? Did you list more than one activity in which you have not participated for more than one year? Do you frequently spend money on your activities, or do most of your activities cost little or nothing? Were any of your answers a surprise? We hope you learned something new about yourself.

Let us try another exercise. Complete the following sentences as quickly as possible:

1. School is . . .
2. I like . . .
3. Children are . . .
4. Teaching is . . .
5. Girls are . . .
6. I want . . .
7. Children should . . .
8. Boys are . . .
9. Parents are . . .
10. Teachers should . . .
11. I am . . .
12. Fathers are . . .
13. I should . . .
14. Mothers are . . .
15. Teachers are . . .
16. Parents ought to . . .
17. School ought to . . .
18. Aggressive children make me . . .
19. Shy children make me . . .
20. Whiny children make me . . .

Did you find this activity easier or more difficult than the first? This exercise is less structured than the first. You had to shift your thinking from statement to statement. We hope it made you take a thoughtful pause as you were forced to shift your thinking, as verbs changed from simple or declarative to the more complex conditional or obligatory forms. Present-tense forms such as "is" or "are" encourage concrete, factual responses. With the conditional *should* or obligatory *ought*, your response may have become more a reflection of what you feel an ideal should be. In addition, with the present tense, a response is usually short whereas with the conditional or obligatory phrasing, you may have used more words to explain your response.

Look at your answers. Do you find you have different responses depending on whether the present, conditional, or obligatory form of the verb was used? What do these differences tell you about yourself? Van Leuvan (1997) believes an initial step and essential component in the development of reflective processes in teaching is the examination and clarification of one's belief about what constitutes and contributes to effective teaching.

● **Figure 2-1**
Family teachings and traditions influence children who absorb values through observation and imitation.

● **Figure 2-2**
Nurturing young children is one of the appealing aspects of a teaching career.

● THE ACQUISITION OF VALUES

Let us reflect on how we acquire our values. Logically, many of our values reflect those of our parents. As children, we naturally absorbed our first values through observing our parents and family members and through direct parental teaching (see Figure 2–1). Few children are even aware that they are being influenced by their parents; they take in parental attitudes and values through the processes of observation and imitation. We want to be like our fathers and mothers, especially because they appear to have the power over the rewards we receive. Smiles when we do something they approve of, hugs, and "that's right," said over and over, shape our behavior so that we begin to accept what our parents accept. Wedman, Espinosa, and Laffey (1998) point out that a person's beliefs about teaching are well established before entering college.

Why are you attracted to the profession of teaching? Is there a teacher in your family? Does your family place a value on learning? Did you enjoy school yourself? Were your parents supportive of school when you were young? The chances are that you answered positively to at least one of these questions. One reason many people teach professionally is that they truly enjoyed being a student themselves. Learning has been fun and often easy. As a result, an education is highly valued. Teachers frequently come from families in which the profession was valued, not because it pays well but, more likely, for the pleasure received in working with young children and the intangible experience of influencing young lives (see Figure 2–2).

Grant and Murray (1999) suggest:

Teachers of both genders choose teaching for the intrinsic satisfactions and joy of the work. They feel whole and connected and engaged in meaningful work in a way that many in modern society do not. The leading reasons teachers say they chose the profession are that they like to work with children (66 percent), that they like the inherent meaning and value of the job (38 percent), and that they are interested in a specific subject-matter field (36 percent).

Other surveys show that most teachers (87 percent) find their greatest satisfaction in reaching students and knowing they have learned.

Vartuli (2005) notes that teachers beliefs are often implicit and unarticulated, yet, they influence the teacher's perceptions, judgments, and decisions, and direct their actions in many ways. Teachers views of their competencies may determine the amount of effort they expend, their perseverance when confronted with obstacles, their resilience when faced with adversity, their interactions with children, and, consequently, children's educational outcomes.

One problem many teachers face is accepting negative attitudes from parents or caregivers who do not place similar values on education. It is difficult to relate to them. You need to remember that some parents may come from cultures where educational opportunities were denied. In addition, some parents may feel that an education never did them any good; they may be products of education systems that failed them. These parents may not share your values. What can you do? Always show, through your actions—which speak louder than your words—that you care for their children and that you want to help them. Assuming that the parents want the best for their children, and want them to have better opportunities, you can earn the parents' respect and cooperation.

On a separate sheet of paper, judge the following as true or false:

1. Your ethnic background was not an issue when you were a child.
2. Your neighborhood was multicultural.
3. People treated you differently because of your ethnic heritage.
4. You were financially secure most of your childhood.
5. Religion is important in your life.
6. You're proud of your racial group.
7. Life was full of hope rather than despair in childhood.
8. You have been the object of discrimination.
9. Your ethnic group is minimally understood by most Americans.
10. Your identity and sense of self are well formed.

Many of our most enduring values were formed through contact with our family, when we were too young to remember. Others were acquired through repeated experience. Let us use an example. Assume that you were raised in the city and lived in apartment houses your entire life. Because you never had a yard of your own, you have had little experience with plants beyond the potted variety. You are now renting a house with a yard, and you enjoy puttering around in the garden. Because your experiences with gardening have been pleasurable, you have acquired a positive value for it. If your experiences had been bad, you could have acquired a negative value just as easily.

Krathwohl's Hierarchy

One way of looking at the acquisition of values is to look at Krathwohl's taxonomy (1984). Krathwohl and his associates were interested in looking at the *affective domain*, or the field of knowledge associated with feelings and values.

Krathwohl arranged the affective domain into a hierarchy as follows:

1. Receiving (attending)
2. Responding
3. Valuing
4. Organization
5. Characterization by a value or value complex

For you, as a teacher of young children, the first three levels are the most important. Suppose you had not been willing to receive the stimulus of potted plants being a pleasure to see? Being aware of the aesthetics of having plants and enjoying their presence is the first sublevel of receiving; that is, becoming sensitive. Becoming interested in them and enjoying their beauty moves one beyond mere awareness to the next sublevel: willingness to receive. There is a third sublevel of receiving: controlled or selected attention. What does this mean? How is this demonstrated? Looking at potted plants and remarking on their growth, need for water, and flowers are all examples of selected attention.

If you saw that the plant needed water and proceeded to water it, you have moved to the second level of the hierarchy: responding. If you water the plant after being asked to do so, you have reached the first sublevel; acquiescence in responding. If you do it without being asked, you are at the second sublevel; willingness to respond. Noting satisfaction in the growth of the plant because you have been a part of its care moves you into the third sublevel of responding: satisfaction in response.

Valuing, the third level, also has sublevels. The first is acceptance of a value. When you buy your own potted plants, for example, you are revealing a value. You like potted plants enough to buy and care for them. The second sublevel is showing a preference for a value. For example, if you chose to rent a house with a yard instead of an apartment because of the opportunity to work in the yard, you have shown preference for a value. Taking care of the yard then moves you into the third sublevel: commitment. (From Awareness to Action, Project Wild, 1986, Western Regional Environmental Education Council.)

Let us use the hierarchy in another exercise. Write your answers on a separate sheet of paper.

1. What types of awareness do you want your students to have? List those things you want the children to notice. (Examples: books, a terrarium, a piano, puzzles, blocks, and so on.)

2. What types of behaviors do you want your students to develop? Describe the behaviors you hope to see. (Examples: listening to stories, sitting quietly, showing curiosity, sharing.)

3. What do you want students to recognize about classroom procedures? (Examples: the predictability of routines, the bell schedule, when recess comes.)

4. What responses do you want to encourage? (Examples: willingness to answer questions about a story read to them, smiling and laughing at a humorous poem, showing excitement.)

5. What responses do you hope to see that may indicate a student has developed a value? (Examples: asking to take home a book read in class, sharing the book with a friend, bringing a book from home to share.)

We will not continue further with this exercise because you may not know if students have absorbed your stimulus into their value systems until after they move on from your class. For yourself, however, go back over this exercise and ask yourself the following:

1. Why did I choose that particular example as the stimulus I wanted my students to receive and respond to?

2. What does this reveal about my own value system?

3. Is this value a part of *me*, a part of my character?

If you cannot answer these questions, we suggest that you go back and repeat the exercise with another stimulus. For example, your choices may range from some facet of the curriculum, like story time and books, to some facet of behavior, such as paying attention, sharing toys, or not fighting.

YOUR VALUES

Why is it important for you, as a student teacher, to be aware of your values? We hope you already know the answer. In many ways, the answer lies in what Rogers (1966) calls *congruence*. Self-knowledge should precede trying to impart knowledge to others. By looking closely at your values, you will be able to develop a philosophy of teaching more easily. Your particular life stories can be the starting point for reflection and dialogue (Jones, 1994).

Let us move on to another exercise. Take a sheet of 8×11 unlined paper. Divide in half vertically. Then divide in thirds horizontally. In the top left-hand section, draw a picture of what you believe is your best asset. Next to it in the top right-hand section, draw a picture of something you do well. In the middle left-hand section, draw a picture of something you would like to do better. In the middle right-hand section, draw a picture of something you want to change about yourself. In the bottom left-hand section, draw a picture of something that frightens you. In the bottom right-hand section, write five adjectives that you would like other people to use to describe you.

Look at your drawings and think about what your **affective** responses were to this exercise. Did you find it easier to draw a picture of something that frightens you? Was it easier to draw than to list five adjectives? Did you feel more comfortable drawing or writing your responses? What does this say about you? Were you able to write the first two or three adjectives quickly and then forced to give some thought to the remaining two?

affective—caused by or expressing emotion or feeling.

Some of us have more difficulty handling compliments than negative criticism. Some might find it easier to draw a picture of something we do well. Some of us have negative feelings about our ability to draw anything; being asked to do an exercise that asks for a drawn response is a real chore. Did you silently breathe a sigh of relief when you came to the last part of the exercise and were asked for a written response? Does this suggest that you are more comfortable with words than with nonverbal expressions?

If you are more at ease with words, what are the implications regarding any curriculum decisions you might make? Would you be inclined to place a greater emphasis on language activities than on art activities, especially those involving drawing? If you can deal more easily with the negative aspects of yourself than with the positive aspects, what are the implications for your curriculum decisions? Is it possible that you would find it easier to criticize rather than compliment a student? Is it possible that you are inclined to see mistakes rather than improvements? Think about this.

How do the activities you enjoy reflect your personal values and thus influence your classroom curriculum? Go back to the first exercise you completed in this chapter. What were the first five activities you listed? List them on a separate piece of paper. Next to this column, write five related classroom activities. Does your list look something like this?

Activity	Related Curriculum Activity
Playing the piano	Teaching simple songs with piano accompaniment
Jogging	Allowing active children to run around the playground
Skiing	Climbing, jumping, gross motor activities

 ## PERSONAL VALUES AND ACTIVITIES

What is the relationship between activities and personal values? Van Leuvan (1997) believes that teachers who aim to improve their professional practice must recognize not only what they are doing but also must understand the origins and effects of their actions. In this way, they might consider alternative approaches to teaching and learning. It seems obvious that we would not become involved in an activity that did not bring us some reward or pleasure; we have to be motivated (see Figure 2–3). Usually, that motivation becomes intrinsic because significant people in our lives provided an extrinsic reward, usually a smile or compliment. Given enough **feedback** in the form of compliments, we learn to accept and even prize the activity.

Many of us want to teach young children because we genuinely like them. When did we learn this? Some teachers, as the oldest of many siblings, learned to care for and enjoy being with younger brothers and sisters. Others had positive experiences from babysitting. Kennedy (Raths, 2001) asserts that the reasons a person chooses to teach might be a product of his upbringing, a reflection of his life experiences, and a result of the

feedback—information given and deemed to be a true and accurate account of what happened. May be evaluated as positive, negative, or otherwise by the informant or listener.

● **Figure 2-3**
Because she enjoys music, this teacher incorporates musical experiences in her program.

socialization processes of schooling. Nevertheless, we frequently have strong beliefs about the role education can play, about explanations for individual differences in academic performance, about right and wrong in a classroom, and many other areas.

Kennedy states further that these beliefs are used to evaluate new ideas, so that those which square with beliefs are recognized and used, whereas those that challenge beliefs are dismissed (Raths, 2001). Deal and White (2006) point out that students entering a teacher preparation program come with many beliefs, based on their previous experiences. They call these entering beliefs *naïve*. They further assert that reflection, often a part of any teacher preparation program, encourages students to think about their own teaching and may encourage change.

Perhaps we want to teach young children because they are less threatening than older children. What does this say about us? In addition, young children are often more motivated to please the adults in their lives than are teenagers.

Attitudes toward or against something are often formed when we are so young that we do not know their origin. We only know that we have a tendency to like or dislike something or someone. Because these attitudes arouse a strong *affect*, or feeling for or against, they can influence our values. People of different backgrounds who do not share similar ideals often find their values being challenged.

Other student teachers in your class or group will demonstrate individual degrees of teaching experience, background knowledge, teaching skill, and technique. You are urged not to compare what you have to offer children with what you perceive others possess, but rather to stretch and advance in your own directions.

We urge you to be thoughtful, open-minded, and reflective concerning your training experiences, stepping back at times to think or reflect about your conclusions and experiences in child classrooms, and to participate in discussions that clarify and enlighten. This is called **reflective teaching**.

Some college supervisors require student teachers to write personal or life histories and mission statements. They recommend including sections describing experiences as pupils, as scholars preparing for teaching, as members of ethnic and cultural groups, and as members of unique and diverse families.

 ## PROFESSIONAL ETHICS

Katz (1992) defines *ethics* as a set of statements that helps us deal with the temptations inherent in our occupations. **Ethics** may also help us act in concert with what we believe to be right, rather than what is expedient. Making decisions in the best interests of children and their families may take courage and commitment to professional excellence. One may risk losing a job or license, or risk other serious consequences by sticking to one's ethical standards.

How do values impinge on ethics? Obviously, if we value being honest, we might do what we know is right rather than what is expedient. Likewise, if we value creativity as a process, we might protest to teaching in a back-to-basics school that emphasizes children's use of photocopied worksheets to learn reading, writing, and mathematics, with few opportunities for creativity. We might, in fact, choose not to take a position in a school whose values are in opposition to ours.

reflective teaching— a serious effort to thoughtfully question teaching practices, perceptions, actions, feelings, values, cultural biases, and other features associated with the care and education of young children.

ethics—a set of moral principles or values that serves as the basis for conscientious, sound, professional decision making or judgment.

Educators have considerable power over children's daily lives and general welfare, and often are seen as experts by parents. This occupational situation enables teachers to influence lives and impact self-esteem. It also gives them the opportunity to cause short- and long-term damage.

So many situations may test ethics in student teaching. Cecile, a student teacher, faced a situation that unfortunately may not be unique. Cecile's cooperating teacher often made comments about the occupation and community status of the children's parents. It seemed to Cecile that some children received special and more attentive teacher treatment if the cooperating teacher was awed by parents with perceived high status and income. Cecile thought "Who cares if children's parents are doctors, mayors, or lawyers!" After discussing the situation with her college supervisor, she was able tactfully to approach the subject with the cooperating teacher. Cecile decided to risk a retaliatory cooperating teacher evaluation but, as it turned out, that fear was not realized during or at the close of her placement.

Other examples of student teacher dilemmas (encountered by the author's student teachers) include student teachers who:

- saw other student teachers cheating on exams.
- noticed licensing law violations at their placement site.
- accidentally broke, damaged, or lost some type of classroom equipment.
- saw others in an act of theft.
- overheard a teacher lying to a parent.
- received sexist advances from a fellow teacher.
- heard discriminatory classroom comments.

When faced with some dilemmas, you may be able to make an equally strong argument for each of the opposing sides. In other cases, your initial position may be clear, but with further explanation or new information, you may mediate or change your position.

Speaking of the power a teacher exerts over the children they care for, Stephens (1999) notes the following:

> I possess tremendous power to make a child's life miserable or joyous. I can be a tool of torture or an instrument of inspiration. I can humiliate or humor, hurt or heal. In all situations it is my response that decides whether a crisis will be escalated or de-escalated, a child humanized or de-humanized.

Recognizing that ethics apply to the education of adults, as well as to the relationships among teachers, children, parents, and staff, the National Association of Early Childhood Teacher Educators, and the American Associate Degree Early Childhood Teacher Educators (ACCESS), "jointly adopted the *Code of Ethical Conduct: Supplement for Early Childhood Adult Educators. . . .* [D]esigned to be used with the existing Code, [i]t addresses the particular ethical issues faced by those preparing the next generation of early childhood professionals" (Freeman & Feeney, 2004). Ward (1992) would certainly be in agreement, as she insists that "members of a profession monitor themselves."

Figure 2–4 lists a segment of NAEYC's *Code of Ethical Conduct* (revised April 2005), which is concerned with ethical responsibilities to colleagues. (See also a reprint of the entire code in the Appendix.)

SECTION III ETHICAL RESPONSIBILITIES TO COLLEAGUES

In a caring, cooperative workplace, human dignity is respected, professional satisfaction is promoted, and positive relationships are developed and sustained. Based upon our core values, our primary responsibility to colleagues is to establish and maintain settings and relationships that support productive work and meet professional needs. The same ideals that apply to children also apply as we interact with adults in the workplace.

A—Responsibilities to co-workers

Ideals

I-3A.1—To establish and maintain relationships of respect, trust, confidentiality, collaboration, and cooperation with co-workers.

I-3A.2—To share resources with co-workers, collaborating to ensure that the best possible early childhood care and education program is provided.

I-3A.3—To support co-workers in meeting their professional needs and in their professional development.

I-3A.4—To accord co-workers due recognition of professional achievement.

Principles

P-3A.1—We shall recognize the contributions of colleagues to our program and not participate in practices that diminish their reputations or impair their effectiveness in working with children and families.

P-3A.2—When we have concerns about the professional behavior of a co-worker, we shall first let that person know of our concern in a way that shows respect for personal dignity and for the diversity to be found among staff members, and then attempt to resolve the matter collegially and in a confidential manner.

P-3A.3—We shall exercise care in expressing views regarding the personal attributes or professional conduct of co-workers. Statements should be based on firsthand knowledge, not hearsay, and relevant to the interests of children and programs.

P-3A.4—We shall not participate in practices that discriminate against a co-worker because of sex, race, national origin, religious beliefs or other affiliations, age, marital status/family structure, disability, or sexual orientation.

● **Figure 2-4**
Reprinted with permission from the National Association for the Education of Young Children. © Copyright 2005.

When Values Clash

In our diverse society, individual values are bound to clash. Some parents may advocate spanking, others may feel their daughters should not participate in active sports, and a staff member may feel it appropriate to accept an expensive personal gift from a parent. The I–2.4 section of the NAEYC

code bids teachers to respect families' child-rearing values, and their right to make decisions for their children. The P–1.1 code section states:

> Above all, we shall not harm children. We shall not participate in practices that are emotionally damaging, physically harmful, disrespectful, degrading, dangerous, exploitative, or intimidating to children (2005).

The code notes *"this principle has precedence over all others in this Code."* It is clear that when ethical dilemmas arise, teachers are first to consider what is best for the child. If parental values are inflexible, parents can choose to terminate a child's attendance. Centers may be able to propose other, less final, solutions. The center or school has the responsibility to communicate clearly its ethical and professional position to parents and to try, *if possible*, to problem-solve difficulties. Principle 2.2 states, "We shall inform families of program philosophy, policies, curriculum, assessment system, and personnel qualifications, and explain why we teach as we do, which should be in accordance with our ethical responsibilities to children."

Yet it is more often in the differences between a center's or school's values and those of a family where difficulties arise. In a recent article, Luo and Gilliard (2006) explore perceptions by Chinese graduate students of American early childhood education programs, both in preschool and elementary school. They point out some of the critical differences. Chinese students come from a society where children are raised on policies based on Confucian ideals, which emphasize obedience to parents and respect for elders. Education brings honor to the family, and there exists an expectation that children should learn at a very young age. Luo and Gilliard summarize, "Confucianism remains a part of the Chinese social fabric and way of life." So what are teachers in the United States to do? Ideal 2.5 helps: "To respect the dignity and preferences of each family and to make an effort to learn about its structure, culture, language, customs and beliefs."

Remembering principle 2.2, we will respect our differences and explain why we teach as we do. Still, as Luo and Gilliard write, the philosophies of many programs in the United States "tend to have less structural learning and play time with more fluid boundaries between children and teachers. . . .American and Chinese early care and education philosophies are vastly different, as they shape children to be citizens in two very different societies." Tan (2004) also stresses the high value Chinese families place on education. She states, "Chinese parents and Chinese society… equate children's academic achievement with parental success." This may, in part, account for the high achievement of Chinese American students throughout their school years, from preschool to graduate school.

Looking at preschool programs in China, Tang (2006) highlights the difficulties Chinese early childhood teachers experience when they attempt to utilize the project approach in kindergartens in Shanghai. The major barrier comes from the teachers' attitudes toward the children. The traditionally held view is that children are dependent on adults. To accept children as active learners challenged this view. Tang writes, "There is a gap between kindergarten teachers' knowledge about children's learning and applying that knowledge into kindergarten activities. This has led to a gulf between the concept of the child as an active learner and the practice . . . in the kindergarten."

TEACHING STYLE

What is meant by teaching style? It is the vehicle through which a teacher contributes his or her unique quality to the **curriculum**. Much has been written about teaching style, in particular, the phenomenon of teachers modeling themselves after the teachers who influenced them in the past.

Placing a student teacher with a master (cooperating) teacher has its advantages and disadvantages. Most college supervisors try to place student teachers with those cooperating teachers who are willing to allow the student teacher to practice and will provide a positive model. However, there are many excellent teachers who are unwilling to work with student teachers. This is because it takes much energy and time to work with student teachers; they have to be watched, referred to resources, conferenced with, and encouraged. In addition, most colleges and universities do not compensate cooperating teachers in any tangible form for their time and energy. As a result, some student teaching placements may be less than desirable.

Of course, this situation sometimes works out well. A student teacher with experience as a teacher aide may do quite well in a classroom where the cooperating teacher is less than an excellent model, providing little supervision or guidance. In some cases, the student teacher may even act as a positive role model for a mediocre cooperating teacher.

Good cooperating teachers will offer suggestions about different lessons to try. They will introduce the student teachers to all areas of the curriculum, usually one area at a time (see Figure 2–5). Most cooperating teachers will allow a certain amount of time for student teachers to observe and become acquainted with the children. Before the end of the student teaching experience, however, most strong cooperating teachers will expect a student teacher to handle the whole day, and all parts of the curriculum. All student teachers will inevitably borrow or copy their cooperating teachers' styles; this results from having worked so closely together.

Sometimes, though, a cooperating teacher's style is so unique, so much a part of himself, that it is too difficult to copy. We are reminded of a male cooperating teacher who stood 6 feet 4 inches tall and weighed around 240 pounds. Female student teachers had problems using his behavior control techniques; the difference in their sizes precluded the use of physical presence as a guidance tool. One complaint the college supervisor heard regularly was, "Of course Mr. Smith has no problems with control! Look at him!" What many student teachers failed to recognize initially was that Mr. Smith used other techniques as well, such as close **observation** of the classroom, moving toward the source of potential trouble before it erupted, quietly removing a child from a frustrating activity, and firm and consistent application of classroom rules.

A cooperating teacher may be so gifted that a student teacher feels overwhelmed. In this situation, the student teacher should be directed to look at only one facet of the cooperating teacher's expertise at a time. For

curriculum—overall master plan of the early childhood program, reflecting its philosophy, into which specific activities are fit.

observation—the process of learning that comes from watching, noting the behavior of, and imitating models.

Figure 2-5
At first, student teachers will work in areas where they are most comfortable. Later, they will be expected to handle all parts of the curriculum.

example, in focusing on how the teacher begins each day, the student teacher may find a model that is not quite as difficult as the total model appears. It may be that the cooperating teacher takes time each morning to greet each child with a smile and a personal comment.

There are also situations where the cooperating teacher is unable to explain how something is done, like the mathematician who can solve a complex problem without knowing how. Intuitive teachers and those who are very involved have this difficulty; they are unable to explain why they do one thing and not another.

Teaching styles are also an extension of the teacher's self. Rogers and Freiberg (2004) contend that the teacher must know the self before effectively teaching another. This means that you have enough self-knowledge to judge from observing your cooperating teacher what activities and techniques will work for you, which ones you may have to modify, and which ones are best not used. Techniques with which you are truly uncomfortable are best put aside until you can become comfortable with them.

Rogers and Freiberg (2004) emphasize the need for teachers to be *congruent*, *acceptant*, and *empathic*. Being **congruent** means that your actions are a reflection of who you are as a person (see Figure 2–6). Being *acceptant* means that you accept or *prize* (to use another term Rogers and Freiberg employ) each and every one of your students. Every child deserves to be accepted, but it is important to differentiate between acceptance of a child's value as a fellow human being and his behavior, which you may or may not accept. *Empathy* means that you are able to put yourself in the child's place, to understand why she is acting as she is. The Native American expression about withholding judgment until you have walked in another's moccasins relates to having empathy.

Another way of remembering these characteristics is to use the acronym *CARE*. To congruence, acceptance, and empathy we add *reliability*; children need to know that their teachers are reliable, that boundaries exist, and that certain behaviors are acceptable and others are not. Remember, safety for your students rests in your ability to *CARE*.

Cartwright (1999) lists the following characteristics as those which are desirable for early childhood teachers: knowing yourself, or self-awareness; good physical health; integrity; a grounding in theory; a strong background in general knowledge; trust in children; unconditional caring; intuition; detachment; laughter; and the ability to be a model. Do some of these not remind you that *CARE*ing counts?

congruent—refers to the similarity between what a person (the *sender*) is thinking and feeling and what that person communicates; behaving in agreement with or as a reflection of inner feelings and values.

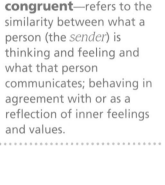 **Figure 2-6**
This obstacle course reflects the teacher's desires to provide her toddlers opportunities to be physically active.

Specific Models of Teaching Style

Miss Noelle is the teacher in a small child development program of 17 children, between the ages of two and a half (toilet trained) and five. The program employs a full-time assistant teacher, Mrs. Quandt—called Mrs. Q by all—and a volunteer, part-time lunch aide, Mrs. Swanson. Mrs. Swanson and her husband are called Grandma and Grandpa by the children, and she often reads stories and he frequently helps with woodworking projects. The program is located in a small house owned by the Swansons, remodeled for use as a child development center. The front door is not used; teachers, volunteers, and families enter through a fence on the side, to a screened back porch with tables and chairs for snacks and lunch (weather permitting) and cubbies for the children along the wall to the house.

The door opens into a large room, remodeled from the former back bedroom and dining area off the old kitchen. This room has shelves with all kinds of toys and puzzles. Blocks are located in a carpeted corner on the left; two double-sided easels are on the right. Cars and trucks can be found on the remaining wall area, neatly arranged on shelves. All shelves are within reach of the children, and the older ones frequently help the younger ones. This room opens into a hall that leads to the front rooms of the house, with a bathroom with child-sized toilets on the left and the kitchen on the right. The kitchen is protected from entry by a cottage door, usually left open at the top.

Miss Noelle's desk and file cabinet can be found in the kitchen. The other door from the kitchen, to what used to be a small dining room, is always closed for safety reasons. In the front, Mr. Swanson has remodeled the front bedroom with a large archway providing access into what is now the dramatic-play center. The former living room is the gathering place for circle time and quiet activities. Two large beanbag chairs can be found in the back corner beside a bookshelf with several picture and picture story books for children to peruse. The front room opens into the former dining room, now used as the discovery center. It houses shelves containing a variety of attractive junk for children to explore and the resident hamster, in his cage.

Miss Noelle has a BA in child development from a local university; Mrs. Quandt is completing her AA in early childhood education from the local community college. Mr. and Mrs. Swanson are retired, she from elementary school, he from a career as a union carpenter.

Miss Noelle's program begins with free play as children enter at irregular times, from 7:30 to 9:00 in the morning; at nine, she gathers the children in the front room for group time. Miss Noelle calls the children by singing a few notes or playing a few chords on her guitar. She uses music to indicate transitions and has taught the children many simple songs. After asking the children what day it is and what the weather is like, Miss Noelle usually reads a story, stopping every so often to ask the children what they think will happen next. Often the story is a familiar one and the children enjoy shouting out the familiar repetitive lines they remember well. Many times the older children will request a book they love; at other times children will bring a book from home for Miss Noelle to read.

After group time, the children are free to go where they wish—to the dramatic-play center, now arranged as a grocery store, or to the discovery room, to see what new materials may be there. Some are intrigued by the change in the celery stalks that were placed in colored water two days ago. Miss Noelle asks them what they think has happened, and asks them to draw a picture of the changes. A few will go to the back room to play with manipulatives, such as cars, trucks, and blocks. Mrs. Q oversees the activities in the back room and Miss Noelle those in the front part of the house. One or two children will choose a favorite book and settle down on one of the beanbag chairs to "read."

After awhile Miss Noelle picks up her guitar to signal the transition to snack time. She reminds the children to use the toilet and wash their hands.

Then the children go to their cubbies, take out their lunch boxes, and sit at the tables on the porch to eat. Mrs. Swanson has poured juice into small pitchers and placed cups on the tables. The older children generally will pour for the younger ones.

After snacks, children are again reminded to use the toilet if they need to and to wash their hands. Then comes free play outside—climbing on the large structure built by Mr. Swanson; playing in the large sand box with many available sand toys to use; riding on the tricycles along a path painted on the driveway, which is protected by a fence and gate. Mrs. Swanson arrives to fix the day's hot lunch and arranges plates, napkins, and cups on the tables on the porch. The children again wash hands and come to the porch to eat. Nap time follows lunch, and free play follows, until children leave. Some leave as early as 3:30, and others depart at various times until the center closes at 5:30.

Miss Noelle sees herself as a model for her children. She rarely raises her voice and usually speaks softly to the children. When there are disagreements between children, she attempts to guide them to a resolution, reminding older children that they are models for their younger peers. Miss Noelle is looking forward to marriage and having children of her own. She and her fiancé enjoy dining out on Friday evenings and occasionally going to a movie on Saturday. They both enjoy music and, when they can afford it, attending concerts.

Further exploration reveals that Miss Noelle is an avid gardener and has several pots of African violets in her apartment. Only a little careless about housekeeping, Miss Noelle knows exactly where anything she needs is located, regardless of the clutter.

It is easy to see that Miss Noelle values all the children in her care. It is also apparent that she is able to empathize with them. She is gentle with those who have experienced a serious loss and refuses to allow an angry child to bait her. In one case when a child tried to kick another and was out of control, Miss Noelle simply picked him up, held him gently on her lap, and spoke soothingly to him until he was calm.

If a student teacher were to ask Miss Noelle about her teaching style, she would answer that it was based on her belief in the inherent goodness of all children, and in their innate need to explore their world. She would mention that she has been working on a parent handbook that includes a statement of her beliefs and her curriculum goals. She would ask families and the children themselves for ideas. "I'm still learning and growing myself," she would confess.

Miss Noelle's teaching seems very much a part of who she is: calm and imaginative, with a desire to create a total learning environment for her children. In looking at Roger's and Freiberg's criteria, it is clear that Miss Noelle is congruent, acceptant, reliable, and empathetic, and that her children perceive these characteristics in her as well. One can tell that each child is as important as the next. She uses many nonverbal responses, touching one child on the shoulder as a reminder to settle down, giving another a sympathetic hug, and getting down on her knees to speak directly and firmly to an angry child. From all her words and actions, it is obvious that Miss Noelle thoroughly enjoys teaching the children in her care.

Let us now look at another teacher, Ms. Trinh, a first grade teacher with 17 years experience and a class of 25 children. Many of the families, whose older children have been in Ms. Trinh's room previously, request that younger siblings be placed there also. They understand that Ms. Trinh expects parents to help in the classroom in some way. They may bake cookies for a party, sew costumes for a play, or read a story to their child at least once a week. One working mother with computer competencies set up a page on the Internet for Ms. Trinh. On it Ms. Trinh includes assignments, work completed by the students, requests for materials she may want, and includes a column written by the families. Ms. Trinh regularly e-mails those families with computer access and keeps in touch informally when children are brought to and picked up from school each day.

Ms. Trinh starts each day by having children line up outside the door, walk quietly into the classroom, sit on a carpet square at the front of the room, and form a semi-circle around her by the white board. She then takes roll and assigns jobs to various children; this is done on a rotating schedule to ensure that all children have an opportunity to perform each task. One child looks at the calendar and announces what day of the week and month it is; another places a sun sticker on the calendar to indicate sunny weather; four more share the topics they have chosen to share. Children then go to the centers to which they have been assigned. Four go to the math center to work on the pattern blocks; six go with the teacher's assistant, Mrs. Hansen, to listen to the next chapter in a book she has been reading to them. Two go to easels to paint pictures designed to be placed in a story they are dictating to one of the cross-age fourth graders. (Older children come into the room once a week, to buddy with the first graders.) Six of the children go to the large group table and wait for Ms. Trinh to tell them how they are to complete the craft project they have been working on. Three go to a U-shaped table at one side of the room to work with the bilingual teacher on a social studies report they will present to the class about their home country and culture. The remaining four go to the writing center where one of the parent volunteers writes down the stories they dictate. Later they will sit at one of the tables and illustrate the story.

Although Ms. Trinh does not like the assertive discipline policy the school uses, she reluctantly does use it when necessary. She has the classroom rules posted prominently in the front of the room next to one of the white boards; interestingly, there are only three. The first, *I have the right to express myself in the classroom*, is illustrated by a picture of a raised hand placed next to the words. *I have the right to be heard in my classroom* is portrayed with several children's heads, listening to a child standing and speaking. The rule *I have the right to feel safe in my classroom* has with it a picture showing the international sign for *no* with two children fighting.

Upon entering Ms. Trinh's classroom, the visitor is impressed by how quiet it is. All of the children seem to be busy at the assignments they have been given. Two parents are busy assisting, one at the reading center and the other at the art center, where children are busy constructing papier-mâché figures for a puppet show that they will present later to their peers. The bilingual teacher is assisting two Hispanic children with their Spanish language arts lesson, and Ms. Trinh is circulating throughout the room, checking on the progress of those working independently on math and science assignments.

What kind of teacher does Ms. Trinh appear to be? In talking to her, it is obvious that Ms. Trinh sees herself as a good teacher. She is proud of the fact that most of her children meet the end-of-the-year goals set by her district. Her children obey class rules and respect each other. As one listens to Ms. Trinh and observes more closely, it becomes more apparent that, in spite of the seeming flexibility of the center and the assistance of the bilingual teacher, an assistant teacher, and parents, the classroom is more teacher-oriented than student-oriented. Children are assigned to the centers, albeit on a rotating basis; they do not have a choice.

Although most of the children appear content, during the observation period, an incident occurred that made the visitor uncomfortable—one of the first grade boys argued with his seat-mate about how to construct a figure with the pattern blocks, and called him a name. Ms. Trinh's face became angry; she pointed to the rules said sharply, "We work cooperatively in our classroom, Justin. If you can't cooperate with Jaime, go to the time out chair until I tell you to return." Justin replied that he thought the time out chair was stupid, and Ms. Trinh quickly put his initials on the white board, followed by a check mark. "You get your initials on the board for arguing, and you receive a check for talking back to me. Remember . . . one more check and you'll be sent to the principal's office." Later, she explains to the visitor, "I simply will not tolerate disrespect from any of my students. Even though I don't like to use assertive discipline, I have to admit that it does work."

Is Ms. Trinh a congruent teacher? As a child, Ms. Trinh's family emigrated from Vietnam. She is proud of her citizenship, and of owning her own home. She generally socializes with family and is quiet and deferential to her parents and their friends. Because Ms. Trinh expects her students to be respectful towards her and quiet in the classroom, she is a congruent teacher.

Ms. Trinh is respected by many families. They are pleased that most of her students are already reading and completing first grade mathematics assignments. They like her use of asking the fourth grade teacher for buddies to help her students in writing. They admire the fact that she is calm, soft-spoken, and a strict disciplinarian.

If one inquired about Ms. Trinh's philosophy of education and curriculum goals, she would respond, "I follow district guidelines and state standards. I expect students to respect each other and me; I expect them to behave; I expect them to put effort into their learning, just as I had to when I came to the United States."

Another way of studying these two teachers is to look at their leadership styles. As we know, Miss Noelle runs as child-centered preschool program, with a flexible curriculum that offers much free choice and emphasizes play. We also know that the children's needs come first. What is her leadership style? One might conclude that it is **authoritative**. The children all have a say in choosing what they will do from day to day. Miss Noelle respects all opinions and ideas, and she models this to her children.

There is an obvious difference between teaching in a child development center and in an elementary school, and both teachers seem to like children. However, Ms. Trinh runs a teacher-centered classroom and seldom deviates from requirements set by district and state guidelines. In terms of leadership style, Ms. Trinh is more **authoritarian**, or teacher-centered.

Although she uses centers in her classroom, Ms. Trinh developed them when she was placed on a first grade teaching team as a newly hired teacher. All three teachers from the school's first grades designed the centers cooperatively.

authoritative—
substantiated, supported, and accepted by most professionals in the field of early childhood education, or having an air of authority therefore the classroom is child oriented.

authoritarian—
characterized by or favoring absolute obendience to authority, therefore the classroom is teacher oriented.

OTHER TEACHING STYLES

We presented examples of two teaching and two leadership styles. With most teachers, however, you will find variants of these extremes. Between these two contrasting styles—student-centered and teacher-centered, or authoritative and authoritarian—lie others. The styles of most teachers lie somewhere between Miss Noelle's and Ms. Trinh's, and a few may lie at an even further extreme. Many elementary school teachers follow a more or less set schedule from day to day. Free play usually starts the day in preschool; a *sponge* activity, such as journal writing or a few simple math problems, frequently starts the day in elementary school. Sharing activities and attendance follow. Outdoor play and recess follow indoor activities. Quiet play alternates with active, noisy play. Rest follows lunch. Free play, and less structured activities such as art, music, or physical education, occur before dismissal time.

Many elementary teachers follow a more or less rigid schedule with such curricula as reading and math, as these disciplines are sequential; children must know *A* before they can proceed to *B.* Many teachers allow more flexibility with activities such as the social sciences and fine arts. Thus, many curriculum choices may be a reflection of student and/or teacher interest (see Figure 2–7). A teacher who is proficient in art will provide many art activities; a teacher with interests in music will provide many musical experiences for students.

While observing as a student teacher, you will find there are almost as many different teaching styles as there are teachers. Teachers tend to emphasize those areas of the curriculum that they feel are more important; they also tend to emphasize those areas in which they have greater expertise. The major characteristic of all truly great teachers is their ability to empathize with their students. Look closely; does the teacher show evidence of really liking the students? Does that teacher *CARE*? *CARE*ing is the secret to good teaching.

Figure 2-7
This area was developed as a result of the teacher's and children's interests.

No matter what teaching style your cooperating teacher displays, you will want to display student teacher behaviors that will be valued (see Figure 2–8).

Stereotyping Good and Bad

In order to fully understand a teacher's style, one has to understand the teacher's philosophy and underlying attitude toward the students. Does this teacher accept the children? Does this teacher feel that children are inherently good? Some teachers believe that all children are essentially bad and have to be taught to be good. Their teaching style reflects this attitude. Usually authoritarian, they have rigid classroom rules. Children are told that they will behave in a particular way; any infringement on the rules will usually bring swift punishment.

Does the teacher feel that children can be trusted? The teacher's style will reflect this belief. Classroom rules will be elicited from the children, with the teacher reminding them of a rule they may have overlooked. Children who misbehave are not considered bad but as needing more socialization time in which to learn. Punishment often takes the form of physical removal from the situation, and isolation until the child feels ready to rejoin the class.

COOPERATING TEACHERS VALUE STUDENT TEACHERS WHO:

- remember staff names and their pronunciation.
- introduce themselves to center support staff.
- share lunch time with staff in staff rooms or with children if on duty.
- make phone calls when ill or late.
- clean up after themselves.
- return or replace supplies and/or equipment.
- ask before using supplies.
- respond when asked for comments and contribute to discussions when appropriate.
- are watchful for needed assistance and pitch in.
- live up to student teacher responsibilities.
- are prepared and timely.
- treat other's opinions with respect; are open-minded and reflective.
- refrain from interrupting.
- ask questions when unsure.
- are friendly and communicative.

Figure 2-8
What most cooperative teachers value.

Does Miss Noelle believe children are good or bad? Does Ms. Trinh believe children are good or bad? From the information presented so far, you can only guess that Miss Noelle believes children are inherently good and that Ms. Trinh may or may not.

A teacher may believe that most children are good and then have an experience with a psychologically damaged child who challenges this belief. At this point, the teacher may accept the fact that most, but not all, children are good. The danger is that the experience with the psychologically damaged child can lead the teacher to formulate a stereotype about all children who look like this child, who come from the same socioeconomic background, who belong to the same racial or ethnic group, or who are of the same sex. Of Miss Noelle and Ms. Trinh, who is most likely to use stereotypic thinking? Stereotypic thinking occurs more often in rigid people than in flexible people.

Flexibility

flexible—willing to yield, modify, or adapt; change or create in a positive, productive manner.

Let us also look at another factor: curriculum planning. The amount of planning needed is often overlooked in a classroom like Miss Noelle's. The visitor does not realize how much work goes into the arrangement of the learning centers. The classroom looks open, free, and **flexible**. Indeed, it is all of these. None of it is possible, however, without a great deal of careful planning. Ask Miss Noelle how long it has taken to develop her classroom and how much work she still does during free time to maintain the atmosphere. You will find that she is continually trying out new things. Evenings and weekends are often spent designing new activities Miss Noelle thinks her children will enjoy.

In contrast, observe Ms. Trinh. During questioning, you will discover that she is still using some of the materials she developed during her student teaching years, and those designed by the first-grade teachers with whom she worked when first hired by her district. If she makes a change, it is usually at the request of her principal or at the suggestion of one of the other first grade teachers, with whom she has established a friendship. She sometimes may make changes on her own but is quite comfortable with what she has always done.

SUMMARY

In this chapter, we discussed the relationships between our attitudes and values, the curriculum choices that might be made as a result, and how these could reflect our developing teaching style. Several learning exercises were included, to help you define more clearly some of your personal values and the curriculum choices to which these might lead.

We observed Miss Noelle, a model authoritative preschool teacher with a clearly stated (and soon-to-be-written) curriculum philosophy and goals of education. We have also looked at what is perhaps a typical teacher, Ms. Trinh. Although more authoritarian than Miss Noelle, and perhaps less acceptant of all children, Ms. Trinh's teaching style, with its emphasis on meeting district and state standards, is admired by many parents.

We also suggested that there is a relationship between a teacher's ability to CARE and her philosophy of education, which leads her to establish clear curriculum goals for students. Of the two teachers described, Miss Noelle obviously CAREs; Ms. Trinh would protest that she does CARE; however, from the visitor's observation she appeared to lack empathy for one assertive boy in her room.

What should you, as a student teacher, do? Perhaps of greatest importance is to discover your own teaching style. With what areas of the curriculum are you most comfortable? Why? Do you see yourself as a CAREing person? Do you have a philosophy of education? In our two examples, do you see the relationship between each teacher's beliefs and curriculum practices? Think about your curriculum goals; consider how your feelings about working with young children influence these goals. Remember, especially, the positive attributes of both Miss Noelle and Ms. Trinh. Think, especially, of how Miss Noelle looks at herself as a learner, how she looks at each child, how she listens to them, how flexible her curriculum is, how student-centered her curriculum style is, and how authoritative her leadership style.

HELPFUL WEB SITES

http://www.nl.edu
The Center for Early Childhood Leadership (National-Louis University).This site publishes research notes on critical issues facing early childhood practitioners.

http://www.selectsmart.com
Values Assessment. Presented here are tests and assessments to help people get to know themselves, containing dozens of multiple-choice exercises.

http://www.zerotothree.org
Zero to Three. Investigate a publication entitled *What Grown-ups Understand about Child Development*.

ONLINE COMPANION   Additional resources for this chapter can be found by visiting the Online Companion at www.earlychilded.delmar.com.

SUGGESTED ACTIVITIES

A. Complete the following exercises in small groups of three to five. Discuss the processes involved in making any decisions. What did you learn about your self and your peers as a result?

1. Draw a picture of what you collectively believe to be an effective teacher and label each part of the drawing to indicate what characteristics are being exemplified.

    For example, a picture of an extremely large ear might indicate a willingness to listen to children; an apron with many pockets, including several labeled *objects*, might indicate the many different items an effective teacher needs at his fingertips. Use your collective imaginations; nothing is too extreme, but you must justify why the item is included.

2. Draw a picture of your collective vision of an ideal child/student. As in the above exercise, label each part of the drawing that exemplifies a desired characteristic.

3. Referring to the first exercise in this chapter, discuss among yourselves any insights learned.

4. Look at your responses to the exercise that involved listing activities you enjoy and the related curriculum activities. What does this tell you about your developing teaching style?

B. Write your developing philosophy of education. Describe it in relation to your curriculum style. Discuss it with your peers and supervisor.

C. In small groups, discuss the following:

1. Following your cooperating teacher's directions, you have always placed your purse and coat in the teachers' closet. The closet is locked after the teacher, assistant, and any parent volunteers have arrived. Only the teacher and assistant have keys. One day, after you have left the center and stopped at a store to buy a few groceries before going home, you discover that ten dollars is missing from your wallet; only a five and a one remain. Your immediate reaction is. . . .

2. You are a student teacher in a preschool classroom for four-year-old children.

    One day, Mike arrives with a black eye, wearing a long-sleeved sweater in spite of the pleasant weather. He winces when you approach him to give him a good morning hug. When you ask him what's wrong, Mike shakes his head and doesn't answer.

    Later in the day, as the weather has turned sunny and warmer, you are able to persuade Mike to remove his sweater. Almost immediately, you notice bruises on his left arm. Quickly, you report to your cooperating teacher. "Sarah, would you come and look at Mike? I think he's been abused. What are the procedures we should follow?" Sarah replies, "Leave it to me; I'll talk to Mrs. R. (the director). She needs to know about possible child abuse and she'll take care of it." By the time the children are being picked up by their parents, no one from either Child Protective Services or from the police has arrived to look at Mike or interview anyone.

    What should you do?

3. You have recently been hired as the afternoon kindergarten teacher at the ABC School. The DEF District policy stipulates that the morning teacher assists the afternoon teacher and vice versa. You feel that this will provide you with wonderful support from the older, more experienced morning teacher, Mrs. Sexton.

    On your first day of work in late August, you are surprised to see that there are no interest centers arranged in the kindergarten room. There are only five tables with six chairs at each, a bookshelf and two desks for the teachers.

    "Mrs. Sexton," you inquire, "don't we have blocks, easels, or dramatic play materials?" "We have the reading workbooks on the shelf over here," she responds, "and the math workbooks on the shelf by the desk. DEF District has a curriculum for kindergarten that we follow; haven't you read it?"

You confess that although you received the district guidelines two days before, when you were hired, you had not had enough time to read through them.

"Well," Mrs. Sexton says, "you'll see that there are specific goals in reading and math that we must reach this year. The children all have their workbooks, and we use direct teaching to achieve the goals. By the way, you do know that Mrs. Maier, the principal, expects you to have your lesson plans ready for her perusal on Friday of each week, and you do understand that DEF District uses the five-step lesson plan format?"

You begin to have doubts about having accepted the position, but you need a job to pay off the student loans you acquired while going through college. You know that this classroom is not developmentally appropriate according to NAEYC guidelines. You hope, however, that maybe you can at least do more developmentally appropriate activities in your afternoon class. You decide to spend some money borrowed from your parents to buy some unit blocks, and you visit the local public library for some picture books, for an in-class library. You also visit the local teacher supply house to price items like unifix cubes, dramatic-play materials, an easel, and paint. You estimate that you may be able to afford different items with each month's paycheck.

You remain in the classroom late on the day before school opens, to arrange a reading corner with the books from the library, and you shift the bookshelf to form a protected corner. You place two, large beanbag chairs you used at college in the reading center. Then you bring in the blocks and place them in the opposite corner of the room, on a shelf you also had in college. A carpet you retrieved from the city's once-a-month clean-up day is cleaned and placed in the block area to reduce noise.

When school opens the next day, Mrs. Sexton exclaims, "What have you done to my room? You had no right to change anything!" What do you do now?

4. A parent of one of the three-year-olds in the parent-participatory preschool where you are student teaching has formed a close relationship with you; you are both about the same age, and you both have experienced financial stresses, which you've shared. One day, Ms. Sharif confesses that she's just discovered she's pregnant again (she has a baby now, as well as a three-year-old in your class) and that she's thinking of having an abortion. What is your reaction?

D. Answer the following with a group of peers:

1. Do people often mispronounce your name?

2. Do you sometimes feel pressure to dress differently to fit in?

3. Have you had teachers that share your ethnic group?

4. Have you been told you cannot do something because of your gender?

5. In social groupings, have you felt uncomfortable because of your perceived difference?

6. Have you been asked to speak about or present an opinion that you feel is held by the majority of individuals in your cultural or ethnic group?

REVIEW

A. List five personal values.

B. Write an essay describing how the values you listed in question A, above, influence what you do in the classroom.

C. Read the following descriptions of classroom interaction. Identify each teaching behavior as student-centered or teacher-centered. If a behavior is neither, identify it as such.

1. Teacher A is standing to one side of the playground during outdoor free play. She is busy talking to her assistant. One child approaches another who is riding a tricycle. The first child wants to ride the tricycle and attempts to push the rider off. Teacher A quickly calls, "How many times do I have to tell you to wait until I blow the whistle? You won't get your turn until you learn to wait!"

2. Teacher B is busy assisting four children on a cooking project. The bilingual assistant teacher is working with six children on a reading worksheet. A parent volunteer is working with five others on an art project, and the student teacher is overseeing the remaining children with their unfinished reading assignments. A child with the student teacher complains in a loud voice, "This is a dumb assignment! I want to cook! Why can't I?" Teacher B looks up and signals the student teacher to try and resolve the problem alone.

3. Two boys are arguing loudly as they enter the preschool. Teacher C, who is standing by the door greeting each child, quickly takes a boy in each hand. She quietly asks, "What's the matter with you two today?" After listening to each boy and insisting that each listen to the other, she suggests a separate active play, based on the knowledge of what each enjoys doing. They comply, and minutes later they and another child are spotted playing cooperatively with the large blocks.

4. Teacher D is standing in front of her class. The children are watching as she explains the activity: making pumpkins out of orange and black paper. After the children go to their assigned tables, it is apparent that at least two children do not know what to do. They sit glumly with their hands in their laps. Teacher D comes over and says, "Don't you two ever listen to directions?"

5. During roll, one of the boys in Teacher E's room begins to cry. Another child yells, "Crybaby." Teacher E quietly speaks, "Sean, remember that we agreed we wouldn't call each other by names that can hurt. Elijah, come over here by me so we can talk. The rest of you can choose what activities you want to do. Mrs. Montoya, will you take over so I can talk to Elijah?"

6. The children are all sitting on the floor in a semicircle facing Teacher F when he asks, "Who has something they want to share today?" Several hands go up. "Let's have George, Ana, Mike, and Jan share today." Noting a look of disappointment on Mary's face, he says, "Mary, I know you're disappointed but remember, you shared something with us yesterday. Don't you think we ought to give someone else a chance today?" Mary nods in agreement, and George begins to speak.

7. Deerat is standing at the front of the class reading a story from the basic reader. The other children are following along, reading silently. It is obvious that Deerat is a good reader and tries to vary her tone of voice. The child fluently reads the paragraph, but something is wrong. Teacher G interrupts her. "You are reading carelessly. It's not *the* coat, it's *a* coat. Now, start over again, and read every word correctly."

8. Ron is a new child in preschool. After greeting him and walking with him to the table with crayons and paper, Teacher H goes back to the door to greet more children. When Teacher H thinks to look back at Ron, he notices Ron is busy drawing all over the top of the table. He quickly goes over to Ron, hands him another piece of paper, and says quietly, "Ron, use paper for drawing." He later comes back with a wet sponge and shows the child how to clean up the marks.

CASE SCENARIO

Setting: Nate, a student teacher, is talking to his university supervisor about student teaching in a kindergarten class for his yet-to-be-assigned student teaching placement.

Nate had always wanted to be a kindergarten teacher. His university supervisor, Mrs. Castillo, however, suggests that he might be more employable in an upper grade.

"But I really enjoy music and art, and I think I'd have more opportunity to infuse them into my lessons in a kindergarten. I can bring my guitar into the classroom, teach some songs, relate what the children are singing to art, language, reading, and even dance. I've already collected several picture and story books, with themes that involve music and other fine arts."

"I understand why you feel the kindergarten placement would be better than the primary grade one, but I'm still concerned about whether a school district would hire you for a kindergarten class. Think your options over, okay?"

Nate thought about what Mrs. Castillo said over the next few days. He then sought her out for further discussion.

"Mrs. Castillo, I've given a lot of thought to what you said about my student teaching placement and I still want to student teach in a kindergarten for the next assignment."

"I'll try to accommodate your desires as I check with the schools I know, to see if there is a principal and supervising teacher who will accept you," Mrs. Castillo answered.

Questions for Discussion:

1. Are you as in touch with your values, as they relate to your future teaching, as Nate is?

2. Could Mrs. Castillo be somewhat biased regarding kindergarten teacher gender, or was she just being realistic about males being hired more for upper grades?

3. If you could advise your supervisor concerning a second student teaching placement, what would you request? Why?

REFERENCES

Cartwright, S. (1999, November). What makes good early childhood teachers? *Young Children, 54*(6), 4–7.

Deal, D., & White, C. S. (2006, Summer). Voices from the classroom: Literacy beliefs and practices of two novice elementary teachers. *Journal of Research in Childhood Education, 20*(4), 313–329.

Feeney, S., & Kipnis, K. (1998). Code of ethical conduct and statement of commitment: Guidelines for responsible behavior in early childhood education. (Brochure). Washington, DC: National Association for the Education of Young Children.

Freeman, N., & Feeney, S. (2004, November). The NAEYC Code is a living document. *Young Children, 59*(6), 12–17.

Grant, C., & Murray, C. (1999). *Teaching in America: The slow revolution.* Cambridge, MA: Harvard University Press.

Jones, E. (1994). Constructing professional knowledge by telling our stories. In J. Johnson & J. McCracken (Eds.). *The early childhood career lattice: Perspectives on professional development.* Washington, DC: National Association for the Education of Young Children.

Katz, L. G. (1992). Ethical issues in working with young children. In *Ethical behavior in early childhood education.* Washington, DC: National Association for the Education of Young Children.

Krathwohl, D. R., Bloom, B. S., & Masia, B. B. (1984). *Taxonomy of educational objectives: The classification of educational goals. Handbook II: Affective domain.* New York: David McKay.

Luo, N., & Gilliard, J. L. (2006, April-June). Crossing the cultural divide in early childhood teacher education programs: A study of Chinese graduate students' perceptions of American early care and education. *Journal of Early Childhood Teacher Education, 27*(2), 171–184.

Raths, J. (Spring, 2001). Teachers' beliefs and teaching beliefs. *Early childhood research and practice, 3*(1).

Rogers, C. R. (1966). To facilitate learning. In M. Provus (Ed.). *Innovations for time to teach.* Washington, DC: National Education Association.

Rogers, C. R., & Freiberg, H. J. (2004). *Freedom to learn* (4th ed.). Upper Saddle River, NJ: Pearson/Merrill/Prentice Hall.

Stephens, K. (1999, January). Bringing light to darkness: A tribute to teachers. *Young Children, 49*(2).

Tan, A. L. (2004). *Chinese American children & families: A guide for educators & service providers.* Olney, MD: Association for Childhood Education International.

Tang, F. (2006, International Focus Issue). The child as active learner: Views, practices, and barriers in Chinese early childhood education. *Childhood Education, 82*(6), 342–346.

Van Leuvan, P. (1997, Summer). Using concept maps of effective teaching as a tool in supervision. *Journal of Research and Development in Teacher Education, 30*(4).

Vartuli, S. (2005, September). Beliefs: The heart of teaching. *Young children, 60*(5), 76–86.

Ward, E. H. (1992). A code of ethics: The hallmark of a profession. In *Ethical Behavior in Early Childhood Education.* Washington, DC: National Association for the Education of Young Children.

Wedman, J. M., Espinosa, L. W., & Laffey, J. M. (1998, Winter). A process for understanding how a field-based course influences teacher's beliefs and practices. *The Teacher Educator, 34*(3), 189–214.

CHAPTER 3

Being Observed: Discovering Your Competencies

OBJECTIVES After reading this chapter, you should be able to:

1. List two important goals of student teacher observation, discussion, and evaluation.

2. Describe five observation techniques.

3. Identify three possible observers who might be able to evaluate student teacher competencies.

4. Describe the major areas of teacher competency.

5. Complete a self-assessment process.

6. List five desirable dispositions or abilities of teachers.

7. Develop a plan that identifies your priorities for future competency development.

Comments of student teachers:

Peer evaluations were valuable and eye-opening. The skills fellow student teachers displayed and the way the room looked and the on-going activities gave me lots of ideas. I think I obtained more insight into the role of a supervisor.●

Joan Chang

I believe being observed is a necessary evil. How else would it be possible to really improve what you may not even know needs to be improved?●

B. K. Sutton

I could have kissed my college supervisor! She noticed my cooperating teacher really wasn't letting me teach. So she asked her to join her in the teacher's lounge for a mid-morning cup of coffee. Finally I was teaching!●

Legretta Banks

Why is it I do poorly when I'm watched? Things ran smoothly as long as I didn't know I was being observed. Fortunately, both my strong points and growth areas were talked about in daily evaluations. The problem finally disappeared except for the tiny knot I get now. Maybe I'll always have it.●

Casey Morgan

assessment—the act of appraising, judging, or evaluating another's efforts, performance, or actions.

A process combining observation, feedback, and discussion is often necessary to acquire new skills or expand existing ones. It is assumed that professional teaching practice can be recognized, identified, and measured through direct observation. Methods of observation vary with each training program, but they all are basically a record of what was seen and heard. An analysis of this record is called an **assessment** or evaluation. Observation, analysis, evaluation, and discussion can be described as a continuous cycle. It starts during student teaching and ends at retirement.

Professional teaching involves lifelong learning and continuous efforts to improve. Tyminski (2006) reports that it is customary for all practicing teachers to receive formal, written feedback yearly.

As more discoveries are made about the process of human learning, and as our society changes, teachers assess existing teaching methods, try new ones, and sometimes combine elements of both new and old methods. Observation is important to this process. The student teacher begins by being watched and ends up watching herself as a practicing teacher.

Teaching competency can be viewed as a continuum—you can have a little of it, some of it, or a lot of it—and there's always room for more competency growth.

As student teachers gain experience, they may feel teaching is more of an art and craft than a science. Beginning teachers are problem solvers, who experiment by trying one action and then another. They learn from mistakes and overcome embarrassments. Many things can be taught *and learned* by practitioners of any craft, along with experiencing intuitive insights. The act of teaching involves the heart and the mind.

The National Association for the Education of Young Children's (NAEYC) *Standards for Early Childhood Professional Preparation, Associate Standards Summary* for a two-year degree (Hyson, 2003) are presented in Figure 3-1. These are the recommended skills and abilities successful candidates are to display before graduating. *NAEYC's Initial Licensure Standards* for a baccalaureate degree (Hyson, 2003) are included in the Appendix.

GOALS OF OBSERVATION, EVALUATION, AND DISCUSSION

Important goals of the observation, evaluation, and discussion process for student teachers include:

- making valid assessments of performance through specific, descriptive feedback
- collaborating in a fashion that generates helpful suggestions and ideas
- creating a positive student teacher attitude toward self-improvement and gaining self-knowledge
- establishing the student teacher's habit of self-assessing teaching performance

Keeping standards and ethics in mind while core competencies emerge is also an important goal in some training programs.

Through observation and evaluative feedback, the student teacher receives objective data she cannot collect herself. *Evaluation* may sound ominous to the student teacher, because that word is usually connected to

STANDARDS SUMMARY

These core standards are identical to NAEYC's initial licensure core standards, however, associate programs distinguish themselves from initial licensure programs in the scope and depth of preparation. In addition, the term *students prepared in associate degree programs* is used rather than the term *candidates* that NCATE uses in accrediting initial licensure and advanced programs.

Standard 1. Promoting Child Development and Learning

Students prepared in associate degree programs use their understanding of young children's characteristics and needs, and of multiple interacting influences on children's development and learning, to create environments that are healthy, respectful, supportive, and challenging for all children.

Standard 2. Building Family and Community Relationships

Students prepared in associate degree programs know about, understand, and value the importance and complex characteristics of children's families and communities. They use this understanding to create respectful, reciprocal relationships that support and empower families, and to involve all families in their children's development and learning.

Standard 3. Observing, Documenting, and Assessing to Support Young Children and Families

Students prepared in associate degree programs know about and understand the goals, benefits, and uses of assessment. They know about and use systematic observations, documentation, and other effective assessment strategies in a responsible way, in partnership with families and other professionals, to positively influence children's development.

Standard 4. Teaching and Learning

Students prepared in associate degree programs integrate their understanding of and relationship with children and families; their understanding of developmentally effective approaches to teaching and learning; and their knowledge of academic disciplines to design, implement, and evaluate experiences that promote positive development and learning for all young children.

Sub-Standard 4a. Connecting with Children and Families

Students know, understand, and use positive relationships and supportive interactions as the foundation for their work with young children.

Sub-Standard 4b. Using Developmentally Effective Approaches

Students know, understand, and use a wide array of effective approaches, strategies, and tools to positively influence children's development and learning.

Sub-Standard 4c. Understanding Content Knowledge in Early Education

Students understand the importance of each content area in young children's learning. They know the essential concepts, inquiry tools, and structure of content areas, including academic subjects, and can identify resources to deepen their understanding.

Sub-Standard 4d. Building Meaningful Curriculum

Students use their own knowledge and other resources to design, implement, and evaluate meaningful, challenging curriculum that promotes comprehensive developmental and learning outcomes for all young children.

Standard 5. Becoming a Professional

Students prepared in associate degree programs identify and conduct themselves as members of the early childhood profession. They know and use ethical guidelines and other professional standards related to early childhood practice. They are continuous, collaborative learners who demonstrate knowledgeable, reflective and critical perspectives on their work, making informed decisions that integrate knowledge from a variety of sources. They are informed advocates for sound educational practices and policies.

Source: Hyson, M. (Ed.) (2003) *Preparing Early Childhood Professionals: NAEYC's Standards for Programs.* Washington, DC: NAEYC p.106. ©The National Association for the Education of Young Children

● **Figure 3-1**
NAEYC Associate Standards Summary

making a grade, or passing a class or training program. A breakdown in trust may occur. Actually, evaluation is a chance for improvement, a time to realize that all teachers are a combination of strengths and weaknesses.

The quality of the feedback given to a student teacher is an important factor, and feedback needs to be consistent and constructive throughout a student teacher's placement.

Observational feedback may pinpoint behaviors the student can then examine while teaching (see Figure 3–2). Discussions following observations usually include:

- identifying what went well
- descriptive analysis
- examination of situational factors
- the creation of action plans
  - additional analysis of written records
  - child behavior particulars
  - action/reaction relationships
  - other features of the observation related to the discussion

Ideally, when a supervisor builds trust during discussions, student teachers are able to:

- develop a clear picture of the supervisor/student teacher evaluation relationship.
- feel that they are supervised by an educator who listens well, clarifies ideas, encourages specificity, and takes time to understand the student's perspective.
- feel free to request value judgments.
- become convinced their supervisor is an advocate for their success.

However, time can be a limiting factor. Colleges and other training programs vary greatly, in both the expected number of visits to observe student teachers in action and the amount of time available for consultation. Whereas one supervisor may have the luxury of being assigned only a few student teachers, another may have many. College and other training program decisions are influenced by budgets, state supervision formulas, accreditation standards, politics, philosophy, and other factors.

Figure 3-2
Most teachers look for effective ways to help children handle their strong emotions.

OBSERVATIONS

Observations can be categorized three ways: informal, co-educator, and formal.

An *informal* visit is best described as a casual, unfocused visit by a supervisor in which a general, overall picture of the classroom emerges. The student teacher's style, the cooperating teacher's style, staff interactions, room organization, children's behavior, classroom routines, and the learning environment are all observed. The supervisor may pitch in or not. Notes may be written later and can include a supervisor's questions about room particulars, unique child behaviors, or features that are uncommon, unusual, or unexpected.

In a *co-educator* observation, the supervisor, like the cooperating teacher, is an active participant in the classroom, sharing teaching responsibilities. Together, they spend enough time in the classroom to determine its dynamics. They focus on the children, program, and the student teacher's involvement in child learning. Supervisors gain experience with the diversities and problems that exist, and may be able to understand the classroom from the student teacher's point of view. They are also able to model techniques and step in during student teacher difficulties. Many college supervisors cannot spend this kind of time with their individual student teachers. In some placement classrooms college supervisors may prefer formal observation.

Formal observation is defined as the observation of a student teacher that happens when a supervisor slips in, noticed or unnoticed, and remains unconnected to classroom action. Some type of recording takes place, whether it be a narrative, a **checklist**, tally, or one of the other types described in this chapter. Many training programs embrace formal observation as a more reliable and accurate method, because the observer, exempt from teaching responsibility and able to catch details, can see events unfold from beginning to end. Often, a supervisor focuses on a different dimension of students' work during subsequent observations. Some supervisors take copious notes as they try to capture the total picture, so enough data are collected to provide quality feedback. Others may use a self-created note system similar to shorthand.

checklist—a method of evaluating children or teachers that consists of a list of behaviors, skills, concepts, or attributes that the observer checks off as the child or teacher is observed to have mastered the item.

Training programs collect data on student teachers' actions in many different ways. The most common collection techniques follow.

Direct Observation

Direct observation is usually accomplished by means of a recorded specimen description, time sampling, and/or event sampling. This can be either *obtrusive*, where the observed individual is aware of the process, or *unobtrusive*, where data collecting occurs without the subject's knowledge, perhaps from an observation room (see Figures 3–3 and 3–4).

time sampling—a quantitative measure or count of how often a specific behavior occurs within a given amount of time.

Supervisors who use direct observation often tell their students that they will enter the classroom quietly and sit where they can best observe. They may provide an observation schedule or drop in without notice. If scheduled, the student teacher will be able to alert the cooperating teacher. Your supervisor may have discussed the observation method to be used, such as **time sampling**, and whether the cooperating teacher will join the observation discussion.

Many supervisors feel one-on-one conferencing is best for a number of reasons, including not wanting to make the student teacher apprehensive about having two pros in attendance. Other supervisors may feel that two pros can give more feedback and advice, or offer different perspectives. Either way, evaluative conferencing is a professionally private matter.

During an observation, the observer may use any or all of the following observation techniques and instruments, or may develop their own personal style of viewing and recording.

◉ Figure 3-3
You will be observed while working with children.

Figure 3-4
Your college supervisor will be instrumental in promoting a successful student teaching experience.

Time sampling. An observer watches and codes a set of specific behaviors within a certain time frame.

Specimen description or narrative. A *stream of consciousness* reporting that attempts to record all that occurs. It involves recording everything that the individual does or says, with as much information about the context (people involved, circumstances that might be influencing the behavior, and so on) as possible.

Event sampling. A detailed record of significant incidents or events.

Criterion-referenced instrument. An analysis of whether the observed person can perform a given task or set of tasks (see Figure 3–5).

Additional Observational Techniques

A specific set of questions can be prepared during an observation or after an observation. These questions can be used in an evaluation interview (see Figure 3–6).

The observer can also use a rating scale that sets a point value on a continuum to evaluate a characteristic or skill (see Figure 3–7). Videotaping, audio recording, or digitally recording a student teacher are other common observation techniques. These have the advantage of being replayed or stopped at certain points during conferencing.

Combinations of observational techniques are possible. Some supervisors and cooperating teachers prefer to work alongside their student teachers, and make mental observation notes rather than written ones.

SAMPLE OF A CRITERION-REFERENCED OBSERVATION INSTRUMENT

I Field-Based Assessment of Competencies

The 10 competency areas include:

1. Child Development Principles
2. Program Planning and Curriculum Development
3. Program Implementation and Classroom Management
4. Program Administration
5. Family and Community Relations
6. Cultural Pluralism
7. Children with Exceptional Needs
8. Assessment of Children
9. Evaluation of Program Effectiveness
10. Professional Behavior

II Program Planning and Curriculum Development

Knowledge

1. Demonstrates knowledge of child development principles in planning programs.
2. Demonstrates knowledge of factors to consider in planning an appropriate environment, indoor and outdoor, which enhances the development of children.

Application

1. Implements a curriculum based on child development principles, including the following areas: large and small motor activities, language arts, science and math, creative arts, social sciences and personal development.
2. Demonstrates the ability to work as an effective member of a team in program planning.
3. Helps provide an environment that meets the needs of young children.
4. Selects and utilizes alternate teaching techniques and curriculum materials in situations that would stimulate and encourage active child participation.
5. Demonstrates the ability to interpret and use collected data in planning curriculum to meet the individual needs of the child.

III Program Implementation and Classroom Management

Knowledge

1. Demonstrates knowledge of appropriate teaching techniques in the learning environment.
2. Demonstrates knowledge of how to facilitate effective child-adult relationships.
3. Demonstrates knowledge of play as an appropriate teaching technique.
4. Recognizes the unique contributions of staff.

Application

1. Provides children opportunities for making choices in learning, problem solving, and creative activities, whenever appropriate.
2. Utilizes play as an appropriate teaching technique.
3. Plans daily schedules that include a rhythm of physical and intellectual activities.
4. Utilizes positive suggestions in child-adult and staff interfaces.
5. Recognizes the importance of setting limits for children that are appropriate to their developmental level.
6. Models teacher behavior in accordance with set expectations.

 Figure 3-5
Sample of a Criterion-Referenceed Observation Instrument.

Area	Percentage				
	Almost always	Usually	Undecided	Sometimes	Seldom
1. Does the student teacher plan adequately for classroom experience?					
2. Does your student teacher utilize up-to-date teaching methods effectively?					
3. Does your present student teacher provide adequately for individual differences?					
4. Is your student teacher able to manage the behavior of children?					
5. Does your student teacher meet class responsibilities on time?					
6. Is your student teacher able to evaluate children adequately?					
7. Does your student teacher cooperate with you?					
8. Is your student teacher willing to do more than minimum requirements?					
9. Does your student teacher attend extra classroom-related social and professional functions?					
10. Does your student teacher seem ethical in his relationships with staff, children, and parents?					
11. Is your student teacher able to motivate children?					
12. Does your student teacher demonstrate facility in oral communication?					
13. Is your student teacher able to organize?					
14. Does the student teacher seem to believe in developmentally appropriate practice?					
15. Does your student teacher demonstrate an adequate background in early childhood education?					

● Figure 3-6
Sample of interview instrument used for cooperating teachers' evaluation of student teachers.

NAME _____

The professional qualities of each student teacher will be evaluated on the following criteria:

A four-point scale is used:
(1) needs improvement
(2) satisfactory
(3) above average
(4) outstanding

PERSONAL QUALITIES

	1	2	3	4
1. Attendance and punctuality	___	___	___	___
2. Dependability	___	___	___	___
3. Flexibility	___	___	___	___
4. Resourcefulness	___	___	___	___
5. Self-direction, sees what needs to be done	___	___	___	___
6. Sensitive to other people's needs and feelings	___	___	___	___
7. Tact, patience, and cooperation with others	___	___	___	___
8. Sense of humor	___	___	___	___
9. Attitude toward children	___	___	___	___
10. Attitude toward adults	___	___	___	___
11. Attitude toward administrators	___	___	___	___
12. Well-modulated voice, use of language	___	___	___	___
13. Ability to evaluate self and benefit from experiences	___	___	___	___
14. Dressed appropriately	___	___	___	___

Comments: _____

_____

WORKING WITH CHILDREN

1. Aware of safety factors	___	___	___	___
2. Understands children at their own levels	___	___	___	___
3. Finds ways to give individual help without sacrificing group needs	___	___	___	___
4. Skill in group guidance	___	___	___	___
5. Skill in individual guidance	___	___	___	___
6. Listens to children and answers their questions	___	___	___	___
7. Consistent and effective in setting and maintaining limits	___	___	___	___
8. Encourages self-help and independence in children	___	___	___	___
9. Sensitive to children's cues in terms of adding to their knowledge or encouraging verbal skills	___	___	___	___
10. Aware of total situation, even when working with one child	___	___	___	___
11. Sensitivity to a developing situation in terms of prevention rather than cure	___	___	___	___
12. Sense of professional ethics	___	___	___	___

Comments: _____

_____

WORKING WITH OTHER TEACHERS, PARENTS, AND VOLUNTEERS

1. Willingness to accept direction and suggestions	___	___	___	___
2. Is friendly and cooperative with staff members	___	___	___	___

continues

● Figure 3-7
Student teacher responsibilities and evaluation form (rating scale)

3. Observes appropriate channels when reporting on school matters ___ ___ ___ ___
4. Respects confidential information ___ ___ ___ ___
5. Establishes good working relationships ___ ___ ___ ___
6. Does not interfere in a situation another teacher is handling ___ ___ ___ ___
7. Shows good judgment in terms of knowing when to step into a situation ___ ___ ___ ___
Comments: _____
_____

PROGRAMMING
1. Provides for teacher-directed and child-initiated activities ___ ___ ___ ___
2. Plans in advance and prepares adequately ___ ___ ___ ___
3. Makes routines and transitions valuable and interesting ___ ___ ___ ___
4. Plans and implements age-appropriate, attractive activities and materials
   in the following areas:
      Self-Esteem/Self-Help ___ ___ ___ ___
      Music/Movement ___ ___ ___ ___
      Health/Safety ___ ___ ___ ___
      Science/Discovery ___ ___ ___ ___
      Cooking/Nutrition ___ ___ ___ ___
      Art/Creative ___ ___ ___ ___
      Outside Environment/Play ___ ___ ___ ___
      Cultural Awareness/Antibias ___ ___ ___ ___
      Language/Literature ___ ___ ___ ___
      Dramatic Play ___ ___ ___ ___
      Math/Measurement ___ ___ ___ ___
      Other Areas ___ ___ ___ ___
5. Creative and problem-solving activities are interesting and appropriate ___ ___ ___ ___
6. Plans developmentally appropriate activities ___ ___ ___ ___
Comments: _____
_____

Figure 3-7 (continued)

CLINICAL SUPERVISION

Clinical supervision was initially promoted as a method to improve instructional practices by providing supervisors with a structured and cooperative approach.

Underlying clinical supervision is the assumption that if the student teacher and his supervisor cooperatively define the focus of each supervision visit, the student teacher has the opportunity to address specific problems rather than global ones. A supervisory visit might focus, for example, on the student teacher's questioning strategies, or on the answers the teacher makes to student questions. It might also focus on interactions among specific students in the class, or on management techniques used by the student teacher. The advantage of using clinical supervision is thought to lie in the reduction of stress for the student teacher and increased ability to address specific, mutually agreed upon problems.

The steps in clinical supervision are as follows:

    1. the pre-observation conference, where the focus for the upcoming observation is decided

2. the observation itself

3. analysis by the supervisor, with consideration of possible strategies for improvement

4. the post-observation conference

5. the post-conference analysis by the student teacher and the supervisor, at which time strategies for improvement are elicited from the student teacher and confirmed, or counseled for change, by the supervisor

Lacey, Guffey, & Rampp (2000) describe clinical supervision as a goal oriented model that assumes a professional relationship exists between a student teacher and a supervisor, in an environment characterized by a high degree of mutual trust, understanding, support, and commitment.

Reflective Supervision

Reflective supervision is a refinement and outgrowth of clinical supervision. It attempts to bring the student teacher and college supervisor together in a collaborative way, to help the student teacher develop a disposition and ability to construct knowledge (Titone, Sherman, & Palmer, 1998). It is characterized by supervisor and student teacher interactions that practice collegiality and that demonstrate teaching as a reflective, inquiry-based, and knowledge-producing activity.

The method assumes the following to be the basic needs and rights of the student teacher:

1. to be treated professionally

2. to have an opportunity to develop self-understanding in a non-threatening atmosphere

3. to learn to analyze curriculum

4. to learn to understand the sociocultural dynamics present in every classroom

5. to work in an intentionally collegial relationship with an experienced teacher and full-time faculty member (Titone, et al., 1998)

The ultimate goal of the relationship between the student teacher and supervisor is to enable the student teacher to develop the disposition and ability to self-assess accurately, in every context in which she works.

Cognitive Coaching

Cognitive coaching is a process that involves (student) teachers exploring the thinking behind their practices (Garmston, Linder, & Whitaker, 1993). This type of evaluation process helps student teachers talk about their thinking and also become aware of teaching decisions.

A supervisor skilled in cognitive coaching asks probing questions. Student teachers may feel uncomfortable working out questions for themselves rather than being given immediate answers. When faced with self-analysis, teachers experiencing a cognitive coaching evaluation search their own minds, unlocking ideas that might not have presented themselves.

RELIABILITY

Observations must serve as a reliable and accurate source of information. In student teaching, the participants understand that each observation record covers only a short space of time compared to the length of the student teacher's placement. Areas of competence that receive similar interpretations, from different observers, over a period of time, should be of special interest to student teachers.

While all observers have different points of reference, depending upon their individual life experiences in the student teaching situation, their goals are similar. They honestly attempt to examine, interpret, and reflect on what they have seen, and possibly recorded, to improve student performance through follow-up dialogue.

Any attempt to interpret meaning brings with it the possibility of misinterpretation, based on the limits of what one can perceive and the observer's **biases**. Observers may have a mind-set that predisposes them to look at particular teaching skills and overlook others. Using a variety of observation tools and forms can help remedy the situation.

Reliability refers to the extent to which observations are consistent over time and "the extent to which a test is consistent in measuring over time what it is designed to measure" (Wortham, 1995). The similarity of information in data gathered in different observations confirms the reliability of the measurement. For example, if both a videotaped observation and a time sampling seem to point to the same measurement of skill or teaching behavior, the reliability of the data is greater.

The degree of obviousness of the collection method also merits consideration. Videotaping may produce unnatural behavior. Hidden cameras and tape recorders raise ethical questions. Observation rooms and one-way screens are familiar and unobtrusive methods commonly used in laboratory training centers. Objective recording of teaching behavior is a difficult task. Observations can be subjective and reflect the observer's special point of view.

Supervisors and cooperating teachers try to keep all observations objective during student teaching. Discussions between the observer and the observed can add additional factors for consideration, before analyses and evaluations occur.

To remove subjective comments from teacher observation, observers should attempt to describe precise teaching episodes, using extensive note-taking that leaves little doubt.

Observers can use the following steps as observation guidelines:

1. Noting the physical layout of the class, by observing such things as the arrangement of tables, instructional aids (bulletin boards, resource centers, and other areas or items of interest), and storage areas for child and adult materials, is often helpful.

2. Observing the cordiality of verbal greetings between teacher and children, and data on the number of children present, sex of the children, and diversity of the group adds further depth to the information gathered.

3. Noting the patterns of action in the classroom, like how children move about the room (getting water, for example), provides information regarding both organization and management.

biases—particular tendencies or inclinations, especially ones that prevent impartial consideration; prejudices.

reliability—a measure indicating that a test is stable and consistent, to ensure that scoring variations are due to the person tested, and not the test.

4. The verbal and nonverbal interactions between teachers and children, and between children, are a crucial part of the observation process. How does the teacher approach children? What tone of voice and choice of words does the teacher use? How do children react? Are teacher comments distributed equally among the children?

5. How are rules established and adhered to? How does the teacher respond to disruptive behavior? What preceded the behavior? How do students respond to the teacher's actions?

6. An important aspect of classroom life that is crucial to teacher performance is the tracking of time and sequencing of activities (see Figure 3–8). What do teachers use as transitions? What are the frequency and smoothness of transitions?

7. As in most supervisory settings, the importance of the post-observation conference cannot be overstated. The student teacher should present personal impressions of activities viewed, prior to discussing the supervisor's observation. This facilitates self-evaluation and recall of salient aspects. The additional information provided by the supervisor's narrative aids the student teacher in clarifying and understanding the antecedents, and the consequences, of classroom events.

Ongoing and cumulative evaluations of students' performances are designed to verify their competencies. In student teaching, these evaluations allow students to discover, plan, and ponder. Without outside assessment and evaluation, assessment is limited to self-assessment.

● **Figure 3-8**
Posted schedules help observers to see student teacher actions during transitions.

Observers and Evaluators

It is possible to be observed and assessed by many people during your student teaching experience. Some students prefer only the supervisor's and cooperating teacher's assessments (see Figure 3–9). Others actively seek feedback from all possible sources.

A wide base of observational data on competency seems best. Other possible observers in most student teaching placements are:

- self (see Figures 3–10 and 3–11)
- classroom assistants, aides, and volunteers
- other student teachers
- the center or school's support staff (cooks, nurse, secretary)
- children
- parents
- community liaison staff
- administrative staff or consulting specialists (see Figure 3–12)

Student teachers can develop their own rating systems based on teaching characteristics that are important to them. Simple tallies are helpful in recording changes in behavior.

Student Name _____ Evaluator Name _____

Date _____ Center _____

Time of Observation _____ Activity Planned _____

Rating Scale: 1 = Unsatisfactory   2 = Needs Improvement   3 = Satisfactory   4 = Good   5 = Excellent

Principle	Possible Evidence—Teaching Behaviors	Rating
The student teacher can create learning experiences that make subject matter meaningful for children.	Explains skills or concepts accurately. Engages children in discovery opportunities. Relates skills or concepts to students' lives. Links skills or concepts to children's prior knowledge. Integrates various fields of knowledge. Prepares hands-on activities and opportunities.	
Further evidence:		
The student teacher understands how children learn and develop, and can provide learning opportunities that support their intellectual, social, and personal development.	Converses with individual children effectively. Identifies and uses learning strategies that are developmentally appropriate for children. Uses a variety of approaches to aid child's discovery and experimentation. Monitors and adjusts activities to fit students' needs. Follows and supports children's self-initiated activities.	
Further evidence:		

 Figure 3-9

Sample of a student teacher evalution form. (Full form is included in the Online Companion)

Instructions:

Evaluate your own performance on this form. To the left of each characteristic listed below, write a W if you are working on it, M if it happens most of the time, or an A if it happens always.

Relationships

_____ 1. I share my positive feelings by arriving with an appropriate attitude.

_____ 2. I greet children, parents, and staff in a friendly and pleasant manner.

_____ 3. I accept suggestions and criticism gracefully from my coworkers.

_____ 4. I can handle tense situations and retain my composure.

_____ 5. I make an effort to be sensitive to the needs of the children and their parents.

_____ 6. I am willing to share my ideas and plans so that I can contribute to the total program.

Goals

_____ 1. The classroom is organized to promote a quality child development program.

_____ 2. I constantly review the developmental stage of each child so that my expectations are reasonable.

_____ 3. I set classroom and individual goals and then evaluate regularly.

_____ 4. I have fostered independence and responsibility in children.

Classroom Skills

_____ 1. I arrive on time.

_____ 2. I face each day as a new experience.

_____ 3. I can plan a balanced program for the children in all skill areas.

_____ 4. I am organized and have a plan for the day.

_____ 5. I help each child recognize the role of being part of a group.

_____ 6. I help children develop friendships.

_____ 7. I maintain a child-oriented classroom, and the bulletin boards enhance the room.

Professionalism

_____ 1. I understand the school philosophy.

_____ 2. I maintain professional attitudes in my demeanor and in my personal relationships while on the job.

_____ 3. I assume my share of joint responsibility.

Personal Qualities

_____ 1. I have basic emotional stability.

_____ 2. My general health is good and does not interfere with my responsibilities.

_____ 3. My personal appearance is suitable for my job.

_____ 4. I evaluate my effectiveness as a member of my teaching team in the following manner:

– 0 1 2 3 4 5 +

(Low)   (High)

My Teaching Team

_____ 1. I've earned the respect and acceptance of team members.

● **Figure 3-10**

Student teaching self-evaluation form

STUDENT SELF-EVALUATION

Put a check on the number in each line which best describes your performance.

1	2	3	4	5	
I often think critically about how my behavior affects children and other adults.	Sometimes I try to analyze classroom interactions.	From time to time I think about how I affect others in the classroom.	I rarely rehash what happened during the day in the classroom.	I give little thought to classroom interactions.	REFLECTION
I have a clear idea of important goals with children and work daily to accomplish them.	Some of my goals are clear; others are still being formed.	My goals are not always clear, but at times I think about them.	I use my center's goals for planning and have a few of my own.	I mainly handle each day by providing activities that teach specific concepts and making sure children behave.	CLARITY OF GOALS
I'm always responsible for what I do and say.	Most of the time I take responsibility for what happens.	At times I feel responsible for my actions.	I can't control all that happens—that's my attitude.	What goes wrong is mostly others' fault.	RESPONSIBILITY
I do what's assigned and needed before deadlines, and check to see it's completed on time.	I usually complete jobs in a timely manner.	I finish jobs that I choose to finish mostly on time.	I start, but often something happens before I finish assignments.	I'm late, and often don't finish what's expected of me.	DEPENDABILITY
I always find what I need and create when necessary in activity planning.	I'm pretty good at getting what needs to be secured.	I sometimes can find or create what is necessary.	I rarely know how to go about getting things I need for the classroom.	I expend little effort at locating hard-to-find items or materials for child instruction.	RESOURCEFULNESS
I rarely need others to direct my work.	Most of the time I don't need the help of my supervisor.	I ask for help when the going gets rough and that's not often.	I need advice frequently and depend on others to solve my problem.	Lots of help and supervision are necessary.	INDEPENDENCE
I'm active in teacher associations and attend nearby conferences.	Sometimes I attend professional association meetings and training opportunities.	I go to the library occasionally to consult the experts.	Haven't the time now to join or attend professional group doings but plan to in the near future.	I don't wish to become a member of a professional group.	PROFESSIONAL GROWTH
I change and create new happenings in my classroom and try new ways joyfully.	I will try some new ways and strategies.	If it's suggested, I try new ways to do things.	I'm pretty stressed about trying something I've not done before.	The old routines and ways are comfortable. Why change them?	CREATIVITY
I respect and enjoy being a helpful team player.	I do help others on my team.	I will share ideas and give time to other team members.	I don't really function well with others; I'd rather do it myself.	Teams don't accomplish much and waste time. Not helpful at all.	TEAM MEMBERSHIP
I'm aware of children's cultural backgrounds.	I'm sensitive to the cultural learning styles of attending children.	I've developed the skill to promote multicultural respect and dignity.	My students' cultural diversity is reflected in classroom displays and materials.	I've expended time and effort to become knowledgeable concerning the culture of attending children.	CULTURAL SENSITIVITY

 Figure 3-11
Rate yourself

Emotionally mature and well-adjusted personality
Alert and enthusiastic
Professional competency
Genuine interest in people, children, teaching
Professional attitude
Good appearance and grooming
Above-average scholastically
Wide interests and cultural backgrounds
Leadership qualities
Sense of humor
Willingness to learn and desire to grow professionally
Success in directed teaching
Creativeness
Understanding of children
Interest in community participation
Moral character
Cooperative
Good health
Ability to communicate effectively
Good penmanship
Interest in curriculum development
Flexibility
Sincerity
Appropriate humility
Ability to organize

● **Figure 3-12**
Administrators' response to the question, "What would you like to know about student teachers?"

Discussion

Discussions held after data are collected are keys to growth. The meeting's tone, format, location, time of day, and degree of comfort can be critical. The communication skills of both participants contribute to success in promoting student teacher skill development.

Two types of discussions, *formative* and *summative*, occur during student teaching. An initial, *formative* discussion sets the stage for later discussions. Goals, time lines, and evaluative procedures are explained. Additional formative discussions will follow placement observations. A *summative* conference finalizes your total placement experience and scrutinizes both the placement site and your competencies.

During discussions, you will examine the collected data, add comments about extenuating circumstances, form plans to collect additional information, and consider initiating new actions that could strengthen your existing skills through change or modification. Suggestions for improvement are self-discovered and formed jointly with the cooperating teacher or supervisor.

Child behavior resulting from student teacher behavior is a focal point for discussions. Influencing factors such as room settings, routines, child uniqueness, and the student teacher's techniques, methods, and behaviors are examined closely.

Discussions that are descriptive and interpretative and involve value judgments about child education and professional teaching are common.

Giving criticism is as much a skill as receiving it. Instructional criticism is given with the intent to improve, and usually specific ideas are offered for the listener's consideration. Evaluation sessions need to be viewed by student teachers as opportunities for growth, and met with a determination to get as much as possible from the supervisor. It is a time to listen and understand, rather than a time to respond.

Ideally, when you know and value yourself, and have a strong sense of your individual identity and self-worth, criticism can be taken at face value, in stride, and can be seen as providing helpful suggestions that can lead to reflection concerning new ideas, changes, and professional growth possibilities. You may hear yourself saying, "I'll take that into consideration. Thanks for sharing it with me."

Teachers are committed to lifelong learning, and student teachers begin to gauge the complexities inherent in working in the career field during their practicum experience. During **formative evaluation** discussions, student teachers can discover career skills they want to investigate, try out, or polish.

We have met student teachers who become angry, even aggressive, taking suggestions as personal attacks, and others who have melted in tears, and still others skilled enough to walk away when strong emotions overcome them, saying, "I need to think about what you've said, and I'll get back to you." Asking questions to better understand, paraphrasing to clarify points, taking notes, and adding unknown information about a viewed situation were also common student techniques to help us—their college supervisors—see things in a more complete light.

formative evaluation— ongoing assessment to ensure that planned activities and methods accomplish what the teacher intended.

Pre- and Post-Conference Supervisor Evaluations. More and more supervisors are conducting pre-observation conferences, so student teachers can brief them about classroom details, and the activities or lesson plan the supervisor will observe. Post-conferences, after supervisor observation, are a standard procedure, and the review of observation notes helps student teachers reflect on their skills. Tips, resource ideas, and possible areas for growth are discussed. Sometimes, discussions and **summative evaluation** meetings lead naturally to pre-conference ones.

summative evaluation—an assessment that follows a specific lesson or unit to evaluate whether the children have met the objectives.

Dealing with Evaluations

Student teachers should try to develop a positive attitude about what may appear to be an emphasis on their weaknesses. However, this attitude may come slowly for some student teachers. Conferencing covers student teachers' strengths but sometimes brings with it that lingering feeling of having just received a report card.

As a preparation for discussion, it is a good idea to get into the habit of self-evaluation early in your student teaching assignment. The following weekly questions are helpful:

- What did I learn this week?
- Have I identified goals for myself?
- Are my goals realistic, or do they need modification?

- Am I expecting perfection, or am I satisfied with an honest attempt?
- Am I communicating effectively?
- Do I seek help when I need it?
- Am I falling behind or keeping up?
- What improvements or adjustment do I need to make?

SkillPath (1997) offers additional pointers in Figure 3–13.

- Be your own best critic
- Know your strengths and weaknesses
- Predict what the person might say before the person says it
- Rehearse your responses to anticipated feedback
- Assume the best intentions
- Recognize that everyone needs feedback to grow
- Separate yourself from the criticism
- It's OK to dislike your behavior and still like yourself
- Think about improving, not labeling yourself
- Deal with the issue, forget personalities
- You are the only person responsible for your behavior, not others
- When the intention to learn from our mistakes overcomes our fear of failure, we're less likely to view criticism as a personal put-down

Figure 3-13
Receiving criticism. Used by permission of Skillpath Seminar.

When handling evaluator comments, one strategy a student teacher will find useful is saying, "Yes, I understand your concern. I had concern as well. Let me tell you about the circumstances that occurred. Tell me what you would have suggested in that case." Discussions can describe a wide range of student and teacher behaviors. Clarification of terms can be helpful to student teachers. Keeping records of discussions will aid your planning; they can be reviewed prior to follow-up conferences. Action plans resulting from previous discussions are usually the primary focus of later talks.

College supervisors have the ultimate and final burden of approving a candidate for graduation from training programs. If one questions a gathering of supervisors, one hears both anguish and elation; elation that they have had a small part in an individual teacher's development and anguish because they are forced to make tough decisions.

Their goal as supervisors is to assure that each candidate possesses the knowledge, skill, and competency necessary to interact sensitively, creatively, and successfully, with both children and adults. The task of assessing individual students involves observing human relations. Some student teachers of diverse cultural and language backgrounds may be tremendously talented and insightful with children, but they may find readings and academic testing in student teaching classes particularly difficult, and may need tutoring assistance.

PEER EVALUATIONS

After graduating, many student teachers feel that peer evaluations were tremendously helpful, for a number of reasons.

1. They are non-threatening because a grade is not at issue.

2. A peer may have greater empathy or understanding because they are experiencing many of the same or similar problems.

3. Peers know how it feels to be observed and evaluated, so they tend to tread softly.

4. Suggestions offered may have recently been field tested. A student teacher's successes are passed on to another student teacher for consideration.

5. When one becomes the evaluator, one experiences increased insight into the role of the college supervisor and cooperating teacher.

6. Seeing a peer's assigned classroom and cooperating teacher offers new data, new techniques.

7 Additional teaching methods, activities, and so on, are observed and possibly considered and tried in the peer observer's own classroom.

8. There is something in assuming the role of an observer/evaluator that makes one feel competent and professional.

All the positive aspects of peer evaluation have not been mentioned in this discussion, and there have been unfortunate instances of friction between peers.

It is wise to follow college instructor guidelines closely. Often, peer evaluators are asked to stick to the positive aspects of a peer's behavior, and suggest growth areas carefully. A rating form used by a peer can focus on a variety of teaching skills (see Figure 3–14).

Post-evaluation discussions center on the observed explaining to the observer what was happening during the observation, and what student teacher intentions were present. The assignment may involve turning in both peers' notes of the evaluation discussion, rather than observation particulars.

Increasingly, peer evaluations are seen as aiding student teachers' reflective thinking and their ability to analyze of skills. Student teachers observing others often ask themselves important questions about their own teaching styles (see Figure 3–15).

Constructive Evaluation

Evaluation should be viewed as a critique promoting positive change. The following are suggestions designed to provide maximum evaluating benefits:

● Start your debriefing by asking the evaluator (cooperating teacher, college/university supervisor, director/principal) to identify what she thought were the best parts of the lesson/activity and what parts needed improvement.

● Ask for specific examples to clarify what the evaluator means.

● An "I hear what you're saying" response is better than a defense or argument.

Student teacher's name _____ Peer's name _____

Date _____

STUDENT TEACHER EFFECTIVENESS SCALE

Excellent Above Average Average or Adequate Needs Improvement Unacceptable Unable to Determine
  1   2   3   4   5   6

Place rating on continuum line.

A. Feeling Tone

Warm _____ Cool
Friendly _____ Withdrawn
Supportive _____ Authoritarian
Interacts often _____ Interacts rarely
Accepts dependency behavior _____ Does not accept dependency
                                                         behavior
Physical contact often _____ Rare physical contact
Open to suggestion _____ Rigid

B. Quality of Presentation and/or Interactions

Organized _____ Seems disorganized
Enthusiastic _____ Neutral
Flexible _____ Rigid
Clear _____ Vague
Reasonable age level _____ Unreasonable age level
Appropriate child expectations _____ Inappropriate expectations
Promotes problem-solving _____ Furnishes all answers
Motivates _____ Turns off
Rewards attention to tasks _____ Ignores or negatively reinforces
                                                         attending behaviors
Sensitive to Cultural diversity _____ Ignores
Expands interests _____ Ignores expanding
                                                         opportunities
Provides developmentally appropriate activities _____ Activities limited by lack
                                                         of understanding
                                                         of appropriateness
Manages time well _____ Poor time management
Discovery centers planned and prepared _____ Poor or little planning/
                                                         preparation
Child-initiated activities _____ Teacher-dominated activities
Plans outdoor activities _____ Ignores outdoor planning
Activity smoothness _____ Poorly sequenced
Activity cleanup _____ Little or no cleanup

C. Child Behavior Management Techniques

Positive _____ Seems negative
Firm _____ Lax
Supervises all _____ Supervises only a few
Uses modeling _____ Few models provided
Notices accomplishments _____ Ignores accomplishments
Restates rules _____ Rarely restates rules
Uses redirection _____ Rarely uses redirection
Uses many methods to change behavior _____ Limited strategies used
Promotes child resolution _____ Teacher resolution frequent

continues

● **Figure 3-14**
Peer rating sheet

D. Verbal Interaction
Enjoys child conversation _____ Ignores
Clear _____ Unclear
Receives children's nonverbal communication _____ Ignores
Specific directions _____ Vague directions
Appropriate questioning techniques _____ Inappropriate questions
Encourages concept formation _____ Limits concept formation
Voice volume appropriate _____ Inappropriate volume
Frequent eye contact _____ Limited eye contact
Negotiates _____ Rigid
Promotes child discovery _____ Stifles discovery

E. Housekeeping
Promotes child clean-up _____ Ignores child ability to clean up
Replaces _____ Leaves out
Sees housekeeping tasks _____ Needs to be directed
Spends appropriate time _____ Seems to spend more time than
                                                          necessary

F. General
Good attendance _____ Poor attendance
Well-groomed _____ Questionable grooming
Dependable _____ Unreliable
Total area supervision _____ Close focus
Flexibility _____ Rigid
Takes constructive suggestions _____ Ignores suggestions
Could easily recommend as early childhood education teacher ___ Limited recommendation possible
Greatest Strengths:
Areas for Future Growth:
Additional Comments:
_____
_____
_____

 Figure 3-14 (continued)

- Separate specific comments from other teaching areas where you are functioning well; try to remember that it is the lesson being critiqued, not you as a person.

- Think of suggestions as being constructive, not as being negative criticisms.

COMPETENCY-BASED TRAINING

competencies—the knowledge and skills desired in education professionals in various staffing positions in early childhood care.

Federal funds have provided for the identification of the Child Development Associate (CDA) **competencies**. A CDA is a person who is able to meet the physical, social, emotional, and intellectual growth needs of a group of children in a child development setting. These needs are met by establishing and maintaining a proper child care environment and by promoting good relations between parents and staff.

CDA competencies are a widely distributed and accepted listing of early childhood teacher competency goals (see Figure 3–16). Your training

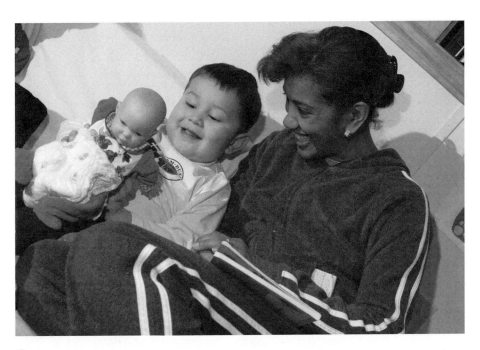

Figure 3-15
"Am I able to develop the close, intimate relationships with children?"

program may use CDA competency guidelines in your training; if not, you may wish to view them for your own purposes.

If your placement is a Head Start classroom, *Head Start Program Performance Standards* clearly defines expectations for all Head Start programs. The standards are a built-in system for ensuring Head Start goals are accomplished. They reflect sound practice, research, and a focus on quality (U.S. Department of Health and Human Services, 1996).

Core Knowledge and Competencies

To promote quality, early childhood teacher training programs, which subsequently affect the quality of child programs in their state, many states' legislatures have adopted their own early childhood educator career development systems. Some states have established articulation agreements between two- and four-year colleges. Core knowledge areas are identified, and specify which knowledge and what skills are to be accomplished, in which college or training courses. This includes student teaching coursework. Ask your supervisor whether your state has written, core knowledge and skill guidelines that affect your training program. And if so, what college classes promote the successful development of state-identified competencies?

National Association for the Education of Young Children's Developmentally Appropriate Practice

NAEYC's **Developmentally Appropriate Practice in Early Childhood Education (DAP)** (Bredekamp & Copple, 1997) is a tremendous accomplishment. Identifying competent teacher behaviors in a detailed fashion, it

Developmentally Appropriate Practice in Early Childhood Programs (DAP)— guidelines developed by the National Association for the Education of Young Children, as a response to the growing trend toward more formal, academic instruction of young children. The primary position of the guidelines is that programs designed for young children should be based on what is known about their development. DAP also reflects a clear commitment regarding the rights of young children, to respectful and supportive learning environments and to education preparing them for participation in a free and democratic society.

CDA Competency Goals	Functional Areas	Definitions
I To establish and maintain a safe, healthy learning environment	1. Safe	Candidate provides a safe environment to prevent and reduce injuries.
	2. Healthy	Candidate promotes good health and nutrition and provides an environment that contributes to the prevention of illness.
	3. Learning Environment	Candidate uses space, relationships, materials, and routines as resources for constructing an interesting, secure, and enjoyable environment that encourages play, exploration, and learning.
II To advance physical and intellectual competence	4. Physical	Candidate provides a variety of equipment, and intellectual competence activities, and opportunities to promote the physical development of children.
	5. Cognitive	Candidate provides activities and opportunities that encourage curiosity, exploration, and problem solving appropriate to the developmental levels and learning styles of children.
	6. Communication	Candidate actively communicates with children and provides opportunities and support for children to understand, acquire, and use verbal and nonverbal means of communicating thoughts and feelings.
	7. Creative	Candidate provides opportunities that stimulate children to play with sound, rhythm, language, materials, space, and ideas in individual ways and to express their creative abilities.
III To support social and emotional development and provide positive guidance	8. Self	Candidate provides physical and emotional security for each child and helps each child to know, accept, and take pride in himself or herself and to develop a sense of independence.
	9. Social	Candidate helps each child feel accepted in the group, helps children learn to communicate and get along with others, and encourages feelings of empathy and mutual respect among children and adults.
	10. Guidance	Candidate provides a supportive environment in which children can begin to learn and practice appropriate and acceptable behaviors as individuals and as a group member.
IV To establish positive and productive relationships with families	11. Families	Candidate maintains an open, friendly, and cooperative relationship with each child's family, encourages their involvement in the program, and supports the child's relationship with his or her family.
V To ensure a well-run, purposeful program responsive to participant needs	12. Program Management	Candidate is a manager who uses all available resources to ensure an effective operation. The Candidate is a competent organizer, planner, record keeper, communicator, and a cooperative co-worker.
VI To maintain a commitment to professionalism	13. Professionalism	Candidate makes decisions based on knowledge of early childhood theories and practices, promotes quality in child care services, and takes advantage of opportunities to improve competence, both for personal and professional growth and for the benefit of children and families.

Figure 3-16
CDA competency goals and functional areas. Reproduced from *Essentials for Child Development Associates Working with Young Children* by permission of Carol Brunson Day, Ph.D.

serves as a guidebook for many early childhood educators and teacher training programs. (Excerpts from the volume are found in the Appendix.) We suggest student teachers become familiar with the entire volume.

THE WHOLE TEACHER

Teaching competency growth can be compared to child growth. Teachers develop intellectually, socially-emotionally, physically, and creatively, as do children. Skills often omitted on competency listings, yet ones becoming more and more important to early childhood teachers in our society, are stress management techniques, holistic health awareness and practice, moral and ethical strength, researching skill, parenting education and family guidance counseling, public relations, and political know-how. Job situations can create the need for skills not covered in your teacher training. As society changes, the early childhood teacher's role as a partner to families in child education also changes.

Personal Abilities and Characteristics

What personal characteristics, dispositions, traits, abilities, or gifts are described in early childhood teachers? Many writers in the field of education believe effective teachers have few **discipline** problems, possess a sense of humor; are fair, empathetic; more democratic than autocratic; and are able to relate easily and naturally to pupils on any basis, in groups or one to one. Teacher behaviors that exemplify the effective teacher include:

discipline—generally considered a response to children's misbehavior.

- a willingness to be flexible, and to be direct or indirect as the situation demands
- an ability to perceive the world from the child's point of view
- the ability to personalize their teaching
- a willingness to experiment, and try new things
- skill in asking questions, to draw answers from the child, as opposed to seeing themselves as a kind of answering service
- knowledge of subject matter and related areas
- the ability to assess child growth and development
- the ability to reflect back an appreciative attitude, as evidenced by nods, comments, smiles, and the like
- use of conversational manner in teaching, and informal, easygoing teaching styles (see Figure 3–17)

CDA training materials specify the following personal capacities as essential:

- to be sensitive to children's feelings, and the qualities of their thinking
- to be ready to listen to children, to understand them
- to use nonverbal forms and adapt adult verbal language and style, to maximize communication with children
- to be able to protect orderliness without sacrificing spontaneity and childlike exuberance
- to be perceptive to individuality, and make positive use of individual differences within the group
- to be able to exercise control without being threatening

- to be emotionally responsive, taking pleasure in children's successes, and being supportive in their troubles and failures
- to bring humor and imagination into the group situation
- to feel committed to maximizing the child and family's strengths and potentials

Other descriptions of the characteristics and qualities displayed by an effective early childhood educator include inner security, maturity, self-awareness, integrity, a theoretical background, general knowledge, warmth and respect for children, intuition, professional behavior, laughter, and the ability to model emotion.

REFLECTIVE BEHAVIORS IN STUDENT TEACHERS

Not all educators agree on what exactly constitutes reflective teaching, as it is still under study, but Schoonmaker (1998) has identified three possible elements:

1. cognitive functioning, which includes information processing and teaching decisions
2. background, which includes individual past experiences, goals, values, and social interactions
3. individual perceptions, feelings, and interpretations of classroom events and happenings

Teacher training programs that emphasize reflective teaching are based on a desire to help student teachers move toward serious and thoughtful questioning, and provide an understanding of their own and others' teaching practices, perceptions, actions, feelings, values, and cultural biases.

Figure 3-17
Using a conversational tone at child eye level is a competency.

A myth among some student teachers promotes the idea that teaching success can happen if someone will only tell them how to do it, or point them to a book containing all the answers. Reflective teaching behaviors, on the other hand, lead student teachers to construct their own, personal theory of teaching and learning, through hands-on classroom experiences, careful and keen observation, and social interaction with children and other adults. Loranger (1997) lists and describes these reflective teacher behaviors (see Figure 3–18).

Whatever preparatory classes have been completed prior to the student teaching assignment will influence teaching behavior, as the student teacher weaves this knowledge into practice. Beginning teachers are also influenced by their concepts of what an effective or good teacher is and does. These perceptions are frequently based on our own remembered experiences, of teachers we had when we were students ourselves.

Schoonmaker (1998) believes that learning to deal with the wide range of emotions that children can evoke in student teachers, and the thought of being in charge, are so overwhelming that "it colors almost everything they do."

Dispositions

Dispositions are associated with the writings of Katz (1993) and are used to describe desirable teaching behaviors. Various attempts to define the term

Behaviors	Descriptors
Risk-taker.	Open to change; willingness to try new approaches to learning; willing to change direction in the middle of a lesson; willing to consider new evidence; invites evaluation of teaching.
Flexible/thinks on feet.	Knows when to change direction during a lesson; seizes "teachable moments."
Willingness to confront.	Willing to explore conceptions of self as a teacher, not so secure as to not want to learn and grow; willing to confront conceptions of self squarely and openly.
Considers context when making decisions.	Carefully examines context when making decisions; understands that contexts either enable or limit educational activity.
Accepts multiple perspectives.	Views an issue simultaneously from the perspective of several people (teacher, student, researcher, parent).
Accepts responsibility for success/failure of lesson.	Recognizes decisions she makes; looks to herself for explanations when something goes awry; accepts responsibility for choices.
Ability to recognize dilemmas and make rational choices.	Ability to use practical, pedagogical, and ethical criteria when making choices; ability to assess consequence of choices.
Links theory and practice/makes connections.	Knows how to use research and integrate it into instruction; comes to value theory as a means for expanding understanding.

Figure 3-18

List of reflective behaviors with descriptors. Originally published in Ann L. Loranger's article titled "Exploring Reflective Behaviors with Preservice Teachers" in the fall 1997 issue of *Teaching and Learning: The Journal of Natural Inquiry*, Vol. 12, No. 1. It is reprinted here with permission from the publisher.

include words like *inclinations*, *traits*, *tendencies*, *propensities*, *proclivities*, and *predilections*. Katz believes usage of the term *dispositions* is ambiguous and inconsistent. She believes dispositions are habits of mind, or tendencies to act or react to events, people, situations, or happenings in ways unique to the individual. Descriptors such as kind, friendly, assertive, thoughtful, curious, and so on might apply, rather than descriptors associated with skill or specific knowledge.

A student teacher can have a goal to strengthen certain desirable teaching dispositions and weaken undesirable ones. Having skill and knowledge of professional practices may not mean one actually uses them. Katz uses the example of a children's curriculum that presents early, formal instruction in reading skills during preschool that may undermine children's dispositions to be readers.

What teaching dispositions do you as a teacher wish to strengthen? Probably:

- curiosity and wonderment about classroom happenings and experiences.
- enthusiasm concerning the challenges of teaching.
- a desire to observe and uncover children's needs and interests.
- a realization that one can continually learn, develop, and sharpen teaching skills and abilities.
- working to gain children's trust and confidence, and to promote each child's self-realization.

Perhaps you can think of many others.

 ## CRITICAL THINKING

Kress (1992) designed a course of study and subsequent class activities to help early childhood college majors become aware of and use critical thinking skills. Kress's study concluded that critical thinking skills or use of them could be increased through training exercises. Ennis (1985) identified thirteen dispositions, which were defines as attitudes and motivations, of critical thinkers. These include the ability to:

1. take an open-minded approach.
2. take a position, and change it when the evidence and reasons are sufficient to do so.
3. take into account the total situation.
4. try to be well informed.
5. seek as much precision as the subject permits.
6. deal in an orderly manner with the parts of a complex whole.
7. look for alternatives.
8. seek reasons.
9. seek a clear statement of the issue.
10. keep in mind the original or basic concern.
11. use credible sources and mention them.
12. remain relevant to the main point.
13. display sensitivity when faced with the feelings, level of knowledge, and degree of sophistication of others.

Let us look at a couple of classroom situations and decide what critical thinking skills could be modeled by this teacher.

Situation 1. A posted chart keeps slipping off the wall. Children bring it to the teacher's attention, and Jamie asks, "Why won't it stay? What can we do to fix it?"

Situation 2. Large wooden blocks are being carried outside for play on a cement patio. Children are busily making structures. Teacher knows these blocks were donated by the parent group and now are being scratched and damaged. She decides to discuss the problem with the class.

Situation 3. Everyone wants a turn looking at a new book read at story time. The waiting list is long, and some children are anxious that they won't have a turn before having to leave for home.

Many classroom environments may encourage teacher action prior to thinking or taking the time to process a decision. As a student teacher, you will take on an increasing number of daily decisions. Would you use the thoughtful, reflective approach of a critical thinker in the situations above?

In the first situation, a critical thinking approach to the falling chart problem would begin with the teacher recognizing the alertness and help-fulness of the children. Jamie might be answered, "Let's find that out, Jamie. Why might the chart keep slipping?" If nothing is offered by the children, the teacher could think out loud, giving a few possible reasons using dis-position #8 above, and also might involve #3, #5, and #12.

The teacher's behavior would suggest he enjoys the quest for answers. If children do offer ideas such as "The tacks fell out," "The glue came off," or "Johnny did it," each idea is accepted and investigated. Analyze the last two situations to determine how many critical thinking skills might be modeled by the teacher, or promoted in children.

How does a student teacher become proficient in critical thinking skills? Many times teachers learn through conscious effort, practice, exper-imenting, making mistakes, and by using reflective thinking.

SELF-PERCEPTION

Researchers have attempted to probe how effective teachers view their abilities and the abilities of others. If a teacher likes and trusts himself, that teacher is more likely to perceive others the same way. A excerpt from Hamachek (1992), whose writings are dated but still valuable, follows:

> They seem to have generally more positive views of others—students, colleagues, and administrators. They do not seem to be as prone to view others as critical, attacking people with ulterior motives: rather they are seen as potentially friendly and worthy in their own right. They have a more favorable view of democratic classroom procedures. They seem to have the ability to see things as they seem to others— from the other's point of view. They do not seem to see students as children "you do things to" but rather as individuals capable of doing for themselves once they feel trusted, respected, and valued.

Students entering the field of teaching have their own ideas regarding qualities important for success. Most include being able to communicate ideas, having interest in people, having a thorough knowledge of teaching skills, having a pleasing manner and creative ability, and being able to get along well with colleagues.

You have received feedback from your cooperating teacher, your supervisor, and perhaps others. This input is the basis of your understanding of how your competencies are viewed by others. Your perception of your teaching competencies is formed based on your own self-analysis and others' feedback.

 SELF-ANALYSIS

Self-analysis will increase your awareness of discrepancies and inconsistencies between your competency goals and your present teaching behavior. As you become more accurate in self-perception, your professional identity and confidence will grow. You may even be able to predict how others will react to your teaching behaviors. You will resolve the tendency to center on yourself (a common tendency of beginning teachers), and develop the ability to focus more on children's learning and teacher and child interactions.

1. Do I work within the policies and procedures established by the placement site?
2. Do I make use of knowledge and understanding of child development and curriculum in early childhood education?
3. What are my relationships with each child?
4. How do I manage small and large groups?
5. Do I use good judgment in situations?
6. Do I plan for appropriate blocks of time indoors and outdoors?
7. Do I make good use of indoor and outdoor space?
8. Do I provide for transitions and routines?
9. Do I add to the attractiveness of the playroom?
10. Do I take care of equipment?
11. Do I consider health and safety factors in planning my activities?
12. Do I offer a wide range of experiences so that children can make choices according to their interests and needs?
13. Do I allow for various levels of ability among children?
14. Do I know how and when to ask questions?
15. Do I talk too much?
16. Do I make adequate provisions for variety in planned activities?
17. Do I see myself as a member of a team?
18. Do I coordinate my efforts with those of my coworkers?
19. Am I able to assume full responsibility in the absence of coworkers?
20. Do I participate in staff meetings?
21. Am I able to transfer concepts from theoretical discussions at staff meetings and workshops to action in my own program?
22. Do I find ways to help children understand the roles of other adults at school?
23. Do I maintain good professional relationships with parents?
24. Do I recognize the importance of seeing the child as a member of the family?
25. Do I share a child's experiences with the parents?
26. Do I know when to refer parents' or a child's problems to an appropriate person?

continues

 **Figure 3-19**
Student teachers' self-evaluation guide

27. Do I experiment with note-taking systems to assist in planning, to evaluate growth, and to form the basis for written records?

28. Do I use the information in records appropriately?

29. Am I a member of at least one professional organization in the field?

30. Do I attend meetings conducted by professional groups?

⬤ **Figure 3-19** (continued)

Using a 1–5 rating scale—1 meaning possesses much skill in this area to 5 meaning little skill displayed. Rate both yourself and how you feel others rate you.

	Self	Others
1. Clear explanations	_____	_____
2. Leads children to self-conclusions and discoveries	_____	_____
3. Verbal interaction	_____	_____
4. Gives reasons	_____	_____
5. Motivates children's desire to find out	_____	_____
6. Demonstrations	_____	_____
7. Promotes comparisons	_____	_____
8. Enthusiastic encounters	_____	_____
9. Accepts children's limitations	_____	_____
10. Plans effectively	_____	_____
11. Guidance techniques	_____	_____
12. Organizes time	_____	_____
13. Developmentally appropriate activities offered	_____	_____
14. Parent interactions	_____	_____
15. Directing work of others	_____	_____
16. Keeping records	_____	_____
17. Observing children	_____	_____
18. Awareness of child needs	_____	_____
19. Awareness of adult needs	_____	_____
20. Cultural sensitivity	_____	_____
21. Accepts responsibility	_____	_____
22. Knows routines	_____	_____
23. Builds effective relationships with children	_____	_____
24. Attracts children's interests	_____	_____
25. Liked by children	_____	_____
26. Liked by adults	_____	_____

⬤ **Figure 3-20**
Rate yourself

Numerous self-rating scales exist; Figures 3–19, and 3–20 are examples.

After assessment, you can decide what additional skills you would like to acquire. Put these skills in the order of their importance to you. You are the director of your learning and the designer of your plan for future accomplishment.

When trying to assess your progress, it may be difficult to isolate how you feel about yourself from how you feel about how others view you.

ADDING TO YOUR PROFESSIONAL PORTFOLIO

A portfolio is a container for documenting one's learning over time. Teachers adapt to change as they become conscious of their ability to address the evolving needs of children. You will reflect on your student teaching, and the resulting changes you have considered and acted on, and add this to your portfolio.

Assessments by others will focus attention on teaching strengths and areas of possible development. Former student teachers, evaluating portfolio usefulness, make comments like the following:

"Developing a portfolio . . .

. . . enabled me to evaluate my strengths and weaknesses."

. . . helped me recognize what to work on."

. . . involved compiling a complete record of my growth."

. . . promoted the recording of daily critiques of my teaching day and helped me recognize priorities."

Davis (2000) suggests student teachers need to peer through the looking glass, as did Alice in Wonderland, to evaluate what they want to accomplish in their careers.

> "Would you tell me, please, which way I ought to walk from here?"
> "That depends a good deal on where you want to get to," said the Cat.
> " I don't much care where . . ." said Alice.
> "Then it doesn't matter which way you walk," said the Cat.
> ". . . so long as I get somewhere," Alice added as an explanation.
>
> (from *Alice's Adventures Through the Looking Glass*, Lewis Carroll, 1923)

An additional end-of-year or end-of-semester self-evaluation appears in the Appendix.

SUMMARY

Observation, evaluation, and discussion are integral parts of student teaching. Different methods are used to observe the student's progress. The realization of professional growth through the use of an evaluative method and subsequent discussion depends on a number of different factors, including the process and method of measurement and the people involved.

It is important for the student teacher to maintain a positive attitude and consider self-evaluation a vehicle for improvement. Both formative and summative discussions are part of an analysis of the student teacher and placement experience. Planning to enhance strengths and overcome weaknesses takes place during discussions and is a growth-promoting part of student teaching.

The complete teacher emerges from of a vast array of possible teaching skills and abilities. Teaching competencies, or performance objectives, have been identified by individuals and groups, based on value judgments concerning appropriate or desirable teaching behaviors. There are many teaching competency lists in circulation.

Each student teacher gathers feedback on teaching skills from others and from self-analysis. Examples of self-rating scales were presented to aid the student's development of a plan of priorities for future competency growth.

HELPFUL WEB SITES

http://www.cdacouncil.org
Council for Professional Recognition. This site provides information about Child Development Associate (CDA) credentialing.

http://www.ncate.org
National Council for Accreditation of Teacher Education. Search for information concerning national standards and accreditation.

http://www.ascd.org
Association for Supervision Curriculum Development (ASCD). An easy to use, organized listing of Web sites is available.

Additional resources for this chapter can be found by visiting the Online Companion at www.earlychilded.delmar.com.

SUGGESTED ACTIVITIES

A. Form groups of four. On slips of paper, write down your fears about being observed and evaluated. Put the slips in a container. Each student takes a turn drawing a slip of paper and describing the fear and the possible cause.

B. Complete the following statements:
  1. My present strengths (teaching competencies) include . . .
  2. My plan for developing more competencies includes working on . . .

C. On the continuum between each extreme, where do you belong? Draw a stick person at that spot.

Talkative	Quiet
Eager to please	Self-assured
Outgoing	Shy
Punctual	Late
Accepting	Rejecting
Leader	Follower
Flexible	Rigid
Sense of humor	Serious
Organized	Disorganized
Studious	Non-studious
Patient	Impatient

Warm	Cold
Enthusiastic	Apathetic
Active	Passive
Open	Secretive
Direct	Indirect
Good communicator	Poor communicator
Autonomous	Conformist
Creative	Conservative
Animated	Reserved
Talented	Average
Sexist	Nonsexist
Specialist	Generalist

D. As a class, try voting on the validity of the statements that follow. Use a thumbs-up signal if the statement is true; remain still if you believe the statement is false, or if you can not decide. When voting on the more controversial statements, ask your instructor to turn away from the class and elect a student to count the votes and record the final tally.
  1. It is unfair to compare one student teacher to another.
  2. It is a wise move to have one student teacher tutor another.

3. Peer evaluations should be part of everyone's student teaching experience.
4. Confidentiality in rating student teachers is imperative.
5. Sharing discussion notes with other student teachers may be helpful to both students.
6. Evaluations by supervisors or cooperating teachers should never be shown to employers of student teachers.
7. A student teacher's placement could inhibit the growth of professional teaching competencies.
8. One can experience considerable growth without evaluative feedback.
9. Criticism is threatening.
10. Being observed and evaluated is really a game. Self-discovery and being motivated to do your best are more important.
11. An individual's manner of dress, hairstyle, and the like should not be included in an evaluation, because these have nothing to do with effective teaching.
12. Observation and evaluation can increase professional excellence.
13. Every student should receive a copy of all written performance evaluations.
14. There is no such thing as constructive criticism.
15. Evaluators tend to see their own teaching weaknesses and inadequacies in the student teachers they observe.

E. Read the statements below and briefly describe your reactions by making comments. Share your ideas with the class.

Statement 1. There is no *perfect* early childhood educator, rather only individual teachers, with varying degrees of competence. Teacher training should magnify strengths and produce teachers who differ greatly.

Statement 2. Celebrate your uniqueness;. you may offer children what others cannot. Your weakness may be another's strength, and their weakness your strength. Feeling middle-of-the-road in everything? Middle-of-the-road may provide stability, safety, familiarity, and feelings of comfort around certain people.

F. How do you react to criticism in performance evaluation discussions? Using the key below, respond to the following statements and discuss your responses with a small group of your peers:

M = most often, S = sometimes, and R = rarely

1. I'm quiet while supervisors talk about my performance.
2. I refrain from defending myself.
3. I'm aware of messages I send with facial expression and body language.
4. I ask for feedback frequently.
5. I discuss my evaluations with peers.
6. I feel disliked when criticized, as if something about me makes others act unfavorably.
7. I tend to think things over before reacting.
8. I tend to gauge whether criticism is well-intended and has some basis in truth.
9. Inside, I'm immediately angry when criticized.
10. Inside, I'm immediately hurt and crestfallen when my weaknesses are pointed out.
11. I feel criticism is a personal attack.
12. I ask for suggestions to improve.
13. If I'm not sure what is meant, I ask for clarification.
14. Examples of my behavior help me see myself through supervisors' eyes.
15. I'd rather have honest feedback than none at all.
16. I can say "thank you" after a less than excellent rating by a supervisor.
17. I look at evaluation discussions as necessary and helpful but still unpleasant.
18. I feel that there is no such thing as constructive criticism.
19. I'm motivated to improve my professional skills.
20. I'll never like criticism, but when it's honest and well-intended, it's really an opportunity.
21. I can tactfully add information that may give supervisors additional insight into my behavior.
22. I can talk my way out of most situations.

G. Read and discuss the following statement. Give examples from your own life and mention some of your own teaching joys.

"A man rarely succeeds at anything unless he has fun doing it. I've known men who succeeded because they had a rip-roaring good time conducting their business" (Carnegie, 1936).

H. Read about Vivian Paley in "Princess Annabella and the black girls" in *The need for story: Cultural diversity in classroom and community* (*pages* 145–154). Urbana, IL: National Council Teachers of English. (Dyson & Genishi, Editors.)

Form groups of four to five classmates. Role-play by assigning the following roles:
1. *Paley's supervisor.* Pretend Paley is a student teacher who has been observed and is now having a follow-up conference.
2. *Paley as a student teacher.*
3. *An African American parent*, who has volunteered in the classroom and has questions about the intent of Paley's storytelling.
4. *Paley's cooperating teacher*, who wonders why Paley (her student teacher) persists in telling daily stories.

◉ REVIEW

A. Name three methods of observational data collection. Give examples.

B. Select the answer that best completes each statement.
1. The process of observation, evaluation, and discussion:
   a. includes observations from supervisors and employers.
   b. usually ends when the student teaching experience ends.
   c. continues after the student teacher graduates and is valued by teachers and employers.
   d. ends when improvement occurs.
   e. can be best performed by the student teacher alone.
2. One of the primary goals of observation, evaluation, and discussion is to:
   a. stress the student teacher's weaknesses through peer evaluation.
   b. increase control.
   c. judge how quickly a student can respond to suggestions.
   d. criticize student teachers.
   e. do none of these.
   f. do all of these.
3. Feedback can be defined as data:
   a. collected through observations and evaluated and communicated to the one being observed.
   b. recorded by a student teacher during discussion.
   c. that include a free lunch.
   d. withheld from a student teacher.
   e. that are none of these.
4. If interviews are used to collect data on student teaching, each interviewee should:
   a. answer only the questions he wishes to answer.
   b. always be asked the same questions in the same manner.
   c. be asked for factual data only.
   d. be asked for opinions only.
   e. be given a specified length of time to answer each question.
5. One benefit of videotaping for the purpose of observation is that:
   a. the student teacher and supervisor can evaluate the tape together.
   b. it is less frightening than other methods.
   c. a camera captures a more natural view of a student teacher.
   d. it saves time.
   e. all of these are true.
6. If a student teaching skill is evaluated using three different observational methods, and each confirms the same level of competency, the three tests would probably be:
   a. rated as reliable.
   b. rated as highly valid.
   c. rated as accurate.
   d. standardized.
7. The collection technique that records a series of significant incidents is called a(n):
   a. time sampling.
   b. rating sheet.
   c. specimen description.
   d. event sampling.
   e. questionnaire.

8. An unobtrusive method of observation might involve:
   a. hidden microphones.
   b. an observer with a tape recorder.
   c. an observer viewing from a loft.
   d. an observer in an observation room.
   e. all of these.

9. To assess the rapport that a student teacher has developed with a group of children, one could:
   a. observe how many children initiate conversation with the student teacher during a given time period.
   b. record and analyze what the children say.
   c. count how many times a child touches the student teacher during a given time period.
   d. observe how many times a child shares an interest or concern with a student teacher.
   e. do all of these.

10. A final discussion that informs the student teacher about his teaching skills is called a(n):
   a. formative discussion.
   b. initial discussion.
   c. summative discussion.
   d. incidental discussion.
   e. alternate discussion.

C. Complete the following statement.

The five individuals who could probably provide the most reliable and valid data concerning my teaching competency are . . .

D. Five individuals observed the same traffic accident. Match the person in Column I to the feature in Column II that he or she would be most likely to have observed.

I	II
1. Car salesperson	a. driver's license and/or license plate numbers
2. Police officer	b. children involved in the accident
3. Doctor	c. damage to the automobiles
4. Teacher	d. make and model of the automobiles involved
5. Insurance adjuster	e. injuries of those involved

E. What five skills would most cooperating teachers want to observe before a summative discussion?

F. Write three pieces of advice to student teachers, to help them accept constructive criticism.

G. Choose the answer that best completes each statement.

1. A student teacher:
   a. needs to develop all the competencies that experts recognize.
   b. should strive to display all competencies.
   c. should develop an individualized plan for competency development.
   d. should rely completely on feedback gained through the comments of others when developing a professional growth plan.
   e. can ignore competencies others consider important.

2. Lists of teacher competencies are based on:
   a. research studies that correlate teacher behaviors and child accomplishment.
   b. value judgments of individuals and/or groups.
   c. recognized teacher abilities and skills.
   d. the qualities parents feel are desirable in teachers.
   e. what teacher training programs produce in student teachers.

3. Well known and accepted lists of teacher competencies for teachers of children under age five are:
   a. Head Start teacher competencies.
   b. NEA graduating level competencies.
   c. NAEYC competencies.
   d. PTA competencies.
   e. CDA competencies.

4. A student teacher's view of competency forms best when:
   a. others comment on student teaching episodes.
   b. children are watched for growth through the student teacher's planned activities or behavior.
   c. self-evaluation and feedback are combined.
   d. parents assess the student teacher's effectiveness.
   e. feedback includes comments from the entire staff.

5. The main purpose of developing plans to acquire other teaching skills is to:
   a. facilitate growth.
   b. have student teachers learn all listed competencies.
   c. make student teachers realize their limitations.
   d. make student teachers realize their strengths.
   e. make sure the profession maintains quality performance.

CASE SCENARIO

Setting: Morgan is a student teacher in a four-year-old class. Her college supervisor has just arrived to observe.

Morgan's cooperating teacher suggests she take a quick look at her activity plan, which includes collecting leaves in the play yard and returning to sort them.

Unfortunately, rain has made the plan unusable. Remembering that physical activity seemed necessary for the group at this time of day, Morgan starts a substitute activity.

She gathers the group and initiates a discussion of children's names. Morgan draws the letter B on a chart-sized piece of newsprint, and a child offers that his is a B name. "B is the first letter of your name, Brent. I see the B on your name tag."

Morgan then asks the group to watch where she puts the B chart. She quickly crosses the room, tapes the chart to a wall, and returns. She

then discusses how she can go and touch the chart using baby steps, then return and sit down. She demonstrates.

"Can anyone think of another way?" Morgan asks. A child suggests using elephant steps, which he demonstrates, followed by the rest of the children. The game proceeds with other names and other suggestions about different ways to cross the room. The activity holds the children's interest and encourages them to create clever ways to cross the room.

Questions for Discussion:

1. What do you think of Morgan's alternate activity?

2. Do you feel the alternate activity was planned as a back-up or created on the spot? Why?

3. Acting as the college supervisor, what teaching skills would you commend? Why?

REFERENCES

Bredekamp, S., & Copple, C. (Eds.). (1997). *Developmentally appropriate practice in early childhood programs* (rev. ed.). Washington, DC: National Association for the Education of Young Children.

Carnegie, D. (1936). How to win friends and influence people. New York: Simon and Schuster.

Carroll, L. (1923). *Alice's adventures in wonderland and through the looking glass.* New York: Winston.

Davis, M. A. (2000, Summer). Through the looking glass: Pre-service professional portfolios. *The Teacher Educator*, 37(1), 27–36.

Ennis, R. H. (1985). A logical basis for measuring critical thinking skills. *Educational Leadership*, 43 (2), 56-64.

Garmston, R., Linder, C., & Whitaker, J. (1993, October). Reflections on cognitive coaching. *Educational Leadership*, 51(2), 38-41.

Hamachek, D. (1992). *Encounters with the self* (4th ed.). New York: Harcourt Brace.

Hyson, M. (Ed.). (2003). *Preparing early childhood professionals: NAEYC's standards for programs.* Washington, DC: National Association for the Education of Young Children.

Katz, L. C. (1993). *Dispositions, definitions, and implications for early childhood practice.* Champaign, IL: ERIC Clearinghouse on Elementary and Early Childhood Education.

Katz, L. G. (1993, September). Dispositions as educational goals. *ERIC Digest*, EPO–PS–93–(10), 13-18.

Lacey, C. H., Guffey, J. S., & Rampp, L. C. (2000, Spring). Clinical supervision using interactive compressed television. *The Teacher Educator*, 35(4), 97–107.

Loranger, A. (1997, Fall). Exploring reflective behaviors with pre-service teachers. *Teaching and Learning*, 12(13), 45.

National Association for the Education of Young Children, (2001). *NAEYC Standards for Early Childhood Professional Preparation: Baccalaureate or Initial Licensure Level.* Washington, DC: Author.

Paley, V. G. (1994). Princess Annabella and the black girls. In A. H. Dyson and C. Genishi (Eds.). *The need for story: Cultural diversity in classroom and community* (pp. 145–154). Urbana, IL: National Council of Teachers of English.

Schoonmaker, F. (1998, Spring). Promise and possibility: Learn to teach. *Teacher's College Record*, 99(3), 27-32.

SkillPath Seminars (1997). *Conflict management skills for women.* Mission, KS: SkillPath.

Titone, C., Sherman, S., & Palmer, R. (1998, Winter). Cultivating student teachers' disposition and ability to construct knowledge. *Action in Teacher Education, XIX*(4), 43-49.

Tyminski, C. (2006). *Your early childhood practicum and student teaching experience: Guidelines for success.* Upper Saddle River, NJ: Prentice/Hall/Merrill/ Prentice Hall.

U.S. Department of Health and Human Services. (1996). *Head Start program performance standards.* Washington, DC: Author.

Wortham, S. C. (1995). *Measurement and evaluation in early childhood education* (2nd ed.). Englewood Cliffs, NJ: Prentice-Hall.

CHAPTER 4

Review of Child Development and Learning Theory

OBJECTIVES   After reading this chapter, you should be able to:

1.... Identify four major child development theories that influence early childhood education.

2.... Describe how children learn.

3.... List five ways in which the student teacher can help a child learn.

Comments of student teachers:

> " *I'm attracted to some children more than to others. I purposely try to spend equal time with every child and give equal attention to all. The active child's the hardest.* ●
>
> **Mia Mendonca**

> " *One of my instructors said, "the hardest thing about being a teacher is figuring out how individual children learn." During student teaching I found many learn quickly from other children, some learn by doing something over and over again, and some learn by observing and asking questions. I found if I wanted to teach something, I definitely had to capture their attention first. I often did this by being enthusiastic.* ●
>
> **Doreen Liu**

> " *Play really is the work of the young child. They become so focused, so serious, so excited at times. It's great fun to accompany them, to watch their enthusiasm and sense of wonder.* ●
>
> **Shelley Ochoa**

THEORIES OF CHILD DEVELOPMENT

Historical Background

Historically, three theories of child development have been prevalent in developing educational programs for young children: the *nativist*, the *nurturist*, and the *interactionist*.

The **nativist** tradition, based on the philosophy of Rousseau (1742, 1947), takes the view that children are like flowers, unfolding in a natural way. Out of the nativist tradition has developed the concept of children's natural development or maturation as the determinant of their ability to learn, with little direction from parents or teachers. Gesell, Ilg, and Ames (1974), as proponents of the maturation theory, best exemplify the nativist point of view. The traditional nursery school of the 1920s, '30s, and '40s, and still seen today in some programs, is based on this nativist philosophy.

Another variant of the nativist tradition can be seen in the psychoanalytic theories of Erikson (1993) and Freud. Erikson's **psychosocial theory** stressed eight stages of human development and posited a specific task to be resolved at each stage. For example, the task of infancy is the resolution of basic trust versus mistrust; for toddlers, the task is autonomy versus shame and doubt. During the preschool years, the task is initiative versus guilt; and for elementary school-age children, industry versus inferiority. The concept that the major tasks of toddlers and preschoolers are autonomy and initiative has evolved into the philosophy of child-directed learning, seen in such programs as those in some traditional preschools and Montessori programs.

The **nurturist** tradition, based on the philosophy of Locke, looks at development from the point of view that the minds of children are a *tabula rasa,* or blank slate. From the nurturist tradition have evolved programs based on the theory of **behaviorism**. The concept that children are much like Locke's blank slate, upon which adults write or impress learnings, has led to traditional, teacher-directed elementary school programs and the use of **behavior modification** as both a teaching technique and a classroom management tool.

Interactionists view development and learning as taking place in the interactions between children and their respective environments. Programs exemplifying this point of view are those of the **constructivist theory**. Jean Piaget (1952), although influenced by Rousseau's concept of children as active explorers of their respective environments, extended the concept of natural unfolding by maintaining that children create their own knowledge as they interact with their social and physical environments. Piaget calls this interaction **assimilation**, **accommodation**, and **equilibration** (Seefeldt & Barbour, 1998). Programs based on Piaget's point of view are best exemplified by Lavatelli (1973), High/Scope (Hohmann, Banet, & Weikart, 1979), and Kamii and DeVries (1978). In each of these programs, Piaget's theory is translated in somewhat different ways: Lavatelli tends to emphasize the structural aspects; High/Scope, the relationship between the theory and children's spontaneous activities; and Kamii and DeVries, the constructivist aspects.

The National Research Council (2000) points out that, although theories differ in important ways, they share an emphasis on considering children as active learners, who are able to set goals, plan, and revise. They recognize that children's **cognitive** development evolves gradually, as they acquire strategies for remembering, understanding, and problem-solving.

---

nativist—one who adheres to the theory that children are born with biological dispositions for learning that unfold or mature in a natural way.

psychosocial theory—the branch of psychology founded by Erik Erikson, in which development is described in terms of eight stages that span childhood and adulthood.

nurturist—one who adheres to the theory that the minds of children are blank or unformed, and need educational input or direct instruction in order to develop knowledge and appropriate behavior.

behaviorism—the theoretical viewpoint, espoused by theorists such as B. F. Skinner, that behavior is shaped by environmental forces, specifically in response to reward and punishment.

behavior modification—a form of systematic training that attempts to change unacceptable behavior patterns. It involves reinforcing acceptable behavior rather than paying attention to and, thus, rewarding unacceptable behavior.

interactionists—those who adhere to the theory that language develops through a combination of inborn factors and environmental influences.

constructivist theory—a theory, such as that of Jean Piaget, based on the belief that children construct knowledge for themselves rather than having it conveyed to them by some external source.

What Student Teachers Should Know

It has been said that a teacher training program is successful if its graduates know just one thing well: how children learn. Feiman-Nemser, Carver, Schwille, and Yusko (1999) believe beginning teachers have two jobs: to teach and to learn to teach. Current learning theory is based on experts' differing views of human development. The concept that each child is a unique individual, who learns in his or her own way, further complicates the issue. How does a beginning teacher begin to understand how children learn?

There is basic knowledge about children's learning that forms the foundation on which theories have been built. Feeney, Christensen, and Moravcik (2006), have identified the following:

- The child develops as a whole.
- Development follows predictable patterns.
- Rates of development vary.
- Development is influenced by maturation.
- Development is influenced by actual experience.
- Culture affects development.

To these, Hendrick (1985, 1993) would add:

- Children utilize play to translate experience into understanding.
- Parents are the most important influence in the development of the child.
- The teacher must present learning within a climate of caring.

The traditional approach by nativists who believe maturation is key emphasizes discovery by the child. This approach is the basis of learning at the traditional nursery school. The approach of **cognitive developmental theory**, notably by Piaget and Montessori, has led to programs such as Weikart's cognitively oriented curriculum.

The studies of Erikson, a psychosexual interactionist, are less concerned with cognitive development and more concerned with social-emotional development. Emphasis is placed on social interaction and discovery (Stevens & King, 1976). In view of these different approaches to child development, it is obvious that no one theorist has the final word on how children learn.

assimilation—according to Jean Piaget, one form of adaptation, which takes place when the person tries to make new information or a new experience fit into an existing concept.

accommodation—according to Jean Piaget, one form of adaptation, which takes place when an existing concept is modified, or a new concept is formed, to incorporate new information or a new experience.

equilibration—according to Jean Piaget, the state of balance each person seeks between existing mental structures and new experiences.

cognitive—pertaining to the mental processes of perception, memory, judgment, and reasoning.

cognitive developmental theory—the theory formulated by Jean Piaget that focuses on how children's intelligence and thinking abilities emerge through distinct stages.

HOW DO CHILDREN LEARN?

Learning occurs as a child interacts with the environment using the five senses. Some theorists include a sixth sense, called the *kinesthetic*, which is a sense of where the body is in relation to space. The human child is a goal-directed individual who actively seeks information (National Research Council, 2000).

What does a toddler do when presented with a new toy (see Figure 4–1)? He looks it over carefully, he may shake it to see if it makes any noise, he puts it into his mouth, and likely turns it over and over in his hands. It seems that the toddler uses all of the senses to discover all there is to know about the toy. Then look at how the preschooler is concentrating on the computer screen (see Figure 4–2). He stares intently and grasps the mouse tightly. We may assume the child is listening closely, with the mouth open and the

Figure 4-1
Infants and toddlers use all of the senses to discover.

reinforcement—in behavioral theory, any response that follows a behavior that encourages repetition of that behavior.

tongue pressed against the teeth to improve concentration. All of these actions show us that the child is learning. A learning sequence may proceed as follows:

- The child attends and records.
- The child experiences and explores.
- The child imitates actions, sounds, words, and so on. The child becomes aware of similarities and differences and/or matching events.
- The child responds appropriately to actions and words, and discusses and questions.
- The child talks about what has been learned or discovered.
- The child remembers and uses knowledge (see Figure 4-3).

When something is learned, the child may respond with appropriate, nonverbal behavior. In addition, the child may name or talk about what has been learned, and may apply the knowledge.

Discussions of child learning may include the following statements:

- If a child's action receives positive **reinforcement** immediately, there is a strong possibility that the act will recur.
- If a child's action receives negative feedback or is ignored, repetition of the act will be discouraged.
- Habit behavior is difficult to change.
- Periodic positive reinforcement is necessary to maintain children's favorable actions.
- Motivation level may increase persistence in learning tasks.
- For each child, all classroom experiences have a feeling tone, ranging from pleasant to neutral to unpleasant.
- Motivation may contain a degree of tension, which may aid or inhibit success.

Figure 4-2
Nonverbal behavior tells us this child is concentrating and learning.

There are two types of motivation: intrinsic and extrinsic. *Intrinsic* motivation comes from within; children act in certain ways because of their interest in any given activity. *Extrinsic* motivation is imposed from without; children act because of a perceived reward or punishment.

For example, a child may play with puzzles simply because he enjoys the activity (intrinsic motivation), but may resist coming to circle time when asked because he then cannot continue with what he has been doing (a punishment in his eyes, so he avoids coming to circle time due to extrinsic motivation).

The emotions that exist within individuals during learning experiences may enhance or retard how much learning takes place. Infants and children have anxiety levels ranging from overload (extreme agitation or excitement) to underload (boredom) in life situations. If overwhelmed, the infant will tune out and turn away. Learning is best accomplished when anxiety is low and the excitement about finding out and knowing is high, but not too high.

A teacher's technique or way of interacting, which includes pressuring, embarrassment, or increasing a child's self-doubt or feeling of inadequacy, can limit a child's learning. Unfortunately, student teachers may only need

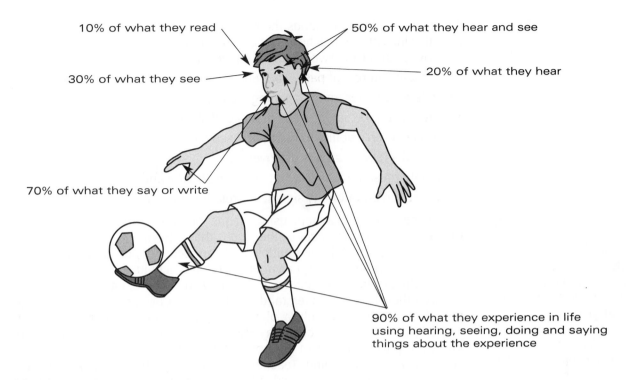

10% of what they read

50% of what they hear and see

30% of what they see

20% of what they hear

70% of what they say or write

90% of what they experience in life using hearing, seeing, doing and saying things about the experience

Figure 4-3
What a child generally remembers.

to look back into their own schooling experience to find examples they do not want to repeat.

On the other hand, we all remember teachers who accepted our ideas as important contributions, smiled at us, appreciated our sometimes feeble attempts, noticed our efforts, and made us feel unique and special.

What else do early childhood educators know about child learning?

1. Children have curiosity and are motivated to know and find out more about what has captured their attention, or what they have experienced.

2. Knowledge is constructed internally, when children move, act, explore, and talk about their environment and life experiences with other children and adults.

3. A social-emotional feeling tone is present in most learning situations, and is accompanied by shared narrative that is meaningful to the child.

4. Questions are welcomed, and answers are thought-provoking, leading to discovery.

Neuroscientists studying human memory theorize that two types of memory exist: *working* memory, which is memory of the present moment, and *long-term*, or *extended period* memory (Cowley & Underwood, 1998). Every perception a child experiences is not stored as memory; only mentally well-connected experiences are retained and survive. Additional experiences connecting the first memory to additional ones become more deeply embedded in brain tissue, strengthening the memory. A specific area of the brain is believed to be responsible for filtering the vast amount of child perceptions that can occur. An encounter with emotional significance, or one related to things already known, stands the best chance of storage as memory. What does this indicate for teachers as they plan activities?

Cowley and Underwood (1998) suggest the following:

- Review and repeat past experiences to strengthen mental associations.
- Relate activities and happenings to children's lives.
- Provide opportunity for the practice of skills.
- Aid children's ability to put their discoveries into words.
- Verbally repeat what is discovered.
- Relate present ideas to what children already know.
- Create an emotionally significant relationship with each learner.

Those student teachers using theme or *unit* planning (discussed in Chapter 5) will appreciate the idea that **thematic teaching and instruction** gives children multiple and connected opportunities to experience new material, through a variety of related activities.

A critical feature of effective teaching involves eliciting from young children their existing understanding of a subject at hand. This knowledge provides possible curriculum planning opportunities (National Research Council, 2000). When a child says "Milk comes from the store," teachers know a trip to a dairy farm or another type of planned activity concerning cows would be expanding. Teachers pay close attention to the knowledge, skills, and attitudes possessed, plus how children are affected by their cultural backgrounds.

Problem-Solving

In a rapidly changing world, the ability to solve problems becomes a survival skill. Problem-solving involves and includes convergent and divergent thinking skills, classification, patterning, and evaluation skills (see Figure 4–4). To become a more effective problem-solver, the child must:

1. have a general knowledge of the properties of objects.
2. have the ability to notice incongruities or inconsistencies, and define the problem (the "what is wrong here").
3. have the ability to think of new and unconventional functions for familiar objects.
4. have the ability to generate many possible solutions.
5. have the ability to evaluate various solutions.
6. have the ability to implement a solution she thinks will best fulfill the requirements of solving the problem.

Early childhood student teachers need to analyze whether problem-solving is a priority in their planning and daily interactions with young children.

Elder and Paul (1998) imply that critical thinking is enhanced when one develops a questioning inner voice that routinely asks such questions as:

- "In this situation, what do I really know? What do I think I know but am not completely sure of? What do I need to learn? What do I still need to figure out?" (intellectual humility)

thematic teaching and instruction—a theme approach to child program planning, including theme identification, environmental needs, activities, presentation, and evaluation, usually designed for a selected period of study. It can encompass a wide range of curriculum areas including art, music, mathematics, language, science, motor, social, and other development opportunities.

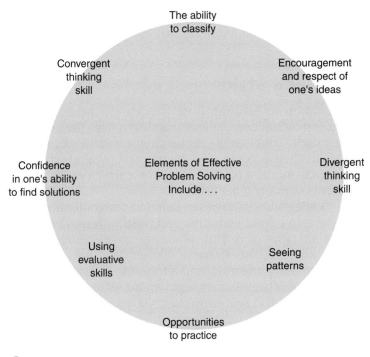

The ability
to classify

Convergent
thinking
skill

Encouragement
and respect of
one's ideas

Confidence
in one's ability
to find solutions

Elements of Effective
Problem Solving
Include . . .

Divergent
thinking
skill

Using
evaluative
skills

Seeing
patterns

Opportunities
to practice

Figure 4-4
Solving problems

- "Am I uncritically accepting what I have learned, or do I have the courage to question what I have learned? Am I afraid to question certain beliefs or practices because I may be rejected for questioning them?" (intellectual courage)
- "Am I honestly trying to imagine this situation from this other person's point of view? Can I accurately state another person's point of view that is in conflict with my own?" (intellectual empathy)
- "Am I thinking through this issue in a way that does justice to its complexity, or do I come to a conclusion too quickly? Do I give up when figuring things out becomes frustrating?" (intellectual perseverance)

Learning Modalities

Recent studies have tried to identify children who learn more efficiently through one sense or modality than through others. A child who enjoys looking at books and notices your new clothes may be a *visual learner*, as opposed to the child who listens intently during story time and is the first to hear a bird chirping outside the window. The second child may be an *auditory learner* (see Figure 4–5). The child who enjoys playing with materials of different textures—for example, fingerpaint, clay, feelie-box games—may be a *kinesthetic learner*, or one who learns best through touch and body motion (see Figure 4–6). Many children are visual learners, but most, especially preschoolers, use a combination of all the senses to gather impressions. A teacher can expect greater retention of knowledge if all senses are

Figure 4-5
A child who enjoys listening activities may be an auditory learner.

Figure 4-6
Children who enjoy playing with materials of different textures may be kinesthetic learners.

field sensitive—a child who needs encouragement from the teacher and peers for motivation, does not trust himself, and looks for reassurance from others.

field independent— a child who works independent of distractions in the surrounding environment; a child who is self-motivated and self-monitoring.

involved. (See the Appendix for a learning modalities exercise for attempting to assess elementary school students.)

Learning Styles

In addition to learning from the use of the senses, or learning modalities, children also learn from the adults in their lives. Traditionally, some children learn as apprentices to their parents. The Native American child's parents may model a particular type of learning mode, as do parents of many other cultures.

Some children, however, demand more attention than others as they learn. The terms **field sensitive** and **field independent** can be used to describe certain types of children. Field-sensitive children like to work with others, and ask for guidance from the teacher. They have difficulty completing an open-ended assignment without a model to follow. The field-sensitive child waits until the other children begin an art lesson to see what they are doing, and then starts. The field-sensitive child asks questions of the teacher, and enjoys working one-to-one with her. In contrast, the field-independent child prefers to work alone, is task-oriented, rarely seeks guidance from the teacher, and prefers open-ended projects. The field-independent child will try new activities without being urged to do so. In terms of learning, this child enjoys the discovery approach best. Which children at your center or school are field sensitive or field independent?

Learning Styles and Learning

Since the publication of Howard Gardner's book, *Frames of Mind*, in 1983, there has been a new look at the influence of learning style on how children learn. Initially Gardner posited seven types of intelligences: *linguistic*, *logico-mathematical*, *spatial*, *bodily-kinesthetic*, *musical*, *interpersonal*, and *intrapersonal*. Gardner (1988), rightfully perhaps, accuses schools, particularly in elementary settings, of teaching only to those children with linguistic and logico-mathematical intelligence, largely ignoring the other five types.

Gardner (Moran, Kornhaber, & Gardner, 2006) now believes that there are eight types of intelligence, and possibly nine, adding *naturalist* intelligence, or "the ability to distinguish and categorize objects or phenomena in nature," and *existential* intelligence, or "the ability to contemplate phenomena or questions beyond sensory data, such as the infinite and infinitesimal." As yet, however, we do not have any solid indication that existential intelligence exists in the nervous system, which is an important criterion for typing as an intelligence (Checkly, 1997; Gardner, 1999; Meyer, 1997).

Using Gardner's theory, early childhood educators are able to look at children in a new and yet already recognized way: in a *global* fashion. *Intelligence*, or *human cognitive competence*, Gardner believes, can be described in terms of sets of abilities, talents, or mental skills called *intelligences*, with all normal individuals possessing each of these skills to some extent, degree, or combination (Gardner, 2000).

As we age, most of us become aware that there are some learning areas where learning is easy and others where one may struggle to comprehend what others grasp rapidly. Areas of human growth encountered in life can be described as being multiple, diverse, unknown, perhaps limit-less, and as yet untested because one has neither encountered nor been introduced to them. People often discuss having gifts that enable them to do, or easily learn, some intelligence-connected life pursuit. People also speak of the "gift" of an opportunity in their lives that resulted in a positive outcome, allowing them to grow or excel.

Moran, Kornhaber, and Gardner (2006) state that as educators trying to put into daily practice the theory of multiple intelligences, we should look closely at each child, seeing that child as unique, complex, perhaps gifted, or with strengths not easily discovered. Educators should then encourage, appreciate, accommodate, promote, enjoy, develop, and offer help and opportunity. They would understand that a child observed with skill in one area may not have skill in another, but that most children have a combina-tion of intelligences. They would not let a child's culture, physical appear-ance, economic circumstance, color, or any other external factor cloud their observations. However, they caution that there is "[n]o need to create nine different lesson plans. Instead, design rich learning experiences that nurture each student's combination of intelligences."

Tomlinson and Jarvis (2006) would strongly second Moran and her associates. They stress five principles for teachers to keep in mind as they plan lessons designed to teach to student strengths:

1. Teachers who see student strengths teach positively.
2. Teaching to student strengths helps students see themselves positively.
3. Teaching to student strengths helps students see strengths in one another.
4. Teaching to student strengths helps students see learning positively.
5. Teaching to student strengths helps students overcome weaknesses.

One of the reasons that some methods of teaching to learning styles have not been addressed in schools is because they are difficult to evalu-ate, and too much emphasis has been placed on discrete, item-to-item, day-to-day evaluation. Another reason is related to our own biases as teachers; we teach in the way we learn best. Many teachers are strong visual, experiential learners.

Preschool, kindergarten, and primary grade teachers, using the state-ments in Figure 4–7, can observe their respective students and learn more about their children's preferred learning styles. (For other learning-style questionnaires, see the Appendix.)

Multiple Intelligences in the Classroom

Preschools involve children's abilities to use multiple intelligences. Playing with blocks, both large and small, involves spatial, bodily-kinesthetic, lin-guistic, and sometimes logico-mathematical intelligences. Learning asso-ciated with height, length, weight, number, inclines, size relationships, and other concepts, which are difficult to grasp without firsthand experience, can be understood in the course of play. Big, bigger, biggest is often dis-cussed by block-playing children. During dramatic play, by using linguistic and interpersonal intelligences, children learn role-playing skills depend-ing on how the dramatic-play center is arranged. Art activities can focus children's attention on color, and the properties of different media, while

	Yes	No

IN THE CLASSROOM THE CHILD:

1. Usually chooses to play/work in a quiet area.
2. Usually chooses to play/work in the noisier areas.
3. Prefers to work/play with music in the background.
4. Becomes distracted if music is played in the background.
5. Is able to concentrate, even if others are talking or are noisy.
6. Prefers to work/play near window areas or in brightly lighted ones.
7. Usually chooses to play/work at a table or desk.
8. Usually chooses to play/work on the floor, or a chair.
9. Concentrates for longer periods of time in the morning.
10. Often appears more tired in the morning than in the afternoon.

IN RELATING TO ADULTS AND OTHER CHILDREN, THE CHILD:

1. Prefers to work/play alone.
2. Prefers to play/work with only one friend.
3. Works/plays better if the teacher/peer helps.
4. Likes clear directions regarding how to complete any specific task.
5. Prefers to play/work with several friends.
6. Looks to teacher/peers to reinforce directions as a task is being completed.
7. Frequently starts an activity but seldom finishes.
8. Has difficulty following spoken directions unless a demonstration, with an example, is given.
9. Notices whenever teacher or playmates have a new hair style, glasses, or are wearing new clothing.
10. Follows spoken directions easily.

⬤ **Figure 4-7**
Observation checklist to assess child's preferred learning style.

children explore using spatial, linguistic, and bodily-kinesthetic intelligences. At circle times, linguistic and interpersonal intelligences come into play when young preschoolers learn appropriate student behaviors, such as raising one's hand to speak in a group.

In elementary schools, more focus may be placed on linguistic and logico-mathematical intelligences. However, as exemplified in the example of the Key School (Gardner, 1993), children may learn new vocabulary words by composing a rap-style song (linguistic and musical intelligences). They dissect owl pellets in small groups, trying to match pieces of bone found to a chart of mice bones, all the time talking to each other and using linguistic, interpersonal, spatial, naturalist, and bodily-kinesthetic intelligences at the same time.

temperaments—
children's inborn characteristics, such as regularity, adaptability, and other dispositions that affect behavior.

Temperament

Children also reveal different **temperaments**. These can also determine how a child relates to the environment. Examine Figure 4–8, which lists the characteristics of temperament. Where do you fit on the lines between the extremes? Are you more or less active? Are your body rhythms regular or irregular? Do you tend to be impulsive or cautious in making decisions? Do

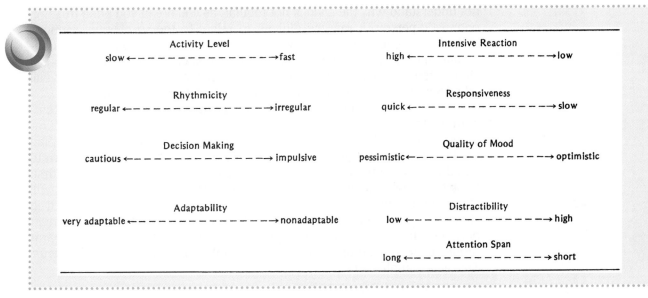

Figure 4-8
The nine characteristics of temperament.

you see yourself as an adaptable person? Do you have a quick or slow temper? Are you generally an optimist or a pessimist? Are you easily distracted, or could the house burn down around you when you are reading a good book? Your answers to these questions describe your temperament.

Chess and Thomas (1999) have undertaken longitudinal studies looking at the nine characteristics of temperament identified by Thomas, Chess, Birch, Hertzig, and Korn (1963). These studies suggest that there are three general types of children, depending on where they fall among the nine characteristics: the easy-to-get-along-with child, the feisty one, and the slow-to-warm-up child.

Children who are easy to get along with have moderate activity levels and regular rhythmicity. They are moderate in decision making, adaptable, slow to anger (without being so slow that they do not assert themselves when appropriate), more optimistic than pessimistic, and both quick and slow to respond, depending on the situation. They tend to have low levels of distractibility and lengthy attention spans. These children may also be more field independent than field sensitive.

The behavior of children who are feisty goes to extremes. The children have fast activity levels and irregular rhythmicity. They are cautious, nonadaptable, quick to anger or prone to temper tantrums, generally negative, and easily distracted. They have short attention spans. Children who are slow to warm up tend to be so cautious in making a decision that they will often wait for a decision to present itself before they move. They are slow to respond, have low adaptability levels, and are generally more pessimistic.

You should be aware that there are no good or bad temperaments; there are only different ones (see Figure 4–8). Take another look at where you fall on the line between the extremes. Generally, you will have difficulty relating to children at opposite extremes from yourself. For example, if your body rhythms are very regular, you may have less patience toilet training a child who does not have regular body rhythms. This can happen because you may not understand why the child is not regular, as you are. If you are a trusting, optimistic person, it may be difficult to relate to the suspicious, cautious child. The teacher with a lengthy attention span and low level of distractibility may have less patience with the child who is easily distracted and has a short attention span. In planning, the teacher may feel that an activity will take 15 minutes only to discover that this child flits through it in 3.

What is the teacher's role in working with children of different temperaments? First, be careful not to label a child with a different temperament as good or bad. Second, take a cue from the characteristics and plan the lessons accordingly. The child with a short attention span can learn to lengthen it. Give the child activities that can be completed quickly at first. Look to see what activities the child prefers. Then plan an activity that will take a little longer to finish, and encourage the child to remain with it. Gradually, you can persuade the child to attend to the activity for a longer period of time. Culpepper, Aldridge, and Sibley (2005) state that it is paramount to recognize and accommodate children's various temperaments. This is accomplished by:

- observing children's behavior.
- considering the physical arrangement of the classroom (more about this in Chapter 6).
- providing a variety of activities.
- investigating non-school-related influences, for example, stress in the family.
- assessing our own temperament.
- evaluating our curriculum and teaching methods (see Chapter 5).
- choosing appropriate guidance techniques (covered more completely in Chapter 6).
- sharing information with parents.

Culpepper and her colleagues (2005) conclude that "[t]emperament and goodness of fit are important concepts for early childhood professionals. . . . Healthy social and personality development occurs in young children when there is compatibility between the child and the demands and expectations of the teacher and center environment."

All teachers soon realize that children do not accomplish the lesson or skill at the same speed, and they differ in the amount of time and attention they devote to activities. The number of repetitions needed for children to learn or memorize varies. In general, the memory of an experience will become stronger each time it is encountered.

REVIEW OF SELECTED CURRENT RESEARCH

Research on Brain Development

Although much of the research on brain development and its implication for caregivers and teachers is almost 30 years old, the ability to see the brain in action with magnetic resonance imaging (MRI) has dramatically pointed out the validity of the earlier findings. Life experiences are believed to control both how the infant's brain is architecturally formed and how intricate brain circuits are wired. Brain development hinges on a complex interplay between inherited genes and life experiences (Shore, 1997). Prenatal conditions, as most of you already know, also affect brain development.

Shortly after birth, a growth spurt in the brain occurs as the axons, which send signals, and dendrites, which receive them, explode with new connections, called *synapses*. The number of brain cells is not as important as the number of connections these cells can make (Sullo, 1999). Bloom, Nelson, and Lazerson (2001) posit that larger numbers of synapses allow an increased number and variety of messages in the brain.

Electrical activity, triggered by a flood of sensory experiences, fine-tunes the brain's circuitry, determining which connections will be retained and which will be pruned or cut off. Pruning is a lifelong process and does not result in the loss of brain function. Brain neurons remain intact and available for later learning (Cashmore, 2001).

Sensitive periods, or *windows*, are felt to exist (for example, in the learning of language, this period is from birth to approximately age three). At these times, certain types of input create or stabilize long-lasting structures. As Kantrowitz (1997) states:

> Every lullaby, every giggle and peek-a-boo, triggers a crackling along his neural pathways, laying the groundwork for what could someday be a love of art or a talent for soccer or a gift for making and keeping friends.

Most cognitive science researchers accept the following as key findings:

- Learning changes the physical structure of the brain.
- Structural changes alter the functional organization of the brain; in other words, learning organizes and reorganizes the brain.
- Different parts of the brain may be ready to learn at different times. (National Research Council, 2000).

The world is in the midst of an extraordinary outpouring of scientific work on brain function, processes of thinking and learning, neural processes that occur during thought and learning, and on the development of competence (National Research Council, 2000).

Open-ended art and musical experiences in early childhood are believed to facilitate learning concepts in math, science, language, and reading later on. Activities that prompt mental imaging, such as family storytelling, art, and music, are deemed important to the brain's ongoing development of mental connections (learning). They are also crucial to the child's development of self-confidence and aid in the development of social relationships, personality adjustment, and the child's natural creative ability (Archilles, 1999; Sylwester, 1998; Szyba, 1999; Weinberger, 1998).

Just as the above-mentioned authors believe that brain research shows how very early experiences influence brain development, Bruer (1998) argues that overstatement, and at times distortion and hyperbole, have led parents and educators scurrying to ensure that children receive the *right* types of enrichment, before age three. Bruer also suggests that the same misinformation has led legislators to develop educational policy based on misinterpretation and hype. A difference of opinion exists concerning deterministic and lifelong effects of early nurturing by parents and care providers (Harris, 1998). Harris, heavily criticized by well-respected child development scientists for the extreme position she holds, bases her assumptions on a behavioral genetics viewpoint. She believes that parenting has

● **Figure 4-9**
This child reveals a low
level of distractibility and
lengthy attention span.

been oversold, and that parents have been led to believe they have more influence on their child's personality than they actually do.

Another difference of opinion exists between Bruer's (1998) contention that "the specifics of home or preschool environments matter little, if at all, to how children's sensory and motor systems develop" and Lowery's (1998) belief that they do. Lowery presents examples from research on how the brain constructs knowledge, perceives relationships, and how carefully planned, sequential activities and curriculums allow children to explore, thus facilitating brain connections.

Whether Lowery's analysis is correct or not, what is certain is that state lawmakers are connecting recent research, which emphasizes the early and rapid development of infants' brains, with the need for quality programs for young children. Over a dozen state legislatures have passed early childhood initiatives that directly reference brain development. Other state initiatives were approved after legislators were specifically informed about brain research (Groginsky, Robison, & Smith, 1999).

Perhaps the one point that we all should remember is Levine's (2002) counsel that different brains are wired differently, but that all brains are wired to learn (see Figure 4–9).

Brain-Based Learning

All learning is brain-based, and teachers can become more effective with some knowledge of how the brain senses, processes, stores, and retrieves information (Perry, 2000). Perry believes that the following is necessary teacher knowledge, especially for elementary grades, when teachers attempt lecture presentations:

- Learning requires attention, and neural systems become fatigued quickly. In three to five minutes of sustained brain activity, neurons become less responsive and need to rest.
- Neurons respond to patterned and repetitive events rather than sustained, continuous stimulation.
- In familiar and safe environments, children's brains will seek novelty.
- A factual lecture can be tolerated four to eight minutes before the brain wanders. If a teacher is not providing novelty, the brain focuses elsewhere.
- When concepts are presented in isolation, and are unrelated to what the child knows, a fatiguing effect ensues.
- Information is easiest to digest when there is "emotional seasoning." Humor, empathy, and other emotions, coupled with factual concepts, make assimilation easier.
- Linking related concepts facilitates the formation of brain connections.
- A presentation that bobs and weaves between facts, concepts, and narrative in a lecture presentation is a prudent approach.
- Human beings are storytelling primates, both curious and fond of learning (Perry, 2000).

Early childhood educators can use the preceding information when giving directions and explanations, leading discussions, trying to develop emotional rapport, and planning activities.

The teacher who wishes to end an activity on a satisfying, high note, before children's lack of ability to attend sets in, will watch the timing of activities, consider the novelty factor, and consider repetition useful. She also will notice which activities children enjoy the most. These are ones children request, or ask you to do again. When reading certain picture books, children will know words, actions, or the story well. Repeated favorite book readings are commonplace in pre-kindergarten classrooms. Children's genuine feelings of pleasure and accomplishment can be displayed in both indoor and outdoor curriculum activities.

Research on Emotional Intelligence

Since the publication of Goleman's *Emotional Intelligence* in 1995, there has been a renewed interest in how children's emotions impact their learning. Greenspan (1997) emphasizes that certain kinds of emotional nurturing propel infants and young children to intellectual and emotional health and suggests that affective experiences help them master a variety of cognitive tasks. Early childhood educators, alert to new research-based data on emotional intelligence, are provided with additional fuel to advocate for the importance of and need for quality child care.

Public school teachers and administrators, recognizing the impact of emotional and social well-being on their students' abilities to learn, have begun to develop programs to help (Cummings & Haggerty, 1997; Elias, Bruene-Butler, Blum, & Schuyler, 1997; Weissberg, Shriver, Bose, & DeFalco, 1997). Although some criticism has been provoked by the thought of teaching a social-emotional program, Elias and his associates contend that social-emotional learning ties several areas of the curriculum together like AIDS education, drug-abuse education, stress prevention, and so on (Elias, et al., 1997).

Pool (1997) cites Goleman as positing five dimensions of emotional intelligence:

1. self-awareness
2. the ability to handle emotions (impulse control, for example)
3. motivation
4. empathy
5. social skills

As you can see, Goleman believes that social skills are a component of emotional intelligence. How can a child with little self-awareness or self-control—even if motivated—develop social relationships without empathy? Is emotional intelligence related to IQ? Goleman (1995) provides several examples from research to demonstrate how emotional skills are essential, not only for school achievement, but also for success in life.

Research on Self-Esteem and Learning

After much research in the 1960s and 1970s on the relationship of **self-esteem** to learning, the 1980s saw little being done. A new interest emerged in the 1990s, however, and researchers were again impressed with the interrelationships between how children view themselves and their abilities to learn. Initial work by Coopersmith (1967) and others has shown that children who perceive themselves as capable and competent,

self-esteem—children's evaluation of their worth in positive or negative terms.

and who have a feeling of belonging in terms of the classroom atmosphere, are more likely to do well in school than those who do not. For teachers, then, the task is clear. We need to help children feel that they:

● are competent and valued as persons
● have control over their own behavior
● can make valid choices within the classroom structure
● can learn to respect others as their own self-respect develops

We must be aware of any hidden biases we might hold and learn to treat all of our children fairly and honestly, to encourage individual responsibility (Curry & Johnson, 1990). Our curricular goals must value the thinking processes children use as much as any product of that thinking; we need to emphasize what Katz and Chard (1989) call *positive dispositions*, such as curiosity, resourcefulness, independence, initiative, responsibility, and others.

Some self-esteem curriculums have been developed, such as Magic Circle, Quest, and Tribes. Preschools, child care programs, and elementary schools using these programs have reported increased interest in cooperation and learning among their children.

Teachers familiar with the need children have to see themselves as capable and belonging to their classroom group often provide opportunities, within the curriculum as a whole, for building self-esteem. These teachers offer children viable choices, and utilize cooperative learning groups and modeling, among other techniques, to boost children's self-esteem (see Figure 4–10).

Violand-Sánchez and Hainer-Violand (2006) stress how crucial it is to ensuring the success of Latino students that teachers acknowledge the strengths they bring to school. Using the phrase *positive identity*, they emphasize the need for schools to:

● foster a positive ethnic identity, by viewing bilingualism and biculturalism as an asset, and immigration as a source of pride.
● empower Latino students through leadership roles within the school and community.
● encourage student voice by having students speak and write from experience.

Violand-Sánchez and Hainer-Violand conclude, "By honoring the complexity of language and culture as well as the tenacious spirit that Latino students bring to the classroom, schools can teach to Latino students' strengths. This will not only enrich our lessons but also our schools, our communities, and our world." Those of us who teach in multicultural, multilingual classrooms and communities prevalent today in the United States would do well to pay heed.

● **Figure 4-10**
Children are allowed to choose child-authored books during silent reading (first grade classroom).

Research on Levels of Representation

According to Piaget's theory, children go through four stages of cognitive development. Gonzalez-Mena (2005) reviewed these stages in her textbook, *Foundations: Early Childhood Education in a Diverse Society*. Piaget posited the four stages as follows:

1. **Sensorimotor stage.** From birth to age two or three. Starting at birth, infants and toddlers learn primarily through their senses, seeing, hearing, touching (manipulating), smelling, and tasting everything, as in the example of the toddler with the new toy, discussed earlier.

2. **Preoperational stage.** From age two or three to eight or nine. At this stage, beginning with the development of language approximately at age two, the preschooler develops what Piaget terms *preconcepts,* and learns by using intuition. Thus, a three-year-old child makes typical mistakes in conceptual learning and may call a cow, seen for the first time, by the name of the only large animal with which he has any experience: "horsie."

Adults can see children's intuition at work, as they make grammatical errors in overgeneralizing plurals. For example, *mouse* becomes *mouses*, just as *house* becomes *houses*. *Foot* becomes *foots* or *feets*. "I don't got no more cookies" becomes standard emphasis for the three-year-old, with the use of the double negative considered normal.

Piaget often called children in the preoperational stage *perception bound*, meaning that they are limited by what they can see, hear, touch, manipulate, and so on, and that they have difficulty seeing comparisons when differences are dramatic. A child at this stage may not understand that a Chihuahua and a Great Dane are both dogs. One two-year-old, for example, called a Scottie dog a "funny cat" because her only acquaintance with small, furry black animals had been her own large, female Persian cat.

3. **Concrete operational stage.** From ages six to eight, to age eleven and even to adulthood. At this stage, the child begins to be able to form classifications and to see the similarities among categories despite their differences. All dogs and all cats, for example, become "animals." Birds that fly, such as sparrows and cardinals, can be grouped with chickens, and sometimes with difficulty, ducks, and geese.

Also during the concrete operational stage, the child begins to understand the principle of **conservation**, which is essential to the understanding of mathematics. This includes examples such as understanding that the mass of clay does not change when it is rolled from a ball into an elongated shape; that the amount of liquid in a tall, thin glass may be the same as in a short, fat glass; that area does not change where there are the same number of objects placed on a field, even though one field looks more crowded because the objects are scattered and the other field *seems* to have more area, because the objects are aligned along one side.

4. **Formal operational stage.** From age eleven to adulthood. According to Piaget, during this final stage in intellectual development, the child begins to be capable of abstract thinking. At this stage, the child can formulate hypotheses and learns to monitor his own thinking, called *metacognition*.

conservation—the ability, usually acquired during the concrete operational stage, to recognize that objects remain the same in terms of size, volume, and area despite perceptual changes.

The Importance of Speech and Language

Much of the research developed by Vygotsky (Berk & Winsler, 1995), a contemporary of Piaget, was kept unknown to Western psychologists and educators by the USSR. After *perestroika* and the breakup of the USSR, many of the former Soviet researchers came to the United States, and a wide distribution of Vygotsky's research became available.

Considered a sociocultural theorist, Vygotsky saw learning as taking place through social contact and the development of what he termed

zone of proximal development (ZPD)—in Vygotsky's theory, this zone comprises tasks a child cannot yet do by herself but that she can accomplish with the support of an older child or adult.

scaffolding—a teaching technique helpful in promoting language, understanding, and child solutions, that may include supportive and responsive teacher conversation and actions following child-initiated behavior.

private speech. Children talk to themselves, either silently or vocally, in the attempt to internalize learning, monitor themselves, and solve problems. Vygotsky emphasized the importance of language in the development of socially shared cognition, in which adults or peers assisted the child to move ahead in development, by noticing what the next logical step might be. The term **zone of proximal development (ZPD)** was applied to the adult's or peer's recognition of when the child needed assistance and when the child did not. This assisted learning is called **scaffolding**.

Understanding Vygotsky's theory in teaching has led to the emphasis on cooperative learning, scaffolding or assisted learning, and teaching children to use private speech to help in their problem-solving. A teacher might notice that a child is having difficulty placing one piece of a puzzle in the right place, and suggests that the piece be rotated. A peer familiar with the same puzzle might do the same. Likewise, a teacher might suggest that the child verbalize as she is putting the pieces into the puzzle, saying such words as, "I see the yellow piece here and I see more yellow there; maybe the piece fits in here."

Translating Theory into Practice

Beliefs about educational practice are shaped both by training coursework and personal experiences in working with children (Brown & Rose, 1995; Vartuli, 2005). Discrepancies between theory and practice may exist in workplaces and in the placement classroom of a student teacher. Over-reliance on experience may not lead to the best practice (Cassidy & Lawrence, 2000). Student teaching requires *sustained examination* of classroom practice and *reflection*, if a student teacher hopes to understand or articulate the relationship between theory and practice (Kvernbekk, 1997). Over time, it is believed that the ability to explain a rationale for a teacher's classroom behaviors may represent a form of *grounded theories*, in which the theories to which teachers have been exposed are supported through experience and become the bedrock of their teaching philosophy and beliefs (Cassidy & Lawrence, 2000).

INTELLIGENT BEHAVIOR

Costa (1991) suggests that there are several characteristics of intelligent behavior displayed by children. These behaviors apply to adults as well so, in this case, student teachers can gain insight into their own behaviors. Costa notes that these are *suggested* intelligence characteristics and are not meant to represent a complete listing. He urges teachers to discover additional indicators through "kid-watching and self-analysis."

Costa's characteristics of intelligent behavior follow:

- persistence or persevering when the solution to a problem is not immediately apparent
- decreasing impulsivity
- listening to others with understanding and empathy
- using flexibility in thinking
- *metacognition*, defined as awareness of one's own thinking

- checking for accuracy and precision
- questioning and problem-posing
- drawing on past knowledge and applying that knowledge to new situations
- using precision in language and thought, rather than confused, vague, and imprecise language to express ideas (this includes using complete sentences, providing supportive evidence for ideas, elaborating, clarifying, and defining terminology in written and oral expression)
- using all the senses
- displaying ingenuity, originality, insightfulness, and creativity
- displaying wonderment, inquisitiveness, curiosity, and the enjoyment of problem-solving; displaying a sense of efficacy as a thinker

Other characteristics of intelligent behavior Costa mentions, which are not found in the above listing, are a sense of humor and ethical/moral reasoning.

⊙ SUMMARY

Several identified theories currently influence views and decisions about child learning. Individuality in learning is apparent; children learn at different rates and learn from different techniques. The teacher's understanding of child development and learning theory, and the idea of how children will learn best, should serve as the basis for children's guidance and growth.

The senses gather information, which is stored mentally and subject to continual revision as new situations are met. There is a definite sequence to the learning processes, and teachers need to be aware of individual styles and preferred learning modalities, to make the experience easier for each child. Many learning behaviors seen in early childhood remain our preferred learning styles throughout our adult lives.

⊙ HELPFUL WEB SITES

http://www.ed.gov
National Institute on Early Childhood Development. This site sponsors comprehensive and challenging research.

http://www.fpg.unc.edu
National Center for Early Development and Learning. Search research and select on-page summaries of the latest research.

http://ericae.net
ERIC Assessment and Evaluation Clearinghouse. Look for readings.

http://www.srcd.org
Society for Research on Child Development. This is an excellent source for the latest research on child development; this organization publishes the journal *Child Development*.

Additional resources for this chapter can be found by visiting the Online Companion at www.earlychilded.delmar.com.

●SUGGESTED ACTIVITIES

A. After reviewing Costa's (1991) 12 characteristics, and then envisioning the kind of preschool or primary grade environment that would promote or allow children's intelligent behavior, it is easy to see that providing time for child-initiated activities, discovery, experimentation, and free choice within a dynamic and interesting classroom suits Costa's characteristics. What opportunities for intellectual behavior and growth are possible in situations where "listen and learn" group instruction dominates? Discuss with a few classmates.

B. Rate the following situations as *A* (appropriate; justified by current learning theory) or *I* (inappropriate). If appropriate, cite the theory that supports the answer. Discuss your choices with four or five others in a class group meeting.

1. Marilee, a student teacher, encounters two children who want to learn to tie their shoes. Because she realizes shoe tying is a complex skill, Marilee says, "When you're a little bigger, you'll be able to do it."

2. Thien, a student teacher, would like to tell a group of three-year-olds about the country of his birth, Vietnam. However, Thien realizes they probably would not be able to grasp the concept of a foreign country, so he presents a simple Vietnamese song he learned as a child instead.

3. A cooperating teacher presents an activity in which she names and appreciates children who give correct answers.

4. Elena, a student teacher, notices that Jessica, an independent child, always hides when inside time is announced. She decides to interest Jessica in an indoor activity before inside time is called, to avoid having to find Jessica and coax her in.

5. Johnny refuses to attend any group activities. Laura, a teacher, suspects that he has had negative experiences at previous group times, and decides to make group time so attractive Johnny will want to join in. Laura has planned an activity with large balloons that children sit on and pop.

6. Lisa, Garrett, and Thad often gather at the reading corner and read new books. Stephanie, the student teacher, sees this as an example of intrinsic motivation.

7. Bud notices that his cooperating teacher always calls on each child by name in any conversation at group or discussion times.

8. Carolyn, a student teacher, feels she needs only to set out activities for the children and they will select the ones they need for their intellectual growth.

9. Gregorio, age three, has just poured water on the floor. The student teacher approaches, saying, "You need to tell me why you poured water on the floor."

10. There is a new child in the classroom. This child has a tattoo, which fascinates other children. The cooperating teacher feels it is best not to ask the child about it at group time because it might embarrass the newcomer. When a child asks about it, the teacher answers, "I can see you're really interested in the mark you see on our new friend's arm."

C. Read the following quote. Then in groups of four, discuss what interests, passions, and aspirations you think might exist in a class of six-year-olds living in (1) an inner city, (2) a rural area, and (3) a small town near the Mexican border. List your ideas and share with your training group.

> If teaching is conceived as constructing a bridge between the subject matter and the student, learner-centered teachers keep a constant eye on both ends of the bridge. The teachers attempt to get a sense of what each student knows, cares about, is able to do, and wants to do (The National Research Council, 2000).

What did you discover from this exercise?

D. Think back to your first days in your assigned classroom. What elements made the classroom feel safe and comfortable for you, the adult? What cooperating teacher actions made you feel at home, capable, and encouraged? Did you feel that you would learn something and do well in student teaching? Were there situations in which you felt like an outsider? What events and features would you replicate in your future classrooms, to have children feel part of the group, capable, and at ease? Discuss with your training class.

E. With a small group of fellow student teachers, discuss student teaching situations that have called for intelligent action and how you or others in your student teaching assignment proceeded or behaved. Share significant conclusions with your training group.

◉REVIEW

A. Choose the best answer to complete each statement.
1. Beginning teachers should:
   a. have a clear idea of how children learn best, because research has discovered the learning process.
   b. realize that there are a number of learning theories.
   c. expect children to learn in their own unique ways, making similarities between the children's learning patterns insignificant.
   d. look to their own learning experiences for clues on child learning.
   e. both b and c above.
2. A theory is someone's attempt to:
   a. gain fame.
   b. help instructors teach.
   c. make sense of a vast series of events.
   d. control others.
3. It is generally accepted that children should:
   a. be grouped according to ability.
   b. be grouped according to age.
   c. be asked to practice and recite learnings.
   d. play because it promotes learning.
4. When one hears that children pass through stages in their development, it means that:
   a. all children pass through stages in an orderly, predictable way.
   b. children should tour theaters.
   c. there seem to be phases in growth that teachers and parents can expect.
   d. most children will return to previous stages at times.
5. Children generally remember a concept best when they:
   a. see a picture of the concept.
   b. watch a demonstration of the concept by the teacher.
   c. hear the teacher describe the concept.
   d. use the concept in the discovery center.
6. Gardner (1988) believes that in elementary schools, teachers too often teach only to children with:
   a. logico-mathematical and intrapersonal intelligences.
   b. logico-mathematical and spatial intelligences.
   c. logico-mathematical and linguistic intelligences.
   d. logico-mathematical and bodily-kinesthetic intelligences.
7. According to research into temperament, the easy-to-get-along-with child has the following characteristics:
   a. a regular rhythmicity, adaptability, positive mood, low distractibility, and a long attention span.
   b. a regular rhythmicity, adaptability, intense reactions to environmental stimuli, and a negative mood.
   c. an irregular rhythmicity, a fast activity level, adaptability, negative mood, and a long attention span.
   d. a regular rhythmicity, negative mood, high distractibility, a long attention span, and intense reactions to stimuli.
8. Field-sensitive children tend to:
   a. want to work and play alone.
   b. seek reinforcement frequently from the teacher.
   c. like to work and play in large groups.
   d. like math and science better than concepts related to personal interests.
9. Costa (1991) suggests that among the intelligent behaviors displayed by children (and adults) are:
   a. persistence.
   b. impulsivity.
   c. questioning and problem-posing.
   d. flexibility in thinking.
   e. a, b, and c.
   f. a, c, and d.

...lren with a strong sense of self-esteem
generally:

a. do poorly in school.
b. do well in school.
c. are resourceful.
d. are dependable.

e. a and b.
f. c and d.

B. List any accepted learning theories you feel were excluded from this chapter. Cite your source (text, individual, etc.).

CASE SCENARIO

Setting: In a first grade classroom, the student teacher, Leah, is observing the children during the first week of her assignment. After the children leave, she talks with her cooperating teacher, Ms. Hails.

Leah wonders about the behavior of the little boy who was sitting under the table when children were doing table work, and whether he should be allowed to sit there while the other children were doing their assigned work.

Ms. Hails explains that Carlos is new to the classroom and comes from a Spanish-speaking family. She is not sure if his grasp of English is strong enough for planned activities. She suggests Leah choose Carlos for her case study assignment.

A week later, Ms. Hails asks Leah what she has learned from observing Carlos. Leah says she feels Carlos knows little English. She explains that even when she spoke a few Spanish phrases, she got a weak response. Carlos just ducked his

head. Leah thinks he is shy or has another problem.

"Based on your understanding of child development, what are the possible difficulties with Carlos?" Ms. Hails asks.

Leah mentions Carlos has not connected with any of the other children who are Spanish-speaking. Leah believes he goes under the table to hide whenever he's faced with something he doesn't understand.

Ms. Hails responds. "I'm going to call for an evaluation by the school psychologist. Until we have further information we'll have to work with Carlos as best we can. I'm going to ask you to check on how Carlos seems to learn best. What does he do on the play yard at recess?"

Leah responds, "Most of the time, he kicks the soccer ball around." She relates that she asked him once, mostly using body language, if he would like to climb on the climbing structure, but he shook his head. But then when the other children had

continues . . .

. . . continued

gone on and left the structure empty, Carlos did climb on it and seemed to enjoy going as high as he could, even balancing dangerously on the top bars, so he obviously enjoys physical activities using his whole body. And she noticed he has good eye-foot coordination; he kicks the soccer ball well and seems to have past experience. Leah believes that if Carlos has a preferred way of learning, it may be bodily-kinesthetic, thinking of Gardner's multiple intelligences. His behavior on the climbing structure would also suggest spatial intelligence.

Leah also remembers he liked playing with the pattern blocks, and one day, arranged them in the pattern shown on the card.

Ms. Hails suggests that as Carlos becomes more familiar with the classroom and the children he will open up. She tells Leah she has scheduled a parent conference. "I want you to work with him on a one-to-one basis whenever you can," she instructs.

Questions for Discussion:

1. What do you think might be some of the problems Carlos is experiencing?

2. If you were his student teacher, what activities might you try?

3. Does language appear to be Carlos' principal difficulty? What indications in this scenario would suggest so?

○ REFERENCES

Archilles, E. (1999, January). Creating music environments in early childhood programs. *Young Children, 54*(1).

Berk, L. E., & Winsler, A. (1995). *Scaffolding children's learning: Vygotsky and early childhood education.* Washington, DC: National Association for the Education of Young Children.

Bloom, F. M., Nelson, C. A., & Lazerson, A. (2001). *Brain, mind, and behavior* (3rd ed.) New York: Worth.

Brown, D., & Rose, T. (1995). Self-reported classroom impact of teachers' theories about learning and obstacles to implementation. *Action in Teacher Education, 17*(1), 20–29.

Bruer, J. T. (1998a). Brain science: Brain fiction. *Educational Leadership, 56*(3).

Bruer, J. T. (1998b). *The myth of the first three years.* New York: Free Press.

Cashmore, J. (2001). Early experience and brain development. *Journal of the HEIA, 8*(3), 16–19.

Cassidy, D. J., & Lawrence, J. M. (2000). Teachers' beliefs: The "whys" behind the "how to's" in child care classrooms. *Journal of Research in Childhood Education, 14*(2), 193–204.

Checkly, K. (1997, September). The first seven . . . and the eighth: A conversation with Howard Gardner. *Educational Leadership, 55*(1).

Chess, S., & Thomas, A. (1999). *Goodness of fit: Clinical applications from infancy through adult life.* New York: Bruner/Mazel/Taylor & Francis Group.

Coopersmith, S. (1967). *The antecedents of self-esteem.* San Francisco: Freeman.

Costa, A. L. (1991). The search for intelligent life. In *Developing minds: A resource book for teaching thinking.* Alexandria, VA: Association for Supervision and Curriculum Development.

Cowley, G., & Underwood, A. (1998, June 15). Memory. *Newsweek*.

Culpepper, S., Aldridge, J., & Sibley, J. (2005, May/June). The temperament trap: Recognizing and accommodating children's personalities. *Early Childhood News, 17*(3), 17–21.

Cummings, C., & Haggerty, K. P. (1997, May). Raising healthy children. *Educational Leadership, 54*(8).

Curry, N. E., & Johnson, C. N. (1990). *Beyond self-esteem: Developing a genuine sense of human value.* Washington, DC: National Association for the Education of Young Children.

Elder, L., & Paul, R. (1998, Spring). Critical thinking: Developing intellectual traits. *Journal of Developmental Education, 21*(3).

Elias, M. J., Bruene-Butler, L., Blum, L., & Schuyler, T. (1997, May). How to launch a social and emotional learning program. *Educational Leadership, 54*(8).

Elias, M. J., Zins, J. E., Weisberg, R. P., Frey, K. S., Greenberg, M. T., Haynes, N. M., et al. (1997). *Promoting social and emotional learning: Guidelines for educators.* Alexandria, VA: Association for Supervision and Curriculum Development.

Erikson, E. (1993). *Childhood and society.* New York: Norton.

Feeney, S., Christenson, D., & Moravcik, E. (2006). *Who am I in the lives of children? An introduction to early childhood education.* Upper Saddle River, NJ: Pearson/Merrill/Prentice Hall.

Feiman-Nemser, S., Carver, C., Schwille, S., & Yusko, B. (1999). Beyond support: Taking new teachers seriously as learners. In M. Scherer (Ed.). *A better beginning: Supporting and mentoring new teachers* (pp. 3–12). Alexandria, VA: Association for Supervision and Curriculum Development.

Gardner, H. (1983). *Frames of mind: The theory of multiple intelligences.* New York: Basic Books.

Gardner, H. (1988). Beyond the IQ: Education and human development. *National Forum, 68*(27).

Gardner, H. (1993). *Multiple intelligences: The theory in practice.* New York: Basic Books.

Gardner, H. (1999). *Intelligence reframed: Multiple intelligences for the 21st century.* New York: Basic Books.

Gardner, H. (2000). *The disciplined mind: Beyond facts and standardized tests: K–12 education every child deserves.* New York: Penguin Books.

Gesell, A., Ilg, F. L., & Ames, L. B. (1974). *The child from five to ten.* New York: Harper & Row.

Goleman, D. (1995). *Emotional intelligence: Why it can matter more than IQ.* New York: Bantam Books.

Gonzalez-Mena, J. (2005). *Foundation of early childhood education: Teaching children in a diverse society* (3rd ed.). Boston: McGraw Hill.

Greenspan, S. I. (1997). *The growth of the mind and the endangered origins of intelligence.* Reading, MA: Addison-Wesley.

Groginsky, S., Robison, S., & Smith, S. (1999). *Making child care better: State initiatives.* Washington, DC: National Conference of State Legislators.

Harris, J. R. (1998). *The nurture assumption: Why children turn out the way they do.* New York: Free Press.

Hendrick, J. (1985, 1993). *Total learning for the whole child.* New York: Merrill/Macmillan.

Hohmann, M., Banet, B., & Weikart, D. (1979). *Young children in action.* Ypsilanti, MI: High/Scope Press.

Kamii, C., & DeVries, R. (1978). Physical *knowledge in preschool education: Implications of Piaget's theory.* Englewood Cliffs, NJ: Prentice-Hall.

Kantrowitz, B. (1997, Spring/Summer). Piaget for early education. In M. Day & R. Parker (Eds.). *Preschool in action.* Boston: Allyn & Bacon.

Katz, L. G., & Chard, S. C. (1989). *Engaging children's minds: The project approach.* Norwood, NJ: Ablex.

Kvernbekk, T. (1997, May). What can we learn from experience? (Paper presented at the California Association of Philosophers of Education, Stanford, CA).

Lavatelli, C. (1973). *Piaget's theory applied to an early childhood curriculum.* Boston: American Science and Engineering.

Levine, M. (2002). *A mind at a time.* New York: Simon & Schuster.

Lowery, L. (1998, November). How new science curriculums reflect brain research. *Educational Leadership, 56*(3).

Meyer, M. (1997, September). The GREENing of learning: Using the eighth intelligence. *Educational Leadership, 55*(1).

Moran, S., Kornhaber, M., & Gardner, H. (2006, September). Orchestrating multiple intelligences. *Educational Leadership, 64*(1), 23–27.

National Research Council (2000). *How people learn: Brain, mind, experience and school.* Washington, DC: National Academy Press.

Perry, B. D. (2000, November/December). How the brain learns best: Easy ways to gain optimal learning in the classroom by activating different parts of the brain. *Instructor, 110*(4), 34–35.

Piaget, J. (1952). *The origins of intelligence.* New York: International Universities Press.

Pool, C. R. (1997, May). Up with emotional health. *Educational Leadership, 55*(1).

Rousseau, J. J. (1947). L'Emile ou l'éducation. In O. E. Tellows and N. R. Tarrey (Eds.). *The age of enlightenment.* New York: F. S. Croft (Original work published 1742).

Seefeldt, C., & Barbour, N. (1998). *Early childhood education: An introduction* (4th ed.). New York: Merrill/Macmillan.

Shore, R. (1997). *Rethinking the brain.* New York: Families and Work Institute.

Stevens, J. H., Jr., & King, E. W. (1976). *Administering early childhood programs.* Boston: Little, Brown.

Sullo, R. A. (1999). *The inspiring teacher.* Annapolis Junction, MD: National Education Association of the United States.

Sylwester, R. (1998, November). Art for the brain's sake. *Educational Leadership, 56*(3).

Szyba, C. M. (1999, January). Why do some teachers resist offering appropriate, open-ended art activities for young children? *Young Children, 54*(1).

Thomas, A., Chess, S., Birch, H. G., Hertzig, M. E., & Korn, S. (1963). B*ehavioral individuality in early childhood.* New York: New York University Press.

Tomlinson, C. A., & Jarvis, J. (2006, September). Teaching beyond the book. *Educational Leadership, 64*(1), 16–21.

Vartuli, S. (2005, September). Beliefs: The heart of teaching. *Young Children, 60* (5), 76-86.

Violand-Sánchez, E. & Hainer-Violand, J. (2006, September). The power of positive identity. *Educational Leadership, 64*(1), 36–40.

Weinberger, N. M. (1998, November). The music in our minds. *Educational Leadership, 56*(3).

Weissberg, R. P., Shriver, T. P., Bose, S., & DeFalco, K. (1997, May). Creating a district-wide social development project. *Educational Leadership, 54*(8).

Programming

CHAPTER 5

Instructional Planning

OBJECTIVES

After reading this chapter, you should be able to:

1. Complete a written activity or lesson plan form.
2. Identify three ways of assessing child interest.
3. Describe three different approaches to curriculum development.
4. Describe the benefits of written activity/lesson plans.
5. Identify factors to consider when planning settings for teacher-guided activities.
6. Plan a group activity.
7. Describe a teaching unit (theme) approach to early childhood instruction.
8. Cite two possible benefits and limitations of theme-centered curriculums.
9. Outline preparation steps in theme construction.
10. Prepare a lesson plan for a teacher-guided activity.

Comments of student teachers:

> The most memorable part of student teaching has been the daily experience in my placement classroom. The lessons I have learned and the information shared has been a storehouse that will take years to exhaust. Being forced to write lesson plans has helped me with my planned classroom activities. It has also widened the activities I present in my employment classroom. I'm more aware of my own capabilities and knowledge. ●

Judy Mabie

> I can remember by the end of the day I was completely exhausted. I remember how surprised I was when we did a week's worth of carefully planned ideas in the first day. I remember feeling panic-stricken; what am I going to do tomorrow? ●

Calli Collins

> My supervisor suggested I plan activities in areas of my own personal interests. Since I'm an avid needlework enthusiast, I planned an activity in which I taught simple stitchery. The children (even the boys) loved doing sewing. Some went on to do long-term projects. ●

Amanda St. Clair

> My first day of student teaching was easy. My cooperating teacher didn't ask much of me, so I made a point of being helpful, handing out papers so she could continue talking, et cetera. Later she said, "If you have any ideas of things you'd like to do, feel free . . ." That filled me with dread. I didn't know what to do with first graders, and I was hoping she'd clue me in to the sorts of things we'd be doing the next few weeks so I'd be able to figure out how to fit in. I remember thinking that the kids seemed older, bigger than I expected, but I was soon reminded of their age when they were trying to do any reading or writing. ●

Fononga Pahula

LOOKING AT ACCEPTED CURRICULUM STANDARDS

All professional, early childhood teachers face a dilemma in designing daily activities for young children. They will, no doubt, plan based on their own philosophy, or a teaching team's philosophy, concerning what is best and right. They will consider recognized and accepted professional standards. Well-known standards are found in the following publications:

- The Association for Childhood Education International (1997) published position papers on the preparation of early childhood and elementary teachers.
- Bredekamp and Copple (1997) *Developmentally Appropriate Practice in Early Childhood Programs*, a publication of the National Association for the Education of Young Children.
- The Head Start Bureau, Administration for Children and Families, Department of Health and Human Services (1975) published *Head Start Performance Standards*.
- The National Association for the Education of Young Children (2003) published *Early Childhood Program Standards and Accreditation Performance Criteria*.
- The National Association for the Education of Young Children and the National Association of Early Childhood Specialists in State Departments of Education (2003) published a joint position statement titled *Early Childhood Curriculum, Assessment, and Program Evaluation*.
- The National Association for the Education of Young Children and the National Association of Early Childhood Specialists in State Departments of Education (2002) published a joint position statement titled *Early Learning Standards: Creating the Conditions for Success*.

In addition to those listed above, national and state legislatures have also established early childhood standards. State standards may exceed a state's licensing regulations in an effort to improve the quality of that state's early childhood programs. The No Child Left Behind Act, an education reform act passed by Congress in 2001, and a federal administration initiative, *Good Start, Grow Smart (2002)*, were both designed to help children achieve the goal of reading at grade level by the end of the third grade. Both of these, and other factors, have promoted the planning or development of early learning guidelines or standards in one-fifth of the states in the United States.

Educators in many states are aligning these state, early-learning guidelines with their states' K–12 education standards (Child Care Bureau, 2005). States, such as Massachusetts in 2003, published and copyrighted their early childhood program standards. The standards for Massachusetts and many other states are available from states' Departments of Education. Geist and Baum (2005) point out that standards do not dictate how goals should be met, but give schools and teachers the freedom to create their own curriculum and implement it. Helpful Web sites, which contain links to both national and state standards in all content areas, are http://www.educationworld.com and http://www.edstandards.org.

You may have worked at a facility using local, state, national, or independently created standards during your training, if the school was publicly funded. And you may have been required to cite what standard was used to create a lesson or activity plan.

The dilemma facing educators creating program curricula is to put philosophy and standards to work in curriculum design and daily lesson planning, and to weigh or insert parental and perhaps community concerns and input into that curriculum. An additional task is to decide *what to teach* and *how to teach. What* can be defined as the scope of information, experiences, and skills to be presented, promoted, and attempted. The *how* is defined as the teaching techniques and teaching vehicles to be used.

Wolverton (2000) describes Head Start and Early Head Start curriculum development:

> No two curricula in Head Start and Early Head Start look exactly the same. There are two basic approach programs used to determine the curriculum. Staff and parents may base a curriculum on an already developed model, and adapt or "tailor" it for the group of children being served. Or staff and parents may develop a local curriculum. Either way, the curriculum must be in keeping with all the requirements of the Head Start Performance Standards and based on sound child development principles.

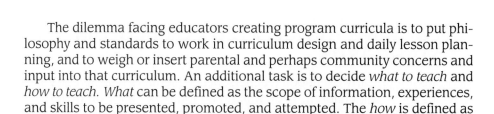

IDENTIFYING CHILD INTERESTS AND NEEDS

You will plan, prepare, and present classroom activities. The teaching day may contain structured (teacher-planned) and unstructured (child-initiated) activities. The cooperating teacher's philosophy, the school's philosophy, the identified program goals, and the classroom setting determine the balance between child-initiated activities and teacher-planned activities. In activity-centered classrooms, student teachers arrange room centers to invite and promote child discovery and learning.

Hyson (2005) notes the National Education Goals Panel, the National Center for Educational Statistics (Kagan, Moore, & Bredekamp, 1995), and others are finding that young children's attitudes and learning behaviors are the foundation of children's success. She states that children's positive approaches to learning include at least four dimensions. These are:

1. initiative, engagement, and persistence.
2. reasoning, planning, and flexible problem solving.
3. curiosity and eagerness to learn.
4. invention and imagination.

Hyson believes adults can encourage and discourage these positive approaches, and teacher observation can discern children's needs for special support and assistance. Observation is complex because children have diverse ways of displaying competencies, which may be influenced by unique temperaments, cultural conditioning, innate characteristics, and individual family configurations.

Using Child Interest and Improvising

Teaching is a complex task requiring continual, on-the-spot decision making (Carter & Curtis, 1994). Carter and Curtis believe master teachers have certain qualities that distinguish them from teachers who depend on curriculum activity books, follow the same theme plans year after year, or struggle daily to get the children involved in anything productive. Master teachers possess a set of attitudes and habits of mind, to respond to classroom dynamics and multiple needs of children with the readiness of an improvisational artist.

An example of the master teacher mind-set can be seen in the actions of one student teacher, Fredrica, in the following:

> A book about cats was brought to school by a child. After being previewed, Fredrica shared the book with a group of the child's friends. Susan, a four-year-old, went to the scrap paper and craft table later in the afternoon and cut long, paper claws for one hand. She then asked Fredrica for tape to secure them to her fingers. They again looked at the book's illustrations to look for cats with long claws. Susan enjoyed meowing, pretending to scratch a tree trunk, and climbing on the outdoor structure. Other children wanted to cut and color cat claws of their own. Fredrica supplied the materials and soon a number of children were pretending to be cats! Fredrica was prepared to intervene if claws were used aggressively.

The following day Fredrica set up a discovery area, which included taped domestic animal sounds, cat figures to manipulate, and pictures of different house cat varieties. Poems about cats were part of story times, a cat visited the school, and cat-care particulars were listed by the children on a wall chart, printed with child ideas. Fredrica and the children explored how the cats' sharp claws helped them climb trees in one activity, and how cats use their claws to protect themselves in another.

You will be searching for activity ideas that will interest and challenge the group of children to which you are assigned. Observing children's play choices and favorite activities will give you ideas (see Figure 5–1). Children's conversations provide clues as to what has captured their atten-

Figure 5-1
Children discuss ways to use classroom materials.

tion. Watch for excitement among the children and make comments in your pocket notebook concerning individual and group curiosity and play selections. What are they eager to try? How much time is spent exploring or concentrating on an experience (see Figure 5–2)?

Living in the Pacific Northwest, teacher Maggie Meyer (1997) noticed that her students were interested in water-quality monitoring. Her school was involved in an integrated watershed curriculum which was a part of a larger national effort—the Global Rivers Education Network (GREEN). Based on the children's interests in what was happening around them in their home environment on the Budd/Deschutes Watershed in south Puget Sound, Meyer had her students take samples of aquatic organisms on the Deschutes River and submit them to chemical analysis.

Although Meyer's students were in a sixth grade classroom, any preschool or primary grade teacher fortunate enough to have a creek or pond nearby, and noticing that children are interested in them, could have children collect samples of the water to look at under a microscope, which the teacher could set up and focus.

Effective teaching includes being observant of children's interest in their environment, and using your own interests and enthusiasm to excite and motivate them. After the children's interests are identified, you can use the three-W strategy to discover **w**hat is known, **w**hat is unknown but can be known, and **w**hat has been learned. This format provides an easy way to engage children in learning.

Many times, a teacher piques children's interests by focusing their attention on a new feature, event, object, or occurrence. What is unknown serves as the basis for teacher activity planning, and the teacher's supportive assistance. The spontaneous or creative planning ability of an educator striving to adjust classroom circumstances, to lead children to answers with or without teacher's help, is part of the joy of teaching. The third *W* aims to promote putting what is learned into words, acts, or representations. It is a kind of recap, or solidifying activity that reinforces what has been discovered or experienced.

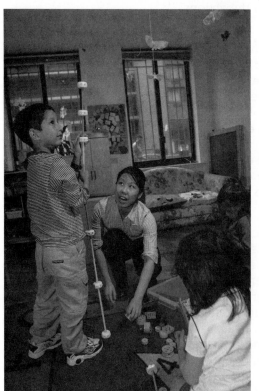

 Figure 5-2
Discovering together is an enjoyable aspect of teaching.

CURRICULUM MODELS

Early childhood educators have been interested in preschool *curriculum models* for a long time, but especially since federal funds were first devoted to preschool intervention programs, such as Head Start in 1965 and Project Follow Through in 1967. In these early years, available research seemed to discount the idea that one, best method could impact preschoolers' academic readiness, or that different curriculum models could contribute to different outcomes. Goffin (2000) notes that renewed interest in early childhood curriculum models has occurred because of the rapid growth of state-financed prekindergartens.

Goffin and Wilson (2001) point out that well-studied curriculum models are being promoted by school districts and state officials, as a means to obtain consistent child outcomes and to provide accountability for public investment in early education for three- and four-year-olds.

CONSTRUCTIVISM AND DEVELOPMENTALLY APPROPRIATE PRACTICE

It is difficult to read any written material dealing with early childhood curriculum development pedagogy that does not mention the terms *child-centered*, *child-initiated*, *active learning*, *constructivist*, and *developmentally appropriate practice*.

The first three terms are self-explanatory. **Constructivism**, as a cognitive-developmental notion, has direct roots within the structuralism that underlies Piaget's theory of intellectual development (O'Loughlin, 1991). A *constructivist* takes the position that learners must have experiences with hypothesizing and predicting, manipulating objects, posing questions, researching answers, imagining, investigating, and inventing for new *constructions* to be developed (Fosnot, 1989).

What distinguishes the constructivist approach is the mental action that takes place as children infer from what they are experiencing and create a system of knowledge from the activity (Epstein, Schweinhart, & McAdoo, 1996). A secure, rather than coercive, classroom environment is believed to allow children to cooperate, develop respect for one another, exercise their curiosity, and gain confidence in their ability to figure things out on their own and become autonomous. Kamii and DeVries (1975, 1977) describe the teacher's role as having the following four components:

1. Creating an environment and an atmosphere in which the child is independent, uses his own initiative in pursuing his interests, says exactly what he thinks, asks questions, experiments, and comes up with a variety of ideas.

2. Providing materials, suggesting activities, and assessing what is going on inside the child's head from moment to moment; the teacher proposes ideas, rather than imposes.

3. Responding to children in terms of the kind of knowledge involved; the teacher shares a child's pleasure, frustration, and disappointments when the child seeks her company, and encourages the child's construction of logical knowledge; social knowledge is stated and reinforced.

4. Encouraging children to extend their ideas without intruding or interrupting.

Early childhood educators realize the importance of teacher interaction in classrooms. Child-initiated activities and social communication take place in many learning situations, particularly with three-, four-, and five-year-olds.

Developmentally Appropriate Practice (DAP)

The National Association for the Education of Young Children's (NAEYC's) Developmentally Appropriate Practice (DAP) in Early Childhood Programs (Bredekamp & Copple, 1997) has been highly praised and acclaimed as one of the field's most respected guides to activity planning. Regarded by some

 constructivism—a term relating to constructivist theory based on the belief that children construct knowledge for themselves rather than having it conveyed to them by some external source. Often attributed to the work of Jean Piaget.

educators as a curriculum model and by others a guide, it has been revised and expanded. It is a must-read-*and-study* for educators who plan curriculums for young children. Vander Wilt and Monroe (1998) believe DAP is neither curriculum nor method, but rather a way of thinking and working with children, and they have outlined what they feel are DAP's central principles and practices:

1. *Wholeness of the child.* Children are whole persons, in whom physical, social, emotional, and cognitive development are integrated. Each area of development is important and affects every other area of development.

2. *Active involvement.* Children must be active participants in their own learning. Manipulation of real, concrete, and relevant materials contributes to children's understandings.

3. *Interaction with adults and peers.* Learning occurs when children interact with people in their environments. Interactions with both adults and other children facilitate the mental manipulation and ownership of ideas.

4. *Authentic experiences.* Children learn best from personally meaningful experiences that flow from the reality of their lives. When school experiences reflect the reality of life beyond the school, learning is more purposeful and relevant.

5. *Appropriate learning activities.* Appropriate learning activities include projects, learning centers, and such activities as building, drawing, writing, discussing, and reading. Research, exploration, discovery, problem solving, and excursions are examples of recommended educational experiences.

6. *Integrated curriculum.* Integrated thematic units form the foundation for an appropriate curriculum, enabling children to make connections among and between ideas and knowledge. Distinctions among the various traditional subject areas are arbitrary and not very meaningful for children.

7. *Intrinsic motivation.* Fostering intrinsic motivation has the potential to support the development of responsible and autonomous learners—that is, learners who develop a passion and love for a lifetime of learning. When learners are reliant on extrinsic motivators, they become distracted and experience reduced interest in their learning.

8. *Authentic assessment.* Evaluation of children's progress should flow directly from the tasks and experiences in which they have been engaged. Evaluation and instruction must be integrally related so that each informs the other.

9. *Inappropriateness of grade retention.* Grade retention is inappropriate. The assumption in developmentally appropriate practice is that each child grows and develops at his or her own pace. And because children do not grow at the same pace, the classroom is expected to meet and accommodate the unique learning needs of each child, making retention inappropriate except in rare cases.

A commitment to DAP's pedagogy, teacher enthusiasm, and administrative support are important factors as teachers introduce DAP in their classrooms. Dunn and Kontos (1998) suggest teachers often struggle with implementation.

Developed through the efforts of many individuals and groups under NAEYC's leadership, DAP has been widely accepted, although it is not without its critics. (A further discussion of differing opinions and the early childhood field's progress in adopting DAP is found in the Online Companion that supplements this text.)

Teacher-written activity or lesson plans are covered later in this chapter to aid student teachers whose placement classrooms suggest their use. We believe that in trying to expand already noted child or group interests, written lesson planning, skill, and practice are useful and necessary.

 # ADDITIONAL CURRICULUM APPROACHES

A program may be planned based on an **emergent model**, with activities developed out of child, parent, teacher, and community interests and focuses. One activity may meld into a logical sequence of others. This can be described as a teacher weaving a web of interconnected activities to follow children's emerging queries for further information, solutions, or skills. The emergent curriculum model is sometimes connected or associated in early childhood literature with the terms *child-centered* and *reflective* (Curtis & Carter, 1996), *responsive*, and *child-initiated* (Edwards, Gandini, & Forman, 1993), *project approach* (Helm & Katz, 2001) (Katz & Chard, 1993), and *creative curriculum* (Dodge & Colker, 1992).

A teacher's ability to listen continuously, observe children's chosen courses of study, gain insights, and transfer these into daily activities, complete with needed classroom media or materials, is viewed as crucial. Behind-the-scenes staff collaboration, to identify ways to enrich, extend, and promote children's discovery and experience, and also assess or document child growth, makes using this curriculum model a professionally challenging and time-consuming task.

Advocates mention the possible staleness and teacher-centered nature of traditional, preplanned and prepackaged curriculums. They feel these may squelch child curiosity, initiative, and enthusiasm for learning.

The Italian *Reggio Emilia* model has captured the attention of a sizable group of early childhood educators. Many of the well-documented aspects of *Reggio Emilia* programs appeal to American educators.

Rinaldi (2001) describes *Reggio Emilia* as a combination of social services and education that focuses on the child in relationship to the family, the teacher, other children, and the broader cultural context of the society. She states that fundamental to the philosophy is an image of the child, who experiences the world and feels a part of it from birth; this child is full of curiosities, desire to live, and able to communicate from the start of his life. This child is fully able to create maps for his personal, social, cognitive, affective, and symbolic orientation.

Curriculum emerges as the teacher, who acts as a participant-observer, closely monitors children's ideas and interests and then shapes what the teacher thinks will contribute to children's growth (Gandini & Goldhaber, 2001). Documentation of children's activities and learning furthers a teacher's understanding of the concepts children are building, the theories

emergent model—a program of instruction, based on child, parent, teacher, or community interests or concerns, in which there is a logical sequence of study using interconnected activities and experiences.

skill-based model— refers to a curriculum model that identifies specific physical, social, or intellectual knowledge, skills, goals, or objectives, and then plans learning activities that promote the attainment of expected child behavior, information, or action.

balanced curriculum—a curriculum that takes into consideration and reflects a broad spectrum of cognitive, physical, socio-emotional, linguistic, and creative development opportunities for young children. It attempts to neither slight nor sacrifice one developmental area for another.

integrated curriculum— a curriculum in which concurrent learning is possible by focusing on more than one ability, developmental skill, or subject matter area at the same time in the same activity. It is believed to promote children's problem solving and aid the children's ability to see relationships among a variety of ideas or events.

they are constructing, and the questions they are posing (Gandini & Goldhaber, 2001).

As Montessori has captured and held many early childhood teachers' attention, *Reggio Emilia* also seems to have generated enthusiasm, and may become a special, unique segment or widely imitated model of early education in the United States.

A **skill-based model** suits the philosophy of other early childhood curriculum designers. Activity planning starts with the identification of specific physical, social, or intellectual knowledge, or goals or objectives. Activities focus on a planned attempt to help children attain expected behavior or action through teacher co-exploration, guidance, or instruction.

Balanced and Integrated Program Planning

A **balanced curriculum** approach to program planning assures all possible growth areas for children are fully promoted. Cognitive, physical, social-emotional, linguistic, and creative development opportunities are included, and individual areas are not slighted or sacrificed, but given appropriate program-planning attention. Advocates believe that demands to increase program planning that enhances children's intellectual abilities should not crowd out other planning areas. Balance is also planned in small and large motor skill activities, active and quiet offerings, individual and group experiences, child-initiated and adult-led activities, indoor and outdoor experiences, and approaches to learning using different learning modalities, such as linguistic, kinesthetic, visual, auditory, and spatial experiences.

The goal of an **integrated curriculum** is to create a planned program that focuses on more than one ability, developmental skill, or subject matter area at the same time, or in the same activity. Recognition is given to the idea that development in cognitive, physical, social-emotional, linguistic, and creative abilities can be interconnected and integrated in both planned and spontaneous activities. An integrated learning approach is believed to aid children's problem-solving skills and their ability to see relationships between a variety of ideas and events.

A theme or project organization of planned activities can include and promote both a balanced and integrated approach to child discoveries and learnings.

A Curriculum Continuum

Educators tend to envision curriculum approaches, and practice along a continuum between child-centered or child-based to traditional, teacher-decided activities (see Figure 5–3). An instructional approach, not mentioned fully thus far, that is popular with many early childhood teachers is a discovery center-based curriculum. Classroom areas designated as activity centers, such as table tops and other areas, are set up daily or weekly for children to choose and explore and consequently discover concepts and experience skill growth. The practice of skills and the extension of children's understanding can also be promoted.

Teacher Controlled Curriculum	Instruction (including theme instruction or other approaches)	Child-Initiated Curriculum
Activity plans primarily grow out of teacher decisions concerning the appropriate content of activities based on the teacher's idea of children's educational, social, and physical needs and interests.	Activity plans usually grow from child interests and needs. Teacher both instructs and plans child-choice opportunities around a central topic, content area, theme, or learning center.	Children follow their own search for answers while teacher plans to support children's investigation and discussion. Teacher provides materials and settings to aid discovery and further child research and discussion.

 Figure 5-3
Instructional approach continuum

Teacher Attitudes and Beliefs

You will be trying to match your planned activities to what your child group and individual children can profit from physically, socially, and educationally. Lumsden (1998) urges teachers to realize that teacher decisions are based on assumptions of child potential and have a tangible effect on child achievement. Children tend to internalize the beliefs teachers have about their ability, and they generally rise or fall to the level of expectation of their teachers.

Effective teachers can be described as planning activities that exhibit both high and appropriate expectations of child performance for all children. Studies of teacher behaviors tend to confirm that teachers engage in affirming, nonverbal behaviors such as smiling, leaning toward, and making eye contact with students more frequently when they believe they are dealing with high-ability students.

Treating children in ways that imply children share the teacher's enthusiasm for wanting to know and wanting to find out is more than an admirable teaching skill. Lumsden (1998) points out that to the extent that one treats young children as if they are eager learners, they will be more likely to become eager learners.

Jablon and Wilkinson (2006) suggest that as pressures mount to emphasize academic standards, teacher reflection on effective practice is essential. These authors note that some factors related to children's achievement are outside a teacher's control, but creating a climate of *engagement* in a classroom is not one of those. What is engagement? During activities, it includes active child behaviors like attentiveness, and commitment to the task at hand. This happens when a child finds some inherent value, displays enthusiasm, and perceives the task to be associated with a near-term payoff the child values (Schlechty, 2001). Even a beginning teacher recognizes this type of engagement when it happens during one of her planned activities. Child focus seems complete, an eagerness to know, do, and participate is present and causes an excitement that can be observed in the child's demeanor. This feels very good, as if the teacher's planning or providing was right on target. Jablon and Wilkinson have identified some activity features associated with engaged child behavior. They include activation of prior knowledge, active investigation, group interaction, collaboration, choice, games and humor, mastery, independent thinking, and not making children wait.

When planning activities, these characteristics can be kept in mind. In preschool practice, teachers often see child engagement in child-selected activities, such as trying to learn how to pump a swing, building the highest block tower possible, or making a snack on their own with offered choices at snack time. Notice each of these activities has a personal payoff.

ACTIVITY RESOURCES

Files, resource books, and activity ideas you collected during training may now come in handy. You will have to discern whether the ideas fit your situation. Teachers' and children's magazines often have timely, seasonal activity planning ideas.

Draw on your own creative abilities. All too often, student teachers feel that tried-and-true ideas are superior to what they invent. The new and novel activities you create will add sparkle and uniqueness to your teaching. Do not be afraid to draw from or improve upon a good idea, or to change successful activities your children have already enjoyed. Some classroom activities are designed because of an overabundance of scrap or donated material. Take another look at materials in storage that are not receiving much attention or have been forgotten. Perhaps these can be reintroduced in a clever, new way.

CURRICULUM

When curriculums are designed, planned daily activities follow. Curriculum design groups usually go through a series of steps. First, discussion takes place with all concerned individuals. Discussion can include philosophies of education, theories, standards, principles, values, research, views on how children learn best, and many other topics. Usually the group considers social, emotional, intellectual, physical, and even spiritual growth, in faith-based programs. Next, goals and objectives are written and attention is given to how these will be recognized, assessed, and realized. A plan for inside and outside environment comes next, along with the creation of activities. At this point, many programs plan a periodic review procedure, so all steps can be revisited if goals and objectives are not being accomplished.

Most prekindergarten curriculums include arts and creativity, music and movement, language, science, large and small motor skill development, cooking and nutrition activities, numbers and measurement, perceptual motor activities, health and safety activities, social understandings, multicultural awareness activities, and plant and animal studies. Snow (2006) reports that despite the National Research Council's study, *Adding It Up: Helping Children Learn Mathematics,* early mathematics has been and continues to be largely absent from some early childhood programs. Primary classrooms often follow district-approved guidelines.

Areas of study with different degrees of acceptance include anti-bias, conflict resolution, social justice, economics and consumer awareness, ecology and energy study, moral and ethical values, changing sex role responsibilities, changing family patterns, introduction to photography, introduction to technology, structure games, and tolerance, nonviolence, and peaceful solution training. These may or may not be integrated and combined in a single planned activity, but usually areas overlap. Gardening, for instance, may involve counting, small motor skills, science, and language.

In planning activities, you will be striving to provide for active exploration integrated with each child's previous out-of-the-classroom experiences. You will attempt to match age-appropriate developmental needs, and characteristics of the group, with activities. Children will

SECTION I ETHICAL RESPONSIBILITIES TO CHILDREN

Childhood is a unique and valuable stage in the human life cycle. Our paramount responsibility is to provide care and education in settings that are safe, healthy, nurturing, and responsive for each child. We are committed to supporting children's development and learning; respecting individual differences; and helping children learn to live, play, and work cooperatively. We are also committed to promoting children's self-awareness, competence, self-worth, resiliency, and physical well-being.

Ideals

I-1.1—To be familiar with the knowledge base of early childhood care and education and to stay informed through continuing education and training.

I-1.2—To base program practices upon current knowledge and research in the field of early childhood education, child development, and related disciplines, as well as on particular knowledge of each child.

I-1.3—To recognize and respect the unique qualities, abilities, and potential of each child.

I-1.4—To appreciate the vulnerability of children and their dependence on adults.

I-1.5—To create and maintain safe and healthy settings that foster children's social, emotional, cognitive, and physical development and that respect their dignity and their contributions.

I-1.6—To use assessment instruments and strategies that are appropriate for the children to be assessed, that are used only for the purposes for which they were designed, and that have the potential to benefit children.

continues

● **Figure 5-4**
Selected Section of NAEYC Code of Ethical Conduct. Section I: Ethical Responsibilities to Children.

I-1.7—To use assessment information to understand and support children's development and learning, to support instruction, and to identify children who may need additional services.

I-1.8—To support the right of each child to play and learn in an inclusive environment that meets the needs of children with and without disabilities.

I-1.9—To advocate for and ensure that all children, including those with special needs, have access to the support services needed to be successful.

I-1.10—To ensure that each child's culture, language, ethnicity, and family structure are recognized and valued in the program.

I-1.11—To provide all children with experiences in a language that they know, as well as support children in maintaining the use of their home language and in learning English.

I-1.12—To work with families to provide a safe and smooth transition as children and families move from one program to the next.

Source: Copyright © 2005 by the National Association for the Education of Young Children

● **Figure 5-4** (continued)

explore, manipulate, converse, move about, play, and freely talk about what is happening and what it means to them. Activities will provide for heterogeneous child abilities. NAEYC's Code of Ethical Conduct (2005) cites ideals that further guide curriculum development (see Figure 5–4).

Your previous, early childhood education training courses have promoted your sensitivity to and awareness of cultural pluralism. Activities and interactions with children are also designed to eliminate practices and materials that discriminate on the basis of race, sex, age, ethnic origin, language, religion, or special needs.

The social-emotional emphasis in activity planning has gained additional status. Social skills involve cooperation, assertion, responsibility, empathy, and self-control and are viewed as key, both to acceptable behavior and academic achievement.

In developing activities, remember that each class is unique and that each child is an individual. What is or is not learned depends on classroom materials and interactions between adults and children, or between children, as they attempt to understand what is experienced and how it relates to them and to others.

Look at your placement classroom in a different way. What do children seem to be learning? What have they already mastered? What line of learning could be extended by provision of materials or a planned activity? The answers to these questions may enhance your ability to customize activities. There has been some type of assessment of participating children's abilities and their knowledge, skills, and dispositions. Your cooperating teacher may have attempted to share this information with you. If so, you have a much better basis for activity planning.

Assessment and Curriculum Planning

There are broad categories that constitute the major functions of assessment in the early years: assessment to inform instruction, assessment for diagnostic and selection purposes, and assessment for accountability and program evaluation. When assessment is used carefully and appropriately, it is used to adjust instruction and promote educational benefits.

With increased state and federal legislation affecting the early childhood years, there appears to be more pressure on educators to use standardized tests. The issue of using standardized testing is a controversial one. Advocates believe this type of assessment identifies atypical developmental patterns, determines whether children are reaching program goals, and makes instructional programs accountable.

Others with opposing views, such as Kohn (2001), suggest young children are rarely able to communicate their understanding when standardized assessments are used. He points out tests often create stress. Wesson (2001) notes that children whose English is limited invariably score lower in language fluency areas when testing is conducted in English. Most educators acknowledge that the younger the child, the more likely they are to be incorrectly labeled.

In early childhood, strategies other than standardized testing are often preferred, professionally accepted, and widely used. These include observation, child portfolio development, and the documentation of children's accomplishments. These approaches can allow instruction planners to tailor curriculum to individual children's needs, and to do so without labeling children unfairly.

State Standards for Public School Kindergartens

Kindergarten teachers in many states are under pressure to prepare children for testing. Children's test scores have been used to rank schools, judge individual teacher performance, and reward or withhold funding. Educators fear that developmentally appropriate practices and classes offering hands-on, flexible curriculums are being sacrificed or compromised for drill-and-skill approaches and structured academic content (Harrington-Lueker, 2000).

Spotting reading readiness and reading problems early is being given top priority. A number of school districts have adopted kindergarten workbooks that require kindergartners to complete tear-out page exercises. Child-centered practices may conflict with school district policy that mandates showing students' progress toward specific goals. In North Carolina, a few public schools have initiated pre-K programs for at-risk four-year-olds. These schools have discovered that 20 percent of attending kindergartners entered school unprepared to learn. These new programs have attempted to combine developmentally appropriate practice with a focus on language and literacy.

Early childhood educators intent on preparing children to meet the challenges of kindergarten realize social skill is a critical factor in child success. Gamel-McCormick (2000) surveyed kindergarten teachers regarding what they felt were the most important skills entering kindergartners could possess and found teachers' top skill choices were:

- exhibits self control
- interacts cooperatively
- communicates needs and preferences

- cares for own bathroom needs
- attends to peer or adult talking

Gamel-McCormick also noted a significant minority of the teachers surveyed included pre-academic and academic skills in their definitions of readiness.

Supporting Self-Regulation

Keeping the factual content of their planned activities in mind, along with children's opportunities for discovery, student teachers may underrate promoting child self-regulation during their planned activities. Lewit and Baker (1995) describe self-regulated kindergartners as being able to:

- sustain attention and enthusiasm
- display curiosity in new activities
- inhibit impulsivity
- follow directions
- take turns
- be sensitive to other children's feelings

How can educators promote these skills and feelings? They do so through teacher modeling, monitoring activity time length, children's sitting endurance, and children's ability to sustain focus. They provide clear explanations and directions that can be easily followed. They move from one-part to two- or three-part directions, if child capacity warrants. They have rules and high expectations, and they reinforce children's self-regulating behaviors when these behaviors appear. Giving choices within activities and promoting children's reflective thinking are additional strategies. All of this may take place in a student's planned activity, if the student teacher is consciously aware of his or her goal of helping children self-regulate.

Being Aware

On any given day, certain classroom events evolve naturally, as children react to the weather, the setting, the choices set out, activities, people encountered, and so on. The dynamics and personalities present influence children. Student teachers need to be curious, watchful, and ready to support child discoveries, rather than closely focusing on planned, teacher-directed efforts.

Some early childhood programs are mapping their communities for possible learning opportunities. Figure 5–5 cites examples of sources of community-based, natural learning opportunities.

 GOAL STATEMENTS

In the first chapter, you were asked to secure and read your center's handbook. Handbooks can include program and content standards, goal statements, and curriculum objectives. Study these if available.

Natural Land and Water Features

Mountains	Desert Areas	Rivers
Forests	Lakes, Ponds, and	Oceans
Farmland	Other Water Bodies	Sand Areas

Outdoor Activities

Swimming	Farming	Jogging
Boating	Hiking	Walking
Biking	Riding	Skiing
Camping	Horseback Riding	Local Walks and Races
Fishing	Skating	Kite Flying
Gardening		

Parks and Recreational Activities—Federal, State, County, City, and Community Attractions and Amusement Facilities

Public and Commercial Enterprises	Monuments Planetariums	Zoos Historical Sites
Aquariums	Museums	Cultural Happenings
Bird Sanctuaries	Science Centers	Plays, Ballets, and Concerts
Displays	Trains	

Club and Organization Sponsored Events, Community and City Celebrations Learning and Educational Activities

Art Classes	Dance Classes	Nature Center Activities
Book Store Story Hours	Drama Classes	Parent Education Classes
Bookmobile	Enrichment Classes	Petting Zoos
Ceramics Classes	Gymnastics/Tumbling	Puppet Shows
Children's Museum Activities	Library Story Times, Movies, and Activities	Religious Education Science Center Activities
Creative Movement Classes	Magic Shows Music Classes	Storytellers

Sports Activities

Baseball/T-Ball	Ice Skating/Sledding	Softball
Basketball	Karate	Swimming
Bowling	Roller Skating	Tennis
Football	Soccer	Track and Field
Golf/Miniature Golf		

Note: Each geographic location is unique. You may find your locale offers opportunities not listed above. This figure does not attempt to list all possibilities.

 Figure 5-5
Community learning opportunities

When the proposed outcomes of a center's planned instruction are stated in written form, center handbooks may identify fields of study and also mention the cultivation of children's talents and dispositions, such as perseverance in tasks, responsibility, self-control, self-esteem, empathy, honesty, problem solving, cooperation, inventiveness, kindness, friendliness, social connectedness, creativity, and so on. The procedures to assess how well a center's instruction has attained its goals may also be specified, along with the timelines in which to do so.

Monthly, Weekly, and Daily Schedules

Schedules alert teachers to planned events. Children's needs dictate what takes place so food, rest, and toileting times are inserted in time slots. Active periods alternate with quiet ones. Group times include announcements of that day's events and activities and also recognize and welcome each child.

With a schedule, teachers and children can anticipate what comes next. Teachers plan in advance for necessary room settings, materials, equipment, furniture, and staffing needs. Each center and school decides on the flexibility of its daily schedule, and most deviate often when the unexpected occurs so children can benefit from a newly created activity. Schools are rarely slaves to schedules, but rather capitalize on unplanned learning opportunities, or immediately revise a schedule when planned activities in some way fizzle or fail to capture interest.

Play and Learning

Children often use play to translate experience into understanding. Teachers often see in child's play the reenactment of behaviors the child has viewed in others. Behaviors that may be puzzling or significant in their lives are tried on for size. They step inside the other person's shoes and seemingly gain insight through the reliving.

In children's random and investigative play, discoveries are made. Happenings are tested, retested, varied, and extended. Focus may be keen, and at times children are eager to talk about what they understand and experience.

Peers often function as tutors or providers of information. During play, adults observe, supply, talk about, encourage, and appreciate without interfering, except when safety is a factor. Adults do ask provocative questions and give suggestions but guard against inflicting their own directions or intentions concerning the child's choice of play.

Reynolds and Jones (1997) use the term *master player* to describe the young child who plays well. They note that experiences and feelings represented in children's play involve symbol making and aids their understanding. They see master players as both master dramatists and master artist-builders, and note that children's play includes many forms, styles, and types of expressions. For a long while, educators have been concerned about young children who are unable to play, or who play poorly. Play, a developmental task of preschool years, is accomplished when young children are able to lose themselves, spontaneously and enjoyably, with and without peers.

Reynolds and Jones have also coined the term *response-ability*, and have defined it as a teaching skill, possessed when an adult notices and responds to the initiative a child has shown in play.

Teachers search for ways to support and sustain children's self-selected and/or self-initiated play themes. Besides watching closely for safety, the teacher considers what teacher interventions might support a child's needs, interests, inquiry, or discovery, and at the same time, encourage classroom goals such as nonviolence, negotiation, cooperation, and individual rights. It is not an easy job. Many times, teacher response-ability involves helping a child enter into an existing play group, helping a group get along by making concessions, starting negotiations, or promoting other social play skills. Helping children discover or creatively search for information is another common teacher undertaking.

Planning for Play

You will most likely be asked to plan and set up varied play opportunities, including providing well-equipped play areas with abundant materials for props. The importance of child make-believe play is not overlooked in child-appropriate curriculums. At times, you will join child play with small groups or individual children and make-believe yourself, carefully avoiding directing, overpowering, or stifling child initiative and control. Most often, you will zip in and out, providing additional materials, redirecting damage or aggression, and asking leading questions that might add depth, while still being interested, enthusiastic, supportive, communicative, responsive, warm, and understanding. Not an easy teaching task!

HOW LANGUAGE INSTRUCTION FITS INTO ALL ACTIVITY PLANNING

Federal legislation has proposed teacher retraining, to facilitate explicit, early reading instruction involving alphabet knowledge, letter sounds, early emergent writing experiences, and carefully designed group projects (Kantrowitz & Wingert, 2002). Early childhood educators have mixed feelings about how to incorporate literacy activities into diverse curriculums and developmentally appropriate practice. Some educators fear children will be pushed into early reading exercises. Others fear not enough will be done for preschoolers living in poverty, those just learning English, and those with special needs. But most educators would agree that teacher-child verbal exchanges should be warm, engaged, and responsive.

Student teachers should focus on their ability to be conversational partners, who promote children's oral speech development, increase children's vocabulary, increase the understandings behind words, promote more complex grammar, and recognize when language development or social integration is not proceeding as expected. They value extended conversations that are cognitively challenging, and realize some children may need explicit phonics instruction to succeed when reading instruction begins.

Federal funds have supported Title One preschool programs since 1965. These programs are designed to prevent skill deficiencies and the need for remediation, by offering an intensive, high-quality literacy curriculum to eligible children living in lower-income families. To see what educational activities Title One preschool programs offer to increase literacy (see Figure 5–6).

Title 1 literacy goals include the children's:
- learning the letters of the alphabet;
- learning to hear individual sounds in words;
- learning new words and how to use them;
- learning early writing skills;
- learning to use language to ask and answer questions;
- learning about written language by looking at books; and
- becoming familiar with math and science.

In what ways do Title 1 teacher daily work to reach literacy goals? They:
- Promote growth in children's listening and speaking skills.
- Read aloud with children and emphasize meaning while involving children's active participation.
- Promote print-recognition and children's understanding that it has meaning and many purposes.
- Offer activities to experience print through writing.
- Teach about books—how to handle, recognize book features, recognize authorship and created illustrations, left to right reading progression of letters and words across page plus top to bottom reading direction.
- Teach about letters—recognizing, naming, capitals and lowercase, knowing letters in own name, and relating some letters to their sounds.
- Build background knowledge and thinking skills by introducing new concepts and words.
- Have engaging conversations that promote discussions. Plan and present activities that help children rhyme, and break words apart into their separate sounds (segmenting).
- Plan and present activities that put sounds together to make words (blending).
- Read to children every day.
- Offer listening opportunities with stories.
- Teach about numbers and counting.

Source: U.S. Dept of Education (2004).

◉ Figure 5-6
Title 1 Literacy goals and ways to reach them.

Neuman and Roskos (2005) have listed some key points, found in an International Reading Association and National Association for the Education of Young Children's research-based, joint position statement on developmentally appropriate practice and literacy instruction. The list includes the following ideas:

- children need to engage in meaningful experiences
- reading and writing should be viewed as a continuum
- teachers should understand normal variation in developing literacy skills and *extraordinary* variation

- teachers should respect and use children's home language as a base on which to build and extend language and literacy
- teachers should engage in regular and systematic use of multiple indicators, to assess and monitor children's progress in reading and writing

Neuman and Roskos also mention that the position statement perceives young children to be active constructors of meaning.

Prekindergarten teachers will continue to plan, present, and promote a language arts curriculum that includes listening, speaking, print awareness, and reading readiness components. They attempt to ensure a love of books by reading aloud a wide range of quality literature, using techniques that make the experience pleasurable to each child. Classrooms that are conversational and print-rich, with alphabet activities, child dictation, and word labels, are commonplace. Inclusion of activities involving oral letter sounds is occurring, promoted by current research. The challenge for early childhood educators is how to make these activities interesting, engaging, interactive, fun, and useful to preschoolers.

If we examine America's schooling historically, we might find it was not the general rule to educate students to think and read critically, to express themselves clearly and persuasively, and to solve complex problems in science and mathematics (National Research Council, 2000). Today, these literacy skills are necessary to participate successfully in contemporary life pursuits.

Learning language is a natural part of young children's play and exploration. Listening, speaking, and becoming aware of print and books happens throughout a school day. Teachers are urged to help young children discover the functional use of language and the integrated nature of language arts in meaningful settings. Language will be involved with whatever you plan for young children. Teaching strategies can facilitate emerging literacy, both functional and literary.

Instructing Non-English-Speaking Children

Census figures predict that by the year 2025, more than half of the children enrolled in U.S. schools will be members of minority groups not of European American origin (U.S. Bureau of the Census, 1995). The new immigrants arriving are expected to be primarily from Asia and Latin America.

Early childhood teachers, regardless of their preparation or background, will have the task of helping these children learn English and making it a successful experience (Genishi, 2002).

Plutro (2000), noting a study of the diversity of Head Start families, found that enrolled families spoke more than 150 languages and dialects. In nearly 20 percent of children's homes, a language other than English was spoken, the most common being Spanish, followed by Chinese, Hmong, and Vietnamese.

There are two opposing positions concerning a teacher's need to be fluent in a child's home language, to be able to plan an effective curriculum for a particular child. Kuster (1994) suggests teachers become fluent in the attending children's language and become knowledgeable about their culture. What has been offered in the past in education in the United States was a standard English-speaking teacher. Some schools with multilingual school populations preferred to hire bilingual teachers, when they could find them. Each early childhood program will plan instruction based on its own opinion.

Working with Hispanic Families

In the United States, the largest group of children with limited English is Hispanic. Eggers-Pierola (2005) advises teachers to involve Hispanic children's extended family, along with parents, in early childhood program activities and operations. Collaborating with families includes meeting to define goals and program planning. Familiarity with families, she believes, can result in an educator's increased ability to refer to and portray family routines, activities, environments, traditions and so on, in center learning activities. Padron, Waxman, and Rivera (2002) define *culturally-responsive teaching* as teaching that incorporates the day-to-day concerns of attending children, such as important family and community issues, into classroom learning opportunities.

Second language instruction requires special skills, and centers and schools decide between accepted program strategies. A variety of program types exist, including bilingual programs, transitional bilingual programs, newcomer programs, developmental bilingual programs, immersion programs, tutor-assisted programs, and others. Whatever program or combination of programs is selected, children's attitudes toward the second-language child, and that child's attitude about himself, are of paramount importance. Teacher training programs are making every effort to equip teachers and prepare them for second-language learners.

Diversity and Citizenship

Many educators work in classrooms where children's ethnic, cultural, and economic living situations are different. Children's homes may or may not have displayed acceptance or respect for others, whom they judge to be different. To deal with this common situation, acceptance and respect are accorded at school and the teacher becomes a model of behaviors, some of which her students may not have experienced previously. Some programs give attention to displaying America's founding strengths in the classroom. This approach used to be called *teaching citizenship and building civic pride*. It is an old concept in American education. Alexander (2006) describes a current, non-partisan movement in elementary schools: the First Amendment Schools Movement, as follows:

> The idea behind the five-year-old program: To keep America strong, children must be trained to respect many points of view, weigh complex issues, and understand the five freedoms (speech, religion, press, assembly, petition) guaranteed by the Constitution's First Amendment.

To reach this goal, the 97 First Amendment Schools in the United States commit to adding hands-on lessons in civics and community building. Teachers in these schools have learned, through training conferences, to include debate and critical thinking in classroom routines. Students accept the responsibility of speaking up in classroom discussions and keeping their school clean and safe. Often parent groups, which are promoted at First Amendment schools, become active and vocal, and the school's approach has resulted in more parent involvement in children's school lives.

Might this approach be applicable to preschool classrooms? Part of it is already there, but it is not called *civics*. Prekindergarten classes emphasize children's individual rights and responsibilities. They promote free speech, but not hurtful speech. Voting activities take place, and children's ideas and diverse opinions are given dignity. Most classrooms solve problems with a *together-we-can-fix-this* attitude. Each child is felt to be a valued individual. Diverse faith-based and cultural events happen, and American citizenship and culture is considered preeminent. Children are free to assemble in groups and invite others to join them. They are encouraged to express complaints and petition for change if necessary. Keeping the classroom safe and clean is emphasized. Although debating skill is not formally taught, it happens frequently in children's conversations. Early childhood educators promote critical thinking throughout the school day, and democratic ideals and freedoms are put into practice.

Delpit (1995) suggests teachers appreciate the "wonders of the cultures" represented in their classrooms (page 43).

> If we are to successfully educate all of our children, we must work to remove the blinders built of stereotypes, monocultural instructional methodologies, ignorance, social distance, biased research, and racism. We must work to destroy those blinders so that it is possible to really see, to really know the students we must teach. Yes, if we are to be successful at educating diverse children, we must accomplish the Herculean feat of developing this clear-sightedness, for in the words of a wonderful Native Alaskan educator: "In order to teach you, I must know you." I pray for all of us the strength to teach our children what they must learn, and the humility and wisdom to learn from them so that we might better teach.

Social justice activities are not new to early childhood curriculum designers. Williams and Cooney (2006) define social justice as follows:

> For us, social justice means that all children have the right to expect mutual respect, fair treatment, and equal access to resources and experiences, and experience a willingness to learn about others' perspectives.

Written Activity or Lesson Plans

Activity plans are useful devices that encourage student teachers to think thoroughly through the different parts of their planned activities. Beginning teachers try to foresee possible problems and find solutions. With adequate preparation through written planning, the student teacher can approach each planned activity with a degree of confidence and security. Cooperating teachers and supervisors often contribute ideas on the student's written plans, or collaborate with the student, sometimes making plans a team effort. Written plans are a starting point from which actual activity flows, depending on the children's reception and feedback. Monitoring the children's interest is a teaching task (see Figure 5–7), and will often result in improvising and revising the activities to suit their needs. Written **lesson plans** proceed one step further and isolate a teacher's or student teacher's plan for what will happen during a specific time block, in a specific location.

 Figure 5-7
This activity captured and held child interest.

lesson plans—the working documents from which the daily program is run, specifying directions for activities.

schedule—a planned series of happenings for a specific time period, to accommodate needs and goals.

A weekly classroom plan, or **schedule**, is usually developed to pinpoint specially planned activities that will take place in different learning centers or room areas. The plan includes which classroom adult has responsibility for preparation, providing necessary materials and equipment, supervision, and cleanup.

The activity plan guide in Figure 5–8 is one of many possible forms that can be used by student teachers. It is appropriate for most, but not all, planned activities. Story times, finger plays, flannelboard stories, songs, and short-duration activities usually are not written in activity-plan form. Activity plan titles are descriptive, such as Sink and Float, Making Farmers' Cheese, or Tie Dyeing. They quickly clarify the subject of the planned experience.

1. Activity title _____
2. Curriculum area _____
3. Materials needed _____
   _____
   _____
4. Location and setup of activity _____
5. Number of children and adults _____
6. Preparation _____
   _____
   _____
   _____
7. Specific behavioral objective _____
   _____
   _____
   _____
8. Developmental skills necessary for success _____
   _____
9. Getting started _____
   _____
   _____
10. Procedure (step by step) _____
    _____
11. Discussion (key concepts, attitudes, facts, skills, vocabulary, etc.) ____
    _____
    _____
    _____
    _____
12. Apply (or additional practice of skill or learning) _____
13. Cleanup _____
14. Terminating statement _____
15. Transition _____
16. Evaluation: activity, teacher, child _____
    _____
    _____
    _____
    _____

Figure 5-8
Activity plan guide

Filling in the curriculum area space sometimes leads to indecision. Many early childhood activities are hard to categorize. Subjects seem to fall into more than one area. Use your own judgment and designation; it is your plan.

Identification of materials, supplies, and tools comes next. Some activities require visual aids and equipment for teachers, as well as those materials used by children. Make sure you, as the student teacher, know how to use the visual aids and operate the equipment. Estimating exact amounts of necessary materials helps calculate expenses and aids preparation. You will simply count out the desired quantities. Student teachers generally know what classroom supplies are available to them and what they will have to supply themselves.

The location of a planned activity has much to do with its success. The following questions can help decide the best locations:

- What amount of space will children need?
- What room or outdoor features (for example, windows, water, flat floor, storage or drying areas, rug, lighting, grass, shade) are necessary?
- Will electrical outlets be necessary?
- Will noise or traffic from adjacent areas cause interference?
- Will one adult be able to supervise the location?

Self-help and child participation in cleanup are necessary considerations. Cleanup might involve a sorting game, with teacher and children working together, or a teacher might provide containers, strategically placed for small item storage or throw away. Adjacent soapy water and sponges help take care of messes. Cleanup often will not proceed smoothly if a student teacher does not prepare beforehand. Seeing cleanup as an integral part of the ending of any planned activity is the key.

Activities that actively engage children and invite exploration suit young children's needs. Random setups can lead to confusion and conflict over work space and supply use. A good setup helps a child work without help; it also promotes proper respect for classroom supplies and equipment and facilitates consideration for the work of others. Each setup reflects a teacher's goals and philosophy of how children learn best.

Student teachers usually begin planning for small groups before tackling larger groups and the total-room activity plans. A number of fascinating early childhood activities call for close adult supervision and can happen safely or successfully only with a few children at a time (see Figure 5–9). Instant replays or ongoing activities may be necessary to accommodate all interested children. Waiting lists are useful in these cases, and children quickly realize they will be called when it is their turn. The number of children on activity plan forms could read "Two groups of four children," for example.

Preparation sections on lesson plans alert the student teacher to tasks to be completed prior to actual presentation. This could include making a number of individual portions of paste, moving furniture, mixing paint, making a recipe chart, or a number of other, similar teacher activities. Preparation includes attention to features that minimize child waiting and decrease the need for help from the teacher (see Figure 5–10 and 5–11).

Figure 5-9
Some art activities are more successful with just a few children at a time under close supervision.

● **Figure 5-10**
The trays used in this activity set-up invite exploration and delineate child space.

● **Figure 5-11**
This student teacher of toddlers has prepared for easy clean-up and is deciding on the best arrangement of materials to promote self-help.

Writing Lesson Plans for Elementary Schools. There are several ways to approach lesson plans and each is based on a different theoretical model. One of the more popular models, based on behaviorist theory, is the *six-step lesson plan*, a direct instruction model (Gunter, Estes, & Schwab, 1990). Used in many elementary schools, the six-step plan consists of:

1. a review of previously learned material.
2. a statement of objectives for the lesson.
3. a presentation of new material.
4. guided practice with corrective feedback.
5. independent practice with corrective feedback.
6. periodic review, with corrective feedback if necessary.

As teachers of young children, however, the six-step model is not necessarily a developmentally appropriate one. More applicable to elementary school students is the *cooperative learning* model. Slavin (1987, 1988) has looked extensively at cooperative learning and has conducted research that indicates its efficacy. Some of the steps included in this model will look familiar. As in any lesson plan, a cooperative learning lesson begins with a statement of the *performance objective*, written in terms of observable behaviors, such as "Students will explore in cooperative learning groups a lesson on health and safety. As they participate in the activity, they will discover why cooperative learning groups are helpful. We will allow 30 minutes for group time." The steps of the lesson follow.

Step 1. Anticipatory set: A motivational question or statement intended to pique student interest, such as, "Wouldn't it be neat if someone else helped you with your homework?"

Step 2. Instruction: Generally, beginning with a follow-up question or statement to the anticipatory set, and intending to motivate further student curiosity, the instruction step involves listing any materials needed and the procedures to be followed.

Example (following from the above question): Materials needed are health texts and related reference materials from the in-classroom library.

Motivation statement: "Today we are going to look at a way that you can help each other get ready for your health and safety test. I know you'd rather do this by yourselves . . . No? . . . Okay, Let's try this then. . . ."

Procedure: A step-by-step look at what happens next. "Please do not move until I ask you to. The first thing I'm going to do is to put you into six groups, with five people in each group. Each group will study one of the parts you need to know for our health test tomorrow. This way no one group has to do it all. How does this sound? Each group will report its findings to the class as a whole, and I'll write down all the important facts you'll need for the test on the board."

The student teacher arranges the groups heterogeneously, with a leader designated for each group. Other roles, such as recorder (appointed for his handwriting ability) and researchers (who look up in books and notes any material relating to the subject they are to present), may be designated by the student teacher or, in groups accustomed to the process of cooperative learning, chosen by the students in the group. The critical difference in cooperative learning as opposed to what has often been called a

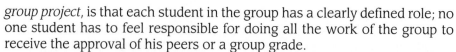

group project, is that each student in the group has a clearly defined role; no one student has to feel responsible for doing all the work of the group to receive the approval of his peers or a group grade.

In the example illustrated here, students would not be receiving a grade; however, it is possible that some reward would be given to the best group report, by the rest of the students in the class. In another example, each member of the group might grade both herself and also each other member of the group. In this way, the student teacher is able then to arbitrate in cases of disagreement.

Step 3. Guided practice: At this point, the student teacher circulates from group to group and checks to see that each group has the materials it needs and that each student in the group is working. She may have to intervene in a group having difficulty, praise a group working smoothly, or give help to a student researcher trying to obtain more information about the topic under study, and so on. In this example, each group studies one aspect of the material to be learned for the test, rather than all of the material. When the groups report back to the class, notes on all important concepts will be written on the chalkboard and copied by each individual student for further study at home.

Step 4. Closure: As the time for the lesson draws to a close, the student teacher alerts the groups to the end of the group study period and the need to prepare for their reports to the class. If the reports are to be presented on the same day, as in this example, they should be, the student teacher possibly needs to have the groups make their respective presentations after a recess. So closure might consist of the following reminder: "In 10 minutes it'll be time for recess. When we come back, we'll have our oral reports from each group. Recorders, make sure your notes are legible. Reporters, be sure to read the recorder's notes so you can ask for clarification on any words you're unsure about."

Step 5. Independent practice: After recess ends and the oral reports have been given, the student teacher will need to remind the class that they are responsible for information in the reports from each group. The student teacher should carefully print all essential information on the board as the reports are presented and have the cooperating teacher circulate to make sure that each student copies them down. At the end of the oral reports, the student teacher should then remind the class, "For homework tonight, I want you to study the notes you took during the group reports. Remember, we're going to have a test on the information tomorrow." Homework, in this example, is independent practice.

Step 6. The test that follows:

(Thank you to Colleen Sequeira, student teacher at California State University, Hayward, for this third grade lesson plan. Colleen might have used Figure 5–12 during her initial planning.)

In the lesson plan, the cooperative learning model is an example from the social learning theory, which recognizes that children often learn best from one another, especially in some cultures.

Other models for lesson planning include *concept attainment*, *concept development*, and *inquiry*. A student teacher should keep in mind that sometimes the purpose of a lesson dictates the type of plan to be used.

Name: _____ Date: _____

School: _____ Grade: _____

Objectives: _____

_____

Materials needed: _____

	Teacher Activities	Student Activites	Time

Anticipatory set

1.

2.

3.

4.

5.

6.

7.

8.

9.

10. Use fewer steps or add more, if needed.

Independent Practice

Evaluation: _____

_____

_____

_____

_____

_____

_____

● **Figure 5-12**
Lesson plan format

In many mathematics lessons, for example, the student teacher may want to use the social learning model as frequently students can better explain a process to a peer than can an adult. Paired learning teams are another variant of the social learning model. Inquiry lends itself well to science, especially when the student teacher wants his class to explore a scientific phenomenon.

LESSON PLAN GOALS AND OBJECTIVES

Planned and unplanned activities and experiences have some type of outcome. Written student teaching plans include a section where **objectives** are identified, and this serves as the basis for planning, presentation, and all other form sections.

Cooperating teachers and supervisors differ in requiring activity plans with specific behavioral or instructional objectives. **Instructional objectives (IO)** are more general in nature and may defy measurement. Examples of **specific behavioral objectives (SBO)** and instructional objectives follow:

SBO: When given four cubes of different colors (red, blue, green, and purple), the child will point to each color correctly on the first try when asked.

IO: The child will know four colors: red, blue, green, and purple.

SBO: When given a cut potato, paper, and three small trays of paint, the child will make at least one mark on the paper using a printing motion.

IO: The child will explore a printing process.

SBO: After seeing the teacher demonstrate cutting on a penciled line and being helped to hold scissors with the thumb and index finger, the child will cut apart a two-inch strip of pencil-lined paper, in two out of five attempts.

IO: The child will learn how to cut on a line.
Note: Written specific behavioral objectives use verbs that clearly describe **observable behavior** (see Figure 5–13). They consist of three parts:

1. conditions and circumstances in which learning takes place
2. the child's observable behavior
3. acceptable performance or criteria for success

It is best for beginning teachers to accomplish one objective per activity, do it thoroughly and well, and keep the activity short and lively. Student teachers tend to plan activities involving multiple concepts or skills. Usually,

objectives—aims; specific interpretation of general goals, providing practical and directive tools for day-to-day program planning.

instructional objectives—aims or goals, usually set for an individual child, that describe in very specific and observable terms what the child is expected to master.

specific behavioral objectives(SBO)— clearly describes observable behavior, the situation in which it will occur, and the exact outcome or the criteria of successful performance.

observable behavior— actions that can be seen rather than those that are inferred.

ask	count	hold	paint	return	take
attempt to	cut	jump	paste	say	tell
choose	dry	look at	pick	select	touch
close	empty	make motions	point to	sequence	turn
collect	explore	mark	pour	show	use
color	find	mix	put hand on	sing	use two hands
comment	finish	nail	put in order	solve	wait
complete	follow two directions	name	remove	sponge off	wash
contribute	guess	open	replace	state a favorite. . .	weigh

● Figure 5-13
Verbs used in writing specific behavioral objectives.

none of these skills is accomplished because of the amount and diversity of learning. Objectives of any kind may or may not always be realized. Evaluation sections analyze whether the student teacher achieved what he set out to do. Centers with clearly defined objectives, combining their teaching team's efforts, have a greater chance of realizing their objectives.

DEVELOPMENTAL SKILLS

Each activity builds on another. A child's skill and knowledge expands through increased opportunity and experience. Knowing the children's developmental skills makes student teachers aware of their capacities and levels. The ability to sit and focus for a period of minutes can be the requirement in a planned preschool activity, and having the ability to pick up small objects can be part of another. Planning beyond children's capacities may occur because of the student teacher's eagerness to enrich the children's lives and try out different ideas. A close look at the children's achievements and abilities will help the student teacher plan activities that are successful for both the children and the student teacher.

Planning for Skill Attainment

Petersen (1996) discusses skill-focused activities as follows:

> There are certain skills that every teacher wants children to master before they leave the program. These are skills agreed on in the early childhood field as appropriate to the development, limitations, and capabilities of children with whom the teacher is working. They are probably skills that the early childhood program and the children's parents believe are important for teachers to teach. These skill-focused activities should consistently appear in daily lesson plans.

Skills can be divided into intellectual, social-emotional, and motor skills, and some skills seem to overlap and fit more than one category. Intellectual skills are skills such as memory, problem solving, sorting, ordering, categorizing, predicting, and making hypotheses. Motor skills may deal with eye-hand coordination, balance, and strength in both small and large body muscles. There is an individual timetable and a natural sequence in the appearance of children's motor skills. Muscle systems develop and become controllable with use, practice, proper nutrition, and, at times, adult guidance. Take riding a tricycle as an example. It is a definite motor skill that many but not all children master during preschool years, depending on their life circumstances and their individual physical developmental capability.

As mentioned previously, social-emotional skills deal with interaction with others, sharing, group living, playing, impulse control, negotiation, self-regulation, cultural and accepted manners, and so on, and cannot be ignored when lesson planning.

Getting Started

Some student teachers find that a lesson plan outlined on a 3 x 5 card, kept on the lap or in a pocket, acts as a cue card reminding them step by step how the activity unfolds. Planning a first statement that motivates children, by creating a desire to know or do, increases their attention. Motivational statements need to be studied for appropriateness. Statements that create competition ("The first one who . . .") or are threatening ("If you don't try it, then . . .") cause unnecessary tensions. Appropriate motivational statements strike a child's curiosity and often stimulate the child to action or exploration. They capture attention, and hopefully, engage the child's mind, like the examples that follow:

"John brought a special pet. I think you'll want to see him."

"There are some new items in the collage box for pasting today. Where have you seen a shiny paper like this?"

"Today you'll be cooking your own snack. Raise your hand if you've seen your mom or dad make pancakes."

"Do you remember the sound our coffee-can drums made yesterday? There's a bigger drum with a different sound here today. Let's listen."

Focusing activities such as finger plays, body movement actions, or songs are often used as a getting-started routine. When planned, this is written in the "getting started" section of the lesson plan. Many teachers find helpful the practice of pausing briefly for silence that signals that children are ready to find out what will happen next. The following types of statements are frequently used:

"When I hear the clock ticking, I'll know you're listening."

"If I see your eyes, I can tell you're ready to find out what we're going to do in the art center today. Martin is ready, Sherry is ready. . ."

Lowering the volume of your voice can motivate children to change their behaviors so they can hear. This creates a hushed silence, which is successful for some teachers. Enthusiasm in a teacher's voice and manner is a great attention-getter. Children are quick to notice the sparkle in the teacher's eyes or the excitement reflected in her voice's tone, stress, or pitch.

During an activity's first few minutes, expectations, safety precautions, and reminders concerning class or activity rules should be covered if necessary. Doing so will avoid potential activity problems.

Procedure

If an initial demonstration or specific instruction needs expressing, this can be noted and written briefly in a step-by-step fashion. Because active involvement is such an important aspect for the young child's learning, participation is part of most planned activities.

This section of the plan outlines sequential happenings during the activity. Student teachers identify important subcomponents chronologically. The student teacher mentally visualizes each step and its particular needs and actions.

Discussion

Although teacher discussion and questioning is appropriate for many child activities, it can be intrusive in others. When deeply involved, children do not usually benefit from a break in their concentration. Other activities lead to a vigorous give-and-take, question-and-feedback format that helps children's discovery and understanding.

The following three questions clarify the written comments that may be included in this lesson plan section:

1. What key points, concepts, ideas, or words do you intend to cover during conversation?

2. What types of questions, inquiries, or voluntary comments might come from the children?

3. Are you going to relate new material to that which was learned previously?

Application

Sometimes, an activity leads to an immediate application of a new knowledge or skill. If the idea of a circle was introduced or discovered, finding circular images or objects in the classroom can immediately reinforce the learning. Repetition and practice are key instruments in learning.

Evaluation after Presentation

Hindsight is a valuable teaching skill. One can evaluate many aspects of a planned and conducted activity. Goal realization, a close look at instructional techniques or methods, and student teacher actions usually come under scrutiny. The following questions can aid both activity- and self-evaluation:

1. Was the activity location and setup appropriate?

2. Would you rate the activity as high, middle, or low in interest value and goal realization?

3. What could improve this plan?

4. Should a follow-up activity be planned?

5. Was enough attention given to small details?

6. Did the activity attempt to reach the instructional objectives?

7. Was the activity too long or too short?

8. If you planned to repeat the activity, how would you change it?

9. Were you prepared?

10. Which teacher-child interactions went well? Which ones went poorly?

11. Was the size of the group appropriate?

12. Was the activity a success with the children?

13. Were my reactions to boys and girls nonsexist?

14. Was the activity above, at, or below the group's developmental level?

15. What did I learn from the experience?

16. What seemed to be the best parts of the activity?

17. Did I learn anything about myself?

18. How good was I at helping children put into words what they experienced or discovered?

19. In what ways do I now know more about the children involved in the activity?

Evaluation and comments from others will add another dimension. Team meetings usually concentrate on a total day's happenings, but may zero in on the student teacher's supervision and planned activities (see Figure 5–14).

⬤ **Figure 5-14**
Team meetings often scrutinize the day's events.

⬤ OTHER ACTIVITY PLAN AREAS

Many activity plans pay close attention to cleanup. Usually, both children and adults clean up their shared environment. Drying areas, housecleaning equipment, and hand washing can be important features of a plan.

In a **terminating statement**, a teacher may summarize what has been discovered and enjoyed, and tie loose activity ends together, bringing activities to a satisfying group conclusion.

> After watching Roddie, the hamster, eating celery and lettuce today, Leticia noticed Roddie's two large teeth. Leticia wonders what other foods he might like. Sam plans to bring some peanut butter on toast for Roddie tomorrow, to see if he likes it. Ting wants to telephone the pet store to ask the storekeeper what hamsters eat. Shawn thinks a library book would tell.

Unforeseen Distractions

The best-prepared activities can often go awry because of events beyond the teacher's control. Although the true-to-life example given below is humorous, the educator's quick thinking and open-ended questioning is to be commended.

> A kindergarten teacher thought it a good idea to have a live mouse visit the classroom. The children's favorite storybook that year involved a small boy's pet mouse and the reactions of family members. The teacher secured a mouse from the sixth grade science teacher. He assured her the mouse was tame and friendly. She introduced the mouse to her class by gathering the children in a circle with children's

terminating statement—an ending summary or recap of what has been discovered, discussed, experienced, enjoyed, and so on, after a learning activity.

legs outstretched, touching the feet of a peer. The mouse was in a cage at the circle's center. She unlatched the cage door and the mouse immediately ran up her leg. She stifled a scream, clamped down, and caught the mouse through her pant's leg about knee high. In a barely controlled voice she asked, "Can anyone think of a way we can get the mouse back in the cage?"

Skilled teachers often creatively draw child attention back to focus with a statement when interruptions occur. They also decide to follow group interest with discussion or unplanned actions, determining on the spot when to pursue an educational opportunity.

TRANSITIONS

Transitions are used to move children in an orderly fashion, from one activity to the next. To end group times, a **transition statement** or transition activity is used. The transition statement should create an orderly departure, rather than a questionable or thundering-herd ending. There are thousands of possibilities for disbanding groups. Some examples are:

"Raise your hand if your favorite ice cream is chocolate. Alfredo and Monica, you may choose which area in the room you are going to now."
"People with curly hair please stand up."
"Put your hand on your stomach if you had cornflakes for breakfast. If your hand is on your stomach, walk to . . ."
"Peter, Dana, and Kingston, pretend you are mice and quietly sneak out the door to the yard."
"After you've placed your clay pot on the drying rack, you can choose to play in the block area or the yard."
"Raise your hand if you're wearing long pants that touch your shoes. If your hand is up, get your jacket and meet Carol near the door. Raise your hand if you're wearing a belt today."
"Suzette, I can see you're finished. If you look around the room, you'll see something else you may want to do. Bill is in the loft reading to Petra and Alphonso."

In the preschool and lower primary grades, a teacher may ring a bell five minutes before recess. A teacher may also remind children of what is expected, as in, "Be sure to put away your math **manipulatives**," or "Try to finish your stories with Mrs. Chandler in the writing center. The rest of you need to shelve your books and get ready." Another teacher may blink the classroom lights, still another may play a few chords on the piano. You will want to try different techniques to decide what works best for you.

Warnings or alerting bells or whistles are used with large groups of older children. Teachers of young children use softer signals sufficient to gain the attention of small groups.

Promoting Cognitive Skills

You know from child development classes that young children often rely heavily on what they see.

When you interact, you can expect some children will begin to pause, reflect, think about and try out more than one idea or attend to more than one factor. Children are problem-solvers by nature, and through curiosity,

transition statement—planned verbalization that moves young children from one activity to another.

manipulatives—toys and materials that require the use of the fingers and hands, for instance, puzzles, beads, and pegboards.

generate questions and pursue answers. They attempt to solve problems and also seek novel challenges, and persist because success and understanding are motivating in their own right (National Research Council, 2000). Many tasks or experiences presented to young children are purposely open-ended, with different ways available to proceed. Many activities promote diverse and individual courses of action, or ways of using, thinking about, or creating things. These types of activities promote reflective thinking and child planning.

The dialogues teachers have with young children often involve imagining, observing, predicting, brainstorming, and creative problem solving. Discussions can be lively. Child answers are accepted and further discussions welcomed and promoted. Child comments are based on child experience, consequently correct in light of what the child knows.

Educators intent on promoting children's thinking should listen closely, and interact with pertinent comments, acknowledgments, and questions following children's line of thinking and focus. Questions that only test the children's memories rarely ask for higher thought processes. Thought provoking teacher questions call for children's conjecture, mental choices, opinions, judgments, cause-and-effect identification, predictions, solutions, reasoning, hypothesizing, and creative expression. These types of questions require effort to formulate, and teachers must learn restraint, resisting urges to jump ahead in conversations, rather than allowing conversational silences and pauses as the child mulls over mentally, cogitates, and processes the question toward a response. Rephrasing or paraphrasing by the teacher may help clarify child meanings, or alert one child to another child's ideas on a given subject, perhaps encouraging interaction between children.

Using Community Resources

The whole community is a learning resource for young children. Each neighborhood has unique features and people with special talents and collections. Industries, businesses, and job sites may provide field trip opportunities, speakers, or activity material giveaways. Cultural events and celebrations, ethnic holidays, buildings, and parks and recreation areas easily integrate into the school's activities to promote a reality-based children's program.

Pitfalls

The biggest pitfall for the student teacher is the tendency to stick to the plan when children's feedback during the activity does not warrant it. Teachers should take their cues from the children's behavior; expanding their interests may mean spending additional time providing additional opportunities and materials. In some cases, it can mean just talking if the children want to know more.

If children's avid interest cuts into another planned activity that follows, it might be postponed or revised to fit into the schedule. The unforeseen frequently happens. Getting the children to refocus on a new, planned activity may mean having to clear the children's minds of something more important to them.

Teachers usually try to relate unexpected occurrences to the planned activity. For example, "That was a loud booming noise. We can listen for another while we finish shaping our bread before it goes into the oven." If efforts to refocus fail, a teacher knows the written plan has been preempted.

A real teaching skill involves using unplanned events to promote specific, identified curriculum objectives, or objectives that were not even considered but are timely and important.

Going out on a Limb

In planning activities and reviewing results, expect successes and failures. You may well experience more growth from activities that flopped; they will need analyzing and could stimulate your creativity. Don't forget that taking risks—within safety limits, of course—and trying new ideas and new ways of doing things may temporarily create uncertainty, but also may offer challenge, excitement, and growth.

Approaching child curriculum in unique ways is part of the fun of teaching. When college and university supervisors and cooperating teachers see students branching out in new directions, they see serious effort. Adults, like children, explore, experiment, fail, create, invent, talk about, and follow their own curiosities to grow.

Teaching Tips

As mentioned before, your enthusiasm while presenting the lesson plan must be emphasized. When your eyes sparkle and your voice sounds excited when you talk about what your class is accomplishing, the children will likely remain interested and focused. Your level of enthusiasm needs to be genuine and appropriate. Langness (1998) believes one of the most powerful services a teacher can deliver is to help children anticipate each day as an exciting learning opportunity. She states that an educator's enthusiasm promotes children's seeing the pursuit of knowledge as a gift that they open with pleasure.

You will be eager to start the activities you have designed, anxious to see whether you have captured the children's attention and stimulated their developmental growth. When you feel that the group joins in your excitement and discovery, no other reward is necessary.

Children see things that you do not, ask unexpected questions, and make statements you will be challenged to understand. Listen closely to children's responses; if you cannot understand them, probe further. More often than not, you will understand the wisdom of their thoughts, which are based on their unique past experiences.

Do not panic when a child corrects you or when you do not have an answer. Develop a we'll-find-out-together attitude. A teacher who has all the answers often fails to notice the brilliance, charm, and honesty of children.

Planning back up activities, for situations when interest lags or an activity finishes before the time expected, is another great idea. Many students have devised an emergency bag with fill-in activities that can be easily introduced and set up, such as a favorite book or art activity.

Room Environments

Looking closely at room environments will be a challenging aspect of student teaching. You may be asked to take over a particular area, redesign or restructure it, or create a new interest or discovery area. In other classrooms, the cooperating teacher may not want anything moved or improved. In this case, you cannot help but evaluate its arrangement.

You will be looking at child behaviors affected by physical surroundings and you will notice popular and unpopular room areas. Problem room areas may be immediately apparent. Some room spaces will appear designed for special purposes, accommodating the needs of one or many children.

Experimentation in placement of furniture, equipment, and supplies is an ongoing teacher task in most classrooms (see Figure 5–15). Prekindergarten classrooms may change dramatically from week to week, depending on the course of study. Many pieces of preschool furniture have been designed for multi-use flexibility and utmost mobility.

Effective classroom arrangements do not just happen. They are a result of much hard work and planning. Considerable thought and observation of child play pursuits is involved. Because of budget (usually for lack of it), creative solutions to classroom environments abound.

 Figure 5-15
Bookcases are angled to create an instructional corner with an element of privacy.

Student teachers will find that some room areas need their constant attention. Analyzing the possible provoking factors may lead to one reason or many, including the room arrangement itself, furnishings, activities, *setups* (the way individual activity materials are arranged), storage, supplies or a lack of them, and cleanup provisions.

In some placement classrooms, student teachers may notice and recognize the cooperating teacher's priorities and individuality. A musically inclined teacher's room might have considerable space devoted to children's experiences and exploration of music-related activities. Another child center or classroom may emphasize gardening activities, both indoors and outdoors, and so on. You are probably already aware of your own favorite instructional areas and envision your own future classroom, which will incorporate your own creative ideas.

WORKING WITH GROUPS

group times—also called circle or story times; time blocks during the day when all of the children and teachers join together in a common activity.

Group times are covered in detail in this chapter because student teachers frequently need help planning and conducting them. We do not intend to suggest that planned group gatherings are the best or most efficient vehicles for child learning. Play and spontaneous child activity offer equally excellent opportunities.

Group Size

More and more early childhood teachers prefer planning and working with small groups of young children within their classrooms. Consequently, large gatherings consisting of the entire class may only happen when a group is formed early in the morning or at closing. These larger groups tend to facilitate information passing rather than instruction. Think about your former training classes and classroom discussions, and your feelings about group meetings and consultations in your own training classes. Most teachers admit they were comfortable offering their ideas and felt listened to when groups were kept small.

Successful Group Times

It pays to think about and analyze elements that promote success. Student teachers will tend to imitate their cooperating teachers' group times and will carry techniques learned there into their own future classrooms.

Identifying the purpose of group times precedes their planning. During such times, children not only learn but draw conclusions about themselves as learners.

Child Characteristics and Group Times

How can group time become what you would like it to be? Go back in your memory to age and stage characteristics. Group times are based on what a teacher knows about the children for whom activities are planned. The children's endurance, need for movement, need to touch, enjoyment of singing or chanting, ability to attend, and other factors are all taken into consideration. The dynamics of the group setting and the children affect outcomes. Two friends seated together could mean horsing around. Maybe some children have sight or hearing problems. Perhaps there is a child who talks on and on at group times. All situations of this nature should be given planning consideration.

Planning

The following are questions you might ask yourself when planning a small-group activity:

- Is this the best format for the lesson?
- How will I promote child self-help and independence?
- Why or how will children be motivated to want to know or find out about planned group subject matter?
- How will I minimize waiting?
- Will my materials attract them?
- Are materials or tools to be shared? How will children know?
- If a demonstration is necessary before children proceed, will materials be temptingly close to them during the demonstration?
- How does my setting provide for active participation?
- Who will clean up? How?
- How will children know what will happen next or where to go?

Whether it is group time or any other time during the day, you will want to promote discussion and elicit children's ideas. Lively interchanges promote comprehension and clarify what everyone is experiencing. Most often, discussions pursue what is of interest to children, and teachers find that one topic leads to another.

Student teachers often plan their group times with other adults. The following planning decisions are usually discussed:

- Which adults will lead? Which adults will be aides?
- When, where, and how long is the activity? How will the children be seated?

- What will be the instructional topics, activities, and goals?
- How many adults and children will attend?
- Will there be one presentation or instant replays?
- What materials or audiovisuals will be needed?
- Who will prepare needed materials?
- How will children be gathered?
- Will children be asked to raise hands before contributing?
- In what order will events happen?
- Can the children actively participate?
- Will a vigorous activity be followed with a slow one?
- Will children share in leading?
- How will the results of group time be reviewed?
- How will children leave at the conclusion?

There seem to be distinct stages in group times. For example, there is the gathering of children and adults. This then leads to a focusing of the children's attention. There is a joint recognition of the persons present at group time. At that point, someone begins to lead and present the activity. This is followed by the children participating and reacting. In the final stage of group time, there can be a brief summary and then a disbanding.

Building Attention and Interest

Teachers use various methods to gather the children and get their attention. A signal, like a bell or cleanup song, helps to build anticipation: "When you hear the xylophone, it's time to . . ." A verbal reminder to individual children lets them know that group time is starting soon: "In five minutes we'll be starting group time in the loft, Tina. You need to finish your block building."

In order to help the children focus, the teacher might initiate a song, finger play, chant, or dance in which all perform a similar act. Many group leaders then build a sense of enthusiasm by recognizing each child and adult. An interesting roll call, a name tag selection activity, or a simple question like "Who is with us today?" are good techniques. Children enjoy being identified. Using a playful approach makes things interesting: "Bill is wearing his red shirt, red shirt, red shirt . . . Bill is wearing his red shirt at group time today. Katrina has her hair cut, hair cut . . ."

To build motivation or enthusiasm, some teachers drop their voice volume to a whisper. Others light up, expressing enthusiasm with their face or body. The object is to capture interest and build a desire in the children to want to know or findout something. Statements like "We're now going to read a story about . . ." or "You're going to learn to count to six today" do not excite children much. In contrast, statements like "There's something in my pocket I brought to show you . . ." or "Raise your hand if you can hear this tiny bell . . ." build children's interest and curiosity. Manner and tone of voice will be a dead giveaway as to whether wonder and discovery are alive in the teacher. Teachers use natural conversation. Presenting age-appropriate materials or topics close to the heart of the presenter is a key element. Experiences from one's own love of life can be a necessary ingredient. New teachers and student teachers should rely on their own creativity and use group times to share themselves.

Sheinman (2000) describes one elementary school teacher's method of gaining attention, so directions are clear and better understood. It follows:

> When I need to gain children's attention, I ask them to stop and give me "five." They have to do five things for me to give out my directions: (1) look at me, (2) close their mouths, (3) stop what they are doing, (4) open their ears, and (5) raise their hands. They are to indicate they have done all five by raising all five fingers showing that they completed what they are expected to do. When all hands are up, I give my directions (Sheinman, 2000).

Practice

If memorized songs, finger plays, or chants are part of the group time, practice is necessary. Time spent preparing and practicing makes for a relaxed presenter (see Figure 5–16). Lap cards may be used as insurance if the student teacher forgets under pressure.

Feedback

Feedback from children and adults needs to be monitored while presenting. For example, seeing a child hesitate may cue the presenter to repeat and emphasize words. It is worthwhile to see what really interests the children and spend additional time with that activity. Sometimes, even the best group time plans are discarded, revised, and another created based on feedback.

● Figure 5-16
A teacher can move easily, relax, and enjoy when she knows the story well and is prepared beforehand.

Recognition

One technique that helps recognize individuality is giving credit to each child's idea. "LeGrand says he saw a fox in the woods, Ryan thinks it was a wolf, and Emma says it looked like a cat." Bringing a child back to focus by naming him or asking a question is common. "Todd, this dog looks like your dog, Ranger," or "Todd, can you show us . . . ?"

Guidance

Handling child behaviors during group time can distract a student teacher and upset the sequence of thought. Quick statements, such as "If everyone is sitting down, you will be able to see" or "Mei-Lee and Josh are waiting for a turn," help curb distracting behaviors. A group leader can be very grateful for an alert aide or assistant teacher to handle group or individual behaviors so the group time can proceed.

Evaluation

If time and supervision permit, you should analyze your group activity after you have relaxed and reflected on its particulars. Hindsight is valuable now. If possible, you might consider videotaping your group time. This offers tremendous growth opportunities. Listen closely to the supervisor's and cooperating teacher's objective comments and suggested improvements.

THEMATIC TEACHING

theme approach—a popular child program planning approach that involves a course of study with identified child activities focused on one subject, idea, or skill such as butterflies, friendship, biking, or a picture book.

The **theme approach** to child program planning is popular in many early childhood centers and classrooms. A theme includes a written collection of activity ideas on one subject, idea, or skill, such as a picture book, butterflies, homes, neighborhood, kindness, friendship, biking, swimming, or animals. Activities within the theme encompass a wide range of curriculum areas including art, music, numbers, science, small and large motor development, and so on. A theme's course of study involves a day, week, or longer period; one week is typical but not always appropriate because this may not allow in depth study of a topic.

Though usually preplanned, themes can be developed after a child's or group's interest is recognized. Curtis and Carter (1996) make a clear distinction between traditional and developmental themes. *Traditional theme* topics are teacher-chosen, rather than those selected by a teacher *after* uncovering topics of interest by observing child play and exploration. In *developmental theme* planning, the teacher bases her approach on inquiry and learning, which focuses on the realities of children's lives, relationships, and issues. Materials and planned activities are designed to elicit curiosity, promote the exploration of the new ideas, and pursue the questions children generate. Themes differ from teacher to teacher and school to school; each offers a unique collection and presentation of activities.

Possible Instructional Benefits

There are a number of reasons for using the theme approach in young children's instruction. Some major ideas follow:

- A theme tackles instruction through a wide variety of activities that reinforce child learning as the same new ideas, facts, skills, and attitudes are encountered through different routes. Discovery and deductions happen in varied activities, keeping classrooms enthusiastic and alive.
- The classroom environment can be saturated with activities and materials on the same subject, reinforcing learning.
- A theme approach lets children gather, explore, and experience the theme at their own pace and level of understanding, because of the number of choices in room activities and materials.
- Planned group times offer shared experiences and knowledge.
- Teachers can identify and gather theme materials for future use, saving time and energy.
- Teachers can best guide child discovery through knowledge gained from their research during theme preparation and construction.
- Community resources become classroom materials, and community uniqueness is incorporated into instruction.
- The teacher collects and develops audiovisuals and real objects.
- A theme can evolve from the unplanned and unexpected, giving curriculum flexibility.
- The teacher's and children's creativity and resourcefulness are encouraged and challenged.
- Once the environment is set, the teacher is free to help uninvolved individuals and interact intimately with the highly focused children.
- The classroom environment becomes a dynamic, changing, exciting place for both children and adults.
- A theme can provide a security blanket for new teachers outlining a plan for one week's activities or longer.

Elementary Grades

An integrated curriculum's goals for language and literacy programming are for children to expand their ability to communicate orally, and through reading and writing, and to enjoy these activities. The teacher might read part of a stimulating story to the class and ask the children what they think will come next. After listening to several examples of what might come and writing them on the chalkboard, the teacher might then assign the students to cooperative groups to write their own endings. Children who may have difficulty reading or writing because of a learning disability may be good at generating ideas or illustrating the final product. As briefly explained in the previous section, it is also important to understand that cooperative groups have been shown to be remarkably effective for children of all ability levels.

Another way to integrate across the curriculum is to use a theme approach. Such topics as dinosaurs or family are immensely popular, and can be introduced with a book. Children are asked to work together in groups to write their own version of the book, or to write a sequel. An in-class library can house several books about dinosaurs or families that children can use for reference and for enjoyment. The books should encompass several different grade levels, so each student can have the opportunity to read independently. In listening, writing, and reading activities, language is strengthened. Spelling and mechanics are an integrated part of the final stories the children write and illustrate.

Each cooperative group needs to have a good editor, maybe two creative thinkers, at least one logical sequential thinker to keep his peers on target, and a good illustrator. After groups have created book covers and flyleaf synopses, the creative teacher will then teach students bookbinding. Finally, card pockets can be affixed to the inside covers, and students can literally "check out" the efforts of their peers. Students can also be invited to go to another class and share their stories, a real self-esteem booster.

How would a family theme relate to the other curricula? Let us look at a first grade social studies example, "We Are All Unique and Special."

Reading, including language arts: Reading and writing about the children's own families and telling stories about family traditions, special events, favorite foods, and so on.

Art: Illustrating their stories about their families.

Math: Counting the number of girls and boys in the class and graphing the results. Counting the number of children with various characteristics, like eye color, hair color, clothing colors, and so forth, then graphing the results and posting them on the bulletin board. Counting the number of siblings in each student's family and preparing a graph of the results. Predicting the number of siblings a new child coming to the class would most likely have.

Science: As an extension of eye, hair, or skin color, have students talk to family about where their ancestors lived. Bring a globe into the classroom and post a world map for children to use. Have them point out where their grandparents and great-grandparents lived. Use colored thread and map pins for each child to place on the map, to indicate where her grandparents or ancestors came from. Have the children stretch a thread from one area of the map to the area where your school is located. Have books available in your in-class library that illustrate life in several different parts of the world.

(The preceding section was based on materials and suggestions in *Project Reach*.)

One way of planning a thematic unit is to use a process called *webbing*. Figure 5–17 presents a web based on an unplanned event that evoked considerable child interest. The teacher then developed a question-and-comment web based on children's queries and comments, as an initial step to developing a subsequent web to reflect children's specific areas of interest. In making a web, the student teacher is laying out the central theme of the plan and illustrating how the pieces fit together in a diagram that might resemble a spider web, thus the name. Webbing may provide the student teacher with a picture of how one topic integrates across curricular areas (see Figure 5–18). An early childhood educator could use the same webbing techniques with a picture book or topic of interest, using other early childhood curricular areas or categories.

A baby robin is found dead on the play yard prompting child interest and discussion. The web is based on children's subsequent comments and questions.

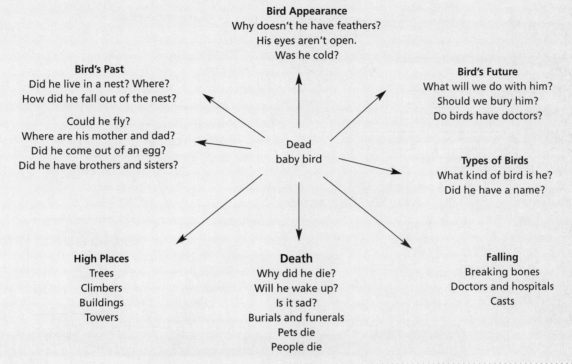

Bird Appearance
Why doesn't he have feathers?
His eyes aren't open.
Was he cold?

Bird's Past
Did he live in a nest? Where?
How did he fall out of the nest?

Could he fly?
Where are his mother and dad?
Did he come out of an egg?
Did he have brothers and sisters?

Bird's Future
What will we do with him?
Should we bury him?
Do birds have doctors?

Dead
baby bird

Types of Birds
What kind of bird is he?
Did he have a name?

High Places
Trees
Climbers
Buildings
Towers

Death
Why did he die?
Will he wake up?
Is it sad?
Burials and funerals
Pets die
People die

Falling
Breaking bones
Doctors and hospitals
Casts

⬤ **Figure 5-17**
Unplanned event web—initial planning

Possible Limitations or Weaknesses

Critics of thematic teaching mention several limitations of this type of programming, for both preschool and elementary school.

- Once developed, thematic units tend to become a teacher-dictated curriculum.
- A reliance on this crutch produces dated programs.
- Themes may not be closely evaluated or critically analyzed for appropriateness during construction.
- Theme teaching promotes the copying of teaching techniques rather than the developing of individual styles.
- A dependence on commercial materials can add expense and lose child interest.
- Thematic unit teaching promotes the idea that preplanned units are a preferred way to teach.
- Themes often overlook geographic, socioeconomic, and cultural factors.
- Themes impose one child's or teacher's interest on the whole group.
- Thematic units may be used to compare teachers.

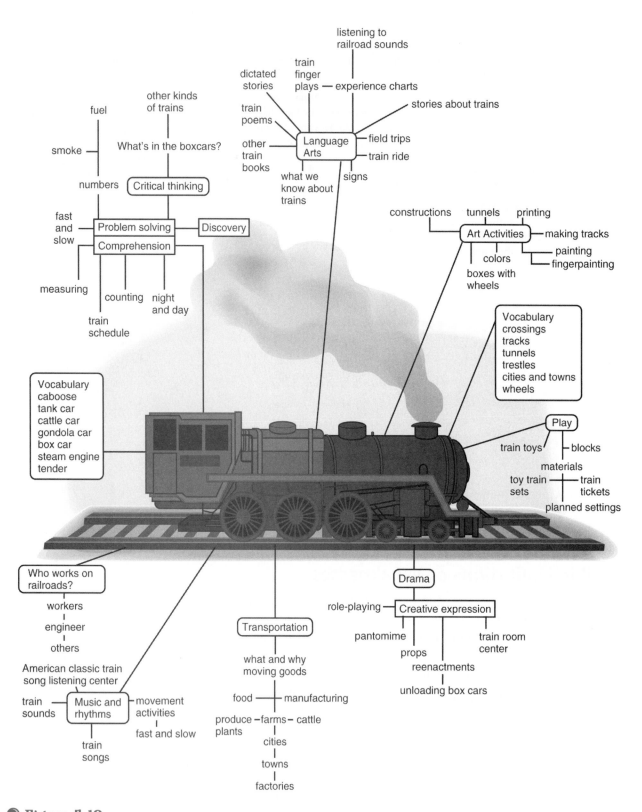

● **Figure 5-18**

This webbing example suits a theme based on a picture book about trains such as Donald Crew's book, *Freight Train*.

Thematic Subsections

This analysis of a thematic unit is provided for student teachers who may need to compile a written unit. Some of you will not be required to do so, and your preparation for unit or thematic teaching will not be this detailed. Nevertheless, what follows will be helpful to those intending to try this type of instructional approach.

Thematic units may have many subsections. Based on teaching preferences and teacher decisions, each section is either present or absent. Subsection listings contain a description of the contents.

- *Title page* includes theme identification, writer's credit line, ages of children, classroom location, and descriptive and/or decorative art.
- *Table of contents* lists subsections and beginning pages.
- *Instructional goals description* contains writer's identification of concepts, ideas, factual data, vocabulary, attitudes, and skills in the unit.
- *Background data* are researched background information, with theme particulars useful in updating adults on the subject. Technical drawings and photos can be included.
- *Resource list* includes teacher-made and commercially available materials and supplies, with names and addresses of where to get them. It also contains audiovisuals, community resources, consultants, speakers, field trip possibilities, and inexpensive sources of materials.
- *Weekly time schedule* pinpoints times and activities, supervising adults, and duration of activity.
- *Suggested activities* include activity plans, procedure descriptions, and plans for room settings, centers, and environments.
- *Children's book lists* identify children's books related to the theme.
- *Activity aids* describe patterns, finger plays, poems, storytelling ideas, recipes, chart ideas, teacher-made aids and equipment, ideas and directions, and bulletin board diagrams.
- *Culminating activities* offer suggestions for final celebrations or events that have summarizing, unifying, and reviewing features.
- *Bibliography* lists adult resource books on theme.
- *Evaluation* contains comments concerning instructional value, unit conduct, and revision needs.

How to Construct a Thematic Unit

Initial work begins by choosing a subject and possibly webbing it. Then data are collected and researched. Next, brainstorming to generate ideas and envisioning saturated classroom environments occurs. Instructional decisions concerning the scope of the proposed course of study are made. The search for materials and resources starts, instructional goals and objectives are identified, and activities are created. A tentative plan of activities is compiled and analyzed. After materials, supplies, and visual aids have been made or obtained, a final written plan is completed. The unit is conducted, concluded, and evaluated. Each aspect of instruction is assessed. Notes concerning unit particulars are reviewed, and unit revisions, additions, or omissions are recorded. The unit's written materials are stored in a binder for protection. Other items may be boxed.

Units can be an individual, team, or group effort. Developing a unit during student teaching creates a desired job skill and may aid in preparing for the first job. A written theme, finished during student teaching, can display competency and become a valuable visual aid for job interviews or for an addition to your professional portfolio.

Saturated Environment

When thinking of ways to incorporate a unit's theme into the routine, room, yard, food service, wall space, and so on means using your creativity. Background music, room color, the teacher's clothing, and lighting can reflect a theme. The environment becomes transformed. Butterfly-shaped crackers, green cream of wheat, special teacher-made theme puzzles, face painting, and countless other possibilities exist. Do not forget child motor involvement and child and adult enactment of theme-related concepts and skills.

A moderate number of activity choices on a theme at any given hour is deemed best, rather than a large or overwhelming array of activities (Stipek, 1996). Because themes are spread out over time, this can be decided, depending on the teacher's logical sequencing of activities, on what activities seem to grow out of stimulated child interest and questions, or what activities complement each other.

Project Approach

Katz and Chard's (1993) text, *Engaging Children's Minds: The Project Approach*, sensitized teachers to the idea that children in most early childhood classrooms had no active role in deciding what they wanted to learn. Activity planning can include both teacher- and child-generated activities, if teachers listen and provide ways for children to follow their own line of inquiry. Elliott (1998) starts with an introduction to a theme and works with kindergarten children to develop a themed child interest project. She states that during project work, children ask thoughtful questions, engage in focused investigation, use problem-solving skills effectively, discover the power of teamwork, and take ownership of what they are learning.

A *project* is an in-depth investigation of a topic. The investigation is usually undertaken by a small group of children within a class, sometimes by a whole class, and occasionally by an individual child. The key feature of a project is that it is a research effort deliberately focused on finding answers to questions about a topic posed, either by the children, the teacher, or the teacher working with the children. The goal of a project is to learn more about the topic rather than to seek right answers to questions posed by the teacher.Projects evolve out of child curiosity and questions. The teacher supports the children's activities and helps children proceed in their investigations and problem solving while keeping them safe. Answers are not supplied by the teacher; he only suggests avenues toward answers. Children's hypotheses may not turn out as expected, and they learn from their mistakes. In presenting a discussion on a unit about birds to preschoolers, and probing what they are curious about or what they may want to find out, many possible child investigative projects can be discovered.

Teachers who strongly believe in young children's innate ability to pursue information, solutions, and answers, given adult assistance, will find this educational approach attractive. Children will no doubt learn many things the teacher had not planned.

Planning Outdoor Activities

Student teachers are expected to use all existing space for children's play, discovery, and learning opportunities. Each yard area has a number of givens, which could include boundaries, traffic patterns, and many other features.

One can think of each given as an instructional asset. Mentally list ways that fences or walls could be used for a child activity. Did you include child water painting? Displaying child work, or using a fence as a base for child easels? Using it as a base to tie on ropes that could, with old blankets, enclose an area for a playhouse, stage, or special activity area?

Your creativity in using givens for the children's activities must always consider child safety and supervision first.

Think about what play areas add beauty, and create a state of relaxed alertness, or else can be classified as warm, cozy, child-friendly places. Look at what yard features have a significant effect on the children's behavior. Movable and mobile furnishings and equipment will have many possible uses. Adding tires, boxes, signs, and donated items to the yard should be explored. Animal and insect study takes place in many centers. A great number of science discoveries can happen that are not possible in indoor settings.

Griffin and Rinn (1998) encourage teachers to add obstacle courses to play yards for variety, developmental value, spatial awareness, adventure, cooperative and gross-motor skill development, creative expression, dramatic play, self-esteem, and challenge. Make sure you consult with your cooperating teacher about outdoor plans for child activities.

Work Ethic Activities

Remember the status that went along with being selected as the wastebasket-dumper or chalkboard-eraser? Cleaning, cooking, room maintenance, material repair, and similar activities are planned regularly in some classrooms. These work-related activities can offer opportunities for children to develop work skills and attitudes, a sense of accomplishment, independence, and feelings of competency. Working alone or in groups is possible. Polishing shoes, cleaning silverware, and shelling peas belong in this work category. Often, these activities are a popular choice. Curtis and Carter (1996) suggest developing cleanup kits using a window cleaning theme. Kits may include spray bottle, sponges, squeegees, paper towels, window-cleaning fluid, tubs, and buckets.

●SUMMARY

Planning, presenting, and evaluating activities are a part of student teaching. Written activity plans are usually required and encourage student teachers to examine closely all aspects of their curriculum. Guidelines and criteria for planning activities promote overall success. Consultation with teachers often aids in the development of written plans. Learning objectives can be written as instructional objectives or in measurable, specific behavioral objective terms.

A number of lesson plan forms exist; this text provides two. Preparing a written plan increases student teacher confidence and reduces stress, and often it averts potential problems. A lesson plan is only a starting point and has the flexibility to change or be discontinued during its presentation, depending on interest and need among the children.

Many planned activities are not to be put into lesson plan form because of their simplicity or their focus on creative expression. Lesson plans are a beginning teacher's attempt to be thoroughly prepared.

Each classroom's group times differ in intent and purpose. Student teachers plan and present group instruction and carefully analyze goals and the group's particular dynamics, needs, and learning levels. Many decisions affect the smooth, successful flow as different stages evolve. Technique, preparation, presentation, and goal realization are all factors that should be evaluated.

Thematic unit teaching is a popular instructional approach. However, there are different views of the benefits and limitations of unit teaching. Construction of a teaching unit includes theme identification, research, decisions concerning instruction objectives, activity development in a wide range of curriculum areas, and gathering of materials, supplies, and teaching aids. Each thematic unit is a unique collection of activities planned for a specific group of young children, and their particular geographic, socioeconomic, and cultural setting should be taken into consideration. The choice of a theme's sequence, and whether it has subsections, is up to the individual teacher. After a thematic unit is presented, it should be evaluated by the writer for possible improvement.

This chapter started with the identification of standards that have served as the basis for curriculum development in early childhood programs. It alerted the reader to a variety of current curriculum models, and the steps curriculum developers follow in constructing a curriculum.

● HELPFUL WEB SITES

http://www.naeyc.org
National Association for the Education of Young Children (NAEYC). Search for a position statement on school readiness or one dealing with early childhood curriculum.

http://www.naeyc.org
NAEYC/SDE. An executive summary, outlining the essential elements of early learning standards, is available.

http://www.teacher.scholastic.com
Scholastic Magazine is a resource for lesson planning and links to other professional sites.

http://www.doe.mass.edu
State of Massachusetts. To obtain copies of early childhood program standards information choose this Web site.

http://www.headstartinfo.org
Head Start: Search publications for standards available in English and Spanish.

http://www/fpg.unc.edu
National Center for Early Development and Learning (NCEDL). Investigate links to research reports. Click "index."

http://members.aol.com
Reggio Emilia. A bibliography of reading material is available.

http://www.whitehouse.gov
United States Government: Read more about the *Good Start, Grow Smart* initiative.

 Additional resources for this chapter can be found by visiting the Online Companion at www.earlychilded.delmar.com.

● SUGGESTED ACTIVITIES

A. In groups of two to four, identify which activity plan section needs greater attention by the student teacher in the following situations.

1. Danielle is presenting an activity with her collection of seashells. She has repeatedly requested that children look while she explains the details of the shells. Most of the children who started the activity are showing signs of disinterest.

2. Francisco introduced a boat-floating activity that has children excited to try it. The children start pushing, shoving, and crowding.

3. Dean prepared an activity with paper airplanes landing on a tabletop landing strip. Children are zooming loudly and running about the room, interfering with the work of others. The situation is getting out of hand.

4. Claire's activity involves making a greeting card. Many children are disappointed because Claire has run out of the metallic paper used for her sample card. Others are requesting help because their fingers are sticky with glue.

5. Kate's activity making cinnamon toast works well until Joey burns his finger on the toaster oven.

6. Spencer has given a detailed verbal explanation of how the children should finish the weaving project he has introduced. However, the children seem to have lost interest.

7. During Jackie Ann's project, paint gets on the door handles and the children are unable to turn on the faucets because of slippery hands.

8. Boris and Katrina have combined efforts during an activity. They have spent 10 minutes returning the area to usable condition for the next activity.

B. Plan and present a group activity.

C. After the class has been divided in half, select either the *pro* or *con* views on theme teaching as an instructional approach. Use 20 minutes to plan for a debate in a future class.

D. Develop a web or outline on the topic of houses, or on a subject of your own choosing.

E. Examine your assigned classroom's curriculum. Try to cite specific incidences of the following. How do children:
1. anticipate consequences of their actions or anticipate elements in instructional activities?
2. gather information?
3. recognize and pinpoint problems?
4. generate theories or ideas that might solve problems?
5. gain control over strong emotions?
6. make choices between different courses of action?
7. evaluate the outcomes of their choices?
8. participate in problem-solving discussions?

REVIEW

A. List two ways to identify children's interests.

B. Write three examples of motivational statements for activities you plan to present or could present.

C. Match items in Column I with those in Column II.

I	II
1. A curriculum area	a. ethnic dance group
2. A specific behavioral objective	b. "Those with red socks may wash their hands."
3. A transitional statement	c. four out of five times
4. A motivational statement	d. "Snails have one foot and excrete a slippery liquid."
5. An activity plan criterion	e. nutrition
6. A setup	f. has three parts
7. A community resource	g. "Have you ever touched a feather?"
8. A performance criterion	h. too many concepts attempted
9. A summary statement	i. paper left, then patterns, crayons, and scissors at the far right
10. A pitfall in student teacher lesson planning	j. child safety

D. List considerations for group instruction planning.

E. Describe five important considerations for a student teacher planning to conduct a 20-minute group time with 15 four-year-olds.

F. Complete the following statements.
1. Two ways to improve a teacher's skill in conducting groups are . . .
2. Activities that approach the same knowledge through art, music, science, cooking, measurement activities, and language activities can reinforce . . .
3. A *saturated* environment might be described as . . .
4. Using a thematic unit developed in another section of the country is . . .

G. List four possible thematic unit subsections.

H. Describe three curriculum models and include three identifying characteristics for each model.

I. What concerns and benefits may be present when teachers undertake assessment prior to activity planning? List your key points in a few sentences.

CASE SCENARIO

Setting: Outdoor play area. Inge, a student teacher in an urban cooperative preschool, is about to present an outdoor science activity.

Inge has planned an exciting outdoor science activity. After turning in her lesson plan, securing her cooperating teacher's approval, and collecting her visuals at a local creek, she takes a group of three-and-a-half-year-olds to a shaded, grassy area outdoors.

She has prepared a small table and a covered tub with air holes. Children's paint aprons are waiting on a chair. At this time of day, other mixed-age classes are using the play yard. Inge gathers her group of seven children, and tells them she has a surprise in the tub but they are to put on paint aprons first. The group stands around the tub. Inge has children guess what is in the tub. Then with a flourishing "Ta Ta" she removes the cover. Small creek frogs start to jump from the tub. Pandemonium, panic, and fear break out immediately. Some children run away screaming. Other children in the yard approach and crowd around the tub, delighted with the frogs. Inge tries to assure the children left in her group that the small frogs will not hurt them. Other teachers in the yard come to help.

Questions for Discussion:

1. What step or steps on Inge's lesson plan form were poorly conceived (see Figure 5–8)?

2. Think about Inge's educational intent. What would you say to Inge if you were her cooperating teacher?

3. Can anything positive be salvaged from Inge's disaster?

4. Does Inge's cooperating teacher share some responsibility for the lesson's outcome?

REFERENCES

Association for Childhood Education International. (1997) Position papers on the preparation of early childhood and elementary teachers. *Childhood Education* 73 (3) 18-23.

Alexander, M. (2006, May). Ahead of the curve: Three schools. Three fresh ideas for getting kids hooked on learning. *Reader's Digest,* 89–93.

Bredekamp, S., & Copple, C. (Eds.). (1997). *Developmentally appropriate practice in early childhood programs* (rev. Ed.). Washington, DC: National Association for the Education of Young Children.

Carter, M., & Curtis, D. (1994). *Training teachers: A harvest of theory and practice.* St. Paul, MN: Redleaf Press.

Child Care Bureau (2002) *Good start, grow smart.* Retrieved September 19, 2005 from http://www.nccic.acf.hhs.gov/pubs/stateplan/execsum.html.

Curtis, D., & Carter, M. (1996). *Reflecting children's lives: A handbook for planning a child-centered curriculum.* St. Paul, MN: Redleaf Press.

Delpit, L. (1995). *Other people's children: Cultural conflict in the classroom.* New York: The New Press.

Dodge, D. T., & Colker, L. (1992). *Creative curriculum for early childhood.* Washington, DC: Teaching Strategies.

Dunn, L., & Kontos, S. (1998, March/April). Developmentally appropriate practice: What does research tell us? *Journal of Early Education and Family Review 5*(4), 19–25.

Eggers-Pierola, C. (2005). *Connections and commitments: reflecting Latino values in early childhood programs.* Portsmouth, NH: Heinemann.

Edwards, C., Gandini, L., & Forman, G. (Eds.). (1993). *The hundred languages of children: The Reggio approach.* Stamford, CT: Ablex Publishing.

Elliott, M. (1998, July). Great moments of learning in project work. *Young Children.* 53 (4) 28–32.

Epstein, A., Schweinhart, L., & McAdoo, L. (1996). *Models of early childhood education.* Ypsilanti, MI: High/Scope Press.

Fosnot, C. T. (1989). *Inquiring teachers, inquiring learners: A constructive approach for teaching.* New York: Teachers College Press.

Gamel-McCormick, M. (2000). *Exploring teachers' expectations for children entering kindergarten and procedures for sharing information between Pre-K and K programs.* Conference presentation, the National Association for the Education of Young Children, Atlanta, GA.

Gandini, L., & Goldhaber, J. (2001). Two reflections about documentation, In E. Gandini & C. P. Edwards (Eds.). *Bambini: The Italian approach to infant/toddler care* (pp. 124–145). New York: Teachers College Press.

Geist, E., & Baum, A. C. (2005, July). Yeah, buts that keep teachers from embracing an active curriculum: Overcoming resistance. *Young Children 60*(4), 2836.

Genishi, C. (2002, July). Young English language learners: Resourceful in the classroom. *Young Children.* 57 (4), 66–72.

Goffin, S. G. (2000, August). The role of curriculum models in early childhood education. EDO–P–00–8, *ERIC Digest.*

Goffin, S. G., & Wilson, C. (2001). *Curriculum models in early childhood education: Appraising the relationship.* Upper Saddle River, NJ: Merrill/Prentice Hall.

Good Start, Grow Smart. (2002, April). Washington, DC: The White House.

Griffin, C., & Rinn, B. (1998, May). Enhancing outdoor play with an obstacle course. *Young Children 53*(3), 43–51.

Gunter, M. A., Estes, T. H., & Schwab, J. H. (1990). *Instruction: A models approach.* Boston: Allyn & Bacon.

Harrington-Lueker, D. (2000, January). High stakes or developmental practice? MAYBE BOTH! *The School Administrator, 57*, 6–11.

Head Start Bureau, Administration for Children and Families, Department of Health and Human Services (1975). *Head Start performance standards.* Washington, DC: U. S. Department of Human Services.

Helm, J. H., & Katz, L. C. (2001). *Young investigators: The project approach in the early years.* New York: Teachers College Press.

Hyson, M. (2005, November). Enthusiastic and engaged: Strengthening young children's positive approaches to learning. *Young Children, 60*(6), 68–70.

Jablon, J. R., & Wilkinson, M. (2006, March). Using engagement strategies to facilitate children's learning and success. *Young Children, 61*(2), 120–16.

Kagan, S. L., Moore, E., & Bredekamp, S. (Eds.). (1995). *Reconsidering children's early learning and development: Toward views and vocabulary.* Report of the National Education Goals Panel, Goal 1, Technical Planning Group, (Publication No. ED391576). Washington, DC: Government Printing Office.

Kamii, C., & De Vries, R. (1975/1977). Piaget for early education. In M. Day & R. Parker (Eds.) *Preschool in action.* Boston: Allyn & Bacon.

Kantrowitz, B., & Wingert, P. (2002, April 29). The right way to read. *Newsweek, CXXXIX*(17), 6–66.

Katz, L., & Chard, S. (1993). *Engaging children's minds: The project approach.* Norwood, NJ: Ablex.

Kohn, A. (2001, March). Fighting the tests: Turning frustration into action. *Young Children, 56*(2), 19–24.

Kuster, C. A. (1994). At the core: Language and cultural competence. In J. Johnson and J. McCracken (Eds.).

The early childhood career lattice: Perspectives on professional development. Washington, DC: National Association for the Education of Young Children.

Langness, T. (1998). *First-class teacher: Successful strategies for new teachers.* Santa Monica, CA: Canter and Associates, Inc.

Lewit, E., & Baker, L. S. (1995). School readiness. *The Future of Children, 5,* 128–139.

Lumsden, L. (1998, Jan/Feb.). Teacher expectations: What is professed is not always practiced. *The Journal of Early Childhood and Family Review, 5*(3), 29-33.

Meyer, M. (1997, September). The GREENing of learning: Using the eighth intelligence. *Educational Leadership, 55*(1), 56–58.

NAEYC Code of Ethical Conduct. (2005). In S. Feeney and N. Freeman (Eds). *Ethics and the early childhood educator: Using the NAEYC code.* Washington, DC: National Association for the Education of Young Children.

National Association for the Education of Young Children and the National Association of Early Childhood Specialists in State Departments of Education (NAECS/SDE) (2003). *Early childhood curriculum, assessment, and program evaluation.* (joint position statement) Washington, DC: Authors.

National Research Council. (2000). *How people learn: Brain, mind, experience and school.* Washington, DC: National Academy Press.

Neuman, S. B., & Roskos, K. (2005, July). Whatever happened to developmentally appropriate practice in early literacy? *Young Children, 60*(4), 22–26.

O'Loughlin, M. (1991, April 3–7). *Beyond constructivism: Toward a dialectical model of the problematics of teacher socialization.* Paper presented at the Annual Meeting of the American Educational Research Association, Chicago.

Padron, Y. N., Waxman, H. C., & Rivera, H. H. (2002, August). Educating Hispanic students: Effective instructional practices. *Practitioners Brief 5.* Santa Cruz, CA: Center for Research on Education, Diversity and Excellence, University of California.

Petersen, E. (1996). *A practical guide to early childhood planning and methods and materials* Boston: Allyn and Bacon.

Plutro, M. (2000, March). Planning for linguistic and cultural diversity: We must continue to respond. *Head Start Bulletin, 67,* 19.

Reynolds, G., & Jones, E. (1997). *Master players: Learning from children at play.* New York: Teachers College Press.

Rinaldi, C. (2001). Reggio Emilia: The image of the child and the child's environment as a fundamental principle. In E. Gandini & C. P. Edwards (Eds.). *Bambini: The Italian approach to infant /toddler care* (pp. 55–56). New York: Teachers College Press.

Schlechty, P. (2001). *Shaking up the school house: How to support and sustain educational innovation.* San Francisco: Jossey-Bass.

Sheinman, A. J. (2000, August). Six behavior tips that really work. *Instructor, 110*(1), 24.

Slavin, R. E. (1987). Cooperative learning and the cooperative school. *Educational Leadership, 47.*

Slavin, R. E. (1988). The cooperative revolution catches fire. *The School Administrator, 44.*

Snow, K., Connecting the early child care worker professional development with child outcomes. In M. Zaslow & I. Martinez-Beck (Eds.). (2006). *Critical - issues in early childhood professional development* (pp. 137–140). Baltimore, MD: Paul Brooks Publishing Co.

Stipek, D. (1996). Motivation and instruction. In D. Berliner & R. Calfee (Eds.). *Handbook of educational psychology.* New York: Macmillan.

United States Bureau of the Census. (1995). *The foreign-born population: 1994.* Current Population Reports. Washington, DC: Government Printing Office.

Vander Wilt, J., & Monroe, V. (1998, July). Successfully moving toward developmentally appropriate practice: It takes time and effort! *Young Children, 53*(4) 29–33.

Wesson, K. A. (2001, March). The "Volvo effect": Questioning standardized tests. *Young Children, 56*(2), 16–18.

Williams, K. C., & Cooney, M. H. (2006, March). Young children and social justice. *Young Children, 61*(2), 75–82.

Wolverton, E. D. (2000, March). The curriculum: A written plan for action. *Head Start Bulletin, 67,* 4–5.

Working with Children

CHAPTER 6

Classroom Management: Beyond Discipline

OBJECTIVES   After reading this chapter, you should be able to:

1.... List the five major management areas.
2.... Discuss the effects of the classroom environment on children's behaviors.
3.... Define the role of the guidance function, commonly called *discipline*, in the management of the classroom.
4.... List and describe five common guidance/disciplinary techniques.
5.... Identify the different behaviors children display when resisting adult authority.
6.... Analyze what guidance/disciplinary techniques work best, and state why.

Comments of student teachers:

> 66   *I once heard in a beginning class what one teacher tried when a child picked up a large tree branch and brandished it threateningly at other children. The teacher went to the child and said, "What a marvelous branch, could I hold it?" That led into a discussion about the branch hurting someone, and the child's deciding it needed to be given to the custodian. The teacher later had the custodian carry it in at a small group time for discussion. The child received attention and status for considering the safety of others.*
>
>   *I tried this technique with a child who'd picked up a playground rock. It worked well for me, too. I'm sure it won't always work but it might work most of the time.* ●
>
> **Peter Mills**

CLASSROOM MANAGEMENT

What comes to your mind when you hear the words **classroom management**? Many student teachers, and many teachers themselves, associate the phrase with another word: *discipline*. Classroom management goes far beyond discipline, although the guidance function is certainly a part of what is involved in managing the classroom. Classroom management, in the fullest sense of the meaning, involves five separate parts:

1. the physical arrangement of a classroom
2. curriculum choices
3. time management
4. classroom routine management
5. the guidance, or disciplinary, function

Guidance, in turn, has two facets: managing routine behavior problems and managing serious behavior problems.

Flicker and Hoffman (2002) believe that although teachers and child educators come to work, in some cases with years of training and experience, classroom management continues to be daunting. One major difficulty lies in the fact that in our multicultural, multiethnic society the disciplinary function is viewed differently by different families. Although state laws forbid spanking as a disciplinary technique, there are families who typically use spanking to control their children's negative behaviors. As early childhood professionals, our task then becomes a delicate one to explain center or school and state laws and policies.

classroom management—consists of supervising, planning, and directing classroom activities and the room environment. It also involves making time-length decisions, providing appropriate direction, and guiding child behavior to enable children to live and work effectively with others.

The Physical Arrangement of the Classroom

What is the *best* arrangement for a preschool classroom? Curtis and Carter (1996) remind teachers that environments have a great influence on how people feel and behave. Put yourself at children's eye level when evaluating a classroom. Questions such as the following should be considered:

- Where should blocks be located? Are they easy to reach?
- Where should the art area be located? On an easy-to-clean floor area? Near a water supply?
- Should there be a clothesline on which to hang paintings?
- Is the dramatic-play area attractive? Are there enough changes of clothing and other props to stimulate a variety of roles?
- Is there a quiet corner where children can look at books (see Figure 6–1)?
- Is there plenty of space, especially outside, for active play?
- Do children have an opportunity to climb, run, and ride wheeled toys without endangering each other's safety?
- Given an empty room of 20 feet by 30 feet, where should different areas be located? How can the teacher define each?
- Are children's physical needs and safety considered?
- Is there a sense of order?

 Figure 6-1
Notice the abundant pillows for children to sit on in this book corner.

● **Figure 6-2**
Does your classroom promote child curiosity, wonder, and intrigue?

● Would the room promote child curiosity, wonder, and intrigue, or beg to be physically explored (see Figure 6–2)?

● Is the room aesthetically pleasing and does it offer elements of natural beauty?

● Are room retreats designed to offer feelings of soft, cuddly, calming textures, seating, and privacy?

● Is the room set up for child self-help?

● Do thought-out storage areas exist?

● Do classroom furniture and equipment arrangements encourage crowded conditions in some classroom areas?

● Is child comfort a priority?

● Are creative materials and toys open-ended?

● Is there a secluded, escape-hatch area?

● Are room arrangements and areas flexible? Can they expand if need be?

● Are there smooth, flowing pathways in and out of room areas?

● Do visual displays reflect children's lives, interests, and cultural experiences?

Room features sometimes overlooked include background noise level, smells, temperature, and lighting.

Look at Figure 6–3. Is this the best possible arrangement this first-grade teacher could have made? What flaws can you see? Was the teacher wise in placing the reading area next to the water fountain? Where should the math manipulatives be stored? Given the configuration of the desks, what circulation problems might you anticipate? Can you think of what you might do if this classroom were yours to rearrange? You may want to discuss this with your fellow student teachers.

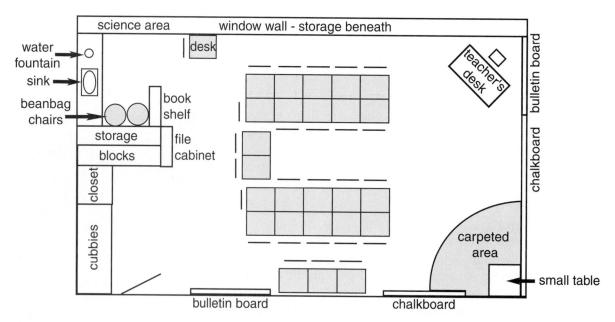

● **Figure 6-3**
Why might the arrangement of this first-grade classroom lead to management problems?

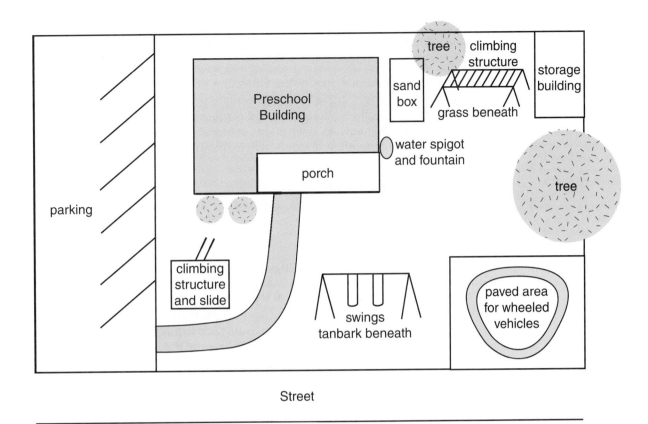

◉ Figure 6-4
What might be the possible problems with the arrangement of this preschool play yard?

Now look at Figure 6–4. Is this the best possible arrangement for this preschool play yard for three- and four-year-olds? Can you point out any possible areas of difficulty related to the placement of the play equipment in the yard? Was it wise of the person who designed the yard to have placed the sand area by the water spigot and fountain? Should the storage shed be located where it is? Is the paved area for wheeled vehicles large enough and stimulating enough? Again, you may want to discuss this play yard arrangement with your peers and describe any changes you feel would be justified, and why.

Curriculum Choices

Each choice you make regarding curriculum is another part of classroom management.

- First, choose the materials you will set out for children to explore.
- Second, decide which materials, such as scissors and glue sticks, can be used only under your direct supervision.
- Third, decide how you will equip the dramatic-play and discovery centers.
- Fourth, develop colorful bulletin board displays that are informative and attractive.
- Finally, decide which materials will be used every day and which will change after children have had ample opportunity to explore them.

Keeping children adequately motivated with new curricular choices, while retaining those materials children clearly love, contributes to effective classroom management.

> The National Association for the Education of Young Children's position statement on developmentally appropriate practices stresses the importance of child-initiated or child-centered learning . . . [T]he importance of involving children in curricular decisions and allowing them to be responsible for their own learning is vital across all age groups (Vartuli, 2005).

It goes without saying that motivated children, exploring curricular areas of their own choice, rarely display problem behaviors.

Time Management

Time is a limited resource. Time management involves more than simply following a schedule; it includes observing each child closely, to recognize when a child may need to use the toilet, or when he may need to be redirected from playing with a child with whom he has had altercations. Time management means knowing how long children in your care can sustain interest, so you can choose books for story time that not only pique their curiosity but are also short enough to sustain their attention. Time management means planning activities that are neither too long nor too short and giving children more opportunities to engage in activities. Sometimes, there never seems to be enough time to accomplish everything we would like to do.

At the elementary school level, time management also means acknowledging *time on task*. How much time is actually spent on learning activities? In one study of time allotted to mathematics in a second-grade classroom, students were actively engaged in learning math only 30 percent of the total time. What happened to the other 70 percent? Some of the time was spent reminding students to get out the math manipulatives they were to use that day. Some of the time was spent telling students to pay attention. In fact, the student teacher in the study had to remind some students three times to take the manipulatives off the shelves where they were stored. How might he have better used the time? One simple solution to the problem of lack of attention, and some students moving too slowly, would have been to have designated only one student from each group to be the "materials manager" for that day.

A word of caution: not all of the time spent off-task that seemed to be wasted actually was. Students used part of the time, when they appeared to be off-task or even day dreaming, to *think*: a critical part of problem solving and unlocking their creative potential. Can you remember times when you might have taken time to withdraw, in a sense, from active participation in a classroom, just to think? Your children or students do likewise.

As mentioned in Chapter 4, recent research on the activities of the brain, together with the burgeoning influence of schools that have implemented brain-based learning, has shown what happens in the brains of people when they think. When the material to learn is new, children and adults both need more time to reflect or think about what it is they are learning. Young children need to be taught how to talk about what they are doing because that helps them develop the capacity to reflect. Later, they can be encouraged to speak silently to themselves as a part of developing the ability to think about thinking, or *metacognition* (Abbott, 1997).

A further note of caution: McCarthy (1997) admonishes us to remember that thinking involves both reflection and action. Although some children will sit quietly while they process newly presented material, others will want almost immediately to act on the material, or experiment with it. Our classroom needs to support both types of children. Classroom experiences with teaching to children's multiple intelligences also supports brain-based learning (Caine & Caine, 1997).

Time management also implies the wise use of your own time; try to balance your work, preparation, home and family, relaxation, and recreation times. Set priorities and try not to become so overwhelmed with preparation for school that you have no time for other things.

Managing Classroom Routines

For student teachers, it is essential to your success that you carefully observe your cooperating teacher's routines. Should you want to introduce a change in routine, clear it with your college supervisor first; then check with your cooperating teacher. One may say no, but another may suggest that you try, but be aware of what a change in the routine may do to some of the children. Always remember that for some children, especially younger ones and those new to the classroom, routines offer predictability and, therefore, safety.

THE GUIDANCE OR DISCIPLINARY FUNCTION IN CLASSROOM MANAGEMENT

When we think of the guidance function and its role in classroom management, what do we mean? **Guidance** can be the act of guiding or it can mean leadership, as in directing someone to a destination or goal. In the classroom, guidance is the teacher's function, to provide leadership and more often is defined as discipline. How do the terms *guidance* and *discipline* differ? *Guidance* is a less specific, more generic word; *discipline* derives from the Latin word for *pupil* and is defined as *training designed to produce a specific character or pattern of behavior*. In particular, discipline is the act of assisting the child to grow toward maturity. This is the major goal.

Guidance can also be looked at as a

> . . . system, one in which people are interdependent and each action taken by one person influences the others. What is expected of children, the schedule and routines of the adults, all contribute to the system of discipline (Boulden, Hiester, & Walti, 1998, with Tertell).

Flicker and Hoffman (2002) advocate taking a positive approach to discipline "through discussion, explanation, limit setting, and enforcement of consequences."

To Boulden, Heister, and Walti (1998), it often seems that some people are born with a natural talent for being able to set appropriate guidelines for children, whereas others have to work at it, learning by trial, error, and a few hard knocks before gradually improving. Yet Boulden and her colleagues admit that when they ask these naturally talented people how they do what they do, they invariably hear that they, too, once struggled with learning what worked and what did not. Walti states that one of the problems she sees today is that "we are exposed to literally dozens of

guidance—ongoing process of directing children's behavior based on the types of adults children are expected to become.

options and hundreds of articles on the subject," all of which make it sometimes difficult to know what to choose at any one time. Schoonmaker (1998) agrees, suggesting that until student teachers feel confident that they can control or manage children's behaviors, they may be preoccupied by discipline issues.

Conflicts Arise

Conflict among preschoolers is an expected part of social development (Killen & Turiel, 1991). When children's different needs and wishes collide, feelings erupt. Play partner selection can be a factor. Transitions from one activity to another may provoke problems if transitions are abrupt. Anger, frustration, and disappointment may trigger child outbreaks, and violence may have become a learned behavior. Browning, Davis, and Resta (2000) remind teachers that children may frequently witness verbal and physical aggression in their homes or neighborhoods, and emulate that model.

Outcomes. Educators who study children's conflicts observe four common outcomes:

1. *Lack of resolution*, which happens if the issue is dropped, children leave the area, select different toys or different activities, or seek other play partners.
2. *Mutual solution,* which is achieved through discussion, bargaining, compromising, settling on a creative alternative, or making the conflict into a game.
3. *Submission,* which happens if a child yields or children give in willingly or unwillingly.
4. *Adult intervention,* which may impose or suggest a solution or otherwise settle the conflict.

As Gillespie and Chick (2001) point out, submission is an undesirable outcome because a clear winner or loser is established, creating or promoting bullying and victimization. Adult intervention, though sometimes necessary, is not the educators' primary goal, which is to minimize the need for adult intervention. When adult intervention is minimized, children negotiate and resolve conflicts themselves. The practice of problem-solving skills may be necessary, and educators take the time to offer practice opportunities by providing supportive assistance (Nelsen, Lott, & Glenn, 1997). Froschl, Sprung, and Hinitz (2005) advocate training children in techniques designed to avert conflict and prevent bullying.

Managing Routine Behavior Problems

What is meant by "routine behavior problems?" Can any misbehavior be considered routine? Obviously, two-year-old children may present several routine behavior problems as they struggle with trying to establish their autonomy. But it isn't just two-year-olds who struggle with autonomy. To a certain extent, all children struggle with it. What do you see then? You see children who push against limits and test boundaries. When you first take over the class from your cooperating teacher, you will often see children who seem to misbehave deliberately. You ask them to come to the circle-time area and some children say, "No." You ask others to pick up the blocks and replace them on the shelves prior to snack time and again you hear, "No" or, "Why should I?" or, "I don't want any snack today."

So what is the student teacher to do? One set of guidelines is called the *four Cs*: *consistency, consideration, confidence,* and *candor.* What is meant by *consistency*? It means that you understand yourself well enough to respond to children in a fair and impartial manner. It means consistency of adult behavior, expectations, limits, and rules, which means reliability; your behavior does not change from day to day and remains reasonably predictable to the children. For children, there is safety in knowing that the adults in their lives are predictable. Such reliability gives children feelings of security and safety. This becomes especially important when you, as a student teacher, are responsible for children who may be inconsistent and unpredictable.

The second *C* is *consideration.* This means that you are considerate of the children you teach and of the adults with whom you work. You respect the children and are aware of their needs, their likes, and dislikes. You are considerate by taking time to listen, even to the child who talks constantly. It means watching all of the children closely and noting which child needs an extra hug and which one needs to be removed from a group before a temper tantrum erupts. All of these actions show children that you care and will help you establish a warm relationship with them. Consideration helps to build rapport.

The third *C* is *confidence.* You need confidence to make decisions that reflect careful thought on your part, decisions that are free of bias and based on all evidence. Confidence implies that you realize you like some children better than others, and you know why you react differently to identical actions involving different children. Confidence is knowing when to stand up for your opinions and decisions and when to compromise. It means understanding when to be silent, knowing that waiting is the more mature action to take.

Candor, the fourth *C*, means that you are open and honest in your actions with children, fellow workers, and yourself. It means being frank and fair; you may inevitably put your foot in your mouth, but you will gain a reputation for being honest in your relations with others. Candor is the ability to admit a mistake and the courage to apologize.

Like the four *Cs*, the acronym *CARE* can also spell success in guiding children. As Rogers and Freiberg (1994) wrote, good teachers possess three qualities: congruence, acceptance of others, and empathy. As mentioned in Chapter 2, these can easily be expanded to four: *congruence, acceptance, reliability,* and *empathy,* or *CARE* (see Figure 6–5).

Congruence, as Chapter 2 states, is Rogers' term for understanding yourself. Always remember that with truly great teachers, their teaching is such an extension of themselves that you see the same person whether that person is in the classroom, the office, the home, or the supermarket. These people radiate self-confidence by knowing who they are and what they want from life. It is sometimes difficult for the student teacher to copy the congruent teacher because the methods the teacher uses are so much a part of the person that the student teacher may not be able to emulate them. This relates to the second goal of guidance: knowing oneself.

● **Figure 6-5**
Student teaching offers many opportunities to show children you CARE.

What you as a student teacher must learn is what methods are congruent with your inner self. The best methods are always those that seem natural to use, those that are an extension of how you feel about yourself.

Remember that *acceptance*, as Rogers uses it, means truly caring about each child you teach. It means that all children deserve your respect regardless of how they act. The aggressive child, who acts-out, is just as deserving of your acceptance as the star pupil of the class.

As mentioned before, *reliability* means that your children know you and they know the routine for the class. Being reliable also implies fairness.

According to Rogers, *empathy* implies being able to place yourself in the child's shoes, to see from that perspective. It is the ability to see that the hostile, aggressive child may need love and acceptance more than the happy, easygoing child. Empathy also means knowing that the happy child needs attention, too, even though attention is not demanded. Learn to be empathetic; it is worth the effort.

Let us assume that you have learned how to *CARE*. Does that mean you will not have any behavior problems? Does that mean you will automatically have rapport with all your children? Of course not. It means only that you can, perhaps, understand children's behavior more easily and can plan to teach self-discipline to those who need to learn it.

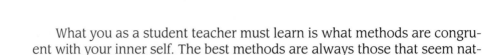

CHILD EMPOWERMENT

empowering—helping parents and children gain a sense of control over events in their lives.

Your previous classes have no doubt dealt with the issue of child choice and responsibility for behavioral actions. **Empowering** children in classrooms can mean giving them the opportunity to think about and guide their own actions, thereby allowing them to choose between possible actions in any given situation. Naturally, all child group arrangements have rules to guard the safety of children and limit behaviors unpleasant to others.

It may be all too easy for a student teacher to do everything for children. It makes the student teacher appear busy and productive, in control, and active rather than passive. Giving choices within limits takes time and is usually more work, and sometimes it creates disorder. Is it easier to pass out paper at art times, or have children help themselves? Is it easier to assign a "materials manager" to hand out the paper at each table group? Is it easier to write names on the children's papers than to ask children if they want to write their own names on their work? Is it easier to promote children's taking turns as group leaders or helpers or to do the task yourself? Most teachers answer that it is *easier* to do it themselves, but sharing tasks to promote children's experiences and self-esteem is the preferred, more educative practice.

Hiester (Boulden, & Walti, with Tertell, 1998) would agree and states, "children's self-esteem is centered around how they were disciplined, the things that do or do not happen to children." She writes about the need for us to "face our monsters," those actions by children that most annoy and upset us. To Hiester, communication is the key, both with the children and the other adults, as is being aware of how much is communicated through nonverbal behaviors. Allowing children to take part in the management process (as with nutrition breaks and cleanup times, for example) and asking them to help in deciding how to store materials in the classroom proved to reduce the times Hiester needed to intervene or be concerned.

Teachers strive to make rules consistent and clear. There are times in classroom life when a child is not allowed to choose, so these times are not presented as choices. As adults, we usually abhor, avoid, and sometimes rebel in situations in which we lose our autonomy; so do young children.

At this point in your student teaching, an update and review might be useful. Unfortunately, there is no magic formula. This text aims to provide you with the possible *whys* of children's behavior (presented in Chapter 7) and the techniques used successfully by effective early childhood teachers.

Character Guidance

Ryan (1993) points out that schools and teachers consciously and unconsciously attempt to educate children:

- to be concerned about the weak and those who need help.
- to help others.
- to work hard and to complete tasks promptly and as well as they are able.
- to control violent tempers.
- to work cooperatively.
- to practice good manners.
- to respect authority.
- to respect the rights of others.
- to help resolve conflict.
- to understand honesty, responsibility, and friendship.
- to balance pleasure and responsibility.
- to ask themselves and decide what is the right thing to do.

Student teachers may experience many learning situations in the classroom that are also guidance situations, and may be concerned with one or more of the above-listed goals of the guidance function in classroom management.

Guidance as Social Development

Social behaviors are sometimes seen as difficult to teach, because so often they involve the *absence* of doing, rather than doing. In other words, we teach prosocial behavior by *not* doing. We choose *not* to grab; we choose *not* to spank; we try to model in our own behaviors how we would like children to behave. But what can we do actively? Honig and Wittmer (1996) suggest the following:

- Provide an environment sensitive to the needs of the children.
- Emphasize cooperation rather than competition. Teach cooperative and conflict-resolution games and sports.
- Set up classroom spaces and play materials to facilitate cooperative play.
- Use **bibliotherapy**: Incorporate children's literature to enhance empathy and caring in daily reading activities.
- Actively lead group discussions on prosocial interactions.
- Encourage social interaction between normally developing children and children with special needs.

bibliotherapy—the use of books that deal with emotionally sensitive topics, in a developmentally appropriate way, to help children gain accurate information and learn coping strategies.

- Develop class and school projects that foster altruism.
- Move very young children with peers to the next age group.
- Arrange regular viewing of prosocial media and video games.
- Invite moral mentors to visit the class.
- Work closely with families for prosocial programming.
- Establish a family-resource lending library.
- Establish a bias-free curriculum.
- Require responsibility: encourage children to care for younger children and classmates who need extra help.
- Become familiar with structured curriculum packages that promote prosocial development.
- Implement a comprehensive, school-based, prosocial program that emphasizes ethical teaching.
- Train older children as peer mediators.
- Cherish children: create an atmosphere of affirmation through family, classroom, and community rituals.

Gartrell (2006) emphasizes that

> The objective is to teach children to solve problems rather than to punish children for having problems they cannot solve. The outcomes of guidance—the ability to get along with others, solve problems using words, express strong feelings in acceptable ways—are the goals for citizens of a democratic society.

To achieve this objective, Gartrell reminds teachers, first of all, that social skills are complex and may take a lifetime to learn. Second, he stresses the need for the teacher to reduce children's needs for what he terms *mistaken behavior*. Third, he states that teachers themselves must cultivate positive teacher-child and teacher-adult relationships. Whether we recognize it or not, we are role models of behavior for children. How we handle anger, distress, frustration, fear, sadness, and so on does have an effect on the children in our charge. Fourth, it is important to remember that any intervention method chosen should be solution-oriented. Fifth, and you have heard this before: We need to build partnerships with parents. Last, teachers should use teamwork with adults. Gartrell states that it is a myth to think we can handle all situations alone.

The Role of Families

Gartrell (2004) maintains that building partnerships with children's families produces the best results. When conflicts arise, as they inevitably do, nurturing mutual respect, listening actively (more about active listening in Chapter 9), being patient, modeling reflective listening, inviting continued involvement, and collaboration are the critical ways in which conflicts may be resolved. Gartrell suggests that discipline policies should be in any handbook prepared for families and should be part of any family orientation or initial meeting.

The best resolutions to any behavior problems experienced by children are those wherein families and schools have established mutual goals. School-family partnerships work smoothly when communication channels have been established, mutual respect is evident, and families are welcome in the classroom. More than once we have noted a change of behavior, from negative to positive, when the parent was present.

Helping Children Understand and Express Emotions and Feelings. Researchers have attempted to identify the stages in children's understandings of their own emotions, as well as the language and actions children use to express emotions. One major conclusion derived from these studies is that conversations about feelings provide an important context for learning about emotions and how to manage them (Kuebli, 1994). In everyday interactions, teachers have the opportunity to help children gain insight into emotions—their own and those of others—and develop socially acceptable expressions.

Kuebli suggests:

- evaluating the classroom climate, for staff acceptance of children's expression of feelings and for the appropriate adult responses.
- considering classroom features and settings where emotions and children's reflections on feelings can be experienced. Well-stocked play centers, and adults who prompt their vicarious exploration, can be part of the dramatic-play area.
- providing art materials conducive to emotional responses, where adults promote discussion and child reflection concerning emotional happenings.
- using storybooks dealing with emotions, asking children how they would feel in a similar situation, and discussing causes and consequences.
- using audiovisual equipment. Children can recreate emotions they have seen and then dramatize a situation for themselves; choices children have made in responding to their own and others' emotions can be discussed.
- dealing with children's quarrels and disputes in a way that develops their understanding, giving children time to tell their respective sides without interruption. Teachers can reflect back and ask for clarification while also urging each child to examine his personal contribution to the conflict. Talking about how they feel and what could be done differently next time helps children manage feelings, rather than suppressing or denying them.

Staffing almost always determines how much time individual teachers have to spend on children's disputes. Student teachers may play a special preventive and interactional role in social-emotional development, supplementing the cooperating teacher's efforts.

Rules

Wherever you work with children, there will be rules. Some will be unique because schools and centers vary immensely in physical structures and staffing patterns. Some rules are defined by state law, such as the no-spanking rule. Check with the laws of your own state to ascertain what they are. Economics, too, can influence rules for children. In an earlier chapter, you were asked to read the written rule statements in existence at your placement site. By now, you have probably discovered rule revisions and rules unique to your classroom that were not included, so-called *unwritten* rules. Rules are not secret, but for them to be effective, each child needs a clear picture of the teacher's expectations of classroom behavior. Any new rules need to be discussed with the children.

All rules in an early childhood center, kindergarten, or primary classroom are related to four basic categories of actions:

1. Children will not be allowed to hurt themselves.
2. Children will not be allowed to hurt others.
3. Children will not be allowed to destroy the environment.
4. Everyone helps with the cleanup tasks.

Another category enters the picture when group instruction begins, and that is:

5. Children will not be allowed to impact other children's access to instruction.

In other words, children cannot interrupt, hamper, impede, or delay the smoothness or flow of the educational program with disruptive actions.

Student teachers need to examine rules closely (see Figure 6–6). If rules become picky or ultra-specific, it often indicates an overuse of teacher power. One student teacher shared with her student teaching class an incident where a child was admonished for eating his "pusher" first at lunchtime. The student teacher could not understand what a "pusher" was, or second, why the adult was interfering with the child's choice of what he wished to consume first. She learned that "pusher" was the adult's word for a piece of bread. Another student teacher shared another unbelievable mealtime rule. She observed that the children were not allowed to eat just the frosting off their cupcakes. You will need to keep tabs on whether rules are reasonable or too numerous as you student teach.

A student teacher is an authority figure, one who assures rules are followed for the safety and welfare of all concerned. Authority figures expect that there may be occasions of child anger because the teacher's actions can block a child from her desire or goal. It is not realistic to expect children to always be happy with you. Do remember that children will test you, to see if rules established by your cooperating teacher still apply when *you* are in charge.

Outdoor Rules

1. Walk across cement to get to lawn or climbing area.
2. Always walk on cement.
3. Sand stays in sandbox, along with the sand toys.
4. On figure 8 side of yard. *Only for bikes *children are not allowed on that side.
5. Children go through the door of the playhouse only!

● **Figure 6-6**
The rules posted on the door to the yard in this classroom helped the many adults who worked there to know what was expected.

Age of Child

Some loose guidelines will be discussed next concerning guidance techniques for children of different ages. Teachers of infants and toddlers find that techniques requiring the physical removal of objects or the child from a given situation are used more frequently, although words always accompany teacher action. To help preschoolers with rule compliance, teachers often focus on changing environmental settings, their planned, instructional program, or the way they interact or speak. It is common in preschool, kindergarten, and lower elementary school grades to have teacher-child and teacher-group discussions about classroom rules, and the reasons behind them, so classroom difficulties may be solved together. Teachers are still the ultimate authority, but children have a greater feeling and understanding that rules protect everyone. Rules become "our rules" rather than "the teacher's rules."

Ethnic, Racial, and Family Differences

Children taught to be assertive in their own culture may be viewed as aggressive by a child of another culture (Gonzalez-Mena & Shareef, 2005). The outgoing boy, who grasps another playfully around the neck as an invitation to play—a behavior appropriate at home with his brothers—may be perceived as aggressive by some teachers and peers. Gonzalez-Mena and Shareef suggest that differences among racial or ethnic families and teachers can best be worked through by setting aside judgments and challenging ourselves to be open to explore the possibilities our differences offer.

Walker-Dalhouse (2005), in her review of literature on the discipline of children from minority and low-income backgrounds, points out the discrepancy of expectations held and management techniques used by teachers. One well-documented explanation is that teachers perceive the behavior of African-American and Hispanic males as more aggressive than the same behavior among their white peers, and their treatment is more likely to be harsher, resulting in suspensions and explusions. Aggressive behaviors by white children are often handled by conferencing with them and/or isolating them in a time-out area of the classroom. Walker-Dalhouse calls for teachers to be aware of their own prejudices and biases, pointing out how "critical it is for the teacher to establish a caring and supportive relationship with African American [and other racial and ethnic minority] children." Does this not sound like *CARE*ing? She concludes by stating, "we must challenge ourselves to make cultural diversity an integral part of our discussions about classroom management as we strive to become multiculturally competent."

Carlson (2005), in citing the works of previous researchers, notes that these authors indicate that American children may be touched by their teachers to be restrained or corrected, whereas caring and playful teacher touches may be less frequent. Carlson urges teachers to reflect on acceptable forms of touching, consider the context of any given situation, decide what touching is developmentally appropriate, determine individual children's sensitivity and preferences regarding touch, and understand that a child's permission is necessary. Carlson believes that adults do not have the right to touch children at will, but if a child's immediate safety is involved, a teacher must act, with or without consent from the child.

Teachers understand that some children may have been raised by parents or caregivers who have been overly lenient or inconsistent when it came to setting limits. Family rules might have been stated but not enforced. Other children might not have received any guidance but might have been allowed to do whatever they wished. These children frequently may display inappropriate behaviors in preschool centers, elementary schools, and after-school programs.

CLASSROOM MANAGEMENT OR DISCIPLINARY TECHNIQUES

Now let us look at specific techniques you might use to manage some of the problems you may encounter in a typical classroom.

In its narrower sense of classroom or **behavior management**, discipline refers to those things you do to teach or persuade the children to behave in a manner of which you approve. There are many ways to

behavior management—behavioral approach to guidance, holding that the child's behavior is under the control of the environment, which includes space, objects, and people.

behavior modification—the systematic application of principles of reinforcement to modify behavior.

manage behavior, but there are six that have proven to be more effective than others:

1. **behavior modification**, achieved by applying principles of reinforcement to change a child's behavior
2. setting limits and insisting they be kept
3. labeling the behavior instead of the child
4. using the concept of logical consequences
5. teacher anticipation and intervention
6. conflict resolution

Behavior Modification

With behavior modification, it is important to be objective. The term has acquired a negative connotation that is unfounded. Everyone uses behavior modification, whether recognized or not, from turning off the lights when children are to be quiet, to planning and implementing a behavior modification plan. (See the Appendix for an example of a behavior modification plan.)

Setting Limits

Rules must be stated, repeated, and applied consistently (see Figure 6–7). The aggressive, acting-out child must often be reminded of these rules, over and over again. You may have to repeatedly remove the acting-out child from the room, or to a quiet area in the room. You may have to insist firmly and caringly that the child change the negative behavior. A technique that works one day, such as removing the child to a quiet corner, may not work the next. A technique that works on one child may not work on another.

● **Figure 6-7**
These children know that helmets are required if they ride the bikes.

There are several difficulties facing the student teacher regarding behavior management. One of the difficulties is the problem of developing a repertoire of techniques with which you are comfortable. A second difficulty is developing an awareness or sensitivity to children, so that you can almost instinctively know what technique to use on which child. The third difficulty is recognizing, usually through the process of trial and error, what techniques are congruent with your self-image. If you see yourself as a warm and loving person, do not pretend to be a strict disciplinarian. The children will sense your pretense and will not behave.

Perhaps the most critical error made by many student teachers is putting the need to be liked by the children, driven by the fear of rejection, ahead of their need for limits. As a result, the student teacher may fail to set limits or fail to interfere in situations, often allowing things to get out of hand. When the student teacher must finally intervene, he may forget to *CARE*; or fail to be congruent, and not accept the child causing the problem. The student teacher may not be consistent from day-to-day or child-to-child, and may not take the time to develop empathy.

The children, in contrast, know perfectly well the student teacher's need to be liked, but they do not know whether the student teacher can be trusted. Trust is acquired only when the children discover that the student teacher *CARE*s. It is more important that the children respect, rather than love, the student teacher. In fact, no child can begin to love without having respect first.

It is easier to explain your limits at the beginning of your student teaching experience than to make any assumptions that the children know them. They know what limits your cooperating teacher has established, but they do not know that you expect the same. To reassure themselves that the limits are the same, they test them. This is when you must insist that your rules are the same as the cooperating teacher's. You will have to repeat them often. Most children will learn rapidly that your expectations are the same. Others will have to be reminded constantly before they accept the rules.

Labeling the Behavior

What is meant by the phrase "labeling the behavior, not the child?" Essentially, we are referring to what Gordon (1974) calls *I messages,* in contrast to *you messages*. In an *I* message, you recognize that it is *your* problem rather than the child's. For example, if one of your three-year-olds accidentally spills the paint, you are angry—not because the child spilled the paint, but because you do not want to clean up the mess. Unfortunately, you may lash out at the child and say something like, "For goodness sake! Don't you ever look at what you're doing?" or "Why are you so clumsy?" The result is that the child feels that spilling the paint is his fault when it is possible that you could have foreseen and prevented it. The paint may have been placed too close to the child's elbow. The spilled paint is your problem, not the child's. How much better to say something like, "I really hate to clean up spilled paint!" This is what is truly annoying you, not the child. Even children can understand a reluctance to clean up a spill. And we can see how much better it is to label the behavior, not the child.

There are times, of course, when you will honestly feel you do not like a child. Then, it is especially important to let the child know that it is the behavior you do not like, rather than the child. Continue to look for other times when you can give an honest compliment. Do not try to use positive reinforcement unless the child's behavior warrants it. All children know whether they deserve a compliment; do not try to fool them.

Sending *I* messages is a technique that even young children can learn. As the teacher, you can ask children to say, "I don't like it when you do that!" to other children instead of shouting, "I don't like you!" By labeling the action that is disliked, the child who is being corrected learns what is acceptable behavior, without being made to feel bad. The children who are doing the correcting also learn what is acceptable. Eventually, they also learn how to differentiate between who a child is and how the child behaves. It is a lesson even adults need to practice.

Logical Consequences

logical consequences—Rudolf Dreikurs's technique of specific outcomes that follow certain behaviors and are mutually agreed upon by teacher and children/students.

Developed by psychiatrist Rudolf Dreikurs, the concept of **logical consequences** is based on his long association with family and child counseling. Eventually relating his theories of family-child discipline to the classroom, his landmark books, *Psychology in the Classroom* (1968), *Discipline without Tears* (co-authored with P. Cassel, 1972), and *Maintaining Sanity in the Classroom* (co-authored with B. Grunewald & F. Pepper, 1982) introduced teachers and administrators to his concepts of natural and logical consequences.

For example, a natural consequence of not coming to dinner when called might be the possibility of eating a cold meal. In the classroom setting, however, natural consequences are not easily derived, so logical consequences are generally used instead. With older preschoolers and primary school children this can be done effectively in the group. For example, if children forget to replace puzzles on the rack after playing with them and pieces are lost, they may decide that the logical consequence should be that no puzzles should be used for a week.

Dreikurs' key ideas relate to his beliefs that all students want recognition, and if unable to attain it in ways teachers would consider socially acceptable, children will resort to four possible *mistaken goals*: *attention getting*, *power seeking*, *revenge seeking*, and *displaying inadequacy*. To change the behavior, teachers need first to identify the student's mistaken goal. This is accomplished by recognizing the student's reaction to being corrected.

time-out—technique in which the child is removed from the reinforcement and stimulation of the classroom.

If the student is seeking attention, she may stop the behavior for a short time, but then repeat it until she receives the desired attention. If seeking power, she may refuse to stop or may even escalate the behavior. In this case, a teacher may want to ignore the behavior as much as possible, to avoid provoking a power struggle with the student. Or the teacher may want to provide the student with clear-cut choices: "You may choose to go to the **time-out** area until you feel able to rejoin the group, or you may go to the math center and work on the tangrams." A student wanting revenge may become hostile or even violent; a teacher may have no recourse but to isolate the student or send her to the office. A student displaying inadequacy may refuse to cooperate, participate, or interact unless working one-to-one with the teacher.

To change student behavior, Dreikurs has several suggestions, some which reinforce what has already been said.

> Provide clear-cut directions of your expectations of the students . . . [and] develop classroom rules cooperatively with students, especially those [rules] related to the logical consequences for inappropriate behaviors.

Logical consequences should relate as closely as possible to the misbehavior, so the students can see the connection between them (Charles & Senter, 2004).

Demond, a second grade student, just sits in class when it is time for math. Given a set of problems to finish after a demonstration at the board, he lowers his head, refusing to look at you when you suggest that he should begin working. Fifteen minutes later, he still has not begun to respond. What does Demond's mistaken goal appear to be? If you identify it as inadequacy, you might say, "Demond, I know you can do this lesson. Take a look at the first problem. What does it ask you to do?"

One way to avoid the problem altogether might be to ask your cooperating teacher if you might pair the students for learning tasks, or group them in blocks of four where the primary rule is *three-before-me*, a technique that means students are responsible for teaching each other, before they raise their hands for help from you.

As Eaton (1997) points out, "[l]ogical consequences are more complicated [than natural ones], yet they are still effective." She cites the need for the teacher to give the child the choice of following a rule ("We put on our coats before we go to play outside") or accepting its logical consequence ("If you don't put on your coat, you'll have to remain inside. You decide what you want to do"). In another example, where a child continually interrupts during story time, the logical consequence of not listening might be to give the child the choice of going to a time-out area, or to a table where he can become involved in some quiet behavior, such as drawing a picture. Again, the child is given choices of what he may do. Eaton stresses that the reason for suggesting to the child that he could go to a time-out area is not to punish the child, but rather to provide the child with an opportunity to change his behavior. She continues, "A logical consequence makes clear the connection between the child's behavior and the resulting disciplinary action." It is too late if not attended to immediately.

Eaton also states that adult follow-through is another essential step in what she calls *positive discipline*. She cautions teachers to remember that guiding a child's behavior "is a process, a developing skill." Critical to the child's learning are three behaviors a teacher needs to model in following through:

1. The teacher should get down to the child's level when speaking to the child.

2. The teacher should always use the child's name, to attract and hold her attention.

3. The teacher should remain focused on the child when speaking to him and must encourage him to learn that consequences will result from his choices.

Eaton (1997) concludes by reminding us how important it is "for children to develop clear values that enable them to grow up being fair and considerate of others." To this end, a part of what children need to learn is to understand their own feelings, and to express these in socially acceptable ways. Another part of the process is learning how to make choices and learning to understand the natural and logical consequences of those choices, because these consequences will follow throughout adult life.

Marion (2002) stresses four points for the use of logical consequences to be successful:

1. the adult has delivered an *I* message
2. the consequence is logically related to the unsafe or inappropriate behavior
3. the consequence is one the adult can readily accept and that the child would likely view as fair
4. the consequence is well timed

Marion illustrates each point with concrete examples that are easy to follow and understand. For example, if a child has repeatedly left toys and a bicycle in the driveway, and the parent has had to move them to park or to bring the car into the garage, the parent first would state an *I* message, followed by the logical consequence should the behavior repeat itself. "I can't park the car with all the toys lying around. So I'll put them in the shed if you decide not to pick them up tomorrow." In this situation, the parent has stated her point of view and a logical consequence; the child would probably view the consequence as fair, certainly more fair than if the parent had said, "If you can't pick up your toys from the driveway, I may run over them another time."

Gartrell (2006) suggests three levels of mistaken behavior, instead of Dreikurs's four. Gartrell urges teachers to drop ideas about *misbehavior*, which connotes willful wrongdoing, and look at inappropriate child behavior as *mistaken*. In the process of learning such complex life skills as cooperation, conflict resolution, and acceptable expression of strong feelings, children, like all of us, make mistakes. Taking this view helps teachers see their role as mediators, problem solvers, and guides.

In Gartrell's three levels of mistaken behavior (see Figure 6–8), level-three behavior, or *survival behavior*, is difficult for the teacher to accept because of its nonsocial and, at times, antisocial aspects. Strong needs result from psychological and/or physical pain beyond the child's ability to cope, so survival behavior should be interpreted as a cry for help. At level three would be the one or two or three children who misbehave because they have a need to exert power or to express hostility; these children typically would be misbehaving with the cooperating teacher or with you as their student teacher.

Suggested level-three techniques include:

● non-punitive intervention
● building a positive child-teacher relationship
● gathering more information by observing
● seeking additional information through conversations with the child, families, and caregivers
● creating a coordinated individual guidance plan with other adults through consultation
● implementing, reviewing, and modifying guidance plans as necessary

Gartrell (2006) believes that level two, *socially influenced mistaken behavior*, is based on pleasing peers, adults, or others. Children exhibiting this behavior seek high levels of teacher or peer approval; they seem to lack self-esteem and the strength to use their own judgment. The teacher's task is to nudge the child toward autonomy and observe whether one child or a group is involved in the mistaken behavior. As previously mentioned, a common problem for many student teachers is such a strong desire to be

Motivational source	Relational pattern	Level of mistaken behavior
Desire to explore the environment and engage in relationships	Encountering	One: Experimentation
Desire to please and identify with significant others	Adjustment	Two: Socially influenced
Inability to cope with problems resulting from health conditions or the school or home environment	Survival	Three: Strong needs

Figure 6-8
Common sources of motivation, relational patterns, and levels of mistaken behavior (Gartrell, 2003).

liked by the children that classroom rules are assumed or relaxed. The result is that children misbehave, because they have not yet learned to respect the student teacher, and the student teacher fails to understand that *respect* must precede liking. At level two, then, the behavior becomes intentional.

At the elementary school level, Gartrell (1995) suggests that class meetings are a useful technique in handling level-two behaviors. The children are asked for their suggestions about how any given problem might be resolved. The teacher then monitors progress and, if needed, calls additional meetings. Teacher follow-up is necessary to acknowledge progress and new appropriate behavior and to provide reminders concerning agreed-upon guidelines.

At level one, Gartrell (1995) suggests that young children may misbehave simply to experiment. The children who unintentionally test the limits of classroom rules when the student teacher takes over from the cooperating teacher are displaying level-one mistaken behaviors; they are experimenting to see whether the student teacher has the same rules as the cooperating teacher. Disagreements over toys also fall into this category. Gartrell (1995) states:

> The teacher responds in different ways to different situations. Sometimes he may step back and allow a child to learn from experience; other times he will reiterate a guideline and, in a friendly tone, teach a more appropriate alternative behavior.

Depending on the situation, Gartrell (2006) offers the following suggestions to teachers:

- Increased levels of teacher firmness are necessary with level-two and three mistaken behaviors, with the element of friendliness retained.
- Serious mistaken behaviors occur when life circumstances make children victims.
- Aggression is a nonverbal request for help.
- In guidance situations, the victim (wronged child) gets attention first and the teacher's assistance in calming down.

- Empathy-building is done by pointing out the victim's hurt.
- Stating that the teacher won't let anyone be hurt at school is necessary.
- Child-teacher discussions about how the problem could be avoided in the future take place.
- Asking how the aggressor could help the hurt child feel better is an appropriate technique.
- Assisting the aggressor to choose a positive activity is another teacher endeavor.

See Figure 6–9 for additional information showing how similar behaviors could be classified at different levels.

It is important to remember that the goal of discipline is to help children learn to assume greater responsibility for their own behavior. This is best accomplished by:

- treating them with respect
- distinguishing between what students do and who they are
- setting limits from the very beginning and consistently applying them
- keeping demands simple
- responding to any problems quickly
- letting students know that mistakes, once corrected, are forgotten
- *CARE*ing

Incident of mistaken behavior	Motivational source	Level of mistaken behavior
Child uses expletive	Wants to see the teacher's reaction	One
	Wants to emulate important others	Two
	Expresses deeply felt hostility	Three
Child pushes another off the trike	Wants trike; has not learned to ask in words	One
	Follows aggrandizement practices modeled by other children	Two
	Feels the need to act out against the world by asserting power	Three
Child refuses to join in group activity	Does not understand teacher's expectations	One
	Has "gotten away" with not joining in	Two
	Is not feeling well or feels strong anxiety about participating	Three

Figure 6-9

Classifying similar mistaken behaviors by level (Gartrell, 2003).

It is also important to remember that "[w]hen there is serious mistaken behavior, the teacher meets with parents and other adults to develop and use a coordinated plan. Through coordinated assistance, children can be helped to overcome serious problems and build self-esteem and social skills" (Gartrell, 1997).

Anticipating Behavior, or "With-It-Ness"

The technique that takes time and experience to learn is anticipating aggressive behavior to intervene before the situation erupts (see Figure 6–10). By studying patterns in the child's behavior, you can learn to anticipate certain situations. Many children are quite predictable. Some children can be in a social atmosphere for only a short time before being overwhelmed by the amount of stimuli (sights, sounds, and actions) and may react in a negative way. If you conclude, from observing a child, that the child can play with only one other child before becoming aggressive, you can take care to allow that child to play with only one child at a time. If you know that another child really needs time alone before lunch, you can arrange it. Likewise, if you know a third child becomes tired and cross just before it is time to go home, you can provide some extra rest time for that child.

Learning to anticipate behavior is not easy and requires much practice. Keep trying; it is worth the effort and the children will be happier.

 Figure 6-10
Learning to take turns is not easy. This child does not like to wait.

Conflict Resolution

As Wheeler (1994) points out, past pedagogy has viewed child-child conflict and confrontation as undesirable, and has urged teachers to intervene or use preventive measures. Newer theory, supported by current research, suggests growth in social skill is acquired when peer conflict-resolution strategies enable children to solve problems without adult help. Now used in many public and private elementary schools, conflict resolution techniques are taught by school counselors to older students, typically in grades five and six. They then monitor play yards when the primary grade students have recess. Having older students monitor the behavior of younger students has proved beneficial to both.

Conflict resolution involves teaching children positive alternative and socially acceptable ways to solve problems. It includes physical and verbal tactics that can be both aggressive and non-aggressive (Wheeler, 1994). Verbal interactions to resolve a conflict may be child statements opposing the other child's actions or verbalization, such as saying, "No! Don't," "I had it first," "My turn," or "My toy," or similar statements. They can also take the form of verbal negotiation, clever reasons to support one child's position, and more mature and complex reasoning attempts to solve the problem. Children can agree on their own to seek teacher help.

A student teacher will also notice that a teacher still needs to monitor and step in to encourage and support conflict resolution, especially with preschoolers who use physical **aggression** in disagreements. Teacher-generated solutions may be to wait, to give children the opportunity to gain skill in using verbal, conciliatory behavior that can lead to nonviolent, satisfying, cooperative play and peaceful conflict resolution.

conflict resolution— promoting child-child or child-adult problem solving through verbal interactions, negotiation, compromise, and use of acceptable physical tactics. It may include teacher support and assistance.

aggression—behavior deliberately intended to hurt others.

Wheeler (1994) offers these suggestions to teachers:

- Teachers need to be aware of children's intentions. Is this conflict one that the children are truly trying to resolve, or is it verbal play? Teachers should help children make clear their own understanding of the conflict.

- Children's ability to resolve conflicts increases as their verbal competence and ability to take other perspectives grows. If the children involved in a dispute are verbal and empathic, teachers should let them try to work things out themselves.

- Teachers' decisions to intervene should be made after they observe the issues of children's conflicts. Possession issues and name-calling generate less discussion than issues about facts or play decisions.

- Children who explain their actions to each other are likely to create their own solutions. In conflicts characterized by physical strategies and simple verbal oppositions, teachers should help children find more words to use.

- Teachers should note whether the children were playing together before the conflict. Prior interaction and friendship motivate children to resolve disputes on their own.

- Teachers can reduce the frustration of constant conflict by making play spaces accessible and providing ample materials for sharing.

- Children often rely on adults who are frequently happy to supply a fair solution. Teachers should give children time to develop their own resolutions and allow them the choice of negotiating, changing the activity, dropping the issue, or creating new rules.

- Many conflicts do not involve aggression, and children are frequently able to resolve their disputes. Teachers should provide appropriate guidance, yet allow children to manage their own conflicts and resolutions.

Gartrell (2006) also urges early childhood teachers to use conflict resolution as a guidance technique. Many of the suggestions he mentions are covered in the previous discussion of Gartrell's views on logical consequences and need not be repeated here.

Holden (1997) cautions us as that once we understand conflict resolution techniques, we should also realize that:

- Teachers can't do it all. There may be one or two children you really cannot reach. You may have to seek the help of others.

- It takes time for behavior to change; learning takes place only through repetition. In fact, changes you may begin when the child is in preschool may not be realized fully until kindergarten.

- The difficulty to see the other person's point of view is difficult for adults as well as children.

- Violent behavior may have any number of causes, and in a specific incident, we may not know what the student is thinking. However, our ability to *CARE* can alleviate stress and may help establish rapport with the student.

- Conflict is unavoidable. As much as we would like for our classrooms to be happy and positive all the time, it simply is not realistic. Children become angry, frustrated, and unhappy, just as adults do.

- Remember that every conflict is not serious, so don't overreact.

- Adults must model ways of handling conflicts peacefully and compliment children who are doing so as well.

Holden (1997) is a firm believer that young children can learn conflict resolution techniques, that they need adult supervision to learn how, and that they need to practice. As a result of her inability to find materials appropriate for the elementary grades, Holden has written her own program, *Students Against Violence* (Holden, 1997), which is geared for grades one through five.

ADDITIONAL MANAGEMENT AND DISCIPLINE STRATEGIES

Child behavior may always remain puzzling challenge your efforts to help each child learn socially acceptable behaviors. A review of common strategies used by other teachers may be helpful. Naming strategies, describing them, and discussing when they are most appropriate and effective will sharpen your professional guidance skills.

In this chapter, you have studied goals and techniques, the origins of behavior, and ways to promote self-control in children. One goal in guiding child behavior is the idea that the child will learn to act appropriately in similar situations in the future. This can be a slow process with some behaviors, speedy with others. There is a change from external "handling" of the child, to the child monitoring her own progress, and then feeling and acting on what it is the right thing to do.

Environmental Factors

Where misbehavior is concerned, it is easy to conclude that it is the child who needs changing. A number of classroom environmental factors can promote inappropriate child behaviors in group situations. A limited variety of dull activities, an above-comprehension program, meager or frustrating equipment, and a defense-producing teacher elicit behavior reactions to unmet needs. Close examination of the classroom environment may lead to changing causative factors rather than changing child behavior. School programs, room environments, and teaching methods can fail the children, rather than the children failing the program.

As a student teacher, you should carefully examine the relationship between the classroom environment, the daily program, your teaching style, and children's reactions. Fortunately, your training program has developed your teaching skill as well as an understanding of quality environments. An analysis of your placement may lead you to discover that child appeal is lacking. Rearranging or creating new areas may add interest. Remember, however, that any changes need the cooperating teacher's approval.

Rapport

Rapport is an important element of guidance. Trying to develop rapport, trust, or a feeling relationship with each child can be tricky. Mitchell, the active, vigorous explorer, may be hard to keep up with, or even to talk with. He may prefer the company of his peers; so how can one establish rapport? When it does happen, you will be aware of the "you're okay, I'm okay" feeling, and experience pleasure when he says, "I enjoy being with you" with his eyes. Children respond to straightforward, genuine teachers in a positive way.

How important is child-teacher rapport during the prekindergarten years? Data collected from Howes (2000) suggest that children with close child-teacher relationships are also socially competent with their peers. Children perceived as difficult four-year-olds tended to build child-teacher relationships that were high in conflict, through the second grade in elementary school. They also tended to be less able to establish social closeness. Academic content mastery, through the use of a close child-teacher relationship, was also more difficult for these children.

Same Behavior, Different Strategy

Child individuality can still result in unexpected reactions. The boy who finally swings at another child after letting others grab his toys and the child who slugs at every opportunity are performing the same act. You will decide to treat each incident differently. The ages of children, their stages of growth, and the particulars of the situations will have to be considered. You have already learned that what works with one child will not necessarily work with another. In time you will develop a variety of strategies, focus often on the child's intent, and hypothesize underlying causes.

You will be able to live with child rejection, come to expect it, and realize it is short-lived. Act you will; and the child will react. Sometimes, you will choose to ignore behavior and hope it goes away. You will find ignoring is appropriate under certain conditions.

Using Proximity

Many times, the teacher's physical presence will change a child's behavior. When the teacher becomes interested in a child's activity and asks questions concerning what the child is trying to accomplish, it may head off undesirable child behavior.

Other Common Strategies

Stating rules, in a positive way, serves two purposes. It is a helpful reminder and states what is appropriate and expected. "Feet walk inside, run outside" is a common, positive rule statement. Statements such as "Remember, after snack you place your cup on the tray and any garbage in the waste basket" and "books are stored in your desk before we go to lunch" clearly indicate the students' tasks.

Cause-and-effect and *factual statements* are common ways to promote behavior change. "If you pick off all the leaves, the plant will die." "Sand thrown in the eyes hurts." "Here's the waiting list; you'll have a turn soon, Mark." Each of these statements gives information and helps children decide the appropriateness, or realize the consequences, of their current actions.

Using **modeling** to change behavior entails pointing out a child or teacher example of desired behavior: "The paint stays on the paper. That's the way, Kolima." "See how slowly I'm pouring the milk so it doesn't spill?" "Nicholas is ready, his eyes are open, and he is listening." These are all modeling statements (see Figure 6–11).

Always using the same child as a model can create a "teacher's pet." Most teachers try to use every child as a model. When children hear a modeling statement, they may chime in "me, too," which opens the opportunity for recognition and reinforcement of another positive model. "Yes, Carrie Ann, you are showing me you know how to put the blocks in their place on the shelf."

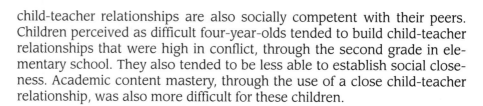

modeling—in social learning theory, the process of imitating a model.

Figure 6-11
When lunching with children, teachers model appropriate behavior.

Redirection is a behavioral strategy that works by redirecting a child to another activity, object, or area. Some examples of redirecting statements follow:

"Here's a big, blue truck for you to ride, Sherilyn."

"While you're waiting for your turn, Avraham, you can choose the puzzle with the airplane landing at the airport, or the puzzle with the tow truck."

"I know you would have liked to have read one of the dinosaur books, Bokko, during SSR [*sustained silent reading period*], but they're all taken. Since you like trains and airplanes, why don't you read one of these two books instead?"

"Mieko, while you're waiting for Tina and Maria to finish the *Spill 'n Spell* game, why don't you and Jennifer look at some of the other games we have on the shelf and choose another one?"

Statements like "Let's take giant steps to the door," "Can you stretch and make giant steps like this?" and "We're tiptoeing into snack today; we won't hear anyone's footsteps" may capture the imagination and help overcome resistance. The key to redirection is to make the substitute activity or object desirable. A possible pitfall is that every time the child cannot have her way, she may get the idea that something better will be offered. Offering a pleasurable alternative each time a difficulty arises may teach the child that being difficult and uncooperative leads to teacher attention and the provision of a desirable activity or object.

Younger preschoolers (two- and three-year-olds) intent on possessing toys and objects usually accept substitutions, and their classrooms are equipped with duplicate toys to accommodate their *I-want-what-he-has* tendencies.

In kindergarten and the primary grades, however, the use of redirection can indicate to children that they have an opportunity to make a second or third choice when blocked on their first.

Giving a choice of things you would like the child to do appeals to the child's sense of independence. Some examples are:

"Are you going to put your used napkin in the trash or on the tray?"

"Can you walk to the gate yourself or are we going to hold hands and walk together?"

"You can choose to rest quietly next to your friend or on a cot somewhere else in the room."

"Remember, Matti, we agreed that class would line up promptly when the bell rang. You have a choice now either to line up quickly or to be the last student to leave for recess."

Setting up direct communication between two arguing children works as shown in the following:

"Use your words, Xitlali: 'Please pass the crackers.'"

"Look at his face; he's very unhappy. It hurts to be hit with a flying hoop. Listen, he wants to tell you."

Taking a child by the hand and helping confront another, to express the child's wishes or feelings, lets the child know you will defend his rights. It also lets the child know that you care that rules are observed by all.

Marshall (1995) cautions teachers to remove "I like the way . . ." statements in teacher attempts to praise or reinforce child behavior. She points out that using I *like* focuses the child on whether the teacher likes them rather than the learning task. As examples of more appropriately worded teacher statements, Marshall suggests the following:

"Let's see who is ready to listen to the story."

"Latasha is ready to learn about frogs."

"Remember to find a place where you can be comfortable, where no one will disturb you."

"You've made a four. What do you think of it? Compare it with the four on the wall."

"Let's sing our Good-Morning song while Erlinda and Duane finish putting their things away so we can start sharing."

Kohn (2001) explains the unfortunate outcome that may occur when teachers overuse praise.

In short, "Good job" doesn't reassure children; ultimately, it makes them feel less secure. It may even create a vicious circle such that the more we slather on the praise, the more kids seem to need it, so we praise them some more. Sadly, some of these kids will grow into adults who continue to need someone else to pat them on the head and tell them that what they did was okay . . .

and

The most notable feature of a positive judgment isn't that it's positive, but that it's a judgment.

It is sometimes difficult to change "good job" to something more specific because it may have been used extensively in one's own upbringing. Saying "Look at how that table shines! You scrubbed every spot. Now it is clean and ready for the next person, Willy!" gives the child specific knowledge concerning his well-done job.

Self-fulfilling statements, such as "You can share, Molly. Megan is waiting for a turn" and "In two minutes, it will be Morris' turn," imply something will happen. Hopefully, you will be nearby with positive reinforcement, and statements that help the child decide the right behavior and feel good about it. Positive reinforcement of newly evolving behavior is an important part of guidance. It strengthens the chances that a child will repeat the behavior. Most adults will admit that, as children, they knew when they were doing wrong, but the right and good went unnoticed. The positive reinforcement step in the behavior-change process cannot be ignored if new behavior is to last. Positive attention can be a look of appreciation, words, a touch, or a smile. Often, a message such as "You did it!" or "I know it wasn't easy" is sent.

Calming-down periods for an out-of-control child may be necessary before communication is possible. Rocking and holding help after a violent outburst or tantrum. When the child is not angry anymore, you will want to stay close until the child is able to become totally involved in play or a task.

Ignoring is a usable technique with new behaviors that are annoying or irritating but of minor consequence. Catching the adult's attention or testing the adult's reaction may motivate the behavior. One can ignore a child who sticks out his tongue or says, "You're ugly." Treating the action or comment matter-of-factly is ignoring. Answering "I look ugly first thing in the morning" usually ends the conversation. You are attempting to withhold any reaction that might reinforce the behavior. If there is definite emotion in the child's comment, you will want to talk about it rather than ignore it. Children can be taught the ignoring technique as well when they find someone annoying them.

When all else fails, the use of *negative consequences* may be appropriate. Habit behavior can be most stubborn and may have been reinforced over a long period. Taking away a privilege or physically removing a child from the group is professionally recognized as a last-resort strategy.

Isolation involves the common practice of benching an aggressive elementary-age student, sending her to a desk segregated from the rest of the class, at the extreme front or back of the classroom, or short periods of supervised chair-sitting for a preschooler. Many educators use this technique only when a child is wildly out of control or is an imminent threat to others.

Teachers refer to this practice as *time-out.* Zabel (1986) notes that if applied immediately and consistently, time-out has been determined to be useful in the reduction of both verbal and physical aggressive behavior. Critics of the practice acknowledge it can reduce undesirable behavior but it fails to teach desirable behavior (Betz, 1994). Because of its effectiveness, the technique may be overused when relatively trivial child behaviors occur. Some children, in a study by Readdick and Chapman (2000), who perceived themselves to be in time-out often, felt isolated, sad, scared, and thought they were disliked by their peers. Fewer than half of the preschoolers questioned could accurately recall what they had done before time-out occurred (Readdick & Chapman, 2000).

Teachers need to be careful not to shame or humiliate the child in the process. Statements such as "You need to sit for a few minutes until you're ready to . . ." allow the child an open invitation to rejoin the group and live up to rules and expectations. The isolation area needs to be supervised, safe, and unrewarding. Teachers quickly reinforce the returning child's positive, socially acceptable new actions.

ignoring—a principle of behavior management that involves removing all reinforcement for a given behavior to eliminate that behavior.

Removal of privilege can restrict the child's use of a piece of play equipment or a play area for a short period. After the off-limits time, the child is encouraged to try again, with a brief, positive rule statement to remind the child of limits.

Using statements that accept the child's reasons for actions show the child you recognize his need or desire. "You want to play with the puzzle." This is followed by "*but* Brianna is using the horse puzzle now." The comment helps the child realize others' rights. Saying "Soon it will be your turn" or "I'll tell you when it's your turn" can encourage children to wait and delay gratification. A teacher might add "You can wait while Brianna finishes or choose another puzzle to work while you're waiting." This indicates your confidence in the child's ability to wait. You will constantly try to increase each child's independence and growing decision-making ability, so you must stay close enough to the situation to assure that what you stated will happen.

Your goal is promoting each child's self-controlled behavior, which satisfies his unique personal needs and yet allows membership and inclusion into today's society. Encourage the development of the child's self-concept as a valued, worthwhile, capable, and responsible person.

Out-of-Control Children

Student teachers often say that the worst part of any day happens when a child loses control and has a tantrum. Bakley (2000) suggests the following techniques:

- *Resist telling an upset child to calm down.* Because the lack of control occurs below the level of consciousness, the child cannot willingly calm himself down.

- *Redirect an escalating child to a sensory activity*, such as play dough, water play, or bins of sensory materials. More vigorous physical activities, such as digging, jumping, and running, can also help. Some children will naturally gravitate to the calming motion of a swing or rocking chair. Others may want to retreat to a safe, quiet place, away from busy activities.

- *Offer a firm hug or a lap to curl up in.* When a child is agitated, the external control provided by your enveloping physical presence can help restore inner control. Some experts believe a firm hug reaches deeply into the subcortical level of the brain, overriding reactions of rage and aggression.

- *Wait for the child to calm down before talking about what happened.* When a child is agitated, your physical approach may trigger a fight-or-flight reaction, with the child striking out or running away. Wait for the child to regain composure. The calmer the child is, the more likely the child will learn from the experience.

- *Maintain a calm, cool demeanor when discussing misbehaviors.* Avoid no-win confrontations. Your composure sets the tone for the child's success in learning from his mistakes. Remember, although this is a child who will surely test your patience, the child desperately needs your help to learn acceptable behaviors.

- *Allow children to avert their gaze when you talk about their behavior.* Because so much effort is required to make and sustain eye contact, there is little energy left for listening. Children with sensory integration problems are likely to listen better if allowed to avert their gaze.

- *Use simple, direct language.* Give brief, specific directions. Say "Put your hands in your lap" instead of "Keep your hands to yourself." Help the child remember what you've said by asking him to repeat it.
- *Keep the family informed and involved.* If a collaborative relationship with the family has been established, encourage them to implement similar discipline techniques at home.

Violent Play

Television, current events, young children's observations of older children, and community occurrences often influence the initiation of violent, aggressive play actions. The student teacher is faced with an immediate decision, concerning children's safety and the prudence of allowing—which may be seen as approving—this type of play. Most teachers feel deeply about peaceful solutions to individual and world problems. New curriculums have been purposely designed by some early childhood professionals to promote peace and acquaint young children with the concept of the brotherhood of humanity.

Experienced teachers know that even if guns and other play weapons are not allowed at school, some children will still fashion play guns from blocks or other objects and engage in mock battles or confrontations.

Schools and centers make individual decisions concerning guns, superhero, and war play. It is best for student teachers to question their cooperating teacher if such play develops. Of course, an unsafe situation is stopped immediately and discussed later.

In looking at violence in the elementary school, Johnson, Johnson, Stevahn, and Hodne (1997) suggest that we can make our school safe by using the *three Cs*: *cooperation, conflict resolution,* and *community values*. To encourage cooperation, teachers should have students work in cooperative learning groups and plan cooperative activities. In addition, they stress the need for schools to work cooperatively with families to establish mutual goals, participation in a division of labor, and shared resources.

Conflict resolution empowers students to learn how to resolve their own conflicts, reestablishes cooperation when the conflict appears within the group, and, according to Johnson and his colleagues, "provides a source of creativity, excitement, motivation, energy, insight, synergy, synthesis, fun, and renewed support and caring for both teachers and students."

By using the terms *community* or *civic values*, Johnson and his co-authors stress that "A community cannot exist if its members have a variety of different value systems, believe in only their own self-interests, or have no values at all." The writers firmly believe that values such as caring, respect, responsibility, and other core values such as integrity, compassion, commitment, and appreciation of diversity must pervade the classroom, and that "civic values are the glue that hold the school together."

Froschl, Sprung, and Hinitz (2005) presented a review of the research on violence in early education environments. They insist that it is essential to establish a classroom environment based upon cooperation, and one that supports children with diverse abilities, to avoid possible violent reactions from children making comparisons about or competing with one another, and drawing inaccurate conclusions.

Superhero Play

In conducting research on the incidence of *superhero*, or violent, play in preschoolers, Boyd (1997) discovered that "superhero play accounted for less than one percent of the 300 minutes of play observed." She suggests that teachers look at the developmental function of such play before banning it. She further believes that superhero play may offer children an opportunity to have power, which may help them to overcome feelings of powerlessness in an adult-dominated world. In addition, it involves children in good-guy versus bad-guy scenarios. Boyd concludes by stating that "educators should consider the best means for making positive use of this play . . . and decide . . . on the basis of information about their students and their needs, whether this sort of play is acceptable."

Child Strategies

Child strategies to remain in control are natural and normal. Rules can be limiting. Crying, whining, pleading, screaming, and arguing are common. Anger, outrage, and aggression may occur. Suddenly going deaf, not meeting adults' eyes, running away, holding hands over ears or eyes, becoming stiff, or falling to the ground may help the child get what is wanted. The child may also use silence, tantrums, changing the subject, bargaining, name-calling, threats to tell someone, or threats to remove affection; talking you to death and ignoring rules are not uncommon strategies.

Much of the time, young children function well in groups, showing consideration for others. Empathic and cooperative interaction between preschoolers in classrooms leads adults to admire both their straightforward relationships and their growing, sensitive concern for others.

Managing Serious Behavior Problems

Many of the techniques and strategies already described may help you with children who display serious behavior problems. What do we mean by the phrase *serious behavior problems*? Depending on the age of the child, serious problems range from biting and hitting (by a two-year-old), to superhero play that is physically aggressive, or destroying another child's work, and fighting on the play yard (by four- to eight-year-olds). And please do not overlook the overly quiet child, who tries to disappear into the background of the classroom or play yard. She may need as much help as the overly aggressive child.

What should you try to do? First of all, you want to defer to your cooperating teacher; she may have already developed plans to help the child acquire more socially appropriate behaviors. Additionally, the cooperating teacher may ask you to speak to the school psychologist, who may be seeing the child once or twice a week; or talk to the PIP (*Primary Intervention Program*) consultant working with the child; or even sit in on a parent conference with the school's student-study team. All of these resources may give you some more ideas of how to work more effectively with the child in question.

Consider how you might handle the following situation:

> Sandor, a student teacher in a third grade classroom, was faced with a male child, Rory, who was getting into fights during the first recess of every day. Upon his return to the classroom, the principal would call over the intercom, "Rory, please come to the office at once!" The result of this behavior was that Rory inevitably missed at least half of the mathematics lessons that were taking place after the first recess. Sandor

discussed the problem with Ms. Olivados, his cooperating teacher. She reassured him that Rory's behavior was not new and suggested that Sandor might observe Rory during the next morning's recess and try to determine why Rory got into fights with the other children.

Following Ms. Olivados' suggestion, Sandor accompanied the class to the first recess the next day. Rory went with two or three other boys from his class to a corner of the play yard; Sandor discretely followed. Suddenly, Rory yelled, "You can't call my mother that!" and hit Derek, the boy standing next to him.

Sandor intervened by placing himself between the two and asked, "What did you say, Derek?" The boy answered, "Oh, we were just playing the dozens; Rory knows that! And besides his mother is a _____!"

"How do you know that?" Sandor asked Derek. "Oh, everybody knows," replied Derek, who attempted to kick Rory from under Sandor's arm. "What do you think you might do instead of calling each other names or calling your mothers names?" Sandor asked both boys.

Neither boy replied, and the bell announcing the end of recess sounded before Sandor was able to take the discussion any further. Both Derek and Rory continued to yell at each other as they lined up to go back to the classroom.

Sandor again placed himself between the two boys in the line to prevent any further hitting or kicking. Upon entering the classroom, Ms. Olivados noticed the angry faces of Rory and Derek, and Sandor's distraught one. Before she could ask what had happened, the intercom clicked on and the principal said, "I want Rory and Derek in my office immediately!"

What might Ms. Olivados and Sandor try the next day, to prevent further altercations between Rory and Derek? How might we look at Rory's misbehavior? What might be his mistaken goal, according to Dreikurs? Does Rory seem to be vying for attention? For power? For revenge? It seems clear that he's not acting from a sense of inadequacy. Looking at Gartrell's levels of mistaken behavior, at what level of mistaken behavior does Rory's behavior appear to be?

Should you conclude that Rory's mistaken goal is revenge or power in his relationship with Derek, what intervention might be the best one to try? Should Sandor keep the boys separated during recess? Should Rory and Derek be involved in a role-reversal exercise? Should Mrs. Olivados involve the principal? The school's PIP professionals? What might be most appropriate?

Introducing Harmony Models in Literary Activities

Many picture books offer peaceful solutions to human conflict. Kreidler (1994) suggests using the following techniques:

- Read the book up to the point of conflict.
- Ask children how they think the book's characters are feeling.
- Have children identify the conflict.
- Brainstorm ways characters could solve the conflict. Discuss which one the children think the characters in the story will use.
- Read the rest of the story. Discuss the characters' solution to their conflict. Ask children "Was it a good solution? Why? How do the characters feel now?"

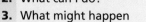

 Figure 6-12

assertive discipline—a
form of behavior
management used primarily
in elementary schools. The
consequences of behavior
are clearly stated,
understood by children, and
consistently applied.

A few picture book titles follow:

Big Al, by Andrew Clements (1997, Aladdin)
No Bad News, by Kenneth Cole (2001, Albert Whitman)
Erandi's Braids, by Antonio Hernandez Madrigal (1999, Puffin)
Hoppy and Joe, by Betty ParaSkevas (1999, Simon & Schuster)
Somewhere Today: A Book of Peace, by Shelley Moore Thomas (1998,
Albert Whitman)
It's Mine, by Leo Lionni (1996, Random House)

Using pictures and problem-solving steps (see Figure 6–12), and acting
out make-believe role-plays, in which children practice conflict resolution,
is suggested by Adams and Wittmer (2001).

GUIDANCE TECHNIQUES USED IN ELEMENTARY SCHOOLS

Assertive Discipline

Many elementary schools use a form of behavior management called
assertive discipline (Canter, 1976; Davidman & Davidman, 1994). While
an inappropriate technique for preschools, assertive discipline has been
widely used in elementary school settings. Assertive discipline has been
shown to work best when an entire school staff is committed to using the
technique. In assertive discipline, teachers must initially set their classroom rules—best done at the beginning of the year, elicited from the children themselves, and posted prominently in the classroom. Teachers must
then consistently apply the rules and learn to use *I* messages indicating
their displeasure or pleasure. "I don't like it when someone interrupts
another student, Aisha." "Most of your classmates are all listening politely
to Mustapha."

Consequences of misbehavior must be clearly understood and consistently applied. At the first incidence, the teacher places the child's initials
on the board in a place reserved and consistently used for assertive discipline markings. At the second incidence of misbehavior, a check mark
goes by the child's name, and a specific and reasonable consequence is
related to it. The consequence may be having to remain in the room during a recess, or having to move to an isolated area of the classroom. After
a second check, the consequence may be a phone call to the student's
family and a request for a conference. After the third check, the child is
generally sent to the office, and the family is called and notified that the
child must serve detention the next day, or that the child must serve an
in-house suspension. (This may involve assigning the child to another
classroom, attended only by other in-school suspension students. The
students are expected to complete assignments their teachers send with
them, and the classroom is monitored by either another teacher or a
teacher assistant.) The child is usually assigned to the in-house suspension class until the family makes an appointment for a conference with
the teacher and principal.

Crucial to the success of assertive discipline is following through with
the predetermined consequences; empty threats cannot be allowed.

Although assertive discipline has been highly successful, it has also
been criticized. Canter, however, maintains that the "assertive teacher is

one who clearly and firmly communicates needs and requirements to students, follows those words with appropriate actions, responds to students in ways that maximize compliance, but in no way violates the best interests of the students" (Charles & Senter, 2004).

Glasser's Model

Another classroom management model commonly used in elementary schools is the Glasser model (1985). Glasser strongly believes that students have unmet needs that lead to their behavior difficulties, and that if teachers can arrange their classes in such a way that these needs are met, there will be fewer control problems. Student needs are identified as (1) the need to belong, (2) the need for power, (3) the need for freedom, and (4) the need for fun.

By breaking the class into small learning teams, the teacher is able to provide students with a sense of belonging, with motivation to work on behalf of the group, with power to have stronger students help weaker ones, with freedom from over-reliance on the teacher for both weaker and stronger ones, and with friends for all students, shy and outspoken. Two precautions: groups should be heterogeneously arranged, and groups should be changed at regular or irregular intervals. Changes might occur as units or themes change, or they might change every six weeks. Teachers should decide for themselves which tactic works best in their respective classrooms.

●SUMMARY

Throughout this chapter, you have been able to formulate an idea of the scope of the classroom management or disciplinary function. Remember that in actuality everything you do—planning activities, arranging the environment, planning the length of activities, planning how much direction you will provide—is part of the management function.

Another part of management is managing behavior. In this chapter, you were given two guidelines to use in managing behavior: the *four Cs* (consistency, consideration, confidence, and candor) and *CARE* (be congruent, acceptable, reliable, and empathetic). In addition, six specific techniques were explained: behavior modification, limit setting, *I* messages, logical consequences, anticipating behavior, and conflict resolution. Try them; experiment with others of your own. Discover which disciplinary techniques work best for you and analyze why they work best.

The involvement of the family in establishing disciplinary goals was stressed. Collaboration with families and the teaching team was mentioned.

Helping children satisfy needs in a socially acceptable way and helping them feel good about doing so is a disciplinary goal. Classroom environments can promote self-control, especially when rapport, caring, and trust are present. Examination of behavior, its intent, and circumstances may lead student teachers to different plans of action with different children. There is no "recipe" for handling guidance problems, but a review of common disciplinary strategies was covered in this chapter.

They are as follows:

- positive rule statements,
- cause-and-effect and factual statements,
- modeling,
- redirection,
- giving a choice,
- setting up direct communication,
- self-fulfilling statements,
- positive reinforcement,
- calming-down periods,
- ignoring, and
- negative consequences.

Children's strategies to circumvent rules and limits cover a wide range of possible actions; yet, obedience to rules and sensitivity to others are present most of the time. Check your responses to Figure 6–13, and you will be doing fine.

Students' Aptitudes	Instructional Treatments	Learning Outcomes
What do I know about the general developmental characteristics of the students I am teaching?	In what varieties of ways can I present instruction on a topic?	Do I consider both cognitive and affective learning outcomes for my students?
What cognitive development abilities can I expect them to exhibit?	What types of learning tactics and strategies can I teach?	Do the cognitive outcomes include higher-level thinking skills as well as basic knowledge?
Which learning style does each student seem to prefer?	What is the best way to organize and sequence the presentation of a lesson?	Do I explicitly share these learning outcomes and their purpose with students?
What social/emotional characteristics must I consider?	How can I present instruction at an appropriate ability level for students to achieve success with effort?	Do I connect these outcomes to students in meaningful ways?
What are the social behaviors that each student exhibits?	How can I present instruction that will be interesting and motivate students?	Do I specify how students will be assessed on their mastery of the outcomes?
What are the academic strengths and weaknesses that each student possesses?	What textbooks and other instructional materials best engage students in active learning?	Is my system of grading a valid evaluation of the content students have learned?
What are the special needs of students that I must take into account?	How can I help students better understand the connections between topics?	Do I provide nongraded formative evaluation to students to monitor their progress?
Who has influence on the students? Their peers? Their parents? Their teachers?	How can I help students develop problem-solving skills?	Do I allow multiple opportunities for students to achieve the learning outcomes?
What ethnic and cultural factors influence the way students communicate with others?	How can I instruct students at higher levels of cognition?	
What are the interests of each student?	How can I plan instruction that fosters creativity?	
What level or degree of prior knowledge does each student possess of a subject?	How can I maintain high expectations for all students?	
	How can I help students attribute their success to their abilities and efforts?	

Figure 6-13
Analysis checklist in establishing a well-managed elementary school classroom.

◉HELPFUL WEB SITES

http://www.acei.org
Association for Childhood Education. Check for readings. ACEI publishes the journal, *Childhood Education*, and several newsletters and books.

http://www.naeyc.org
National Association for the Education of Young Children. Search for readings. NAEYC publishes the journal, *Young Children*, and many other brochures, books, and videos.

http://www.fpg.unc.edu
Frank Porter Graham Center at the University of North Carolina. Search for readings.

http:/www.ncedl.org
National Center for Early Development and Learning (NCEDL). Try child care designations.

http://www.nncc.org
National Network for Child Care. Search social and emotional development.

http://www.ascd.org
Association for Supervision and Curriculum Development (ASCD). This source offers readings on social and emotional growth. Click "reading room."

 Additional resources for this chapter can be found by visiting the Online Companion at www.earlychilded.delmar.com.

◉SUGGESTED ACTIVITIES

A. Analyze your placement classroom's rules. Do many rules fall into the four basic areas mentioned in this chapter? Are there any rules that need a new category?

B. Go back to your own childhood. What techniques did you use to avoid punishment when you had broken a family rule? What parental guidance techniques or punishments remain vivid today? What guidance techniques used on others have you observed that created strong emotions in you? If you received but one unforgettable message from your parents concerning your behavior as a child, what was that message? Report the message to the group.

C. Roger, a student in your kindergarten room, is in his usual negative mood. During morning planning time, he refuses to choose what interest center he will go to during the morning, center-choice period. Your reaction is to offer him a choice between the manipulatives center and the storytelling one. Roger tells you to f—— off. Your anger aroused, you are tempted to send him to the office immediately; instead you say quietly, "Roger, we don't use those words at school." He glares at you defiantly, and you realize that the other students are looking expectantly at you to see what you'll do next.

According to Dreikurs, what does Roger's mistaken goal appear to be? Discuss with your peers what responses might be most effective.

D. Discuss the following story with three to four classmates. Report key ideas, observations, and conclusions to the class.

Mrs. Xavier, the college supervisor, visited Miss Yates, a student teacher, at her preschool placement classroom, a private proprietary preschool program. The yard looked spacious and well equipped. Miss Yates was a paid employee doing her student teaching at her place of employment. Mrs. Xavier entered a small hallway with a desk and wall phone, then approached the doorway to the classroom and hesitated. Miss Yates motioned her supervisor to enter.

A free-play period was in progress. Children were busy at small desks or playing in groups. One child stood by the wall, seemingly trying to push himself against it.

Children looked at Miss Yates frequently, as if checking for some signal. Two small girls wanted to lean against Miss Yates and followed her around the room. One patted her arm periodically. The telephone in the hall rang. Miss Yates went to answer it, leaving Mrs. Xavier in the room.

After a minute or so, a boy tried to grab a toy and another boy was running back and forth across a small table. The running boy attempted to push the toy-grabber away. He knocked over both the table and the other child. Miss Yates entered just in time to see the child falling.

"We don't hit," she said sternly. "You know what happens now."

The running child who pushed said, "He did it," and pointed to a third child.

Other children seemed tense and frightened. The accused boy, hugging the wall, turned and faced it. Miss Yates picked up the boy who had pushed the child, who tried to grab his toy, and headed toward the door. One girl put her head down on a desk and covered her eyes.

At this point, Mrs. Xavier said, "It was an accident."

Miss Yates put the child down and said, "Mrs. Xavier said it was an accident."

After watching another half hour, Mrs. Xavier could finally consult with Miss Yates on the play yard, because another teacher had come on duty. Asking her to step to an area where they wouldn't be overheard, the supervisor said, "I can see this school uses spanking. How do you feel about that policy?"

Miss Yates answered, "Oh, it works very well. I don't have but rare acts of hitting now, and I've noticed the children are much more affectionate toward me."

Mrs. Xavier asked, "You've been present in classes where guidance techniques were studied. Was spanking a recommended technique?"

The student teacher replied, "No, but it sure works well!"

"You've seen no child behavior that bothers you?" Mrs. Xavier asked.

"No," Miss Yates answered.

"Have you noticed children accusing other children of things they might have done themselves?" (The supervisor had seen this a number of times during her observation.)

Miss Yates responded, "Well, that always happens. I did it myself when I was a child."

Mrs. Xavier asked, "Did you know spanking was against the law in preschools in this state?"

Miss Yates said, "Yes, but we have a form parents sign approving spanking, and my director and I think spanking works."

"Can I give you permission to break the law and speed at 70 miles per hour?" asked the supervisor.

"No, I don't think that would work," answered Miss Yates.

"Can parents give you permission to break the law?" Mrs. Xavier asked.

"Well they have," retorted Miss Yates.

After a discussion in which Mrs. Xavier asked for another meeting, she left the school. Later in the day, Mrs. Xavier telephoned the licensing agency responsible for licensing Miss Yates's place of employment.

E. Plan a discussion with a small group of four-year-olds. Have a picture of a child who might want to join the children's classroom handy. Start your discussion with "We have a rule in our classroom. The rule is we ask for a turn if we want a toy someone else has chosen to use. Here's a picture of Suzy. She wants to come to school with us. What will Suzy need to know about our classroom?"

Ask students questions like "If Suzy plays in the block center, what should we tell her?" "If Suzy wants to join us at snack time, what should we tell her?" Share the results of your discussion group with classmates.

F. Role-play the following situations with a small group of classmates. After each situation, have the students playing children explain any insights or feelings they discovered when stepping into the child's shoes. Critique the role-playing reaction according to the child's behavior and the guidance techniques used.

1. Tonette says Renata pushed her down. You observed the incident, and Renata just happened to trip Tonette as she ran to pick up the ball.

2. Conner is large and muscular. He delights in terrifying other children by standing

directly in their paths. He rarely physically hits, pushes, or touches the children he is frightening. You see Conner standing in front of the outside water faucet intimidating children who wish to drink.

3. Angela is telling your aide she's ugly and fat. The aide, being new, is distressed.

4. Scott cries every time he is not chosen to be first in line, or when some other child gets a job he wants. You asked Geoff to go to the aquarium to feed the fish and now Scott is crying because Geoff got the job. Geoff turns to Scott and says, "Okay, stop crying. You can do it."

5. Sierra is on a painting binge. It's time to clean up. You've told her it's cleanup time. "No way," says Sierra, as she threatens you with a wet paintbrush.

6. Shania plays well with others until pickup time. As soon as she spots her parent arriving, she will either throw a tantrum or cry. Her arriving parent is typically faced with an angry or an unhappy child.

7. Forrest, a four-year-old, disappears each time he has a bowel movement.
   Teachers try to monitor his problem and watch him closely, but are usually unsuccessful in steering him to the bathroom in time.

8. Stanton runs from one area to the next, dumping toys to the floor while smiling in satisfaction. So far, he has no pals who help him, but Lance seems to be on the verge of joining.

G. Go back to situations one through eight in the previous exercise, but think about the child's needs, feelings, and point of view. Is there any way for the child to solve the inherent difficulty in the situation? Are there setting or time factors teachers could manipulate, so the same problems will not happen again? What are *your* feelings in each situation? Discuss these with your group.

⦿REVEW

A. List four classroom factors that might promote inappropriate child behaviors.

B. Complete the following statement:
   The reason teachers may use different techniques in guiding aggression is. . .

C. List four positive rule statements. List four redirection statements. List four modeling statements.

D. List six strategies a child may use to get around an adult who has just announced that it is time for all the children to come inside.

E. Select the answer that best completes each statement.

1. Roberta, a student teacher, feels sure a textbook or a cooperating teacher will be able to describe guidance strategies that work. Roberta needs to know that:
   a. children are different but the same strategies work.
   b. teachers handle behaviors based on examples their parents and teachers modeled in their own childhood.
   c. there are no techniques that always work.
   d. books and practicing teachers agree on best methods.

2. Withholding of privilege is:
   a. a technique that may work.
   b. used before rule statements.
   c. not very effective.
   d. a rather cruel punishment.

3. When a teacher notices inappropriate child behavior, the teacher should immediately realize that:
   a. parents created the behavior.
   b. the child may need to learn school rules.
   c. her teaching technique is ineffective.
   d. the director should be consulted.

F. Complete the following statements. Analyze your responses and write a short paragraph about what you have just learned about yourself.

1. The ideal classroom should. . .

2. When a fight breaks out, I want to. . .

3. As a teacher, I want to control. . .

4. Aggressive children make me. . .

5. Shy children make me. . .

6. Children who use bad language ought to be. . .

7. Little boys are. . .

8. Little girls are. . .

9. Whiny children make me. . .

10. Stubborn children make me. . .

G. List the steps in conflict resolution.

CASE SCENARIO

Setting: A child care program for two-year-olds. Marcia is the student teacher, Mrs. Rice is the cooperating teacher, and Christina is the aide. It is late afternoon; most of the children have been picked up by their parents and Christina is watching the few who remain. Mrs. Rice is talking to Marcia about an incident that happened during the morning activity period.

"Marcia, did you notice what Ramon and David were doing while you were working with the children at the crafts table?" asks Mrs. Rice.

"I'm not sure I'm following you," Marcia responds.

"Did you notice that David and Ramon were arguing about who was going to use the large red truck over by the block center and that David was biting Ramon?"

"Oh, yes, I turned to look when I heard Ramon scream," Marcia says, "but I have to admit that I didn't see what was happening because I was so busy at the crafts table. Besides, I had my back to the block and truck area. Of course, I thought David was at fault; I missed Ramon's hitting him first, and I didn't see the two of them tugging at the same truck."

"You know, we teachers have to place ourselves so we can get an overview of the entire classroom every time we plan an activity that has to be supervised. I don't mean this in a negative way, Marcia. Part of the reason you are a student teacher is to learn. Always place yourself so you can see the whole classroom, or ask Christina or me to supervise where you can't see," Mrs. Rice says gently. "Had you seen the two boys pulling at the same truck, you might have been able to leave the crafts table and quickly intervene."

"I understand, Mrs. Rice. I know I'm here to learn but it seems so hard at times," Marcia sighs. "I remember our college supervisor saying that we had to develop eyes in the backs of our heads; now I understand why!"

Questions for Discussion:

1. How do you feel about what happened to Marcia? Has anything similar happened to you?

2. How might Marcia feel after her talk with Mrs. Rice? How might you feel in her place?

3. Do you think Mrs. Rice could have handled the situation differently? Why or why not?

●REFERENCES

Adams, S. K., & Wittmer, D. S. (2001, Fall). "I had it first": Teaching young children to solve problems peacefully. *Childhood Education, 77*(5), 10–15.

Abbott, J. (1997, March). To be intelligent. *Educational Leadership, 54*(6).

Bakley, S. (2000, November). Through the lens of sensory integration: A different way of analyzing challenging behavior. *Young Children, 56*(6), 70–76.

Betz, C. (1994, March). Beyond time out: Tips from a teacher. *Young Children, 49*(2), 10–14.

Boulden, K., Hiester, K., & Walti, B. (with Tertell, L.). (1998). *When teachers reflect: Journeys toward effective inclusive practice.* Washington, DC: National Association for the Education of Young Children.

Boyd, B. (1997, Fall). Teacher response to superhero play: To ban or not to ban? *Childhood Education, 74*(1).

Browning, L., Davis, B., & Resta, V. (2000, Summer). What do you mean "Think before I act?" Conflict resolution with choices. *Childhood Education, 76*(2), 232–238.

Caine, R. N., & Caine, G. (1997). *Education on the edge of possibility.* Alexandria, VA: Association for Supervision and Curriculum Development.

Canter, L. (1976). *Assertive discipline: A take-charge approach for today's educator.* Seal Beach, CA: Canter & Associates.

Carlson, F.M. (2005). *Essential touch: Meeting the needs of young children.* Washington, DC: National Association for the Education of Young Children.

Charles, C. M., & Senter, G. W. (2004). *Building classroom discipline* (8th ed.). Boston: Allyn and Bacon.

Clements, A. (2001). *Big Al.* New York: Aladdin.

Cole, K. (2001). *No bad news.* Morton Grove, IL: Albert Whitman.

Curtis, D., & Carter, M. (1996). *Reflecting children's lives: A handbook for planning a child-centered curriculum.* St. Paul, MN: Redleaf Press.

Davidman, L., & Davidman, P. (1994). *Teaching with a multi-cultural perspective: A practical guide.* New York: Longman.

Dreikurs, R. (1968). *Psychology in the classroom.* New York: Harper & Row.

Dreikurs, R., & Cassel, P. (1972). *Discipline without tears.* New York: Harper & Row.

Dreikurs, R., Grunewald, B., & Pepper, F. (1982). *Maintaining sanity in the classroom.* New York: Harper & Row.

Eaton, M. (1997, September). Positive discipline: Fostering the self-esteem of young children. *Young Children, 52*(6).

Flicker, E. S., & Hoffman, J.A. (2002, September). Developmental discipline in the early childhood classroom. *Young Children, 57*(5), 82–89.

Froschl, M., Sprung, B., & Hinitz, B. (2005, June 8). Start early to stop violence: Turning critical theory research on diversity into practical action. Presentation at NAEYC's National Institute for Early Childhood Professional Development, Miami, FL.

Gartrell, D. (1995, July). Misbehavior or mistaken behavior? *Young Children, 50*(5).

Gartrell, D. (1997, September). Beyond discipline to guidance. *Young Children, 52*(6).

Gartrell, D. (2004). *The power of guidance: Teaching social-emotional skills in early childhood classrooms.* Washington, DC: National Association for the Education of Young Children and Delmar Learning.

Gartrell, D. (2006). *A guidance approach for the encouraging classroom* (4th ed.). Clifton Park, NY: Delmar Learning.

Gillespie, C. W., & Chick, A. (2001, Summer). Fussbusters: Using peers to mediate conflict resolution in a Head Start classroom. *Childhood Education, 77*(4), 192–195.

Glasser, W. (1985). *Control theory in the classroom.* New York: Perennial Library.

Gonzalez-Mena, J. & Shareef, I. (2005, November). Discussing diverse perspectives on guidance. *Young Children, 60*(6), 68–70.

Gordon, T. (1974). *T.E.T.: Teacher effectiveness training.* New York: David McKay.

Holden, G. (1997, May). Changing the way kids settle conflicts. *Educational Leadership, 54*(8).

Honig, A. S., & Wittmer, D. S. (1996, January). Helping children become more prosocial: Ideas for classrooms, families, schools, and communities. *Young Children, 51*(2).

Howes, C. (2000, Spring). Relationships: Child, and teacher. *Early Development, 4*(1), 12–13.

Johnson, D. W., Johnson, R. T., Stevahn, L., & Hodne, P. (1997, October). The three Cs of safe schools. *Educational Leadership, 55*(2).

Killen, M., & Turiel, E. (1991). Conflict resolution in preschool social interactions. *Early Education and Development, 2*(3), 240–255.

Kohn, A. (2001, September). Five reasons to stop saying "Good job!" *Young Children, 56*(5), 24–28.

Kreidler, W. J. (1994). *Teaching conflict resolution through children's literature.* New York: Scholastic Professional Books.

Kuebli, J. (1994, March). Young children's understanding of everyday emotions. *Young Children, 49*(3).

Lionni, L. (1996). *It's mine.* New York: Random House.

Madrigal, A. (1999). *Brandi's braids.* New York: Puffin.

Marion, M. (2002). *Guidance of young children* (6th ed.). Upper Saddle River, NJ: Pearson/Merrill/Prentice Hall.

Marshall, H. H. (1995, January). Beyond "I like the way . . ." *Young Children, 50*(2).

McCarthy, B. (1997, January). A tale of four learners: 4MAT's learning styles. *Educational Leadership, 54*(6).

Nelsen, J., Lott, L., & Glenn, H. S. (1997). *Positive discipline in the classroom.* Rocklin, CA: Prima Publishing.

Paraskevas, B. (1999). *Hoppy and Joe.* New York: Simon & Schuster.

Readdick, C. A., & Chapman, P. L. (2000, Fall/Winter). Young children's perception of time-out. *Childhood Education, 15*(1), 81–87.

Rogers, C., & Freiberg, H. (1994). *Freedom to learn* (3rd ed.). New York: Merrill/Macmillan.

Ryan, K. (1993, November). Mining the values in the curriculum. *Educational Leadership, 51*(3).

Schoonmaker, F. (1998, Spring). Promise and possibility: Learn to teach. *Teachers' College Record, 99*(3).

Thomas, S. M. (1998). *Somewhere today.* Morton Grove, IL: Albert Whitman.

Vartuli, S. (2005, September). Beliefs: The heart of teaching. *Young Children, 60* (5), 76-86.

Walker-Dalhouse, D. (2005, Fall). Discipline: Responding to socioeconomic and racial differences. *Childhood Education, 82*(1), 24–30.

Wheeler, E. J. (1994, September). Peer conflicts in the classroom. *ERIC Digest*, EDO-PS-94-(13).

Zabel, M. K. (1986). Time out with behaviorally disabled students. *Behavioral Disorders 21*, 15–20.

CHAPTER 7

Using Case Studies to Understand Behavior

Comments of student teachers:

66 *The hardest part of student teaching involved the children's understanding that I would enforce rules. I hated it when children cried or threw a wingding. A teacher is an authority figure. Children will not always like you.* ●

Ke-Chang Wang

66 *I had been warned by the previous student teacher that a certain child would make my life miserable. I gleaned the best information on power-seeking children from a management book I knew. Lucky for me, I over-prepared because the child was not nearly as difficult as I anticipated.* ●

Catherine Millick

66 *My placement class-room was a Montessori school. Each child automatically pushed his chair under the table when he got up. It was habit behavior. They also returned each child game activity to its own special place on shelves. It's the first class-room where I've worked where children picked up after themselves so effortlessly. I wish my placement had started in the fall so I could have seen how my cooperating teacher accomplished it.* ●

Marlis McCormick

To analyze the behavior of any child, you, as the student teacher, need to remember two important concepts:

1. All behavior is meaningful to the child, even that which an adult might call negative.

2. All behavior is reinforced by the environment (people, places, and things).

Then the question arises: Why does the child act as he does? Why does she repeat behavior?

Let us begin this chapter by looking at some of the typical reinforcers of behavior. Perhaps the easiest ones to understand are physiological in nature: the need to eat when hungry, drink when thirsty, sleep when tired, dress warmly when cold, stay out of the sun when hot, and so forth. It is less easy to understand the psychological ones, although they control more of our actions. In an attempt to understand them, there are a few major theories that would be helpful.

ERIKSON'S THEORY OF PSYCHOSOCIAL DEVELOPMENT AND ITS RELATION TO SELF-CONTROL

Erikson's (1993) theory of psychosocial development is relevant to our understanding of behavior and self-control. According to Erikson, there are eight developmental stages people go through during a lifetime. The child goes through the first four from birth into elementary school age These are: the resolution of basic trust, autonomy, initiative, and industry. The remaining four, usually resolved from approximately age 12 and continuing through the adult years, are: identity, intimacy, generativity, and integrity. Each stage has its developmental task to achieve (see Figure 7–1).

Age	Task	Outcome ("Good Me")	Outcome ("Bad Me")
0–1 year	Acquiring a sense of BASIC TRUST	Child develops the ability to TRUST the significant adults in her life	Child develops a sense of MISTRUST in all adults and a sense of HOPELESSNESS
	PARENTAL/CAREGIVER ROLE:	Meeting physical needs, nurturing emotional and social needs; providing stimulation of intellectual and language needs; providing unconditional LOVE	
1–3 years	Acquiring a sense of AUTONOMY	Child develops SELF-CONTROL and willpower; learns give-and-take (leadership-follower roles)	Child develops SELF-DOUBT and a sense of SHAME
	PARENTAL/CAREGIVER ROLE:	Emotional support; firm, but gentle, limit setting; gradual granting of freedom; consistency in expectations and in establishing boundaries; providing simple choices	

continues

● **Figure 7-1**
Erikson's developmental stages

3–5 years	Acquiring a sense of INITIATIVE	Child develops a sense of direction and purpose; is unafraid to explore new or changed settings	Child feels a sense of GUILT; becomes uneasy with new settings; only involves self in activities he knows well
	PARENTAL/TEACHER ROLE:	Communication; joint problem-solving; sharing of values and ideals; continued emotional support	
6–12 years	Acquiring a sense of INDUSTRY	Child learns that he is competent; experiments with methods to become competent; fully develops leadership-follower roles	Child develops feelings of incompetence and INFERIORITY; lacks understanding of leadership-follower roles
	PARENTAL/TEACHER ROLE:	Encouraging realistic goals; helping child become open to criticism; accepting criticism from child; answering child's questions; being open to all kinds of questions from child	

● **Figure 7-1** (continued)

First Stage of Development

For the infant (birth to approximately one and one-half to two years), the task is to develop basic **trust**. If the infant is fed when hungry, changed when wet, dressed to suit the weather, and given much love and attention, the infant will learn that adults can be trusted. The infant who is not fed regularly and feels rejected or neglected may learn that adults cannot be trusted.

Look at a small baby. What do you see? If the child is younger than six months, you will notice almost immediately that this infant is constantly using the senses and the mouth. The presentation of a toy brings a multiple reaction. The child puts it into the mouth, tastes it, takes it out of the mouth, looks at it, turns it over in the hands, shakes the toy, listens to see if it will make a noise, and holds the toy to the nose to see if it smells. The child uses all of the senses to understand this toy that has become a part of the immediate environment (see Figure 7–2). Eyes (sight), mouth (taste), hands (touch), nose (smell), and ears (hearing) all come into action.

What does this have to do with learning self-control? Think about the interaction between the infant and the toy, and among the infant, toy, and significant adult, usually the mother. Think also about why the infant uses all of the senses to learn about a new toy or about anything in his environment. Why is this important? In learning about the environment, a baby feels safe in that environment and learns to control it. Can you see why it is important for the infant to sense some control over the environment? How does the child feel when experiencing cause-and-effect relationships? What does the child learn from tasting, shaking, looking at, and manipulating an object? The child is learning that he has some influence on what is happening. It is this feeling of influence or control that is important to the child's learning of self-control.

● **Figure 7-2**
The toddler "scientist" yearns to feel things firsthand.

trust—the first stage of development described by Erik Erikson, occurring during infancy, in which the child's needs should be met consistently and predictably.

Think about what can happen if the child feels no control over the environment. Suppose the significant adult in the infant's life holds out a new toy toward the child, shakes it in front of her eyes, and, as the infant reaches for it, takes it away? Suppose the infant reaches for an object over and over, only to have it always withdrawn? How long do you think the child will continue to reach? Ultimately she will stop trying. The child will also learn to feel helpless and not in control over the environment. This child, then, will have difficulty in acquiring self-control. This is the child who becomes either under-disciplined or over-disciplined.

Experiencing some influence on the environment leads the child to understand that she affects the environment. An awareness of cause-and-effect relationships develops in this manner.

Second Stage of Development

autonomy—the second stage of development described by Erik Erikson, occurring during the second year of life, in which toddlers assert their growing motor, language, and cognitive abilities by trying to become more independent.

As the child becomes mobile and begins to talk, he enters the second stage of development. Erikson calls this the **autonomy** stage. (Its contrasts are shame and self-doubt.) Two-year-old children are motor individuals; they love to run, climb, ride, move, move, and move (see Figure 7–3). They are so active—they almost seem like perpetual motion machines! The developmental task of the two-year-old toddler is learning autonomy and self-discipline. It is this age in particular that is so trying for both the parents and preschool teachers.

This stage coincides with two physiological events in the toddler's life: the ability to crawl and walk and learning how to use the toilet. Much has been written about the problems of training a child to use the toilet. (The subject is covered in more detail in Chapter 14.) Many parents, child care workers, and family child care providers do not understand that most children will essentially train themselves, especially if given an appropriate model, such as an older sibling who is toilet trained or a loving, caring parent who anticipates the child's need to use the toilet, and in an unthreatening way, sits the child on the seat and compliments the child on success. The adult needs to allow the child to look at, and even smell, what his body has produced. It is not uncommon for toddlers to play with their bowel movements, an action sure to bring down on them the wrath of the adult. What needs to be remembered is that the child is pleased and curious about what his body has done. Instead of becoming angry, adults should understand the child's interest and simply state that the playing is not approved of and direct attention to playing with clay, for example, as a substitute.

Figure 7-3
This child has become an autonomous bike rider.

Problems arise when adults overreact to the child's playing with fecal matter. Many parents who try to toilet train what appears to be a stubborn, willful child fail to understand that the child is simply attempting to develop control, over the parent, in part, but over herself as well.

At this time, the child reinforces the sense of having an effect on the environment. Assume that the toddler, as an infant, was allowed some degree of freedom, in which to crawl and explore safely. Assume that within this safe environment the infant had a variety of toys and objects with which to play and manipulate, and a loving adult to supervise. This infant then becomes an active, curious toddler, ready to expand her environment. Assume also that the parents, early childhood caregivers, and family child care providers with whom this toddler comes into contact continue to provide a safe environment, in which the child can explore. What is the child then learning? At this age, the child is continually learning that she has some control over the immediate environment. This helps the child learn and practice self-control. To allow for practice, the environment must be physically safe, stimulating, and offer choices.

It is this third factor—offering choices—that is critical in terms of helping a child acquire self-control. Even an infant crawling around in a playroom can make choices about which toys he will play with and when (see Figure 7–4). As the child begins to feed himself, the child can make a choice between slices of apple or orange for a snack. The toddler can make the choice between two shirts that may be laid out. In the center setting, a toddler can easily make the choice between playing with clay or climbing on an indoor play structure. As we talk about older infants and toddlers, we are also talking about allowing the child a choice between two alternatives chosen by the adult. The young child cannot handle a choice of six different activities; this is overwhelming. Too much choice is as bad as no choice at all. In either case, one child may become confused, anxious, and angry, whereas another child will withdraw and do nothing.

But one concern that family and teachers share is that young toddlers often seem to be breaking limits deliberately. We fail to understand that one of the ways the child can be reassured that we care is to test the limits repeatedly, to see if we really mean what we say. What sometimes happens is that on days when we are rested and time is plentiful, we tolerate behavior that would not be tolerated under different circumstances.

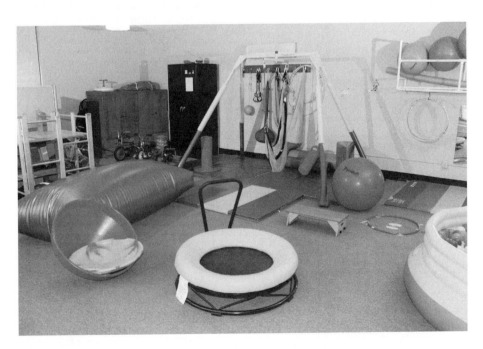

● **Figure 7-4**
Toddlers become autonomous as they explore in this brightly equipped activity room.

If it is okay to throw a ball to another child, why is it wrong to throw a rock? If it is okay to run down the driveway in one instance, why is it wrong in another? Boundaries are not understood very well by toddlers, especially when the child can go somewhere *with* supervision but not without it. In the toddler's mind, these are seen as inconsistencies regarding adult expectations. The child cannot differentiate safe from unsafe, so for parents and preschool teachers it means repetition of rules and limits. Eventually, of course, the child does learn: "I don't go down the driveway without holding Mommy's hand," or "I don't leave the yard unless Miss Jan holds my hand."

For some parents and teachers, the two-year-old child becomes too difficult to handle in a caring way. Two courses of action are frequently taken. Some parents confine the child rather than tolerate the need to explore. As a result, the child's basic motor needs are squelched, and she becomes fearful and distrustful of her motor abilities. She develops self-doubt rather than self-confidence. The child also learns to feel ashamed about the anger felt toward the adults. Because these adults are still responsible for the child's primary needs, for food, water, and love, the child feels there must be something wrong with her if the adults inhibit her natural desire to explore. Thus, the child learns to be ashamed of the anger and represses it. In the classroom, this child is the timid, shy, fearful one, with poor motor abilities due to a lack of opportunities to practice them.

Other families may refuse to assert their responsibilities and allow the child to do anything. Think of how terrifying it must be for the child to have such power over the adults in his life. As a result, the child's behavior becomes progressively worse until the parents finally have had enough and resort to punishment. A different result may be a child who fights against any kind of limits and becomes shameless in attempting to do the opposite of what adults expect or want, especially regarding motor restrictions. Just as the physically restrained child learns to feel ashamed, so does the unrestrained child. This child really wants to have reasonable limits set but cannot accept them without a struggle. This struggle of wills makes the unrestrained child feel just as ashamed as the overly restrained child. Both children lack the inner controls that the emotionally healthy child has developed. Both lack self-discipline: the overly restrained child through a lack of opportunities to practice, the under-restrained child through a lack of learning any standards.

In the primary school setting, difficulties with autonomy can be seen in two very different types of behavior. One is overconfidence, a willingness to try anything (the more outrageous, the better), characterized by frequently unrealistic expectations of physical prowess. Overconfident students appear to have leadership qualities but become angry if thwarted in their attempts to lead, and may then heap scorn on ideas that originally might even have been theirs. The opposite is the child who lacks self-confidence, a student who continually asks if he is completing an assignment the way you want him to, one who seems to need additional cues before starting a creative writing or art project; this child will check what his peers are doing before beginning his own work.

Third Stage of Development

The next stage roughly approximates the usual preschool years, from three to five. Erikson believes that the developmental task of the preschooler is to develop initiative, to learn when to do something by himself, and when to ask for help. The result of practice in asserting his **initiative** results in a self-confident, cheerful child.

Again, as with the overly restrained toddler, the five-year-old who has been denied a chance to exert initiative learns instead to develop feelings of guilt. The child learns that any self-made decisions are of no importance; the adults in the child's life will make decisions. For example, if the child attempts to dress without help, the parents are likely to criticize the result. "Your shirt's on backwards. Don't you know front from back?" Sometimes, the correction is nonverbal; the parent or teacher will simply reach down toward the child, yank the T-shirt off the arms, turn it, and put the arms back through the sleeves. The child learns that he does not know how to dress and eventually may stop trying altogether. As the teacher, you then see a child of six or seven who cannot put on a jacket without help, who mixes left and right shoes, and who often asks, "Is this the way you want me to . . . ?"As with the child who lacks autonomy, this child, too, needs constant reassurance that an assigned task has been completed the way the adult wants it done. Unstructured assignments, such as a blank piece of paper on which to draw, can be frightening. Because such children have little self-confidence, they frequently look to peers, or come to you, for ideas.

The under-restrained toddler grows to be an under-restrained preschool child and becomes your most obvious classroom problem. This child enters preschool like a small hurricane, spilling blocks, scattering puzzles, and tearing up a classmate's drawing, because it is perceived as either not as good as or too much better than the child's own. The under-restrained child is the one who pushes another child off the tricycle so she can ride it, or who grabs the hammer out of the hand of another child when she wants it for herself.

The under-restrained child is also under-socialized. This child has never learned the normal give-and-take of interpersonal relationships, and does not know how to take turns or share (see Figure 7–5). This child has

initiative—the desire to do something by oneself. Identified as the third developmental stage of three- to five-year-old children by Erik Erikson.

 Figure 7-5
Learning to wait for a turn is not easy.

had few restrictions regarding what to do, when to do it, and where. At the same time, this child often *wanted* the adults in her family, caregivers, and teachers to tell her what to do and what not to do. A word of caution: some perfectly normal children who have little or no preschool experience will act like the under-socialized child simply because they lack social experience. They learn rapidly, however, and some quickly become acclimated to classroom procedures and rules.

Remember, the child who appears unlovable is the one most in need of your love. What are some of the ways you can help this child? Use the four *Cs* and *CARE*. Although it is difficult to accept this child, all children deserve your respect and acceptance, regardless of how unlikable they may be. In fact, this particular child will probably sense your dislike; therefore, it is important to be scrupulously fair. Do not allow yourself to be caught in the trap of assuming that this child will always be the guilty party in every altercation. It does not take other children long to realize that they have the perfect scapegoat in their midst; it is too tempting for them to break a rule and blame it on the child who is expected to break rules. Remember to be firm. The under-restrained child needs the security of exact limits. Rules should be stated repeatedly and enforced. This is the child who will constantly need to be reminded of the rules and of his need to adhere to them, like everyone else.

Ask your cooperating teacher about the child's family background. You may discover there is little security. Bedtime may occur whenever the child finally falls asleep, whether on the floor in front of the television, on the couch, or in bed with an older brother, sister, or cousin. You may discover that mealtimes are just as haphazard. Breakfast may come at any time in the morning, or only if there is food in the house. You may find out that family members eat as they each become hungry. This child may open a bag of potato chips for breakfast and eat whatever can be found in the refrigerator for dinner. Sometimes, the child's only meal is the one served at school. Life for this child is simply not very safe or predictable. Mom may or may not be home when the child returns from school. Dad may come home and may work, or not, as opportunity presents itself. There may be no one primary caregiver for this child. It is even possible that this child has always been unwanted and has been sent from relative to relative, or from foster home to foster home.

In terms of Erikson's theory, this unwanted child may never have learned to trust. This possibility is easy to check. As you try to be friendly, does this child's behavior worsen? As you reach out, does the child draw away or wince? Think of the consequences of not being wanted. If the child perceives that no one, especially the significant adults in his life, likes him, how can the he learn to like himself? How can the child learn to love without first receiving love from others, preferably from the significant adults in his life? The child cannot do these things for himself. An unwanted or unlovable child is a real challenge to any caring teacher. Because the child feels so little self-worth, attempts at friendliness on your part may be perceived as weakness. To deal with this child, you first will have to acquire a tough skin. This child has learned how to read adult behavior; this is how he protects himself. This child knows what you are going to do before you do it. On the other hand, the child's behavior will seem less predictable to you. One day he will obey the rules, another day he will not. This youngster will make friendly overtures to another child in the morning and kick that same child in the afternoon. He will help a group of peers build a city with blocks, only to knock them down when the project is finished.

You will have to repeat limits and rules continuously. You may have to physically remove this child from the center of action to a quiet corner or room. There is no magic wand that can change this child overnight. In fact, you have to remember that it has taken two, three, or four years to shape the child into the person you are seeing. It may take weeks, even months, to properly socialize the child. In rare cases, it may even take years.

Uncaring, neglectful families may have been warm and loving occasionally, and this child may have learned how to trust, at least in part. Still, if this child has not resolved Erikson's second task of early childhood, learning autonomy, the child may frequently get into trouble. Never having learned how to live with limits, this child is constantly going beyond them. If the roof is off limits, this child finds a way to climb on it. If the kitchen is off limits, this child continually goes there. This child will continue the escapades, even if an injury results. The child accepts a hurt as the correct punishment. In fact, this child seeks punishment. When you speak to the child's family, the answer often given is, "Just give him a good spanking. He'll behave then!" One mother we remember fondly responded, "Oh, my good Lord! I never know what to do with that boy!" Was it any wonder that we didn't know either? Or that he had us figured out faster than we could understand him?

Similar behaviors may be exhibited by the child who is overindulged at home and smothered with attention. This child expects to be the center of attention at school.

Children with this type of behavior test every resource you have. Again, remember to use the four *Cs* and to *CARE*, even though it may be difficult. Repeat the limits and expectations over and over. Physically remove the child whenever necessary; isolation sometimes works best.

Another technique is to say what the child is thinking. "You want me to tell you that I hate you, but I'm not going to." Sometimes, the shock of hearing you put into words what she is thinking is enough to change the behavior. It may work for a day, anyway. You will have to do this repeatedly. When the child hits another, you can say, "You expect me to yell at you for hitting Jada. Well, I'm not going to. I'm going to ask you to sit here with me until you think you can go back with the other children. You know we do not hit in this room." Insist again that limits be respected; the child must follow the rules like everyone else.

Speak to the family but be careful. Try not to speak down to them, or in an accusing manner. Try to use the "I want to help your child" approach. Most families want to help their children; however, some do not know how. You may have to explain why you have limits and rules, and suggest that the family have some limits for the child at home. You may have to give many tips to some families, and you will have to be tactful and show them that you care. If you sense a non-caring attitude, you can easily understand why the child has problems. In this case, you will have to work only with the child, but keep trying.

One technique that sometimes works with the aggressive, under-disciplined child is to call the child on the behavior. What is meant by *call*? One way to look at interactions between two or more children is to find the underlying motivators. Does this sound familiar? Some children are motivated by a desire to control, because they have learned that their own safety lies in their ability to control their environment. This can provoke a tug-of-war between the child's need to control and yours. At this point, there is no sense in trying to reason, especially verbally. Simply isolate the child, repeat the rules or limits, and leave. Tell the child as you leave that you know what the child is doing and why. Be specific: "I'm not going to argue with you," or "Sit here until you feel ready to rejoin us."

Be prepared to understand that you will not be successful with every child. There will always be one or two children who will relate better to another teacher.

Once in a while you will see a child who is so psychologically damaged that the regular classroom may not be an appropriate setting. The child may be underfed, poorly clothed, uncared for, and unloved. Or he may be fed whenever he fussed, well-clothed and seemingly well-cared for; but the care may have been cursory and unloving. Erikson would suggest that this child has never resolved the task of basic trust as an infant, much less having resolved the tasks of autonomy and initiative. Being unwanted and unloved makes it extremely difficult for a child to acquire any sense of self-worth.

As the teacher, your job is to provide the kind of environment in which the child is able to resolve these early developmental tasks, especially if the child has not yet done so. It is never too late to learn to trust, or to develop autonomy; it is never too late to undo earlier, negative outcomes, even while working toward resolution of a different stage's positive outcome.

Fourth Stage of Development

industry—the fourth stage of development described by Erik Erikson, starting at the end of the preschool years and lasting until puberty, in which the child focuses on the development of competence.

For school-age children, there is probably no more important task than to learn that they are capable of learning. Erikson called this stage **industry**. (Its negative outcome is inferiority.) Unfortunately, even children who have progressed through the earlier stages of development smoothly, who enter school trusting in others, knowing the give-and-take expected of group life, feeling confident in their own abilities, may stumble when they reach kindergarten and first grade.

For some children in kindergarten and the primary grades of elementary school, the fine motor tasks, such as writing manuscript, shaping numerals, and coloring within specified lines, are difficult. These children may have already learned that they do not have abilities that are rewarded by their teachers (see Figure 7–6).

School, instead of being a place of joy and learning, may become a place where children fail. Inferiority is the obvious result. A secondary result can be that the child develops feelings of helplessness. Successful students generally believe that they are responsible for their successes and attribute any failures to lack of effort. Unsuccessful students, however, often attribute successes to luck and failures to factors beyond their control, or to lack of ability. The unfortunate consequence in students who feel helpless is that they often give up and stop trying. It then becomes extremely difficult for teachers to change the behavior.

In a classroom that offers developmentally appropriate materials for children to interact with actively, there is little difficulty with industry. A developmentally appropriate classroom is likely to have centers to allow for active exploration, and enough physical space to allow for movement opportunities, at different times.

● **Figure 7-6**
Choosing their own books shows initiative.

For example, a school may have a carpeted reading area, with pillows where children can go to look at and read books; a science area, with attractive junk to explore; floor space, for the children who may wish to work on the floor; a math center, with Cuisenaire rods, unifix cubes, tangrams, and other manipulatives; a writing area, managed by an **assistant teacher**, or a family or other volunteer, where children can dictate stores or write and illustrate their own; and so on. In the classroom with many options for working alone, in pairs, or in cooperative groups, children discover that learning is enjoyable; and industry is the result.

Erikson and the Professional Development of Student Teachers

Gratz and Boulton (1996) look at Erikson's stages of development as they might apply to you as student teachers, and to your futures as teachers and caregivers in general. At stage one, for example, *trust* develops as a student teacher feels prepared to handle the classroom and is confident in her abilities. At stage two, a student teacher develops *autonomy* as he successfully moves from teaching one small group of children to working with the entire class. At stage three, the student teacher develops *initiative* as she designs and implements her own activity or learning center. Stage four student teachers manifest *industry* by becoming involved in their professional organizations and attending conferences.

Stage five student teachers develop an *identity* as a teacher "through the cumulative activities that have helped the teacher to achieve a sense of initiative and industry and eventually a sense of self as an early childhood educator." *Intimacy*, the developmental task of stage six, can be seen as the student teacher establishes relationships with his cooperating teacher, other adults in the classroom, and his college supervisor. At stage seven, the student teacher, now actively working as a teacher, becomes what can euphemistically be called a contributing member of society. In other words, she has become *generative* and may be asked to mentor to another student teacher or a beginning teacher. Or she may plan a presentation for a professional conference. Generativity can be seen in many ways. At stage eight, the former student teacher, now a teacher for several years, feels a sense of *integrity* as a professional and "trusts in her own mature professional judgment." Where do you see yourself in relationship to Erikson's developmental stages as posed by Gratz and Boulton?

BURTON WHITE AND SELF-CONTROL

White (1975) divides the child's first three years into seven phases, each with its unique characteristics, needs, and preferred child-rearing practices.

> Phase I: birth to six weeks
> Phase II: six weeks to three-and-a-half months
> Phase III: three-and-a-half to five-and-a-half months
> Phase IV: five-and-a-half to eight months
> Phase V: 8 to 14 months
> Phase VI: 14 to 24 months
> Phase VII: 24 to 36 months

According to White, the primary need of the infant in Phase I is to feel loved and cared for and to have the opportunity to develop certain skills, such as holding up her head while on her stomach, and tracking objects held 8 to 24 inches from her face. The newborn baby does not need much

assistant teacher—also called aide, helper, auxiliary teacher, associate teacher, or small-group leader; works under the guidance of the head teacher in providing a quality program.

stimulation other than a change of position from back to stomach, or to the caregiver's arms.

During Phase II, helping the infant achieve certain skills, such as holding up the head, becomes more important than during Phase I. Phase II infants also need hand-eye activities, such as crib devices.

Phase III infants have attained head control and are beginning to attain torso control. At this age, the child learns to turn from stomach to back and from back to stomach. Also, the child's leg muscles are strengthened. Infants at Phase III enjoy being held so they can press their feet against a lap and practice standing. They are quite social and respond to tickling and smiling with their own coos and smiles. These infants soak up all the attention from family and strangers alike and respond easily.

Phase IV infants begin to show an understanding of language. *Mama*, *daddy*, *bottle*, and *eat* may all be understood by the child. The child cannot say the words but can respond, indicating an understanding of the words. Phase IV babies are beginning to develop real motor skills such as sitting independently, getting up on hands and knees, and rocking. A Phase IV child may even pull to a standing position. Phase IV babies need freedom in which to move and practice these growing skills. They can also grasp toys quite well and need suitable, small objects that they can practice picking up and holding. Toys like crib devices to kick at, stacking toys, stuffed toys, balls to pick up, and objects that are two to five inches in size that cannot be swallowed all help the Phase IV child learn about the world and gain mastery over the immediate environment.

During Phase V, the infant usually comes into direct conflict with significant adults for the first time. This is due to the child's growing mobility. Soon there is no area in the house or center that is safe from the child's active exploration. Knick-knacks, books, ashtrays, electrical cords, pots and pans, utensils, and pet-food dishes are stimuli to the active Phase V child, and bring the child into conflict with the parents or caregivers.

It is at this age that the child begins to develop self-control. It is important that the child have a childproof area in which to play. Parents, early childhood teachers, and family child care providers need to know that the Phase V child is safe from harm in that area.

If the Phase V child does not get into trouble, the Phase VI child will. At this point, mobility has been established. Phase VI children can walk and begin to run, climb, ride, push and pull objects, reach for and pull down, and talk. *No* becomes a favorite word, mostly because they hear it so often. *Mama*, *daddy*, *bye-bye*, and *baby* are spoken. The Phase VI child begins to pay less attention to the people in the environment and spends more time looking, listening, practicing simple skills, and exploring.

It is the exploring that causes difficulty for both the Phase V and the Phase VI child. Most houses and yards are not childproof. Children will pull flowers off stems, grab dirt pebbles and throw them, toddle down driveways and out into streets, climb up ladders, and push and pull at furniture. This struggle to experiment with growing motor skills comes into continued conflict with needs for the child's safety. Instead of complimenting the climber who has mastered the front steps and is now crying to be picked up so he can start over, we may scold the child and insist that the steps are off limits. The Phase V and Phase VI child simply cannot comprehend this. It would be more beneficial to our peace of mind, and the child's need to climb, if a portable gate is placed across the third stair to allow the child to practice going up and down. If the child falls down three steps, he will not be hurt and will approach the climb more carefully the next time.

Self-control grows from experiences like these. The Phase V and Phase VI child will become an autonomous, able Phase VII preschooler if allowed to experiment with what the body can do and given opportunities to practice growing motor skills. As a Phase VII preschooler, the child will be able to:

- get and hold the attention of adults
- use adults as resources, after first determining that a job is too difficult
- express affection and mild annoyance
- lead or follow peers
- compete with peers
- show pride in accomplishments
- engage in role-playing activities
- use language with increasing competence
- notice small details or discrepancies
- anticipate consequences
- deal with abstractions
- see things from another person's viewpoint
- make interesting associations
- plan and carry out complicated activities
- use resources effectively
- maintain concentration on a task while simultaneously keeping track of what is going on (dual focusing)

According to Burton White, most babies grow at essentially the same rate until Phase V. Most family environments provide reasonably positive experiences for Phase I through Phase IV children. As mentioned, conflicts arise as the child's mobility increases. As a teacher of young children, you must provide the kind of environment in which the children have as much opportunity as possible to grow and learn safely about their environment and themselves.

Emotional Development of Infants and Toddlers

Butterfield, Martin, and Prairie (2004) suggest that there are certain key concepts that teachers should be familiar with for children at different ages. With infants, for example, one key concept is that *early experiences shape our ability to communicate through emotional signals.*

Lally (1995) refers to research conducted by Greenspan and Greenspan (1985) and posits six stages of emotional development:

1. *Regulation and interest in the world (from birth).* This stage lasts until infants are approximately four months of age. Infants take an interest in sights, sounds, smells, and other inputs from their environments, and attempt to understand these sensations. What the infant is learning is that he can regulate some of his needs: when he wants to sleep, for example, or nurse.

2. *Falling in love (from four months).* At this age, infants establish strong, loving relationships with their primary caregivers, usually the mother and father, and often do so with a secondary caregiver if the parents work. This stage lasts until about eight months, to the beginning of language skills. Infants between the ages of four and eight months are often seen as euphoric; they are generally happy,

smile frequently, and coo at themselves and others. They begin to realize that they can affect their environment and are interested in their bodies. Some will watch their hands for several minutes.

3. *Purposeful communication (from eight months).* At this age, infants react to language, and family and caregivers realize that the baby understands what is being communicated. Some infants will begin to repeat babbling sounds, and a few may even articulate a sound such as *bu* for *book*, and *ba-ba* for *bottle* or *bye-bye*. Infants now understand that the adults in their lives react to them, and that they can cause a reaction with certain sounds, words, and activities.

4. *The beginning of a complex sense of self (from 10 months).* "By 10 to 18 months, babies need to be admired for all the new abilities they have mastered," to enable toddlers to begin to expand their sense of self, as competent individuals.

5. *Emotional ideas (from 18 months).* Around 18 to 24 months, toddlers begin to use fantasy play and begin to express emotions, sometimes intensely, as with tantrums. It is important then to help toddlers put feelings into words and allow them to explore how they feel on any given day.

6. *Emotional thinking (from 30 months).* "When children are about 30 months old, their emotional development involves shifting gears between make-believe and reality." It is important at this stage to set clear limits for children, yet allow them freedom to indulge in creative, dramatic play.

Goleman (1995, 1997) and Mayer and Salovey (1995) address what they call *emotional intelligence* and the skills associated with it. The key skills include:

- *self-awareness:* being able to recognize and name emotions, and understand why the child feels as she does.

- *self-regulation of emotion:* being able to verbalize and cope with emotions, such as anxiety, anger, and depression, and being able to control impulses, aggression, self-destructive and antisocial behavior, and recognize her strengths and her ability to handle emotions, both positive and negative.

- *self-monitoring and performance:* being able to focus on the task at hand, set short- and long-term goals, modify performance after feedback, and mobilize positive motivation to work toward optimal performance states.

- *empathy and perspective taking:* becoming a good listener (see Figure 7–7), being able to empathize with others, increasing sensitivity to the feelings of others, and understanding another child's perspective, point of view, or feelings.

- *social skills in handling relationships:* the ability to express emotions in relationships and express them effectively, to harmonize diverse feelings and viewpoints, work as a member of a team or cooperative learning group, exercise sensitivity to social cues, and respond constructively, in a problem-solving manner, to interpersonal obstacles (Elias, et al., 1997).

Elias, et al. (1997) emphasize that "acquiring an integrated set of skills such as these often occurs in an experiential context, where the skills are

Figure 7-7
As friends, these girls
enjoy being together.

learned through practice and role modeling." They further stress the developmental nature of the acquisition of emotional skills, and the fact that emotional skills are best learned through experience and repetition during early childhood.

Goleman (1995, 1997) states that effective programs to promote emotional intelligence include emotional, cognitive, and behavioral skills development. As student teachers, you may be able to help children acquire these.

Emotional Skills

- identifying and labeling feelings
- expressing feelings
- assessing the intensity of feelings
- managing feelings
- delaying gratification
- controlling impulses
- reducing stress
- knowing the difference between feelings and actions

Cognitive Skills

- *self-talk*, or the conducting of an inner dialog, as a way to cope with challenge or reinforce one's behavior
- reading and interpreting social cues, for example, recognizing social influences on behavior and seeing oneself as a part of a larger community
- using steps for problem solving and decision making, controlling impulses, setting goals, identifying alternative actions, and anticipating consequences
- understanding the perspectives of others
- understanding behavior norms, and what is and is not acceptable

- a positive attitude toward life
- self-awareness, including developing realistic expectations about oneself

Behavioral Skills

- nonverbal-communication, through eye contact, facial expressions, tone of voice, gestures, and so on
- verbal communication, making clear requests, responding effectively to criticism, resisting negative influences, listening to and helping others, participating in positive peer groups (Goleman, 1995, 1997)

In agreement with Goleman, Hyson (2004) lists the following five components of emotional intelligence:

1. self-awareness
2. adaptive coping
3. an ability to discern others' emotions
4. an ability to use words to express emotions
5. empathy

Teacher Priorities

Teachers realize that emotions and cognitive development are intertwined and inseparable. In an earlier article, Hyson (2002) listed ways in which teachers can help every child develop emotional maturity. She identifies six *priorities* in promoting emotional competence:

1. *Creating a secure emotional environment.* If teachers build close relationships and an emotionally secure climate, children are able to explore and learn.

2. *Helping children understand emotions.* If teachers promote emotional understanding, children have insight into their own and others' feelings, thereby becoming more empathic and socially competent.

3. *Modeling genuine, appropriate emotional responses.* If teachers themselves show real emotions, and if they are effective models, children are likely to adopt appropriate ways of showing their feelings.

4. *Supporting children's regulation of emotions.* If teachers gradually guide children toward expressing and regulating their emotions in appropriate ways, children will gain powerful tools that lead to healthy development in social, emotional, and academic areas.

5. *Recognizing and honoring children's expressive styles.* If teachers respect individual and cultural differences in how children express their feelings, while promoting appropriate expressions, children feel affirmed and supported.

6. *Uniting children's learning with positive emotions.* If teachers give children many opportunities to experience the joys and overcome the frustrations of new learning experiences, children become able to tackle hard work, persist at tasks, and seek out challenges.

Young children, progressing toward the emotional growth and control needed in kindergarten, often display secure and trusting feelings for their teachers and peers. They are able to control, express, regulate, and understand a wide spectrum of their own feelings. They display problem-solving abilities, persistence, positive relationships with others, and an eagerness to experience classroom activities. They are headed toward academic success.

Self-Esteem and Self-Control

Although much of the research on self-esteem was completed in the late 1960s and throughout the 1970s, the new millennium is bringing about a renewed interest. With the noticeable changes that have occurred in families in the past twenty years—due to the problems of divorce and subsequent single-parenthood, mobility, the rise in the incidence of substance abuse, remarriage and blended families, teenage parenthood, smaller family size, homelessness, the two-working-parent family, and difficulties with child care or after-school care—child caregivers and teachers are seeing more and more stressed and even "damaged" children. Characteristic of such children is low self-esteem. Children of divorced parents typically blame themselves for the divorce, a phenomenon that exists even in the most friendly of divorce cases.

Children raised in single-parent homes, over 90 percent of them headed by a woman, often live in reduced economic circumstances. It is well known that most single-parent females are not able to command the salaries that the single-parent male can; the result has been the feminization of poverty, and the consequent cost to children living in poverty. Housing, if there is any, in less desirable and often in more dangerous neighborhoods; there is little medical or dental care, insufficient clothing for the weather conditions, lack of proper nutrition, and plain lack of care, in too many instances.

What you see in the classroom then is the damage to these children's self-esteem: families too stressed, and parents too busy and too often suffering from low self-esteem themselves to parent their children properly, or nourish their children's self-esteem. One word of caution: not all single parents are overstressed; some children are less stressed after the divorce of parents who constantly argued; some single-parent women do earn substantial salaries, are emotionally and psychologically healthy, and are able to build their children's self-esteem. As always, be wary of applying stereotypes.

In his landmark research, Coopersmith (1967) cited three factors in the home that contribute to children's feelings of self-esteem:

1. unconditional acceptance of the child, although not necessarily accepting all of the child's behaviors
2. setting clear expectations for behavior and consistently reinforcing the need for adherence to them
3. respecting the child's need for initiative within the set limits

Some children you see in child care and school may have a parent's acceptance only when they do exactly what is demanded of them. A parent tired from working may abandon their job as a parent and allow children to essentially raise themselves, or may allow the TV to raise them. Other parents may feel threatened by their children's desires for autonomy and initiative and may not respect the need children have to exert their wills.

For the caregiver and teacher working with children with low self esteem, the task is to attempt to provide the missing elements of acceptance,

self-control—restraint exercised over one's own impulses, emotions, or desires.

clearly defined limits, and respect for the child's need to assert autonomy and practice initiative within those limits. If this sounds like *CARE*ing, it should.

Self-control can be defined as *the ability to resist the inappropriate and act responsibly.* Acting responsibly includes respecting the rights of others, showing compassion, being honest, and at times exhibiting courage. It entails dealing effectively with anger and other strong emotions, and having patience.

The suggestions for promoting children's social development and social skill, cited by Honig and Wittmer (1996) (listed in Chapter 6), are still relevant here. You may want to refer to them.

MASLOW'S HIERARCHY OF NEEDS AND ITS RELATION TO SELF-CONTROL

Maslow (1968) attempted to develop a hierarchy of needs, by which people are motivated (see Figure 7–8). He grouped these needs according to whether they were *deficiency* needs or *growth* needs, based on whether the individual was growing in a positive direction. For anyone to grow positively, Maslow felt that the deficiency needs must be filled for the growth needs to be met.

The implications for the children you teach are manifold. The child who is hungry, cold, and—more importantly—unloved, may not be able to grow and learn as we would wish them to. Such a child may be afraid to grow, for fear of losing the security of what is already known. Regardless of how severe or unwholesome that child's current environment may be, there is a certain safety in the known. For this child, growth comes with anxiety.

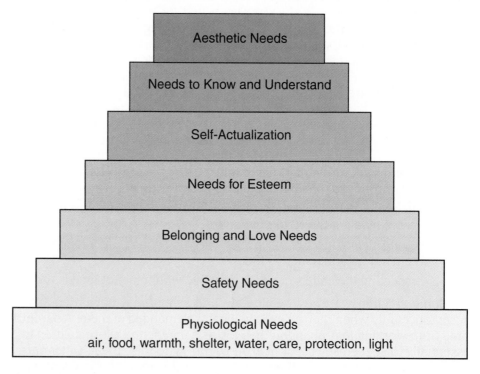

 Figure 7-8
Maslow's hierarchy of needs.

Just as children are different, anxiety and fear in the child may be expressed differently. One fearful, anxious child will withdraw physically from the environment. The child may cling to the mother or the teacher, refuse to try a new activity, and limit participation to what he knows and can do best. Another fearful, anxious child will lash out verbally or physically, sometimes both.

Maslow's hierarchy of needs presents another way of looking at what motivates behavior. The child who is hungry, poorly clothed, and unloved may have difficulty in becoming *self-actualized*, a term Maslow uses to describe the attainment of a certain potential. The same child may have difficulty in developing the natural desire to explore and understand the environment. As stated before, both the overtly aggressive child and the fearful child are under-disciplined.

In studying Maslow's hierarchy, we find that if the goal is to help the child become self-actualized, the child's deficiency needs must first be met. The child's belongingness, love, and esteem needs must be met. Belongingness carries the implication of *family identity*, of belonging to a particular adult or group, and feeling that one is a part of this group. There is psychological safety in having a group to belong to; witness the popularity of cliques and gangs among older students in elementary school. The group is the one that takes care of the physiological needs and makes sure that the environment is safe. The group also allows the growing child to develop self-esteem.

How is self-esteem developed? According to Maslow, it is developed in interaction with the important people in the environment. Look at the following sequence of events. It is morning. The infant cries; the mother goes to the crib, smiles, speaks softly to her, and picks her up. Mother changes the diaper, goes to the kitchen to warm a bottle, or sits down in the rocking chair with the infant to nurse. As the infant feeds, mother coos and speaks to the child and plays with her hand. What is the infant learning? Besides learning that mother is reliable and loving, the baby is learning that she is important to the mother. Later, the child turns over from her stomach onto her back. The mother smiles, claps her hands, and says, "My, aren't you getting big! How smart you are to turn over!" The child is learning that he is physically competent. Self-esteem is developed through the continual interaction between the family, child care workers, and the child. Every time you give positive attention to a child, smile, and notice achievements, you are helping to build the child's self-esteem (see Figure 7–9).

A child from this type of environment will have no difficulty in becoming self-actualized. In contrast, the child whose home environment has not provided for these *deficiency needs* may have difficulty. For this child, you will need to provide those experiences that the child has missed: attention to physiological needs, safety needs, and the need to belong. The loving early childhood teacher or family child care provider can do much to help the child whose own family group has been unable to help.

How does self-actualization relate to self-control? One aspect of self-actualization *is* self-control. The child who is able to self-actualize is able to make choices, accept leader or follower roles, and has a good sense of self. Having a sense of self enables the child to be assertive when appropriate, or to accept directions from another.

Maslow's hierarchy of needs—a theoretical position which attempts to identify human needs and motivations. It describes the consequences of need fulfillment and the consequences of unmet needs on growth.

● **Figure 7-9**
A large part of teaching is giving attention to individual children.

Resiliency

Children are remarkably resilient; they can survive situations that seem almost impossible. Even given a poor beginning, if a child comes into contact with a warm, loving, accepting adult, the child will be able to self-actualize. Children who seem invulnerable or untouched by negative family environments (alcoholism, criminality, poverty, and/or mental illness) are also those children who, during their first year, had at least one significant adult in their lives who cared (Werner & Smith, 1992). This adult could be trusted, thus enabling the children to resolve the question of basic trust. According to Werner and Smith, these children are able to find other adults to whom they can relate in terms of resolving the other tasks of early childhood. These adults meet the children's deficiency needs so that they can self-actualize in spite of negative environments.

Today's world is full of change, uncertainty, and challenge, for everyone, and Breslin (2005) maintains that resiliency must be a primary concern. She states, "Resiliency is not a fixed attribute. Rather it is a set of protective mechanisms that modify a person's response to risk situations." She identifies four factors for teachers to examine in resilient children:

1. they have a heightened sensory awareness
2. they have high, positive expectations for themselves
3. they have a clear and developing understanding of their strengths relating to any accomplishment
4. they have a heightened, developing sense of humor

Implications for Teachers

To summarize theorists' suggestions regarding the promotion of self-control, let us briefly look at each. Erikson relates self-control with resolving the question of autonomy, the task of toddlers. According to Maslow, self-control relates to the resolution of deficiency needs and the beginnings of self-actualization. Burton White's theory indicates that self-control develops as the child passes from Phase V to Phase VI in a healthy, positive environment with caring, loving parents and caregivers. The child who has gained mastery over the environment gains self-control. Goleman, Mayer and Salovey would suggest that the child with emotional intelligence, who can self-regulate, has self-awareness. Furthermore, her empathy for others and ability to monitor her behavior all exhibit self-control. Gillespie and Seibel (2006) would also agree.

Self-esteem theory would suggest that self-control is related to self-worth; when provided with acceptance, respect, and clearly stated classroom rules, children who feel good about themselves will also exhibit self-control. Often, families of these children begin changing and showing interest when their children begin to feel good about themselves.

Sometimes words like *empower* and *belonging* are used to indicate that teachers who empower their students and provide them with a sense of belonging are also teaching them self-control. *Empowerment* means allowing children control over certain aspects of classroom life, choices such as deciding at which learning center they want to study, or what the logical consequences might be for breaking certain classroom rules. For a child, being given the opportunity to feel like a part of the classroom group satisfies the universal need to belong.

What does this mean to you as a teacher? First, you will need to provide the kind of environment where children feel safe and which allows children to grow positively. You must use guidance techniques prudently and recognize, through keen observation, which children need more help than others to learn self-control.

What is meant by saying that you must provide for a safe environment? Aside from the fact that the physical arrangement of the rooms must be safe, it also means consistency of expectations and predictability regarding the schedule and your own behavior. You must remember to use the four *Cs* of discipline. You must *CARE* so that the psychological climate is warm and loving. It means recognizing a child's developmental level in terms of self-control.

If a child has not learned to be autonomous, you will need to provide opportunities that allow the child to practice. As mentioned, it means providing guided choices and allowing practice in decision making. Does the child have a low self-image? Is the child's need to belong unfulfilled? You will need to provide success experiences for this child and a lot of tender, loving care. If this child has at least a sense of belonging in class, this is a start.

You may encounter a negative-acting child who appears to be at Burton White's Phase V and Phase VI stages. What has happened to this child? Most likely, if you check with the family or other primary caregivers, you will find that the child's attempts to explore at Phase V were thwarted. This child was not encouraged to explore the physical environment and master emergent motor abilities. This child may either be too fearful and shy or too aggressive. This child needs opportunities to explore and use motor abilities but needs to be told the limits over and over. This child must be urged ever so gently to try again.

Self-control and self-discipline are learned only through the initial imposition of controls from the significant adults in the child's life, and the opportunity to practice the child's own controls secondarily.

Self-Respect

Young children often want to share accomplishments with peers and caregivers. Requests to "Look at me!" pervade daily teacher-child interactions and help children respect themselves if given teacher attention. Many children take satisfaction in their appropriate behavior and accomplishments and notice the inappropriate behavior of peers. When classrooms model respect, compassion, and concern for others, children gain self-control and self-respect with greater ease. Teachers genuinely try to model the sort of person they hope children will become.

Talking through complications or problem situations with children is one way to help them understand the consequences of different choices. Story discussions also bring to light what choices and consequences occurred for story characters. Most teachers attempt to draw from children what choices exist in life situations and what consequences might follow. This promotes the child's own ability to reflect.

CULTURAL DIFFERENCES

In analyzing student behavior, how do you see cultural differences reflected? The most important factor to remember is to avoid using **stereotypes**. All Asians are not quiet, nor are they all straight-A students, nor are all Asians

 stereotype—a simplified conception or image of a person or group based on race, ethnicity, religion, gender or sexual orientation.

from a single cultural group. All African Americans are not inner-city dwellers, nor do they all speak nonstandard English. All Hispanics are not Mexican or Puerto Rican or Cuban; they come from as many different, separate Hispanic cultures as do Africans, Asians, or Europeans. Among Native Americans, you will note the same great variations, depending on individual cultural backgrounds.

As a teacher, it will be important for you to remain as open-minded as possible, to avoid being tempted to ascribe to culturally diverse students behaviors that may not apply to them as individuals; being open-minded is also the most important factor in establishing a good relationship with the families of culturally diverse children. Listen carefully to what a parent may say. Even if you initially disagree, try to place yourself in the parents' shoes, to see from their perspective. Cultural differences are often immediately apparent. Even an offer to shake hands may not be appropriate. Some parents from India typically greet another person with clasped hands and a bow of the head. A parent from Japan may often bow to his child's teacher, as a sign of respect. A Latina mother may not look you in the eye as she may feel that to do so is disrespectful. Parents from Vietnam may, although legally married, have different names (Berger, 2004).

Certainly one reason for the existence of stereotypes is that when we do not have information, we rely on the news media, typically television, for the "facts." However, bad news sells better than good news, so stories of homicides, robberies, and assaults abound. Because many more of these occur in inner cities than in suburbs, the stereotype develops that because the inner city or barrio or wherever the violence is happening has more people of color living within its confines, all people of that particular race or ethnic group must be prone to violence.

We need to remember that the first African Americans to come to what is now the United States came with Columbus and Coronado, and many more arrived, as did many European Americans, as indentured servants. It was only later that they were brought as slaves (Banks, 2002). We need also remember that Latinos had settled in the southwestern parts of the United States before the first Puritans settled in Massachusetts. If there is any one thing you should always remember about children from minority families in your classroom, it is to recognize their diversity (Berger, 2004). For some excellent ideas of how to avoid stereotyping and bias in your classroom, look at Derman-Sparks's (1989) book, *The Anti-Bias Curriculum: Tools for Empowering Young Children.*

 ## CASE STUDIES

As a student teacher, you may be asked to complete a case study on a child. The assignment frequently requires an in-depth analysis and recording of the child's achievements, development, and learning. Data collection can involve:

- systematic observations
- work samples
- assessments and test results
- samples of creative artwork
- videos, photographs, or tape recordings

- dictations
- anecdotal records (factual notes recording spontaneous events and happenings)
- checklists, inventories, or rating scales
- interviews with the child or others
- home visits and other activities

The kinds of data collected may depend on both your college instructor's assignment criteria and the purpose of the child study. Any materials and data are arranged in chronological order, so assessments can compare earlier with later work and happenings. If student teacher evaluation is required, records document the child's progress and the student teacher's hypotheses. Case study development can often provide the basis for planning a parent-teacher conference.

A strict code of confidentiality and anonymity concerning the child's identity is observed whenever student teachers collect data or share evaluations. A family's presence in the school or classroom makes confidentiality crucial. The temptation for student teachers to discuss their case studies with other adults has led to a few unfortunate and emotionally charged discussions.

Assignments may require a view of the child as a whole, or narrower aspects of the child's development or behavior may be considered. Most training programs assign in-depth case studies, so student teachers can begin to realize the benefits accrued from watching one child intently, and attempting to satisfy curiosity about the *hows* and *whys* of that one child's actions. Student teachers, then, become researchers who reserve judgment, interpret carefully, hypothesize, explore many possible reasons for the observed behavior, and begin to see child development theories in the flesh.

OBSERVATION FORMS

You may have already had a course on observing children, and you may have learned how to use a variety of observation forms. We are going to focus on three: the *narrative* or *anecdotal*, *event sampling*, and *fixed interval* or *time sampling forms*. Then, more importantly, we will demonstrate how to use the information to ask yourself questions and analyze the child's behavior.

Narrative

This is one of the simplest forms to use when observing a child. A narrative describes the child's behavior as it occurs. As an observer, you can sit to one side of the room or yard with a small notebook (see Figure 7–10). After consulting with your cooperating teacher, pick a child to observe and simply record what you see. Your narrative might look something like this:

Case Study 1: Chris
Background

Chris is a four-year-old child whose mother brought him to the preschool during a spring registration period. School policy invites fall registrants to attend class with the current children for a part of the morning session.

● **Figure 7-10**
Observation can take place inside the classroom.

Narrative Observation

(Note: This was written after the events occurred but as accurately remembered as possible.) Chris arrived this morning with the housekeeper. She explained that Chris's mother and father were at work. I said, "Hello. Chris, I have a name tag for you to wear. That way the rest of the children in the class will know your name. See, they all have picture name tags on, too, so you will know who they are." Before I could stick on the name tag, Chris ran through the room to the block center where Jordan and Roberto were building a castle. Before I could turn around, Chris had knocked down the castle and Jordan and Roberto were angry. "Hey!" they shouted, "Watch what you're doing!"

Chris responded, "I want to build a garage for those trucks over there," and pointed to the corner containing several cars and trucks.

"Well, we were building a castle; you'll have to wait your turn. Anyway, why did you knock down our castle? And, hey! Don't you know the rules?"

"Rules, smules, tools, bules! Who cares!" Chris replied. Then he shrugged and ran to the easels where Anya had been painting. To her dismay, Chris grabbed the paint brush from her hand and smeared the painting, causing Anya to break out in tears. My cooperating teacher went to comfort her and nodded at me to follow Chris.

With a smile on his face, Chris ran to the science center, where we keep a hamster, and quickly opened the cage and searched through the wood shavings for the sleepy animal. I chased after him and cautioned him to handle the hamster carefully, but Chris grinned at me and brought his hand out with the hamster in it. Then as I watched, he squeezed it. I immediately removed the hamster gently from Chris's hand, placed it back in its cage, and held Chris by the arm and firmly pulled him to an empty chair near the teacher's desk to talk to him about the rules of the class.

Obviously, the difficulty of a narrative observation is that it either must be re-constructed after the event or the student teacher must remove himself from the action and sit on the side while writing down what he sees. The narrative can be abbreviated somewhat, through the use of an *anecdotal form*. (For an illustration of this narrative in anecdotal form, see Figure 7–11.)

Name of school: <u>ABC Preschool</u> Date: <u>May 14</u>		Student Teacher: <u>MK</u> Class: <u>Four-year-olds</u>
Description of behavior	Time	Comments
C enters, won't wear name tag	9:07	
Runs to block center	9:08	
Knocks down castle J & R had built	9:09	
J & R protest		
C runs to easel, grabs A's paint brush	9:10	What gives w/C?
C smears A's painting	9:10	A cries; CT consoles A
C runs to science center	9:10	I follow
C searches for hamster, picks it up		
and squeezes it	9:12	What a challenge! I intervene. In 5 mins., he almost destroys the room!

Figure 7-11
An anecdotal record form of Chris's Behavior.

Event Sampling

Assuming Chris is one of the regular students in your preschool class, you might want to prepare an event sampling of his daily behavior. The narrative and anecdotal forms presented only a five-minute sampling of Chris's total behavior. Is it always so disruptive? Perhaps completing an event sampling of disruptive versus constructive behavior would give you a clearer picture of Chris's typical behavior.

Take a three by five card and divide it into two columns, label one "Disruptive Behavior" and the other "Constructive Behavior." The recording is simple; throughout the day you simply note each time Chris behaves or misbehaves. At the end of the day you can add the number of times each kind of behavior is observed. You do this for a week. Your purpose in doing this series of event samplings is to determine a baseline of Chris's typical behavior. Once the baseline is determined, you can develop a behavior modification plan to change the behavior. (See the Appendix to Chapter 6 for a sample behavior modification plan.) At the end of the week, you can make a chart that summarizes the event samples taken. It might look something like Figure 7–12.

Analysis of Chris's Behavior

First of all, what do the observations of his initial five minutes in the classroom tell you about Chris? Questions you may want to ask:

- Is this typical behavior?
- What is Chris like at home?
- Has Chris attended any other preschool? If so, where?

Let us assume that the answers are as follows:

- Yes, Chris typically runs from one area of the classroom to another and frequently destroys or tries to destroy the work of the other children. It is only when riding one of the trikes and playing with the large trucks that Chris attends to a task for more than three to five minutes.
- The housekeeper relates that she is unable to control Chris and simply allows him to do whatever he wants. She explains that she is new to the household and that there have been several previous housekeepers. When asked, she did not know how many. Attempts to schedule a parent conference have proved unsuccessful so far. The parents protest that they are too busy. Chris's father owns a successful business and his mother is the financial secretary for the father.
- The housekeeper says that Chris has been enrolled in another preschool but the parents had been asked to remove him because of his behavior.

In considering the different theories introduced, what hypotheses come to mind?

Monday		Tuesday		Wednesday		Thursday		Friday		Average.	
+	-	+	-	+	-	+	-	+	-	+	-
3	10	5	7	6	6	7	9	2	14	4.6	9.2

Figure 7-12
Summary of event sampling of Chris's behavior.

Analysis of Chris's Behavior

Erikson. In looking at the developmental milestones Erikson proposes, it seems reasonably clear that Chris is under-restrained. He has not resolved the task of initiative. It is also likely that he has not resolved the earlier task of autonomy. Chris is showing too much initiative and autonomy; he needs and probably wants clear limits. Being in charge as a four-year-old is frightening; it makes a child feel that something must be wrong. Guilt and shamelessness have developed in Chris—guilt because he instinctively understands that he shouldn't be in charge, shamelessness because Chris sincerely wants set limits. Whether or not Chris has basic trust is another question; it is possible that he has some trust but may not have totally resolved this most basic of developmental tasks.

Burton White. Obviously Chris knows how to gain the attention of adults, but just as obviously, he does not know how to ask for help. He is willing to try and do everything; he will not admit that he may need help. If he cannot complete a task, he throws a tantrum. Does Chris show affection or mild annoyance? Chris resists being hugged and, when frustrated, usually becomes angry, breaks something, throws a toy, or whatever object may be close at hand, or fights with his peers. Can he lead or follow peers? Here again is a problem: Chris shows some leadership ability but often has difficulty asserting himself without becoming aggressive. And he definitely does not follow others.

Goleman/Mayer/Salovey. Concerning emotional intelligence, Chris has difficulty. He cannot identify his own feelings, much less those of his peers. Just as obviously, Chris is unable to manage his feelings or delay gratification. He does not use self-talk nor is he able to understand the perspective of another child. Many of his verbal comments are demands, criticisms of his peers, and aggressive, non-verbal behaviors.

Maslow. While Chris has his physiological and safety needs met, it is doubtful whether his belongingness and esteem needs have been met fully. He does not talk about his parents, although he brags about his toys, the television programs he likes to watch, and the computer games he knows how to play on his PlayStation and X-Box.

Implications for the teacher. The number one need for Chris is firm limits on his behavior. He needs clear expectations and much *CARE*ing. You will need to make it clear what the rules of the classroom are and repeat them frequently. Your cooperating teacher will follow through on scheduling a conference with Chris's parents and, if possible, gently suggest that they take a more active, decisive role in raising their son. Your cooperating teacher may want you to sit in on a conference with the school psychologist or counselor.

Fixed Interval (Time Sampling)

Case Study 2: Maya
Background

Maya is a bright-eyed, eight-year-old student in the third grade. She is slightly taller than many of her age peers and enjoys excellent health. Her parents are supportive of her schooling and both attend family-teacher conferences. Her father is a computer engineer; her mother is an accountant. She has a brother in the first grade at the same school. The two children usually walk to and from school together and appear to have a close relationship.

Fixed-Interval (Time Sampling) Observation Form

Look at Figure 7–13. Note that the student teacher made an observation—with few exceptions—every five minutes, and tried to describe what was happening. However, she does insert her assumptions more than once but places her comments in parentheses. Based on these observations, what might you conclude about Maya? Has she resolved the tasks appropriate to her age?

Child: Maya
T = teacher
St = Student; Ss = students

Grade: 3rd
Date: 12 October

8:30 A.M.:	Enters classroom, places lunch box & jacket in cubby
8:30 A.M.:	Sits at desk, talks to J. (a student in her group), ignores math "sponge" activity on board
8:40 A.M.:	Still talks to J.
8:45 A.M.:	(Bell rings)
	(I was busy taking roll & lunch count; didn't note what M. was doing)
8:50 A.M.:	Talks to G. (another St. in her group)
	(Should be saying Pledge of Allegiance and completing math "sponge" activity on chalkboard)
8:55 A.M.:	(T. reminds children that 1st activity of the A.M. will begin at 9:00 & that "sponge" problems are to be placed in her "in-basket")
	Maya quickly completes problems & turns in paper
9:00 A.M.:	All Ss sitting quietly on carpet squares, choosing centers; Maya waves hand excitedly; "Writing center! Writing center!"
	T reminds her that she has been in the writing center for the past two days and that others like the writing center, too
	"Why not try the math center, Maya?" T. suggests
9:05 A.M.:	Maya pouts, "But, I want to go to the writing center"
9:10 A.M.:	Still pouting but goes to math center where tangram puzzles and pieces are arranged to stimulate problem-solving
9:15 A.M.:	M. complains, "These tangrams are too easy! Can I make some of my own?" T. says "Of course, Maya; maybe you'd like to have B. work with you?" "No!" . . . emphatically said
9:25 A.M.:	M. working very carefully
9:30 A.M.:	M. still working carefully
9:45 A.M.:	(I'm too busy; unable to check on M.)
9:50 A.M.:	M. looks intent on creating a new design
9:55 A.M.:	T. rings a bell & warns Ss they have five min to finish their center work; reminds those who haven't that they can finish after recess
10:00 A.M.:	M. says, "I'm nearly finished with my design; may I stay in for recess and work on it?" T. suggests to M. that she should get some fresh air and exercise too; M. groans but agrees

(I have yard duty this A.M. recess and I notice that Maya is off by herself drawing in the dirt. I wonder if she's still working on her new tangram design or dreaming up a new one. As I approach her, she quickly erases what she's been working on.)

 Figure 7-13
Fixed interval or time sampling model

Analysis of Maya's Behavior

Erikson. Given her desire to compose her own tangram patterns, it would seem that Maya is clearly working to resolve the task of industry. This also reveals some degree of initiative. Maya also appears to have resolved the task of autonomy. Maya's supportive family and good relationships with her brother would seem to reveal basic trust. Trust can also be seen in Maya's relationships with her teacher and her peers. Her social exchanges with peers in her group may indicate follower and leadership abilities, but this particular set of observations does not.

Burton White. Maya clearly is able to get and hold the attention of adults and is able to express affection and mild annoyance. Certainly she takes pride in her accomplishments and appears to be able to deal with abstractions, as she designs her own tangram patterns. Her use of language is sophisticated for an eight-year-old and likely is a reflection of her parents' language interactions with her, though she converses easily with her table group and other peers.

Goleman/Mayer/Salovey. If we look at what researchers have proposed regarding emotional intelligence, Maya reveals a high degree of self-awareness and the ability to modulate her emotional responses. She can focus on a task for an extended period of time and has a sunny and positive outlook on life. If she has areas that still need to be developed, they are not obvious. We did not note much give and take with her peers except during the sponge activity, but she plays on a youth soccer team; you plan to attend one of her upcoming games to observe more fully her interactions with peers.

Maslow. Maya is well cared for; she looks well fed and you have noticed that the lunches she brings from home are nutritious. She is always clean and dressed well but not ostentatiously. Her deficiency needs are strongly met: she has no physiological, safety, belongingness and love, or esteem difficulties. Her desire to work by herself in the classroom would suggest a need to know and understand, an example of self-actualization.

Implications for the teacher. Maya is one of those students who could easily become the teacher's pet, and the major problem for you as her teacher is to avoid letting this happen. You enjoy her quick mind, her eagerness to learn, her supportive family, and good relationships with both peers and adults. Maya displays a great amount of curiosity and especially enjoys challenges such as math puzzles and experiments in science. More than once her parents have mentioned that Maya has wanted to try at home an experiment completed at school. Maya enthusiastically told you about trying out spraying her mother's perfume atomizer to explore the diffusion of smell in the air and of placing food color in water to see how it diffused. The best advice for a student like Maya is to enjoy her!

Case Study 3: Stevie
Background

Stevie is a late-admit, five-year-old child at ABC School's child care center. He has difficulty separating from his mother, and the teacher is sensitive to this. As the student teacher in the room, you note that your cooperating teacher frequently kneels by Stevie and directs his attention to the block center, where Hiroku is playing. The teacher has mentioned that having Stevie play by Hiroku might help Stevie adjust more smoothly, as Hiroku is one of the more mature children at the center. The cooperating teacher has asked you to prepare an event sampling of Stevie's play behaviors, to provide additional information about the boy and to help understand his behavior at the center. A *two-dimensional play model*, combining event and time sampling, may be found in Figure 7–14.

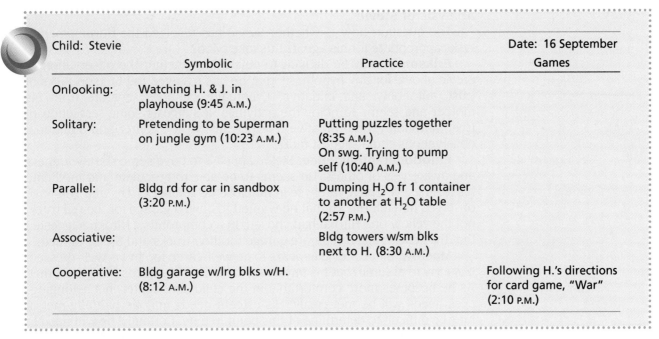

Child: Stevie			Date: 16 September
	Symbolic	Practice	Games
Onlooking:	Watching H. & J. in playhouse (9:45 A.M.)		
Solitary:	Pretending to be Superman on jungle gym (10:23 A.M.)	Putting puzzles together (8:35 A.M.) On swg. Trying to pump self (10:40 A.M.)	
Parallel:	Bldg rd for car in sandbox (3:20 P.M.)	Dumping H_2O fr 1 container to another at H_2O table (2:57 P.M.)	
Associative:		Bldg towers w/sm blks next to H. (8:30 A.M.)	
Cooperative:	Bldg garage w/lrg blks w/H. (8:12 A.M.)		Following H.'s directions for card game, "War" (2:10 P.M.)

Figure 7-14
Two-dimensional play model, combining event and time sampling

In looking at play behavior, two theorists come to mind: Parten (1932) and Piaget (1962). Parten divided play behaviors into the following categories:
- *Onlooking play* (play without reference to another child)
- *Solitary play* (play by oneself)
- *Parallel play* (play in which two or more children may be using similar materials but without personal interaction)
- *Associative play* (play with objects in which two or more children are using the same materials but each child is doing a separate activity; for example, each child is using some of the blocks but building separate structures)
- *Cooperative play* (play in which there is a common goal toward which two or more children are working; for example, the children are using the blocks to build one house)

Piaget suggested that there are three types of play common among preschoolers.
- *Symbolic play* (play in which the objects with which the child is playing become something else; for example, blocks become a garage or a house)
- *Practice play* (play in which the child continuously repeats an activity as though to master it; for example, repeatedly going down a slide)
- *Games* (Play in which children follow a set of agreed-upon rules)

The resulting observation form, Figure 7–14, shows how the play activities of Stevie may be recorded. To provide more information, note the time of each play activity. In looking at Figure 7–14 you can see that on the Parten dimensions Stevie uses solitary and parallel play more than associative or cooperative. Using Piaget's dimensions, we see that Stevie uses symbolic and practice play more frequently than play with games. For a new child in the center these behaviors may not be unusual.

Analysis of Stevie

The question now is whether Stevie has resolved the developmental tasks appropriate for his age. Let us take a look.

Erikson. It may be difficult to determine whether the observation of Stevie allows for any hypothesis that he has resolved the Erikson tasks of trust, autonomy, and initiative. Eventually, he does separate from his mother and seems to enjoy the activities. It suggests some resolution of trust, autonomy, and initiative. Further time in the center and additional observations could suggest more.

Emotional intelligence. Stevie appears to have some self-awareness and awareness of others. He seems to be able to articulate and modulate his feelings; you have rarely seen him lose his temper or cry, and you have observed him tell Hiroku that he wanted to build a garage for the red truck, not the yellow one Hiroku had chosen. In a compromise, Hiroku suggested that they each build a separate garage for their trucks and Stevie agreed.

Maslow. Since Stevie appears to be well-cared for and is well-dressed, it is easy to assume that his physiological and safety needs have been met. As he becomes more comfortable in the child care center, his belongingness needs will be met easily. His esteem needs may be partially met; it may be difficult to determine at this point in time. Certainly, he will need to have opportunities to self-actualize.

Implications for the teacher. As the student teacher in the center, your cooperating teacher may ask you to be a special friend to Stevie. After she greets him each morning, she may ask you to plan an activity with Stevie and another child, Hiroku perhaps initially, adding another child later. Whatever activity is planned, it should be one calculated to stimulate the interests of both. Block play might be a place to start, as you've noticed that both boys enjoy playing and building with them. Later, as Stevie's interests broaden, you can plan something else. In becoming a special friend with Stevie you may help him feel more a part of the group. And as you introduce him to activities with some of the other children, again, Stevie's needs to belong will be met. As his deficiency needs are met, Stevie will have opportunities to self-actualize.

THE ROLES OF A STUDENT TEACHER

One role, already defined, is that of an observer. During your first days of placement, you will often be given opportunities to observe. This is an especially valuable time for both the student teacher and the cooperating teacher. Take advantage of this period. Observe several children carefully; confer with your cooperating teacher, supervisor, and peers. It is a fascinating learning experience to listen to someone else's perceptions of your observations. Often, we become emotionally involved with the children whom we observe; thus, we may receive a different perspective from those who do not know them as well, or who know them better, as might our cooperating teacher. This situation may be reversed. Some cooperating teachers know that their judgments of children may be obscured by the knowledge of the children's backgrounds. A student teacher's judgment, in contrast, may not be affected by this factor.

A second role student teachers frequently play is that of being a friend to a child who, according to your cooperating teacher, needs one. This friendship role may help a newly enrolled child feel more comfortable in the classroom, and may help a shy child become more outgoing.

A third role is obviously to plan activities or lessons and to teach. As do young children, student teachers also learn best by doing.

SUMMARY

In this chapter, we have presented several different theories to help you analyze children's behaviors, together with suggestions to implement in your attempt to help children learn self-control. Among theorists mentioned were Erikson, Maslow, Goleman, Mayer, Salovey, and Burton White.

In terms of the Erikson tasks, the one most closely related to self-control is autonomy. If resolved during toddlerhood, teachers see a child who knows how to play and work within the prescribed limits of any classroom, who understands both leadership and follower roles, who knows when to ask for help and when he can do a task by himself. Ideas for teachers to implement in the classroom for children who have incompletely resolved autonomy were also given: allowing choices and reminding children of limits and rules are two.

Maslow believed that self-control evolved out of self-esteem (as do the self-concept theorists) and self-actualization. Thus, everything a teacher can do to build self-esteem and a feeling of belongingness in the classroom, and, again, to allow choices, all will lead to children with good self-control.

White focuses on infants during their first explorations with mobility, an event that usually comes between 8 and 24 months. Given appropriate toys, and the freedom to explore within safe limits, active babies and toddlers develop into healthy, happy preschoolers.

Theorists, looking at emotional intelligence, would suggest that self-control grows out of the child's self-awareness and ability to self-modulate feelings. Afterwards the child develops awareness of others and gains empathy for others.

Finally, we presented you with the case studies of three children, Chris, Maya, and Stevie and gave some suggestions, related to the different theories, designed to help you understand their behavior. Implications for the teacher and your role as a student teacher were also presented.

HELPFUL WEB SITES

http://www.aecf.org
Annie E. Casey Foundation—Kids Count. Search for *Kids Count* Data Book; state profiles of child well being are included.

http://www.nccic.org
National Child Care Information Center (NCCIC). Search infant and toddler topics.

http://www.ericeece.org
ERIC. Many topics related to early childhood and elementary education are covered here, such as strategies to enhance the achievement of gifted minority children.

http://www.apa.org
American Psychological Association. Look for readings in early childhood.

http://www.zerotothree.org
Zero to Three: National Center for Infants, Toddlers, and Families. This site offers a wide range of material.

 Additional resources for this chapter can be found by visiting the Online Companion at www.earlychilded.delmar.com.

SUGGESTED ACTIVITIES

A. With your cooperating teacher's approval, select a child to observe. Try some of the observation forms presented. Discuss the results of data gathered with your peers, cooperating teacher, and supervisor.

B. Read the following Case Study of Maria (see Figure 7–15, an anecdotal observation). Discuss the case with your peers and supervisor.

Identity Key (do NOT use real name)	Description of What Child Is Doing	Time	Comments
M. — Maria T. — Teacher ST. — Student Teacher S. — Susie J. — Janine B. — Bobby Sv. — Stevie	M. arrives at school. Clings to mother's hand, hides behind her skirt. Thumb in mouth.	9:05	Ask T. how long M. has been coming. I bet she's new.
	M. goes over to puzzle rack, chooses a puzzle, goes to table. Dumps out, and works puzzle quickly and quietly. B. & Sv. come over to work puzzles they've chosen. M. looks at them, says nothing, goes to easels, watches S. paint. S. asks M. if she wants to paint. M. doesn't answer.	9:22 9:30	Her eye/hand coordination seems good. I wonder why M. doesn't respond. Ask T. if M. has hearing problem.
	M. comes to snack table, sits down where T. indicates she should. Does not interact with other children table.	10:15	Is M. ever a quiet child.
	M. stands outside of playhouse, watches S. & J. They don't ask her to join them.	10:47	She looks like she'd like to play.
	M. goes right to swings, knows how to pump.	10:55	Nothing wrong with her coordination.
	During Hap Palmer record M. watches others, does not follow directions.	11:17	Hearing? Maybe limited English? (She looks of Spanish background.)

Student Teacher: _____

Name of School: _____   Date: _____

Figure 7-15
Anecdotal record on Maria

Background: It is the beginning of the school year. As the student teacher, you have just been placed in a bilingual kindergarten. Many parents choose Adelante School because of its attention to providing lessons in both languages. One student intrigues you. Maria arrives each morning accompanied by her mother and a younger sibling in a stroller. She appears to be in good health; her hair is always carefully brushed and she usually wears a bow in her ponytail. Her clothes are always clean. She generally joins in music and art lessons enthusiastically but is reluctant to participate in reading and math activities. You often have had to persuade her to come to the carpeted circle for story time. During recesses she doesn't interact with the other children, choosing instead to go to the swings or stand to one side by herself, watching the others.

What questions come to mind about Maria? Do you think she has resolved the Erikson tasks appropriate for her age? Have her deficiency needs been met (Maslow)? Does she show emotional intelligence in her behavior, or do you need to observe her more closely? Does she show self-awareness? Has she established any relationship with the cooperating teacher, you, or any of her peers?

(Note: There are no absolute answers to the above questions. They are meant solely to direct your thoughts.)

C. You are concerned because Tahira, a student in your third grade room, is frequently absent. An eager-to-learn child, she does poorly on tests, and when she turns in her homework, it is often incomplete. Your cooperating teacher is also concerned, and she suggests that you sit in on a conference she has arranged with Tahira's mother, to help you understand. At the conference, you discover that Mrs. Bhas often keeps Tahira home to take care of her younger brother and sister whenever one or both of them are ill. Your cooperating teacher explains that it is necessary for the child to be in school, but Mrs. Bhas demurs, "Tahira is my oldest girl; she knows she is supposed to help me. I work, and it's Tahira's duty to take care of her younger brothers and sister after school, or when they are sick. I know that education is important but I need Tahira's help at home at times."

In view of Mrs. Bhas's expectations for her daughter, what might your cooperating teacher suggest? How might she try to convince her that she thinks a third grader is too young to babysit, and that there are state attendance laws to obey? Do any of the theories discussed in our chapter help you in understanding your dilemma about Tahira?

Applying Erikson's theory might indicate the satisfactory completion of basic trust, but is autonomy or initiative an expectation set for Tahira by Mr. and Mrs. Bhas? It is more likely that being quiet and obedient (that is, doing as mother and father ask) are practices more valued by her parents than are independence, exploration, and curiosity. One approach your cooperating teacher might take is to ask Mrs. Bhas what her occupation is, to determine whether or not education is needed. Her response could be, "We own several motels in town and my job, and Tahira's and her sister's on the weekends, is to see that linens are changed, beds are made, and rooms are cleaned." Or the response could be, "Mr. Bhas is a software designer and often works at home. My job is to ensure that the house is run smoothly, meals are prepared on time, and that the children are quiet and do not interfere with their father while he's working."

Using Maslow's hierarchy might point out the satisfactory completion of the deficiency needs, but interference with Tahira's need to know and understand, by her parents' expectations.

D. Read the following descriptions of behavior. For each child, analyze his or her behavior using the theories of Erikson, Burton White, Maslow, the emotional intelligence theorists, or the self-esteem theorists.

1. Denise, a five-year-old kindergartner, is sitting on the swing.

"Teacher, teacher, come push me," she demands.

"Try to pump, Denise," responds the teacher.

"I don't know how," Denise whines.

"Push me, Ashley," Denise calls to a child riding by on a tricycle.

"I can't now. Push yourself," answers Ashley.

Ryan comes to the swing. "Get off and let me swing," he demands.

"No! My swing!" Denise cries.

The assistant teacher comes over and says, "Ryan, you can have the next turn. Denise, do you want me to show you how to make the swing go?"

Denise answers, "Please."

2. The following chart, Figure 7–16, was developed by Juan, a student teacher in a second grade classroom. He was interested in Anthony's attending behavior. He developed a simple form to check off observations as he noticed them, throughout the 9:00 A.M. to 10:00 A.M. activity hour. On a 3 x 5 card, which he could hold in his hand, Juan drew a vertical line, dividing the card in half lengthwise. Then he wrote "Attending" on one side, "Nonattending" on the other. Question: How much attending behavior should a teacher expect of a second grade student during a free-choice center activity?

3. Michaela is a three-and-a-half-year-old attending a morning preschool. Look at the two-dimensional play model, combining event and time sampling, which was

		Attending	Nonattending	
Mon.	9:05	yes (t.i.)*		
	9:16		no	(sitting under desk)
	9:27		no	
	9:40		no	
	9:48	yes (t.i.)		
Tues.	9:07		no	
	9:18		no	
	9:25	yes (t.i.)		
	9:34	yes		
	9:40		no	(sitting under the desk
	9:47		no	again)
	9:55		no	
Wed.	9:02		no	
	9:12	yes (t.i.)		
	9:20	yes (t.i.)		
	9:35		no	
	9:42		no	
	9:58		no	
Thurs.	9:05		no	
	9:15	yes (t.i.)		
	9:33	yes		
	9:48		no	(back under the desk again)
	9:55		no	
Fri.	Anthony was absent			
*t.i. = teacher initiated				

● **Figure 7-16**
Attending/nonattending chart

used to gather data in Figure 7–17. Questions: Do three-year-olds do as much onlooking and solitary play as Michaela? Should the teacher be concerned?

4. Angel is a four-year-old at a private child care center. Figure 7–18 is a time sample of his behavior during outside free play. Questions: Is Angel's poor gross motor coordination something that should concern his teacher? Was there any theorist in this chapter whose theory might explain anything about motor development?

E. Read the following excerpt (Grey, 1995). Discuss the questions at the end of the paragraph with a group of classmates.

A kindergarten teacher is trying to reinforce the behavior of a child who has voluntarily carried out a classroom rule.

She says to him, "Good job, Tom! You're doing just what you're supposed to do, aren't you? You're always such a good boy."

The message to Tom is not about his intrinsic worth, but about his value when he does what his teacher wants him to. If Tom's teacher truly wants to affirm Tom's intrinsic worth, as he expressed it through his desire to participate competently in classroom culture, she might say, "I saw you carry all the dirty paintbrushes to the sink, Tom. You had to make three trips to get them all! I sure appreciate your help."

Child: Michaela			Date: 17 Nov.
	Symbolic	Practice	Games
Onlooking:	Watches three girls in playhouse, when asked to join, shakes head no. (9:35 A.M.)	Watches children go up & down slide. (10:22 A.M.)	
	Watches M. & A. at easels. T. asks, "Do you want to paint, M.?" "No." (11:05 A.M.)	Watches children in sandbox, filling cups & pails over & over. (10:35 A.M.)	
		Watches children on swing. (10:45 A.M.)	
Solitary:	"See my cracker? It's a plane!" Zooms cracker thru air; makes plane sounds. (10:03 A.M.)	Sits on swing while teacher's aide pushes. (10:50 A.M.)	
Parallel:	Picks up egg beater at H$_2$O table. Beats H$_2$O. Says, "I'm making eggs for breakfast." (11:12 A.M.)	Picks up paintbrush at easel; lets paint drip. Picks up next brush. Repeats with remaining brushes. (11:35 A.M.)	

● **Figure 7-17**
Observation sample

If Tom regularly hears the unspoken message in the first scenario, how is he likely to apply it to himself? How do you think this message will affect his ability to make judgments for himself?

Would he have a different sense of his competence if he regularly received the message in the second sample?

10:05 a.m.:	A. runs stiffly toward two of his friends on tricycles. "Let me ride!" he shouts.
10:10 a.m.:	A. is happily riding on the back of E.'s tricycle. E. has to stop to let A. climb on. A. first placed his left foot on, lifted it off, placed the same foot on again, took it off; finally he put his right foot on and then successfully put his left foot on.
10:15 a.m.:	A. is still riding on the back of E.'s tricycle.
10:20 a.m.:	A. and E. have switched places. A. had difficulty pedaling up the slight grade. E. pushed from behind.
10:25 a.m.:	E. has suggested that he, A., and S. go to the workbench. A. picks up the hammer and a nail. He hits the nail awkwardly into a block of wood. E. says, "Hey, watch me! Hold the nail like this!"
10:30 a.m.:	E. is holding A.'s hands with his, showing him how to drive the nail into the block of wood.
10:35 a.m.:	A. is sitting in the sandbox, shoveling sand into a bucket. E. is still at the work bench.
10:40 a.m.:	A. is putting sand into another bucket. He looks surprised when the bucket overflows. He reaches for the first bucket. S. says, "I'm using it now," and pushes a third pail toward A.
10:45 a.m.:	A. and S. are smoothing down the sand, calling it a road. They go and get a couple of cars to run on their road. E. joins them, having completed his project at the workbench.
10:50 a.m.:	When called to clean up for activity time, A. climbs out of the sandbox. As he does this, his foot catches on the edge and he falls down. He gives the sandbox a kick and joins the others to come inside.

● **Figure 7-18**
Observation time sample

◉REVIEW

A. According to Erikson, what are the first four stages of psychosocial development? What are the tasks associated with each?

B. Read the following description of behavior and answer the questions at the end.

Cindy, an only child, is a small, assertive three-and-a-half-year-old attending your child center for the first time. Her family recently moved to your community. Her mother and father are both teachers in local school districts. Her mother reported that Cindy's birth was normal, and she has had no major health problems. Coming to your child center will be her first experience with children her own age, except for religious instruction school.

Cindy appears to like child care very much. She is a dominant child despite her small size, and rapidly becomes one of the leaders. She plays with just about all of the toys and materials supplied at the center. Her favorite activities, however, appear to be the dramatic-play center and easel painting when inside, and either the sandbox or swings when outside. She occasionally gets into arguments with her peers when they no longer accept her leadership. Cindy has difficulty resolving these conflicts and frequently has a tantrum when she is unable to have her own way.

1. Would you suggest that Cindy has basic trust? What evidence suggests this?
2. Do you think Cindy has resolved the task of autonomy? What evidence suggests that?
3. Erikson would suggest that Cindy's task at age three-and-a-half is to learn to use initiative. What evidence is there in the brief description of her behavior that suggests she is going through this phase of development in a positive or negative way?
4. Using Maslow's hierarchy of needs, at which level would you place Cindy? Why?

C. List the seven phases of development that occur during a child's first three years, according to Burton White.

D. List five characteristics of an autonomous, six-year-old child with positive self-esteem.

E. Identify each of the following statements as either an observation or an inference (opinion).
1. Jonathon likes to read.
2. Tiffany has a new t-shirt.
3. Brandon can be a mean boy.
4. Kimberly has emotional problems.
5. Stefanie is smiling.
6. Kevin hit Sandel on the playground.
7. Jennifer has a frown on her face.
8. Alexander looks unhappy.
9. Alyssa likes to play with clay.
10. Aaron is an affectionate child.

CASE SCENARIO

Setting: A private parochial school near a residential parochial college. Ron, a student teacher recently assigned to a second grade classroom, is complaining to his cooperating teacher, Mrs. Kuefner.

"I simply don't understand why the kids behave for you but won't for me." Ron says. "What am I doing wrong?"

"Some of the things you are doing are right; don't forget that!" Mrs. Kuefner replies encouragingly. "But just reminding the children the first day you started to teach that you would abide by the same rules that I

continues . . .

. . . continued

had established with them isn't enough. What do you think their talking, snickering, and lack of attention shows?"

"That they don't like me!" complains Ron.

"Didn't you learn about reasons students misbehave?" queries Mrs. Kuefner.

"The classroom management course was a year ago!" Ron states. "Now is when I need it!"

"Do you know where the children come from?" Mrs. Kuefner asks.

"Aren't most of them local?" asks Ron. "I know we have children from various ethnic backgrounds, and some whose families are immigrants, but I think most of them must be middle class, right?"

"To answer your questions, you might want to do a getting-to-know-you activity. And, incidentally, you should answer the same questions you pose for the students, so that they get to know *you* better," Mrs. Kuefner suggests. "And you should know that some of our students are here on a scholarship. Remember, too, I would

need to see any proposed questionnaire prior to your implementing it.

"That still doesn't answer my question about what seems to be their disrespect of me," Ron says. "Before I started taking over for you, I was sure they liked me and thought of me as a friend."

Mrs. Kuefner sighs. "You know the answer to that: before you can be a friend, you first have to be a teacher. And as a teacher, you need to establish your own authority; you can't just ride on mine. Think about that, please. And maybe talk to Dr. To, your university supervisor."

Questions for Discussion:

1. Have you ever had the same problem as Ron? Did you also want to be a friend, and as a result, were reluctant to make students adhere to classroom rules?

2. Is reminding students on your first day of teaching that your cooperating teacher's rules were the same as yours enough? Why?

3. What should Ron do now to establish discipline in his classroom?

REFERENCES

Banks, J. A. (2002). *Teaching strategies for ethnic studies* (7th ed.). Boston: Allyn & Bacon.

Berger, E. H. (2004). *Parents as partners in education: The school and home working together* (6th ed.). Upper Saddle River, NJ: Pearson/Merrill/Prentice Hall.

Breslin, D. (2005). Children's capacity to develop resiliency: How to nurture it. *Young Children, 60*(1), 47–52.

Butterfield, P., Martin, C. A., & Prairie, A. P. (2004). *Emotional connections: how relationships guide early learning.* Washington, DC: Zero to Three Press.

Coopersmith, S. (1967). *The antecedents of self-esteem.* New York: W. H. Freeman.

Derman-Sparks, L. D. (1989). *The anti-bias curriculum: Tools for empowering young children.* Washington, DC: National Association for the Education of Young Children.

Elias M. J., Zins, J. E., Weissberg, R. P., Frey, K. S., Greenberg, M. T., Haynes, N. M., Kessler, R., Schwab-Stone, M. E., & Shriver, T. P. (1997). *Promoting social and emotional learning: Guidelines for educators.* Alexandria, VA: Association for Supervision and Curriculum Development.

Erikson, E. H. (1993). *Childhood and society* (reprint of 2nd ed.). New York: Norton.

Gillespie, L. G., & Seibel, N. L. (2006). Self-regulation: A cornerstone of early childhood development. *Young Children, 61*(4), 34–39.

Goleman, D. (1995, 1997). *Emotional intelligence: Why it can matter more than IQ.* New York: Bantam Books.

Gratz, R. R., & Boulton, P. J. (1996, July). Erikson and early childhood educators: Looking at ourselves and our profession developmentally. *Young Children, 51*(5).

Greenspan, S. & Greenspan, N.T. (1985). *First feelings.* New York: Penguin.

Grey, K. (1995, July/August). Not in praise of praise. *Child Care Information Exchange, 104.*

Honig, A. S., & Wittmer, D. S. (1996, January). Helping children become more prosocial: Ideas for classrooms, families, schools, and communities. *Young Children, 51*(2), 62-70.

Hyson, M. (2002, November). Emotional development and school readiness. *Young Children, 57*(6), 76–78.

Hyson, M. (2004). *The emotional development of the young child: building an emotion-centered curriculum.* New York: Teachers' College, Columbia University.

Lally, J. R. (1995, November). The impact of child care policies and practices on infant/toddler identity formation. *Young Children, 51*(1).

Maslow, A. H. (1968). *Toward a psychology of being* (2nd ed.). Princeton, NJ: Van Nostrand Reinhold.

Mayer, J., & Salovey, P. (1995). Emotional intelligence and the construction and regulation of feelings. *Applied and Preventive Psychology, 4*(2).

Parten, M. B. (1932). Social participation among preschool children. *Journal of Abnormal and Social Psychology, 27* (3), 243-269.

Piaget, J. (1962). *Play, dreams, and imitation in childhood.* New York: W. W. Norton.

Werner, E., & Smith, R. S. (1992). *Overcoming the odds.* New York: Cornell University Press.

White, B. L. (1975). *The first three years of life.* Englewood Cliffs, NJ: Prentice Hall.

CHAPTER 8

Working with Children with Special Needs

OBJECTIVES

After reading this chapter, you should be able to:

1. .... Define *special*.

2. .... List at least five characteristics of *special* children.

3. .... State the categories of special need according to the Individuals with Disabilities Education Act, PL 101–476.

4. .... Discuss the concept of least restrictive environment.

5. .... Discuss the implications of least restrictive environment to the teacher of an early childhood program.

6. .... Discuss the implications of recent special education laws for preschools, child care centers, and elementary schools.

Comments of student teachers:

> *Just when I thought I knew the characteristics of two-year-olds well, along came Gregory! He taught me to look for new ways to reach individual children.*

Danielle Tracy

> *I was asked to work with one of the children who had a learning disability. I really got involved in what was happening in the child's home. I became interested in the child's life.*

Deanna Miller

> *When I started student teaching in Ms. Hessler's first grade class, I wondered who Jessica was. She always had an aide who seemed to work only with her. She wouldn't always look at me when I spoke to her. What a surprise to learn she was supposedly autistic! I never would have guessed!*

Brianna Fitzgerald

> *At first I had real problems understanding Eric; his speech was so full of mispronunciations. It surprised me that his classmates seemed to know exactly what he was trying to say. Before I finished student teaching, though, I too had little difficulty understanding him.*

Samantha Hope Maier

LAWS RELATING TO THE EDUCATION OF YOUNG CHILDREN WITH SPECIAL NEEDS

We know that most of you think all children are special; so do we. However, it is important to recognize that some children have needs beyond those of the average child; some have needs that can be met only by a team of specialists, working together for the welfare of the children. To meet the needs of special children, the federal government has passed several laws related to people with special needs (see Figure 8–1). Although the first law was passed over 40 years ago (PL 89–313, 1965), the primary laws that currently define how preschools, child care centers, and public schools are to serve special needs children are PL 94–142, PL 99–457, and PL 101–476 and its subsequent amendments.

PL 89-313	(1965)	Provided federal funds to establish early intervention programs for "children with disabilities," birth to age five. (Voluntary.)
PL 90-538	(1968)	Established the Handicapped Children's Early Education Program (HCEEP), now the Early Education Program for Children with Disabilities (EEPCD). (Voluntary initially.)
PL 91-230	(1969)	Provided funds to states for the education of "young children with disabilities." (Voluntary.)
PL 93-644	(1974)	Amended Head Start legislation and required that 10 percent of children served must be those with disabilities.
PL 94-142	(1975)	The Education for All Handicapped Children Act; discussed in detail in this chapter.
PL 98-199	(1983)	Provided grants to states to plan, develop, and implement a service delivery system for handicapped children, birth through age five. (Mandatory for states receiving federal funds.)
PL 99-457	(1986)	Again provided funds to states to plan services for children, birth through age five, as a condition to receiving further federal funds. (Essentially, then, became mandatory.) Also discussed in this chapter.
PL 101-336	(1990)	Americans with Disabilities Act: Required that individuals with disabilities, including children, have equal access to public and private services.
PL 101-476	(1990)	The Individuals with Disabilities Act (IDEA); discussed in this chapter.*
PL 102-119	(1991)	Allowed states up to two years to implement PL 101-476 (IDEA), because of differences between fiscal years of some states and federal government.

In 1994 through 2006, PL 101-476 has been evaluated and refunded. Since the passage of IDEA in 1997, the emphasis in making placements for special needs children has been on inclusion, IDEA could be seen as the Inclusion of the Disabled in Education Act (Lewis & Doorlag, 2003).

*This act has been evaluated and refunded. The act (IDEA) has emphasized the inclusion of children with special needs (Lewis & Doorlag, 2003).

Figure 8-1
Public laws related to special education for young children.

Individuals with Disabilities Act, PL 101–476

The provisions of this law reaffirm many of the provisions of PL 94–142, but include amendments related to specific categories of exceptionality, and additional services. The key provisions are:

- Free and appropriate public education will be made available for all children with special needs (included are special education and related services, the use of the term "children with disabilities," and the stipulation of age restrictions of 3 to 21 years; states with programs for children from birth to age three are also covered).

- Each child identified as needing special education or related services must have an **individual education program (IEP)** written by the multidisciplinary team working with the child and with the parents' approval. For children under three, and in recognition of the importance of the family, each identified child must have an **individual family services plan (IFSP)**.

- Parents are to be involved at every step in the process, from identification, assessment, and educational placement, to evaluation of that placement. Furthermore, parents must agree to the assessment procedures used to identify the need for services, and must approve the IEP, and the evaluation.

- Each child is to be placed in the **least restrictive environment (LRE)** (see Figures 8–2, 8–3, and 8–4).

- Due process is guaranteed for every child and family. The parents have the right to sue a district if they feel that the best interests of their child are not being met.

Individual Education Program (IEP)—with children with special needs, an individual education program states the short-term and long-term learning objectives, how they will be accomplished and by whom, and applicable dates. It must be approved by both parents and school.

Individual Family Service Plan (IFSP)—required by the 1986 Education of the Handicapped Act Amendments for handicapped children under the age of three and their families; the IFSP, often developed by a transdisciplinary team that includes the family, any needed specialists, such as a physical therapist, a language therapist, an educator, who cooperatively determine goals and objectives that build on the strengths of the child and family.

least restrictive environment (LRE)—a provision of Public Law 101–476 that children with disabilities be placed in a program as close as possible to a setting designed for children without disabilities, while being able to meet each child's special needs.

Figure 8-2
The "least restrictive environment" may be having the child sit in a special chair . . .

Figure 8-3
. . . or it may be having the physical therapist position the child's head while the child uses his arms . . .

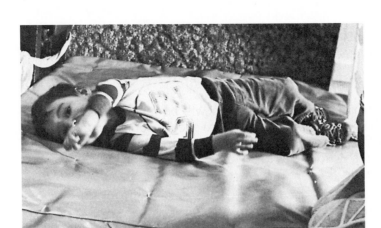

● **Figure 8-4**
. . . or it may be letting the child roll free on a mat.

- Any assessment of a child must be done with instruments that are nondiscriminatory in terms of race and ethnicity. Assessment must also be in the child's dominant language, or in the child's preferred mode of communication (sign language, for example).
- All children and youth between the ages of three and 21 (under IDEA) are to receive the same free services as the earlier law (PL 94–142) guaranteed to those between the ages of 5 and 18.
- State grants for infant and toddler programs are also to be funded, so that states may develop comprehensive, coordinated, multidisciplinary, interagency programs. With infants and toddlers an IFSP is prepared and monitored.

Recognizing the difficulty of being able to pinpoint specific diagnoses with the very young, under PL 99–457 a child did not have to be specifically labeled to receive services. Two more categories of special needs were defined by recent amendments to PL 101–476: children with persuasive developmental disorders, including autism spectrum disorder, and children with traumatic brain injuries. Three additional services were also included: rehabilitation counseling, social work services, and spoken descriptions of on-screen video productions (through descriptive video service (DVS), provided over the second of two audio channels on stereo television sets). Subsequent reauthorizations in PL 105–17 (IDEA '97) and PL 108–446 (Individuals with Disabilities Education Improvement Act of 2004) placed a major focus on maximizing student participation in the general education curriculum (Lewis & Doorlag, 2006).

Both the "special" and "typical" child profit from association with each other. One private preschool has a policy to integrate special and typical children. The director allows four, identified special children in a class of 24. In the 30 years since this policy was put into effect, the school has taught mentally retarded children, children with orthopedic problems, partially sighted children, hard of hearing children, children with behavior disorders, speech- and health-impaired children, as well as other children not as yet identified as having specific special needs. With family permission, other children have learned to help special children with bathroom visits and other activities, and both children benefit.

Implications of Special Education Laws

The major shift mentioned above in providing services in the general education curriculum, is better known as **inclusion**. Inclusion has led to having various kinds of children with special needs, even those with severe disabilities, included in regular classrooms, both at the preschool and public school level. What it means for you, as a student teacher, is that you may be asked by your cooperating teacher to work with a child with special needs.

Student Teaching with Children with Special Needs

Student teachers in two-year degree or other shorter training programs may feel inadequate, because few of their academic classes went into any depth or detail on teaching strategies, goals, specific disabilities, program modifications, and so forth, to prepare them to work with children with special needs. Baccalaureate-level student teachers also may have only encountered one, specific special education course, since many states now require a class on working with children with special needs for certification or licensing.

An understanding of the positive aspects of including young children with special needs in regular classrooms helps (see Figure 8–5).

Advocates of inclusion usually cite the following benefits:

- All attending children, both those with and those without disabilities, make gains.
- Social and play skills of children with disabilities grow and develop.
- Children's sensitivity to and acceptance of disabled peer's results.

The higher the quality of the child development program, the more likely individualized intervention occurs. Severe disabilities require intensive, professional support systems.

What is a student teacher to do? First, accept the disabilities you find. They may range from mild to moderate to severe. Become a team player in helping each child reach their potential. Know that your cooperating teacher may have already:

- assessed the classroom environment and staff requirements.
- developed a routine or schedule for each identified child with special needs.
- developed individual learning objectives and plans.
- made curriculum modifications or adaptations to enhance child participation, which may include special equipment, room arrangement, classroom materials, activity simplification, peer mentoring, or other adjustments, giving attention to child preferences and needs.
- assessed individual children's progress.

Most cooperating teachers will expect student teachers to be instrumental in helping them both observe children with special needs and work toward helping the children reach the goals of their IFSP or IEP. Student teachers also must be aware of any individual adaptations that may be necessary, as well as the teaching team's efforts.

inclusion—a term that has widely replaced the term "mainstreaming" and that emphasizes placement of the child with special needs in the regular classroom with, perhaps, greater assistance from special education services. There is still controversy as to whether total inclusion is best for every child with special needs.

Figure 8-5
This child is attending an inclusive classroom with the aid of her walker.

Ask for specifics on each child if you have questions. Be alert and inquisitive about child behaviors or teaching practices you find questionable. The author remembers, as a new teacher, observing a disabled preschool child who would not pull up her pants after toileting. She was capable of doing so but would not. The teacher, monitoring the child's behavior, would calmly but firmly say, "Just reach down, grab your pants, and pull up. I think that you can pull up your underwear. I will wait. You can do it." The teacher repeated this periodically. The child tried an array of behaviors, including pleading, crying, sulking, calling the teacher names, pulling long sections of toilet paper off the rolls, looking sad, and continually flushing the toilet, but the teacher held her ground. A stranger coming into the classroom might think the teacher cruel, unfeeling, and perhaps obstinate. In the end, after a good half hour, the child finally pulled up her pants. The staff's intent with this child, after family consultation, was to increase the child's independence and self-help skills.

Using book or Internet resources will increase your knowledge of specific disabilities. You will discover resources for families and teachers. A second list of Web sites is found at the end of this chapter. Most communities have local, state, and federal agencies, school districts, and other entities that have been created to help children with special needs, and their families. Investigate. The administrator or director of the school where you are student teaching is responsible, after considerable collaboration with the teaching team and family, to make child or family referrals if necessary.

CHILDREN WITH SPECIAL NEEDS

"Special children are as different from each other as are typical children, but not all children with special needs are easily recognizable (see Figure 8–6). There are signs that can help you identify a special child. Does Johnny hold his head to one side constantly? Does he squint? (He may need glasses.) Does he ignore directions, unless you are close to him and facing him? Is his speech unclear? Does he have frequent bouts of middle ear infections? (He may have a hearing problem.)

Figure 8-6
Not all children with special needs are easily recognizable.

Is Sally not learning to talk at the same rate as her peers? (She may have a language delay problem.) Is she still using baby talk when most of her peers have outgrown it? (She may have a speech problem.) Is she frequently out of breath? Does she sneeze often? (She may have an allergy that should be properly diagnosed by a doctor.)

Fortunately, most health problems are diagnosed by family doctors; your role might simply be to monitor the child's medication, if the supervising teacher asks you to. Children taking medication often have to be observed, to decide if the dosage is appropriate; doctors often must know if a child's behavior changes in any way, such as with increasing drowsiness or irritability. It is more than likely, however, that the supervising teacher or a school nurse, if there is one, would monitor medication reactions.

Is the child extremely aggressive or withdrawn? (He may have a behavior disorder.) Is the child extremely active? Does he have a short attention span? Is he easily distracted? Does he have problems with cause-and-effect relationships? Does he have difficulty putting thoughts into words? (He may have a learning disability.)

Is the child much slower than her peers in talking and completing cognitive work, such as classifying objects? (She may be developmentally delayed.) Does the child have difficulty with social relationships? Does he have problems looking you in the eye when you talk with him? (He may have Asperger's syndrome, a form of autism.) It is important to note that these characteristics are only indications of a problem, not solid evidence that the problem does exist. Only a qualified person can make the actual determination.

In your child care center, do you have a child talking in sentences, at age two or two-and-a-half? Is this child larger and taller than other children of the same age? Does this child enjoy excellent health? Does he already know the names of the primary and secondary colors? Does the child already know the letters in his name? Does this child see relationships between seemingly unrelated objects? This child may be special in the sense of being gifted or talented.

Working with the Special Child in Inclusive Settings

There are few concepts that have been as misunderstood as inclusion. Nowhere in any special needs law does the word appear. As mentioned before, PL 101–476 refers only to LRE. However, the LRE phrase does state that the focus is on maximizing the student's participation in the general education curriculum (Batshaw, 2002).

As Grisham-Brown, Hemmeter, and Pretti-Frontczak (2005) state, inclusive settings are those settings that are designed to address the needs of children who are developing normally, children who are at risk, and children with disabilities. The range of inclusive programs includes child care programs, public school, preschool, and school-age programs, Head Start, and other center-based programs.

What does this mean for you as a student teacher? Can children with special needs be integrated smoothly, all day, into regular programs? Does the mandate mean that you will have to work with disruptive children in a regular classroom (preschool or elementary) or a child care center? If, after you finish your teacher training, you decide to open your own, family child care home or preschool, will you have to enroll children with special needs? According to a question and answer bulletin (October 1997) from the U.S. Department of Justice, Civil Rights division, Disability Rights section, the answer, clearly, is "yes."

Whether you realize it or not, many preschools and child care centers always have had children with special needs, especially those with less obvious disabilities. Many preschool and primary age children do not have obvious special needs and are enrolled before any diagnosis is completed. And, as mentioned before, some preschools have enrolled children with severe disabilities. Typically, children with less severe disabilities, or those with "hidden" disabilities, are frequently diagnosed in preschool and elementary school. You may have had a vision impairment, mild to moderate hearing loss, learning disability, scoliosis (spinal curvature), or **attention deficit disorder** diagnosed in elementary school. Also, children of all ages experience bouts of depression that go undiagnosed.

The implications for teachers and caregivers of young children involve, first of all, the need for collaboration. As Mastropieri and Scruggs (2007) suggest, families, caregivers, and teachers all need to be involved. Existing routines, in both at-home and out-of-home settings, need to be considered, as must the goals in each setting. For the greatest chance of success, all adults in the child's life should plan together for the ultimate good of the child. Building positive, collaborative relationships among team members (families, regular and special education teachers, and other specialists) "can substantially improve the school and life functioning of students with disabilities" (Mastropieri & Scruggs, 2007).

In agreement, Lewis and Doorlag (2006) propose that teachers look at their instructional methods, to see how these might be adjusted to meet the needs of special students. Furthermore, they suggest that the children themselves be involved in any implementation of integration (they use the concept of a "friends helping friends" approach). Lewis and Doorlag also state that inclusion must be planned carefully, and that teachers need to model appropriate behavior. In addition any appropriate behaviors, such as positive interaction between children with special needs and other children, should be praised. Finally, cooperative learning activities have proven to be most successful in integration. Turnbull, Turnbull, and Wehmeyer (2007) caution, however, that successful inclusion requires support from administration and support personnel as well as from the families of the children with special needs.

The research on inclusion does not describe the quality of inclusive practices, nor does it allow for the amount of time spent in inclusive settings, and the extent to which students from culturally and linguistically diverse backgrounds have appropriate respect, support, and accommodations (Turnbull, Turnbull, & Wehmeyer, 2007).

In an earlier study, Schoen and her associates, Auen and Arvanitis (1997), looked at the inclusion of children with special needs in three settings: a public school, a preschool class, and a for-profit child care center. The authors' concluded that

> Not only was the integration plan enriching for the children and the parents, it was a fulfilling experience for all the professionals involved.
> . . . [T]he integration program was about children learning about others and, in turn, learning about themselves.

If you have the opportunity to work and teach in an inclusive setting, you may also find it a fulfilling experience, and in the process learn more about yourself.

---

attention deficit disorder (ADD)—a disorder that causes children to have difficulty sustaining attention in the classroom and concentrating on an assigned task for any length of time.

In general, working with the special child is not much different than working with the typical child. Your cooperating teacher will, in most instances, give you clues for teaching a special child.

Children with Speech Impairments

The child with a speech or language impairment may need one-to-one tutoring (see Figure 8–7). Two early indications of hearing impairment are lack of language skills and unclear speech. If you suspect a child has a hearing loss, you should discuss your perceptions with your cooperating teacher. She may suggest to the family that the hearing be checked. If the child is experiencing language delay, it may be because the family has not spent much time talking to the child. Indeed, some children speak in what sounds like television language. Typically, the child will use words verbatim from his preferred television program. For example, he might talk like his favorite action figure or mimic Bart Simpson. You should provide these children with opportunities to use verbal language. You may need to name objects for them, and provide them with descriptive adjectives. You may engage in a variety of language activities with these children, such as feelie-box games, and guessing games in which they describe and use language.

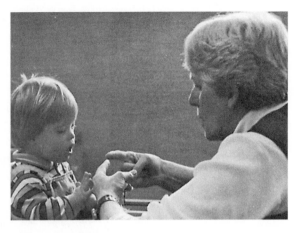

● *Figure 8-7*
It is common to work one to one with a child with special needs.

Children with Cognitive Impairment

The child with cognitive impairment may need no special attention beyond your being attuned to activities that may prove frustrating to the child. Your teacher may ask you to assist the child in certain activities known to be more difficult. For example, during a finger play, you may be asked to hold the child on your lap and to manipulate the child's fingers. The child with cognitive impairment might also need some extra help with language; slow language development is often characteristic.

Children with mild cognitive impairment often integrate well into the preschool setting. They frequently have good social development, and their physical development may appear normal. Their language may be simpler than that of peers, but they often make their needs known through gestures and body language. They may not be able to do some of the cognitive tasks well, but they can derive as much pleasure from painting, role-playing, and playing with clay, blocks, and trucks as any other child. Knowing that this child is less able cognitively than some of the other children, you can work with activities the child *can* do successfully, and reduce the amount of stress associated with goals set too high.

Children with Orthopedic or Health Disabilities

There are many different types of physical disabilities and health problems. In working with children who have orthopedic or health disabilities, the only difficulty you may encounter is whether your setting is wheelchair accessible, and whether you need to be more attentive to health problems on days when air quality is poor. Asthma and allergies are the most common health problems for young children, and affected children are more sensitive to smog and seasonal pollens.

Your cooperating teacher may want you to help a child in a wheelchair go to the bathroom, or may ask you to assist a child with leg braces as he sits at, or rises from, a table or the floor.

Some other specific strategies include:

- acquainting yourself with any special equipment needed by the child
- being alert to medication the child may be taking
- remembering to tell your cooperating teacher about any changes you may have noticed in the child's behavior that may have been missed
- being aware of the fact that a chronically ill child may be absent frequently, and that close contact must be kept among families, the school, and specialists

Children Who Are Hard of Hearing

Children who are hard of hearing may wear hearing aids or, if profoundly disabled, may use sign language. These children will vary in their competencies just as typical children do. Their language may be somewhat delayed, and your cooperating teacher may ask you to work with them on language games. You are not expected to learn sign, but you may find it helpful to learn a few simple signs from the sign language specialist or classroom assistant.

Strategies for working with a child who is hard of hearing include:

- speaking directly to him using normal, well-articulated speech and normal gestures.
- seating the child where she can see you if you are reading a story, doing a finger play, or some other visual activity.
- encouraging others to include the hearing-impaired child in their activities.
- encouraging the other children to follow your examples above.
- being alert to the need for your cooperating teacher to change the batteries in a child's hearing aid if the child seems confused, is rubbing her ears, or uses any other signal to indicate she is not hearing (your cooperating teacher or the specialist may show you how to do this, to save their attention and time).

In one case involving a child who was hard of hearing, all of the children learned sign language in order to better communicate with the child. In fact, the children learned sign language faster than the teacher.

Children Who Are Blind or Have Low Vision

As with hard of hearing children, those with visual problems vary widely in their abilities. Children so affected have frequently been in regular classrooms for years.

The following strategies can be employed with such children:

- Be alert to the child who may not see well, who may be holding books close to his face, placing his head close to the picture he is drawing, or complaining of headaches or nausea after trying to concentrate on a visual work activity (see Figure 8–8).

● Remember that the partially sighted or blind child needs to have a room where furniture and equipment are kept in predictable arrangements. If you bring in a newly designed activity center, be sure to orient the visually impaired child to its placement and use.

● Set the television to a channel that provides a verbal description of what is happening for viewers with visual limitations.

Commercial and public television programs are sometimes closed-captioned (CC) for the hearing impaired, or may employ DVS for the visually impaired.

● **Figure 8-8**
If this boy consistently holds his head this close to the pages of books, he may need to wear glasses.

Children with Behavior Disorders

There is probably no area more controversial than behavioral difficulties affecting children. Many teachers may think a child is emotionally disturbed but do not know how to approach the family. The term "behavior disorders" is now commonly used to indicate children who have problems with behavior but who may not, in terms of a psychiatric definition, be truly "emotionally disturbed."

Often, when you see a young child with behavior problems, you are likely to see a family with problems. The term "dysfunctional" is sometimes used to describe families with problems that affect their children. To many families, even the suggestion of a behavior problem with their child brings about a defensive reaction, such as, "Are you telling me I'm a bad parent? That I don't know how to raise my own child?" Teachers and administrators attempt to avoid value-laden terms that may arouse a defensive reaction in families. Instead, they will substitute terminology such as "acts out," "has no friends," "daydreams," "fights," or "tries to hide in the back of the room." We have to understand how difficult it is for families to accept the possibility that something may be "wrong" with their child. If the family has no idea that their child is not perfectly normal, it becomes extremely difficult to convince them that there may be a problem.

Facing the possibility that their child may not be perfect, some families actually grieve for the lost image of what their child was to have been. They grieve much the same as they would if the child had died. They become angry and often accuse teachers of prejudice and of not really knowing their child. Some families verbally attack teacher skills and the suggested diagnosis; others deny that anything is wrong. Most go through a phase in which they blame themselves for causing the child's problems. In some instances, we may feel that families are indeed responsible for the problems of the child, and we must be careful not to prejudge.

The child with a behavior disorder may or may not present a problem in the classroom. In one example, a child with a (depressive) behavior-disorder was placed in a regular preschool. The children quickly learned to tolerate his temper tantrums and screaming. To a visiting stranger, they would explain, "Don't worry about George. He just needs to be alone now." In many ways, the children were more tolerant than some of the adults.

Certainly, the child who shows aggression presents a challenge and must be watched closely. For this reason, it is not uncommon for the teacher to assign an assistant or student teacher to work on a one-to-one basis with the child, to try to control the child's outbursts. Some good techniques are holding the child on your lap, allowing the child to hit a heavy chair cushion instead of another child or adult, removing a child to the back of a classroom or "benching" them on the playground, allowing the child to punch clay or pound nails into scrap wood instead of hurting others, having the child bite on a leather strap or chew a wad of sugarless bubblegum instead of biting, or having the child run around the playground when it might serve to calm him. Remember that behavior modification works well with children who have behavior disorders.

Be aware that as the withdrawn, depressed child becomes better, he is likely to become aggressive. This is known as the **pendulum effect**. When a depressed child reaches this stage and begins to act out, some families become angry and fearful and stop therapy, not understanding that the child must release the pent-up anger. They may not understand that it takes time for a child to learn how to deal with anger in socially acceptable ways. We can reassure the family that this phase is normal; we can also be alert for signs that the child needs to be alone, to stomp, yell, throw, and hit without hurting anyone. In some schools, the child is directed to go to a room to throw Nerf balls, pound on clay, or hit a weighted clown doll. In others, there are time-out corners, where the child will be told to stay until she feels ready to rejoin the group. Whatever the technique used, you may be asked to remain with the child for safety purposes. At the same time, you can acknowledge the child's anger and suggest better ways to channel their energy.

Burgess and Younger (2006) looked at the self-perceptions of students in middle school with behavior disorders. They found that in comparison to a control group of typical students, shy and withdrawn students tended to internalize problems and chose more negative than positive self-descriptors. Aggressive students tended to externalize problems, but differences were not significant. For teachers of younger children, findings suggest that attempts should be made to integrate shy and withdrawn students into classroom activities, and to build their self-confidence whenever possible.

Children with Learning Disabilities

The child suspected of having learning disabilities presents a challenge. Although some families are willing to accept a diagnosis of possible learning disabilities, others are not. What is a **learning disability**? According to PL 94–142, and reaffirmed by PL 101–476, a "specific learning disability"

> means a disorder in one or more of the basic psychological processes involved in understanding or in using language, spoken or written, which may manifest itself in an imperfect ability to listen, think, speak, read, write, spell, or do mathematical calculations (Federal Register, 1977).

School districts commonly define learning disabilities in terms of a child's actual achievement in relation to the achievement of his age peers. The unfortunate result of this practice has been postponing the identification of a problem until the achievement is two or more years behind, a practice that has meant, in too many cases, three and even four years of failure for the child. The damage to the child's self-esteem can be almost irreparable.

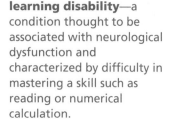

Pendulum effect—a phenomenon observed especially with children in therapy for the treatment of depressive disorders. Children swing from non-expression of emotions to explosive outbreaks.

learning disability—a condition thought to be associated with neurological dysfunction and characterized by difficulty in mastering a skill such as reading or numerical calculation.

Another commonly used definition is that a learning disability is reflected as a significant discrepancy between the child's potential ability and her actual achievement in learning to read, write, or figure. The curriculum areas of reading, language arts, and mathematics are most typically involved.

Does this mean that a preschooler does not have a learning disability? Many preschool teachers, families, and educational psychologists who are capable diagnosticians would disagree.

What are some of the characteristics you might see in a preschooler that could signal the possibility of a learning disability? Typically, you see a child who appears immature; who frequently has difficulties with language, both receptive and expressive; who acts impulsively; and who may seem to be "hyperactive." (Be careful about calling a child hyperactive; be aware that high energy is not necessarily hyperactivity.)

Ask yourself the following questions:

- Does the child in your preschool have difficulty using language?
- Does he use unreferenced pronouns because he can't remember an object's name?
- Is this the child who cannot think of more than one word to describe an object in a feelie box, or repeats a word a playmate has just used, instead of coming up with her own?
- Does this child display poor coordination for her age?
- Does the child have difficulty following simple requests?
- Does he dislike changes in the routines of the preschool?
- Does the four-year-old child prefer interacting with the three-year-olds more than with children her own age?
- Is the four-year-old child unable to tell what letter has been drawn on his back, indicating difficulty transferring a tactile sensation to a visual image?
- Do you have to constantly remind the child of the rules?

None of these characteristics by itself would be symptomatic of a possible learning disability; taken together, and being seen daily, might be cause for suggesting a more formal evaluation by a qualified expert in learning disabilities. In the meantime, the child's family may ask your cooperating teacher to arrange for some one-to-one learning for their child. In turn, the cooperating teacher may ask them to attend a conference, involving everyone who works with the child, to develop an individual learning plan that will involve them all (see Figure 8–9). (See the Appendix for a sample individual learning plan and checklists that can be used to determine modality strengths and weaknesses.)

Dyslexia

Many children with a specific learning disability have a condition known as dyslexia, a problem "manifested by difficulty in learning to read, write, or spell, despite conventional instruction, adequate intelligence, and sociocultural opportunity" (Orton Dyslexia Society, 1988). As a student teacher in an elementary school, you may be asked to work one-to-one with a dyslexic student, to allow the student extra time to finish a written assignment, or to have the student present an oral report instead of a written one. You may be asked to write a story the student dictates.

SCHOOL: ABC Preschool   STUDENT'S NAME: Tommy   C.A.: 43   DATE: 14 Oct

LONG-RANGE GOAL: Tommy will expand his vocabulary both at school and at home.

FUNCTIONAL DESCRIPTION OF THE PROBLEM: Tommy speaks in telegraphic sentences; his language is frequently unintelligible, which has led to interpersonal problems with peers. Assessments by School District DEF shows that Tommy is developmentally normal on all criteria except language. His pediatrician's report shows no difficulty with hearing but a severe case of pneumonia when Tommy was 8 mo., followed by a relapse at 9 mo. Tommy's mother admits overprotecting him and worrying about his frequent bouts with upper respiratory infections. Tommy's attention span appears short relative to peers at ABC Preschool.

BEHAVIORAL STRENGTHS: Tommy is agile and well coordinated.

SHORT-TERM OBJECTIVES	INTERVENTION ACTIVITIES AND MATERIALS	PERSON(S) RESPONSIBLE
(Section 3153, Title V Regulations) (Specify time, specific behavior, evaluation conditions & criteria)		
1. Tommy will use 3–4 word sentences when talking in the classroom. (6 mo.)	ST or aide will model speaking in complete sentences & ask child to repeat model; "Feelie Box" will be used on 1:1	Teacher, with assistance of ST or aide
4. Tommy will retell stories using complete sentences of 3–4 words. (8 mo.)	Mother or father will read to boy each evening before bed, model complete sentence construction & have him repeat or construct his own sentences	Parents
6. Tommy will practice using sentences under guidance of District DEF's speech therapist. Word lotto games, etc., will also be used. (6 mo.)	Peabody Early Experiences Kit	Speech & language therapist
9. Mr. & Mrs. Fabian will be offered an opportunity to participate in LDA (Learning Disabilities Association) support group & to receive counseling. (on-going)	District DEF psychologist gives parents information regarding County LDA support group; may ask LDA to call parents	DEF School Dist. psychologist

CRITERION MEASURE without modeling or prompting. Tommy will be speaking in 3–4 word complete sentences.

Reviewed: _____

_____   _____
                                            Speech Therapist

                                            _____
                                            Teacher

Revision(s) Recommended: _____
                                            School Psychologist

_____   Date: _____
(Parent 1)   _____
                                            (Parent 2)

● **Figure 8-9**
Part of an individual family services plan.

Interventions used by Wadlington, Jacob, and Bailey (1996) involve helping dyslexic students with organizational and study skills, which, of course, are of value to all the students. They also advocate using a multi-sensory approach to reading tasks, providing audiotape books for students to use, together with the standard readers. In spelling, they concentrate on having students learn words that are phonetically regular before introducing any that are not. They accept handwriting that is not perfect, as long as it is legible, and encourage the use of computer word-processing programs. Extra time is allowed for all language arts activities and for test-taking. You may want to talk to your cooperating teacher about some of these ideas.

Children with Attention Deficit/Hyperactivity Disorder (AD/HD)

One category in special education often seen in child care and schools today is **attention deficit with hyperactivity disorder (AD/HD)** and the *Diagnostic and Statistical Manual of Mental Disorders* (DSM-IV, American Psychiatric Association, 2000), recognizes three kinds of attention disorders: the predominantly inattentive type, the predominantly hyperactive-impulsive type, and the combined type. There are some who believe AD/HD labels children whose temperament runs at a faster rate than "normal" (Armstrong,1996; Reid, Maag, & Vasa, 1994; Smelter, Rasch, Fleming, Nazos, & Baranowski, 1996).

Children with AD/HD typically have difficulty concentrating for prolonged periods of time, some even for 5 or 10 minutes. For some of these children, taking a stimulant drug such as Ritalin, Dexadrine, or Cylert appears to help. For others, especially those allergic to drug therapy, specially designed computer games appear to help.

If you have children with AD/HD in your classroom, one proven way to work with them is to keep them busy. Allowing them the freedom to move from one center to another is another way. On the other hand, a room with many choices may be difficult for AD/HD children; in many ways, they need less stimulation rather than more. You may have to suggest gently to the child that he choose one of two options. "I notice no one is painting at one of the easels, and I also notice that your friend Jean Pierre is the only child playing with the blocks. Why don't you paint a picture or join Jean Pierre?" Your room may have a sheltered corner or area where these children may go when over-stimulated.

Hogan (1997) stresses that "like all children, children with AD/HD need love, acceptance, discipline, and the freedom to grow and learn." To that end, she suggests that teachers first learn as much as they can about AD/HD. Then, they can set attention goals for their students. Hogan states that there may be a need to modify assignments, and to tailor academic materials to individual learning styles and abilities. The need to be flexible is paramount (for example, allowing a student to lie on the floor to read, or "hide" under a desk). If an assignment is completed, there may not be a need for a student to sit at a desk. In fact, one of the authors once taught in an L-shaped third grade classroom, where there was a study carrel off to

attention deficit with hyperactivity disorder (AD/HD)—like ADD, it causes attention problems and an inability to sit still and concentrate for very long. Children with AD/HD are said to "bounce off the walls."

the side, where any student could go. Although originally planned for the AD/HD students, many of the so-called typical students would move to the study carrel, where they found it easier to concentrate.

Of concern to many families, teachers, and others is what has been described as the over-prescription to younger and younger children of psychoactive drugs, Ritalin and Prozac in particular. Some educators believe that too many preschool children are being placed on these drugs when the effects of long-term use on the very young are not known.

One interesting finding about AD/HD students is their ability to hyperfocus; that is, they demonstrate intense levels of concentration and attention in completing tasks in which they are totally absorbed. This has been discovered to be one of the "key descriptors in biographies of creative individuals" (Cramond, 1995, quoted by Turnbull, Turnbull, & Wehmeyer, 2007).

Autism Spectrum Disorders and Asperger's Syndrome

Autism spectrum disorder—a persuasive developmental disorder usually seen with qualitative impairments in communication, social interactions, and restrictive or repetitive patterns of behavior that first occur before the age of three.

Children diagnosed as autistic represent a wide range of abilities, as do all children; some are high-functioning, and succeed in inclusive settings, and some are low-functioning, and may be in inclusive settings only for short periods of time, for activities such as art, music, lunch, and recess. Others may attend inclusive settings for part of the day and special settings for the rest. Autism is defined by the American Psychiatric Association in a category of pervasive developmental disorders. The primary characteristics include "a pattern of social aloofness and preservation of sameness" (Batshaw, 2002).

Asperger's syndrome is a term often applied to those children who usually are able to remain in inclusive settings. You will notice their uniqueness by their failure to develop peer relationships and their use of nonverbal behaviors, such as a reluctance to look eye-to-eye with a peer or an adult, awkward facial expression, body posture, and gestures to regulate social interactions. They may have no problem with spoken language, or with cognitive development, but may have difficulty in sustaining a conversation. They adhere to strict routines and often demonstrate narrowly defined interests (DSM-IV, American Psychiatric Association, 2000).

Asperger's syndrome— one of the autism spectra but generally seen at less severe levels. Children with Asperger's often remain in regular classrooms with a sensitive teacher who recognizes the frequently seen delay in the child's social development and subsequent difficulties with peers.

In a classroom setting, you may notice few differences between children with Asperger's and other children, other than the inability of the child with Asperger's to develop friendships, and his desire to regale you with details about his specific interests. One boy we know is totally fascinated with severe weather phenomena. He thoroughly enjoys telling about the latest earthquake or hurricane, and what damage it caused, yet he has problems relating to the interests of his peers and has not established any friendships.

The Gifted Child

gifted children—children who perform significantly above average in intellectual and creative areas.

Teachers are considering new ways to think about and observe **gifted children**. Very young children, culturally and linguistically diverse children, and economically disadvantaged children may escape detection as gifted children, particularly if standardized assessments are used. Smutny (2001) urges educators to consider factors fundamental to a fair assessment of children's abilities, as follows:

- *Look for giftedness in domains other than academic* (for example, creative imagination, wit, improvisation, kinesthetic abilities, and hands-on problem solving). Become aware of your own ideas about what giftedness looks like, or what behaviors indicate high potential. Don't assume that gifted children are early readers or even high achievers. Don't assume that an athletic child with little interest in academics or a bilingual student struggling with English is unlikely to be gifted.

- *Look beyond "good" or "bad" behavior.* Consider the role that good behavior plays in the assessment of a child's ability. Do children who please the teacher get more opportunity, as a reward for their good behavior? While problem behavior needs to be addressed, always remember that some gifted kids act up because of frustration or boredom.

- *Create activities that demand higher-level thinking and creative solutions.* It is obvious that a child who needs hands-on activities to process information and analyze problems will not show these abilities if no such activities occur in the classroom. Be willing to incorporate different learning styles and materials, so that more students can demonstrate their strengths.

- *Allow students to express their ideas in different ways.* For example, a child from another culture may have a novel solution to a problem, but may express this better through diagrams and drawings than through verbal or written expression. Offer students a variety of ways to show what they are learning.

- *Ask children about their work.* Do not assume that you know what a student is trying to do, or whether or not it works. It may be that their ideas are more interesting or sophisticated than are their abilities to express them. Uneven development is common in young children, and cultural differences may enhance this phenomenon.

When assessing the behavior of young children, teachers need to be sensitive to differences in learning style, development, and cultural background, which influence the way they process information and respond to activities in the classroom (Smutny, 2001).

Non-English Proficient Children

Children of immigrant families are increasingly represented in classrooms. Their numbers are expected to grow dramatically during the next decade and include Hispanics, Asians, Pacific Islanders, Haitians, Africans, and others.

Student teachers may face the immediate task of communicating acceptance and respect to children with varying degrees of English proficiency. No single description fits these children; they are widely diverse. Teachers strive to decrease children's feelings of alienation and isolation, if it exists (Lewis & Doorlag, 2006; Mastropieri & Scruggs, 2007). Many of these children have backgrounds and cultural understandings that can be tapped as classroom resources.

Student teachers need to become familiar with planning and implementing programs for students who do not understand and/or speak English. Planning is based on the following assessments:

- How proficient is the child in the language spoken in the home?
- What English words does the child seem to know, if any?
- Is the child's language and speech appropriate for his age?
- What degree of comfort or discomfort is present at school?
- What experiences are developmentally appropriate for this child?

Children Born to Mothers Who Were Substance Abusers

Children born to mothers who have been substance abusers are often born addicted to the drugs the mother abused during pregnancy. These children may appear to be hyperactive, have an attention deficit, or be learning disabled. Caregivers working with these children have noted that they often overreact to stimuli; thus, they need environments that contain fewer, rather than more, curriculum possibilities, and fewer children with whom to interact.

As infants, these children may need constant care. They are frequently born prematurely and often have had to spend their first weeks, even months, in pediatric intensive care units. After release from the hospital, caregivers may still need to use pediatric monitors with these infants when they sleep because sudden infant death syndrome (SIDS) has been observed more frequently in such children. These infants are often difficult to console when crying, and appear to have trouble adjusting to change. Swaddling has proven effective in comforting these infants.

Upon entering the preschool or classroom, these children become over stimulated. They may strike out at anyone nearby—child or adult—and their behavior may be unpredictable. Obviously, this leads to difficulties in establishing friendships with the other children. Children born to substance-abusing mothers have been shown to work better in small groups, and in rooms with minimal stimuli.

For more information, you may want to contact your local children's hospital or large-city school district. School districts in many cities, such as Los Angeles, New York, and Chicago, have suggestions for how to work more effectively with these children. Don't be afraid to contact hospitals or school districts for advice.

WORKING WITH CHILDREN WITH SPECIAL NEEDS

Among the several techniques proven effective for teaching children with learning disabilities, and others with special needs, are:

- providing structure. A well-planned classroom is essential. Classroom rules are posted for older children, and repeated often to younger ones, so everyone understands the limits.
- consistent discipline.
- behavior modification.
- *CARE:* Be *congruent, acceptant, reliable,* and *empathetic*. It works with all children, especially those with special needs.

- alternating quiet time with activities. Provide for enough physical exercise to tire the active child and allow the child the freedom to move around often. Do not expect the child to sit still, unless you are there.
- being openly loving. One parent and educator, Armstrong (1996) questions whether AD/HD exists or whether children so labeled simply need *CARE*ing and love.

Armstrong decried the tendency of parents and educators to ask medical doctors to place the seemingly inattentive, overactive child on drug therapy. He advocates instead that we use diet, physical exercise, relaxation exercises, and proven educational techniques, such as those previously mentioned. We urge you to do the same.

Vulnerable Children

Which children are considered "vulnerable?" Initially, these were children who had a parent or parents who had psychiatric problems or were substance abusers. Children living in poverty, with inadequate housing, clothing, or insufficient food, are also considered vulnerable. Weissbourd (1996) lists the attributes of teachers who work with vulnerable children in Figure 8–10. These attributes, in fact, are important characteristics for any and all teachers.

Attributes of Effective Teachers Working with Vulnerable Children
1. Effective teachers operationalize high expectations for every child.
2. Effective teachers attribute failure to aspects of a child or classroom that can be positively influenced, rather than to intractable aspects of a child, family, or community.
3. Effective teachers provide every student with the elements from which real and durable self-esteem is built, including specific, tangible skills and achievements, progressively increased responsibilities, and opportunities to give to others.
4. Effective teachers view children as having complex constellations of strengths and weaknesses and communicate this understanding to parents.
5. Effective teachers work to develop children's adaptive capacities, their ability to manage disappointment and conflict.
6. Effective teachers pick up on the quiet troubles that undermine children in school, such as mild hunger or wearing the same clothes day after day and respond aggressively to these problems.
7. Effective teachers view the classroom and school as a complex culture and system and seek to understand the difficulties of a child in terms of the interactions between a particular child and a particular culture and system.
8. Effective teachers engage parents proactively and have the skills to work with parents when a child is in crisis.
9. Effective teachers are self-observing and are responsive to feedback and ideas from both other school staff and children—they see children as active partners in their education.
10. Effective teachers know when to respond to a child's problem themselves and when a child needs to see another professional who has specialized training.
11. Effective teachers innovate, take risks, and reshape their activities based on close attention to results.

 Figure 8-10
Attributes of effective teachers working with vulnerable children. From *The Vulnerable Child* by Richard Weissbourd. Copyright 1996 by Richard Weissbourd. Reprinted by permission of Perseus Books Publishers, a member of Perseus Books, L.L.C.

At-Risk Children

Today, we can look at a broader definition of vulnerable children and include any child living in an environment that is not optimal for the child's positive growth. Look again at the attributes listed in Figure 8–10. If you can internalize them, you will have no difficulty with **at-risk children** or any others.

Breslin (2005) suggests that these children not be labeled, as that tends to focus on deficits rather than on the strengths and competencies the children have. She stresses how often these children possess a heightened sensory awareness, stressing the need for teachers to have high, positive expectations for these children. Furthermore, Breslin emphasizes the need for teachers to help the children develop a clear understanding of their strengths and how these strengths relate to the child's respective accomplishments, reminding us to help the child develop a sense of play. "Humor is not an innate gift, but it can and should be cultivated. It is a frame that can keep things in perspective" (Breslin, 2005).

Children Who Fall Through the Cracks

● **Figure 8-11**
A wheelchair-bound child has access to sand play with this specially designed equipment.

Many children you are likely to see in your rooms may have some of the characteristics of a child with special needs but on such a mild basis that they do not qualify under the law for any supportive help. Others may be special because of a recent trauma, like losing a beloved grandparent, having a sibling with cancer, or witnessing an accident that caused injury or death to someone, whether that person was known to them or not. Our best advice: remember that all children are unique, and that all, at one time or another in their lives, are likely to need special love and care (see Figure 8–11).

One descriptive resource that provides profiles of nine special needs children, told from the perspectives of teachers, families, and the children themselves, is *Children with Special Needs: Lessons for Early Childhood Professionals* (Kostelnik, Onaga, Rohde, & Whiren, 2002).

Working with Parents of Children with Special Needs

Research (Chinn, Winn, & Walters, 1985) has shown that families of children with special needs go through a process similar to the grief reactions described by Kubler-Ross in *On Death and Dying* (1969). In interactions with parents, you may see a father denying that his son has a problem, while the mother, wracked with guilt, is blaming herself. Families often project feelings of blame on the elementary or preschool. One reason for the high divorce rate among families of children with special needs is that two parents are seldom at the same step in the grief process at the same time, a fact that obviously can lead to dissension at home.

In cases where the child has a clear disability, diagnosed by a medical doctor at an early age, families have had to adjust, and learn to accept the child and any concomitant problems, earlier than families of a child who has what are often called "invisible handicaps," like learning disabilities, mild retardation, Asperger's syndrome, and behavior disorders. What this means to teachers in both preschool and elementary school settings is that they may have to be especially sensitive to what stage of grieving a child's family is in. Working with these families may require all of a teacher's communication skills, and a teacher still may not be successful in persuading families that their child needs special attention. (This is one reason why elementary schools may assign a child, whose family is "income eligible," to work with a Chapter 1 teacher. (Chapter 1 of PL 95–581, the Education Consolidation Act of 1981, provides federal funds for compensatory education of children from low-income families.) Another child may receive help from a reading specialist, student teacher, teacher assistant, or volunteer.

Commonly Used Tests

Retardation or cognitive impairment is easily measured with any well-known, standard intelligence test. Intelligence testing, often called *IQ testing*, for *Intelligence Quotient*, uses a figure based on standard deviation from the norm, with 100 as the mean or average. Despite the fact that it has come under fire over the past 30 to 40 years, its use is still widespread. As a tool for understanding the child's intellectual development, in regard to predicting possible success in school, the IQ test provides valuable information. Combined with other measures of a child's development, such as the checklist previously referred to (and found in the Appendix), the IQ test can provide a differential picture of the child's school-related abilities.

One major drawback to the **Stanford-Binet intelligence scale**, (1985), developed by Terman and Merrill, is its verbal emphasis. The **Wechsler intelligence scale for children (WISC-III)** (1991) and the **Wechsler preschool and primary intelligence scale-revised (WPPSI-R)** (1989) attempt to provide both verbal and performance measures of intelligence. However, both of these tests may discriminate against children from racial or cultural minorities. Even though both tests have been translated into other languages, there is still the question of appropriateness. For most preschools, a developmental checklist provides as good or better information than an IQ test. The major advantage to the IQ test, of course, is in diagnosing cognitive impairments and giftedness. However, tests seldom provide clues about how to work with the child once diagnosed.

If we use a developmental checklist (as found in the Appendix) which relies on our observation of the child, we can develop a learning plan based on what we see. Noting that a three-year-old child can walk upstairs alternating the feet, but walks downstairs one step at a time, we might have the child hold our hand at first. Then, we can have the child hold onto a railing. Finally, we can urge the child to try without any support. If we note that a child is still speaking two-word sentences, we can provide for more language experiences on a one-to-one basis. In every case, we should not urge the child to accomplish tasks that are not appropriate to her developmental level. The child who cannot gallop will not learn to skip, but perhaps the child is ready to learn how to slide one foot after the other sideways.

Head Start has developed a screening and assessment process (see Figure 8–12) that occurs throughout the program year, on a periodic schedule, rather than only on the child's entrance into a Head Start program. This allows analysis and, it is hoped, reassurance that the child is on track for achieving the expected developmental outcomes, as outlined in the child's

Stanford-Binet intelligence scale—a widely used test that yields an intelligence quotient (IQ).

Wechsler intelligence scale for children (WISC III) –another widely used test that yields an intelligence quotient (IQ).

Wechsler preschool primary intelligence scale-revised (WPPIS-R)— a test sometimes used with young children to determine their ability to learn and which yields an intelligence quotient (IQ).

IEP developed by staff and family. The Head Start screening assessment process is called *Early and Periodic Screen, Diagnosis, and Treatment Program* (EPSDT) (O'Brien, 2001).

The Individual Family Services Plan

You should note that Figure 8–8 represents only selected items that might be listed on Tommy Fabian's IFSP. (Remember, at the elementary school level the IFSP becomes, as required by law, an IEP.) As stipulated in PL 99–457, and continued in PL 101–476, a multidisciplinary approach is taken that involves the preschool, local school district, and a local community resource group. The student teacher, under the direction of the cooperating teacher, has an important role in modeling language and listening to responses; the school district speech therapist and psychologist each have their roles in working both with Tommy and with the family. Finally, a community organization, the local county chapter of the Learning Disability Association (LDA), has been enlisted for family support. It is important to remember that having a child with special needs often leaves families feeling disbelief, anger, and helplessness; a support group can be invaluable in alleviating these feelings.

Unique Challenges in Early Childhood Inclusion

A common myth is that inclusion in early childhood programs is easy, because of the playful nature of many of the programs. However, Cook, Klein, and Tessier, with Daley (2004) point out that in K–12 programs the general education teacher is credentialed at the same level as the special educator, but the same is not always true at the preschool level. The level of education and experience among preschool teachers varies widely. The early childhood special education specialist may have to take on an unfamiliar role, and even when the early childhood staff is highly trained, there may be philosophical differences between the regular staff and the specialist.

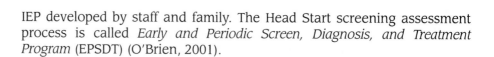

SUMMARY

In this brief introduction to the special child, we presented an overview of current thinking regarding the integration of the child with special needs into the regular classroom. We attempted to show that, in many instances, the child with special needs can do very well there and such integration has almost always been successful. Of course, there can be awkward moments initially, but other children often prove more tolerant than adults in accepting the special child. Children with special needs are no different than any other child; if you meet them with kindness and *CARE*, they will respond.

We presented an overview of the public laws, especially PL 101–476, and listed some of the major provisions. We discussed least restrictive environment, or inclusion, and emphasized that what is least restrictive for one child may not be so for another.

We have presented a sample of short-term objectives, from an IFSP for a family with a preschool child who may have a possible learning disability. We have also explained why working with families who have children with special needs can present difficulties.

Finally, we offered some practical suggestions for working with the special child. We agree that these techniques seem appropriate for all children. Methods that work well with one population are often applicable to another.

HELPFUL WEB SITES

http://cpmcnet.columbia.edu
National Center for Children in Poverty. This organization offers an informative newsletter on the prevention of poverty.

http://www.ncbe.gwu.edu
National Clearinghouse for Bilingual Education. This is a good source for language education information.

http://www.naeyc.org
National Association for the Education of Young Children. Read NAEYC's position statement on school readiness.

http://ericec.org
ERIC Clearinghouse on Disabilities and Gifted Education. Behavior disorders and learning disabilities can be researched on this database, where information on special and gifted education is maintained.

http://www.cec.sped.org
Council for Exceptional Children. The council provides information to teachers, administrators, and others concerned with the education of gifted children and children with special needs.

Additional Web Sites for Student Teachers Working with Children with Special Needs

http://www.nichy.org
National Information Center for Children and Youth with Disabilities. NICHY provides free, on-line publications, case studies, and information on visual and hearing impairments, cerebral palsy, mental retardation, and assessing programs for infants and toddlers.

http://www.kidstogether.org
Kids Get Together. Learn about language disabilities at this Web site, which contains many helpful links.

http://www.aamr.org
American Association for Mental Retardation. Fact sheets are available here.

http://www.autism.com
Autism Society of America. This site provides information about causes and types of autism.

http://www.ccbd.net
Council for Children with Behavior Disorders. Information on behavioral disorders may be found here.

http://www.ici2.umn.edu/preschoolbehavior
Positive Approaches to Challenging Behaviors for Young Children with Disabilities. This is a helpful information resource.

http://tiger.coe.missouri.edu
Center for Innovation in Education. Search cultural and linguistic diversity here; an IDEA guide is available.

http://www.ncela.gwu.edu
The National Clearinghouse for English Language. This site provides information on acquisition and language instruction for linguistically and culturally diverse learners.

http://www.fpg.unc.edu
FPG Child Development Institute. Click publications dealing with disabilities.

http://www.BehaviorAdvisor.com
Behavior Management Advice. This site offers assistance understanding and managing behavior.

http://www.easter-seals.org
Easter Seals. This organization is dedicated to children with special needs.

http://www.modimes.org
March of Dimes. This organization is also devoted to children with special needs.

http://www.chadd.org
Children and Adults with Attention-Deficit/Hyperactivity Disorder. The title tells exactly what you might find at this Web site.

http://ldanatl/.org
Learning Disabilities Association of America (LDA). This is an excellent resource for educators.

http://interdys.org
Formerly the Orton Dyslexia Society, now the International Dyslexia Association (IDA). This site provides information and resources for people coping with Dyslexia.

Additional resources for this chapter can be found by visiting the Online Companion at www.earlychilded.delmar.com.

SUGGESTED ACTIVITIES

A. Visit a preschool or elementary school that has children with special needs in attendance. Spend at least one morning watching the special children, taking notes as you observe. What similarities or differences do you find between the special children and the others? Discuss your answers with your peers and supervisor.

B. Read the following profile of a child. Then read the statement made by the parent. What would you consider to be an appropriate response? Discuss possible responses with your peers, cooperating teacher, and supervisor.

1. You are concerned about Mark's appearance; he arrives at preschool in dirty, torn clothing, his hair is unkempt, and he often smells of stale urine and feces. His peers frequently complain about his odor and choose not to sit or play near him. You have noticed that his underpants look like they have been worn for a month without having been washed. You ask the cooperating teacher if she has made a home visit and she tells you that she had asked, but the mother refused, stating "The mister don't want no one to come when he ain't home." You ask if she shouldn't schedule a conference with the mother and she reluctantly agrees. After the usual opening remarks, the cooperating teacher asks, "Do you have a washing machine at home?" Mark's mother responds negatively, eyes both you and the cooperating teacher suspiciously, and asks, "What business is it of yours if the mister and me has a washing machine?"

2. Kathy caught your attention for two reasons. First, she is always cocking her head to one side and holding it close to the paper when she draws or writes. You notice that she frequently squints when she tries to read material on the chalkboard and has, more than once, copied a math problem incorrectly. One day, she asks to switch seats with Alicia, so she can see the side chalkboard more easily. You have to repeat directions for Kathy, and have noticed that she sometimes asks her seatmate to explain the directions to her again. You do not have the services of a school nurse to check sight and hearing, but your cooperating teacher has called Kathy's mother, scheduled a conference, and has asked you to sit in.

   In the meantime your cooperating teacher has allowed you to look at Kathy's registration form and medical doctor's statement. The doctor has noted slight nearsightedness but no apparent hearing problem. You suspect that Kathy may have deficiencies in both.

   When her mother arrives, your cooperating teacher asks about Kathy's behavior at home. The mother admits that Kathy does sit close to the television and seems inattentive at times. "I thought Kathy might have a problem hearing but her father put an end to that! You know what he did? He sat in the kitchen while she was in the family room and whispered, 'Kathy, do you want some ice cream, honey?' Well, Kathy answered right away! Her father and I both think Kathy just gets too involved in things. She's not deaf!"

3. Josip is one of those children who never sits still for a minute. He moves around constantly from the moment he enters the child care center until nap time, when he must be urged strongly to lie down. Nap time is agony for Josip: he twists and turns, grumbles, sighs, and disturbs everyone around him. Yet, when he does fall asleep, he is difficult to awaken. Sometimes your cooperating teacher has allowed him to continue to sleep. You talk to your cooperating teacher and hypothesize that you think Josip does not get enough sleep at night. She suggests that you call Mrs. Milutin and ask her to come in for a short conference. "Mrs. Milutin," you ask, "when does Josip go to bed? Sometimes he really takes a long nap at school."

   Mrs. Milutin responds, "Well, of course he sleeps at school! That is why his father and I cannot get him to sleep at home! Maybe if you do not allow Josip to sleep at school, he will sleep better at home!"

C. Visit a residential center for children with special needs. Discuss your observations with your peers and supervisor.

○REVIEW

A. List five characteristics of a child with special needs.

B. Read the following descriptions of behavior. Identify the child in each situation who may be special. Discuss your answers with your peers and supervisor.

1. Ladan is a new child in your room of four-year-olds. Her mother says that the family speaks English in the home, but you have doubts. In the classroom, Ladan seems to be more of a spectator than a participant. You note that when playing "Simon Says," Ladan does not appear to know what to do but copies her neighbor.

2. Richie is an abused two-year-old who has recently been placed in a foster home. He enters preschool every morning like a small whirlwind, running around the room, kicking at block structures other children have built, knocking over puzzles others are making, and screaming at the top of his lungs.

3. Even though Kosuke has been in your kindergarten class for nearly the entire year, his behavior has not changed noticeably from the first day. He still clings to his mother's hand when she brings him to school, and he cries for three to five minutes after she leaves. He has only one friend in the room, and efforts to persuade him to play or work with another child are met with tears. He appears totally absorbed by cars and plays with the match box cars or the large truck in the play center to the exclusion of other activities. This absorption continues in his drawings—always of cars.

4. Elena, a pretty, dark-haired seven-year-old in your after-school child care center, complains every day she comes in about her headaches and her queasy stomach. You wonder if she is coming down with the flu (it had been going around), but Elena has no fever, and the complaints are a chronic occurrence.

5. Jorge is a student in a bilingual first grade but seldom talks, in either Spanish or English. When he does speak, he usually speaks so softly that only the students next to him can hear. When you urge him to speak up, Jorge often lowers his head and says nothing. He does appear to understand when given directions, but you are concerned about his non-communicative behavior. When his mother is questioned, she's not concerned because Jorge's older brother, Carlos, had displayed similar behavior when he first entered school.

CASE SCENARIO

Setting: A first-grade classroom in a public school.

Matt is the newly assigned student teacher. Mrs. Levinson is his cooperating teacher, and Dr. Canalas, the university supervisor. After Matt's first week in the room, Dr. Canalas and Mrs. Levinson meet after school with him.

"Well, Matt, how do you like the class?" asks Mrs. Levinson.

Matt answers, "The children sure are little! And what is happening with Carl? He's constantly moving: tapping

continues . . .

. . . continued

his foot, rapping his fingers, sharpening his pencil, asking to go to the boy's room. I've noticed he has difficulty writing; his handwriting is almost illegible, and he moves awkwardly at recess."

"You've observed some of the same behaviors we have," Mrs. Levinson states. "Dr. Canalas, what have you noticed? You've only come once but I know you're pretty observant. Any hypotheses?"

"I'd like Matt to tell us what he thinks might be behind Carl's behavior. Matt, what hypotheses might you suggest?" Dr. Canalas turns toward Matt.

"Well, I've only been here a week but I can't help but think Carl might be hyperactive. In fact, could he be AD/HD? Then again, could he be somewhat slow intellectually? I don't think he has a problem hearing, but I'd want that checked, too. Do you think I'm on the right track?" Matt asks.

Questions for Discussion:

1. Does Matt seem to understand what might be causing Carl's behavior in the classroom?

2. What are some of the symptoms of a child who has AD/HD?

3. Are there other background factors that might cause the same observed behavior displayed by Carl?

4. In a week's time, does a student teacher really have the time to observe an individual child sufficiently? What might you say to your cooperating teacher and college supervisor if you were put in Matt's situation?

REFERENCES

American Psychiatric Association. (2000). *Diagnostic and statistical manual of mental disorders* (4th ed.). Washington, DC: Author.

Armstrong, T. (1996, February). ADD: Does it really exist? *Phi Delta Kappan, 77*(6).

Batshaw, M. L., M.D. (2002). *Children with disabilities* (5th ed.). Baltimore, MD: Paul H. Brooks Publishing.

Breslin, D. (January, 2005). Children's capacity to develop resiliency: How to nurture it. *Young Children, 60*(1), 47–51.

Burgess, K. B., & Younger, A. J. (2006, Spring). Self-schemas, anxiety, somatic and depressive symptoms in socially withdrawn children and adolescents. *Journal of Research in Childhood Education, 20*(3), 175–187.

Chinn, P. C., Winn, J., & Walters, R. H. (1985). *Two-way talking with parents of special children: A process of positive communication.* St. Louis, MO: C. V. Mosby.

Cook, R. E., Klein, M. D., & Tessier, A., in collaboration with Daley, S. E. (2004). *Adapting early childhood curricula for children in inclusive settings* (6th ed.). Upper Saddle River, NJ: Pearson/Merrill/Prentice Hall.

Federal Register. (1977). PL 94–142, 300.5.

Grisham-Brown, J., Hemmeter, M. L., & Pretti-Frontczak, K. (2005). *Blended practices for teaching young children in inclusive settings.* Baltimore, MD: Paul H. Brookes Publishing.

Hogan, D. (1997, Spring). ADHD: A travel guide to success. *Childhood Education, 73*(3).

Kostelnik, M. J., Onaga, E., Rohde, B., & Whiren, A. (2002). *Children with special needs: Lessons for early childhood professionals.* New York: Teachers College Press.

Kubler-Ross, E. (1969). *On death and dying.* New York: Macmillan.

Lewis, R. B., & Doorlag, D. H. (2006). *Teaching special students in general education classrooms* (7th ed.). Upper Saddle River, NJ: Pearson/Merrill/Prentice Hall.

Mastropiere, M. A. & Scruggs, T. E. (2007). *The inclusive classroom: strategies for effective instruction* (3rd ed.). Upper Saddle River, NJ: Pearson/Merrill/Prentice Hall.

National Association for the Education of Young Children. Understanding the Americans with Disabilities Act: Information for early childhood programs. [Brochure]. Washington, DC: Author.

O'Brien, J. (2001, April). How screening and assessment practices support quality disabilities services in Head Start. *Head Start Bulletin*, (70), 20–23.

Orton Dyslexia Society. (1988). *Definition. Perspectives.* Baltimore: Author.

Smelter, R. W., Rasch, B. W., Fleming, J., Nazos, P., & Baranowski, S. (1996, February). Is attention deficit disorder becoming a desired diagnosis? *Phi Delta Kappan, 77*(6).

Smutney, J. F. (2001, Winter). Identifying young gifted disadvantaged children in the K–3 classroom. *Gifted Education Communicator, 32*(4), 35–36.

Terman, L. M., & Merrill, M. A. (1985). *Stanford-Binet scale* (4th ed.). Chicago: Riverside.

Turnbull, A., Turnbull, R., & Wehmeyer, M. L. (2007). *Exceptional lives: special education in today's schools.* (5th ed.). Upper Saddle River, NJ: Pearson/Merrill/Prentice Hall.

U.S. Department of Justice, Civil Rights Division, Disability Rights Section. (1997, October). *Commonly asked questions about child care centers and the Americans with Disabilities Act.* Washington, DC: Author.

Wadlington, E., Jacob, S., & Bailey, S. (1996, Fall). Teaching students with dyslexia in the regular classroom. *Childhood Education, 73*(1).

Wechsler, D. (1991). *Manual for the Wechsler intelligence scale for children (WISCIII)* (3rd ed.). San Antonio, TX: Psychological Corporation.

Wechsler, D. (1989). *Manual for the Wechsler preschool and primary scale of intelligence-revised (WPPSI-R).* San Antonio, TX: Psychological Corporation.

Weissbourd, R. (1996). *The vulnerable child.* Reading, MA: Addison-Wesley.

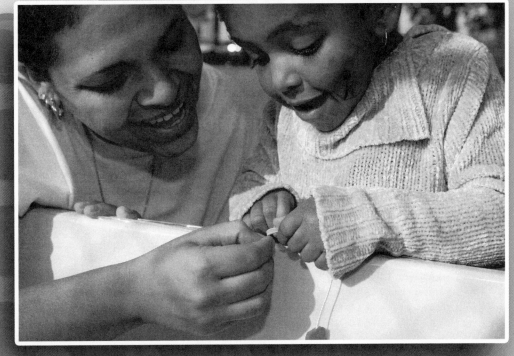

Communication

CHAPTER 9

Common Problems of Student Teachers

OBJECTIVES   **After reading this chapter, you should be able to:**

1.... Identify five common student teacher problems related to interpersonal communication.

2.... List areas of possible conflict between student teachers, supervisors, and cooperating teachers, and their relationship to interpersonal communication.

3.... Describe the goals of interpersonal communication during the student teaching experience.

4.... Identify communication skills that aid in sending and receiving verbal and nonverbal messages.

5.... Define "authenticity" of communication.

6.... Identify a sequential approach to problem solving.

7.... Describe the goals of negotiation.

Comments of student teachers:

> *I was convinced my cooperating teacher didn't like me! I don't take criticism well. After hearing the same comment from different team members, I realized they were trying to help me.* ●

Jonah Hamilton

> *Many of the parents of my placement classroom's children don't speak English. Some are new, struggling immigrants. My cooperating teacher makes all feel welcome. We've a classroom corner where tea and coffee is served and parents can sit and chat at pickup time on sunny days. It's a good idea.* ●

Maylene Hanneford

> *Something that threw me was the fact that the playground rules were different from the school where I work. When I saw a child standing on the big cement tunnel my first thought was "Oh, my goodness! He'll fall and kill himself!" Fortunately my cooperating teacher moved over to the tunnel and calmly asked the child to state how he could get down safely. This was a good lesson, for the technique facilitated problem solving and used child ideas. My first day went faster than greased lightening, and I survived.* ●

Layne Akers

> *I'm working up the courage to tell a fellow student teacher she's not doing her share. My supervisor suggested I tell her how frustrated and angry I am before I explode. It's so easy to say "you" but I plan to stick to "I'm feeling. . . , I'm expecting. . . ."* ●

Glo Hopkings

This chapter is not intended to solve all problems encountered during student teaching, nor is it meant to minimize the many successful and creative solutions student teachers will experience. It will probe possible reasons for difficulties, especially those related to communication, and help alert the student teacher to possible courses of action. Knowing that problems can occur and knowing there are ways to avoid them is stress-reducing. You will relate more strongly to some ideas in this chapter than to others. Knowledge may help you escape some problems, confront others, and cope with ones that cannot be changed. Open communication with others, such as cooperating teachers, college supervisors, and children, is often the key.

KINDS OF PROBLEMS

Do you know of any human relationship that is problem-free and always smooth sailing? Student teaching, involving close human interaction and communication, is no exception. Pressures, feelings, desires, needs, risks, and possible failures are inherent.

Stress

During the first days and weeks of student teaching, **stress** may increase, usually from student teachers desiring to become good practicing teachers, confounded by feelings of self doubt and lack of confidence. As you grasp the challenges through watching your cooperating teacher and attempt to put your own theory into practice, the task seems monumental. Three sequential stages in teacher training are commonplace:

1. focus on self, or self-protection
2. focus on children
3. focus on outcomes of teaching

Initial focus on self appears to be a necessary and crucial element in the first stage of teacher development.

A research study probing student teacher anxieties suggests that supervisors' and cooperating teachers' evaluations of student teacher competency was the most frequently mentioned contributing factor. Program planning, child behavior, class management, and staff relationships were other anxiety producing factors (Morton, Vesco, Williams, & Awender, 1997).

Student teachers without past child care employment experience can feel overwhelmed by a beginning realization concerning teacher workloads. Teaching is hard work, requiring intelligence, preparation, creativity, determination, and perseverance. This reality is quickly understood.

Anxiety

An early focus on oneself may produce **anxiety**. A student teacher can feel uncomfortable until there is a clear feeling of exactly what is expected, and may react to stress in a number of ways. In student teaching, reactions might include becoming defensive, avoiding child guidance, illness, missing class, becoming critical of the placement classroom, looking for faults in others, withdrawing into busy work, undue attention to classroom maintenance, or other behaviors.

 stress—internal or external demand on a person's ability to adapt.

 anxiety—a general sense of uneasiness that cannot be traced to a specific cause.

More positive courses of action are:

- seeking additional written or oral guidelines (see Figure 9–1).
- organizing tasks into time blocks.
- clearly outlining assignments on a calendar, file, or using a binder system.
- seeking the supervisor to communicate anxieties.
- using stress-reduction techniques.

The first three actions can help if lack of information or lack of organization are part of the student teacher's problem. The next actions either express or confront, and will possibly reduce tension. Anxiety can occur when there are changes in life. Change for student teachers occurs with their increasing responsibilities.

What other techniques are helpful? SkillPath Seminars (1997) suggests the following:

- Talk to yourself, emphasizing positive thinking.
- Visualize your success.
- Reward yourself for a job or task well done.
- Take on the responsibility to change situations that cause stress.
- Exercise.
- Learn to play as hard as you work.
- Take care of health concerns.
- Reject perfectionism, yet strive for excellence.
- Maintain optimism.
- Develop a sense of humor.
- Interject fun into your work.
- Seek counseling if necessary.

● **Figure 9-1**
Ask for more information when you need it.

It will be helpful if you continue to pay attention to healthful living, use your sense of humor about the student teaching situation, develop or rely on a support system, obtain an upbeat outlook, exercise, and learn relaxation techniques. It's best to stay away from gossiping if it exists at your workplace, and eliminate destructive self-talk.

Canter (1998) suggests that stressed teachers should look for opportunities to:

- take a walk around the room or yard.
- do some deep breathing exercises to relax.
- identify the source of stress.
- talk to a colleague about it.
- surround themselves with positive-thinking people, who appreciate the challenges of the teaching profession and the significance of a teacher's role in society.

The negative comments of staff at a placement site, and their complaining about lack of administrative support, work overload, parents, and so on, may affect a student teacher's stress level (Canter, 1998). Stress promotes a chemical change in the body, creating tenseness and nervousness that gears the body for action.

Clear, authentic communication of feelings, done with skill and sensitivity, may have not been modeled or taught at home or during schooling. To be effective when expressing feelings, it should be clear that the speaker takes responsibility for the feelings. Feelings should not be confused with thoughts, evaluations, or solutions, but stated with clarity and directness. The speaker avoids implying others are to be blamed or judged for causing the feelings. Using the words "angry," "pleased," "happy," "annoyed," "frustrated," "hurt," "upset," or similar descriptors adds clarity for the listener, who will not have to rely on tone of voice, sarcasm or other implied body messages. The student teaching experience puts student teachers, children, and other adults in close contact, and adds the anxiety-producing element of observing and assessing the student teacher's competency development. If you have already acquired the abilities of speaking openly and frankly without alienating people, being a skillful listener, and receiving and accepting suggestions, this chapter will serve as a review, perhaps providing additional insights and communication techniques.

Keirsey and Bates (1984) offer the following advice for individuals seeking to understand and communicate with others:

> If I do not want what you want, please try not to tell me that my want is wrong.
>
> Or if I believe other than you, at least pause before you correct my view.
>
> Or if my emotion is less than yours, or more, given the same circumstances, try not to ask me to feel more strongly or weakly.
>
> If you will allow me any of my own wants, or emotions, or beliefs, or actions, then you open yourself, so that some day these ways of mine might not seem so wrong, and might finally appear to you as right—for me.

People are different in fundamental ways. They want different things. The importance of relating and communicating with others in early childhood work cannot be overestimated. Many early childhood teachers face cultural diversity daily, which necessitates increased awareness, sensitivity, and skillful communication. The situation is complicated by biases and stereotypes each of us may have about teachers. You may find yourself saying, "All teachers are bad . . . I will save these children and protect them from the teacher. I will do the opposite of what she does. . . ." Or you may say, "All teachers are wonderful, superior people . . . I will copy the words, phrases, voice quality, and gestures of this teacher. Then I, too, will be marvelous." (Danoff, Breitbart, & Barr, 1977)

Very strong feelings can be accepted as natural and to be expected. Once accepted, there is the chance to move on and get past them, or at least cope.

> First of all, students can expect to feel inadequate when they begin participating in the school, and probably for some time after that. They cannot possibly be prepared for all that may happen. No one can give instructions that will cover everything, and certainly not in what time there may have been to prepare. Of course, students will not feel sure of what is expected of them, nor of what they are supposed to do. The teacher who is guiding them may not be sure of these things herself, as she does not know the students yet, nor does she know what is possible for them. What we can do about feelings of inadequacy at this point is to feel normal for having them (Read & Patterson, 1980).

You will find it is possible to be excited, even eager, to try your ideas and activities, ready to develop your own teaching style, and still be somewhat apprehensive. The caring and involvement student teachers bring to their work are commendable. These will further their success in student teaching. Warner (1995) suggests "teachers should never feel guilty at the end of a teaching day, or think of themselves as a failure. If they have made a positive difference in just one child's life, they should view themselves as successful."

A contrast to the anxious approach to student teaching is the relaxed, confident one. This happens after a few successes. Self-confidence and self-esteem are important primary goals of student teaching. They evolve in student teachers as they do in children, through actions resulting in success and through the feedback received from others. A strong feeling of success through child interactions is described by Read and Patterson (1980):

> A child's face lights up when he sees us come into the room, and we know that our relationship with him is a source of strength. He is seeing us as someone who cares, who can be depended on, and who has something significant to give him. It makes us feel good inside to be this kind of person for a child. It gives us confidence (see Figure 9–2).

Hints for dealing with anxiety suggest trying not to worry about being the teacher; instead, reflect on teachers you liked when you were a child. Another method is to relax and treat children your own way, the way you really think about them. This will give you the confidence required to give more, try more, and be more effective. One of your authors still meets with elementary classmates who had Mrs. Bertulli as their teacher in fourth grade and agree they share a liking of

● **Figure 9-2**
Building trusting and caring relationships aids communication.

opera music. Mrs. Bertulli, an opera buff, used it frequently to calm her class during rest periods.

Putting student teaching in perspective, and being able to laugh at the situation, or at yourself, helps reduce anxiety.

Time Management

As mentioned in Chapter 6, time management is a part of total classroom management. For some student teachers, time management is a continuous problem. A date book, file, or pocket and desk calendar help. Organization is a key element. Devise a system that puts what you need within reach; it will save time. Plan ahead and break large tasks into small, specific pieces. Use daily lists and give tasks priorities. Think of "must do first," medium priority, and "can wait" categories. Do not waste time feeling guilty. Working with a colleague or friend is a strategy that often gets difficult tasks accomplished.

Cooperating teachers sometimes complain that students are not prepared, are tardy, or are unreliable. Already having a job may limit the hours necessary for the preparation of class assignments. Assignments should involve planning ahead and analyzing task time lengths. Last minute desperation increases tension, destroys composure, and creates stress. Only the student teacher can make adjustments to provide enough time and rest necessary for student teaching. Standards of teacher training are rarely relaxed for just one individual.

Von Bergen (2003) believes disorganization sends out "ripples of difficulties." Every time you can't find what you need, stress mounts and time is wasted. One can miss deadlines, feel frustration, and become less comfortable and less confident. With organization one becomes more productive, efficient, and usually maintains a more positive work/life balance. It pays to not only organize available time, but also schoolwork, materials, schedules, and so on, using your own system of organization.

If you have not discussed with your family and friends how your practicum may affect your relationship and time with them, do so. Solicit their supportive understanding, so they will be aware of the possible mental and physical stress you may experience because of your workload. Fortunately, you can assure them that student teaching is a temporary experience.

Worry

Practicing teachers, and some student teachers, tend to mull over their teaching day, worrying about particular children or some other feature of their classroom. Von Bergen (2003) suggests that on-the-job stress may be replayed during sleep. This, she feels, allows thoughts and emotions to rise and fall in different parts of the brain, perhaps to produce solutions to problems that might not emerge any other way. Though not a research-proven theory, we mention it here because rarely is there mention of any positive effects of worrying. We, in fact, would urge you not to worry, but rather have faith in your ability.

Seeking Help

It is difficult for some student teachers to ask for help or suggestions. The risk involves having either the cooperating teacher or supervisor realize your limitations. Therefore, student teachers sometimes turn to other student teachers. Trust is an important element in this dilemma. Fortunately, one builds trust through human interactions, and seeking help usually becomes easier as time passes. Self-doubt may cause a student teacher to resist asking questions, for fear of looking dense, needy, or vulnerable. Leeds (2001) suggests asking "smart questions." She believes the following types of questions are effective problem solvers:

● *Pose a question that lets the other person answer what you want to know.* "Would you like me to plan another physical development activity or branch out to another area?"

● *Begin conversations with open-ended questions.* "What kinds of words or actions might I use to calm Rocky down?"

● *End conversations with closed-ended questions.* "Am I making sense? Have I addressed everything?"

● *If you are dealing with a problem, explain what you have done so far, and pose your question.* "I read the label on the powdered paint can and mixed in more powder, but I'm wondering if the paint is still too runny. What do you think?"

● *Ask questions at a neutral time, when the problem can be separated from strong emotions.*

● *Avoid asking negative questions.* For instance, instead of saying, "You didn't like the way my lesson went, did you?" ask questions such as, "How could I have improved my planned activity?"

It is important to seek help quickly in many instances, and to use consultation times and meetings to pick the brains of others and seek assistance.

The role of both the supervisor and cooperating teacher includes on-site mentoring and advice (see Figure 9–3.) A beginning teacher needs encouragement, reassurance, comfort, guidance, instruction in specific skills, and insight into the complex causes of behavior. In the English primary school system, it is customary for a beginning teacher to receive advice and supportive assistance on a daily basis, throughout the first full year of teaching. Some school districts in the United States provide mentor teachers to newly hired teachers.

● **Figure 9-3**
Mentoring is an important part of a supervisor's job.

The Half-a-Teacher Feeling

During their experiences, many student teachers are led to feel, either by the children, cooperating teachers, or other staff members, that because of their position, they are not quite students and not quite teachers. Because of this neither-here-nor-there attitude, student teachers are not always treated as figures of authority. Read the poem in Figure 9–4. It may bring a knowing smile. Children in many instances may not recognize you as a teacher, but may refer to you as a student teacher. Some student teachers have had the experience of being treated as a "go-fer," and being asked to do things a teacher is not required to do.

Sometimes early in student teaching, a strong team feeling has not been established, yet its development is critical, for all involved. It may be best to consult with your supervisor first; cooperating teachers have a number of factors to consider in relinquishing control of their classroom.

Often they feel uneasy when their routines, or classroom behavior standards, are threatened. They may also feel like they are asking too much too soon of their student teachers, and may be unclear of their role in giving assignments. It may be difficult for cooperating teachers to interchange their roles and become co-teachers instead of lead teachers. They can also be worried about child safety.

Most cooperating teachers get a real sense of teaming with student teachers as the semester progresses. One cooperating teacher describes her experience as follows:

> One student teacher was so perceptive that she would anticipate what I wanted or needed without my having to ask. As a result, we worked as a team and the children really accomplished a great deal (Sanders, 2002).

Student teachers may feel frightened about taking risks, and torn between being eager to try new things but afraid of observer feedback if they differ significantly from their cooperating teacher's style (Brighton, 1999). They may decide to play it safe, not realizing they are losing opportunities for growth in doing so. New and beginning teachers are usually enthusiastic and optimistic, with a passion for teaching. Most hope to change children's lives, and existing practice, for the better (Hurst & Reding, 1999).

Guidance

Student teachers often find that the children will obey the rules when the cooperating teacher is present, or is the one who asks, but not when the *student teacher* asks. Children test and question the authority of a new adult. Student teachers may tend to force issues, or completely ignore children when classroom rules are broken. These situations may be temporarily troublesome. In time, the children will realize that the student teacher means what he or she says, and consistency and firmness will win out.

When student teachers feel they cannot deal with these situations, they tend to stay close to self-controlled or affectionate children. This type of behavior indicates a possible withdrawal from the total room responsibility. If you are experiencing difficulty, look back at the ideas in Chapters 6 and 7, and consult with both your cooperating teacher and supervisor for suggestions.

Attachments

At times, a child may form a strong bond or attachment with a particular student teacher. The child may be inconsolable for some time after the student teacher's departure. Most student teachers worry about this behavior, and their supervisor's and cooperating teacher's reactions to it. It is an important topic for team meetings.

Male student teachers often have a unique experience while student teaching, based on children's lack of experience with males as teachers. After a short period, the children will view the male student teacher as just another teacher, with his own individuality. If this does not happen, further study of the child or children is in order.

Male student teachers may experience family bias and suspicion concerning their choice of a career with young children. This may be voiced and is a difficult issue to deal with. Highly publicized cases that have been in the media can lead to family fears. Most center directors face the issue of new, male student teachers head on, and as early in the placement as

Not Quite

Her classroom

Her rules

Her kids

And ———

She's "the teacher" here.

I'm just an almost, a "not quite"

Who's working hard to get it right.

But wait and see

A real teacher I'm beginning to be!

 Figure 9-4
"Not Quite"

possible, with parent group meetings that focus on father figures and parenting skills that relate to men.

Philosophic Differences

Sometimes the cooperating teacher's view of child education, and how children learn, is quite similar to the student's; in other placements, it is not. Gleaning an understanding of methods, techniques, curriculums, goals and objectives of classrooms is the task of the student. When conflicting views are present in a supportive atmosphere, they are respected. Student teachers can gain a chance to clarify their own ideas when confronted with differing ones. New and diverse views result in the growth and clarification of the student's idea of what is best for children and families.

It is disconcerting and uncomfortable for both students and cooperating teachers when their teaching styles clash. Open discussion, particularly when done in a caring way that preserves the dignity of each teacher's opinions, is the best course of action.

Students should not surrender their philosophical values, but tenaciously retain what they feel is best for children. Every wave of newly trained preschool and primary school teachers has its own contribution to make. The old or established way is always subject to questions in education. Practicing teachers continue to try innovative approaches; some are used in a complete or modified form, others are tried and discarded. Thoughtfulness and open-mindedness help student teachers, as does a "win-win" attitude.

Personality Conflicts

Whether or not you believe everyone has their own "vibe," you probably readily admit that you work much better with some people than with others.

Communication skill is critical in working relationships. Most difficult situations can at least become bearable through open communication.

Being Held Back

Very often, student teachers are not given the opportunity to work with children as much as they would like. As a result, they can become frustrated and feel that their potential for growth as teachers is being stifled. This can also happen when a cooperating teacher steps in during an activity or incident and assumes the student cannot handle the situation. These occurrences reduce the student's opportunity to work out of tight or uncomfortable spots. In the first example, the student is not allowed to start; in the second, to finish.

The student needs to know the thinking behind the cooperating teacher's behavior; the cooperating teacher needs to grasp the student's feeling. Neither can happen without communicating.

> Your master teacher is not able to read your mind. The only way he is going to know the things you are worried about, any feeling of inadequacy or uncertainty you may have, as well as your positive feelings, is to tell him. (Gordon-Nourok, 1979).

A special, agreed-upon signal can be used by the student teacher to alert the cooperating teacher to her need for help, in the form of immediate consultation, or suggestion.

Sensing a Need for Child Activities and Using One-Day Wonders

One way to avoid misunderstandings and difficulties with your cooperating teacher is to come prepared with a number of short activities that could be called **one-day wonders**. These preplanned activities are a sort of insurance policy, and relieve the panic of possibly being asked to do a last-minute activity, or when sensing the need for children's engagement in an activity at certain times of the day. One can fit a number of preplanned activities, stored separately, in a large tote bag or cardboard file that can be stowed somewhere in the classroom (see Figure 9–5).

A simple lesson, appropriate for fall, might be to come to class with the following materials for each child: a two-inch ball of clay (carefully wrapped in plastic so the clay won't dry out), paper plates to define work space, and lunch bags for gathering leaves and seeds lying on the ground. This lesson has been successfully used with preschoolers and primary-age children. During free play or recess, children can be directed to pick up and place in the bags items from the play yard that remind them of fall. Typically, students will gather all kinds of leaves, twigs, seed pods, dry weeds, and even stones and pebbles.

On returning to the classroom, the following directions can be given:

"At the science (or discovery) center, you will find a stack of paper plates and a large plastic bag with balls of clay. You may choose the science center as one of your options to explore this afternoon. Place one of the paper plates on the table; carefully take one of the balls of clay from the plastic bag and place it on your plate. Shape the ball of clay into any form you wish, and use any of the materials you brought in from the play yard as decoration. When you finish, leave your sculpture on its paper plate and place it on the shelf by the window." You may want to demonstrate the process as you give the directions.

one-day wonders— preplanned and often prepackaged collections of materials that student teachers can easily set up or use on the spur of the moment to engage young children.

● **Figure 9-5**
Student teachers may test activities with other student teachers watching. Courtesy of Iowa State University Child Development Laboratory School.

Do you enjoy stories? Another example of a successful one-day wonder is the following first-grade language art lesson. Introduce as follows:

"I've brought you one of my favorite stories to share during story time today. It's called *Rosie's Walk*, by Pat Hutchins (1968)."

After you finish reading, you might tell the children, "Those children choosing the writing center activity may dictate to me or Mrs. Nguyen (or write) your own versions of *Rosie's Walk* (Hutchins, 1968). When you have finished, you may illustrate your story. Remember, only four students can come up at once, but the rest of you will have a chance later this afternoon."

Other possibilities for one-day wonders are limited only by your imagination. Many cooperating teachers who may be reluctant to turn over large segments of time to a student teacher are willing to do so with one-day wonders that fit smoothly into the curriculum. Any area of the curriculum can work, but it is always best if you can agree with your cooperating teacher on one specific area, perhaps one that she does not particularly enjoy.

Other one-day wonders designed by former student teachers follow:

- Provide colored, gummed paper worker hats (precut chef, cowboy, firefighter, police officer, nurse, sailor, farmer, doorman, cab driver, and so on), art paper, and crayons. Children lick and stick, add a face if they wish, and possibly share a story about their hat, or give their created person a name.

- Provide tongs, blunt tweezers, chopsticks, three colors or more of colored cotton balls (shake powdered tempera and balls in *closed* plastic, zippered bags), small containers. For this activity, children sort colors by picking up the cotton balls with the variety of tools provided.

- Provide mounted photos of children, snapped in action in the classroom. This causes lots of discussion and excitement. Say, "Tell me about the photograph you've chosen." This works especially well if children can stand in front of the group of photos, giving all a good look before commencing.

- Provide small plastic cars and roads, drawn on shelf paper by the student teacher beforehand, with other features such as houses, stop signs, trees, dead-ends, railroad tracks, parking spots, and the like. Use your imagination. A roll of masking tape secures the road to table tops or floors. This wonder is good for outside as well as inside, as shelf paper can be rolled and ready. Many children will want to talk about what they are doing and where they are going.

One-day wonders for elementary school can most easily focus on activities related to one of your favorite children's books. If you want a book that also ties into topics associated with the social studies curriculum, your cooperating teacher or college supervisor may have some suggestions. We have found children's librarians to be of great help when asked for books on given topics, such as families, pets and wild animals, and different countries. Always make sure you have a range of books, from those that can be read in a day to those read in chapters. When it comes to art, music, and creative writing, children are often naturals.. They can illustrate their own endings to any story, suggest a song to sing on the topic, or even create their own, additional adventures for the story's characters.

One-day wonders for math can relate to graphing months in which children have birthdays, then asking them to predict your birthday, or your cooperating teacher's birthday. Their predictions can be pasted on a prepared calendar chart. Favorite foods, numbers of brothers and sisters, which student is wearing what colors: all of these lend themselves to graphing. How children get to school opens up the topic of modes of transportation, which is another graphing possibility.

Science activities can be as simple as having magnets and cartons (we prefer egg cartons) filled with all kinds of attractive "junk," ranging from paper clips, buttons, and other magnets to screws, nuts, bolts, and keys. It is best if some of your paper clips, buttons, and keys are not magnetic, whereas others are, as this leads to hypothesizing about why similar objects can be magnetic or nonmagnetic. Probing magnetism can extend to having children discover which items around the classroom will hold magnets and which will not.

Other science lessons can relate to classifying a variety of leaves and flowers and discussing their similarities and differences. Do not expect children to classify in exactly the same way a botanist would, but do expect them to be able to justify why they have formed the classification they have. As with many things you might use as activity ideas, you are limited only by your imagination, and your ability to predict what will interest children.

Site Politics

One of the most difficult placement situations is one that is consumed with conflict. Power struggles between teachers, the director or principal, parents, community, or any other group make the student feel as if he is being pressured to take sides. The student teacher is usually afraid to join either faction and tries to be a friend to all. This situation should be discussed with your supervisor—quickly. Make sure to convey that you are willing to work through any difficult situation, but that you want her to be aware of your placement site's tensions.

Developing Supportive Staff Relationships

Just as you **role model** behaviors for children, you will consciously or unconsciously model behaviors for colleagues. These behaviors may include empathy, friendliness, kindness, concern, and **collaboration**.

Professional conduct encompasses valuing staff diversity, in special abilities, talents, and educative ideas and approaches. Working together to accomplish goals may require acceptance of differences, careful listening and observation, the ability to communicate effectively and honestly, and the elimination of any need to change others, or to defend any position on issues (See Figure 9–6). These attributes, along with the use of reflective thinking to find the many avenues to reach goals, skillful collaboration, and the development of team spirit, give staff an edge in goal realization.

The National Association for the Education of Young Children has developed a position statement: The *Code of Ethical Conduct and Statement of Commitment*. The Code of Ethical Conduct provides suggestions for maintaining healthy, positive, and professional relationships. Although it was not designed for student teachers, it can be used as a helpful guide. Figure 9–7 is an excerpt from section III, "Ethical Responsibilities to Colleagues."

role model—a person whose behavior is imitated by others.

collaboration—parents and teachers working together for the ultimate good of the children or students.

Figure 9-6
The teaching team can be small or have many members.

SECTION III ETHICAL RESPONSIBILITIES TO COLLEAGUES.

A—Responsibilities to co-workers

Ideals

I-3A.1—To establish and maintain relationships of respect, trust, confidentiality, collaboration, and cooperation with co-workers.

I-3A.2—To share resources with co-workers, collaborating to ensure that the best possible early childhood care and education program is provided.

I-3A.3—To support co-workers in meeting their professional needs and in their professional development.

I-3A.4—To accord co-workers due recognition of professional achievement.

Principles

P-3A.1—We shall recognize the contributions of colleagues to our program and not participate in practices that diminish their reputations or impair their effectiveness in working with children and families.

P-3A.2—When we have concerns about the professional behavior of a co-worker, we shall first let that person know of our concern in a way that shows respect for personal dignity and for the diversity to be found among staff members, and then attempt to resolve the matter collegially and in a confidential manner.

P-3A.3—We shall exercise care in expressing views regarding the personal attributes or professional conduct of co-workers. Statements should be based on firsthand knowledge, not hearsay, and relevant to the interests of children and programs.

P-3A.4—We shall not participate in practices that discriminate against a co-worker because of sex, race, national origin, religious beliefs or other affiliations, age, marital status/family structure, disability, or sexual orientation.

 Figure 9-7

Selected Section of NAEYC's Code of Ethical Conduct. Copyright © 2005 by the National Association for the Education of Young Children.

THE ROLE OF COMMUNICATION AND CONFLICT RESOLUTION

communication—giving or receiving information, signals, and/or messages.

Communication is a broad term that we define as giving and/or receiving information, signals, or messages. Human interactions are full of nonverbal signals, accounting for 60 to 80 percent of most human encounters. Some of the more easily recognized nonverbal communications are facial expression, body position, breathing tempo, and voice pitch, volume, and inflection (see Figure 9–8).

A two-way process of sending and receiving information occurs in true communication, and communication skill can be learned. Burke (1998) estimates that only seven percent of communication is actually influenced by the words of a communicator, with tone of voice and body language making the largest impact on the listener.

Being conscious of what messages people are conveying as they speak with body gestures and tone of voice is an important first step. The whole climate of interpersonal relationships in an educational setting can be affected by an individual's ability to read nonverbal cues and communicate.

Conflict Resolution

Conflict resolution usually refers to strategies that enable individuals to handle conflicts cooperatively, possibly attaining win-win situations. Mediation by a neutral third party can be part of the process. Skills enlisted by conflict resolution participants include, among others, communication, cooperation, tolerance, and positive expression of emotions (see Figure 9–9).

All conflicts may not be resolvable using the recommended conflict resolution techniques. Some problems do not have immediate fixes or short-term solutions, and it is unfortunate if student teachers hold that expectation. Teacher training programs are introducing conflict resolution classes because the coursework is viewed as essential.

Student teacher growth and self-realization can depend on the communication skill of the student teacher and others. According to Rogers and Freiberg (1994), it is through a mutually supportive, helping relationship that each individual can become better integrated and more able to function effectively. Student teachers can model appropriate communication behaviors, increasing effectiveness for other adults and children.

No doubt your student teaching group contains people with diverse opinions and backgrounds. Your placement site may also reflect our multiethnic and multicultural society. Delpit (1995) believes we all carry worlds in our heads, and those worlds are decidedly different. She feels it is the responsibility of a dominant group member to attempt to hear the other

 Figure 9-8
Clint loves to make faces that cause peers and teachers to laugh.

conflict resolution—a process to resolve disputes between people with different interests. This resolution process can have constructive consequences if the parties air their different interests, make trade-offs, and reach a settlement that satisfies the essential needs of each.

WHAT MAY RESULT IN CONFLICT RESOLUTION EFFORTS IS:

• the *recognition* that a problem exists, which focuses attention and motivates individuals to take action.
• a *clarification* of one's values, points of view, goals, wants, and ethics, and to what degree and intensity one cares.
• an *understanding* of others' goals, wants, values, and ethics.
• a *focus* on change.
• a *confidence* in oneself and the conflict resolution process when resolution is successful.
• a *feeling* that personal relationships with other staff can weather problems and disagreements.
• a *clearing of the air* and *reduction of stress*.
• an *emotional release*.
• a *new outlook* about conflict being a part of many working group situations.
• a *wake up call* regarding how one's actions and ideas can create problems with others.
• a *realization* that confrontational techniques can be scary, yet may lead to positive outcomes.
• a *realization* that boredom or staleness may be a problem in itself and a "ho-hum" attitude changes nothing.

 Figure 9-9
Possible positive outcomes in conflict resolution attempts.

side of an issue, and after hearing, to speak in a modified voice that does not exclude the concerns of minority colleagues. When a conflict exists, all participants in a discussion should state their perspective so that all the individual perspectives held can be understood. This affords an opportunity to gain a broader view before jumping into a solution.

Working productively with other staff members requires a mutual exchange that takes place in an atmosphere of openness, respect, and honesty (Caruso & Fawcett, 1999).

Communication: Reacting to Bias

With the multicultural representations in many early childhood classrooms and staff members, a teacher may encounter bias. What one adult deems appropriate and worthwhile, another may see as inappropriate. Carter and Curtis (1994) suggest teachers have seven choices when responding to adults who express bias:

1. Attacking
2. Defending
3. Empathizing
4. Investigating
5. Reframing
6. Excusing
7. Ignoring

Some of a responding teacher's communication choices can come as an assault to others or be perceived as defensive, whereas others may foster awareness and sensitivity (Carter & Curtis, 1994). Analyze the following teacher responses and decide which promote the early childhood goal of working as a supportive partner with parents.

Situation: Alfredo's mom tells you most of the activities planned at school, and much of the equipment, don't allow Alfredo to be a real boy, and are more suited for girls. A teacher's seven choices of statements might be:

1. "Alfredo chooses his own activities, Mrs. Santos. You don't want us to force him to play more vigorous games, do you?"
2. "We're an accredited school; we've been approved by experts."
3. "You are distressed over Alfredo's behavior at school."
4. "You are concerned that Alfredo will not learn to play like a real boy."
5. "Alfredo chooses many sedentary activities over more vigorous play right now. He is really enjoying books and exploring writing tools. Your feeling is that this behavior might not allow him to develop the physical skill necessary for play with other boys his age. Our program offers vigorous outdoor play, but at the moment, Alfredo is following his own interests."
6. "Well, Alfredo is just being Alfredo."
7. "Mrs. Santos, has this been a good day for you?"

Which choices may identify the problem appropriately? What bias is present? Could the parent's cultural expectations cause her feelings?

Caring and Sharing: A First Step in Communicating

What makes a person interesting or easy to talk with? Why do we discuss problems with some individuals and not with others? Perhaps it is because the person with whom we can talk freely loves and accepts us as we are at that moment. Love and acceptance can be demonstrated a number of ways. Saying it may be the easiest way; showing it through actions may be the toughest. With children, giving attention and not interfering with their freedom of choice helps develop their feelings of self-worth and value. Touching also usually reinforces rapport; a pat, hug, or open lap for young children expresses love and acceptance. A wink, a notice of accomplishment, or a sincere recognition of a special uniqueness in an individual helps feelings of caring and sharing grow.

Setting the stage for easy approaching and interacting also helps. NAEYC's *Early Childhood Program Standards (2005)* state that warm, sensitive, and responsive interactions help children develop a secure, positive sense of self, and encourages them to respect and cooperate with others. It also notes children who see themselves as highly valued are more likely to feel secure, thrive physically, get along with others, learn well, and feel part of a community.

Student teachers plan ways to establish rapport with children and adults during their first working days (see Figure 9–10). Being an upbeat person and making sincere, appropriate remarks when first meeting others is recommended. Impressions depend on first contacts and interactions. There are definite skills beginning teachers can acquire to establish an easy flow of daily conversation with children. Some suggestions follow:

● **Figure 9-10**
Student teachers establish rapport on their first working days.

- Offer a personal greeting to each child.
- Take time to listen and respond to the child who is bursting to tell a story.
- Make a point of giving a special greeting to the shy child; verbalize the child's actions.
- Help children plan for the day by building on prior experiences and introducing new ones.
- Find time to talk personally with each child during the day about important events or experiences in their lives.
- Explain requests to children so that they will understand.
- Talk to the children more than to classroom adults.

Children's communication skill and degree of cooperation may affect how a student teacher relates to and views them. Student teachers tend to gravitate toward conversation with children who respond, use the student teacher's name, establish eye contact, and to those children who are most like them, or who make them feel at home. They also interact with the child who gains their attention. Popular, well-liked children usually fit this description. Seeing the challenge in developing trust and open communication with each child, student teachers will notice some children who may ignore conversational overtures, change the subject, say something irrelevant, or otherwise reject them. They sometimes find that approaching a small group of children or a child in solitary play works best to initiate conversation.

Children who feel good about themselves and experience caring teachers usually communicate successfully with newcomers such as student teachers.

Armstrong (1994) offers additional guidelines:

1. Build solid, trusting relationships before seeking information from children.

2. Keep conversation on subjects that are strongly relevant to children's interests, or part of their everyday experience.

3. Try role-playing with manipulative toys that allow the relationship between early language and activity to flourish.

4. Use words and styles that "belong" to the children, and that take into consideration their competence level.

5. Be empathetic; try to see situations from the child's point of view.

6. Probe for responses by asking questions a new way, but avoid suggesting answers.

7. Select times to talk that do not interfere with children's favorite activities.

Authenticity

Much has been written about being *"real"* with children and adults. This means honestly sharing your feelings without putting down or destroying anyone's feelings of competency and self-worth. The term "congruent sending" was coined by Gordon (1972), well known for his work in human communication. His definition follows:

> Congruence refers to the similarity of what a person (the sender) is thinking or feeling inside, and what he communicates to the outside. When a person is being congruent, we experience him as "open," "direct," or "genuine." When we sense that a person's communication is incongruent, we judge him as "not ringing true," "insincere," "affected," or just plain "phony."

The resulting risk in sending real messages without skill is that we may experience rejection. Student teachers can learn to express a wide range of real feelings in a skillful way. Anger is perhaps the hardest to handle skillfully. Ginott (1972) has advice for dealing with anger:

> The realities of teaching make anger inevitable. Teachers need not apologize for their angry feelings. An effective teacher is neither a masochist nor a martyr. He does not play the role of a saint or act the part of an angel. He is aware of his human feelings and respects them. Though he cannot be patient, he is always authentic. His response is genuine. His words fit his feeling. He does not hide his annoyance. He does not pretend patience. He does not demonstrate hypocrisy by acting nice when feeling nasty.
>
> An enlightened teacher is not afraid of his anger because he has learned to express it without doing damage. He has mastered the secret of expressing anger without insult.
>
> . . . When angry, an enlightened teacher remains real. He describes what he sees, what he feels, and what he expects. He attacks the problem, not the person. He protects himself and safeguards his students by using "I" messages.

The following tips may help when you become aware of strong emotions or anger:

- Listen and nod while maintaining eye contact.
- Show acceptance.
- Make empathy statements.
- Acknowledge the person's feelings.
- Remain calm by deep breathing.
- Arrange a specific time to discuss and negotiate the matter if the emotions occur in a setting that is not conducive to conversation. With a child, wait until strong emotions abate and then talk it through.

It is wise to remember that not all situations, problems, or conflicts can be solved; anger and strong emotions directed toward you may be displaced. Your function may be that of a "listening board" who suggests the conflict would be best resolved if the speaker were to address the problem with another.

A student teacher's idea that the perfect teacher is always calm and cool may inhibit communicating and produce feelings of guilt. A multitude of emotions will be present during student teaching days; a daily diary or journal helps students pinpoint feelings in early stages, and written expression is often easier than speaking with a supervisor. Usually, pleasant feelings are the ones most easily described and discussed. Recognizing the buildup of angry feelings may take a special tuning-in to the self. Common tension signals include:

- Shrill, harsh, or louder voice tone.
- Inability to see humor in a situation.
- Withdrawal or silence.
- Continual mental rehashing of an emotionally trying encounter.

Sharing feelings, including those you consider negative, may help develop a close feeling with others.

"I" Messages

Message-sending takes practice and is only one part of a communication sequence. A series of teacher-sent *I* **messages**, which communicate the sender's feelings without blaming or judging others, follow. You will probably be able to picture the incident that evoked them.

I **messages**—Thomas Gordon's term for a response to a child's behavior that focuses on how the adult feels rather than on the child's character.

"I'm very sad that these pages in our book about horses are torn and crumpled. Book pages need to be turned with care, like this."

"I get so upset when materials I had planned to use with the children disappear."

"Wait a minute. If all the student teachers take a break together, there will be only one adult in the classroom. I'm frustrated; I thought there was a clear statement about taking separate breaks."

"I'm confused about this assignment. I feel like I missed an explanation. Can we talk about it sometime today?"

"I'm feeling very insecure right now. I thought I sensed your disapproval when you asked the children to stop the activity planned for them."

One should guard against "I" messages that are destructive; they sometimes send solutions, or involve blaming and judgmental phrases. These are false "I" messages:

"I feel frustrated when you behave so stupidly."

"I am angry when you don't keep your promises. No one will be able to trust you."

The ability to send "I" messages is a communication skill that follows recognition of feelings and an effort to communicate directly with the individuals concerned. At times, we provoke strong feelings within ourselves, and an inner dialogue ensues. *I* messages do not tend to build defensiveness, as do **you messages**. With *I* messages, the communication starts on the right foot.

Exercising integrity during moments of choice is an important consideration. Moral dilemmas are frequently faced by student teachers who may or may not weigh decisions before responding to stimuli. It is sometimes so easy to give defensive responses during periods of growth, like student teaching. This type of response may stretch or cloud the truth.

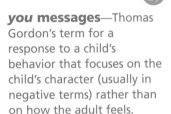

you messages—Thomas Gordon's term for a response to a child's behavior that focuses on the child's character (usually in negative terms) rather than on how the adult feels.

LISTENING: THE ABILITY TO RECEIVE

We listen with our ears, of course,
But surely it is true
That eyes, the lips, and hands, and feet
will help us listen, too.

Though commonly used with children, this poem may aid student teachers' communicative listening skills. The poem is describing **active listening**, a term also attributed to Gordon (1972), who notes:

> In recent years psychotherapists have called our attention to a new kind of listening, "active listening." More than passively attending to the message of the sender, it is a process of putting your understanding of that message to its severest of tests—namely, forcing yourself to put into your own words to the sender for verification or for subsequent correction.

March (2002) points out the need to closely attend to speakers:

> Positive attention is the most valuable tool we have for enriching the quality of our relationships. Positive attention is *listening without distraction*.

Think of everyone as a person who needs attention. Then you will automatically begin to treat others with more compassion and respect.

We encounters four basic types of verbal communication from other adults:

1. Communication, for *building relationships*
2. *Cathartic* communication, for releasing emotions and relating our troubles
3. *Informational* communication, for sharing ideas, information, and data
4. *Persuasive* communication, for reinforcing and changing attitudes or producing a desired action

active listening—the process of putting into your own words a message you received from another based on your understanding of what you thought you heard.

People who listen interact with others more effectively and make fewer mistakes.

To practice good listening, try the following tips:

- Focus on content and ideas.
- Do not prejudge or second-guess.
- Listen for feelings.
- Jot down facts when appropriate.
- Make eye contact; watch nonverbal cues.
- Avoid emotional rebuttals by keeping an open mind. Realize there are emotionally laden words.
- Give signs to the sender that you are actively receiving.
- Try to identify main and supportive ideas. Store key words; they'll make messages easier to remember.
- Rephrase, ask, and/or answer questions, whether explicit or implied.
- Understand that there are times when not responding is best.

The active listening process is probably more difficult to learn than "I" message sending. Most individuals have developed listening habits that block true listening (see Figure 9–11). Lundsteen (1976) has labeled four chief listening distortions:

1. *Attitude cutoff* blocks the reception of information at the spoken source because expectation acts on selection. For example, if a student has a strong negative reaction every time he hears the word "test," he might not hear the rest of this message: "The test of any man lies in action."

WHY WE DON'T HEAR OTHERS

If you want to listen so you really hear what others say, make sure you're not a:

- Mind reader. You'll hear little or nothing as you think "What is this person really thinking or feeling?"
- Rehearser. Your mental tryouts for "Here's what I'll say next" tune out the speaker.
- Filterer. Some call this selective listening—hearing only what you want to hear.
- Dreamer. Drifting off during a face-to-face conversation can lead to an embarrassing "What did you say?" or "Could you repeat that?"
- Identifier. If you refer everything you hear to your experience, you probably didn't really hear what was said.
- Comparer. When you get side-tracked assessing the messenger, you're sure to miss the message.
- Derailer. Changing the subject too quickly tells others you're not interested in anything they have to say.
- Sparrer. You hear what's said but quickly belittle it or discount it. That puts you in the same class as the derailer.
- Placater. Agreeing with everything you hear just to be nice or to avoid conflict does not mean you're a good listener.

Source: *The Writing Lab*, Department of English, Purdue University, 1356 Heavilon Hall, West Lafayette, IN 47907.

 Figure 9–11

Hearing others. From Communications Briefings, (1997) Vol. XVI, NO. IV, Alexandria, VA: Capitol Publications. Reprinted with permission from Communication Briefings.

2. *Motive attributing* is illustrated by the person who says of a speaker, "He is just saying that for public relations," and by the child who thinks, "Teachers just like to talk; they don't really expect me to listen the first time because they are going to repeat the directions 10 times anyway."

3. *Organizational mix-up* happens as one is trying to put someone else's message together: ["]Did he say 'turn left, then right, then right, then left,' or. . . ?" or "Did he say 'tired' or 'tried'?"

4. *Self-preoccupation* causes distortion because the listener is busy formulating his reply and never hears the message: "I'll get him for that; as soon as he stops talking, I'll make a crack about how short he is, then . . ."

Preoccupation with one's own message is a frequent distortion for young listeners. Hanging onto their own thoughts during communication takes a great deal of their attention and energy. Some teachers help out by suggesting that young listeners make small, quick pictures to help cue their ideas when their turn to speak arrives. That way, they can get back to listening. Older children may jot down "shorthand" notes, to help them hold onto ideas while returning to the line of communication.

New, active listening habits can change lives and communicating styles, giving individuals a chance to develop closeness, insight, and empathy.

> To understand accurately how another person thinks or feels from his point of view, to put yourself momentarily into his shoes, to see the world as he is seeing it—you as a listener run the risk of having your own opinions and attitudes changed. (Gordon, 1972)

Many authors suggest that listening is much more than hearing. To develop new listening habits, it is necessary to make a strong effort. The effort will pay off dramatically, because it provides an opportunity to know others at a deeper level. It is a chance to open a small inner door and catch a glimpse of the authentic self. By listening closely, a new perception of an individual can be revealed; our own thoughts about how we might answer are secondary.

> Before that, when I went to a party I would think anxiously "Now try hard. Be lively. Say bright things. Don't let them down." And when tired, I would drink a lot of coffee to keep this up. But now before going to a party, I just tell myself to listen with affection to anyone who talked to me, to be in their shoes when they talk; to try to know them without my mind pressing against theirs, or arguing, or changing the subject. No! My attitude is: "Tell me more. This person is showing me his soul. It is a little dry and meager and full of grinding talk just now, but presently he will begin to think, not just automatically talk. He will show his true self. Then he will be wonderfully alive." (Ueland, 1941/1966).

The student teacher hopes others recognize her teaching competencies. Being anxious to display what you know can focus communication on sending messages that concentrate on self rather than really listening to others. New listening skills will take conscious practice. To gain skill in reflective listening, an exercise called *mirroring* is often used. The following examples mirror back to the child the feeling the listener believes he received.

1. *Child, pleading:*"I don't want to eat these baked potatoes. I hate them."

   Listener: "You don't like baked potatoes."

2. *Child, pleading and forlorn:* "I don't have anything to do today. What can I do? I wish there was something to do!"

   Listener: "You're bored and lonely."

3. *Child, angry and confused:* "I hate Julie. She always cries and tries to get her way. If I don't do what she wants, she goes home."

   Listener: "You're angry and confused."

4. *Child, stubborn and indignant:* "I don't want to take a bath. I'm not even dirty. I hate baths anyway. Why do I have to take a bath every day?"

   Listener: "You don't want to take a bath."

5. *Child, crying:* "Fran won't let me play with her dolls. She's mean. Make her give me some of them to play with."

   Listener: "You're angry with Fran."

6. *Child, crying because of a hurt finger:* "Ow! Ow! It hurts! Ow!"

   Listener: "It sure hurts."

Adults often find mirroring and reflecting back feeling statements easier with children than adults. With use, mirroring statements feel more comfortable, and the sender, whether a child or an adult, feels he has been heard. With adults, clarifying mirroring-type *questions* seems more natural. This is done as follows:

"Am I hearing you correctly, that you're really angry right now?"
"Is frustration what you're feeling?"
"You're saying you don't want to be told what to do?"

Communication Tips

Harris (1995) suggests the following tips to improve staff communication:

● Beware of kicking and stroking at the same time. When we tell someone something positive, then reprimand, then end with a positive, we call that sandwiching. Some workshops teach this as a soft technique, but it does send conflicting messages.

● Whenever possible, plan the message. Think of what the message is, along with how, where, and when you want to send it.

● For communication to be effective, spend as much time listening as talking. Be attentive.

● Do not imply a choice if there is not one. Tentative language and manner are fine in some circumstances, but they often suggest an option that may not exist.

● Record an hour or so of routine, day-to-day conversations on a tape or digital recorder. Look for hidden agendas, soft or padded language, and other indicators that you are not sending clear messages.

● Say what you mean, mean what you say.

● Feedback is a continuous process, not just a one-time action. Learn to give and elicit feedback on a regular basis.

● Look at the person you are talking to and establish eye contact throughout the conversation. (But do be aware that in some cultures this may be considered rude.)

● If it appears that no one is listening, the problem may be exactly that; no one *is* listening.

Additional suggestions follow:

- Try to think of two possible ways to resolve the problem at hand before speaking to a coworker or supervisor.
- When weighing possible solutions, identify possible joint benefits.
- Paraphrase differing opinions to clarify ideas.
- Admit to changing your mind, and view it as appropriate and mature.
- Admit doubt and error. Be seen as a collaborator.

Warner (1995) notes there is not much that can be done about negative or unprofessional teachers except to smile, be pleasant, minimize contact, and seek out professional, positive-minded colleagues.

Copeland (1997) outlines three choices in dealing with problems important to staff members. (This chapter concentrates on choice two.)

Choice 1: I am satisfied with things the way they are. I can live with what's going on, so I won't worry about it.

Choice 2: I am unhappy with my situation, and I am on a path of trying to resolve the conflict. If my first effort doesn't succeed, I will try something else.

Choice 3: I will quit my job.

 A PROBLEM-SOLVING PROCESS

Most problems can be faced in a sequential manner. This text suggests problem solving in a rational manner, when emotions are under control. Take some time alone to cool down or physically burn off excessive tension before you try to use it. Substituting new behaviors into your problem-solving style takes time and effort. Practice is necessary.

Sending *I* messages and active listening will avert conflict buildup. However, you do have the choice of living with a problem and not working on it. This can work for short periods, but usually erodes the quality of your relationship with others or with yourself. Alienation occurs in most instances, but you may prefer this course of action and be prepared for its consequences. Most often, you will choose to confront others or yourself and work toward solutions that eliminate the problem. Familiarize yourself with the following steps, which suit many different situations.

Step 1. The recognition of tensions, emotions, or an expression of a problem occurs.

Step 2. Analysis takes place. (Who and what are involved? When and where is the problem happening? Whose problem is it?)

Step 3. *I* messages are sent. (This step includes active listening *and* reflecting messages.)

Step 4. Discussion takes place. (This involves probing for more data. Who owns the problem?)

Step 5. Both sides of the problem are clearly stated.

Step 6. Possible solutions are proposed.

Step 7. An agreement is secured to try one of these solutions, and if the solution does not work, an agreement is made to meet again.

Step 8. Individual respect for willingness, time, and effort to solve the problem is expressed, in an attempt to reinforce positive behaviors.

This process can be attempted, but will not work if one party refuses to talk, mediate, or look for courses of action that will satisfy everyone involved. Refusing to act on solutions also hinders the process. Problem solving can be two-sided, even when only one person is involved.

At step two, you may realize the problem belongs to another, and the best course of action is to help that person communicate with someone else. It may be that only one person can own the problem, such as when the issue is with using inappropriate exclamations. Often a problem may disappear at step three.

The discussion in step four, can include "I'm really interested in talking about it" or "Let's talk; we'll examine just what's happening to us." However, there is a tendency to blame rather than identify contributing causes. Getting stuck and not moving past step four stalls resolution of the problem. Statements like "You're right; I really avoid cleaning that sink," or "I'm really bothered by interruptions during planned group times," all involve owning the problem.

Before possible solutions are mentioned, a clear statement of conflicting views in step five, adds clarification.

With a child: "You'd like to paint next, and I told Carlos it's his turn."

With a fellow student teacher: "You feel the way I handle Peter is increasing his shyness, and I feel it is helping him."

With a cooperating teacher: "I think my activity was suitable for the group, but you believe it didn't challenge them."

With a supervisor: "You feel I tend to avoid planning outdoor activities; I think I've planned quite a few."

Your confrontation might start at step six. ("Let's figure out some way to make the noisy time right before nap a little calmer and quieter.") Finding alternate solutions admits there are probably a number of possibilities. "Together we'll figure a way" or "That's one way; here's another idea." A do-it-my-way attitude inhibits joint agreement. Thinking alternatives over then getting back together is helpful at times. Seeking a consultant who offers ideas can help solve problems that participants see as hopeless.

When all parties decide to try one solution, as in step seven, consideration should be given to meeting again if that particular alternative does not work. ("We'll try it this week and discuss whether it's working next Monday.")

Step eight reinforces both sides. "We figured it out." "Thanks for taking the time to solve this." "I appreciated your efforts in effecting a solution." This process is not to be used as a panacea; but it does provide helpful guidelines.

Classroom problems can involve any aspect of the student teaching situation (see Figure 9–12). Interpersonal conflicts will take courage to resolve, as well as consideration of the proper time and place to confront the issues.

> The teacher is sometimes afraid to confront a child who is hostile, caustic, or vengeful. Such a teacher avoids and avoids until the accumulation of feelings becomes so unbearable an explosion occurs, and the teacher loses control. Once out of control, there is no possibility of bringing about a positive resolution. But when the hateful, rejection emotions subside, there is always hope that the teacher can come to terms with the child and reach a depth of relatedness and mutuality (Moustakas, 1966).

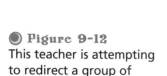

● **Figure 9-12**
This teacher is attempting to redirect a group of children's 'rowdy' behavior in the play yard.

Arrange to problem-solve when participants have no classroom responsibilities, and where there will not be any interruptions or non-involved observers.

Using Problem Solving with Children

Gartrell (2006) defines conflict mediation in early childhood classrooms as happening when a third person assists others to resolve conflicts. This usually happens when two children work with a mediator who is most often the teacher or a student teacher. It falls in the curriculum area called [*social-emotional learning*], and it involves learned skills and behaviors that work successfully when conflict takes place.

When faced with children in disagreement, student teachers often hesitate if the children are showing signs of working toward resolution, negotiation, or tempers are calming rather than escalating. They monitor whether bullying is involved, and notice if a particular child is having trouble sticking up for her rights. They watch before deciding to become the neutral, third party who attempts mediation, unless harm is eminent. When they do attempt to intervene, they realize volatile and strong emotions may be present. A good first step can be for the teacher to bend to eye level and circle the children with her arms at their waists. This act in itself may assuage children's feelings somewhat, but most often other techniques to help the children calm down and listen are used.

Gartrell suggests having children take three big breaths. Another technique is to ask children to sit down together with the teachers, then saying "Please wait until I count to 10 before you tell me what happened. Then both of you will have a turn to tell me."

Then the teacher plugs in step one, by recognizing child emotions and saying, "Looks like we have a problem." She then gives one child a chance to state his case while she reminds the other to listen and he will be next.

("It is your turn to speak, and your time to listen.") Both sides of the problem are then stated by the mediator. Step four, active listening has occurred, and the mediator moves on to steps five and six, during which she promotes negotiation and ideas for solutions by saying something like, "What might we do now?" or "Can you think of a way to solve this problem?" The mediator then works toward a solution that satisfies both children. In a stalemate, she suggests a solution, but chances are the children will think of something. When children agree, she verbally applauds their problem solving, and reinforces the behavior with, "That is a fine idea; both of you were able to talk about ways that felt right to both of you and you solved your problem. If this idea does not work, we will come back together and try another idea."

It may take many mediated sessions for some children to resolve differences, and some may have a hard time breaking behavior habits that have been successful in getting them their way in the past. The process is offered here because it depends a great deal on a teacher's ability to communicate.

Negotiation Skills

It has been said that we do not get what we deserve in life, but what we negotiate, and that negotiation is not about fairness.

After an individual or staff conflict is apparent, one usually decides if it is worth resolving and then identifies who has the power to make a resolution decision. The goal in negotiation is to uncover a solution that contending participants feel comfortable with: in other words, win-win or get-give resolutions.

Negotiating a series of steps can aid progress and create an attitude of "How are we going to work together on this?" It is important to clarify your position, know what is desired, what options could be considered, and what you might settle for. Many times, options that are acceptable to both parties depend on the creative brainstorming that ensues during the negotiation process. Active listening is mandatory. Thinking about settings conducive to negotiating and the comfort of participants can enhance outcomes. Taking a walk together in a secluded area may work, as may going to relaxed staff or meeting rooms when groups of people are involved.

Written materials by negotiation experts suggest opposing sides speak in tune with the other side's interests, mentioning why options offered might benefit one or both sides. Face-saving solutions are seen as important considerations.

Negotiations end with a commitment, an agreed-upon plan, or a follow-up date to try again for an amicable solution.

It is easy to see that staffs with a sense of community, who respect diversity and diverse opinions, have an advantage in the negotiation process. Groups that believe conflict is natural and healthy may more effectively handle problems.

Unfortunately, negotiation breaks down when attitudes include an unwillingness to confront conflict or even admit it exists, or when an unwillingness to listen or accept others' ideas characterizes behavior. Delpit (1995) suggests teachers must learn to be vulnerable enough in their thinking to turn upside down to allow others' ideas to enter consciousness.

Resistance

Resistance to rules and not conforming to what is expected can be seen both in children and adults. It is usually viewed as negative behavior. Moustakas (1966) believes it is healthy:

> Resistance is a way for the child to maintain his own sense of self in the light of external pressures to manipulate and change him. It is a healthy response, an effort of the individual to sustain the integrity of the self.

Resistance and controversy can become challenges that develop our understanding and let us know others at a deeper level. Though confrontations may frighten student teachers in early days, later they are seen as opportunities to know more about children and adults.

> The anxiety in facing an embittered, destructive child can be eliminated only in actual confrontation with the dread child because until we actually meet him, we cannot know him (Moustakas, 1966).

◉ SUMMARY

Student teaching is a miniature slice of life and living. Problems arise and are common to all. Some situations change with time; others need extended communication to be resolved.

Growth and change are experienced sometimes easily, sometimes painfully. It is helpful to maintain a caring and sharing feeling, open communication, and a sense of humor. Time and successful experience take care of most initial difficulties. The supervisor's and cooperating teacher's roles are to provide supportive assistance. Team status may evolve slowly and depends on student effort.

Skill in sending and receiving oral and written messages is a necessary one for student teachers. The whole climate of the student teaching experience depends in part on communication know-how. Developing rapport with adults and children during the early days helps student teachers become relaxed and comfortable.

Love and acceptance are established in a variety of ways. Authenticity in communication is deemed highly desirable and effective. *I* messages are an integral part of effective communication skill. Skill in sending *I* messages and active, reflective listening increase with practice and become a natural part of the student teaching experience.

Problem-solving skills are important for student teachers. There seem to be definite styles of relating to others during problem-solving situations. Students are urged to practice new techniques in negotiation. Early fears of confronting tend to disappear as communicative problem solving becomes a way to know and understand others. In problem solving, teachers model the skills for children; therefore, the children may also learn to use them.

◉ HELPFUL WEB SITES

http://www.peace-ed.org
Peace Education Foundation. Take a look at classroom-tested curricula.

http://www.clas:uiuc.edu
Early Childhood Research Institute. This is a good source for those working with culturally and linguistically diverse children and families.

http://www.apa.org
American Psychological Association. Search for violence issues.

http://www.nea.org
National Education Association. Read about standards and recommendations promoting professional relationships.

http://www.ericeece.org

ERIC Clearinghouse on Elementary and Early Childhood Education. Discussion groups that let you dialog with others are available.

http://www.csefel.uiuc.edu

The Center on Social and Emotional Foundations for Early Learning. Use "social outcomes" and "emotional outcomes" as search phrases, also "communication techniques."

http://www.suebaldwin.com

Lifesavers and *Lighten Up* are two inexpensive resources for student teachers wishing to use humor for their stress reduction.

Additional resources for this chapter can be found by visiting the Online Companion at www.earlychilded.delmar.com.

SUGGESTED ACTIVITIES

A. Briefly describe three possible courses of action for the following student teacher situations. Of the three, which do you feel is the best course of action?

1. Amy, a fellow student teacher, confides in you that she objects to the way her cooperating teacher punishes children.

2. Jonas, a four-year-old, says, "You're not the teacher. I don't have to do that" when you ask him to return blocks he has played with to the bookcase.

3. You have a great idea about rearranging the room and do so in the morning before the children or cooperating teacher arrive.

4. You tried very hard to encourage Qwan to complete a task, and the cooperating teacher quickly finishes the task for him to make sure he is not late for snack.

5. You cannot seem to get any feedback on your abilities as a student teacher from either the cooperating teacher or the supervisor.

6. You notice you are spending an increasing amount of time straightening, table wiping, sink cleaning, and maintaining the block area.

7. You realize you do not know any parents' first names, and half the semester is over.

8. Manuela and Colleen are student teaching in the same classroom. Manuela feels Colleen is insensitive to the children of Hispanic heritage and rarely builds their sense of ethnic pride.

9. Carol, a student teacher, plays the guitar and is a talented folksinger. She has not planned a classroom activity to share her talent.

10. Your supervisor gives you credit for setting up a new activity area that the children are exploring with enthusiasm; however, the cooperating teacher was the one who set up this activity. Because your supervisor has encouraged you to add new activities, you did not correct the mistake. The next day, you feel badly about taking credit but are reticent to approach your supervisor with the truth.

B. Answer the following questions. If you don't know an answer right away, ask someone who knows you well.

- How do I behave when I'm feeling over-stressed? (Some people get angry, others withdraw, some cry more easily, others become forgetful, and so on.)

- What are some of the warning signs that indicate I am about to go beyond the amount of stress I can handle? Analyzing your reactions to stress can be eye-opening.

- What do I do that helps relax me and release my stress?

- Are my ways of relaxing healthy for me?

- Do I have time in my life that is just for me? If yes, how often during the week?

- Do I take my own need for relaxation and time out seriously enough?

- Do I know any relaxation techniques that I can practice?

- Am I aware of how I talk to myself inside my own mind? Am I telling myself negative or hopeless things that contribute to my stress level?

- Am I aware that I have a choice about how I want to deal with my own stress?

C. Form groups of six for the following role-playing activity. Select two members to role-play; others will be observers. Switch between role-playing and observing until all group members have had two turns.

Role-Playing in Active Listening

Directions: Analyze each of the following role-played statements or situations. Offer suggestions for active listening responses.

1. *Student teacher to cooperating teacher:* "Your room needs more organization."
2. *Cooperating teacher to student teacher:* "Jennifer, have you been having problems at home lately?"
3. *Irritated cooperating teacher to student teacher:* "Taylor, you've been ill too often. We rely on our student teachers to be here every day."
4. *Critical parent to student teacher:* "My daughter needs her sweater on when she goes out of doors."
5. *One student teacher to another:* "Mrs. Brown, the director, only sees what I do wrong, not what I do right."
6. *One student teacher to another:* "You always leave the sink a mess."
7. John, a preschooler, is dumping paint on the floor.
8. *Student teacher to child who is not going to the wash area:* "It's time to wash hands."
9. Mary, a four-year-old, hit you because you insisted that she share a toy.
10. *College supervisor to student teacher:* "Filomena, I'm confused. Your assignments are always late. Weren't my directions clear?"
11. *Cooperating teacher to student teacher:* "When you were doing your activity, I had a difficult time not stepping in. The boys were destroying the girls' work."
12. *First child:* "Give me back my paint brush." *Second child:* "You can't have it."

D. Consider the following statements:
1. A teacher saying to a child "I liked the way you helped your friend button his coat." This is an appropriate statement.
2. Rough-and-tumble play prepares preschool boys to be successful in later competitive sports and life in general.
3. By becoming a mediator, the student teacher may teach children that they need an adult whenever there is a problem.

In a group, allow three to five minutes to agree with the first statement verbally. In the next three to five minutes, have group members disagree. Do the same with the second and third statement. Follow this exercise with a discussion centered on the difficulties encountered, if any, in really listening and giving value to opinions that conflict with individual viewpoints.

E. Answer the following questions anonymously on a piece of paper using the number scale below. Collect and tally slips from a group of classmates and discuss the results.

1 = Never; 2 = Infrequently; 3 = Sometimes; 4 = Often; 5 = Always

1. I am anxious about spending too much of my time and attention with some children and consequently neglecting others. _____
2. I am not sure my behavior management techniques are always appropriate. _____
3. I am not certain my planned activities are developmentally appropriate. _____
4. Unruly children cause me problems. _____
5. My lesson planning makes me doubt my ability. _____
6. I am anxious about creating a good working relationship with my cooperating teacher or other staff members. _____
7. I am anxious about having lesson plans flop. _____
8. I am anxious about creating classroom chaos when planning creative activities. _____
9. I am anxious about getting all my paperwork done in time. _____
10. I am nervous about what lesson the college supervisor will come to see. _____
11. I am stressed about having time to study in other college classes. _____
12. I am worried about developing a portfolio. _____
13. I get sweaty when I make contact with upset parents. _____
14. I am nervous about working in the neighborhood where I have been assigned. _____
15. I worry because I am from a different culture or ethnic group than the children. _____
16. I suspect my cooperating teacher doesn't like me. _____
17. I am unsettled because of the staff friction that exists at my placement site. _____

18. I am afraid of saying the wrong thing to my supervisor. _____
19. I am stressed when being watched. _____
20. I am afraid of the cooperating teacher's assessment of my competency. _____

F. In the following situations, state as clearly as possible what you think are both sides of the problem. Then describe two alternatives that you feel might satisfy both parties in each conflict.

1. Cecelia has been assigned to student teach from 9:00 AM to 2:30 PM on Tuesdays. Her cooperating teacher, Mr. Kifer, notices she has been leaving early. Cecelia has been arriving 10 to 15 minutes early each day. Her cooperating teacher confronts Cecelia one day before she departs. "Leaving early, Cecelia?"

2. Henri, a four-year-old, has been told repeatedly by the student teacher that he must put the blocks he used back on the shelf. Henri has ignored the request continually. The student teacher requests the cooperating teacher ask Henri to replace the blocks because he does not respond to the student teacher.

3. The cooperating teacher has been silent most of the morning. The student teacher can feel tension mounting and says, "I'm really feeling uncomfortable because I sense there is something wrong." The cooperating teacher ignores the remark. At the end of work, the student discusses the situation with the supervisor.

4. Christopher, a student teacher, is fuming. "After all the work I put into the activity, she didn't even mention it," he says to Charlotte, another student teacher.

5. "I'd really like to present this new song to the children," says Robin, a student teacher. "You didn't put it in the plan book, Robin, and I have a full day planned," the cooperating teacher says. "Let's talk about it; I can see the disappointment on your face." Robin replies, "It's not disappointment. I can't see why the schedule is so inflexible." "Let's talk about that after the morning session, Robin."

6. "I sure needed your help at circle today," the cooperating teacher says. "I was in the bathroom with Anthony; he's got those pants that button at the shoulders," the student teacher answers.

7. "I'm really tired today, Mrs. Cuffaro," the student teacher answers, when asked why she stayed in the housekeeping area most of the morning. Mrs. Cuffaro says, "There were lots of children who could have used your assistance, Annette. Will you have time to talk when the children are napping?" "Sure," Annette replies.

8. Miriam, an attractive student teacher, is assigned to an on-campus laboratory school. Male friends often hang around the lobby, or ask the secretary to give her messages and notes. The secretary has told Miriam this is bothersome. Miriam tells the secretary the notes often concern getting a ride home because she does not have a car.

REVIEW

A. Briefly describe what you feel are prime areas or issues of conflict in student teaching.

B. Write a student teacher "I" message for each of the following situations:

1. Fred, your cooperating teacher, stares at you absentmindedly all morning.
2. Your supervisor has given you a failing grade on an assignment. You spent many hours on that assignment, and you feel like dropping the class.
3. You cried during the staff meeting when other adults suggested one of your activities with the children was a flop.

4. Another student teacher in your classroom is not living up to assigned duties, making it twice as difficult for you.
5. A child says to you, "I wish you were my mommy."
6. Your cooperating teacher has asked you not to pick up and hold a particular child. You feel the child needs special attention.
7. An irate parent says to you, "This school policy about bringing toys from home is ridiculous."
8. Your neighbor says to you, "I hear you're going to college to become a baby-sitter. It is so wasteful of your talents."

C. Choose the best answer to complete each statement.

1. Your cooperating teacher has informed your supervisor that you were not prepared for class on the preceding day. This is not the first time it has happened. Your supervisor seems upset because the two of you have discussed this problem twice before. In talking to your supervisor, you want to use active listening techniques in communicating. You say,
   a. "You need to explain assignment dates again, please."
   b. "She's always criticizing me; I'm really upset."
   c. "But I was prepared. I brought in two flannelboard stories and a music game!"
   d. "I can see you're disappointed and perhaps a bit angry, too."
   e. "Isn't there any way I can please the two of you?"

2. Your cooperating teacher is always stepping in and taking over in guidance situations. You have pleaded to be allowed to follow through so children will know you mean what you say. You decide to send a congruent feeling statement at a staff meeting. You say,
   a. "I'm really frustrated. You always take over."
   b. "I've had it. Can't you let me finish what I start?"
   c. "I'm confused. I want the children to know I mean what I say, but it's just not happening."
   d. "You need to step back and let me follow through with the children."
   e. "I know you're trying to help me, but I don't need your help."

3. You feel you can easily handle the whole day's program, but you haven't been given the opportunity. You say to your supervisor,
   a. "Please counsel me about how I should cope with this situation. The cooperating teacher doesn't give me enough to do."
   b. "I feel I'm competent enough to handle a whole day's program."
   c. "I'm just doing cleanup and housekeeping most of the time."
   d. "You could ask my cooperating teacher to give me more responsibility."

   e. "I'll sure be happy when I finish and have my own class."

4. Mrs. Schultz is angry and yells, "Janita wet her pants again. I don't think any of you remembered to remind her!" You respond by saying,
   a. "You're upset because you don't think we reminded Janita."
   b. "All the children wet sometimes, Mrs. Schultz!"
   c. "I didn't see her wet today."
   d. "We remind all the children right before snack time."
   e. "Your loud voice is upsetting everyone!"

5. Congruent sending and authentic sending are
   a. very different.
   b. easy skills for most adults.
   c. similar to active listening.
   d. very similar.
   e. similar to parcel post sending.

D. Arrange the following problem-solving steps in order, based on the eight-step sequence found in the text. You may find that more than one applies to the same step.

1. *Cooperating teacher:* "We'll put paintings without names in this box this week and see what happens." *Student teacher:* "Okay."

2. *Student teacher:* "You feel children's artwork should always have the child's name printed in the upper left corner."

3. *Cooperating teacher:* "You could put names on the artwork when you're the adult in the art area."

4. *Student teacher:* "I feel the child's name should be put on the artwork only when the child gives permission to do so. If the children don't ask to have their names put on, they will learn the consequences when it's time to take the art home."

5. *Student teacher:* "I could tell each child what will happen if there is no name on a painting."

6. *Cooperating teacher:* "There's been quite a bottleneck when parents try to find their child's artwork at departure time. Sometimes, there are no names printed in the upper left corner."

7. *Student teacher:* "You would like to put each child's name on his artwork, and I think each child can learn something if I don't print his name when he does not give me permission to do so."

8. *Student teacher:* "I appreciate your understanding my point of view."

9. *Cooperating teacher:* "You could write the child's name lightly if that child said no."

10. *Cooperating teacher:* "I think the lesson to be learned isn't worth the commotion at closing."

11. *Student teacher:* "This is the way I feel about names on artwork."

E. List as many possible alternative solutions as you can for the following problem.

Winona has been placed with a cooperating teacher who, in her opinion, has created a classroom environment that offers the children few play choices. She has communicated this to her cooperating teacher, who then asks Winona for suggestions.

CASE SCENARIO

Setting: A morning Kindergarten class.

Mrs. Kitayama is Miss Ling's cooperating teacher. To make the names easier for the students, many of whom are second-language learners, Mrs. Kitayama is called Mrs. K and Miss Ling is called Miss L.

The schedule starts with the children writing their names on a sheet of chart paper placed on a table near the door to the room; this is done to facilitate taking attendance and to encourage the children's reading and writing skills. Mrs. K always has a question for the children to answer and the children place their names in a "yes" or "no" column in response. Today Miss L has written the question, "Do you like chocolate ice cream or vanilla?" She has written "chocolate" in one column and "vanilla" in the other.

Mrs. K questions her. "Was there a reason you asked the opening question on the attendance paper as you did?"

"Absolutely," answers Miss L. "I've noticed that several of the students are beginning to read and I thought having "chocolate" and "vanilla" would be different and intriguing. I noticed that Fwasia, who generally comes early, helped those who couldn't read the words. I sometimes wonder why her parents didn't start her in school last year. Do you know why she entered late, Mrs. K?"

"Yes, I do," Mrs. K responds. "Fwasia's family speaks Farsi at home. She had a second year in preschool in order to build her English language skills. She began to read last fall and she enjoys helping those who don't read as well."

"I also want to compliment you on the choice of *Corduroy* (Freeman, 1968) and the art activity you designed to go with it. And you brought your own teddy bear to share; great idea! You made the directions for the drawing of a teddy bear easy enough to follow, and you

continues . . .

. . . continued

found that the children didn't have experience passing out paper."

"I honestly hadn't given thought to the children's knowing how to pass out paper. When I saw their confusion, it seemed logical to ask those at the ends of the lines to stand and pass to the rest of the children on their line. I must admit that coming from a fourth grade assignment last semester to this kindergarten has really been a learning experience."

Questions for Discussion:

1. Have you ever been in a situation where you overestimated what the students in you classroom knew?

2. What do you think about Miss L changing the opening question routine from "yes/no" answers to "chocolate" and "vanilla" choices?

3. How would you characterize the communication between Mrs. K and Miss L?

4. What do you think you could do to facilitate the communication with your cooperating teacher, if it's not really open?

REFERENCES

Armstrong, J. L. (1994, January). Mad, sad, or glad: Children speak out about child care. *Young Children, 49(2)*,19–23.

Brighton, C. M. (1999). Keeping good teachers: Lessons from novices. In Scherer, (Ed.). *A better beginning: Supporting and mentoring new teachers* (197–201). Alexandria, VA: Association for Supervision and Curriculum Development.

Burke, C. (1998, September 17). *Communication skills that matter.* SkillPath Seminar, the Women's Conference, Boise, ID.

Canter, T. (1998). *First-class teacher: Successful strategies for new teachers.* Santa Monica, CA: Canter and Associates, Inc.

Carter, M., & Curtis, D. (1994). *Training teachers: A harvest of theory and practice.* St. Paul, MN: Redleaf Press.

Caruso, J. J., & Fawcett, M. T. (1999). *Supervision in early childhood education: A developmental perspective.* New York: Teachers College Press.

Copeland, T. (1997, January/February). How to help your staff cope with conflict. *Child Care Information Exchange, 182.*

Danoff, J., Breitbart, V., & Barr, E. (1977). *Open for children.* New York: McGraw-Hill.

Delpit, L. (1995). *Other people's children: Cultural conflict in the classroom.* New York: The New Press.

Freeman, D. (1968). *Corduroy.* New York: Viking Press.

Gartrell, D. (2006, March). Guidance matters, *Young Children, 61(2), 88–89.*

Ginott, H. (1972). I'm angry! I'm appalled! I am furious! *Teacher and child.* New York: Macmillan. Reprinted in *Today's Education Magazine,* NEA Journal (Nov. 19, 1972).

Gordon, T. (1972). The risks of effective communication. *Parent Notebook.* New York: Effectiveness Training Associates.

Gordon-Nourok, E. (1979). *You're a student teacher!* Sierra Madre, CA: SCAEYC.

Harris, J. (1995, July/August). Is anybody out there listening? *Child Care InformationExchange, 104.*

Hurst, B., & Reding, G. (1999). *Keeping the light in your eyes: A guide for helping teachers discover, remember, relive, and rediscover the joy of teaching.* Scottsdale, AZ: Holcomb Hathaway.

Hutchins, P. (1968). *Rosie's walk.* New York: Macmillan.

Keirsey, D., & Bates, M. (1984). *Please understand me* (5th ed.). Del Mar, CA: Gnosology Books.

Leeds, D. (2001, September). Good things come to those who ask: The power of questions. *Bottom Line, 22(18) 6–8.*

Lundsteen, S. W. (1976). *Children learn to communicate.* Englewood Cliffs, NJ: Prentice-Hall.

March, A. A. (2002, April). Are you listening? The simple strategy for enhancing relationships: Business and personal. *Bottom Line,* 23(7) 1–2.

Morton, L. L., Vesco, R., Williams, N. H., & Awender, M. A. (1997). Student teacher anxieties related to class management, pedagogy, evaluation, and staff relation, *British Journal of Educational Psychology* 67: 33–39.

Moustakas, C. (1966). *The Authentic Teacher.* Cambridge: Howard A. Doyle.

National Association for the Education of Young Children (2005, Spring).Governing board approves new standards and criteria. NAEYC's *Accreditation Update,* 6(2)1–5.

Read, K., & Patterson, J. (1980). *The nursery school and kindergarten* (7th ed.). New York: Holt, Rinehart & Winston.

Rogers, C., & Freiberg, H. (1994). *Freedom to learn* (3rd ed.). New York: Merrill/Macmillan.

Sanders, J. (2002). Personal Interview. Boxwood Child Center, San Jose, CA.

SkillPath Seminars (1997). *Conflict management skills for women.* Mission, KS: SkillPath Publications.

Ueland, B. (1941, November). Tell me more. *Ladies Home Journal,* 58(51), as quoted by Moustakas, C. (1966). *The authentic teacher.* Cambridge: Howard A. Doyle.

Von Bergen, J. M. (2003, September 7). Dreams can reveal job anxiety and sometimes produce solutions, *Idaho Statesman* 1CB.

Warner, J. (1995). *The unauthorized TEACHER'S survival guide.* Indianapolis, IN: Park Avenue Publications.

Interactions

CHAPTER 10

Student Teachers and Families

OBJECTIVES After reading this chapter, you should be able to:

1.... Describe a family relations philosophy for an early childhood center.
2.... List five or more common home or school involvement activities.
3.... Watch or listen to a taped parent-teacher conference and analyze the interaction.
4.... List five possible goals of home visits.
5.... Discuss four student teacher skills or behaviors that build or strengthen family-friendly relationships.

Comments of student teachers:

> What an education! It was impossible to ignore how individual parents separated from their children each day. Some kids got a farewell kiss and a hug, others seemed shoved into the room. ●

Bing Anza Bohtua

> Deliver me from parent conferences! It's like walking on eggs blindfolded, and talking with someone who expects you to be an expert on a subject (their child) that they know a hundred times better than you do. ●

Shyree Torsham

> I was placed at a parent cooperative preschool for student teaching. The play yard had creative and innovative play materials and structures. I learned what compulsory father involvement could achieve, and marveled at the Saturday father work crew's hard work. It was a terrifically maintained facility. ●

Nana Ghukar

> The politics of some parent advisory group members confused many issues. My cooperating teacher and the school's director were models of professionalism. They seemed to be able to soothe differing factions with ease. This part of student teaching reminded me of something I remembered from previous classes. The school really was a microcosm of our diverse American society. ●

Rae Jean Wittsby

DISCOVERING A CENTER'S FAMILY RELATIONS PHILOSOPHY

Centers and schools differ widely in their philosophy and attitudes toward parents and families. All programs have beliefs and values that guide staff behaviors. Program handbooks usually articulate family relations specifics, and most programs invite, plan, and require family involvement. As a student teacher interested in high quality care, working with families cooperatively as a team member is a primary goal. This supports the best interest of children.

Stephens (2005) suggests that building authentic partnerships with families goes farther than sporadic school-home meetings, visits, and joint holiday celebrations; it requires putting a high priority on family needs. Staff, Stephens believes, should be provided with training in *family engagement* and family-friendly human relations and interactions. Training would encompass skill in rapport building, using a variety of methods to communicate, developing anti-biased communication, planning engaging family meetings or events, constructive problem solving that avoids casting blame, parent-teacher conferencing, professional confidentiality, and gathering accurate, relevant, and timely data for family referrals when called for.

Epstein (2000) identifies six major types of home/school family partnership activities programs can include. These are:

1. providing information on child development and helping parents strengthen parenting skills.
2. increasing and encouraging school-to-home and home-to-school communications.
3. involving families in school activities as volunteers at school, home, or other locations.
4. assisting families in setting up home conditions to support learning.
5. involving families in decision making through participation in advisory or other school operations.
6. collaborating with the community and other local resources.

As a student teacher, your first step is to identify your placement classroom's family relations philosophy and policy. Ask questions if written materials do not articulate it sufficiently.

Most centers adhere to a non-discrimination policy. Children are cared for and belong to unique types of families, and teachers are obligated to facilitate and ensure individual families, no matter how diverse, are accepted and included in center-family interactions. Many centers officially welcome diversity and alert all families to their non-discrimination policy that asserts the center's goal of accepting and validating family uniqueness, and also building a sense of classroom community, to benefit each child's pride in family and learning potential. Figure 10–1 lists possible heads of families, who care for and parent young children. It is not intended to be a complete listing.

- grandparents
- adoptive parents
- foster parents
- step parents
- gay/lesbian parents
- single parents
- teen parents
- AIDS/HIV parents
- parents in rehabilitation
- incarcerated parents
- drug-dependent parents
- immigrant parents
- non-English-speaking parents
- divorced parents
- migrant parents
- relative guardians
- non-relative guardians

* This is not a complete list, and combinations of categories do exist.

Figure 10-1
Possible heads of families

Figure 10-2
Staff will greet Ryan and his grandmother when they enter the classroom.

INTERACTING WITH FAMILIES

Most interactions with parents or family members are informal. The most frequent interaction occurs when people bring and pick up children from the center or school (see Figure 10–2). The person will say something to the teacher, or smile and nod; these constitute interactions. When teachers note an important development during the day, they will often mention it briefly at pick-up time. In preschool and infant/toddler centers, daily written notes are used to share child activities and behaviors, such as food consumption, diaper changes, and a child's general mood, if significant. Likewise, if there has been a problem, teachers often take a few minutes to explain what has happened. Communications such as these are typical of the informal kind. Internet communication is increasingly used for school-home messages, family feedback, and family resource information. In elementary school classrooms, face-to-face contact with parents and family members may be rare.

More formal communication consists of scheduled parent-teacher conferences and home visits. During a parent-teacher conference, a teacher might discuss the developing friendship between two children (see Figure 10–3). In each case, the families will have prior notice about the conference or home visit. They can then plan ahead and anticipate questions they may want to ask on topics of concern or interest.

Kyle and McIntyre (2000) believe that to educate effectively, teachers must reach out to students' families in ways not traditionally imagined, and bridge the ever-widening gap between home and school, so that children realize they are important, cared about, and expected to achieve. Research suggests one of the keys to successful teaching is creating personal connections with children, inside and outside of school.

Figure 10-3
At the next parent-teacher conference the teacher will be sure to mention Alison, a new child, has formed a friendship with Sharie.

THE IMPORTANCE OF HOME-TEACHER PARTNERSHIPS

Although educators agree that relationships between schools and families are important, preservice teachers and student teachers may have received little training or experience working with families. Teachers are the most influential link in school-home collaboration. Communication seems the biggest barrier. Without providing teachers with strategies and techniques, partnerships may not happen.

While teachers may feel completely at home with children and fellow teachers, Winkleman (1999) suggests that collaborating with families can be a frightening and sometimes difficult challenge.

Winkleman surveyed student teachers who soon would become new elementary school teachers. He found their anxieties about parents centered in four general areas:

1. defending curriculum and teaching practices
2. involving families in their child's education
3. deciding how much family participation they want in their classroom
4. communicating children's problems and weaknesses

Family surveys, and interviews with parents or family program volunteers, can gather information that assesses the need for improved relationships. Most families want to be informed about their child's program, educational progress, and what happens at school. Many families are eager to learn how to support their child's growing skills, knowledge, and ability. Validating and celebrating what parents and families do for children, and what teachers endeavor to do, help partnerships thrive.

There are a vast number of levels of family involvement that aid center goal realization. All sorts of discussion groups, workshops, socials, volunteer projects, work parties, and so on between families and schools are possible. Many schools now alert parents during their child's enrollment to the expected level of family participation in school activities. With changing family life patterns, teachers may feel that it is becoming harder and harder to involve the many diverse and work-consumed families.

Student teachers can observe their cooperating teacher's attention to teacher-family relationships, noting the effectiveness of communications and actions.

First impressions of a child center or school facility form as parents and family members observe the outside area, enter, and notice lobby areas. The upkeep and maintenance of the school, grounds, and equipment catch parents' eyes. Sounds and smells are noted. The people and conversations encountered, and staff manner and demeanor, create distinct impressions.

Family member phone inquiries also allow callers to assess the warmth, knowledge, and careful attention to detail provided by the answering staff member. Each center is felt to have a unique personality, as judged by each new family. In primary grades, student teachers may be asked to send a letter or card to families, to introduce themselves and share information about the student teacher's background, goals as a student teacher, and experience or training.

Most cooperating teachers will introduce student teachers to parents, family members, volunteers, and professionals visiting the classroom. If you are meeting a person for the first time, and your cooperating teacher is otherwise occupied and unable to introduce you, introduce yourself and maintain a friendly, professional demeanor.

As the student teacher becomes acquainted and skilled, some cooperating teachers may feel that family contact can be handled by the student. It is wise to discuss this with your college supervisor. Helping people feel at ease is an art.

Home Cultures

Teachers attempt to gain insight by studying children's home cultures, their histories, and the culture's impact on families and children. In California and many other states, this can be a monumental task because of the variety of cultures present and the differences in social class, economic circumstance, and family values. Many centers and schools base their partnership efforts on the following assumptions:

- Parents are children's first and primary teachers.
- Regardless of diversity, parents' support of their child's education is influential.
- To promote children's school success, congruence between home and school is essential.
- A center should take the initiative in eliminating barriers to partnership formation and maintenance.
- Clear messages are necessary in both oral and written communication.
- Classrooms are examples of democratic principles and freedoms in action.

What happens if partnerships are successful? Families become involved, take action, and feel instrumental in their child's learning; and feel respected, capable, and accepted. They have gained insight into their child's growth and development. Families know their child's teacher has a sincere interest in children's school success. They understand the school offers an individualized program that takes into consideration parents' wishes and values. Parents come to see themselves as important teachers, and believe teachers describe their child's educational accomplishments accurately. They recognize the classroom as an example of democratic practice.

Some educational writers, such as Igoa (1995), have alerted educators to a cultural divide that families new to the United States may experience as they struggle to be accepted as insiders, rather than outsiders, at schools and in communities. Other writers warn that family relationships can be stressed or strained when young children do become insiders. Historically in America, this has been a concern with each wave of new families. Most children have been able to separate fairly easily between what is expected and rewarded at school from what goes on at home. In the past, the majority of new families in the United States wanted to join the American mainstream and intended to become citizens. They viewed education as the key to future family success and employment. Many families held onto traditions and religious practices, and congregated in groups of like-speaking others. They anticipated their children's adoption of English, and many learned English from their children.

Today, this supportive attitude and desire to become Americanized as soon as possible may or may not be present, for a number of reasons. Families may wish to return to their homeland, or they may believe the American way is not a model to emulate. This can be a controversial discussion, particularly at a time when immigration issues are debated. It is suggested that you reflect, investigate, and consider your own family background.

Eggers-Pierola (2005) has suggestions for student teachers who wish to become culturally and linguistically responsive teachers when working with Latino children. She suggests that teachers open their hearts, and recognize the community that surrounds children, to establish lasting and supportive partnerships. She notes that extended family and family friends may be key players in a child's upbringing, and she feels that committed teachers engender committed families. Consequently, a culturally and linguistically sensitive educator should:

- know that to understand the child, she must know the community.
- extend her work to the child's family circle and neighborhood.
- welcome members of the child's extended family as co-teachers, co-planners, and initiators of activities.
- prepare to work with parents when there are disagreements.
- provide opportunities for intergenerational engagement that mirror *la familia*.

Boards, Committees, and Councils

Family members may serve on advisory committees, boards, or councils, and may have active administrative involvement, including teacher hiring and dismissal. They may exercise budgetary control and assume legal responsibilities. Each center differs uniquely, with greater parent involvement mandated in publicly funded programs. Church associated, parent cooperative, and nonprofit programs also frequently use parent advisors. Profit-making centers, on the other hand, may rarely seek or depend on family input in administrative decisions, but exceptions do exist.

Establishing a Professional Image and Rapport

Family interaction with student teachers varies. Many classrooms and schools design program features to create as much family involvement as possible. Others may have somewhat limited parental contacts that consist mainly of dropping-off and picking-up conversations, and of formal, evaluation-consultant parent conferences, as mentioned earlier. In either situation, the student teacher's professionalism is displayed by her actions, appearance, and demeanor. Student teachers' friendly, supportive behaviors and conversational skills help families seeking clarification concerning the student teacher's apprenticeship. It is best to explain your position as a *learner*, and a fledgling novice, hopeful of working toward ever greater classroom responsibility and competencies.

In working with other staff, student teachers may wish to make positive comments. Most people know when praise is deserved, and can easily recognize the difference between superficial "stroking" and sincere encouragement, appreciation, and praise (Caruso & Fawcett, 1999). Pointing out specific actions helps: "You moved next to Alfaro at circle and that calmed him. I didn't have to stop reading. That helped, thank you."

Understanding the Cooperating Teacher's Role

Cooperating teachers may have communicated, either verbally or in writing, to enrolled children's families information about their role as a mentor, guide, collaborator, and consultant in the student teacher's placement. The visits of college supervisors may also have been a topic of discussion. The aim is to give families a clear picture of the student teacher's roles and responsibilities, and of the cooperating teacher's role as a work supervisor. Family fears concerning the student teacher's handling of children's behavior, the degree of confidentiality expected, and the student teacher's possible lack of experience, among other concerns, can be allayed through open discussion. Most families see student teachers as a classroom asset, able to offer their children additional attention and educational opportunity.

Daily Classroom Interactions with Adult Staff and Volunteers

In many classrooms, outside observers may have difficulty distinguishing the different roles of teachers, teaching aides, volunteers, and student teachers. Each may possess uniquely individual skills and style. A hierarchy of responsibility may not be readily apparent. The student teacher will understand that the cooperating teacher has ultimate responsibility, and directs and supervises children, classroom adults, and the planned program—no easy task in most busy classrooms.

Pitfalls

Unfortunately, some families may view student teachers as experts, to be quizzed on child development issues, their child's intelligence, talents, educational progress, and so on. This may feel complimentary, but student teachers should refer all such queries to their cooperating teachers. Unfortunate is the student teacher placed in a program where political or conflicting issues have developed. Most supervisors visit and evaluate placements sites, but occasionally an undercurrent of tension escapes detection. The roles of fence-sitter and cooperating teacher's defender are both difficult ones. Our advice is to direct complaints or criticisms to the person or persons involved, and to broach the matter quickly, with the cooperating teacher and college supervisor.

Student teachers in campus laboratory schools may have children's parents as classmates and friends. Parents can view student teachers as inside information resources. Student teachers need to guard their comments closely, avoid gossip, and emphasize the confidentiality expected of them. It can be a difficult situation when the child of one's best friend or one's college instructor becomes part of the student teacher's child group.

Our advice is, again, to direct the friend or instructor to the cooperating teacher if questions exist.

Children's Separation from Parents

Student teachers will observe daily how individual children enter and separate from their adult caregiver at arrival. Separating from family can be painful, even though a child sees preschool as an interesting place. Some children need time to adjust and readjust to group care, and experience **separation anxiety**. Student teachers are often asked to aid entering children by providing attentive, patient support and comfort. This type of child behavior is usually a preschool teacher's problem, but kindergarten teachers sometimes also encounter separation anxiety, in both children and an occasional parent. Words that help could be, "You want your mom, but she needs to go to work. After nap time, she'll come to get you. Let's go see what Lorie and Wong are making at the center table."

Be prepared to stay near, hold, or comfort a crying child when a parent needs to leave, after staying for an additional time to help the child with the transition. Short periods of absence are lengthened, and with teacher coaching, assurance, and parent firmness, most children adjust.

Problems with Reunion at Pick-Up Time

Many systems and ideas have been used to make pick-up time easier for children, teachers, and the person picking up the child. You should know that only certain individuals can leave the room with a child, and that a list or file exists specifying which adults have clearance to do so. This should have been discussed during your beginning days; if not, talk to the cooperating teacher before you release a child to someone you do not know, or to anyone questionable.

Children's belongings, including projects and artwork, are collected beforehand. Children are made ready to be picked up, and at times, are partially or fully dressed for outdoors. Teachers usually step in to help parents with dawdling or obstinate child behavior. If more detailed information about the child is necessary for a parent or family member, a note, follow-up telephone call, or e-mail to arrange a conference is in order. The teacher's goal is to have a smooth transition with established routines. Schools adopt a variety of procedures to make departure times successful and as stress-free as possible.

 COMMUNICATION

One communication model compares the process of communication to a telephone call, in which there is a caller sending a message through a specific channel—the telephone—to a receiver, who has to decode the message (Berlo, 1960). Whether the message is understood depends on five variables (see Figure 10–4):

    1. the *communication skills* of the sender and receiver

    2. the *attitudes* of the sender and receiver

    3. the *knowledge* of the sender and receiver

    4. the *social system* of the sender and receiver

    5. the *cultures* of the sender and receiver

separation anxiety— emotional difficulty experienced by some young children when leaving their parents or other primary caregivers.

Receiver and Sender	Message	Channel	Receiver
Communication skills	Content	Eyes (seeing)	Communication skills
Attitudes	Structure	Ears (hearing)	Attitudes
Knowledge		Hands (touching)	Knowledge
Social system		Nose (smelling)	Social system
Culture		Mouth (tasting)	Culture
		Body in space (kinesthesia)	

● **Figure 10-4**
Variables in a communication model.

Any differences between the sender and receiver, on any of the variables, can lead to misunderstanding. (Communication skills and conflict resolution skills are covered in depth in Chapter 9.)

Nonverbal Communication

We have suggested that nonverbal communication often tells more about how someone feels than verbal communication. Nonverbal communication involves *body talk*, such as gestures, facial expressions, eye expression, and stance (see Figure 10–5). Motions, such as a wave of the hand, a shrug of the shoulders, a smile, standing erect, or slumping, all send messages. Actions, like pushing one's chair closer or away from another, and leaning forward or back, also seem to send messages.

	Nonverbal Physical Expression				
Message sent through body talk	Gesture	Facial expression	Eye expression	Large body muscles	Stance or posture

	Specific Vocal Expression			
Message sent vocally	Tone	Pitch	Rate	Loudness

● **Figure 10-5**
Nonverbal and vocally sent messages.

Just as nonverbal communications give clues, so do some aspects of verbal communication. The tone, pitch, rate, and loudness of a person's voice sends a message. When a person is excited, the pitch of the voice rises, and the rate of speech increases. Excitement causes a person to speak louder. Anger often makes a person speak louder and quicker, but the pitch may become lower and the tone hard. Teachers try to recognize hidden messages, not just words.

Conferencing: Communication Techniques

In two-year college training programs, student teachers may be invited to sit in on home conferences or visits, playing the role of observer. They may be asked to study child behaviors or actions, but conclusions are confidential and discussed only with cooperating teachers. Four- and five-year college training programs may or may not offer student teachers opportunities to conduct parent conferences and home visits.

To grasp fully the different methods of communication, it is a good idea to role-play situations. You should take turns with your peers, role-playing parents or family members and teachers. Try this: on a 3 × 5 card, write a communication problem you have observed at your center or school. Place all the cards in a box. Pair off with another student teacher and pick a problem from the box. Discuss and decide how you both would resolve the problem. Present your results to the class.

The following are guidelines that practicing teachers use to plan and conduct teacher-parent conferences:

 idiosyncratic—a characteristic peculiar to an individual.

- Families and teachers both have time constraints, so time planning is important.

- In working with others, the first rule is to put them at ease. Seat people comfortably. Offer something to eat or drink, especially if the conference is at the end of a workday.

- Try to begin the conference in a positive manner. Even if one needs to report a child's negative behavior, or ask a difficult question, always comment on the child's positive behaviors or actions before stating other concerns or behaviors.

- Try to elicit a description of the child behavior noticed in school from the parents. This is especially appropriate in a parent-cooperative or center setting that encourages parents to observe and then consult with staff (see Figure 10-6). If a child has not been seen in action at school, ask about the child's observed behavior at home or in other social settings. This will allow you to study the degree of parent perceptivity regarding the child's behavior.

- Be specific when describing child behavior. Avoid generalities. Use descriptive, preferably written accounts, taken over a period of at least three consecutive days, with several samplings per day.

- Keep samples of the child's work in a folder, with the child's name and the date the sampling was taken. Actual samples of work can speak louder and more eloquently than words.

- Avoid comparisons with other children. Each child is unique. Most develop in **idiosyncratic** ways that make comparisons unfair.

 Figure 10-6
"Have you noticed CeCeil's interest in books?"

- When presenting negative aspects of behavior, avoid making any evaluation about the goodness or badness of the child.
- Remember that attitude is important. One must choose to *CARE*.
- Keep conferences focused. Remember that most parents are busy and their time is valuable; do not waste it. Discuss whatever is supposed to be discussed and do not stray off course.
- Be cheerful, friendly, and tactful.
- Act cordially. The last thing you want is to appear argumentative.
- Be honest and avoid euphemisms. Do not say "Tony is certainly a creative child" when you should say "Tony often finds ways to avoid listening to directions."
- Be businesslike. In this situation, a teacher is a professional, not a close friend.
- Know facts and the program so well that you can discuss them without defensive statements.
- Be enthusiastic.
- Do not discuss another child unless it is appropriate.
- Do not make judgments before all the evidence is in.
- Do not betray confidences. Children will sometimes tell something that should not be repeated and is best overlooked. If, however, an educator thinks the disclosure is important to the child's welfare, do discuss it.
- Observe body language; it will often tell you more about how people are really feeling than the words they say.

In the rest of this chapter, we will present some ground rules for home visits, as well as some ideas for other family involvement.

PLANNING THE HOME VISIT

Some schools have a policy that the family of each enrolled child must be visited at least once during the school year. Other schools, both public and private, have a policy that teachers should visit the families of every enrolled child, during the latter part of the summer, prior to the opening of school. If you are student teaching in a school where home visits are an accepted feature, planning a home visit usually involves no more than choosing, with your cooperating teacher, which home to visit. Many times, the cooperating teacher may ask you to visit the home of a child with whom you are having difficulty establishing rapport. Other times, you may be asked to visit the home of a child with whom you have had little interaction.

In planning a home visit, teachers and student teachers should familiarize themselves with the neighborhoods in which the home visit will take place. Hildebrand (1993) states, "A home visit is the single most effective act that can be performed for developing harmonious relationships between child and teacher." (page 86)

Successful home visits have brief agendas, but are flexible and responsive to issues the families might raise (Kyle & McIntyre, 2000). Questions a teacher prepares beforehand help guide discussions. Questions can probe child interests, favorite activities, how the child learns best, interactions with other children out of school, what the child talks about having done at school, or other features of the child's school and home life.

Another point that should be made concerns planning home visits at homes of families from different ethnic or social groups. Families may be suspicious of the motive behind wanting to visit, especially at a school or center without a home visitation policy. In some cases, you may accompany the cooperating teacher rather than make a solo visit.

Regarding the question of home visits, in most cases it is best to ask the families when they bring or pick up their child. It helps to watch nonverbal cues in planning how you will ask. Obviously, if the people seem tired, cross, or hurried, one should wait. The longer you are at a center, the better families will know you. With one of these families, you may feel quite comfortable about planning the home visit over the telephone. Your cooperating teacher may even encourage a telephone or e-mail contact, so that you can gain experience making such contacts.

Let us assume that you and your cooperating teacher have discussed which child's home the two of you will visit. Your cooperating teacher will speak to the parents, preferably in person, and may ask if there is a convenient time for the two of you to visit the child at home. The person will most likely ask why, and your cooperating teacher may say, "We'd like to get to know Sandy better."

Most teachers visiting homes consider what the child or siblings will be doing while adults talk. They select child materials to carry with them, such as small objects to manipulate, coloring and other books, crayons, puzzles, and puppets that a child can use without adult help. If other children are to be home, other safe items can also be planned. Teachers can introduce play items as teacher's *traveling toys*, which will go back in the bag at the end of the visit, or if the budget permits, as gifts to remain with the child.

An Account of a Student and Cooperating Teacher's Home Visit

The following is a description of a hypothetical home visit, by a cooperating teacher and her student teacher, narrated using the student teacher's own words and perspective.

You arrive at the Campbells' apartment a few minutes early. You both decide to look around before you go into the apartment. The Campbells live in a lower-income area. The streets are dirty and littered with paper, broken bottles, and empty soda and beer cans. There is little grass in front of the apartment house; the yard is generally unkempt and weedy. The apartment house, like the others on the street, is built in motel fashion. It is badly in need of paint, and you can easily see that local teenagers have used the walls for graffiti. There are at least two abandoned cars on the street. One has no tires and its windows are smashed; the other is resting on its rims and is severely dented, as though it had been hit in an accident and never repaired. Further down the street, a group of youths are playing soccer in the street. Some of them appear to belong to an ethnic minority. A radio or record player is blaring from one of the apartments; a baby is heard crying.

You get out of the car, lock it, and look at the mailboxes to see which apartment is the Campbell's; they live in 2E. You begin to make your way through the cluttered hallway and almost trip over a small, grubby child riding a rickety, old tricycle. "Who ya lookin' for?" she demands. You tell her you are going to visit the Campbells. The little girl responds negatively. "Oh, them! They're sure stuck up. Why dya wanna see them?" You walk past the child, who keeps pestering you with questions. When she sees that you have no intention of answering, she rides off.

You walk up the stairs to the second floor, noting the chipped paint and shaky railings. You go past the apartments with the blaring radio and the crying child, arriving finally at 2E. You ring the bell. Sandy answers. She is spotlessly clean and wearing what appears to be her Sunday dress. She greets you shyly, ducking her head. You enter a sparsely furnished but immaculate apartment. The television is on; Sandy goes into the kitchen and announces your arrival. Mrs. Campbell enters and asks you to sit. She has just made some tea and offers you some. You thank her and accept. She leaves and returns quickly with four steaming mugs, one each for you and your cooperating teacher, one for herself, and a small one for Sandy.

Before your cooperating teacher can ask anything, Mrs. Campbell hesitantly and nervously says, "I want to apologize for making you come all this way on a Saturday, but I dare not ask for time off from work. Your wanting to visit us was such a nice thing; it's good for Sandy to see you're interested in her like that."

Your cooperating teacher murmurs something about wanting to get to know Mrs. Campbell better as well. Mrs. Campbell suggests to Sandy that she show you some of her books. "I think books are so important. Sandy and I go to the library every two weeks, and she picks out six books to bring home to read. You know I read to her every night, don't you?"

You wonder if Sandy and Mrs. Campbell live by themselves or if there are any others who share the apartment. You then remember that Mrs. Campbell listed two parents on Sandy's school enrollment form. "Is Mr. Campbell at work?" your cooperating teacher asks. Mrs. Campbell sighs. "I only wish he were!" she says. Sandy announces, "Daddy's at the races. He thinks Sandy's Dream is going to win today. He told me my name would bring him good luck." Mrs. Campbell admonishes Sandy to be quiet, saying, "Miss Julie doesn't care about what Daddy's doing." Mrs. Campbell smiles slightly and shrugs her shoulders. "Mr. Campbell has been out of work lately and has been going to the races to pass the time." Without thinking, the teacher asks what Mr. Campbell does for a living. "He's a heavy equipment operator; you know, he operates those big road-grading machines they use to build highways. Only, there hasn't been much work lately, and Mr. Campbell doesn't like to take jobs away from home. It makes it real hard on Sandy and me, though, because there's only my salary to live on. You know, we used to have our own home in suburbia, but we had to give it up to pay our bills, after John lost his last job."

You remember that Mrs. Campbell listed her job as a billing clerk for a large corporation, with headquarters in your area. You get the impression that Mrs. Campbell is trying very hard to maintain her small apartment the same way she kept her former home.

A shout from the apartment next door can be heard. "You'll have to ignore the Browns," Mrs. Campbell says. "They always fight when he's had too much to drink." Angry voices can be heard screaming at each other.

Sandy disappears and returns with a dilapidated rag doll in her arms. "Want to see Andrea?" she asks, thrusting the doll under your nose. (Sandy pronounces it like An-*dray*-a.) "Sandy, don't bother Miss Julie when we're talking," admonishes Mrs. Campbell. You say, "That's okay, Mrs. Campbell." You pick up the doll and look closely at it, smiling at Sandy. "Sandy, I think you love your doll very much, don't you?" Sandy enthusiastically nods her head. Mrs. Campbell gives her a quick look and shake of her head. Sandy goes over to her mother, sits down on the rug, and plays with her doll.

The cooperating teacher and Mrs. Campbell continue the conversation for another 15 or 20 minutes. You wonder if Mr. Campbell will come home from the racetrack before you leave, and you decide that Mrs. Campbell chose this time for you to come, knowing that Mr. Campbell would not be there. It makes you wonder about their relationship. Mrs. Campbell has offered no information about Mr. Campbell other than to answer the teacher's question about his work. You sense some underlying feelings of anger and despair, but also feel that it is none of your business.

You both soon rise to leave and thank Mrs. Campbell and Sandy for their hospitality. You and your teacher hand Sandy your mugs. She turns to her mother and asks if she can walk you to your car. Mrs. Campbell replies, "Okay, Sandy, but come right back upstairs. I don't want you playing with the no-good riffraff downstairs." She turns to your cooperating teacher and explains that the children who live below are "real rough and use language I don't approve of, so I don't let Sandy play with them." "They swear," Sandy volunteers, "and use words my Momma and Daddy won't let me repeat." Mrs. Campbell glances quickly at the teacher.

"It's not so bad now, but I worry about when Sandy grows a little older. It won't be easy keeping her away from them when they all get into school together. Her face brightens a little. "But maybe we'll be able to move from here by then. We're trying to save so we can move across Main Street." You understand what she means. The houses and apartments across Main Street are cleaner and better kept; most people own their own homes.

Reflections on the Home Visit

Imagine you are the student teacher in the home visit just described. After returning home, you jot down your impressions of the visit with Mrs. Campbell and Sandy. Your first impression is that they seem out of place in the neighborhood. Mrs. Campbell obviously attempts to keep the apartment clean. Sandy is always clean and wears clean clothes to school. At the age of four, she already knows to wash her hands when she goes to the bathroom; you have not had to remind her as you have the other children. You have also noted that Sandy eats slowly and uses good manners, reflecting good training at home.

Your second impression is that Mrs. Campbell is under great strain where Mr. Campbell is concerned. You understand why Sandy is such a quiet child. Mrs. Campbell is a quiet woman who is training Sandy to be a quiet child at home. You also understand why Sandy rarely mentions her father. It is obvious that Mrs. Campbell disapproves of her husband spending time at the races. You suspect that Mr. and Mrs. Campbell have probably had many arguments about this matter, especially because their finances seem somewhat precarious. You may have also surmised that the couple has had many arguments about Mr. Campbell's unemployment. These disagreements may be another reason why Sandy is quiet and subdued. Sandy may blame herself for the difficulties her parents express between themselves. You begin to realize why Sandy needs emotional support before trying something new and requires much praise when accomplishing something that is fairly simple. In addition, Sandy's desire to please her mother is carried into her relationship with adults at school; she is always seeking adult approval. "Is this the way you want it done?" or "Can you help me?"

As you relate your impressions to your cooperating teacher the next day, you have another thought. Not only did the Campbell apartment seem out of place in the neighborhood, but you suspect that Mrs. Campbell has no friends among her neighbors. You wonder to whom she would turn when and if she ever needed help. The cooperating teacher suggests that Mrs. Campbell might receive support from the pastor at her church. She had listed a church affiliation on the questionnaire that she completed when she enrolled Sandy. You and your cooperating teacher agree that Mrs. Campbell probably attends church regularly. Certainly, Sandy has talked enough about Sunday school to confirm this possibility. You are slightly relieved to think that Mrs. Campbell is not quite as isolated as you had thought.

As you read the home visit account, were there other aspects of the visit and subsequent discussion that concerned you? If so, jot them down, so you can participate in a group discussion with your fellow student teachers.

OTHER SCHOOL-HOME INTERACTIONS

A center may conduct regular, parenting education programs, and may send home frequent information concerning school happenings and planned events (see Figure 10–7). Some preschools, especially those

Kindergarten News

October 24

Language Arts: Reviewing M, F, R, S, N, T, and learning the short sound of the vowel a.

Working on colors, especially purple.

Math: Continue counting, sorting, and patterning, and working with the numbers 2 and 3.

Social Studies: This week is Red Ribbon Week when we talk about keeping our bodies healthy and saying no to drugs.

Science: The sense of touch and taste.

Music: We will be studying the opera Lucia Di Lammermoor.

Art: Halloween art.

P.E.: Working with balls.

We will have a Halloween Party Friday morning. There is a 12:00 dismissal. We will be making a costume, so do not send one.

Progress reports will be given out Friday. Attached to this newsletter is your scheduled time for a conference, either Friday afternoon or sometime Monday. If the time scheduled doesn't work out for you, please let me know and we can reschedule.

Next Tuesday, Nov. 2, we will be privileged to have the San Francisco Opera Guild come to our school and perform a preview of Lucia Di Lammermoor.

Regards.
M. Andreozzi

● **Figure 10-7**
Example of a parochial school teacher's newsletter to parents.

associated with adult education classes offering child development theory, include parent education as a mandatory part of their program. Topics may range from discipline, to problems specific to areas of the curriculum, to planning for emergencies, and a countless number of other topics (see Figure 10–8). Kieff and Wellhousen (2000) caution educators about making assumptions when planning parent meetings, such as assuming that family members:

- can read advanced, take-home announcements.
- are available for the times scheduled.
- have transportation.
- can understand English.
- can bring foods, snacks, and so on.
- are children's biological parents.
- have circumstances, lifestyles, and cultures that are the same as the teaching staff.
- will communicate the barriers they face in attending school meetings.

Figure 10-8
Infant care was the subject of this parent-teacher meeting.

Family planning worksheets may prove helpful as you plan your own strategies to engage families in the learning experiences (see Figures 10–9 and 10–10).

Most elementary schools have regularly scheduled PTA/PTO meetings. Typically, the September meeting is called *Back-to-School Night,* and offers explanations of the class curriculum by each teacher. Generally, teachers arrange displays of the children's work on bulletin boards and explain curriculum goals for the year. Many teachers have sign-up sheets posted for volunteer help, and all teachers attempt to establish rapport with their respective family groups. Student teachers are traditionally introduced at this time also.

Another form of school-home interaction consists of formal and informal written communications. Most public school districts and private schools send newsletters home to parents. These typically include a calendar of upcoming district and school events, and articles for parents on specific parts of the curriculum, ideas for parents to implement at home, and so on. These may be written by the superintendent, headmaster, director, or by curriculum specialists and consultants. Sometimes, individual teachers prepare newsletters to send to families, or for students to take home. They frequently include news about topics taught in class that week, articles written and illustrated by the children themselves, and requests for toys, books, and volunteers for upcoming field trips. Newsletters frequently include curriculum items for people to try at home (especially arts and crafts), recipes for snacks, and a question and answer section. They may also contain a swap column, or notices of toys to exchange, and may even contain a column written by the family members of enrolled children. Some centers, and most school newsletters, advertise parenting education meetings.

In many elementary schools, e-mail goes back and forth regularly. Some schools also maintain chat rooms that families, students, teachers, and the public can access.

Family Involvement Planning Worksheet

Name of activity/event _____

Proposed date and time _____

Location _____

Targeted participants _____

Consider the descriptors below to identify family-related factors that could create barriers, and prevent or limit the participation of families. After identifying possible barriers, adapt the activity or event to incude all families.

Family structures

Consider who are the primary caregivers for the children. Consider the presence of younger and older siblings living at home.

❑ divorced parents	❑ split families	❑ same-sex parents
❑ single parent	❑ foster parents	❑ family member with disability
❑ grandparent(s)	❑ legal guardian	❑ teen parents
❑ blended family	❑ widowed parent	❑ other_____

Possible barriers include _____

Family lifestyles

Consider the daily challenges or routines affecting the children and each family.

❑ income level	❑ unemployment	
❑ employment hours and time of day, number of jobs	❑ caring for an elderly or a disabled family member	❑ incarcerated parent ❑ community ❑ education level
❑ risks or dangers involved in work	❑ latch-key child care ❑ transporation	❑ housing ❑ access to telephone
❑ travel distance	❑ reading ability	❑ resources
❑ migrant status	❑ number of family members or siblings	❑ other_____

Possible barriers include _____

Family cultures

Consider the cultural aspects of each family. Avoid stereotypes.

❑ religious backgrounds	❑ nonverbal communication styles
❑ holiday celebrations	eye contact
❑ dietary restrictions	gestures
❑ views on child-rearing	touching
❑ languages	proximity during conversations
	❑ other_____

Possible barriers include _____

How the activity or event can be adapted to include all families represented in the class or school _____

● **Figure 10-9**

Family involvement planning worksheet. Reprinted with permission from the National Association for the Education of Young Children.

Common Barriers and Possible Modifications Checklist

Barriers	❑ Modifications
Time	❑ breakfast meetings
	❑ weekend events
	❑ one event scheduled over a number of days
	❑ open invitations
Transportation	❑ school bus or van
	❑ car pool arranged by teacher or parent volunteer
	❑ buddy system among families
Child care	❑ school-provided child care
	❑ chid care provided by parent organization
	❑ buddy system among families
Decorations/ celebrations	❑ artwork created by children in the art center
	❑ artwork generated during a theme/project study
Curriculum	❑ opportunities for children to make multiple gifts and cards, and to pick their recipients
	❑ family members share expertise and culture
	❑ bias-free curriculum
Food	❑ multiple menus available
	❑ buffets
	❑ picnics
Printed material	❑ translate copies
	❑ make audiotapes
	❑ make telephone calls
	❑ use voice mail or e-mail
Special guest	❑ guest not specified by role
	❑ a pal or friend
	❑ open invitations to extended family members or a noncustodial parent
Expense	❑ support provided by community businesses underwriting the event or materials needed
Misunderstanding the role as parent volunteer in the classroom	❑ volunteer training sessions
	❑ specific routines created
	❑ recorded or printed instructions
Misunderstanding the parental role in home-extension learning activities	❑ specific routines created for home-extension learning activities
	❑ parent workshops to explain activities
	❑ demonstration tapes
	❑ demonstrations during home visits
Discomfort in school situations	❑ alternative home visits or neighborhood meetings
	❑ buddy systems among families
	❑ small-group meetings

◉ Figure 10-10

Common barriers and possible modifications checklist. Reprinted with permission from the National Association for the Education of Young Children.

Parenting Education Meetings

The following ideas are suggested by Foster (1994):

- Plan together with families and include the children—they have ideas, too. You may want to have a committee of family members, teachers, and a few children do some parts of the planning.
- Assess family needs and interests.
- If the school, center, or child care facility is not close to where families live, ask them for help in locating an alternative meeting place.
- If you have families who do not have cars or do not drive, the meeting place should be accessible by public transportation, or carpools should be arranged.
- During the meeting, arrange activities for children, so families do not have to worry about caring for them or keeping them occupied.
- Plan refreshments and activities.
- Plan for a meeting that will last no more than an hour and 15 minutes.
- Open with a short introduction.
- Decide whether the presentation will be a lecture, a video, a panel discussion, or something else.
- Keep in mind the families' abilities to process English if it is not their primary language.
- If this is the first meeting of the year, think about having an icebreaker so families can get to know each other.
- Remember that people talk more frequently in small groups, so you might want to plan a short presentation, followed with small discussion groups, and ending with sharing from each small group.
- People enjoy handouts and activities that involve making something they can take home.
- Always be sure to thank the people for coming, and have fliers with information about the next meeting—topic, date, and time—available to hand out.

Eggers-Pierola (2005) describes one teacher's observation of the diversity found in parents' and family members' greeting styles at one parenting night meeting:

> With the families we have here—from seven different cultures—I make a point to learn about cultural differences in communication, like eye contact, touching behavior, tone, and the distance people use when talking with each other. One day, at a parents' night, I watched as parents greeted each other when they arrived, and noticed for the first time what amazingly different conventions they had for greeting each other or greeting someone from a culture not their own. Some gave each other three kisses on alternate cheeks, intoning the same greeting words; the same families simply nodded and said "Hello" when greeting someone from another culture. Others kissed on two cheeks, another pair of mothers by one kiss and a hug. The men in two of the cultures hugged and patted each other's backs. When they greeted children, I saw even more differences in style, although many bent down to the level of the children. When I brought this up at circle time

and asked children to play act greeting different people in and outside of their families, even more differences in the "discourse" of greetings became apparent, such as the fascinating subtleties of rhythm of speech and movement as the children role-played the greetings.

Teacher Presentation Skills at Parent Meetings

When conducting a presentation to families, you will use many of the same strategies you use with children. Although many of your child activity presentations concentrate on discovery and exploration, with parents and families you relay clearly stated facts. Depending on the topic, or to further illustrate some learning, hands on and active audience participation may, at times, add insight and create interest.

You will want to show enthusiasm for teaching, and look straight in the eyes of your audience, panning the whole room while using expressive but natural gestures and varying your tone of voice. This will clarify your main points and express your emotions. As with children, use examples, anecdotes, and stories of classroom happenings. Creating curiosity and excitement in your subject matter is well worth the effort. Help your audience visualize how the school's curriculum creates child learning opportunities, and either suggest home activities or prepare a helpful handout, if the presentation's topic calls for it. Teachers frequently plan time for family questions and comments at the end of presentations.

At any meeting, people will naturally want to discuss their child. Many teachers develop the habit of jotting down each day at least one significant observation of each attending child; this, they believe, helps them identify children who may have escaped their attention. This may seem a near impossible task to suggest to a student teacher, but many practicing teachers do it. As a professional student teacher, you will stress again that you are in training, and questions should be directed to the cooperating teacher if they concern children's progress and abilities. If comments were to be made by a student teacher, they would concern positive aspects of a child's individuality. Some people alarm easily, as you will be sure to find when you have full classroom responsibility.

PRECAUTIONS

Single-parent families are also prone to stress, some created by the myths surrounding the stereotype of the minority or single parent. It is a myth, for example, that the child from a single-parent family will have emotional problems. The truth may be that had the parent remained married to an abusive spouse, the child might have been negatively affected. It is a myth that the single parent lacks interest in the school's activities. Because most single parents are women, and women tend to have lower-paying jobs with less personal freedom, they may not be able to participate in the school program. Be very careful not to interpret this as a lack of interest. The truth may be that single parents cannot take time off from work to be more active. The single parent may compensate by talking with the child every evening and sending notes when questions arise. The single parent may not have time to bake cookies for a party but may be willing to volunteer to serve as an adult helper at a Saturday event.

Be aware that single parents may need a support group, especially if they have no family members living close by. If you have several children from single-parent families, you might even want to plan a parenting education meeting devoted to their needs. At one Head Start center, the number one request by families who were asked about preferences for the program's parenting education meeting was the topic of *stress and the single parent.*

Unfortunately, many families cannot exist without the income from two working family members. Be sensitive to ways in which people can involve themselves in the life of the center. Educational meetings are fine, but not if people on limited incomes must hire a babysitter to attend. Knowing this, your cooperating teacher or director may make arrangements for children to be cared for on site. Many families may not have a car and must rely on public transportation. Find out when buses travel and what routes are available. Make sure the meetings end on time so a people do not miss the bus.

However important parenting education may seem to you, it may not seem as valuable to every family. Many will choose to attend when the topic presented meets their needs but be absent when it does not. Others may find it too hectic to try to attend a meeting held in the evening.

There will always be people in families on whom you can rely, regardless of the circumstances. Do not take advantage of this; some people simply cannot say no.

Collaboration

collaboration—a desire or need to create or discover something new, while thinking and working with others. It is a process of joint decision making. It involves discussion, different views and perspectives, shared goals, building new shared understandings, and perhaps the creation of a new outlook or course of action.

The NAEYC revised statement on developmentally appropriate practice, and other newer guidelines, recommend that preschool program goals be developed in collaboration with families (Bredekamp & Copple, 1997). This focus on **collaboration** is a departure from older ideas, which emphasized early childhood educators as supportive assistants, rescuers, or compensators for families with less than ideal home environments. Collaboration affords educators insights that can strengthen home involvement in school activities and family-teacher bonds.

Families Seeking Help

Because of the increasing focus on early literacy and pre-reading skills, brain growth, development during early childhood, and ordinary child-rearing concerns, an increasing number of questions are directed to early childhood personnel. Many people seek direct help concerning what home activities they can provide. (Practical, home literacy-developing activities are found in Figure 10–11.)

Early childhood educators can promote each families confidence in their ability to influence children's literacy. Through center outreach and involvement activities, centers may change reluctant care providers into very active and resourceful ones, who promote children's educational opportunities.

Your student teaching assignments and experiences may involve a higher level of school-home interaction than in previous years, as colleges and training programs give greater emphasis to involvement. Competencies in this area of teaching are increasingly important as teachers assume a leadership role and develop creative strategies to involve families and other community members in the life of the school or center.

HOME LANGUAGE AND LITERACY–PROMOTING ACTIVITIES

Families and teachers working together to identify language and literacy-developing home activities frequently include the following activity suggestions:

- Give each child—no matter how young—*daily* individualized attention that includes talking about what has captured his interest at the moment or describes what the instructing adult is doing. Become a focused listener who tries to understand.
- Be responsive and open to the child's verbal and nonverbal communicative attempts, by answering with positive comments, suggestions, and recognition of each child's efforts.
- Model an interest in books and reading materials in daily life, including the daily mail, magazines, and so on.
- Provide home areas for child activities where books, drawing and writing materials, alphabet letters, and comfortable furnishings are readily available. Include listening activities, puppets, and scratch paper for writing or mark making.
- Read aloud and share such things as labels, instructions, shopping lists, recipe cards, words on objects, phone messages, coupons, notes, signs, calendars, alphabet letters, advertisements, directions, and other printing you find in the home or community environment.
- Be creative in obtaining reading material for the home by investigating yard sales, library sales, used book stores, inexpensive children's book clubs (like Scholastic), and free book offers.
- Make your local library a frequent destination for family outings, encouraging its further use and investigation by children. Check on all available library services and resources. Make books part of family life for all members, infants and elders included.
- Write notes and postcards to your children and be an avid sharer of personal, daily happenings and stories.
- Create meal times that are full of informative conversation, stories, and sharing.
- Play all sorts of games where rules are read and discussed, including board and card games. Check resale and thrift store offerings. Investigate and create spelling and alphabet games as part of daily life.
- Encourage scribbling, printing, drawing, and art. Use child-created products as starting places for discussion, rather than correcting beginning attempts at learning or child-created spellings.
- Probe gently for more information or details when speech or writing seems incorrect to you, knowing that age, time, and experience will correct usage. Focus on keeping child communication attempts coming, rather than focusing on perfection. Correct with subtlety and gentleness, just as you accepted immature speech forms such as *baba* for *bottle* when the child was learning to talk.
- Keep in touch with your children's teachers to find out new and evolving school interests and accomplishments. Request the teacher's suggestions on how to expand these interests at home.
- Explore the community and home neighborhood for opportunities to experience and explore. Record and relive these away-from-home activities, along with children's reactions to them.
- Make family scrapbooks with labels or stories attached.
- Encourage children's efforts to initiate conversation, read words or letters, print, use writing tools or computers, or record their ideas by providing attention and approval.
- Have fun with words. Try playful rhyming, riddles, new captions for pictures, silly naming or spelling, emphasizing certain syllables in words, rhythmic chanting, and so on.

Value children's ideas, perspectives, and opinions so individuality and feelings of self-worth grow. (Machado, 2007).

 **Figure 10-11**

Adapted from Machado, J. M. (2007) *Early Childhood Experiences in Language Arts*. Thomson/Delmar Learning: Clifton Park, NY.

SUMMARY

In this chapter, we discussed a school's family relations philosophy and described interactions between families, cooperating teachers, and student teachers. We mentioned again the importance of communication skill and nonverbal communication. Some specific techniques and recommendations to use when conferencing with people, conducting a home visit, and presenting family education programs were included.

Most family-teacher communication is informal in nature. Therefore, it is important to be aware that the impression you make in informal interactions may often set the stage for how people view and accept you.

We have detailed a home visit, as seen from the student teacher's perspective. We included illustrations, not only of the physical description of the childs' home environment, but also of the feelings experienced by the student teacher.

Awareness of communities can be obtained in various ways, some as simple as a drive through the neighborhood or as complex as a formal, written survey. Such knowledge helps teachers become more sensitive to a child's needs and interests. An important goal of a school's involvement efforts is to promote family engagement with what is going on at the school, and to enlist active support of the educational opportunities offered at school and at home.

HELPFUL WEB SITES

http://www.fape.org
Families and Communities—Families and Advocates Partnership for Education (FAPE). This site includes public information concerning coordinated community efforts.

http://www.nncc.org
National Network for Child Care. Search for children's developmental milestones.

http://www.npin.org
National Parent Information Network. Select information concerning the process of parenting and family involvement.

http://www.asha.org
American Speech-Language-Hearing Association. Activities to stimulate language growth are offered.

http://www.cssp.org
Center for the Study of Social Policy. A program handbook is available for centers and schools interested in supporting and strengthening families.

 Additional resources for this chapter can be found by visiting the Online Companion at www.earlychilded.delmar.com.

SUGGESTED ACTIVITIES

A. Observe the arrival of children and adults at a local preschool program. Who greets them? Are there indications of separation difficulties? If not, why do child easily transition from parent to school? What strategies are used? How are teachers building school-home relationships? Would you change any school entry procedures? If yes, why?

B. With your cooperating teacher's permission, interview some of the parents at your center. What kinds of support systems are present in their lives that aid their ability to parent? What type of school-planned involvement activities do they enjoy or choose not to attend? Why?

C. How are local schools or other public or private agencies in the community helping new immigrants? What kinds of specialized materials are being used, if any? What kinds of specialized services are offered? Discuss your findings with your peers and supervisor.

D. With a small group of peers, share how schools you attended involved your own parents and whether this influenced your education. Or relate incidences in your early education when teachers made your parents aware of your special interests or abilities. Report your findings to your larger training group.

E. Role-play the following parent-teacher confrontational exchanges. In groups of six peers, select members to role-play the teacher and the parent. Discuss scenarios, and share with the entire training group when finished.
1. Mrs. G. decides to have her class of three-year-olds celebrate the birthday of Martin Luther King. Mr. L. complains, emphasizing this is beyond his child's understanding.
2. Miss R., Joshua's mom, feels his teacher takes far too many field trips with the children.
3. Mrs. T. tells her child's teacher that in six months her child hasn't learned one new thing.
4. Mrs. S., a parent, says "Don't ever call me at home!" with considerable anger in her voice.
5. Mr. N., a teacher, asks Mardell's mother to find objects at home that begin with the letter *B*. She glares at him and says, "I'm paying you to educate my daughter. Preschool homework is ridiculous."
6. A parent volunteer, Mrs. P., says, "After watching Raoul today, I can see he is bored in your classroom."

F. Read the following then discuss with a group of peers how the reading relates to you, a student teacher. Share your group's ideas with the entire training group.

Perhaps the greatest challenge of our generation is to be role models for the children of 2010, by demonstrating through our actions, as well as words, that an inclusive democracy is viable in our communities, workplaces, and nation.

This will often require that we grow by reaching out beyond our social enclave to listen, talk, and cooperate with people who are different (Washington & Andrews, 1998, page 44).

G. Examine Figure 10–12. In speaking to this child's parent, what might be one of the parent's concerns?

● **Figure 10-12**
Seeing individuality.

H. Discuss the following child statements with peers and formulate a teacher response. Analyze responses for teacher attempts to give equal status to non-traditional families.
1. On Father's Day, a child says, "I don't have a daddy to make a card for."
2. Megan says, "I have two mommies, and they are both called Mary."
3. Ryan says, "My mom's boyfriend takes me home from school. He lives at our house."
4. Anna says, "My sister is my momma, and grandpa takes care of me, too."

●REVIEW

A. If you were to write a non-discrimination policy statement or a school-home relations philosophy for a prekindergarten or school, what would it include?

B. Rate your knowledge and effectiveness in teacher-family working relationships using the following rating scale:

1 = Very knowledgeable; 2 = Knowledgeable;
3 = Some knowledge; 4 = Meager knowledge;
5 = No knowledge

1. I am able to conduct professional conferences and interviews with parents. _____

2. I could design and develop an adequate parenting education and involvement program for an early childhood center. _____

3. I feel comfortable planning and conducting meetings and workshops. _____

4. I possess the ability to successfully involve people in classroom activities. _____

5. I am aware of a wide range of involvement possibilities and strategies. _____

6. I possess professional communication skills and abilities useful in family contacts. _____

7. I can develop positive relationships with the families of attending children. _____

8. I understand the importance of school-home partnerships concerned with children's growth and education. _____

C. Name five tips for planning a parent-teacher conference, or five suggestions for techniques useful in a student teacher presentation at a parenting meeting.

D. Read the following statements and determine whether they are effective communication statements or blocks to effective communication. If any statement is neither, identify it as such.

1. *To the parent who picks up a child late:* "Mrs. Jones, you know you're supposed to pick up Susan before 6:00 PM."

2. *Quietly, in a one to one with a parent about an upcoming parent education meeting:* "We've followed up on your request, and at Tuesday's meeting, one of the county social workers will talk about applying for food stamps and TANF. We hope you'll be able to attend."

3. *To parent bringing a child to the center in the morning:* "Why don't you go with Randy to the science corner? He has something to show you. Randy, show your Dad what you found yesterday."

4. *To a parent with limited skills in English:* "Mrs. Paliwal, we hope you'll be able to stay today. Anil seems so shy. I think he might feel better if you could stay with him for a few minutes."

5. *On the telephone to a parent whose child has been involved in a fight at school:* "Mr. Smith, we're hoping you might stop by early this afternoon when you pick up Steve. We know how busy you are, but we're busy, too, and Steve needs you."

6. *To a mother volunteer who is berating someone else's child:* "You know we never raise our voices like that in our classroom."

7. *To a parent reading a story to her own child during free play:* "Mrs. Smith, would you please watch the children at the water table?"

8. *To the crying child of a harried mother who arrives later than usual:* "Aiden, I know you like to play with clay; let's go over to the clay table and see what your friend, Sari, is doing."

9. *On the telephone to a parent whose daughter has wet her pants and has no dry ones at school:* "Mrs. Carter, Kalea wet her pants this morning. We put her into a spare pair we had on hand. Tomorrow, you can bring an extra pair so if Kalea has another accident, she'll have her own clothes to wear."

CASE SCENARIO

Setting: A community college laboratory school. Mark, a four-year-old, has been enrolled since age three in the child development center attached to an older community college in a large, metropolitan city.

Observing Mark was a joyful experience for those enrolled as early childhood majors who chose him as a subject of study. He was energetic, with his own pack of special buddies who were willing to investigate or participate in any classroom or outdoor adventure. Physically strong, of average height, and well coordinated, he possessed obvious good health. Mark was often described as a sweet dynamo, quick to offer his ideas in classroom discussions. Mark was also the kind of child his teachers described as progressing above average in all developmental areas.

His single mother, a community college sophomore, expected to transfer to a local university in the fall. She often picked up Mark's older, elementary school-aged brother first, so both came into the center at pick-up time. Mark would excitedly show his brother his school projects, or demonstrate how he could maneuver a new piece of outdoor equipment. It was easy to see that Mark idolized his brother, and a close relationship was apparent with his mom. His professionally employed father had custody on some weekends but never attended school functions. Mark talked, at times, about camping trips and ball games with dad.

Without warning, Mark's behavior changed. He appeared sleepy, withdrawn, uninterested in the activities around him. He sat in one spot for long periods and sought to be alone in the play yard. His friends approached him but he would either not talk or say he didn't want to play when they offered ideas. The staff alerted Mark's mom to his bad day and suggested monitoring his health. Teachers had talked to Mark, asking if he felt sick, but he indicated he didn't hurt anywhere. The staff's plan was to record Mark's behavior the next day and engage him by delicately probing and offering as much close, physical contact as he seemed willing to accept.

continues . . .

. . . continued

A meeting with Mark's mother was set as soon as possible. His behavior led teachers to suspect depression. When the meeting took place, Mark's mother immediately broke down and was extremely distraught. She explained that Mark's father, who had remarried about six month's earlier, had begun a suit for full custody of Mark's older brother, but not for Mark. The father thought that Mark was the result of a relationship Mark's mother had while they were legally separated.

Questions for Discussion:

1. Was the center's handling of Mark's changed behavior appropriate?

2. Is documenting Mark's daily behavior important? Why?

3. Is parent-center communication working effectively? If yes, what brings you to that conclusion? If no, explain.

REFERENCES

Berlo, D. K. (1960). *The process of communication.* New York: Holt, Rinehart & Winston.

Bredekamp, S., & Copple, C. (Eds.). (1997). *Developmentally appropriate practice in early childhood programs* (rev. ed.). Washington, DC: National Association for the Education of Young Children.

Caruso, J. J., & Fawcett, M. T. (1999). *Supervision in early childhood education: A developmental perspective.* New York: Teachers College Press.

Eggers-Pierola, C. (2005). *Connections and commitments: Reflecting Latino values in early childhood programs.* Portsmouth, NH: Heinemann.

Epstein, J. (2000, July 21). The national view of school, family, community partnerships: Current status and future view. Conference presentation, Northwest Regional Laboratory Invitational Conference, Improving student success through school, family, and community partnerships. Portland, OR.

Foster, S. M. (1994, November). Successful parent meetings. *Young Children 50*(1), 37–39.

Hildebrand, V. (1993). *Management of child development centers.* New York: Macmillan.

Igoa, C. (1995). *The inner world of the immigrant child.* New York: St. Martin's Press.

Kieff, J., & Wellhousen, K. (2000, May). Planning family involvement in early childhood programs. *Young Children, 55*(3), 18–25.

Kyle, D., & McIntyre, E. (2000, October). Family visits benefit teachers and families—and students most of all. *Practitioner Brief #1.* Santa Cruz, CA: Center for Research on Education, Diversity and Excellence, University of California Brochure.

Machado, J. M. (2007). *Early childhood experiences in the language arts: Early Literacy.* Clifton Park, NY: Thomson Delmar Learning.

Stephens, K. (2005, May/June). Meaningful family engagement. *Exchange, 163,* 18–24.

Washington, V., & Andrews, J. D. (Eds.). (1998). *Children of 2010.* Washington, DC: National Association for the Education of Young Children.

Winkleman, P. H. (1999). Family involvement in education: The apprehensions of student teachers. In M. S. Ammon (Ed.), *Joining hands: Preparing teachers to make meaningful home-school connections* (pp.79–100). Sacramento, CA: California Department of Education, California Commission on Teacher Credentialing.

Professional Concerns

CHAPTER 11

Quality Programs in Early Childhood Settings

OBJECTIVES After reading this chapter, you should be able to:

1. .... List five of the factors in a quality program, according to the U.S. Department of Education.

2. .... Describe two different types of quality programs in schools.

3. .... Discuss the relationship between a program's philosophy and its quality.

4. .... Discuss the importance of the teacher and director/principal in a quality program.

5. .... List the program standards evaluated under NAEYC accreditation criteria.

6. .... List the types of schools evaluated under state standards.

7. .... Discuss the process of self-evaluation and its relationship to the accreditation process.

8. .... Discuss the impact of the No Child Left Behind Act on the quality of kindergarten and primary grade classrooms.

Comments of student teachers:

> 66 I'll never forget the time I watched my cooperating teacher's enthusiasm at reading group time. She looked as if she enjoyed the story as much as the group of children. At recess I asked if it was a new reading series. She told me the book had been used for three years at her grade level. I marveled at her ability to make reading the story new, alive, and interesting to yet another group of children. ●

Marie Ota

> 66 My cooperating teacher and I became good friends. We still see one another at district meetings. I was privileged to have apprenticed under such an excellent model. ●

Rich Bacon

In looking at the concept of quality, what comes to mind? High quality always suggests something that goes beyond the ordinary. In a program for young children, then, quality suggests that it exceeds minimal standards. We might also want to include the fact that a high-quality program, in general, seeks to employ well-trained teachers, who more than meet the minimal education requirements of their respective states, and usually pays a higher salary and offers more benefits than lower-quality programs. As are many states, California is moving toward requiring all teachers in publicly-funded preschools to have BA/BS degrees in early childhood education (ECE), child development, or related fields. With funding from the state's *First Five Initiative* and other funding sources, representatives from community colleges and four-year universities have been meeting and planning for a seamless transition, from the two-year to four-year institutions, with three goals to consider:

1. Increase, retain, and maximize resources to support students' professional development, tuition, tutoring, mentoring, and book expenses as they transition from high school to Ph.D. in the field of ECE.

2. Promote and develop academic programs in ECE at institutions of higher education that address the current and future needs of the ECE profession.

3. Ensure that the early childhood workforce reflects the racial, ethnic, and linguistic diversity of the population they serve (Thompson, 2006).

Why do we see this move to requiring teachers in preschool settings to have bachelor degrees? One thrust has come from the requirement by the federal government that all teachers in Head Start programs should hold bachelor's degrees. Supporting influences come from researchers like Whitebook (1995). She points out that high-quality centers are those that meet standards that are higher than the minimum standards set by the state. They are also the programs "that have access to extra resources beyond parent fees." In one quality, nonprofit, parent-participation preschool with which we are familiar, the director has a master's degree in ECE, and every teacher but one with a master's has a bachelor's degree in ECE, child development, or a related field. Child development researchers have identified continuity of care from consistent, sensitive, well-trained, and well-compensated caregivers as key ingredients of good quality care (Groginsky, Robison, & Smith, 1999).

In addressing what she calls *quality teaching* in K–12 schools, Kennedy (2006) writes that most states adhere to the hypothesis that teachers are made in "carefully constructed higher education programs where [students] acquire both content and pedagogical knowledge." But then she questions whether or not this is true. Kennedy concludes that there are many factors that affect the quality of teaching, such as unreliable circumstances like the failure of props to support a science lesson, or unresolved discipline problems in the classroom. In the end, the important lesson is to think not just about *teacher* quality but to think about *teaching* quality. We must always remember that teaching is inherently an unpredictable, complex enterprise.

A study by Early, Bryant, Pianta, Clifford, Burchinal, Ritchie, Howes, and Barbarin (2006) indicates that "education and credentials by themselves are not sufficient" to ensure quality. However, these authors caution that it could be harmful to children to cut costs by lowering teacher or educational standards. The key is to properly compensate teachers according to the degrees they hold. Similarly, Pianta, Howes, Burchinal, Bryant, Clifford, Early, and Barbarin (2005) completed a study that failed to show any relationship between program quality and staff-child ratio or length of day. One difficulty lies in the variability among programs and preparation, especially at the preschool level. For example, regulations are stricter in state-funded programs and the ranges of both quality and education are more limited, making associations harder to detect (Early et al, 2006).

◉ MEETING CHILDREN'S NEEDS

Among the factors to consider in evaluating the quality of an early childhood program is whether the program meets each child's developmental needs. There must be an awareness of and attention to the needs of the children.

What are the needs of children during their early years? Accepting the validity of theories discussed in previous chapters, we know that their needs are to self-actualize, to know and understand, and to develop aesthetically. Children need to trust the significant people in their environment, resolve the questions of autonomy and initiative, and learn to become industrious.

◉ **Figure 11-1**
This climbing structure allows room for these four girls to play on it at the same time.

Implications According to Maslow's and Erikson's Theories

Let us briefly return to the theories of Maslow and Erikson. What are the implications, and the factors to consider, for a quality program in regard to these theories? The first factor would be to assure an environment in which the child's physical safety is considered. Quality programs for young children have the physical environment arranged so that children can explore without encountering physical dangers, such as electric cords or unprotected outlets, tables with sharp edges, and so on. In quality programs, the physical environment has been childproofed.

The second factor is attention to the child's need for psychological safety. Essentially, quality programs provide for predictability, decision-making opportunities, and reasonable limits. Predictability teaches the rudiments of learning about time and safety. With predictability comes the safety of knowing that certain activities will happen at certain times with consistency, such as snack time, group time, indoor and outdoor play, and the like (see Figures 11–1 and 11–2).

Children have little control over their lives, and in our modern industrial society, they have little opportunity to contribute to the family welfare. If, however, they have freedom of choice within the limits set, they can and do exert control over this part of their lives and thus learn how to make decisions. They also learn to accept the consequences of their decisions. Limits allow the child the safety of knowing which behaviors are acceptable and which are not. Limits teach children the concepts of right versus wrong and help the child develop inner control over behavior.

 Figure 11-2
The indoor water table is large enough to accommodate several children together.

A third factor is attention to belongingness and love needs. A quality program will provide for these. All children need to feel that they are a part of a social group; a preschool, child care center, elementary classroom, and family can provide the sense of group identity that is so important for the young child's positive growth.

Esteem needs are met in a quality program. Care is taken by all staff members to ensure that the children's **self-concepts** are enhanced. Look to see how the workers in a program relate to the children. Do they *CARE*? Do they take time to listen to the children? Do they compliment children when they have accomplished some goal? Do they make a conscious effort to bolster the children's self-esteem?

Are self-actualization needs met? Quality programs have enough equipment and materials with which the children can interact (see Figure 11–3). Are there enough art materials, books, and cut-and-paste opportunities? Is there a climbing apparatus? Are there plenty of tricycles and swings, so that no child has to wait too long? Are there enough puzzles? Are they challenging? Is the dramatic-play center well furnished? Are there enough props to stimulate sociodramatic play? Are there both large and small blocks? Is there a water table, a sand area, a terrarium, an aquarium, and a magnifying glass? Are there enough small manipulatives? Are the play areas and yard clean and well kept? Do the children look happy?

At the elementary school level, is the classroom physically attractive? Is it uncrowded? Is there a schedule of activities? Are there enough materials for every student? Are rules and consequences decided by the children themselves? Is there a sufficiently large play yard to encourage active play during recesses? Are there structures that encourage climbing and jumping and in a safe way?

self-concepts—
perceptions and feelings children may have about themselves, gathered largely from how the important people in their world respond to them.

● **Figure 11-3**
Exploring what to build with the blocks requires cooperation.

syntax—involves the grammatical rules that govern the structure of sentences.

Where Went On Our Train Ride

(Katie) I went to Disneyland. (Ryan) I think were in jail. (Fatima) thinks she went to Disneyland. (Brandon) I went to here. (Angel) to my casa (Joe) Jail (Gabriel) To Disneyland. (Christine) We go to school. (Angel) hey, I go to school too (Tara) To Disneyland (Joe) would play (Fatima) would see the firework (Gabriel) I would eat pizza. (Joe) Pizza Pizza

The End

● **Figure 11-4**
A wall chart with each child's contribution promotes language use and understanding.

A Balanced Program

A quality preschool or elementary school program will have a balanced curriculum that includes language, mathematics, motor activities, arts and crafts, music, creative movement, and science opportunities; none of these is neglected. Because of its importance, language will be emphasized in curricular areas in a quality preschool program. Look at and listen to how language is used and encouraged. It is during the preschool years, from age two-and-a-half to five, that the child makes the most progress in language. Having an *active* vocabulary—words the child uses—of around 300 words at two-and-a-half years, the preschool child will expand this to perhaps 3,000 words by age five. In *receptive* vocabulary, the 800 words *known* by the two-and-a-half-year-old will grow to approximately 10,000 by age five. At the same time, the child is learning the **syntax** rules of language, such as present, past, and future tenses and the use of the negative, interrogatory, and conditional forms of speech. All of this language ability is, for the most part, acquired without formal teaching. A quality preschool program, however, recognizes this growth of language in the young child and provides opportunities for the child to hear language being used in proper context, to listen to models of language, and to practice growing language competencies. In addition, a quality program affords many opportunities for language enrichment (see Figure 11–4).

A quality program for both preschool centers and elementary schools will have a quiet corner or private space for the children, so that any child can be alone when necessary. Children, especially those who spend long hours in a center or school every day, need time and space to be alone.

Some children live in homes that afford them little or no privacy; the center or school may be the only place where they can experience privacy.

Personnel and Philosophies

Perhaps the most important factor in quality programs is the personality of the teacher and director or principal. As thoroughly as students entering a teacher preparation program or teachers being considered for a position may be screened, it is not always apparent what their personal characteristics or dispositions might be. Cartwright (1999) lists good physical health, integrity, a grounding in theory, general knowledge, unconditional caring, intuition, and laughter as needed characteristics for early childhood educators.

Katz (Feeney, Christensen, & Moravcik, 2006) "describes a number of *dispositions* (relatively stable habits of mind or tendencies to respond to experiences in certain ways) that she believes are crucial—such as curiosity, openness to new ideas, a sincere liking for children, and so forth." But many things should be considered. Is this a person who really *likes* children? Does this person appear to be upbeat? Are there laugh lines in the corners of the eyes? Does this person smile when talking? Does there appear to be a mutual respect between this person and the children? When talking to the children, does this person stoop or kneel in order to be at their level? Is this person *with* the children or *over* the children? Is this a person trained in child development? A warm, loving, knowledgeable teacher and director/principal can make almost any program—public or private—a quality one, given the space and materials with which to work.

The second most important factor is the underlying philosophy of the program, or the basic principles by which the program is guided. Are there stated objectives? Is there a written statement of philosophy? Is the curriculum based on background knowledge of child development principles? Are there printed materials describing the program in terms of what the teacher, director, principal, district, and state want for the children? Or is this a program with no statement of purpose, no written goals, and no clear curriculum? Does the program assume that you know all you need to based on the program label (for example, Montessori, Christian, Reggio Emilia)?

STANDARDS OF QUALITY PROGRAMS

The U.S. Department of Education (2005) includes the following as components of high-quality preschool programs:

1. The program contains a clear statement of goals and philosophy that is comprehensive and addresses all areas of child development, including how the program will develop children's cognitive, language, and early reading skills, the cornerstones of later school success.

2. Children are engaged in purposeful learning activities and play, and are taught by teachers who work from lesson and activity plans (see Figure 11–5).

3. Instruction is guided by a coherent curriculum that includes meaningful content (such as science) and has a strong and systematic focus on cognitive skills, including the language, early reading,

Figure 11-5
Lesson and activity plan preparation is all part of the student teaching experience.

writing and math skills children need to develop before they enter kindergarten (see Figure 11–6).

4. Instruction is always intentional and frequently is direct and explicit. There is a balance between individual, small-group, and large-group activities.

5. The classroom environment is one where children feel well cared for and safe. It also stimulates children's cognitive growth and provides multiple and varied opportunities for language and literacy experiences.

6. Teachers frequently check children's progress. Ongoing assessment allows teachers to tailor their instruction to the needs of individual children, as well as identify children who may need special help.

7. The preschool staff regularly communicates with parents and caregivers so that caregivers are active participants in their children's education.

8. Services are sufficiently intensive to allow more time for children to benefit from cognitive experiences. Preschools that operate for a full day, on a year-round basis, or have provided children with two years of preschool, show better results than those that offer less intensive services.

To access or order the complete report, go to http://www.edpubs.org.

Although intended for preschool programs, the above-listed characteristics can be applied just as easily to elementary programs.

● **Figure 11-6**
Art activities play an important part in a well-balanced preschool curriculum.

Turner (2002a) describes the essential elements of quality, identified by New Mexico's *Comprehensive Professional Development System in Early Care, Education and Family Support*, in the following:

We defined an essential element of quality as a statement that defines a goal of practice, which has a base of legitimacy or validity based on scientific data, or when this evidence is lacking, representing the widely-agreed upon, state-of-the-art, high quality level of practice. Viewed this way, essential elements of quality are not static, rather they are revised and improved as the knowledge base increases and as new scientific findings become available.

The NAEYC is widely recognized for its leadership role in the development of standards for preschool center accreditation (see Figure 11–7). Standards vary somewhat between organizations and agencies, but in studying the above list, it is easy to see that Maslow's hierarchy of needs is considered, although not specifically stated. Erikson's developmental tasks have been considered as well. NAEYC's list, however, goes beyond simply relating conditions to developmental theory. It also introduces the importance of looking at minimum standards, as set by governmental authorities, suggesting that a good program exceeds such minimal standards. For example, federal or state standards may propose that a ratio of 12 children (two- and three-year-olds) to 1 adult is sufficient. A quality program may have 8 to 10 children for every adult.

Although a school cannot become licensed without meeting minimum state standards regarding the number of children per square foot of indoor and outdoor space, there are programs that *average* the number of children throughout the day and so exceed the maximum recommended number during hours of prime use. For example, a center may be licensed for 28 children and may have as few as 10 present at 8 AM and eight at 5 PM; yet, they may have as many as 34 present between 10 AM and 3 PM. The total number of children present throughout the day may be averaged so that a parent may never be aware of the overcrowding at midday. Some centers will employ a nutrition aide at lunchtime to assist in meal preparation. Although this person may never work with the children, she may be counted as an adult when figuring the ratio of children to adults. Many parents are unaware of these types of practices, none of which would be present in a quality program.

Figure 11-7
Programs often display their licenses, awards, and accreditation certificates if they have received them.

Has the No Child Left Behind Act Made a Difference in Quality?

There has been a fair amount of controversy about the efficacy of the No Child Left Behind Act (NCLB) in relation to quality schooling. The NCLB has its proponents and detractors. There are many who decry the emphasis on end-of-year testing; others praise the rating of schools by their Adequate Yearly Progress (AYP). Due to be re-authorized by Congress in 2007, the Center on Education Policy has been gathering information during the four years of the act. Jennings and Rentner (2006) summarize 10 observed effects:

1. State and district officials state that student achievement on state tests is rising. It is not clear, however, that students are really gaining as much as the rising percentages of proficient scores would suggest.

2. Schools are spending more time on reading and math, sometimes at the expense of subjects not tested.

3. Schools are paying much more attention to the alignment of curriculum and instruction and are analyzing test score data much more closely.

4. Low-performing schools are undergoing makeovers rather than more radical kinds of restructuring.

5. Schools and teachers have made considerable progress in demonstrating that teachers meet the law's academic qualifications, but many educators are skeptical about whether this will improve the quality of teaching.

6. Students are taking a lot more tests.

7. Schools are paying much more attention to achievement gaps and the learning needs of particular groups of students.

8. The number of schools on states' "needs improvement" lists has been steady but is not growing. Schools so designated are subject to NCLB sanctions, such as being required to offer students public school choices or tutoring services.

9. The federal government is playing a bigger role in education.

10. NCLB requirements have meant that state governments and school districts also have expanded roles in school operations, but often without adequate federal funds to carry out their duties.

NCLB clearly has impacted education in the United States. "There is more testing and more accountability. . . . Yet, some provisions of the act. . . are causing persistent problems," especially when it concerns testing students with special needs and those who are learning English. As Jennings and Rentner conclude, "The key question is whether the strengths of the legislation can be retained while its weaknesses are addressed."

Certainly the alignment of state standards to curriculum goals and assessment is one positive outcome of NCLB. But Kagan, Carroll, Comer, and Scott-Little (2006) decry the absence of alignment in the transition between preschools and K–12 education. They find that horizontal alignment to standards at the prekindergarten level can be seen as positive, in a variety of programs—public, private, or federally funded and regulated.

> All five domains of early learning and development (approaches to learning, cognition, language development, physical/motor, and socioemotional) show close alignment, from standards to curriculums to assessments. At the kindergarten level, however, there is a lack of horizontal alignment among standards, curriculums, and assessments. They conclude that "early learning standards, curriculums, and assessments [must be] age appropriate and that they [must] address all domains of development. . .[S]tandards, curriculums, and assessments must be aligned vertically as well as horizontally. . . .[And] alignment, as a key component of accountability, [can be] a safeguard that can improve the quality of services and outcomes for young children."

Quality in Family Child Care

A recent study by Doherty, Forer, Lero, Goelman, and LaGrange (2006), of 231 licensed family child care homes in Canada, explored the factors they hypothesized affected quality care: level of provider general education, intentionality (providers are looking for opportunities to learn about child development, for example), training and experience in child care, use of support services, and the work environment. Using the Family Day Care Rating Scale, they found that intentionality was predictive of higher quality, as was a college/university degree in early childhood or related discipline. The authors maintain that "quality child care is a skilled occupation requiring specific knowledge and skills." However, most family child care providers enter the profession without having any child care-related training. Training can be provided in a variety of ways including evening and Saturday offerings, distance learning, and via the Internet.

Another study by the Institute for Women's Policy Research (reported in *ExchangeEveryDay*, September 26, 2006) recommended, among other suggestions, the development of community mentoring programs, conducting needs assessments to determine gaps in service, the creation of a single entry point from which providers can access services and resources, and the development of high standards for licensure. (For more information, go to http://www.childcareexchange.com/ece_orgs/ex_partners.php#41.)

TYPES OF QUALITY PROGRAMS

It is important to recognize that there are many different types of early childhood programs (see Figure 11–8). There are child care centers, state-funded child care programs, Head Start and Montessori programs, **parent cooperatives**, and private, nonprofit, and profit-making preschools and primary schools. In each of these, a student teacher or family can find programs with varying amounts of quality, some good, some mediocre, and some even poor. "[T]here is no precise 'cookie-cutter' model, and parents should have a role in deciding what their child's early education program looks like" (U.S. Department of Education, 2005).

Preschool programs reflect the underlying philosophy of their director, head teacher, or proprietor. It takes time to interview and observe carefully to determine quality. One may discover, on close observation, that children have no freedom of choice as to what toys they will play with, that they are, instead, assigned toys. It is also easy to be deceived by a verbally persuasive director, head teacher, or proprietor. Smooth talk and right answers do not make a quality program. Look carefully when presented with a persuasive director. Is this person putting into action policies that are in the interest of the children?

In elementary schools, a building principal is one of the key factors in assuring a quality program. As Biddle and Saha (2006) indicate, school principals in both the United States and Canada value, know about, and use education research. They strive to keep themselves informed and work to improve their respective schools. Lipsitz and West (2006) looked at what makes a good school. Although they considered criteria for middle schools, the findings are appropriate for the primary grades as well. High-performing schools are academically excellent in that they challenge all of their students to do well; they are developmentally responsive in being sensitive to the developmental levels of their students; they respect student needs and

 parent cooperatives— programs staffed by one professional teacher and a rotating staff of parents.

● **Figure 11-8**
One usually cannot judge quality from a school's exterior.

interests; and they are "socially equitable, democratic, and fair—they provide every student with high-quality teachers, resources, learning opportunities, and support and make positive options available to all students."

WHO DECIDES THE QUALITY OF A PROGRAM?

As we suggested, the director has the responsibility for the quality of a preschool program. Indirectly, families also have a say in a program's quality. Obviously, there would be no program without client families. Thus, if a client buys an inferior service, in this case education, he has the choice to stop using it. The solution is, however, not always so simple. Families may not have many options in terms of an immediate neighborhood. This may be compounded by the family's lack of knowledge; they may judge a program by its external appearance, cleanliness, and their personal perceptions of the director's competence.

In a recent study of family satisfaction with the educational experience of their children, Fantuzzo, Perry, and Childs (2006) showed that families with children in Head Start or kindergarten were more satisfied than were families with children in child care or first grade. The writers believe that the study has "important implications for educational policy and practice. It substantiates that there are distinct dimensions of parent satisfaction" and they urge district administrators to "gather information about satisfaction levels. . .across grades." It would seem that families do recognize whether or not their children are enrolled in a satisfactory program.

Quality is also dependent on the type of program. For example, in a program sponsored by a public school district, quality is determined not only by the principal in whose school the program is located, but also by the local board of education and its policies, and ultimately by district, state, and federal government regulations. A public program must adhere to prescribed standards. However, in most public schools, ultimate quality depends on the individual teacher and the supervising principal.

In a private program, quality may depend on several people. In a proprietary preschool, quality is related to the personality and training of the proprietor. Is this person a loving, caring human being? Does this person have formal training in early childhood education? Does the proprietor hire people who are loving and caring, who have formal training? In any proprietary school, you will find the same range of quality as in a public program.

Who determines quality in a Montessori program, for example? Does the name promise that all its programs will have the same standards and quality? In the United States, there are *two* main approaches to Montessori education, both using the Montessori name. One branch includes schools under the sponsorship of the Associatione Montessori Internationale (AMI), with headquarters in Switzerland and headed by Maria Montessori's family. AMI schools adhere closely to Maria Montessori's original curriculum. Its teachers are trained in the philosophy and the **didactic** (teaching) materials designed by Dr. Montessori herself. In AMI schools, you will generally find the same **Montessori equipment** used, regardless of where the school is located. You will also find that the teachers have basically the same training in philosophy and methodology. Still, there will be differences in quality. Just as in the public schools or in the proprietary centers, quality will depend, to a large extent, on the teacher's personality. Does the teacher really *like* children? Does that person *CARE*? Are the children happy? Look carefully.

The other type of Montessori program is sponsored by the American Montessori Society (AMS), whose headquarters are in New York. AMS schools are less like the original Montessori schools in that, although they use the didactic materials developed by Dr. Montessori, they make use of modern trends toward a greater emphasis on gross motor and social development. AMS programs vary widely, so the personalities of the directors and teachers are the important factors.

Another determining factor for the quality of a program is who or what organization sponsors the school. Many churches sponsor schools and child care programs. In this case, quality depends not only on the personality of the director and teachers but also on the philosophy of the sponsoring church. Church-sponsored schools can also be excellent, mediocre, or poor. The teachers or child care workers always make the difference.

Studies of Quality

The *Cost, Quality and Child Outcomes in Child Care Centers Study* (National Center for the Early Childhood Work Force, 1995b) is described as a landmark study linking data on program costs and quality to child outcomes. Four hundred randomly selected centers in California, Colorado, Connecticut, and North Carolina were assessed. Half the centers were nonprofit and half were profit-making.

The following study conclusions were highlighted by researchers:

- Child care at most centers in the United States is poor to mediocre.
- Children's cognitive and social development are positively related to the quality of their child care experience, across all levels of maternal education, child gender, and ethnicity.

didactic—often applied to teaching materials, indicating a built-in intent to provide specific instruction.

Montessori equipment—early childhood learning materials derived from and part of the Montessori approach.

- Consistent with previous research, the quality of child care is related to specific variables:
  —staff-child ratios

  —staff education

  —administrators' prior experience

  —teacher wages

  —teacher education

  —specialized training
- States with more stringent licensing standards have fewer poor-quality centers. Centers that comply with additional standards beyond those required for licensing provide higher quality services.
- Centers provide higher than average, overall quality when they have access to extra resources that are used to improve quality.
- Center child care, even mediocre-quality care, is costly to provide.
- Good-quality services cost more than those of mediocre quality, but not a lot more.
- Center enrollment affects costs.

Bryant, Maxwell, and Burchinal (1999) stated findings from a study involving 508 children in North Carolina's *Smart Start*. "Overall, only 14 percent of the preschool classes in 1994 were providing good quality care. In 1996, 25 percent of the preschool classes were providing it."

Wiechel (2001) describes *Smart Start's* quality improvement efforts:

> North Carolina's *Smart Start* is a comprehensive public/private initiative to help children enter school healthy and ready to succeed. The North Carolina Partnership for Children provides state-level leadership for the initiative, sets statewide benchmarks for young children and families, and makes grants to county or multi-county collaboratives. These collaboratives assess community early childhood needs and design comprehensive plans to improve and integrate services.

Most professionals agree with NAEYC's National Institute for Early Childhood Professional Development, which holds that "the most important determinant of the quality of children's experiences is the adults who are responsible for children's care and education" (NAEYC, 1994). Freeman and Feeney (2006) note that while more and more early childhood educators are entering the field better prepared, there is great variability between one state and another regarding licensing criteria. Even with the emphasis on having better qualified teachers—that is, more holding bachelor's degrees—the Center for the Child Care Workforce in 2004 found that "salaries of many early childhood educators fell well below those earned by similarly qualified workers in other professions."

Working with experts, Kagan, Brandon, Ripple, Maher, and Joesch (2002) developed five guiding principles as the basis for implementing adequate compensation:

1. Early childhood teachers require training and professional competence.
2. Teachers with comparable qualifications and experience should receive the same salary and benefits, whether teaching in a public elementary school or in early childhood education.

3. Staff compensation should vary by qualifications and by degree of responsibility.

4. Staff should have a range of formal qualifications, with a portion of center teachers and family child care teachers holding bachelor's degrees and administrators holding advanced degrees.

5. Entry-level positions should be maintained so that pre-service qualifications do not become a barrier to individuals from low socioeconomic backgrounds or minority groups seeking to enter the field (Kagan, et al 2002).

Kagan and her colleagues also note that many of the experts they consulted in developing their recommended principles cited the same principles as those many early childhood professionals have advocated for decades: that early childhood staff should earn wages linked to those earned by public elementary school teachers, with salaries varying depending on the locale, experience, degrees held, levels of training, work responsibilities, and professional behavior and skill. Health, retirement, and vacation benefits should also be provided to all staff positions.

Vobejda (1997) believes concerned early childhood professionals feel that a crisis exists in hiring and retaining quality child care employees. With the draw of higher wages in other fields, an exodus of workers exists; consequently, the job applicant pool is often filled with people who lack qualifications and training, and who sometimes possess limited reading, writing, and verbal English fluency. Whitebook (1997) notes half of the country's three million child-care workers were likely to quit their jobs and head for higher pay during 1997. Little has changed since then.

Research has repeatedly confirmed that a key to quality and the prevention of harm in child care lies in the training and qualifications of the people who work with young children (Whitebook, Howes, & Phillips, 1989).

A study by the National Center for the Early Childhood Work Force (1995a), *Cost, Quality and Child Outcomes in Child Care Centers (CQ&O)*, reinforces what was found in the national child care study, in that overall quality of care in center-based child care programs is poor to mediocre (Whitebook, Phillips, & Howes, 1993).

Many factors contribute to poor quality including strong price competition in the marketplace, lack of consumer demand for quality, poor licensing standards, staff-child ratios, staff education, administrator experience, and center revenue and resources, to name but a few.

As mentioned, several of the programs reviewed in the CQ&O study proved to be only poor to mediocre. Those for infants and toddlers were poor enough to raise concern (Cryer & Phillipsen, 1997). But not all were negative, although the negatives were highlighted in the national media. One promising finding about the CQ&O study team programs was that those accredited by the NAEYC (25 of 390 preschools and 14 of 222 infant/toddler classrooms) consistently received higher scores on the Early Childhood Environment Rating Scale (ECERS) and the Infant/Toddler Environment Rating Scale (ITERS) (Cryer & Phillipsen, 1997). As accreditation has become more popular, we do find more quality programs.

The ECERS is a 37-item scale with seven categories: space and furnishings, personal care routines, language-reasoning, activities (fine motor, art, music/movement, blocks, and the like), interaction (supervision of gross motor activities, for example), program structure, and parents and staff. It currently has been revised and tested for reliability and validity (Clifford, 1998). The revised scale has 43 items; attention to cultural diversity and the inclusion of special needs children are now subsumed within the seven categories, rather than being considered separately, as before. The ITERS also has been revised. It includes 35 items, including adult personal area, meals/snacks, personal grooming, furnishings for relaxation, art, dramatic play, space to be alone, and others. As with the ECERS, attention to cultural diversity and inclusion of special needs infants and toddlers are subsumed under the other items.

Greenberg and Springen (2000) report that an ongoing study of early child care by the National Institute of Child Health and Human Development found that children in high-quality, center-based care outperformed children in other kinds of high-quality care (for example, family child care homes, relatives, and so on) in language development and cognitive skills like problem solving and reasoning. They also tended to have fewer behavioral problems.

Most experts and researchers believe high-quality programs have a recommended adult-child ratio, a relatively small group size, age-appropriate activities, a safe environment, and access to comprehensive services as needed, such as health and nutrition and parent involvement.

Head Start Family and Child Experiences Survey (FACES) is a longitudinal study of a nationally representative sample of Head Start programs. Its purpose is to examine the overall quality and outcomes of Head Start using specific program performance measures (see Figure 11–9) (Tarullo & Doan, 1999).

In 1997 and 1998, children and families in 40 national Head Start programs were observed and assessed by teachers and parents in the areas of emergent literacy, numeracy, general cognitive skills, gross and fine motor skills, social behavior and attitudes, positive learning attitudes, emotional well-being, and physical health. Classrooms were assessed on scheduling, the early learning environment, and teacher behavior. Tarullo and Doan (1999) have reviewed preliminary findings and report the following:

> Research has consistently linked aspects of classroom quality such as low child-adult ratio, small group size, responsiveness of teacher-child interaction, and richness of learning environments to better child outcomes. For the first time, using a national sample, FACES tests the same linkages in Head Start. Preliminary data show that the higher the quality of a Head Start classroom, the more likely that children will show higher levels of skills, and over time, display greater gains in developmental outcomes.

Additional study data is available at the Head Start Bureau Web page, at http://www.acf.dhhs.gov.

The Quality 2000 Initiative

The *Quality 2000: Advancing Early Care and Education Initiative* proposes that its "primary goal. . .is that by the year 2010, high-quality early care and education programs will be available and accessible to all children from birth to age five whose parents choose to enroll them" (Kagan & Neuman, 1997).

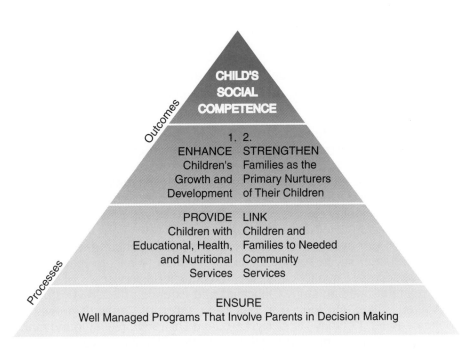

Figure 11-9

Quality ratings in preschool and infant classrooms. From Cost, quality, and child outcomes in child care centers. (1995, May). *Young Children, 50*(4). Reprinted with permission from the National Association for the Education of Young Children, NAEYC, © 1995.

The recommendations made by the people involved in writing the initiative are not simple: each is comprehensive and broad; each is a vision of what might be. Each includes several examples of strategies, which, if followed, are designed to achieve the goal of the recommendation.

The first recommendation concerns program quality:

Imagine a time when we expect and support quality in all family child care and center-based programs. . .allowing staff flexibility in using state-of-the-art strategies, technologies, and resources creatively and cost effectively.

Possible strategies are:

- Promote cultural sensitivity and cultural pluralism.
- Encourage pedagogical inventiveness in family child care and centers.
- Focus on improving the overall organizational climate.
- Increase the number of accredited programs.
- Link programs to networks, supportive services, or other community resources (Kagan & Neuman, 1997).

The second recommendation concerns children:

Imagine a time when clear results and expectations are specified and used to guide individual planning for all three- and four-year-old children, based on all domains of development (social/emotional, physical/motor, cognitive, language) and approaches to learning.

Some of its strategies are:

- Identify appropriate results.
- Develop appropriate strategies and instruments.
- Share results effectively, ensuring safeguards for children (Kagan & Neuman, 1997).

Recommendation three involves the parents and family; four, staff credentialing; five, staff training and preparation; six, program licensing; seven, funding and financing; and eight, governance structures. We will consider more details about staff credentialing, training and preparation in Chapter 12.

Financing, however, is worth a quick look here. Whitebook (1995a) writes, "Higher quality centers [in the CQ&O study] were also those whose teachers had completed more education. . .and were paid higher wages and had less turnover." Kagan and Neuman (1997) concur and state that recommendation seven supports this as essential to ensure that all children have access to quality early care and education services.

A related Canadian study replicated and extended the CQ&O study in the United States and looked at quality in seven of Canada's provinces. Goelman, Forer, Kershaw, Doherty, Lero, and LaGrange (2006) found many of the same phenomena as the U.S. study: staff education levels were significant predictors of child care center quality, as were adult to child ratios and staff wages. Goelman and his associates extended the study to include other variables and found that the number of staff or adults was a significant direct predictor of quality, just as the presence of a student teacher was a significant indirect predictor.

Legislative Efforts

Early childhood researchers know it is not enough to identify problems that contribute to lower-quality programs; we also must advocate realistic solutions that change national polices (Epstein, 1999). Groginsky, Robison, and Smith (1999) cite ways past and present day state legislators and policymakers have upgraded their programs:

> State legislators and other policymakers have addressed this poor to mediocre child care by focusing on improving child care quality in a variety of ways. A base measurement of quality levels is state regulation, which includes licensing standards for child-to-staff ratios, professional qualifications and physical space, among others. These standards represent a minimum level of health and safety for a child. In recent years, state decision makers have gone *beyond regulations* to make child care experiences better for young children.

> Four key ways that legislatures are moving in this direction include:

- ensuring an effective workforce through training, education and career development.
- establishing program quality standards.
- improving reimbursement policies to advance good quality and access.
- developing comprehensive services for young children.

How have states financed legislative and other state efforts to improve quality?

The National Institute for Early Education Research (2006, 2007) believes by thinking "outside the box":

- Arkansas enacted a new surcharge on beer to be earmarked for child care.

- Maine, Kansas, and Kentucky have earmarked tobacco settlement funds.

- Georgia created a lottery and set aside a portion of the proceeds for prekindergarten.

- Missouri earmarked a portion of the Gaming Commission Fund.

- Colorado has an innovative child care contributions tax credit, as well as a voluntary income tax check-off to raise money for quality child care.

- Oregon offers a tax-credit to spur business investment in child care.

- Rhode Island taps into health care funds to help pay the cost of health insurance for child care providers.

- Connecticut makes tax-exempt bonds available to help finance facilities, then uses funds from the Temporary Assistance for Needy Families (TANF) program to underwrite a portion of the debt.

- New York, Washington, Boston, and other local governments have used criminal justice funds to help create child care centers in court buildings.

- Local 1199, the National Health and Human Services Employees Union, raises nearly $9 million each year for child care subsidies through collective bargaining agreements with employers in New York.

- Indiana's Dekko Foundation is building child care endowment funds in six counties.

- Minnesota Governor Tim Pawlenty has proposed an early childhood scholarship program to provide up to $4000 per child for at-risk children to attend certified kindergarten readiness programs.

- New Mexico Governor Bill Richardson has proposed doubling the number of 4-year-olds attending the state pre-K program from 2,200 to 5,000.

- Kansas Governor Kathleen Sibelius has proposed $6.6 million in new funds for Early Head Start and state pre-K.

- Mississippi Governor Haley Barbour has proposed $5 million to fund a new state-preschool program.

Many studies have associated quality child care with positive outcomes for children, including better language, cognitive, and social skills, fewer behavioral problems, and stronger mother-child relationships (Groginsky, Robison, & Smith, 1999). The High/Scope Perry Preschool project found low-income children's attendance in a quality early education program led to children's greater academic success, better adult job achievement, and half as many arrests in later life (Schweinhart, Barnes, & Weikart, 1993; Schweinhart & Weikart, 1997).

The True Cost of Quality Child Care

Family budgets are strained in many households because of child care costs. If child care fees were increased and parents assumed the true costs for quality care, experts estimate the cost for parents would be as much as $8,500 per year (Vobejda, 1997), leaving little left for other family living expenses. Political platforms often include promises to enhance child care quality and access, but child care advocates do not expect an infusion of federal, state, or private monies in amounts necessary to alleviate the present situation in the United States.

Research has just begun to undercover the true costs of operating a quality early childhood program. Hidden costs have been borne by early childhood workers through foregone wages and benefits. The CQ&O study team (Helburn, 1995), after studying 401 child care centers, estimates that 25 percent of the full cost of care and education of enrolled children was covered by some form of subsidy, primarily through low staff wages, but also building, rent, or occupancy aid, volunteers, donated goods, and in-kind contributions.

Conclusions cited in the *Cost, Quality and Child Outcomes in Child Care Centers* public report (Helburn 1995) estimated as much as 19 percent of the center's full costs were borne by workers, who earned less than workers in other fields with similar educational backgrounds and comparable skills.

ACCREDITATION AND ITS RELATIONSHIP TO QUALITY

Accreditation in Elementary School Programs

For many years, schools, colleges, and universities have undergone periodic accreditation by the Accrediting Commission for Schools (2000). The commission divides the United States into several regions that have separate commissioners, who use the same criteria to evaluate programs.

Over the past five years, the commission has worked intensively with an advisory group, composed of representatives from the Western Association, to revise the accreditation process for the region. Input was solicited from schools, colleges and universities, and took into account current thinking and research about teaching and learning. The result has been to shift the focus of **accreditation** from the previously used list of factors to a focus on student outcomes. The Accrediting Commission for Schools' (2000) *Focus on Learning program* specifies four categories of criteria by which schools will be assessed. These are:

1. Organization for student learning
2. Curriculum and instruction
3. Support for student personal and academic growth
4. Resource management and development

The new focus was developed to ensure that the "critical elements of school change were integral to the *Focus on Learning* design" and include the following specific features:

- clarification of the school's purpose and expected school-wide learning results for all students
- the involvement of the school community in self-directed problem solving

accreditation—an official form of approval that a learning institution receives from a recognized review board, usually a state oversight or licensing authority.

- the opportunity for meaningful dialogue, collaboration, and shared decision making
- the use of high-quality criteria to analyze the program for students
- the development of a school-wide action plan to support desired learning results
- the opportunity for an outside perspective regarding proposed changes, through the Visiting Committee's dialogue and findings
- the monitoring of progress in meeting or redefining goals and actions, through accreditation reviews and reports

It is obvious that the new criteria place an emphasis on change, so a school can better serve its students, parents, and community.

Visiting Committee members undergo training each year to ensure that they are up-to-date on any changes involved in the accreditation process, and to provide members with additional practice regarding the application of the criteria prior to the visit. Committee members include teachers, administrators, college and university faculty, students, and community representatives such as school board members and representatives of business and industry. There are generally five or six members on any one committee. After the visit, a written report is forwarded to the commission with the accreditation recommendation. The commissioners meet, usually in the late spring, read all of the Committee reports, and vote either to approve, deny, or amend their recommendations. Accreditation terms are generally for one to six years.

Because many elementary and middle schools do not go through regional accreditation by the commission, several states have instituted their own version of accreditation, commonly referred to as a *coordinated compliance review* (CCR) or a *contract monitoring review* (CMR). In California and some other states, the state board of education requires that all schools in the state undergo periodic CCRs. These involve a self-study—as does accreditation by the commission—and review by a team of evaluators, who look to see how closely the school meets standards set in the Desired Results Developmental Profile for each student. "In this way, California's standards must come alive in its early childhood programs" (Grondlund, 2006). Included on the review team are teachers, administrators, and state board of education representatives who have all received training in how to conduct a CCR. The reviewers prepare a report for the state superintendent of instruction, and the state board of education members, who have the final authority to accept the report, ask that the school undergo further review or reject the report. Reviews are conducted every three years, so it is a continuing process.

Nationwide, both the Catholic Education Association and the Lutheran Schools Accreditation work with the Accrediting Commission for Schools to accredit their respective parochial schools. Christian and private schools may also be accredited by their sponsoring association. Families interested in placing their children in these schools should ask whether the school is accredited. It does not automatically verify quality but it does suggest that certain standards are maintained. Families might be wise to ask for a copy of the last accreditation report to review.

Strader (2006) states that many states have explored ways to look at the issue of quality. Among these are Pennsylvania, Vermont, North Carolina, Montana, Maryland, Colorado, Tennessee, and the District of Columbia. These states have developed a *quality rating system* (QRS) to support their early care and education communities in assessing, improving, and communicating the quality of their programs. Rhode Island is completing two years' work in developing their QRS and will begin implementing it in 2007. In all of the states, staff qualifications was one of the criteria. To check on QRS in your state, go to the National Child Care Information Center Web site at http://www.nccic.org and click on *Popular Topics* then *Quality Rating Systems.*

NAEYC Accreditation

In 1985 the NAEYC, concerned with how to ensure quality programs for young children, especially as they relate to developmentally appropriate practices, established the National Academy of Early Childhood Programs to administer accreditation procedures. These involved some of the same steps used by the Accrediting Commission for Schools. Any program wishing to be accredited must write the NAEYC and request that it be placed on the calendar for an accreditation visit.

Once the date of the visit is confirmed, the program conducts a self-study, involving formal reports by the administrator, staff, and families. The result is a program description that includes a center or school profile, the results of classroom observations (completed by both the teacher and the director), and the results of the administrator report that ties together the results of the ratings of the program by staff and parents.

After completion of the self-study, and its subsequent reception at NAEYC, a trained validator visits the center or school to verify the self-study much in the same manner as the Visiting Committee or the CCR reviewers. The validator's report is then read by at least three commissioners who make the final accreditation decision.

NAEYC's revised Early Childhood Program Standards and Accreditation Performance Criteria (2005) were approved by its governing board in April of 2005. The criteria are believed to be a major step forward and include the following focus areas:

1. Children
2. Teaching Staff
3. Family and Community Partnerships
4. Leadership and Administration

In each of the areas, program standards are listed, together with their rationales and an example of each criterion. There are five criteria in the focus area for children: relationships, curriculum, teaching, assessment of child progress, and health. Under focus area two, Teaching Staff, there is only one criterion, and two criteria each are in the Family and Community Partnerships and Leadership and Administration focus areas. (These are available on-line at http://www.naeyc.org/accreditation/next_era.asp.

It is believed that with implementation of the new criteria in September 2006, "NAEYC-accredited programs will help families, educators, and many others in our communities recognize the value of setting high standards for all programs for young children" (NAEYC, 2005).

As more and more programs implement developmentally appropriate practices, and especially as families begin to demand accredited programs for their children, the number of approved programs has risen. In 2002, there were 8,192 NAEYC-accredited early childhood programs, serving more than 720,000 young children (NAEYC, 2002).

Does accreditation assure quality? In many ways, yes. The self-study alerts teachers, directors, principals, and others involved in the process to any areas of needed improvement, especially those impinging directly on standards required for accreditation. Often, then, when visiting committees, reviewers, or validators arrive, changes have already been instituted to improve an area likely to cause concern. One principal difference, though, between accreditation by the Accrediting Commission for Schools and that of the National Academy, or by coordinated compliance reviews, is the point on philosophy. Where the Commission accredits on how closely the curriculum goals match school philosophy, coordinated compliance reviewers are interested in two things: how closely elementary school curriculum goals and objectives match those set forth in state program standards, and test results obtained on the No Child Left Behind testing program mandated by states and the Federal government. National Academy validators observe to see how closely school goals and objectives match the program standards of the National Academy. Thus, emphasis shifts from school to state to national standards.

In an attempt to understand why quality remains low, with soaring investment in early care and education, and with so many accredited centers, Kagan et al (2002) suggests

> The answer is twofold. Most important, the resources to do the job are simply inadequate. . . .While inadequate resources are absolutely the first and major problem, they are not the only issue. *How resources are spent* is also important.

State lawmakers have turned their attention toward accreditation by promoting voluntary accreditation. The National Conference of State Legislatures publication, *Making Child Care Better: State Initiatives*, notes accreditation legislation in some states often includes language that is broad enough for programs to acquire accreditation by a range of organizations, but other states specify NAEYC accreditation (Groginsky, Robison, & Smith, 1999).

A number of states have chosen to develop differential subsidy rates, to more closely match the cost of providing accredited care, improve quality, and to increase family availability to accredited programs (Warman, 1998). Warman has identified 10 states (Florida, Minnesota, New Mexico, South Carolina, Vermont, Wisconsin, New Jersey, Kentucky, Mississippi, and Connecticut) with higher subsidy rates for accredited care, and two other states (Arizona and Oklahoma) with unfunded systems to pay accredited programs' higher rates. Some states (Arizona, Connecticut, Texas, Wisconsin, and the District of Columbia) provide mini-grants, training, technical assistance, and bonuses to help individual programs achieve accreditation (Warman, 1998). In northern California, funds from Contra Costa County's *First Five* and Alameda County's *Every Child Counts* programs provides, among other things, subsidies for preschool teachers to further their education, and currently are funding articulation programs between two- and four-year institutions (Thompson, 2006).

Also in California, the California Association for the Education of Young Children (CAEYC) established a program in 2004, the Professional

Development Academy, to support the training of early childhood education professionals, caregivers, and parents. The Academy has three major focus areas:

- Professional Staff Development
- Leadership Training
- On-Site Consultation

A variety of delivery options are used, such as a series of one-day seminars, offered at different locations throughout the state, and on-site training for centers and homes that choose to subscribe to the service. Currently, some of the training modules are available though the Internet with follow-up contact by e-mail and telephone (Phipps, 2004).

Believing that quality education begins with preparing quality faculty, the Frank Porter Graham Child Development Institute of the University of North Carolina-Chapel Hill (FPG) has established relationships with several colleges and states, to promote the development and well-being of young children and families. "The institute regularly hosts special conferences and training events that further the knowledge and skills of faculty and in institutions across the state and nation" (FPG, 2003). One model developed by FPG, *Walking the Walk*, seeks to address the nationwide shortage of a culturally and linguistically diverse pool of early childhood teachers. For more information visit the project Web site. A downloadable diversity guide is available at http://www.fpg.unc.edu/walkingthewalk/pdfs/RG10-DWTW.pdf.

In an earlier report on quality (Report on Preschool Programs, 1998) 16 states were promoting child care quality by setting reimbursement rates that reward caregivers for higher quality. To receive the highest rates, centers must have been accredited by the NAEYC or another recognized entity.

A highly trained teaching staff is the strongest predictor of program quality, along with the levels of staff compensation. Teacher and administrator turnover is a problem, and a staffing crisis exists in most areas of the country. *La Ristra*, New Mexico's publication, concludes that ignoring factors that contribute to lack of quality is a poor course of action:

> An acute problem left unattended eventually becomes status quo, yet is no less in need of urgent action. So it is with the child care staffing crisis. For three decades advocates and researchers have sounded warnings that without massive sustained effort to improve child care employment, turnover will continue unabated and children, families, and caregivers will suffer the consequences. . . . At the heart of the crisis lie the insufficient resources to attract and retain a workforce able to sustain developmentally appropriate environments for children (Turner, 2002b).

Whitebook and Sakai (2002) point out centers receiving intensive support—like on-site technical assistance from an early childhood professional, custom-designed training for staff and directors, funds to cover release time for staff participating in training, and an ongoing, facilitated support group for directors—achieved accreditation at more than twice the rate of centers receiving moderate support, or seeking accreditation independently, and at nearly 10 times the rate of centers with only limited support.

THE COMER PROJECT FOR CHANGE IN EDUCATION

Dr. James P. Comer's work in the public schools of New Haven, Connecticut, shows us that change can take years (Goldberg, 1997). The original School Development Project started in the 1968–1969 school year, with two elementary schools in low-income, predominantly African American areas. Test scores were 19 months below grade level and did not reach grade level until 1979—ten years later. By 1984, scores were 12 months *above* grade level. What had happened?

Learning obstacles were identified and remedied. The project focused on what might be called *the ecology of the total school*: children, parents, administrators, custodial staff, and the community in which the school was located. Changes were made: schools were painted and cleaned; staff became a part of the decision-making process; teachers and administrators were retrained or transferred.

Today, the *Comer Project for Change in Education* is now operating in more than 600 schools, in 82 school districts, in 26 states. The results continue to be good, but experience has taught those involved that change, although slow, "can yield to good will and hard work" (Goldberg, 1997). Comer, Ben-Avie, Haynes, and Joyner (1999) state that there are six points that need to be considered if change is to occur:

1. To reform schools we must understand the complex dynamics that affect them.
2. To reform schools we must start where the children are.
3. To reform schools we must keep pace with our changing society.
4. To reform schools we must focus on relationships and child development.
5. To reform schools we must develop group goals, trust, and accountability to standards.
6. To reform schools we must make financial commitments and policy changes.

Comer concludes with the following plea:

> The Agricultural Extension Service helped make America the breadbasket of the world. Today's economy needs to have educated workers, but our schools can't change even when they want to. Rather than turning to radical and unproven formats of schooling, we should create an Education Extension Service that helps all involved in the education enterprise to put child development front and center, and move toward a system of education that will keep the nation in the economic and democratic forefront in the twenty-first century (Comer, et al.,1999).

How well Dr. Comer's vision for schools in the United States might flower, we can only trust that educators, the public, you, and especially the federal government take heed. If it took 10 years to accomplish a turnaround in the two public schools in New Haven, where the Comer project started, it might be wise not to expect immediate changes under the No Child Left Behind Act.

Figure 11-10
A new teacher confers with her mentor.

mentoring—guidance by an experienced and trusted teacher, who is frequently paired with a new, inexperienced teacher or aide, and who assists the new teacher with ideas and advice.

MENTORING PROGRAMS

The more experienced worker, tutoring and serving as an example to the new worker, has always been a way of training (see Figure 11–10). Mentoring programs have emerged as one of the most promising ways to stabilize and support the child care workforce to guarantee more reliable and high-quality care for young children (National Center for the Early Childhood Work Force, 1995a). Some states—including Arkansas, California, Florida, Maine, Maryland, Minnesota, Montana, Ohio, Rhode Island, South Dakota, Utah, West Virginia, and Wisconsin—operate mentoring and apprenticeship programs for early childhood teachers (Groginsky, Robison, & Smith, 1999).

The National Center for the Early Childhood Work Force (1995a) describes the **mentoring** effort:

> Throughout the country, mentoring programs have emerged as one of the most promising strategies to retain experienced teachers and providers and thereby guarantee more reliable, high quality care for young children. Experienced teachers and providers participate in programs designed to give them the skills necessary to teach other adults how to care for and educate infants and young children. Upon taking on the role of mentor teacher, most teachers and providers receive additional compensation for training protégés; gain new respect from their co-workers and parents, and renew their own commitment to working with children in the classroom or home. As dozens of programs develop, the need to share information grows.

The Early Childhood Mentoring Alliance, a newly emerging group, intends to provide a forum for sharing information and providing technical assistance. The alliance is supported by a consortium of foundations.

Teacher-Support Programs for Public School Teachers

Beginning and newly credentialed elementary school teachers are finding that many public school districts are not letting them "sink or swim" in their first teaching year. Many districts realize teacher quality is the single most important factor in improving student achievement (Haycock, 1998). These districts are investing in and designing teacher-induction programs that focus on supportive assistance (see Figure 11–11). American schools expect to hire more than two million teachers in the next decade (Moir, Gless, & Baron, 1999).

California's *Beginning Teacher Support and Assessment* (BTSA) program is a statewide initiative, jointly administered by the California Department of Education and the California Commission on Teacher Credentialing. This program allots $3,000 for each beginning teacher, and some local districts augment that with additional funding. Funds are being used a number of ways, including onsite collaboration, classroom supplies, aids, technical assistance, and so on. Beginning teachers are assigned a mentor teacher, who consults with them on a regular basis, and are given released time to visit their mentor's or other classrooms.

Figure 11-11
These experienced teachers are collaborating with a new teacher at their school.

Most new teachers see themselves as agents of change, and are inspired and committed to the idea that they will make a difference in children's educational lives. Teacher-induction programs hope to sustain and nurture that idealism.

◉ SUMMARY

In this chapter, we attempted to provide guidelines by which you can evaluate the quality of an early childhood education program. We have suggested that a quality program is one that takes into consideration the developmental needs of the children and that exceeds, rather than meets, minimum standards for state licensing. We have also suggested that quality programs may be found in many different settings, ranging from federally-funded programs to parent cooperatives to proprietary, profit-making centers.

We also presented a review of the accreditation processes sponsored by the Accrediting Commission for Schools and by states' boards of education coordinated compliance reviews, as these apply to the provision of quality elementary school programs. NAEYC's National Academy of Early Childhood Programs and its accreditation process were briefly explained, as was the impact on quality programs for children from birth through age eight. (Most accredited programs are for children from birth through age five, with public schools not applying for accreditation through NAEYC but, instead, undergoing coordinated compliance or other quality reviews, such as CMR.)

Quality programs depend on you as student teachers. You need to strive to preserve and improve programs when you enter the field. Quality programs can exist only if quality people fight for them.

◉ HELPFUL WEB SITES

http://www.naeyc.org
National Association for the Education of Young Children. Proceed to *Academy* for NAEYC accreditation information.

http://www.ecs.org
Education Commission of the States. Readings on state funding, teacher qualifications, program standards, legislation, and other early childhood issues may be found here.

http://www.fpg.unc.edu
Frank Porter Graham Child Development Institute, University of North Carolina-Chapel Hill. This site offers readings on quality care. The institute is involved in many different projects such as Walking the Walk and studies of program quality.

http://www.ed.gov
National Institute on Early Childhood Development. Search *research* and *child care* categories.

http://www.edpubs.org
Publications of the U.S. Department of Education, Office of Elementary and Secondary Education. This is a helpful resource, containing much valuable information.

http://www.headstartinfo.org
Head Start. This site provides general information and publications.

http://www.ericeece.org
ERIC database. Search text of *Five Perspectives on Quality in Early Childhood Programs*.

http://nieer.org
National Institute for Early Education Research, a unit of Rutgers University. Publishes newsletter *Preschool Matters*; NIEER supports early education initiatives by providing objective, nonpartisan information based on research. Check for information on quality rating systems (QRS).

http://www.cde.ca.gov/sp/ed/ci/ drdppinstructions.asp
State of California, Child Development Education. See instructions for Desired Results Developmental Profiles.

...esearch for Education and ...L). The mission of this ... a difference in the quality

http://www..._...l/eed

Child Care Information Exchange. If you want to receive the daily newsletter, *Exchange Every*

Day, it is free. Readings are short and helpful Web sites are frequently listed, especially when a synopsis of a longer article is given.

 Additional resources for this chapter can be found by visiting the Online Companion at www.earlychilded.delmar.com.

◯ SUGGESTED ACTIVITIES

A. Visit at least three of these different types of early childhood programs: a Montessori school, a Head Start program, an NAEYC accredited program, a proprietary child care center, or a public school kindergarten, first, second, or third grade classroom. Evaluate them on the standards of a good program from NAEYC, or look at the Accrediting Commission for Schools criteria. Interview the teachers and/or the principal of the school you visit and ask them about their self-study. Are the programs of equally good quality? Why or why not?

B. Summarize your evaluations of the programs you choose to observe. Discuss your ideas with your peers and supervisor.

C. Discuss the following quote in a small group. Report your group's reactions.

The growth in child care and preschool education, along with the need for families to be more informed about quality has spurred the adoption in several states of systems for rating program quality through the assignment of stars or other quality indicators consumers are used to seeing for other services like hotels and restaurants. . . .Thirteen states are now using some sort of quality rating system (QRS) and 30 others are considering them. With numbers like that, it's safe to say the move to QRS is a trend (NIEER, 2007).

◯ REVIEW

A. List five features of a quality early childhood program, according to the Federal government, and six of the program standards listed in the NAEYC accreditation procedures.

B. Read each of the following descriptions of different early childhood programs. Decide whether each paragraph is describing a quality program, a mediocre program, or a poor program. Indicate if you do not have sufficient data to make a decision. Discuss your answers and opinions with peers and your college supervisor.

1. This private preschool/child care center is located in a former public school. Each morning, the director greets every child as they enter. Each child has a wide choice of activities. Clay containers are placed on one table; crayon boxes and paper

on another; scissors, old magazines, and scraps of construction paper are on a third, with sheets of blank paper and glue sticks. Some children prefer to go to the block area, the book corner, or dramatic-play corner. The outside play area beckons those who wish to climb, ride, swing, or play at the water table or in the sandbox.

The director has a degree in early childhood education, as does the only paid aide. Parents are seen often; both fathers and mothers stay with their children for a few minutes. The director speaks to each parent and sends home a monthly newsletter to inform parents of special activities and to solicit help for special projects (both the indoor and outdoor climbing structures were built by parents).

The director carefully interviews every prospective family who wishes to place their children in the center. The director insists on at least one visit by both parents and the child before final acceptance. Prospective parents receive a written statement of philosophy and curriculum. During these meetings, the director has been known to state, "I expect parents to interview me as carefully as I interview them."

2. This after-school program is sponsored by a franchised nonprofit organization. The director of the program has an AA degree in early childhood education. Certified teachers, with the state-required 24 units of early childhood or holding a Child Development Associate certificate, work with the children (ages five to nine). In addition, there are many volunteers, recruited from the local community college and high school. The program is located in unused classrooms in four elementary schools, and in the nonprofit organization's main facility.

Because the main facility does not meet state standards, children are asked to join the organization. As a result, the organization is exempt from having to meet standards. For example, although there is ample outside play area at the school sites, there is little other than a paved basketball court at the main facility site. This after-school program has a written statement of purpose and goals, a conceptual outline covering such items as safety, self-image, adult role models, a stimulating environment, and so on; a parent advisory group; and a daily schedule listing curriculum factors. The child-to-adult ratio is listed as 15:1 but has been known to exceed 25:1 when volunteers have been absent.

The program schedules free time for the first 30 minutes so that the children can unwind from their school day. This is followed by snack time, activity time (arts and crafts, gymnastics, swimming in the facility's pool, field trips), cleanup time, and free time during which quiet activities such as games, reading, homework, and drawing can be done.

3. This first-grade program is located in a large, public elementary school of approximately 900 students, from kindergarten through fifth grade. Having been opened only four years ago, the school is almost new. The primary wing contains 12 classrooms. Each room is carpeted and has regular and clerestory windows that allow for a maximum of natural light to be suffused throughout the room. Each room also has a side area, with linoleum flooring, a sink, water fountain, storage closets, a small refrigerator, and a round table suitable for six to eight students and an aide or parent volunteer. This area also contains a two-sided easel. Children sit at individual desks in small groups of two to four.

The first grade teacher has a guinea pig in a cage on a shelf labeled "Discovery Center." Located on the shelf are books containing pictures of guinea pigs, some requiring little or no reading, others requiring more. A chart depicting the amount of food and water used each day by the guinea pig, Rafael (the name voted on by the class), is maintained by the children assigned, on a rotating basis, to his care. A bulletin board by the entry door has a graph, completed by the children, of drawings of their favorite foods. Another graph posted on the wall contains pictures drawn by the children, illustrating the different ways they come to school.

On your visit, some children are busy writing stories, assisted by a parent volunteer. Two other children are taking care of Rafael. A student teacher has grouped six more children in a small circle at the back of the room, near the teacher's desk, and is doing some one-to-one correspondence exercises with them. The cooperating teacher has assigned different groups math exercises, using the Math Their Way manipulatives, and is circulating around the room responding to questions and posing her own questions, to check on student understanding.

C. Discuss mentoring as it relates to a program's possible quality.

D. How would you describe the quality of our nation's child care? Cite sources.

CASE SCENARIO

Setting: Mrs. Kumar, director of Little Pals Preschool, is interviewing Ms. Perez, mother of four-year-old Andrea. The mother is assessing the school for the possible enrollment of her daughter.

"Here's our brochure, Ms. Perez. We have an excellent program. You are quite lucky because we actually will have one opening next week. Please follow me; I'm sure you would like to see our classrooms."

As they approach a classroom door, Ms. Perez notices that the school's interior is freshly painted and spotlessly clean. As they enter the classroom for four-year-old children, Ms. Perez notes the room is quiet and tidy. All the children are seated, working on what looks to be photocopied paper. Mrs. Kumar whispers that the children all know their ABCs and can count to 50. Mrs. Kumar approaches the teacher, who is applying smiley face stickers on some of the children's papers, and introduces her. Many elaborate pieces of child art decorate the walls, along with alphabet letters, numerals, word charts, and crayoned pages of coloring books. A world globe and a collection of library books are available. A computer and televison set sit along one wall. The center of the room features a large, colorful round rug that Mrs. Kumar says is used for group instruction.

Mrs. Kumar enthusiastically describes extra lessons in dance that take place one day a week. These lessons are available if parents so choose. Mrs. Kumar shows Ms. Perez the play yard. It is full of expensive, commercially designed, large climbing structures, swinging bridges, and slides. It looks like an elaborate, well-tended city park.

Before Ms. Perez leaves, Mrs. Kumar asks if she has any questions. She says, "No," and leaves after thanking Mrs. Kumar for the tour and her time.

Questions for Discussion:

1. Pretend you are Andrea. What questions would you have liked your mother to ask?

2. Would this type of school impress a parent favorably? Why?

3. What reservations might you have concerning the quality of Little Pals Preschool?

○REFERENCES

Accrediting Commission for Schools, Western Association for Schools and Colleges (WASC). (2000). *Focus on Learning.* Burlingame, CA: Author.

Biddle, B. J., & Saha, L. J. (2006, March). How principals use research. *Educational Leadership, 63*(6), 72–77.

Bryant, D. M., Maxwell, K. L., & Burchinal, M. (1999). Effects of a community initiative on the quality of child care. *Early Childhood Research Quarterly, 14,* 449–464.

Cartwright, S. (1999, November). What makes good early childhood teachers? *Young Children, 54*(6), 4–7.

Clifford, R. M. (1998, November 20). *Measuring quality in preschool settings: The development of the revised early childhood environment rating scale.* Paper presented at the National Association for the Education of Young Children Conference, Toronto, Canada.

Comer, J. P., Ben-Avie, M., Haynes, N. M., & Joyner, E. T. (1999). *Child by child: the Comer process for change in education.* New York: Teachers College Press.

Cryer, D., & Phillipsen, L. (1997, July). A close-up look at child care program strengths and weaknesses. *Young Children, 52*(5).

Doherty, G., Forer, B., Lero, D. S., Goelman, H., & LaGrange, A. (2006). Predictors of quality in family child care. *Early Childhood Research Quarterly, 21*(3), 296–312.

Early, D. M., Bryant, D. M., Pianta R. C., Clifford, R. M., Burchinal, M. R., Ritchie, S., Howes, C., & Barbarin, O. (2006). Are teachers' education, majors, and credentials related to classroom quality and children's academic gains in prekindergarten? *Early Childhood Research Quarterly, 21*(2), 174–195.

Epstein, A. S. (1999). Pathways to quality in Head Start, public school, and private nonprofit early childhood programs. *Journal of Research in Childhood Education, 13*(2), 101–119.

FPG Child Development Institute, University of North Carolina at Chapel Hill. (2003, Spring). Elevating the educators: the quest for quality begins with effective faculty. *Early Developments, 7*(1), 14–15.

Fantuzzo, J., Perry, M. A., & Childs, S. (2006). Parent satisfaction with educational experiences scale: A multivariate examination of parent satisfaction with early childhood education programs. *Early Childhood Research Quarterly, 21*(2), 142–152.

Feeney, S., Christensen, D., & Moravcik, E. (2006). *Who am I in the lives of children?* (7th ed.). Upper Saddle River, NJ: Pearson/Merrill/Prentice Hall.

Freeman, N. K. & Feeney, S. (2006, September). The new face of early care and education: Who are we? Where are we going? *Young Children, 61*(5), 10–16.

Goelman, H., Forer, B., Kershaw, P., Doherty, G., Lero, D., LaGrange, A. (2006). Towards a predictive model of quality in Canadian child care centers. *Early Childhood Research Quarterly, 21*(3), 280–295.

Goldberg, M. F. (1997, March). Maintaining a focus on child development: An interview with Dr. James P. Comer. *Phi Delta Kappan, 78*(7).

Greenberg, S. H., & Springen, K. (2000, October 16). Back to day care. *Newsweek,* 61–62.

Groginsky, S., Robison, S., & Smith, S. (1999). *Making child care better: State initiatives.* Washington, DC: National Conference of State Legislatures.

Grondlund, G. (2006). *Make early learning standards come alive: connecting your practice and curriculum to state guidelines.* St. Paul, MN: Redleaf Press; Washington, DC: National Association for the Education of Young Children.

Haycock, K. (1998, Summer). Good teaching matters: How well-qualified teachers can close the gap. *Thinking K–16, 3*(2), 1–2.

Helburn, S. (Ed.). (1995). *Cost, quality and child outcomes in child care.* Center for Research in Economics and Social Policy, Department of Economics, University of Colorado.

Institute for Women's Policy Research, quoted in *ExchangeEveryDay* newsletter, http://www.childcareexchange.com/ece/ex_partners.php#41.

Jennings, J. & Rentner, D. S. (2006, October). Ten big effects of the No Child Left Behind Act on public schools. *Phi Delta Kappan, 88*(2), 110–113.

Kagan, S. L., Brandon, R. N., Ripple, C. H., Maher, E. J., & Joesch, J. M. (2002, May). Supporting quality early childhood care and education. *Young Children, 57*(3), 58–65.

Kagan, S. L., Carroll, J., Comer, J. P., & Scott-Little, C. (2006, September). Alignment: A missing link in early childhood transitions? *Young Children, 61*(5), 26–32.

Kagan, S. L., & Neuman, M. J. (1997, September). Highlights of the *Quality 2000 Initiative*: Not by chance. *Young Children, 52*(6).

Kennedy, M. M. (2006, March). From teacher quality to quality teaching. *Educational Leadership, 63*(6), 14–19.

Lipsitz, J., & West, T. (2006, September). What makes a good school? Identifying excellent middle schools. *Phi Delta Kappan, 88*(1), 57–66.

Moir, E., Gless, J., & Baron, W. (1999). A support program with heart: The Santa Cruz project. In M. Scherer (Ed.). *A better beginning: Supporting and mentoring new teachers* (pp. 106–113). Alexandria, VA: Association for Supervision and Curriculum Development.

National Association for the Education of Young Children. (2005a, July). NAEYC accreditation: governing board approves new NAEYC early childhood program standards and accreditation performance criteria. *Young Children, 60*(4), 50–54.

National Association for the Education of Young Children. (2005b, September). NAEYC accreditation: facts about the new NAEYC accreditation system. *Young Children, 60*(5), 74–75.

National Association for the Education of Young Children (NAEYC). (2002). Our mission. *Young Children, 57*(6), 98–99.

National Association for the Education of Young Children. (1994, March). Professional development. *Young Children, 49*(3).

National Center for the Early Childhood Work Force. (1995a, January). Mentoring programs: An emerging child care career path. *Compensation Initiatives Bulletin, 1*(3).

National Center for the Early Childhood Work Force. (1995b). *Cost, quality, and child outcomes in child care centers.* Washington, DC: Author.

National Institute for Early Childhood Education Research (2006, December 15; 2007, January 26). Online News, Hot Topics, 5 (21) & 6 (2). http://www.info@nieer.org.

National Institute for Early Education Research. (December/January 2007). It's in the stars: More states are using quality rating systems for Pre-K, *Preschool Matters, 5* (1) 4, 11. New Brunswick, NJ.

No author. (1998, August 19). Sixteen states use tiered rates to promote child care quality. *Report on Preschool Programs, 30*(17).

Phipps, P. (2004, Winter). CAEYC launches new professional development academy. *Connections, 32*(2), 17.

Pianta, R. C., Howes, C., Burchinal, M. R., Bryant, D. M., Clifford, R. M., Early, D. M., & Barbarin, O. (2005). Features of pre-kindergarten programs, classrooms, and teachers: predictions of observed classroom quality and teacher-child interactions. *Applied Developmental Science, 9*(3), 144–159.

Schweinhart, L. J., Barnes, H. V., & Weikart, D. P. (1993). *Significant benefits: The High/Scope Perry preschool study through age 27.* Ypsilanti, MI: High/Scope Press.

Schweinhart, L. J., & Weikart, D. P. (1997). Evidence that good early childhood programs work. *Phi Delta Kappan, 66*, 545–551.

Strader, W. H. (retrieved September 29, 2006). *ExchangeEveryDay,* http://www.ccie.com/eed.

Tarullo, L. B., & Doan, H. M. (1999, March). Linking Head Start quality to child outcomes: The *FACES* study. *Head Start Bulletin, 65*, 18–19.

Thompson, S. (2006). Revised Mission Statement and Goals, Early Childhood Education Workgroup. Email received June 27, 2006.

Turner, P. (2002a). Best practices. In P. Turner (Ed.). *La Ristra: New Mexico's comprehensive professional development system in early care, education, and family support* (pp. 77–82). Santa Fe, NM: Office of Child Development, Youth and Families Department.

Turner, P. (Ed.). (2002b). *La Ristra: New Mexico's comprehensive professional development system in early care, education, and family support.* Santa Fe, NM: Office of Child Development, Youth and Families Department.

U.S. Department of Education, Office of Elementary and Secondary Education. (2005, July). ABC serving children under Title 1: Non-regulatory guidance. Washington, DC: U.S. Government Printing Office.

Vobejda, B. (1997, October 22). Employee shortage at day-care to be addressed. *The Idaho Statesman.*

Warman, B. (1998, September). Trends in state accreditation policies. *Young Children, 53*(5).

Whitebook, M. (1995, May). What's good for child care teachers is good for our country's children. *Young Children, 50*(4).

Whitebook, M., Howes, C., & Phillips, D. (1989). *Who cares? Child care teachers and the quality of care in America. The national child care staffing study.* Washington, DC: National Center for the Early Childhood Work Force.

Whitebook, M., Phillips, D., & Howes, C. (1993). *The national child care staffing study revisited.* Oakland, CA: Child Care Employee Project.

Whitebook, M., & Sakai, L. (2002, November). Readers write. *Young Children, 57*(6), 7.

Wiechel, J. (2001, Summer). Eliminating the "non-system" of governance. *State Education Leader, 19*(2), 13–15.

CHAPTER 12

Professional Commitment and Growth

OBJECTIVES After reading this chapter, you should be able to:

1.... Define professionalism.
2.... Explain the importance of acquiring a sense of professional commitment.
3.... List four different activities that promote individual professional growth.
4.... Name two early childhood professional associations and describe membership benefits.
5.... Discuss why advocacy efforts are important to student teachers.

Comments of student teachers:

> " My family and friends complained that I didn't have time for them when I was in student teaching practicum. And I didn't! I barely kept up and turned assignments in late at times. ●

Bill Jackson

> " My most memorable experience in student teaching has been the kindness, help, and cooperation that I received. So much praise and encouragement made it easier. ●

Carole Mehors

> " My dream is to have a school of my own among evergreen trees in a small mountain town. I'll call the school "Tiny Piney" or "Evergreen Academy" or such. ●

Nomsa Ncube

> " I was convinced my cooperating teacher didn't like me! Our teaching styles seemed so different. Her attitude toward teaching made me wonder why she'd kept at it so long. Things got better. She had big problems in her personal life which she struggled to keep out of her classroom manner. It was then that I caught glimpses of her teaching strengths. ●

Carrie Lee Foulkes

professionals—
individuals engaged in
occupations considered
learned endeavors, such as
law, medicine, or as in this
text, education.

As a student teacher, you may already be considered a professional. **Professionals** are those individuals whose work is predominantly intellectual in character. They make constant decisions that call for a substantial degree of discretion and judgment. Some of your skills are new, emerging, and wobbly, whereas others are definitely observable, and you are currently being measured—against standards established by those in your profession.

The No Child Left Behind Act of 2001 (NCLB), and its complementary early childhood presidential initiative, *Good Start, Grow Smart (2002),* have put a new emphasis on early childhood educators' professional development. The act was an effort that assumes that well-prepared early childhood teachers handling young children in prekindergarten programs are critical to children's healthy development, school readiness, and eventual responsible citizenship. Readiness is believed to prepare children for school success. Schools that are publicly funded are now accountable for showing children's progress, and their teachers are accountable for offering the necessary research-based experiences to do so.

Good Start, Grow Smart calls for federally funded early childhood programs to formulate early learning guidelines—goals for the skills and competencies that preschool age children should accomplish before starting kindergarten—and to identify how these should be measured. It also requires prekindergarten staff members to have the necessary qualifications which includes training, certification or degree, and vocational experience. Programs were structured to include professional staff development plans.

If you are employed in a public program, and have been given a professional development plan, you can still follow that plan and also develop a personal growth plan, for career skill improvement. You will most likely do this because you have probably decided on a long-range career goal. If you are working in another type of program, your professional development plan may be self-created. No doubt, you believe, as do other professionals, that you are a lifelong learner.

DEFINITIONS

As early as 1925, in attempting to define professionalism for the business community, Follet stated, "Profession connotes for most people a foundation of science and a motive of service [that must] rest on the basis of a proved body of knowledge [and be] . . . used in the service of others" (Fox & Urwick, 1982). There is no question that early childhood educators are involved in the service of others. Most would agree that child development is a proven body of knowledge.

Maxwell, Field, and Clifford (2006) reviewed studies on the topic of professional development and found no common definition of the term. They created their own definition, which includes three components: *education* that occurs within a formal educational system, *training* that was not for credit, and an educator-earned *credential/certificate/license* that was either institutional or occupational. A simpler definition of professional development is *getting better*—more competent and skilled—in one's chosen profession. Those who attempt to become early childhood professionals develop a conscious commitment, intentionality and concern for excellence. They achieve and maintain the career capabilities that ensure quality, developmental care, and educational opportunity for the young children they serve. In doing so, professional identity develops, and as professionals, there is collaboration with others of like purpose. Professionals devote energy to group efforts that strive to attain goal realization. They realize the value of their contribution to the lives of children, families, and society. They are well-informed and aware of current research, ethics, and standards. They sometimes become the "movers and shakers," the leaders, advocates, organizers, innovators, and reflective thinkers, who apply their talents and knowledge and are vocal about problems facing career professionals, children, and families.

Is it impossible to be that altruistic and dedicated when just starting out in this career field? Possibly, but it takes time and effort, and has its own reward. Improving children's school lives and educational future means living a career that matters. It is hoped that you have encountered one such educator that possesses these qualities.

PROFESSIONAL CONCERNS

Your teaching day includes tasks that may appear custodial in nature, such as helping at cleanup time, supervising the children as they wash their hands, serving snacks, and encouraging them to rest (see Figure 12–1). Each of these is a learning time for children, and your professional skill is at work. Helping a child who is struggling to slip on a sweater is done in a professional way and is an opportunity to help the child become more independent.

Professional status, everyone agrees, is a problem for this career field. Societies award status to trained, educated individuals, who provide valuable services to society. People can easily tick off on one hand the high-status professions and possibly what they consider middle-status professions. Early childhood workers will not be among them.

Increased status is happening in a growing number of places, and it is often the result of an increase in the qualifications necessary to hold such

Figure 12-1
Serving at snack time may appear custodial.

positions. What are the possible reasons for educators not receiving the recognition and status they deserve? There are no simple answers, but rather many conjectures by many writers. Included among those frequently cited reasons are the following:

- a blurred image between parenting and paid child care providers in the public's mind
- public attitudes and perceptions that almost anyone can watch children, and that child care requires little or no specific knowledge, education, or skill
- caregivers' attitudes toward themselves, particularly feelings of personal or collective lack of power
- lack of early childhood teacher self-esteem or assertiveness
- a public perception that children's teachers provide dedicated service, rather than a service for personal gain
- the turnover rate of prekindergarten teachers, as opposed to the life-long careers of other recognized professionals
- a lack of collective political clout for the career group
- lack of employee bargaining power
- low or minimum entry-level requirements or qualifications

Primary school professionals may find some of the above listed reasons applicable to their situation. There often is a general public concern about the quality of primary school education, and the lack of uniformity from one state to another.

In addition, primary-level professionals may notice a general acceptance that public education has failed and private schooling is superior. Another widely held and expressed view is that teacher unions, such as the National Education Association and the American Federation of Teachers, have become too politically powerful and protect incompetent teachers.

Many early childhood staffers' reticence to accept themselves as professionals may be partly responsible for low salaries and job classifications that equate prekindergarten teacher's work with attendants, custodians, and domestics. The babysitter image, in the public's view, has been difficult to escape. Advocacy training is now a recommended part of pre-service training for most early childhood educators.

A teacher's pride in the profession is justified. By participating in student teaching, you now realize that the job of an early childhood or elementary school teacher is demanding, challenging, and complex. It involves constant decisions, and can be physically and emotionally taxing, as well as being highly satisfying and rewarding.

PROFESSIONAL BEHAVIOR AND COMMITMENT

Professionalism entails understanding children and yourself, and practicing your craft diligently. Some of the demands that professionals make on themselves follow:

1. A professional gives a full measure of devotion to the job.
2. A professional follows professional ethics and standards.

3. Professionals accept responsibilities assigned to them, with as much grace as they can muster, and then work in a positive way to change those duties that deter their teaching.

4. A professional joins with others in professional organizations that exchange research and ideas. They act and advocate to benefit all children and families in areas related to children's well-being and education.

5. A professional understands and is aware of prejudices, and makes a concerted effort to get rid of them.

6. A professional treats children and others as people with feelings.

7. A professional speaks up for the child when the child needs somebody to speak out on their behalf.

8. A professional is an educator who is informed about research, issues, and trends in education.

Student teachers may spend long hours both in and out of their classrooms, and may feel that they are barely hanging on. This feeling can continue through the first year on the job. Vukelich and Wrenn (1999) describe a new teacher's inner thoughts, quoting from a journal written by one of the graduates of their elementary teacher education program:

> [I have chosen the] most complex job in the world. . . . How will I possibly remember everything I have learned? . . . There were all the curriculum areas to know. Then there is understanding the children—their learning styles, environments, personalities, disabilities, gifts, and intelligences. The list is endless!

Katz (1972) has proposed that teachers go through three stages of professional development. During the first year, they focus on *survival.* During the next two to five years, they begin to *consolidate* what they know and begin to feel a deeper understanding of what they are doing and why they are doing it. Finally, they reach the *maturity* level and function as a true professional.

Caruso (2000) believes that even cooperating teachers, who have years of experience, may have mixed feelings when their student teacher ends their practicum. These feelings can include a period of reflection, pride in their student teacher, satisfaction, a sense of reward, gratitude and relief, plus feelings about being the only adult in the classroom again, or, if their student failed, questions regarding their suitability to be a cooperating teacher.

Student teachers at the end of their practicum may experience separation difficulty, guilt about not accomplishing all they hoped, anxiety when returning to their campus, and other more positive feelings, including a sense of accomplishment and pride. Most often student teachers will continue to use reflective thought. Caruso sees this as probably the most important aspect of the final phase of student teaching (Caruso, 2000).

Anxieties stem from a desire to become a professional while at the same time having questions about stamina, endurance, and the capability to do so. Your commitment to the profession will be nourished by the supportive adults that surround you in your student teaching experience.

Severe tests of a student teacher's professional commitment may happen if a placement site models attitudes that downgrade the value and worth of the profession. When negative behavior is present in the teachers at any given facility, it is not unusual to see new teachers taking the same negative attitudes as staff who have been there awhile (Moore, 1998). A good grasp on professional conduct and commitment helps the student teacher sort out less than professional behavior. Improved and continued high standards in the profession depend on the newly trained professionals' enthusiasm, idealism, knowledge, and skills, and the experienced professionals' leadership. Unfortunately, some new teachers simply become overwhelmed; in some school districts the beginning teacher's attrition rate is high. To counteract this reality, many school districts adopt mentoring strategies that aid young teachers and support their struggle to put into practice what they have learned in training and on the job. Newly trained professionals can strengthen the field through their identification with practicing, committed professionals (see Figure 12–2).

● **Figure 12-2**
Fortunate indeed is the student teacher who joins a staff of dedicated professionals.

Advocacy

You should view advocacy as a career responsibility that goes way beyond improving conditions at your job site, for it considers all job sites and educational opportunities, for all young children. Gathering more support by identifying, enlisting and convincing policy makers, the business world, and the general public to give a higher priority to early childhood education, or the education of older children, is a common and ongoing advocacy activity. Advocacy efforts include the search for successful solutions to problems. In the past, what has contributed to successful advocacy?

- advocacy by individual educators
- increased understanding of the process by those advocating
- communicating clear messages
- studying ways others have successfully advocated
- organizing and forming liaisons with other concerned individuals and groups
- not giving up, but rather searching for better solutions

Most experts agree that child and family advocating takes time, practice, and skill. By speaking out with substantiated facts, passion, and personal concern, and expressing concerns with clarity, one has a better chance of influencing listeners. Listeners can include family, friends, other educators, the general public, business leaders, manufacturers, developers, legislators, board of education members, and community leaders.

One needs to become knowledgeable and skilled by joining an advocacy group. Advocacy usually involves one or more of the following areas: quality, delivery systems, funding, standards, and research.

Unfortunately, educators can become stale and silent. This may happen if they are not engaged in changes and developments in their professional field, feel overwhelmed with their teaching tasks, feel there is no place to share their concerns and questions, feel isolated and work in facilities full of apathy, or if program administrators withhold support and believe advocacy activities are threatening or out of character for staff members. Well-trained professionals entering the workforce can bring new advocacy energy and dedication to the field and renewed hope and support to other professional's advocacy efforts.

Meyer (2005) notes advocacy action can be simple and private or more bold and public. It can start with a question, a problem, a concern, or something witnessed that doesn't seem right. Migrant programs for field workers' children have come into being because an educator or another individual observed unsupervised young children in a field with adult workers, who were unable to watch children while working. High school child centers for teen parents have been established, because someone noticed teenage parents struggling to stay in school and parent adequately. Many college child centers and training facilities came into existence because concerned faculty noticed that college students, often unable to afford child care, were bringing their young children to campus or to classes. In many cases, the entire faculty advocated for change, and had a difficult time convincing their school board that on-campus child care—or preschool teacher training—should be a college function.

How Student Teacher Advocacy Can Begin

Advocacy usually begins when teaching colleagues meet socially and talk about concerns and conditions in their school, community, or beyond. If there is an on-campus, education major group or club, or an early childhood major group or club, *join it*. If the club is planning *Week of the Young Child* or other activities, join them and gain experience. Advocacy groups can exist anywhere a like-minded group of educators gathers for a safe forum with a sense of purpose. Professional associations are mentioned later in this chapter and many have ongoing advocacy activities.

Advocacy activities can be diverse and involve letter writing, marches, celebrations, fund-raising, t-shirt slogans, bumper stickers, and many other strategies. For tips on writing letters to promote an advocacy issue, see the *Online Companion*. To become familiar with advocacy groups who advocate on child and family issues and worker issues, see Figure 12–3.

GROUPS THAT ADVOCATE
- American Associate Degree Early Childhood Educators {http://www.accessece.org}
- International Reading Association {http://www.reading.org}
- National Association for Bilingual Education {http://www.nabe.org}
- National Association for Early Childhood Teacher Education {http://www.naecte.org}
- National Council f Teachers of Mathematics {http://www.nctm.org}
- Program for Infant/Toddler Caregivers {http://www.pitc.org}
- Zero to Three {http://www.zerotothree.org}
- Council for Exceptional Children {http://www.cec.sped.org}
- Association for Childhood Education International {http://www.acei.org}
- American Federation of Teachers {http://www.aft.org}
- National Black Child Development Institute {http://www.nbcdi.org}

(Note: This is not a comprehensive list.)

 Figure 12-3
Groups that Advocate

How Has Past Advocacy Affected You?

Your course of study, your instructor's credentials and background, your on-campus child center experience, your placement in an actual, functioning classroom for student teaching, and many other aspects of your educational experience have been influenced by someone's, or some group's, past advocacy. Many community colleges with early childhood AA degree programs are in the process of examining their programs, to gain recognition of their excellence by participating in an accreditation process that examines all or most aspects of their training program. Advocacy groups in the recent past have been instrumental in the development of national AA degree training standards, accreditation procedures, and the transferability of your credits to institutions of higher education granting BA degrees.

When you enter the workforce, even more of your work life will be impacted by past and current advocacy efforts, including the amount and kind of funding your center or school receives, your working conditions, compensation, the standards to be followed, the curriculum that was adopted, the factors that protect child safety, the college training and degree you must hold, and much, much more. In San Jose, California, a local newspaper reported that a newly hired prekindergarten teacher was told by her site director that the director would supervise her class at break time so the new teacher could clean, sweep, vacuum, and mop the classroom and the adjoining children's bathroom. The new teacher asked if her break time would follow the cleaning, and was informed that *was* her break time (Rockstroh, 2005). Fortunately, California law sets a duty-free break time, and licensing law prohibits any teacher activity unrelated to the teaching function. Advocacy was instrumental in the creation of both laws.

Student teaching commitments may make advocacy at this time near to impossible. These paragraphs strive to make you aware of the need for future advocacy. In your daily contacts, you will be instrumental in developing opinions of child development and early childhood education. You are, right now, a representative of the profession. What you say and do can influence others' priorities and voting behaviors.

This is a good time to mention that there are sometimes differences between educator's positions on issues. Currently, the No Child Left Behind Act has its advocates and detractors. It is suggested that you give attention to all sides of issues that affect you, children, and families, and that you investigate issues thoroughly.

Becoming Aware

Advocacy means being aware of legislation, the legislative process, and individuals who support child and family issues. Another step in understanding advocacy is identifying groups or individuals who monitor and help author legislation and are politically active. The National Association for the Education of Young Children is well known for its advocacy efforts, as are many other associations, and has set goals, one of which is to make all members politically effective (NAEYC, 2005). Politically effective members can be described as aware, knowledgeable, with the ability to competently discuss and debate issues, and possessing the capacity to act in ways that influence decisions. NAEYC's public-policy efforts include influencing national, state, and local legislators.

Student teachers can view NAEYC position statements online at http://www.naeyc.org/about/positions.asp and find journal articles and other useful resources at NAEYC's Beyond the Journal page, at http://www.journal.naeyc.org.

Students sometimes feel advocacy for compensation is a self-serving activity. But research studies have found that a positive relationship exists between better quality care and teacher compensation (Ghazvini & Mullis, 2003; Philips et al., 2000; Sachs, 2000).

The National Black Development Institute (NBCDI) has developed a unique program, *The Parent Empowerment Project,* which seeks to educate, motivate, and inspire parents to excellence as their child's first teacher. Since 1970, the Institute has worked to improve and protect the well-being of African American children through a variety of innovative programs, advocacy, educational publications, and dynamic training conferences (National Black Child Development Institute, 2006).

PROFESSIONAL GROWTH AND DEVELOPMENT

Early childhood teaching offers each professional a lifelong learning challenge. The goal of professional growth includes the unfolding of abilities and the achievement of greater self-actualization. True self-actualization leads to an increasing sense of responsibility and a deepening desire to serve humanity.

Maslow (1971) has described the conflict individuals face as they struggle toward increasing excellence.

> Every human being has both sets of forces within him. One set clings to safety and defensiveness out of fear, tending to regress backward, hanging on to the past . . . afraid to grow away from primitive communication with mother, , afraid to take chances, afraid to jeopardize what he already has, afraid of independence, freedom and separateness. The other set of forces impels him forward toward wholeness and uniqueness of self, toward full functioning of all his capacities, toward confidence in the face of the external world and at the same time he can accept his deepest, real, unconscious self.

When your future job includes promotional material, or rewarding incentives, it may add impetus. Your attitude toward your profession should include giving a high priority to activities that contribute to your skill development.

As a professional, you will actively pursue growth. Maslow (1971) describes the struggle and possible outcomes of your pursuit.

> Therefore we can consider the process of healthy growth to be a never ending series of free choice situations, confronting each individual at every point throughout his life, in which he must choose between the delights of safety and growth, dependence and independence, regression and progression, immaturity and maturity.

Your efforts to grow professionally will become part of your life's pattern. You will experience the tugs and pulls of finding the time and energy to follow your commitment and still have a balance in your life.

Professional Growth Plans

Many public agencies and school districts are giving new attention to the development of written professional growth plans for their employees, knowing that staff development efforts impact the quality of services.

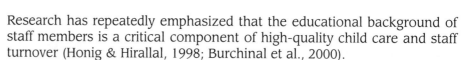

Research has repeatedly emphasized that the educational background of staff members is a critical component of high-quality child care and staff turnover (Honig & Hirallal, 1998; Burchinal et al., 2000).

The majority of early childhood educators, especially those in the private sector, will plan individual courses of action to attain professional growth. They may not have the inducements—like stipends, release time, transportation provisions, or salary schedules—that reward their efforts, as do many public employees.

A California program, *The Child Development Corps*, provides a professional development stipend ($500 to $600 per year) to child care teachers, directors, and home-based providers, meeting certain education and training qualifications, who commit to continuing their professional development and have provided service prior to the receipt of the stipend (Whitebook & Eichberg, 2002).

Kagan, Brandon, Ripple, Maher, and Joesch (2002) have listed experts' recommendations for building professional development systems, to promote a nationally qualified workforce:

- Training and credentialing should be ongoing, so that pre-service formal education requirements do not constitute a barrier to people from low socioeconomic backgrounds and immigrant teachers seeking to enter the field.

- All staff should participate yearly in ongoing professional development activities.

- The costs of professional development should be fully subsidized for low-wage staff including paying the costs of substitutes. As their salaries increase, staff will share in the costs of professional development as do elementary school teachers.

- The costs of expanding and maintaining the institutions that provide the training must be included in the estimates.

Many growth plans recommend using local resources, referral agencies, conferences, continuing education classes, and professional readings as vehicles of growth, besides seeking new information in other ways that can be incorporated into your existing practice.

Individual Learning Cycles

Just as you have watched children take enormous steps in learning one day and just mark time another, your professional growth may not be constant and steady. Harrison (1978) observed the phenomenon of *risk and retreat* in self-directed learning.

> The learning cycle is our name for the natural process of advance and retreat in learning. We observed early in our experiments with self-directed learning that individuals would move out and take personal risks and then would move back to reflect and integrate the experience.

Such risk and retreat relates to what Piaget described as the process of equilibration. You, as a learner, assimilate new material first as an accommodation with past learning (the risk); then, the assimilation becomes play (the retreat). Such a retreat is important to the process of equilibration as you seek to establish connections between old and new learning.

Reflection, or standing still at times, may give ideas time to hatch. Being aware of your own creative thinking can make you more aware of this creative process in children.

NAEYC's Professional Development Position Statement

In an effort to gain public support for the importance of high-quality early childhood programs, and to facilitate the professional development of child care workers, the NAEYC (1994) published a position statement titled "A Conceptual Framework for Early Childhood Professional Development."

Working with a number of other groups, the NAEYC's National Institute for Early Childhood Professional Development fosters the development of a comprehensive, articulated system of professional development for *all* individuals, in *all* early childhood settings. The NAEYC framework includes various components and uses the symbol of a *lattice*, to communicate combining diversity and uniqueness (Johnson & McCracken, 1994). Both vertical and horizontal strands of this lattice system are interconnected in the model, which connects additional preparation and training to increased responsibility and compensation. Figure 12–4 displays NAEYC's professional categories. These are used in a number of state plans. Each state's specific definition of what constitutes completion of each level may differ. Most large centers have career ladders, or lattices, which show up, down, and lateral job positions, necessary qualifications, and an organizational chart. Salary schedules also may be attached.

Standards and Compensation

The rising demand for high-quality child care and education, new standards, and stiffer educational staff qualifications has begun to increase salaries, benefits, and improve working conditions. Bright spots occur in some areas of the career field, including Head Start, military child care, and in states initiating or instituting state-funded preschool or universal prekindergarten programs. There is still a long way to go before equitable compensation becomes a reality for most early childhood educators.

Whitebook and Eichberg (2002) give the career field hope for salary improvement in the following:

> [I]n the last three years, driven in part by a robust economy and a shortage of trained workers, many states—among them California, Illinois, New York, North Carolina, Rhode Island, Washington, and Wisconsin—have initiated or expanded publicly funded programs focused on building a more skilled and stable child care workforce. Initiatives are also being developed in Connecticut, Georgia, Idaho, Kansas, Missouri, Oklahoma, and Pennsylvania. In some states, local governmental entities are establishing programs.

While professional groups strive for excellence, taxpayers and funding sources require accountability. Cunningham (2006) describes the new NAEYC Accreditation Standards for teacher qualifications.

> The new NAEYC Accreditation Standards for teacher qualifications include a time line from 2006 through 2020 for teachers and administrators in accredited centers to meet these requirements. (By

CAREER LADDER CITING CERTIFICATES, CREDENTIALS, AND DEGREES

Doctorate

Master's Degree

Bachelor's Degree in Early Childhood/Child Development**

Associate Degree in Early Childhood Education**

A certficate* awarded after a number of college credits are accumulated in an approved associate degree program.

Completion of a Child Development Associate (CDA) credential at an institution of higher education that articulates into a certificate program or an associate degree program.

Certificate of completion of an entry level early childhood training course with specified hour or unit credit.

*Certification in some states may be undertaken by state departments, associations, training agencies, or private entities.

**Degree granting institutions have different department names such as Family Studies, Human Services, and so on.

Figure 12-4
Career ladder citing certificates, credentials, and degrees.

2020, teachers on staff must have a minimum of an associate's degree and at least seventy-five percent of the teachers must have a baccalaureate degree.) Similarly, Head Start has instituted a time line for increasing staff qualifications, which specifies that fifty percent of all teachers must have a baccalaureate degree by 2011.

NAEYC revised its professional preparation standards in 2003; the revision constructed five critical components, felt to be key elements, that are identical across the three preparation levels: associate degree, initial licensure, and advanced level. This emphasized the underlying supposition that professional preparation of early childhood educators has certain essential or core expectations, for candidate knowledge, skill, and dispositions that are shared and built upon across the three preparation levels mentioned. If you remember, we suggested obtaining *Preparing Early Childhood Professionals*: NAEYC's *Standards for Programs* (Hyson, 2003) for your personal profession library in the first chapter. It is an indispensable career guide. Figure 12–5 displays a sample key element, from NAEYC's third standard "In the area of observing, documenting, and assessing to support young children and families" across the three preparation levels.

STANDARD 3. OBSERVING, DOCUMENTING, AND ASSESSING TO SUPPORT YOUNG CHILDREN AND FAMILIES

Associate degree candidate

Students prepared in associate degree programs know about and understand the goals, benefits, and uses of assessment. They know about and use systematic observations, documentation, and other effective assessment strategies in a responsible way, in partnership with families and other professionals, to positively influence children's development.

(p. 106)

Source: from Hyson, M. (Ed.) (2003) Preparing Early Childhood Professionals: NAEYC's Standards for Programs. Washington, DC: NAEYC. p. 106

Permission of the National Association for the Education of Young Children

Initial licensure (bachelor's or master's degree) candidate

Candidates' work shows knowledge of the important goals of early childhood assessment. Their work generally shows alignment between goals, curriculum, teaching strategies, and assessment. In their work, candidates explain how assessment may be used in positive ways, and they also explain how inappropriate assessment may harm children and families.

Candidates' work shows research-based knowledfe and basic competence in observation, documentation, and other assessment tools. Their work reflects essential knowledge of the characteristics, strengths, limitations, and appropriate uses of the most frequently used assessment tools and approaches, including approaches for children with disabilities and culturally and linguistically diverse children. Candidates demonstrate essential skills in using assessments, interpreting candidates' work shows that they can identify current educational, legal, and ethical issues with respect to assessment practices. Candidates can provide examples of responsible as well as irresponsible assessment. In their practice, they apply responsible assessment practices when working with diverse children. (p. 29)

Advanced (master's or doctoral degree) candidate (Example: accomplished teacher)

Assessment issues are relevant and challenging for all candidates in addvanced programs. Future early childhood leaders should be at the forefront of research, policy, and best practices in the assessment of young children and in program evaluation. Advanced program candidates build on the competencies described in NAEYC's Initial Licensure Standards document, gaining greater depth and specialization related to their current or intended professional role.

Early childhood accomplished teacher

These candidates have great opportunities to articulate and use in-depth knowledge and skills in early childhood assessment and to link assessment to curriculum planning in increasingly skillful ways. Beyond the Initial competencies, candidates must show enhanced skills in analyzing, understanding, and using a variety of sound assessment practices. For all candidates–but to a greater or lesser extent depending on their focus–expertise and interdisciplinary teamwork in assessing culturally and linguistically diverse children, and children with developmental delays, disabilities, or other special needs, are critical. Consistent with National Board standards, candidates also show competence in working with other professionals on assessment issues, and a high level of skill in engaging families in assessment. In addition, advanced program candidates show skills in articulating issues around assessment and advocating within and beyond their workplace for ethical, effective assessment policies and practices. (p. 80)

Figure 12-5

Sample section of Key Element in Standard 3, Across Levels of Preparation.

It is prudent here to clarify terms used in typical standard's statements. You may find these in early childhood education professional literature. *Standards* usually define widely held expectations for young children, programs, teachers, future teachers, and institutions of higher education (Zaslow & Martinez-Beck, 2003). *Professional preparation standards* are widely held expectations for candidates (students in training) like you. *Early learning standards* encompass expected learning and development outcomes for young children, and *benchmarks* refer to child accomplishments at certain points in an offered program of study. *Program standards* and *guidelines* promote the quality of a child curriculum and environment by identifying expected characteristics. And *content standards* refer to what a student (child) should know and be able to do within a particular discipline, such as recognizing 20 alphabet letters before kindergarten, or counting to 10 by age four. Notice content standards mention a particular point in time and they differ from school to school, and many schools may not identify them at all. Some have developed content standards for kindergarten through grade 12. All schools are expected to use them and are measured against them.

 # PROFESSIONAL GROWTH OPPORTUNITIES

Early childhood teachers have a wide range of alternative routes to professional growth. These include additional credit coursework leading to a degree, training without college credit, apprenticeships and exchanging teaching, independent study, visitation and travel, professional group membership (see Figure 12–6), mentoring by other professionals, attending conferences and workshops, in-service training, and skill and study sessions.

SAMPLING OF POSSIBLE ASSOCIATION MEMBERSHIP SERVICES AND BENEFITS
- association Web site may disperse early childhood education news and information
- exclusive access to members-only services
- on-line shopping with member discounts for the latest resources
- on-line registration for events, conferences, institutes, workshops, and training opportunities
- listing of accredited programs
- association position statements available on current topics and issues
- networking with colleagues at an on-line community Web site
- listing of career openings and members seeking employment at an early childhood career forum
- association news delivered to your e-mail address monthly
- affiliate member groups may have local chapters
- association advocacy activities conducted at national, state, and local levels, including legislative alerts and lobbying information
- discounts on conference registrations, books, and other publications
- interest forums that promote collaboration on topics of interest
- on-line discussion groups
- a member service center
- association recommended insurance information
- student discount membership fees

 Figure 12-6
Sampling of possible association member services and benefits.

Administrative Planning for Staff's Professional Growth

After reviewing their former student's journal, Vukelich and Wrenn (1999) proposed the following tenets of quality professional development, affirming that professional development should:

- focus on a single subject.
- focus on participants' needs.
- be ongoing and sustained.
- engage participants in the pursuit of answers to genuine questions, problems, and curiosities.
- provide for participants' meaningful engagement.
- help participants develop collegial relationships.
- encourage participants to reflect on their teaching.

Vukelich and Wrenn (1999) caution administrators and others who plan for the professional development of their teachers to avoid the one-day, one-shot, this-is-good-for-everyone approach. Those who feel the information is valid need far more than one day to change teaching behaviors. An introduction should be followed by opportunities to practice, mentoring by a teacher knowledgeable in the new practice, critiques of attempts to implement the new ideas, and further practice.

A one-day, one-shot approach does not produce change in any teacher whose needs the approach does not meet (Sykes, 1996). Under those conditions, the presentation is usually ignored, and the teacher considers it time wasted which probably doesn't leave them too enthusiastic about future presentations. Your authors know only too well how one-day shots on material in which teachers already have a background, or in which they are not interested, are considered time wasters.

Varying Approaches to Professional Development

To consider what they call a "new vision," Sparks and Hirsh (1997) suggest that a paradigm shift is necessary. Traditional ways of conducting staff development deny the very ways in which teachers want their students to learn: activities that engage, experiences that actively involve, and problems that require solutions. Sitting passively in a classroom before or after a busy workday encourages boredom and sleepiness. Sparks and Hirsh see a need to teach teachers in much the same ways in which they want their students to learn. That requires active learning, opportunities for small-group discussion, and working toward solutions of real problems.

Darling-Hammond (1996) states in her article, "What Matters Most: A Competent Teacher for Every Child," that teachers must recognize that they are learners first and that learning is a lifelong process. When you graduate and receive your credentials, you have just started on a road to competency, a road that will continue throughout your life.

Continuing Education

Credit and noncredit college coursework leads to advanced skill. Coursework frequently results in on-the-job application of ideas, spreading enthusiasm throughout a preschool center. Local college career placement and counseling centers provide a review of college catalogs and bulletins. Coursework descriptions and particulars can be examined. Additional college services often include career guidance, financial aid information, housing particulars, job placement boards, and tutoring assistance.

Articulation Agreements

Examine the transferability of community college coursework credits to baccalaureate degree programs at degree-granting institutions. Although agreements have been developed recently in many geographic locations, it pays to check. If articulation agreements exist, usually both institutions have had representatives meet and tailor coursework so a smooth transition is possible. Credits can be accepted as elective units or as equivalent units. Since institutions differ, it is prudent to consult with college counselors and early childhood department chairpersons at both institutions.

Distance Learning

A number of colleges offer distance learning opportunities, offered on-line, on television, by satellite, by correspondence, and a few by conference call. Questions to ask regarding such programs follow:

- What are the qualifications of the sponsoring institution?
- Are instructors credentialed?
- Is the institution accredited?
- Is financial assistance available?
- Is it a degree-awarding program? Will credits awarded satisfy degree requirements at other colleges?
- What skills will one need to be successful in the course?
- Is what is offered geared for independent study, or are there opportunities to interact with peers?
- What resources does a student need? Must one have a computer, cable television access, satellite access, **software**, or other technology?
- Are reading materials covered in enrollment costs?
- Are any student support systems in place, or are local facilitators or tutors available?
- How and when can one contact the instructor? (Nealy-Shane, 2002)

software—the "instructions" that direct a computer to perform an activity, usually stored on a disk or directly in the computer. Many such programs are available for young children.

Computer Expertise

Many colleges are now insisting students display computer literacy and skill before graduation. Teacher training programs—already full of requirements and electives—have been slow to institute coursework. Most student teachers in two-year community college programs pursue an independent course of study to acquire computer expertise. Many public libraries have developed computer centers where Internet access and help are available. The increasing computer skills preschoolers exhibit surprise most early childhood teachers (see Figure 12–7). Commercial, early childhood program software is abundant and entering young children's lives at an amazing rate. Debell (2005), after studying data from a 2003 U.S. Census Bureau survey of 53 million children, in preschool through the twelfth

 Figure 12-7
Computer skill seems to
come easily for many
young children.

grade, reports that 67 percent of children enrolled in preschool had used computers and 23 percent had also used the Internet.

The teacher with **computer literacy** is able to guide children through computer-based learning and discovery opportunities. The computer then becomes a valuable child and adult teaching aid, and an indispensable adult communication, recording, and researching tool.

computer literacy—
familiarity with and
knowledge about
computers.

Teacher Certification

National certification as an Early Childhood Generalist is awarded by the National Board for Professional Teaching Standards (NBPTS). It is voluntary and requires fees. Applicants who successfully meet rigorous standards, including years of experience, become certified and join a distinguished group of 3,800 others (Guiding & Hyson, 2002). The professional advantages of completing the process and pursuing this credential might be advanced teaching skills, upward mobility, and the ability to become a leader in the field.

Each state has developed policy concerning teacher certification and credentialing but there is a definite lack of commonality. When trying to determine what credentials, certificates, permits, and licenses exist for educators in early childhood programs in a particular state, the best place to consult is that state's department of education. It's best to secure requirements in writing. Often, teacher qualification requirements change, depending on funding sources. Publicly supported centers usually have higher and stricter standards, requiring the completion of additional education and experience.

Unfortunately, many states do not require beginning, early childhood teachers to have successfully completed college-level coursework before entering the career field. This is changing rapidly as parents demand trained caregivers and quality programs.

At the elementary school level, a master's degree is required for permanent certification in most states, and 56 percent of public school teachers hold master's degrees, up from 27 percent in 1971 (Grant & Murray, 1999).

Apprenticing, Demonstrating, and Exchanging Teaching

You may know a teacher with whom you would like to study, whose direction and tutelage could be growth-producing. Volunteering in that teacher's classroom offers opportunities for closer examination of techniques. It may be possible to earn college credit through enrolling in a cooperative work experience program or independent study course; check with your college.

In a demonstration-teaching arrangement, you watch and discuss methods with practicing teachers. Hearing explanations and asking questions give insight into different ways to accomplish teaching goals. Most professionals will provide this type of short-term arrangement.

Exchanging teachers within a school is sometimes considered growth-producing. New partnerships stimulate new blends of techniques. Many schools permit a shifting of staff members, enabling gifted and talented teachers to share their ideas. Cross-matching and lively discussions act as healthy catalysts.

MENTORING

Mentoring programs are an established and increasingly available vehicle to enhance staff professional development and retention. Mentoring for teachers offers an approach to teacher training within the context of the teaching environment and emphasizes excellence in daily practice. Merrill (2002) notes mentoring programs differ, and range from informal buddy-system arrangements to structured meetings with a trained mentor, who may be a fellow employee or a mentor provided through a partnership with another local program or agency. Many mentors have received training in mentoring skills, adult development, observation, and communication. Funding may be provided for both the mentor and the one mentored. Most mentors are chosen for their expertise and are considered master teachers. Increased collaboration in the mentoring process often leads to sharing ideas, reflective thinking, research and implementation, enthusiasm, and improved overall program quality. In other words, it is a dynamic professional growth opportunity for both participants.

The percentage of teachers who experience mentoring in their first year of teaching has tripled in the past 20 years, and 48 percent of mentored teachers report it was beneficial (Grant & Murray, 1999).

Internships

Internships are employed positions, for a designated period of time. Teacher interns work under the direction of experienced practitioners and assume a variety of teaching responsibilities (see Figure 12–8).

Grant and Murray (1999) have this to say about internships:

> Internships are just as important for teachers as for medical doctors. Neither the craft of healing nor that of teaching can be learned at the highest levels without such forms of induction into the profession. Teachers also need more substantial, intellectually challenging opportunities for professional growth throughout their careers, like those architects and professors now enjoy, such as sabbaticals and opportunities for research and learning new techniques.

Independent Study

Self-planned study allows one to choose the subject, sequence, depth, and breadth of professional growth. Your home library will grow yearly, funds permitting! You will spend much time reading books and other professional materials; these resources will be a tribute to your professional commitment. Professional journals and magazines provide research articles and practical suggestions. A brief list of periodicals follows:

- *Young Children* (bimonthly publication of the NAEYC)
- *Childhood Education* (published quarterly by the **Association for Childhood Education International**; they also publish an annual theme issue and an international issue)
- *American Education Research Journal*
- *The Black Child Advocate* (quarterly newsletter)
- *Day Care and Early Education*
- *Child Care Quarterly*
- *Child Health Talk* (quarterly publication)
- *Learning*
- *Child Study Journal*

Organization and association publications carry timely information. A starting point for independent study may be the bibliographies and book titles you collected during your training.

 Association for Childhood Education International (ACEI)— professional organization that focuses on issues of children, from infancy to early adolescence, including those involving international and intercultural concerns.

Visits and Travel

Other teachers' classrooms will always be a valuable resource and study possibility. Observing other classrooms offers good ideas, clever solutions, and provocative discoveries. It is amazing how many early childhood programs extend professional courtesy to visiting early childhood contemporaries if approached. Travelers, contacting administrators and directors beforehand, often are able to tour facilities, interview staff, and observe program activities. A written letter of introduction from a supervisor, to include in a request-to-visit letter along with your email address, is a good idea. For tax purposes, keep records of visits, including notes on conversations, photographs, happenings, and ideas that might help your professional growth. Professional groups' conferences often schedule tours of outstanding local programs.

Almost every country in the world has group child care, and you have probably developed a list of programs in your own community you would like to observe. The professional courtesy of allowing observers is widespread. Directors and staff members frequently provide guided tours that include explanations and discussions of goals, program components, and teaching philosophies.

Professional Group Membership

You will find professional, early childhood group membership to be one of the best ways to locate skill development opportunities. We previously mentioned the advocacy leadership many provide.

Association publications are generally reasonably priced and current. Publication listings are available on request from main office headquarters.

The advantages of local professional membership are numerous. Workshops, study sessions, and conferences provide favorable circumstances for professional development. There are opportunities to meet other professionals, discuss views and concerns, and jointly solve problems. The talents of early childhood experts are tapped for the benefit of all the members.

A fascinating and exhilarating experience awaits the student teacher on first attending a national conference. There will be so much to see and sample, so many inspiring ideas, materials, and equipment to examine; a virtual overdose of stimuli that wholesomely feeds your attempt to grow.

Workshops, Meetings, and Skill and Study Sessions

Workshops, skill sessions, and meetings are smaller versions of state and national conferences. Diverse and varied, they cover topics related to early childhood. Practical and theoretical presentations are popular.

Identification with the spirit of professionalism—which can be defined as *striving for excellence*—motivates many of the attending participants. Most communities schedule many professional growth meetings each year and encourage student teacher attendance.

In-Service Training

In-service training sessions are designed to suit the training needs of a particular group of teachers or caregivers. They are arranged by sponsoring agencies or employers. Typically, consultants and specialists lead, guide, plan, and present skill development sessions and/or assessments of program components. There is usually no fee and attendance is mandatory. Often, staffs decided the nature and scope of the in-service training, and paid substitutes free up staff members from child supervision duties.

LEADERSHIP

Leadership is an outgrowth of professionalism and can take multiple and various directions. One can lead the career field in discovery through research and its application, lead an association's or organization's efforts to increase recognition and compensation, lead by encouraging teachers-in-training to create developmentally appropriate classrooms, lead by becoming an effective liaison with legislators, lead through advocacy actions or involvement in many other possible areas that promote career excellence.

Leadership often begins with achieving expertise recognized by other professionals. The saying "leaders are born not made" may not be true for early childhood career professionals. Many leaders have worked diligently, taken opportunities offered them, or sought out opportunity themselves, through advanced training, coursework, apprenticeships, scholarships, and other leadership-training vehicles. Formal leadership training opportunities for promising individuals have been funded by professional associations, private individuals, foundations, and other entities interested in the welfare of children and families. The funding sources may have recognized potential, or may have put faith in the recipient because of certain criteria, such as a high grade point average or past recognition or awards. Professional associations, along with college and university professors and counselors, are good sources of information concerning leadership training.

Professional excellence entails mastery. Professional mastery affects recognition, position, status, and compensation.

LEADERS KEEP CURRENT

A well-informed professional reads material that identifies what is currently affecting the field of education or educational practice. A good way to do this is by reading position statements that have taken a stand on an issue. Professional journals and books are numerous. The field of education has often been criticized for jumping into the latest educational fad, but professionals look for research-based substantiation and further information before they advocate something new or take a position.

SUMMARY

Student teachers strive for recognition of their professional skills and try to achieve standards established by those in the teaching profession. Pride in the early childhood profession grows as student teachers realize the dedication and skills of those already teaching. *The important contribution this profession makes to children, families, and society cannot be overrated.* The commitment to update continually and gain additional skills begins in training and continues for a lifetime. Each professional teacher is responsible for her own unique, growth-planning schedule.

Many activity choices leading to advanced skills are available, and most professionals engage in a wide variety. Additional coursework and training, professional group membership, conference and workshop attendance, in-service training, school visits, and exchange teaching lead to the learning and discovering of new techniques. Social interactions in educative settings reinforce individual teachers' commitments to professionalism.

The solitary pursuit of a true professional, bent on increasing excellence, includes self-directed study, reflection, and analysis. Visiting education Web sites, and reading professional journals, magazines, and books that present new and classic strategies, practices, techniques, ideas, issues, trends, and research is both never-ending and personally rewarding.

HELPFUL WEB SITES

http://www.hsbbs.org
Head Start. This site offers a calendar of events for Head Start and other early childhood conferences, meetings, and activities.

http://www.naeyc.org
National Association for the Education of Young Children. Lists what this professional organization offers.

http://www.ecs.org
Education Commission of the States. Investigate education and early childhood issues.

http://www.ftj.com
Forrest T. Jones and Company. Information concerning NAEYC's insurance for early childhood workers is available here.

http://www.eclu.uc.edu
University of Cincinnati. Distance degree learning particulars may be found here.

http://www.acei.org
Association for Childhood Education International. Find out what this professional association offers.

http://www.cudenver.edu
Colorado Early Childhood Professional Credential Office. Check out Colorado's five credential levels.

http://www.njpdc.org
New Jersey Professional Development Center for Early Care and Education. Click on *Professional Standards and Articulation* to view New Jersey's seamless education attempts.

http://www.ccw.org
The Center for the Child Care Workforce. This site provides updates of proposed, newly funded, and existing child care compensation efforts.

http://www.nlci.org
National Latino Children's Institute. A clearinghouse and resource center site concentrating on Latino children's issues is available.

Additional resources for this chapter can be found by visiting the Online Companion at www.earlychilded.delmar.com.

SUGGESTED ACTIVITIES

A. Join a professional organization.

B. Read three articles in an issue of *Young Children* or *Childhood Education* and discuss with your peers.

C. In groups of four to six, develop a chart that lists factors that promote professionalism, and those that impede professionalism, in early childhood teachers.

D. Rate each statement based on the scale below. Discuss your results with the class. Strongly agree = 1; agree = 2; cannot decide = 3; mildly disagree = 4; strongly disagree = 5
   1. Being professional includes proper makeup and clothing at work.
   2. It is unprofessional to keep using the same techniques over and over.
   3. Professional commitment is more important than professional growth.
   4. Professional growth can involve coursework that does not pertain to children and/or families.
   5. A teacher can grow professionally by studying children in the classroom.
   6. Professional association fees are so expensive that student teachers can rarely afford to join.
   7. One of the real causes for the lack of status of early childhood teachers is their own attitude toward professional growth.
   8. It is difficult to feel like a professional when salaries are so low.
   9. Most teachers who pursue professional skills receive little recognition for their efforts.
   10. One can learn all one needs to know about handling children's behavior by watching a master teacher.
   11. Sweatpants, T-shirts, and tennis shoes are very comfortable, but they are not very professional looking (Franquet, 1997).

12. The community should see child care as not just a social service but as an income-generating, job-creating industry that is vital to the economic infrastructure of any city (Petersen, 2002).

E. Investigate groups in your community that schedule skill sessions, workshops, or meetings offering growth opportunities to early childhood teachers. Report your findings to the class.

●REVIEW

A. Name four benefits of professional group membership.

B. Match items in Column I with those in Column II.

I	II
1. rate of teacher growth	a. pulling ideas together
2. commitment	b. code of ethics
3. standards	c. advances and retreats
4. consolidation	d. depends on individual's activities
5. learning cycle	e. ranges from high to low
6. professionals	f. constant intellectual decisions
7. apprenticing	g. expert advice
8. classroom visits	h. onsite training
9. workshops	i. studying with another
10. in-service training	j. professional courtesy

C. Select the answer that best completes each statement.

1. The person most responsible for a particular teacher's professional growth is:
   a. the employer.
   b. the parent.
   c. the child.
   d. the teacher.
   e. none of these.

2. Of the following entries, the one that is a well-known early childhood professional magazine is:
   a. *The Whole Child.*
   b. *Child and Learning.*
   c. *Young Children.*
   d. *Helping the Child.*
   e. *The Professional Growth Journal.*

D. Complete the following statement: *Lifelong learning is typical of the professional teacher who . . .*

E. In the following paragraphs, make note of all statements that indicate questionable professionalism.

I made an appointment to observe a class in a community school. As I arrived, the director nodded and indicated that I was to enter a classroom labeled "The Three's Room." The teacher and aide looked at me, and quickly looked away. I sat quietly near the wall. The teacher approached, demanding, "Who sent you in here?" "The director," I answered. She went back to the aide and whispered to him briefly. The teacher began a conversation with Mrs. Brown, a parent, who had just arrived. The teacher mentioned that Mrs. Brown's daughter, Molly, refused to eat lunch and kicked a hole in a cot at naptime. "I told you I'd tell your mother," the teacher said to Molly, who was standing at her mother's side.

Time for outside play was announced. The teacher and aide left the room for the play area. One or two children failed to follow the group outside. I wasn't sure if I could leave them inside so I stood in the doorway and looked out. The children must have headed out the other door, to the director's office, while I took note of the play equipment.

The aide approached. "Looking for a job?" He asked. "I could work afternoons," I answered. "Well, the person who teaches four-year-olds is quitting," he offered. "It's an easy job. You just watch them after naptime until their parents come." "Thanks for telling me about it," I said.

I left the yard to return to the director's office. She was on the phone with a parent and motioned me to sit in a chair opposite her desk. She was describing the school's academic program, and winked at me when she told the parent every child learned the alphabet, shapes, and colors, besides reading a number of words. She hung up the phone and said to me, "Sometimes they're hard to sell." I thanked the director for allowing me to observe. She acknowledged this and asked, "Did you notice the teacher or aide leaving the children unsupervised? I've been too busy to watch them, but we've had a couple of complaints." "No," I lied, not wanting to become involved. Hoping to change the subject, I asked, "Do you have any openings for a teacher in the afternoon hours?" Because I needed money badly, a part-time job would have been welcome. "We will have a

position available starting the first week of October," she answered. The director then proceeded to describe job duties. They ranged from planning the program to straightening the classroom at the end of the day. I told her I needed time to think over the offer. The director insisted she needed to know immediately, so I accepted.

CASE SCENARIO

Setting: An inner city prekindergarten program, in a large metropolitan area.

At the first open house after the fall enrollment period, it was customary for the preschool classes to prepare and present a short child activity during the meeting. The student teacher and cooperating teacher decided on one; the song *Uno, Dos, Tres, Inditos* would be sung in both English and Spanish by the children.

The children worked on self-decorated headbands with colorful feathers for the event. The room would be decorated in a way that the staff felt might welcome their majority of immigrant families. A photo of Cesar Chavez, donated by the parent group, was on display in the classroom along with lots of children's artwork.

Everything went smoothly during the bulk of the parent meeting, and the children's song was a big hit. The refreshments had been well planned and parents had contributed goodies from their homes.

As the meeting was winding up, Mrs. Williams, DeVon's mother, took the cooperating teacher aside. The student teacher watched and listened as heated words entered the conversation. He heard parts of the conversation—"Isn't this America?" and "I don't see Washington, Lincoln, or a flag."

Question for Discussion:

1. After consulting about the incident, the cooperating teacher and the student teacher should do what? Why?

2. The student teacher had another parent at the meeting ask, "Do you teach any patriotic songs to the kids?" He answered, "Didn't you think so?" Was this an appropriate answer?"

3. Should the immigration debate that polarized public opinion in 2006 be considered when early childhood teachers display items in their classrooms? Why? Why not?

⬤REFERENCES

Burchinal, M. R., Roberts, J. E., Riggins, R., Zeisel, S. A., Neebe, E., & Bryant, D. (2000). Relating quality of center-based child care to early cognitive and language development longitudinally. *Child Development, 71*(2), 339–357.

Caruso, J. J. (2000, January). Cooperating teacher and student teacher phases of development. *Young Children, 55*(1), 75–81.

Cunningham, L. L. (2006, Spring). Challenge of an educated early childhood education workforce. *Connections, 34*(3), 24.

Darling-Hammond, L. (1996, November). What matters most: A competent teacher for every child. *Phi Delta Kappan, 78* (3), 39-45.

U.S. Department of Education National Center for Education Statistics. (2005). M. Debell (Ed.). Rates of computer and Internet use by children in nursery school and students in kindergarten through twelfth grade: 2003. Washinton, DC: U.S. Government Printing Office. Reprinted in *Education Statistics Quarterly, 7,* (1, 2), 54–56.

Evans, V. J. (2006). Economic perspectives on early care and education. In M. Zaslow & I. Martinez-Beck (Eds.), *Critical issues in early childhood professional development* (pp. 309–312). Baltimore, MD: Paul Brookes Publishing Co.

Fox, E. M., & Urwick, L. (1982). *Dynamic administration: The collected papers of Mary Parker Follet* (pp. 19). New York: Hippocrene Books.

Franquet, M. (1997, July). R-E-S-P-E-C-T: Can I have some? Please! *Young Children, 52*(2), 36–41.

Ghazvini, A., & Mullis, R. L. (2002). Center-based care for young children: Examining predictors of quality. *The Journal of Genetic Psychology,* (163), 112–124.

Good Smart, Grow Smart. (2002, April). Washington, DC: The White House.

Grant, C., & Murray, C. (1999). *Teaching in America: The slow revolution.* Cambridge, MA: Harvard University Press.

Guiding, R., & Hyson, M. (2002, September). National Board certification: The next professional step? *Young Children, 57*(5), 60–61.

Harrison, R. (1978). *Self-directed learning: Human growth games.* Beverly Hills, CA: Sage Publications.

Honig, A. S., & Hirallal, A. (1998). Which counts more for excellence in childcare staff: Years of service, education level or ECE coursework? *Early Child Development and Care, 145,* 32–46.

Johnson, J., & McCracken, J. B. (Eds.) (1994). *The early childhood career lattice: Perspectives on professional development.* Washington, DC: National Association for the Education of Young Children.

Kagan, S. L., Brandon, R. N., Ripple, C. H., Maher, E. J., & Joesch, J. M. (2002, May). Supporting quality early childhood care and education. *Young Children, 57*(3), 58–65.

Katz, L. (1972, February). Developmental stages of preschool teachers. *The Elementary School Journal 5th edition,* 24–30.

Maslow, A. (1971). Defense and growth. In R. H. Anderson, & H. G. Shan (Eds.), *As the twig is bent,* 54-60. Boston: Houghton Mifflin.

Maxwell, K. L. , Field, C. C., & Clifford, R. M. (2006). In M. Zaslow and I. Martinez-Beck (Eds.), *Critical issues in early childhood professional development* (pp. 21–44). Baltimore, MD: Paul Brookes Publishing Co.

Merrill, S. (2002). Mentoring in Head Start programs. *The Head Start Bulletin, 72,* 32–33.

Meyer, R. J. (2005, May). Taking a stand: Strategies for activism. *Young Children, 60*(5), 80–92.

Moore, M. (1998, May/June). Improving the performance of child care workers: A serious dilemma. *Journal of Early Education and Family Review, 5*(5), 48-53.

National Association for the Education of Young Children. (1994, March). NAEYC position statement: A conceptual framework for early childhood professional development. *Young Children, 49*(3), 28-30.

National Black Child Development Institute. (2006). *Parent Empowerment Project.* Retrieved September 13, 2006 from http://www.nbcdi.org/programs/pep/pep.asp.

Nealy-Shane, D. (2002). Choosing a distance education program. *The Head Start Bulletin, 72,* 25.

No Child Left Behind Act. (2001). PL 107–110. 20 U.S.C. 6302 et seq.

Petersen, D. (Quoted in Corcoran, K.). (2002, November 12). Report: Child care is cog in economy. *San Jose Mercury News,* 1–2B.

Phillips, D. A., Mekow, D., Scarr S., McCartney, K., & Abbot-Shinn, M. (2000). Within and beyond the classroom door: Assessing quality in child care centers. *Early Childhood Research Quarterly, 15,* 475–496.

Rockstroh, D. (2005, December 7). Teacher ordered to use breaks to play janitor. *San Jose Mercury News,* C9.

Sachs, J. (2000). Inequities in early care and education: What is America buying? *Journal of Education for Students Placed at Risk,* (5), 383–395.

Sparks, D., & Hirsh, S. (1997). A new vision for staff development. Alexandria, VA: Association for Supervision and Curriculum Development, 32.

Sykes, G. (1996, March). Reform *of* and *as* professional development. *Phi Delta Kappan, 77*(7), 26–34.

U. S. Department of Health and Human Services Administration on Children, Youth, and Families. (2003). *Child maltreatment: 2001.* Washington, DC: U.S. Government Printing Office.

Vukelich, C., & Wrenn, L. C. (1999, Spring). Quality professional development: What do we think we know? *Childhood Education, 75*(3), 11–15.

Whitebook, M., & Eichberg, A. (2002, May). Defining policies to improve child care workforce compensation, *Young Children, 57*(3), 66–72.

Zaslow, M.& Martinez-Beck, I (2006). *Critical Issues in early childhood professional development.* Baltimore, MD: Paul H. Brookes Publishing.

CHAPTER 13
Trends and Issues

OBJECTIVES

After reading this chapter, you should be able to:

1.... Discuss two facts concerning American families that is influencing or affecting children's care and education programs.

2.... List choices American families are making about their children's place of schooling.

3.... Explain why it may be a perfect time, or not so perfect time, to graduate from an education or early childhood education teacher-training program.

Comments of student teachers:

> 66 I'll be advocating for children and myself as long as I teach. I couldn't believe my cooperating teacher was so concerned about children's rights, laws, and working conditions. I was just trying to become a really good teacher. She's so aware of factors influencing quality care and works in her free time with professional groups and projects. That's dedication! ●
>
> **Dale Wildeagle**

> 66 I think I can say I'm an eclectic student teacher. I grab the best of what I see and it's incorporated into my teaching style. There's also some original, unique, me included. ●
>
> **Ann Ng**

> 66 My cooperating teacher is a baseball buff. You wouldn't believe how he uses baseball-related material to teach children math and science. ●
>
> **Shirley Booker-Maddux**

We will categorize trends and issues in the following ways. We realize some trends lead to issues, and some issues lead to trends in education, so in some cases the line between a trend and an issue may seem blurred. First, we will present facts and figures that we feel are important and cite present day happenings in the lives of American children and families. Following that is a section concerning trends and issues in the education career field with an emphasis on early childhood education. We include facts and figures that concern educators searching for employment, plus tips and suggestions about how to go about actually securing the employment you seek.

Any consideration of trends and issues must be selective; ones you may feel are important may be mentioned briefly or even be omitted. Included in this chapter are the ones we think have primacy; these are not mentioned in any order of priority.

FAMILIES AND CHILDREN: FACTS AND FIGURES

As the 21st century began, family characteristics and the lives of children in the United States were changing, as they have continued to do. Witness the following facts and figures.

- In 2000, three million reports of abuse or neglect were filed, concerning five million children; about one million children were confirmed victims of these crimes. Boys and girls are at equal risk for neglect and physical abuse, although girls are four times more likely to experience sexual abuse, most of which happens within families (U.S. Department of Health and Human Services, 2003).

- In the past 10 years, the United States has seen a dramatic increase in the number of children who live without their parents, in a household headed by a relative (Birckmayer, Cohen, Jensen, & Variano, 2005).

- Child-rearing occupies a smaller share of a person's adult life, because there are longer periods before and after raising children, compared to previous generations (Whitehead, 2006).

- One in 10 women in their forties remained childless in 1979; in 2004, it was one in five.

- In 1999, almost half (48 percent) of all children born to women ages 21 to 24, of all races and ethnicities, were born to single mothers (Will, 2002).

- In some of the nation's largest cities and metropolitan areas, at least half of public school students are students of color; in 2001, 40 percent of all students enrolled in the nation's schools were (Ladson-Billings, 2003).

- More than 7.5 million legal immigrants settled in the United States between 1991 and 1998, most of whom came from nations in Latin America and Asia (Riche, 2000).

- In California, more than half of the state's newborns are Latinos, as were the *majority* of children entering California kindergartens in the fall of 2006 (Figure 13–1).

● **Figure 13-1**
Ethnic diversity in
preschool classrooms is
the norm, not the
exception.

- More than 2.5 million grandparents now raise grandchildren without a biological parent present in the home (Simmons & Dye, 2003).
- More unmarried mothers are choosing to remain single, a rise of over 18 percent since the 1930s.
- The number of fathers who are single-parents, though only 3.4 percent of the total, has risen from less than one percent a decade earlier (Children's Defense Fund, 2002).
- In 2003, 61.3 percent of American four-year-olds were enrolled in a preschool program, compared with 6.6 percent in 1965 (Hull, 2006).
- Preschoolers from white families with an income exceeding $60,000 per year were the most likely to attend some kind of preschool program (San Jose Mercury News, 2006).
- A total of 49.6 million children attended public and private schools in 2003, beating the previous high mark of 48.7 million, set in 1970, when the baby boom generation was in school.
- The majority of children under the age of six received some type of child care or education on a weekly basis, and on average spent 31 hours a week away from parents (National Center for Educational Statistics, 2005a).
- In the early part of the 21st century, minorities will comprise 49 percent of American students but just five percent of their teachers (Marx, 2001).
- More than one half of community college students are first-generation students: that is, neither of their parents attended college (Philippe, 1997).
- It is estimated that one quarter of all children aged three to nine have parents who were born out of the United States (Gadsen & Ray, 2002).
- One in five children in the United States comes from an immigrant family (Sadowski, 2004).

- Children from immigrant families are the fastest-growing segment of the U.S. population (Sadowski, 2004).

- Immigrant families are not confined to just a few states, and their populations have been rising in virtually every state. Many areas have little infrastructure to accommodate newcomer families (Sadowski, 2004).

- Children from immigrant families are more likely than their peers to live in poverty, to be behind in grade level, and to live in overcrowded housing (Sadowski, 2004).

- More than 70 percent of children from immigrant families speak a language other than English at home (Sadowski, 2004).

Child Poverty

Poverty is defined in terms of a family income failing to meet a federally established threshold, living at or below which signifies that the family lacks basic financial resources and, consequently, adequate access to food, health care, and shelter (Leventhal & Brooks-Gunn, 2002). In 2001, almost 12 million children (16 percent) lived in families where the income was at or below poverty level (U.S. Census Bureau. 2002). Poverty during early childhood often affects children's academic achievement, literacy development, and cognitive abilities to a greater degree than poverty experienced in late childhood.

Not all social scientists conclude that family income is of prime importance to child outcomes. Some consider other factors to be most important, such as a strong family work ethic, a mother's educational attainment, a mother's literacy skills, family modeling of reading and writing behaviors, authentic family uses of literacy, family beliefs and attitudes toward literacy, parents' conversational styles, family educational goals for children, and a home literacy environment that includes availability and exposure to print (Britto, Fuligni, & Brooks-Gunn, 2006). All of these are seen to influence young children's educational outcomes.

Both groups of scientists agree that children's basic physical and emotional needs must first be satisfied (see Figure 13–2). Unfortunately, this is often not the case for economically disadvantaged children, who experience more hearing problems, ear infections, dental problems, lead exposure, poor nutrition, asthma, and poor housing arrangements than other children (Rothstein, 2004).

Figure 13-2
Equipment to promote attending children's physical needs can be very important to some children's development.

Kindergartners Repeating or with Delayed Entry to School

Among children enrolled in kindergarten in the fall of 1998, about one in ten was either repeating kindergarten or had delayed entry to kindergarten (had not enrolled the year he or she became age eligible). Both groups were more likely than their on-time classmates to be male, and they were less likely to have attended preschool. Compared with those who entered on time, delayed entrants were more likely to be white and to have parents with bachelor's degrees or higher. Kindergarten repeaters were more likely than on-time entrants to have parents with something less than a high school education (U.S. Department of Education, 2002).

What do all these facts and figures say to you as a student teacher? They suggest that any teacher will need to be sensitive to the diverse circumstances of the children in her care. Many children will not come from traditional families, where both mother and father are the biological parents and live together in the home. Many more will come from homes where only one of the parents is a biological parent. Teachers will also find a number of families headed by a single mother working outside the home. When working with children, you must think twice when talking about families, and plan differently for events such as Mother's Day, Father's Day, and even Grandparent's Day. Some children may have six or more individuals in their family performing grandparent roles.

Family heads are working. The U.S. Census Bureau (2000) reports that the percentage of mothers in the workforce who had children under six more than doubled between 1970 and 2000. Almost seventy percent of all mothers were working in 2000. Close to 20 million children under the age of 13 have experienced some type of non-parent child care arrangement (National Survey of America's Families, 2002).

Where Are the Children?

Quinn (2005) notes a U.S. Census Department report, *Who's Minding the Kids?* (2005), that found that over 22 percent of working mothers had multiple child care arrangements, sometimes called *hybrid care* (see Figure 13–3). Non-parental care includes babysitters, nannies, grandparents, center-based care, preschools, prekindergartens, relatives, friends, and family care providers. Zaslow and Beck (2006) observe that children experience different forms of care as they grow older, and many children experience several types of care daily.

The National Household Education Survey (NHES), a division of the National Center for Educational Statistics (NCES) provided national estimates of the types of non-parental care experiences of children, from birth through six years, who were not yet in kindergarten (NHES, 2001). Approximately half (52 percent) of children under two were in some form of non-parental care arrangement, as compared with 74 percent of three- to six-year-olds. Not surprisingly, younger children (birth to two years) are more likely than older children (three to six years) to receive non-parental, home-based care and less likely to receive center-based care. In addition, the child care arrangements of preschool-age children are more complex than those of younger children, with just under one third of three- to six-year-olds participating in multiple-care arrangements, as compared with one fifth of children under two. Although a large number to children from birth through age six, from families of all income levels, are participating in non-parental care arrangements, there are differences across family income levels in the types of care arrangements families are using.

Every week in the United States nearly five million individuals other than parents care for and educate young children between birth and age five (Lowenstein,Ochshorn, Kagan, & Fuller, 2004).

● **Figure 13-3**
Britney and LaNeta go to a family day home when their classes end at their public school.

Factors Influencing Choice of Care

Many factors seem to influence family selection of child care, including availability. About 35 percent of all public schools in the United States offered prekindergarten classes in 2000 and 2001, and 822,000 children were enrolled (Wirt et al., 2004). Many of these were half-day programs, so many of the working parents choosing them needed additional arrangement for afternoon care. Kirp (2005) points out that middle-class families are insisting on first-rate child care and publicly supported prekindergartens. Meisels (2005) notes that suddenly everyone is interested in universal prekindergarten.

Family income, race, and the mother's educational attainment level are believed to also influence child care selection. Children with more highly educated mothers are more likely to participate in center-based early childhood programs (U.S. Department of Education, 2002). Since 1991, child centers have also experienced an increase in the number of children of mothers with something less than a high school education.

When considering whether the race of the parents influences child care choices, the U.S. Department of Education (2005a) reported that with children aged six and under, about 48 percent of Hispanic children, 60 percent of white children, and 73 percent of black children received care on a weekly basis from people other than their parents. Black infants, toddlers, and preschoolers were shown to be more likely than their white or Hispanic counterparts to experience non-parental care.

TRENDS AND ISSUES THAT AFFECT THE CAREER FIELD

Accountability

Since the mid-1990's, public funds have been used for prekindergarten pro-grams (Pianta, 2006). National surveys indicate that nearly half of all pub-lic elementary schools house a program for children under five (Clifford, Early, & Hills, 1999). With public investment, accountability has become an increasingly voiced issue. Head Start has adopted *outcome accountability assessments*. Standardized assessments and the use of *benchmark* to iden-tify child performance in publicly funded prekindergartens are common-place, because many parents are interested in knowing if prekindergarten enrollment has actually helped their child succeed. Teachers whose classes do not live up to identified outcomes are under pressure to change instruc-tional methodology.

Most educators realize that test reliability and validity at the preschool age has its limitations and dangers, particularly when children are labeled during formative years, when growth spurts occur. Test results may be sit-uation dependent and based upon English language skills. Research has supported the idea that the quality of instruction and adult-child interac-tions in early education and care programs affect child achievement and social skills. A number of states have proposed that accountability may be assessed through the direct observation of a teacher's classroom behaviors and ratings of children's classroom experiences.

Curriculum Content Standards

Roskos, Rosemary, and Varner (2006) observe:

> With title wave force, the standards movement swept into the early childhood education field at the start of the 21st century with the promise of a seamless PreK–12 continuum of cognitive development and learning linked to academic achievement.

This standards movement also includes the push for content stan-dards, which are appearing in state plans. Because teachers will have to adjust their instruction to the needs of diverse children to a greater degree than was formerly necessary, a larger number of individual learn-ing plans will be necessary to meet content standards. If high teacher/student ratios exist, or if teachers are without the necessary resources to provide individualized instruction, teachers may find content standards hard to achieve.

State-Administered and Universal Pre-K

Between 2000 and 2001, state prekindergarten (Pre–K) programs operated by a local district existed in about 19,000 elementary schools (U.S. Department of Education, 2005a). These programs differed dramatically in eligibility requirements, guidelines, children served, hours of operation, teacher qualifications, and compensation. As of 2002, 14 states offered full-day programs (Potts, Blank, & Williams, 2002). About 86 percent of teachers in state-funded programs held a bachelor's degree or higher (National Center for Educational Statistics, 2005a). Evans (2006) believes the realization of nationwide universal education is still in the future, but that the trend is certainly headed in that direction—so much so that Evans feels it appropriate to wonder whether there is or will be enough educators to meet this emergent social demand.

What does all this mean for student teachers just entering the field? More job opportunities, better compensation (in some cases the same pay as public school teachers), higher standards regarding teacher qualifications and training, a chance for increased benefits, stipends for future training, more specialized job titles, a new public image, and a hope that with all the state and federal interest in quality care, the inequities that exist for early childhood educators will, at least partially, disappear.

Elementary Schools

The majority of families in the United States select public school education for their school age children. Others, who can afford to, often select private schooling. A fairly new choice is the charter school. Some charter schools are publicly funded and others are funded privately, by businesses and corporations.

Charter Schools. Public charter schools have been exempted from some local and state regulations, to provide greater flexibility than regular public schools. They differ from one another and from regular public schools in their origins, the authority under which they are chartered, and the students they serve (U.S. Department of Education, 2005b). A public charter school can be chartered by a school district, a state board of education, a post-secondary institution, or a state chartering agency. Minnesota was the first state to establish a charter school, in 1991, followed by California.

There are several management companies operating over 800 charter schools in the United States. The Edison Project of New York has perhaps received the most publicity, but then the company was created by media entrepreneur Chris Whittle. Whittle is the sponsor of Channel One, which has brought child-oriented news and commercials into the classrooms that subscribe to the service (Guthrie, 1998).

As of the fall of 1998, there were 51 Edison Project partnerships throughout the country, and the number of charter schools has grown dramatically. Founder and chairman of the Gap clothing stores, Don Fisher, made an initial pledge of $25 million to help improve the public schools in San Francisco, if they would agree to be taken over and managed as charter schools by the Edison Project. Philadelphia transferred 42 failing city schools to private operators, including Edison Schools Incorporated, and to two nearby universities (*San Jose Mercury News*, 2002).

Some educators are noticing that family and friends want to know more about the charter movement and what educators believe concerning its quality. We recommend a visit and study of charter schools in your vicinity, so you can provide an informed opinion; also, review any current quality studies you can find. When you visit a charter school, ask if a salary schedule is available.

URBAN AND RURAL ELEMENTARY AND SECONDARY SCHOOLS-QUALITY ISSUES

A number of educators consider American education to be at a crossroads or turning point in many of its schools. Many believe a good number of urban and rural schools face difficulties which prevent them from delivering quality education. A variety of causative factors, or reasons for these schooling difficulties, have been identified by professional educators and other analysts. Suspected causative factors include the American family itself, particularly broken homes and family unemployment, children's lessening respect for parents' and teachers' authority, children's inordinate amount of time viewing various kinds of media, children's lack of English and literacy knowledge, parent neglect, and other home characteristics. Also commonly mentioned is the reality of a decline in the quality of life in some American cities, the lack of adequate school funding, burned-out school staffs, and inept administrators, principals, and school boards. Other causative factors include inadequate housing, decaying neighborhoods, lawlessness, drug-infested communities, crumbling school facilities, and a general, pervasive lethargy or lack of pride in environmental surroundings.

Children can arrive at urban, rural, or any other school in the country, unruly, rebellious, without family support of education, with a history of health or physical problems, hungry, without hope, love, or motivation, and with a myriad of other problems promoted by unwholesome living situations and poverty. Communities with the conditions described above usually have a greater number of hurting children. Some families, through force of will, determination, their attitude toward education, and by other means, have overcome limiting conditions to raise children who have escaped what has negatively affected other neighborhood children. These children cope and succeed in school.

Teachers in these poor quality schools may range from energetic reformists—excellent educators who struggle to improve conditions—to apathetic or tired educators, long before beaten down by their teaching loads and lack of support.

Fingers point in all directions when poor schooling exists, and individuals and groups place blame on school administrators, parents, federal, state, or local government funding levels, teachers, teacher training institutions, even the children. This encourages few successful solutions. Educational researchers and policymakers have developed and distributed countless reports and position papers. Government and community leaders, though concerned, have found few solutions for many schools. Some people argue that current legislation may work, and to give it time, and others are not so certain. Educators entering the field are sure to be involved as key players in any improvements or turnarounds that occur.

School-Age Programs

Before- and after-school child care programs are a viable and growing phenomenon. They developed during the mid and late 1970s and blossomed in the 1980s and 1990s. The demand has grown in proportion to the number of employed family members. School-age child care is seen as a regular program, designed for children ages five to twelve, during the times when school is not in session and parents are working, such as before and after school and on school holidays.

Busing is frequently supplied, for children to be transported from their elementary school to another facility, but usually children stay on the grounds of the school they attend. Student teachers occasionally are given student teaching placements in school-age care programs.

After-school programs are specifically designed for kindergartners through fifth graders after they have completed their academic day (see Figure 13–4). Many children above the fifth grade are involved in extracurricular activities that finish later in the day, closer to the time an adult would return home from work. Some families believe these older children are able to fend for themselves at home, so these kids return to empty houses to do chores, homework, or play. These **latchkey children**, as they are sometimes called, may also care for younger siblings. An estimated two to six million school-age children are left at home without adult supervision before and after school, and there seems no end to the pressing and increasing need for low-fee, quality school-age programs.

In a 2001 study of before and after-school programs, the NCES estimated that five percent of children in their representative sample (children in kindergarten through grade eight) had regularly scheduled care (Child Care Bulletin, 2005). The NCES study noted that after-school program activities included art, reading and writing, outdoor play activities and sports, television, video games, music activities, and homework and related educational activities.

Many states are revising their school-age care licensing regulations, and thirteen states have regulations with written standards (Child Care Bulletin, 2005). A University of California at Irvine study concludes California's after-school programs could result in state tax dollar savings equal to or greater than the cost of the program itself. These savings would be realized because of less holding back of children, and repeating of grades, and fewer students enrolled in summer school classes to avoid grade retention (Becker, 2005).

latchkey children— school-aged children who, after school, return to an empty home because their parents are at work.

◉ Figure 13-4
A variety of activities may be available in after-school programs.

Those responsible for school-age programs sometimes struggle to recruit, train, and retain staff. Staff problems can be complicated by a reliance on volunteers, use of split-shift staffing schedules, short program hours, and lack of staff preparation and training opportunities (Child Care Bulletin, 2005).

School-age programs are often good employment choices for teachers-in-training who wish to eventually work in elementary school systems, or for teachers or college education majors who want part-time work. If attached to a public school system, higher than average hourly compensation and some benefits may be available.

Quality in After-School Programs. Because other organizations operate after-school programs besides public schools, there are issues related to quality. The principal issue is whether or not the program meets state licensing standards. Your college supervisor may want to apprise you of your own state's regulations for the before- and after-school care of elementary school children. Some facilities may be exempt from meeting state standards, and may only have to meet the standards of the organization to which they belong.

Growing evidence shows that after-school programs can have significant academic and social benefits, particularly when programs supplement material learned during the regular school day with skills training and recreational activities (Harvard Education Letter, 2002).

Homeschooling

Over 850,000 children nationwide are homeschooled (Toppo, 2001). About one fifth of these children were also enrolled in public or private schools part time. Of all American students, 2.25 percent were homeschooled in the spring of 2003 (U.S. Department of Education, 2005b). About 75 percent of these children were white, and their parents had higher levels of educational attainment than did parents of children enrolled in other types of schools.

The most common reasons parents cited for choosing to homeschool, according to *Homeschooling in the United States: 1999* (U.S. Department of Education, 2001), were parents' beliefs that a better education could be provided at home, faith-based education would not take place in other schools, character and morality development would suffer, poor local schools were unable to deliver quality experiences, family circumstances would not allow other school attendance, transportation was problematic, public school curriculum was limited, accessible schools were not challenging, their child's special needs included behavior problems, and they could not afford private schooling.

Homeschooling families sometimes hire others to provide educational lessons and activities. This includes tutors and specialists in subject matter and study areas such as music, art, mathematics, science, and sports.

Child Abuse Prevention Programs

Earlier in this chapter, facts and figures concerning child abuse in America were cited. Here we will briefly describe reporting particulars, and what is considered to be an *evolving curriculum*, whose goals include preventing abuse before it happens.

To whom do you report abuse? Child protective services and law enforcement agencies receive reports and investigate them. Generally, if abuse does not appear to be life threatening, CPS is called. If, however, the child seems in immediate danger, a law enforcement agency is usually notified because only they can legally remove a child from parental custody.

One caveat here: Professionals and teachers need to be aware of the cultural values and ethnic differences in families of attending children. Newly arrived families may not be aware of abuse laws and may continue to use corporal punishment or other harsh disciplinary practices, or health practices deemed appropriate in their country of origin.

It is usual for a team of school or center staff members to determine through investigation if reporting is necessary. You may have seen this happen at your placement site. Your training may also have covered the protective factors known to correlate with reductions in child abuse and neglect cases. After an intensive research study, conducted in 2003 by the Center for the Study of Social Policy (2006), reduction factors were identified:

- increasing and bolstering parent resilience and social connectedness
- providing knowledge of parenting skill and child development
- providing concrete support in times of need
- promoting the social and emotional competence of children

Early childhood, primary school, and high schools may have long-standing programs using preventive strategies to purposefully facilitate parent friendships and mutual support activities. These include sponsoring parenting classes, outings, and advisory and support groups.

Centers and schools reach out to parents, siblings, and extended family. Efforts are made to strengthen existing parenting skills and to provide information on child-rearing issues selected by participants. Many early childhood programs promote and provide child observation opportunities by changing a classroom's design or by using technology that allows parents to view and then discuss children's behaviors with staff. Parents see how staff respond to behaviors effectively. Centers must also be quick to recognize and support families faced with illness, job loss, housing problems, and other situations, by providing information and referral services and links to networks in the community. Some centers employ family support workers and a mental health consultant. They also attempt to develop an ongoing relationship with child protective services personnel, to ensure child safety and parent access to needed services. Jobs for educators are growing in this area, sponsored by a wide variety of organizations other than public schools.

Obesity Prevention Curriculum

Anderson (2006) points out that since the 1980's, the number of overweight children in the United States has more than tripled, and children are in child programs more hours than ever before. Consequently, more meals and snacks occur at school, and more hours are available to participate in physical exercise. Obesity is often the result of lack of physical activity, poor eating habits, making poor food choices, lack of adult models who display proper eating habits and active lifestyles, and children spending more time inert, before media screens.

Early childhood centers and primary schools are developing obesity prevention curriculums that attempt to educate both children and families. A number of strategies are used. The first strategy is to change the structure of elements under the staff's control. These elements included monitoring food service, providing easy access to water throughout the day, and examining the school's curriculum to increase children's physical activity if necessary. Teachers then team with families, by involving them in school food choices, through discussion of child nutrition and fitness, alerting parents' to their role in modeling food behaviors and choices, and discussing the dangers of long periods of passive media viewing.

For the first time in U.S. history, children are unlikely to live as long as their parents, or enjoy the same quality of life. Effective intervention programs involving families, educators, and children are critical because childhood obesity has become an epidemic (Huettig, et al., 2006).

Second Language Teaching

Consider the data given earlier, taken from U.S. Census reports, for it highlights the cultural and linguistic diversity of America's school-age population.

A future teacher has a good chance of being a second language instructor at some time in his or her career. If you speak a second language, this will be an advantage when teaching children with that native language. Your school district or other employers will be searching for individuals with cultural knowledge and linguistic skill. A greater volume and variety of positions will be offered, especially if you obtain specialist credentials.

Asian Students

Researchers are looking closely at figures that show a steady climb in the enrollment of Asian students from immigrant families in institutions of higher education. In 2006, Asian students accounted for 36 percent of entering freshmen in California's public universities (Krieger & Fernandez, 2006). For the first time, Asian students outnumbered other ethnic groups at the University of California at Berkeley. Factors promoting this trend include Asian students' strong performance in high school. Deborah Reed (2006) believes another factor influencing Asian students' academic achievement is the fact that Asian students are more likely to have a college educated parent, and books and computers are usually found in their homes. Asian families tend to expect their children to attend college, as do many other parents, from all ethnic backgrounds. Reed notes that Asian families seem to be more knowledgeable about both preparing and applying for college admission.

Vaden-Kiernan and McManus (2005) pointed out that the percentage of students—in kindergarten through grade twelve—whose parents reported taking them to a public library in the previous month was higher for Asians (65 percent) than for other races. This alone does not account for Asian students' school success, but it may be an indicator of Asian parent engagement in the education of their children.

Children's Media Usage

Neergaard (2006) notes a 2003 Henry J. Kaiser Family Foundation study, which found that children under the age of six averaged an hour and

58 minutes a day spent using some type of screen media, compared to 48 minutes of reading or being read to. Twenty-six percent of parents in the study reported using screen media activities as a reward for good behavior.

Student teachers need to become book and reading salespeople and advocates, who can effectively sell the idea of early literacy and the benefits of reading books to the families of children. To do so teachers must cite research, share techniques and strategies, and transfer their passion for both books and reading. Each home may have unique circumstances that inhibit attaching pleasure to reading. Finding and circumventing family obstacles is gaining increased importance with thoughtful teachers. Teachers will somehow have to destroy the myth that television programs, videos, and computer activities are superior to reading activities, while promoting the use of quality software that parents and children can discuss to expand reading ability.

Computers and Young Children

There has been much interest in computers and software development for early childhood. As Alexander (2001) pointed out, while school districts are spending huge sums on training adults to speak the language of computers, young children are growing up computer literate (see Figure 13–5). Companies are creating effects on color television screens with voice prompts, musical sounds, and clever picture forms, and have developed simple keyboards. As screen happenings are shared and discussed, child interest and motivation increases.

Contrary to the popular belief that children would become isolated, sitting in their separate cubicles, working at a computer, this has not been the case. You frequently find two or even three children playing or working with any given program.

● **Figure 13-5**
One child often serves as another's guide and consultant.

Haugland (2000), an advocate for early childhood computer use, suggested that when used effectively, computers make an excellent learning tool, imparting to children knowledge and skills far beyond expectations. She believes *how* they are used to be more important than *if* they are used:

> Computers clearly have a powerful influence on children, and thus how we use them is especially important. To integrate computers and maximize children's learning, four steps are critical: selecting developmental software, selecting developmental Web sites, integrating these resources into the curriculum, and selecting computers to support these learning experiences.

Violence in Society Drives Curriculum Development

Early childhood activity planning that promotes kindness and nonviolent problem solving is a curriculum offering that is gaining increased acceptance as a necessary offering. Child activities that emphasize love, empathy, gentleness, respect, friendship, responsibility, self-control, and conflict resolution are valued. Rice (1996) noted the following:

> During the last thirty years, our educational system has shied away from teaching right and wrong because of a view that doing so would restrict personal freedom. Unfortunately, this lack of emphasis on basic values coupled with the stressing of rights over responsibilities has helped produce a less kind and less gentle society.

As a first step, a quality program strives to ensure that children feel safe and loved. Teachers model a peace-loving nature, an ability to calm themselves, and an ability to resolve problems reasonably in their daily interactions. They prevent children from becoming victims of violence in their classroom. Although anger is a normal feeling, teachers believe children can learn to manage it and understand that there are ways to express it that are okay and not okay.

Levin (2003) suggests that there are many ways to create a peaceable classroom. She includes standard ideas, such as teaching conflict resolution and an appreciation of diversity, but also stresses building a sense of safety and community. As a student teacher you may have watched your cooperating teacher attempt to teach through daily interactions, as most all teachers do, but planned activities in this curricular area may not have been undertaken.

Educators Searching For Employment

Feller (2005) reported that 40 percent of America's teachers plan to leave teaching by 2010, and 42 percent of teachers currently practicing their craft are age 50 or older.

Teachers who entered the field during the baby boom years are now retiring. Simon (2005) estimated that a half million teachers will be needed before 2010 (see Figure 13–6). Some teachers in urban school districts have become disillusioned and have left teaching. Still others, especially in the shortage areas of mathematics and science, never take teaching jobs as private industry and other businesses pay substantially more than teaching.

Recruiting Efforts for Elementary School Teachers. To meet what is already a shortage in many districts, some districts encourage paraprofessionals to acquire their teaching credential, and some districts help with financing and adjusted work hours. Other districts have attracted retiring military personnel, especially those trained in one of the sciences, or in mathematics.

Programs involved in recruiting and training teachers are Teach for America, Troops to Teachers, Recruiting New Teachers, and Pathways to Teaching Careers. At the high school level, Phi Delta Kappa sponsors the Future Educators of America (FEA). Like the Future Teachers of America, FEA sponsors an annual summer camp and has a scholarship program.

Suryaraman (2005) reported that California school districts are hiring overseas teachers because their recruitment efforts in the United States have failed. The Philippines, Canada, and some European countries have supplied teachers, with specialties in mathematics, music, special education, science, bilingual Spanish, middle school French, Japanese, and Mandarin. Suryaraman estimates as many as 15,000 elementary, middle, and high school teachers from abroad now work in the United States on temporary work visas. Over the next decade, the pressure on schools to hire from abroad is expected to intensify as teachers retire.

Simon (2005) noted that 500,000 new teachers have been hired in elementary and secondary school classrooms in the past 5 years. Career changers—post baccalaureate degree and mid-career job switchers—are the biggest trend in education employment, with 70,000 entering the profession in the last two years. These "second-act" educators are filling teacher positions, and 47 states and the District of Columbia have created 122 alternative routes to teacher certification.

◉ **Figure 13-6**
Many more teachers will be needed as older teachers retire.

Fredix (2006) researched U.S. Bureau of Labor Statistics, which listed occupations with the largest projected job growth in the United States for 2004–2014. Post-secondary teachers, Fredix found, placed third, following retail salespeople and registered nurses.

From the information provided so far it is easy to see that certain specialties and teaching skills are in short supply, especially in certain geographic locations. Do not overlook using library references to investigate an area's economic growth, housing, and quality of life when considering employment options.

Relocating to areas of high population growth, or to areas in the path of progress, will afford more opportunity and more job openings, but one must investigate to discern credential requirements. The Internet will aid your search but it is beneficial to first become familiar with your college's career center. Sarnoff (2005) points out that campus career centers differ in the services they provide, but most will provide search help and suggestions, resume development, counseling, a Web site for posting and upgrading your resume, and a search library. Many career centers hold job fairs, and some have staff members who work exclusively with alumni and have the ability to put you in touch with alumni living in the geographic area where you are searching. Campus career centers may also schedule meetings with recruiters.

If you are searching for job announcements, the following are the most common places to find them: professional teaching association Web sites, school district's and county education office's human resources departments, and newspaper advertisements (most of which are available on the Internet). A personal visit is always best, but contact via the Internet can also be successful.

You will want to list and examine your skills and abilities thoroughly before submitting an application or creating a cover letter or resume. What you submit needs to be perfect or near perfect to gain the attention you wish. "The better the job, the more the competition" is a general rule of thumb. When you are really in touch with your skills, abilities, talents, accomplishments, qualifications, and experience, the more effectively and convincingly you will be able to describe them in person or on paper. If you have a professional portfolio and letters of reference, these will aid you. If you are making phone calls to unearth job openings or get an interview, practice what you will say beforehand. Your goals are to sound professional while speaking with a friendly ease as you make your first impression.

Many times you will be able find out specific hiring information about the employer, such as whether they will keep your application on file when there are no openings. If applying in person, carry along everything you will need to fill an application. In most cases, you should ask to take the application with you, so you have time to study it, figure out what the employer is looking for, and tailor both the application or your resume to highlight how you match what the employer desires. This involves fact finding, and a smart job applicant takes the time and makes the effort to know as much as possible about the employer's operation. Fact finding includes looking at the job site, neighborhood, and community. Some schools will allow a school tour.

All materials submitted need to be attractive, neat, businesslike, and honest—no truth-stretching or omissions—printed in an easy to read font, on appropriate paper stock, in an acceptable format, using current educational and occupational terms. It is crucial that any submissions be grammatically correct with no misspellings. Libraries, bookstores, and the Internet are the best resources for books on resume writing, and computer programs are plentiful. Our *Online Companion* has a few resumes for you to examine and offers additional tips. Most resources will tell you to adapt your resume to the specific job you seek.

There is definitely an art to interviewing, and practice interviewing is recommended. Interview questions can be direct or situational, and many will be asked by a committee of diverse individuals connected to the school's operation. It pays to do whatever you can to feel relaxed and confident; whether that means a new haircut or new shoes, it is worth the investment. Dress to fit in, rather than catering to the latest style. Appearing well groomed, articulate, professionally skilled, and personable is your objective; being likeable is a real plus. Contained in the *Online Companion* are suggested interview questions to practice.

Will Ethnicity or Gender Matter to Employers?

Herrera-Malone (2005) reported that U.S. companies have finally seen the profit in creating a workforce that looks like their clients and customers. This has been true in many school districts and early childhood programs for a long time, yet there is still considerable need for minority teachers, in light of the ethnicity of the public school student population in the United States (see Figure 13–7). The U.S. Department of Education, in 2000, noted that public elementary school students were 61 percent white but their teachers were 84 percent white. African American students accounted for 17 percent of the student population in public schools, but African American teachers made up only 8 percent of the public school teacher workforce; Hispanic teachers accounted for only 6 percent of teachers, although 16 percent of public school students were Hispanic. The answer to the question of whether or not ethnicity is important is yes; a job seeker from a minority background will possibly find a school district actively seeking to balance their staff, but they will also be searching for the person with the best qualifications.

Nelson (2002) found that the number of males teaching in the field of early education had not changed much since 1979. The U.S. Bureau of Labor Statistics (2005) reported that about 5 percent of child care workers are male and about 2 percent of those are preschool and kindergarten teachers (see Figure 13–7). Men comprise about 9 percent of all public elementary teachers. Male job applicants with ECE degrees, though eagerly sought by most schools and centers, do occasionally encounter interviewers who are suspicious and feel that men are less able to care for and educate young children. During job interviews, male applicants may ask about policies concerning teacher-child physical contact and bathroom supervision, to probe employer's attitudes and policies. Sometimes a double standard exists in these areas. As with minority applicants, qualifications are what matter most.

 Figure 13-7
Many schools search for staff members from the same ethnic group as their enrolled students.

Employment Trends Affecting Early Childhood Educators

Early childhood educators currently looking for work are bound to be surprised by the diverse sponsorship of child care and development programs. Traditionally, educational institutions, charitable and faith-based organizations, the federal government, a small number of industrial employers, and a large number of private, profit-making schools funded, supported, and/or operated facilities that offered the bulk of educational and custodial care for young children. Currently, new sponsors are appearing, including city, municipal, and state governments, hospitals and other health care facilities, an increased number of business and industrial employers, and recreational centers. These newer facilities are in new locations, such as adjacent to health care facilities and rehabilitation centers, discovery centers, city parks, municipal gardens, arboretums, zoos, art centers, community centers, senior housing centers, and business complexes. Child centers formerly found in neighborhoods close to children's homes or near family employment may now be located in urban storefronts, in skyscrapers with terrace or rooftop play yards, in converted warehouses and factories, and even in mobile vans.

There has been a recent proliferation of specialty schools and programs that focus upon a narrow curricular agenda. Dance, music, and other single-emphasis, sport-skill schools, such as for swimming, skating, and skiing, have existed in some areas for a long time, but now they offer instruction to younger children. Families can often find schools that focus on computers, etiquette, arts and crafts, early academic tutoring, cultural and foreign language studies, acrobatics and gymnastics, martial arts, and yoga, among other types of instruction and training for the very young.

Parent-on-the-premises care, often called *drop-in* care, is growing, with centers in large retail stores or malls, restaurants, recreational and sports complexes, cruise ships, casinos, spas, ski lodges, tennis centers, and bowling alleys.

Where to Search

Besides investigating non-traditional places to find work, early childhood educators will discover an increasing number of very different job titles in job announcements, advertisements, and on Internet job listings. Jobs will involve direct service to children, or will be indirect support and administrative positions; public, for-profit, and non-profit sponsors; full-year, partial-year, full-day, or part-time opportunities. Seasonal work and armed services child program positions are also available, as well as overseas work. Self-employment can be another possibility; many self-employed early childhood educators operate a business that offers a service or product for children, families, centers, and schools.

Family Home Providers

Some ECE majors start their training with job experience working in a family provider's home, and are well aware of this type of employment. Other students are relatively unaware of this type of child care (see Figure 13–8).

Most students do not realize that two thirds of all workers in the early education field are self-employed, and that the majority of these are family child care providers (Krantz, 2002). Many make a good living, and their business is profitable. Unfortunately, a good number of people think these providers have no formal training, but this not the case: about 13 percent of these providers have college degrees; an estimated 11 percent have not graduated from high school, and the remaining 76 percent fall somewhere between these two extremes, in educational attainment. Trawick-Smith and Lambert (1995) noted that family day home providers suffer from an image problem, and may be the least respected of all educators.

Where to Start

Networking with family, friends, and professional colleagues seems to be more successful, and many jobs are secured through personal contacts. Let people know you are available for work and ask their advice concerning strategies rather than directly asking for a job. As previously mentioned, local professional association membership is invaluable. Resumes are still necessary, and wording used should reflect terminology common to the field. Cover letters sent with resumes can unearth openings and should interest readers enough to inspire them to want to know more. Cover letters and resumes represent you; both should be written with attention to detail and should display your professionalism. The *Online Companion*, located at http://www.earlychilded.delmar.com, shows a few examples. It might also be beneficial to work up a short opening or conversation starter that quickly tells a job recruiter who you are and what you have to offer; so you are prepared to attend job fairs and meet potential employers.

○ **Figure 13-8**
Family day homes can look similar to care center facilities.

 QUESTIONS MANY GRADUATES ASK FOLLOW. ANSWERS ARE IN PARENTHESES.

- Should I bring a portfolio to an interview? (It is best if the employer has a chance to see it beforehand. Ask about this when you are invited to interview. You should review it yourself before submitting it because interviewers may ask questions about portfolio contents during the interview.)
- When should I ask about salary? (You can ask if a salary schedule is available once you have been asked to interview, or ask when a job has been offered. Many employers tend to probe what salaries have previously been received. Have in mind a range rather than a fixed figure.)
- Can I ask questions during an interview? (Of course, but ask only what you really want to know.)
- Should I negotiate salary when a job offer is made? (Most professionals do this, and it is easier to raise your salary at this time than it will be later. Negotiating rarely jeopardizes the job, as the employer has usually already decided they want you.)
- What is the worst error I can make during an interview? (Badmouthing a former employer is a big one. This makes interviewers uneasy. Most interviewers, who know the early childhood field, know there are many valid reasons for leaving past employment, including unethical employers and poorly functioning programs.)

⊙SUMMARY

Many factors affecting American families and, consequently, early childhood educators were discussed in this chapter, including family's diverse child care arrangements and choices for children's care and schooling. State and federally funded prekindergarten programs, charter schools, school-age programs, and homeschooling were given attention. Poverty, abuse, child obesity, and children's media and computer use came under scrutiny.

An attempt was made to inform readers about career realities that can influence future work in the education field. Changes impacting educators were highlighted.

The employment of early childhood, elementary, and secondary educators was discussed. Search strategies alerted job seekers to the growing and diverse employment opportunities that exist, and the authors provided both suggestions and tips.

⊙HELPFUL WEB SITES

http://www.actagainstviolence.org
ACT Against Violence Project. Learn about a public service advertising campaign that supports adults and children working against violence.

http://www.childrenandcomputers.com
Children and Computers. Investigate descriptions of publishers and prices of developmental software.

http://www.esrnational.org
Educators for Social Responsibility. Readings concerning educational issues are available.

http://www.home-ed-magazine.com
Home Education Magazine. Select *homeschooling* as a search word.

http://www.ibm.com
IBM. Search *KidSmart*. A multimedia guide to computers and early learning is available online, and answers questions regarding computer use to support learning.

http://www.nccp.org
The National Center for Children in Poverty. Search for a publication titled *Ready to enter: What research tells policymakers about strategies to promote social and emotional school readiness among three-and four-year-old children.*

http://www.nieer.org
National Institute for Early Education Research. Working papers, newsletter, events, research, and information are available.

http://www.cssp.org
Center for the Study of Social Policy. Search grants and projects in progress. Check the index.

http://www.naaweb.org
National After-School Association. Click on *Accreditation.*

http://www.emurse.com
Emurse. Provides help for student teachers in preparing and distributing resumes.

http://www.craigslist.org
Craigslist. Check jobs listed, by city and state.

http://www.menteach.org
Men Teach. Information helpful for male teachers may be found here.

http://www.reading.org
International Reading Association. Visit the career center.

http://www.thewomensalliance.org
Women's Alliance. Assists women with career skills and provides interview clothing.

http://www.childcareexchange.com
Child Care Exchange. Click on *Job Opportunities.*

http://www.DirectEmployers.com
Job Central National Labor Exchange. Use key words *educational institutions, teaching,* and *child care.*

http://www.CalWestEducators.com
Cal West Educators. Job listings are available.

http://www.jobs.caeyc.org
California Association for the Education of Young Children. See what one state professional association offers job seekers.

http://www.worldteach.org
World Teach. Overseas employment opportunities are available.

http://www.teachwave.com
Teachwave. A free job posting and search service for K–12 can be found here.

http://www.teachforamerica.org
Teach for America. Provides information on improving outcomes for children living in poverty.

http://www.pdkintl.org
Phi Delta Kappa. Provides information on a variety of topics of interest to professional educators.

http://www.wallacefoundation.org
Pathways to Teaching Careers. This site offers information on teaching careers.

http://www.ed.gov/programs/troops
Troops to Teachers. Provides information for retired military personnel interested in teaching careers.

Additional resources for this chapter can be found by visiting the Online Companion at www.earlychilded.delmar.com.

SUGGESTED READINGS

Grant, C., & Murray, C (1999). *Teaching in America: The slow revolution*. Cambridge, MA: Harvard University Press.

Machado, J. M., & Reynolds, R. E. (2006). *Employment opportunities in education: How to secure your career*. Clifton Park, NY: Delmar Learning.

Sadowski, M. (Ed.). (2004). *Teaching immigrant and second-language students: Strategies for success*. Cambridge, MA: Harvard Education Press.

SUGGESTED ACTIVITIES

A. Make your own list of current issues in early childhood teaching. In groups of three to five, arrange your lists in order of their importance for young children's education and welfare in the United States. Share and compare results with the group.

B. Read an article on a trend or issue in early childhood education (ECE), ECE teaching, or ECE programs. Seek help from library staff to locate articles in the *Current Index to Journals in Education* or ERIC, or some other resource to locate one. On a separate sheet, provide the following information to review the article:
1. title of article
2. author(s)
3. journal or publication name
4. date of publication
5. page numbers
6. general parameters and findings of the study or article, including number of subjects, ages, testing devices or procedures, results, key ideas, points, or conclusions
7. your reactions

C. With a team of four classmates, investigate the funding of preschool programs with federal or state funds in your state. Try to obtain the following:
1. Who administers funds for state-sponsored preschools?
2. Are programs licensed? Are they accredited?
3. What are teacher qualifications?
4. Are reimbursement rates different if preschools are accredited or judged to be of excellent quality?
5. Do written guidelines exist for state preschool programs?
6. Is state public money given to private, profit-making schools for child care?

7. What are the qualifications necessary for parents who wish to enroll a child? Do parents pay fees?

8. Are state or federal funds used to enhance teacher compensation or benefits? Report your findings to the group.

D. Research the ERIC Clearinghouse on Elementary and Early Childhood Education's Web site {http://www.ericeece.org}. ERIC is a nationwide system funded by the National Institute of Education and contains a vast storehouse of information, on all aspects of early childhood education. Print out an article of concern to you. Report your findings to your training group.

E. Share three pieces of job hunting or interviewing advice that you believe would help an education or ECE graduate. Example: Start your job search a few months before you graduate. Share with the group.

◉REVIEW

A. List five current debatable trends or issues affecting families or the ECE field.

B. Describe briefly what you feel should be public policy on child care for young children in the United States. Include children living in poverty and immigrant children.

C. Why might it be a good time to graduate and enter a career in ECE or some other segment of the education field? List your main ideas (at least four).

CASE SCENARIO

Setting: Suzanne, the daughter of an elementary school teacher, was enrolled in a small, private preschool in a suburban neighborhood, with about eighteen children in attendance. Suzanne, an older four-year-old, had attended for over a year.

Suzanne enjoyed activities, particularly music and art, and books were a favorite choice. She was often found in the book loft with pals, pretending to read, laughing, and pointing to illustrations. Able to read a few words, she delighted in sharing these with her teachers. Active in the play yard, she was a sought-after playmate, easily enticing others with her creative play games. Suzanne's mother asked for a conference and described a troubling behavior Suzanne had displayed at home. Suzanne had been stung by a bee a few months earlier, and since had become hysterical at times, screaming, "It's on me! Get it off!" while flailing and flapping her arms as if to remove a bee.

The staff developed a plan of action, contingent on Suzanne experiencing an episode at school. Teachers would remain calm and protect Suzanne and others from harm or distress by gently moving her to a quiet area if possible. When Suzanne quieted, staff

continues . . .

. . . continued

would say something calming, like "I don't see any bees on you, Suzanne," or "There are no bees flying around you," or something similar.

Fortunately, Suzanne was alone with a student teacher when she became highly agitated, trying to slap imaginary bees. The student teacher waited, showing no excitement, and acted as a calm observer. As Suzanne quieted, the student teacher said, "There really aren't any bees. This is a game, isn't it?" Suzanne answered, "My mother thinks there are bees." Suzanne then walked off to play with others.

Questions for Discussion:

1. Do you feel the staff and student teacher listened seriously to the parent's concern?

2. What next step(s) should the staff undertake?

3. How would you describe the student teacher's handling of Suzanne?

4. What might have happened if the student teacher had not had prior knowledge of Suzanne's behavior at home?

REFERENCES

Alexander, P. (2001, Summer). Young children bridge the digital divide. *State Education Leader*, 19(2), 7–8.

Anderson, J. (2006, May/June). A comprehensive approach to addressing child obesity in early childhood programs. *Exchange*, (169), 41–45.

Author. (2005, Summer). Staffing and professional development in programs serving school-age children. *Child Care Bulletin*, 29, 11.

Becker, B. (2005, Summer). California's after-school program: Fighting crime by investing in kids. *The Child Care Bulletin*, 29, 14.

Birckmayer, J., Cohen, J., Jensen, I. D., & Variano, D. A. (2005, May). Supporting grandparents who raise grandchildren. *Young Children*, 69(3), 100–104.

Britto, P. R., Fuligni, A. S., & Brooks-Gunn, J. (2006). Reading ahead: Effective interventions for young children's early literacy development. In D. K.Dickinson and S. B. Neuman (Eds.), *Handbook of early literacy research*, 2, (pp. 311–322). New York: The Guilford Press.

Center for the Study of Social Policy. (2006). *Strengthening families through early care and education*. Washington, DC: Author.

Children's Defense Fund. (2002). *The state of children in America's union*: A 2002 action guide to leave no child behind. Washington, DC: Author.

Clifford, R. M., Early, D. M., & Hills, T. W. (1999). Almost a million children in school before kindergarten: Who is responsible for early childhood services? *Young Children*, 54(5), 48–51.

Evans, V. J. (2006). Economic perspectives on early care and education. In M. Zaslow and I. Martinez-Beck (Eds.), *Critical issues in early childhood professional development* (pp. 309–312). Baltimore, MD: Paul Brookes Publishing Co.

Feller, B. (2005, August 18). 40% of teachers plan to quit by 2010. *Chicago Sun Times*, P12. Retrieved September 6, 2005 from http://www.suntimes. com/output/education/cst-nws-teach.html.

Fredix, E. (2006, September 7). Firms look to avoid labor shortage. *Idaho Statesman*, 3B.

Gadsden, V., & Ray, A. (2002, November). Engaging fathers: Issues and considerations for early childhood educators. *Young Children*, 57(6), 32–45.

Guthrie, J. (1998, October 18). The fisher king. *San Francisco Examiner*.

Harvard Education Letter. (2002, November 19). Schools supplement curricula with after school programs: Author.

Haugland, S. W. (2000, January). Early childhood classrooms in the 21st century: Using computers to maximize learning. *Young Children, 55*(1), 12–18.

Herrera-Malone, A. In Solis, D. (2005, June 19). Diversity slowly seeps into corporate America. *Idaho Statesman,* 1CB.

Huettig, C., Rich, S., Engelbrecht, J., Sanborn, C., Essery, E., DiMarco, N., Velez, L., & Levy, L. (2006. May). Growing with ease: Eating activity, and self-esteem. *Young Children, 61*(3), 26–30.

Hull, D. (2006, February 12). Should California pay for preschool? *San Jose Mercury News,* 1A, 12–13A.

Jayson, S. (2006, July 12). Society switches focus away from children. USA Today, 1D.Kirp, D. L. (2005, July 31). All my children. *The New York Times,* E7.

Krantz, L. (2002). *Jobs rated almanac* (5th Ed.). New York: St. Martin's Press.

Krieger, L. M., & Fernandez, L. (2006, April 20). Asians surpass mark at UC. *San Jose Mercury News,* 1A, 17A.

Ladson-Billings, G. (2003). *Beyond the big house: African American educators on teacher education.* New York: Teachers College Press.

Levin, D. E. (2003). *Teaching young children in violent times: Building a peaceable classroom* (2nd Ed.). Cambridge, MA: Educators for Social Responsibility.

Leventhal, T., & Brooks-Gunn, J. (2002). Poverty and child development *International encyclopedia of social and behavioral sciences, 3*(14), 11889-11893.

Lowenstein, A. E., Ochshorn, S., Kagan, S. L., & Fuller, B. (2004, March). Report #2: The effects of professional development efforts and compensation on the quality of early care and education services. *Child Care and Early Education, National* Conference of State Legislature, #6164–0002.

Marx, G. (2001, May). 10 trends for tomorrow's kid. *Education Digest, 66*(9), 5–10.

National Center for Education Statistics. (2001). *National household education survey: Early childhood program participation.* Washington, DC: Institute of Education Sciences, U. S. Department of Education.

National Center for Education Statistics. (2005, November). *Child care and early education arrangements of infants, toddlers, and preschoolers: 2001.* Washington, DC: U.S. Department of Education.

National Survey of America's Families. (2002). *Assessing the new federalism.* Washington, DC: Urban Institute.

Neergaard, L. (2006, May 25). Parents turn small fry on to the small screen. *Idaho Statesman,* 18 M.

Nelson, B.G. (2002). *The importance of men teachers and why there are so few.* Minneapolis, MN: Men in Child Care and Elementary Education Project.

National Institute of Child Health and Human Development, Early Childhood Child Care Research Network(2001). Non-maternal care and family factors in early development: An overview of the NICHD study of early child care. *Journal of Applied Developmental Psychology, 22*(5), 457–492.

Philippe, K. A. (1997). *National profile of community colleges: Trends and statistics.* Washington, DC: American Association of Community Colleges.

Pianta, R. C. (2006). Standardized observation and professional development. In M. Zaslow & I. Martinez-Beck (Eds.), *Critical issues in early childhood professional development* (pp. 231-254). Baltimore, MD: Paul H. Brookes Publishing Co.

Potts, A., Blank, R., & Williams, A. (2002). *Key state education policies on PK–12 education: 2002.* [Results from the 2002 Council of Chief State School Officerspolicies and practices survey]. Washington, DC: Council of Chief State School Officers.

Quinn, M. (2005, November 10). Juggling child care providers. *San Jose Mercury News,* 1B–2B.

Rice, J. A. (1996). *The kindness curriculum: Introducing children to loving values.* St. Paul, MN: Redleaf Press.

Riche, M. F. (2000). America's diversity and growth: Signposts for the 21st century. *Population Bulletin, 55*(2), 1–43. Washington, DC: Population Reference Bureau.

Roskos, K., Rosemary, C. A., & Varner, M. H. (2006). Alignment in educator preparation for early and beginning literacy instruction. In M Zaslow and I. Martinez-Beck (Eds.), *Critical issues in early childhood professional development* (pp. 255–279). Baltimore, MD: Paul Brookes Publishing Co.

Rothstein, R. (2004). *Class and school.* New York: Teacher's College Press.

Sadowski, M. (Ed.). (2004). Teaching immigrant and second-language students: Strategies for success. Cambridge, MA: Harvard Education Press. (2002, April 18). 42 failing Philadelphia schools to be privatized. *San Jose Mercury News,* 5A.

San Jose Mercury News (2006, February12). Analysis of data from the 2000 Census. *San Jose Mercury News,* 1A, 12–13A.

Sarnoff, A. P, (2005, June 2). Alumni turn to alma mater. *USA Today,* D1, 3.

Simon, C. C. (2005, July 31). Those who can, and can't. *New York Times.* Retrieved from http://www. nytimes.com/2005/07/31.html?ex=1126152000Ben=8 16c1c82bcab7086Bei=5070 July 31, 2005.

Simmons, T., & Dye, J. (2003, October). Grandparents living with grandchildren: 2000. *Census 2000 Brief.* Retrieved from http://www.census.gov/prod/ 2003pubs/c2kbr-31.pdf.

Suryaraman, M. (2005, November 13). Schools look abroad to find needed teachers. *San Jose Mercury News,* 1A, 11A.

Toppo, G. (2001, August 4). Study finds 850,000 American children are homeschooled. *The Idaho Statesman*, 5 Main.

Trawick-Smith, J. & Lambert, L. (1995, March). The unique challenges of the family child care provider: Implications for professional development. *Young Children*, 50(3), 25–32.

U. S. Census Bureau. (2000). P54: *Presence of own children under 18 years of age and employment status for females 16 years and over*. Washington, DC: Author.

U. S. Census Bureau. (2002, March). Current population surveys, 1976–2002. Retrieved May 16, 2002 from http://www.census.gov/prod/2003pubs/p60-222.pdf.

U.S. Department of Education. (2000, Spring). *Teacher profile*. Washington, DC: Author.

U.S. Department of Education. (2001). *NHES Parent Survey for the National Household Education Surveys Program: 1999*. Washington, DC: Author.

U.S. Department of Education, National Center for Education Statistics. (2002). *The condition of education 2002*. NCES 2002-025. Washington, DC: U.S. Government Printing Office.

U.S. Department of Education, National Center for Educational Statistics. (2005b). The condition of education 2005. *Education Statistics Quarterly*, 7(1&2), 281–297.

U.S. Department of Education, National Center for Educational Statistics (2005a). *Child care and early education arrangements of infants, toddlers, and preschoolers: 2001*. Washington, DC: U. S. Government Printing Office.

U.S. Department of Health and Human Services, Administration on Children, Youth and Families. (2003). *Child maltreatment 2001*. Washington, DC: U.S. Government Printing Office.

Vaden-Kiernan, N., & McManus, J. (2005). Parent and family involvement in education: 2002–2003. In U. S. Department of Education, National Center for Education Statistics *Education Statistics Quarterly*, 7 (1 & 2) 79–86.

Will, G. F. (2002, January 7). Schools can't fix family failings. *San Jose Mercury News*, 7B.

Wirt, J., Choy, S., Rooney, P., Provasnik, S., Sen, A., & Tobin, R. (2004). *The condition of education 2004* [NCES 2004-077]. U. S. Department of Education, National Center for Education Statistics. Washington, DC: U. S. Government Printing Office.

Zaslow, M. & Martinez-Beck, I. (2006) *Critical issues in early childhood professional development*. Baltimore, MD: Paul H. Brookes Publishing Co.

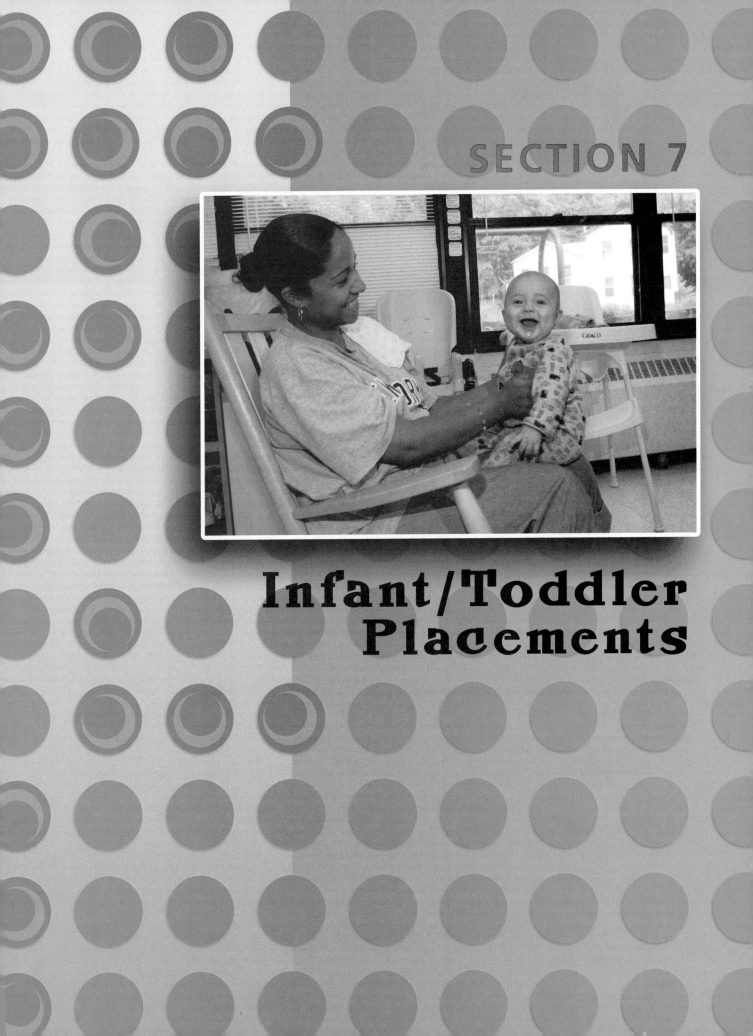

Infant/Toddler Placements

CHAPTER 14

Student Teaching with Infants and Toddlers

OBJECTIVES

After reading this chapter, you should be able to:

1.... List at least three characteristics of a quality infant/toddler center.
2.... Discuss two findings in the research on child care for infants and toddlers.
3.... Describe the general regulations of an infant center, including health concerns.
4.... Cite techniques for approaching and working with children.
5.... Describe care giving as a teaching activity.
6.... Identify activities for infants and toddlers.

Comments of student teachers:

" I asked to be placed in an infant/toddler center. Student teaching there pointed out caregiver skills I hadn't dreamed of. Thank heavens I've a strong back. That's really necessary! ●

Michaela Grossman

" Wash your hands, wash your hands, then, do it again. I think the staff said that hundreds of times! ●

Pat Booth

" One of my friends said I'd never want children of my own if I worked at a toddler program. Wrong! It made me want children of my own even more. ●

Briana DeLong

STANDARDS

Most infants and toddlers today are cared for by relatives or in family child care homes. Many parents feel, rightly or wrongly, that the infant thrives better in an environment most like the home. Family child care homes are popular. State licensing in California mandates adult-infant and adult-toddler ratios. The National Association for the Education of Young Children (NAEYC) has been urging a ratio of 1:4 as a national standard. A quality center may deliberately choose to keep its ratio at 1:3.

One of the reasons for the lack of national standards lies in the belief that all young children, especially infants and toddlers, belong at home with their mothers. This attitude, however, does not reflect what is happening in the workplace. The fastest growing group of new workers is women with children under the age of six.

CHARACTERISTICS OF A QUALITY INFANT/TODDLER CENTER

Many of the quality characteristics mentioned in our discussions of child care centers for preschool and school aged children also apply to infant/toddler centers. A study by the National Institute of Child Health and Human Development (NICHD, 1996) highlighted the following as critical to the provision of sensitive, warm, responsive care:

- A low caregiver-to-infant/toddler ratio was the number one indicator of quality. The closer the ratio came to 1:1, the higher the quality. Thus, high quality care was frequently found in home settings with relatives and sitters.
- A smaller group size provided for higher quality care.
- Caregivers who were less authoritarian were more likely to provide positive interactions with infants.
- A safe, uncluttered physical environment with age-appropriate materials was an important quality indicator.

Reinsberg (1995) lists *security* as the most important factor, so infants can develop a sense of trust. To accomplish this, "primary caregivers and other consistent staff are the single most important factor." At Reinsberg's college center, student teachers were assigned for longer periods of time, to provide for greater consistency and to reduce the caregiver-infant/toddler ratio to 1:2 on most days.

To respond to the NICHD finding about group size, the center kept the group size in the infant/toddler room lower than the number for which it was licensed. To guarantee greater safety for rapidly growing infants, a partition was installed to separate the very young infants from the older, more mobile ones.

Believing that the room had become overstimulating and noisy, Reinsberg, her teachers, and students stopped holding casual conversations with each other and began to listen more for the sounds the infants and toddlers were making. They soon discovered that the infants and toddlers were more relaxed in the quieter setting.

Diapering routines were changed to become more responsive to the needs of the children. Rather than adhering to a strict schedule, caregivers began to wait until they noticed that an infant appeared uncomfortable, or that a toddler was ready for a change. Then, adhering to the principles outlined by Magda Gerber (trained by Dr. Pikler in Hungary prior to her immigration to the United States), caregivers slow down the process of changing diapers. They talk to the child about what they are doing and involve the child in the process (see Figure 14–1). In this the caregivers are modeling similar behaviors as those observed by Gonzalez-Mena (2004) in Hungary when she visited the Pikler Institute. (Gonzalez-Mena was familiar with the work of Gerber who founded the organization, Resources for Infant Educarers.) The same process—going slowly, talking to the child about what was happening, involving them—was followed when feeding the infants and toddlers.

The emphasis must be on responsive caregiving in daily activities, such as feeding, grooming, diapering, and bathing, where the focus is on close, one-to-one interactions with infants and toddlers (Gonzalez-Mena, 2004). Infants essentially need and desire one-on-one interaction with caregivers —physical contact, attention, and sensitive recognition of their attempts to communicate. Relevant, tailor-made caregiver actions and responses lead to early conversation skills, which promote social, intellectual, and emotional development as well as language growth. This happens when adults listen and observe closely and truly believe that infants are constantly-communicating. This happens as they share intimate moments, verbalize, maintain eye contact, smile, and enjoy mutual, playful episodes. The key points at Pikler's Institute include:

- valuing independent activity. Caregivers do not interfere with a baby's ability to discover pleasure in free movement, and they constantly reinforce the activity generated by the child.

- developing a special caring relationship between the adult and the child. Caregivers take a consistent, gentle approach, in which they show respect for each child's personality, and understand his or her needs.

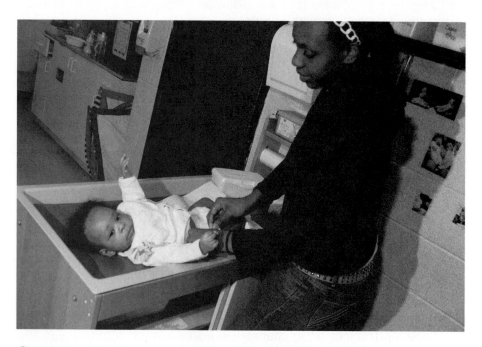

● Figure 14-1
The curriculum in an infant center includes changing diapers.

treating the child like a partner. Caregivers foster children's self-awareness by encouraging them to be active participants in whatever is happening. This helps them to know, express, and assert themselves as individuals. Children become active partners in every interaction. (Gonzalez-Mena & Chahin, 2004)

In agreement with the concept of responsive interactions with infants, Wingert and Brandt (2005) state:

> Science is now giving us a much different picture of what goes on inside [infants'] hearts and heads. Long before they form their first words or attempt the feat of sitting up, they are already mastering complex emotions—jealousy, empathy, frustration—that were once thought to be learned much later in toddlerhood.

The concerns of Wingert and Brandt are seconded by Lally and Mangione (2006), who insist that infancy demands responsive care. Learning by infants begins in the womb, and from conception infants follow developmental paths that are genetically programmed and genetically wired.

> Babies have their own learning agenda . . . to learn language, to become more skillful in their . . . muscle functioning, to construct knowledge about . . . people and things in the world about them, to seek out significant relationships . . . and to use relationships to learn appropriate and inappropriate ways of relating to others (Lally & Mangione, 2006).

Another aspect of responsive care is touching the child. Carlson (2005) reminds us about how much touch matters.

> Humans need nurturing touch for optimum emotional, physical, and cognitive development and health—especially in infancy. Daily touch plays a significant role in early brain development.

Close communication with parents and the need to reevaluate what teachers do at an infant center is essential to assure continuing quality care. Many centers chart feeding times and amounts, sleeping, and diapering times in a notebook that goes home with the parent every day. The parent then enters the feeding, sleeping, and diapering times in the same notebook and brings it back to the center each day. What procedures does your center use?

The following characteristics are needed in an infant/toddler center:

- Kind, leisurely physical and emotional care from one primary caregiver comes first.
- Parents are encouraged to stay and play as much as they can. (This may be one reason for the growing number of businesses with child care facilities on site or located nearby.)
- Caregivers take time to provide the emotional support a baby needs.
- Caregivers have one primary goal: Each baby should have a happy day.

Quality Family Child Care

In the home of one of our former students, three large, sunny rooms in the bottom level of her split-level house serve as a family child care center. A fourth room, the downstairs bathroom, houses the changing table and potty chairs for the preschoolers. A door from the room used by the preschoolers opens to a large fenced backyard, with a climbing structure and covered sandbox. In the infant room, a large playpen serves to separate the older, crawling babies from the very small ones.

Our former student and her daughter are licensed for a total of 12 infants, toddlers, and preschoolers. Although she could take more infants, she will only enroll two, and no more than four toddlers, together with six preschoolers. Of the two infants for whom she cares, one is more mobile than the other and is allowed to roam safely in the carpeted room. A mirror is attached to the wall at floor level, as infants thoroughly enjoy looking at themselves. Electrical outlets are covered and no electrical cords are evident. A rocking chair is in one corner of the room. A bookshelf loaded with appropriate toys for the crawler to reach is along the wall. A second bookshelf contains small board books with brightly colored pictures and minimal stories.

The four toddlers have a second room, separated from the infant room by a gate. In the toddler room are more age-appropriate toys: books, blocks, cars, trucks, trains, puzzles, and other stimulating things, lined on shelves within reach of toddlers and preschoolers (see Figure 14–2). A small table with four chairs is along the window wall and a soft couch is on the opposite one. The walls are brightly painted with Pooh characters, complements of a friend who is a commercial painter.

Preschoolers share a third room, separated from the toddler room by a low partition that allows caregivers to easily monitor activities.

Figure 14-2
In this family care home everything is within reach of older infants and toddlers.

attachment—the child's bond with a teacher or caregiver, established over time through personal interaction. A child's primary attachment is usually to her parents.

Attachment Issues in Infant/Toddler Care

Over the past 20 or so years, there have been many studies of **attachment**. One of the crucial issues in infant/toddler care is whether the children involved will establish bonds with their working parents. Studies have shown that infants do bond with their parents, and in centers where they are consistently assigned to one caregiver for extended periods of time, infants will establish secondary bonds with that caregiver. This is why in some infant/toddler centers, a caregiver will move with the child from the infant to the toddler room. Watson (2003) writes "When primary caregivers are responsive and sensitive to children's needs, these supportive experiences allow children to develop secure attachments and view relationships as reciprocal and cooperative." She continues to explain that as these attachments are developed, children acquire the ability to trust and enlist help from adults, in support of the child's learning and development.

In other words, infants secure in their bonds to parents and caregivers will be able to resolve the Erikson task of learning to trust, and learn to ask for help from significant adults in their lives by age three, as Burton White (1975) has suggested.

Special Issues of Infant/Toddler Care

Separation from Parents. As Daniel (1998) writes, mothers historically stayed home, and those who worked were frequently regarded negatively. Many mothers approach the use of child care with feelings of guilt, even though family finances may dictate that they work. Added to this is *society's* condemnation of working mothers—especially those with infants—and parents' concerns about how to find a caregiver they can trust, in a quality care setting.

Dombro and Lerner (2006) mention that some parents, usually mothers, become concerned that their children will form a primary attachment to their respective caregivers rather than to them. Sharing care with another can and does provoke strong feelings, and Dombro and Lerner caution caregivers to:

- be aware of the impact their words and actions can have on others.
- help families recognize the central, forever roles they play in their child's life. Assure families that no one can take their place.
- acknowledge the feelings that caring can stir up; these can sometimes be difficult to admit and handle.
- communicate respectfully and effectively.
- understand, appreciate, and address differences.

Daniel (1998) stresses some of the points previously mentioned:

- Good infant and toddler programs assign a primary caregiver to each child.

In the former student's home-based child care center, the mother had the primary care of a newly enrolled, two-month-old infant. At nine months, when the child was crawling, she enrolled a second, very young infant (six weeks old). The daughter had the primary care of the second infant and the mother retained the primary care of the older one.

- Caregivers should have formal and informal communication with parents about the details of the child's day, to help form viable partnerships. A notebook—mentioned before, with notations of feeding, sleeping, and diaper change times—that goes back and forth between caregiver and parent is certainly one way of maintaining formal contact. As the infant grows, notations can include such milestones as turning over, sitting up, walking, and so on. Taking a few minutes to converse when the infant is brought in or picked up allows for informal communication.
- Low staff turnover is essential to building emotional trust between caregiver and infant and between caregiver and parent.

Infant/Toddler Child Care and Identity Formation

If, as research states, a baby is emotionally part of his parents, just as he was physically a part of them prior to birth, how does an infant/toddler center deal with the child's developing sense of being *separate* from the parent—his sense of identity? Lally and Mangione (2006) believe that infants develop a sense of self during their first two years. "How they are treated and what they are allowed to do or not to do is incorporated into the infant's developing self." They assert that the way in which adults respond to the infants' needs impacts the child's **identity formation**. In addition, "[b]ecause security, exploration, and identity formation manifest themselves differently during the infancy period," adult responses must fit the child's developmental stage.

Lally and Mangione (2006) further agree on the need for responsive infant/toddler care, with the quality indicators mentioned by Greenberg (1996), Reinsberg (1995), and the NICHD study (1996). Lally and Mangione

identity formation— the way in which a young child separates from his parents and establishes his own character traits and personality.

● **Figure 14-3**
Books are placed in a rack that toddlers can access easily.

assert that infants learn in a holistic way, in that they are continually learning. Furthermore, infants rapidly move from one developmental stage to another. It therefore is essential that caregivers be responsive to infants and toddlers. Caregivers should allow the children to make their own choices as to what toys they want to play with (see Figure 14–3) and what books to peruse or which puzzles to reconstruct, to guarantee their optimal development.

Infants and Toddlers with Special Needs

Batshaw (2002) points out that in the United States, 6.9 babies out of 1000 died during their first year of life in the year 2000. The most common causes were related to prematurity. However, if you are placed in an infant/toddler center, you are more likely to see children whose mothers were substance abusers during pregnancy than you are to see infants with more serious medical needs. As newborns, infants may have had to be withdrawn from the drugs the mother was using. Frequently, a mother abuses more than one substance, and it is often difficult to know which are involved. It is not uncommon for an abuser to use both cocaine and alcohol, for example. Other substances frequently abused are marijuana and nicotine.

Children born to mothers who are substance abusers are often placed in foster care, with a trained foster mother who knows how to care for babies with special needs. "Many of these children qualify for early intervention services . . . [and] the short-term effects of intervention are encouraging in terms of gains in language acquisition and socialization skills" (Batshaw, 2002).

Batshaw then affirms:

● the effectiveness of early intervention.

● the mandate of the law that special needs children be included with their non-disabled peers.

● the need for families to have access to services like quality care, education, and special intervention.

● the fact that increasingly diverse populations of infants and toddlers present great challenges to child care and educational systems.

● the need for action to support child care and education, in meeting the challenges of diversity and inclusion.

● the need to validate the quality of infant/toddler programs, and that these should support full inclusion.

● the necessity for child care, health care, and education to be integrated, and for individualized care and education to be provided to all infants, toddlers, and their families.

● to this end, the need for collaboration among the different fields of early childhood mentioned above.

● the right for all infants, toddlers, and family members to child care, education, and intervention, to be delivered by trained personnel, with appropriate certification or licenses, who are adequately compensated (Sexton, Snyder, Sharpton, & Stricklin, 1993).

Infants Born to Teenage Parents

DeJong and Cottrell (2003) state that child care programs for children born to teenage parents must have some extra features not found in most infant/toddler care settings. She stresses that teenage parents present unique challenges. One frustration for the teacher occurs when the parent appears to be disinterested in her child. Another happens when "a teen appears to compromise the needs of her infant to get on the good side of her boyfriend or when she repeatedly brings an unclean baby or dirty bottles to the center. DeJong and Cottrell assert that they have found Erikson's model of social-emotional development helpful (see Chapter 7). They have noted that many of their teen mothers had not resolved earlier stages of development, as follows:

- Trust versus mistrust (infancy). As a parent the lack of trust may leave the teen without an appreciation for the need to establish a basic sense of trust between herself and her child.

- Autonomy versus shame and doubt (toddlerhood). When a toddler's growing independence is not adequately supported, that toddler may grow into a teenager who lacks a basic sense of responsibility and may fail to show appropriate responsibility for herself or her child.

- Initiative versus guilt (preschool years). Without a world full of rich, exploratory experiences and positive guidance, an adolescent may fail to acquire a basic sense of curiosity, ambition, and empathy for others.

- Industry versus inferiority (school-age years). A child who experiences limited success with school-related tasks can grow into a teenager who feels incompetent and inferior.

- Identity versus role confusion (adolescence). Depending on the extent to which her family and early school experiences supported the formation of trust, autonomy, initiative, and industry, a teenager may demonstrate a range of behaviors that could jeopardize positive identity formation. She may unconsciously believe that early parenthood is a way to gain love, acceptance, and status and, as a result, she may make a parenting commitment before exploring other alternatives for her future.

DeJong and Cottrell believe then that the major goals of programs for these special parents must be to help them:

- stay in school, to earn a high school diploma or its equivalent.
- continue their post-secondary education.
- improve their parenting skills.
- reduce repeat pregnancies.
- deliver normal-birth-weight babies, of at least 5.5 pounds.

STUDENT TEACHING WITH INFANTS AND TODDLERS

An infant/toddler center is an entirely new world, one that is completely different from the preschool environment. Every infant/toddler center is operated a little differently. However, most centers have similar regulations regarding children's health, caregivers' health, feeding, and diaper-changing procedures. A student teacher should request a staff handbook. Read it before you go to the center. Be prepared to ask questions about anything you do not understand. Babies need consistency, and it is important that you be able to fit into the center routines as quickly as possible. Most importantly, relax and enjoy the children!

APPROACHING AND WORKING WITH VERY YOUNG CHILDREN

When working with infants and toddlers, remember that every child is an individual. Even tiny infants have preferences. They may prefer to sleep on their sides rather than their backs, although because of the possibility of **sudden infant death syndrome (SIDS)**, most medical professionals urge parents to place their newborns on their backs, or with specially designed cushioned forms, to allow the infant to sleep on her side. Some infants may like to be burped over your shoulder, rather than across your knees. When caring for infants, take a minute to try and find out what some of their preferences may be.

When working with children of this age, remember:

- your size may be frightening to a child.
- to keep confidential material to yourself. Medical, financial, personal, and family information is privileged information that helps you understand the child more completely.

Working with Infants

Children need to hear your voice; talk to them and sing lullabies to them, softly (Honig, 2005). They need the social contact that only another person can provide. Hearing language is also how children learn to talk. Be sure to use clear, simple language. *Speak softly*. Voice tone and volume greatly affect small children. If you speak in a loud, excited voice, the children are very likely to become loud and excited in response.

Sharing music can be a playful, energizing experience: Think of songs by Raffi, Hap Palmer, Miss Jackie, and Ella Jenkins. On the other hand, cradle songs or lullabies can calm and soothe children and help them relax and sleep (Honig, 2005). In an earlier study, Kemple, Batey, and Hartle (2004) mention that "infancy and early childhood are prime times to capitalize on children's musical spontaneity and to encourage their natural inclinations to sing, move, and play." Play, according to these authors, is the vehicle through which young children best learn, and music and play are difficult to separate, as both are interactive, social, creative, and joyful.

Encourage anticipation by telling children what you are going to do. Say "Now we are going to change your diaper." They will respond and cooperate when you let them know what to expect.

Try to *be at eye level* with children. Sitting or kneeling on the floor brings you closer to their line of vision. *Make eye contact*. When bottle-feeding, playing, diapering, and the like, look directly at children. Meet and hold their gaze when talking to them, and *smile*. You like to have people look at you; babies undoubtedly feel the same way.

Move slowly around infants. Young children do everything in slow motion. They often get upset and overstimulated when adults run around them excitedly. Young infants need time to understand the changes that

sudden infant death syndrome (SIDS)— where death of an infant occurs without warning, generally during the first three months of life and for which there is no known cause.

are happening. Be affectionate and warm but *do not hover*. Be ready to hug, hold, and comfort when they need it, but let them be free to explore. Young children need to be able to move around and experience their environment. They need to find their own solutions to problems whenever they can. Let children experiment with toys and invent new uses for them. Intervene only when they are likely to get hurt, are obviously in distress, or are too frustrated to cope.

Becoming independent, competent, and self-sufficient is hard work; children need loving, secure adults and a safe place to begin the process. *Encourage babies to help you* in care giving. You need to dress them, change them, and feed them. However, they will help if you let them. Recognize their attempts to participate and encourage them. Allowing them to help does not take much longer, and the rewards are many times greater.

There has been an increased use of signing with infants as a result of current attention to infants' and toddlers' communication and pre-reading skills (Meyer, 2005). Early childhood infant educators are much more aware of infants' attempts to communicate with nonverbal hand, arm, facial, eye, and body movements or expressions. Almost all adults realize that arms extended upward means a child wants to be picked up; most adults know to watch children's eyes to find out what has attracted their attention. Skilled caregivers working in infant centers may understand each infant's unique and individual signing attempts, then imitate and pair the child's signs with simple words or phases (e.g., "bottle" or "ball, you want the ball?"). Meyer writes that babies as young as six months are able to learn and use basic signs to tell their caregivers that they would like milk, food, or a diaper change. This gives infants the knowledge that they are indeed communicating, for their signs elicit caregiver actions.

Researchers believe this signing interaction does not inhibit but rather enhances the infants' and toddlers' eventual use of words. Acredolo and Goodwyn (2000) found that successful signing by babies stimulates brain development, particularly in areas involving language, memory, and concept development.

Working with Toddlers

Toddlers are a very special group. They are just beginning to understand that they are people (see Figure 14–4). They are seeing themselves as separate from their parents for the first time. They are compelled to explore and understand their environment (see Figure 14–5). They must assert themselves as individuals. If you can recognize their need to be individuals without feeling personal insecurity, you will have made a giant step in dealing effectively with them.

Toddlers, more so than infants, will challenge your authority. They may test you until they can feel secure in your response. You will need to call on all your reserves of strength, firmness, patience, and love to deal with them. They are loving, affectionate, giving, sharing, joyful, spontaneous people; take pleasure in them.

You may find some of the following ideas helpful when working with toddlers. Read the suggestions and think about them. Try to put them into practice.

Make positive statements. "Feet belong on the floor." When children hear the words *don't* and *no* constantly, they begin to ignore them.

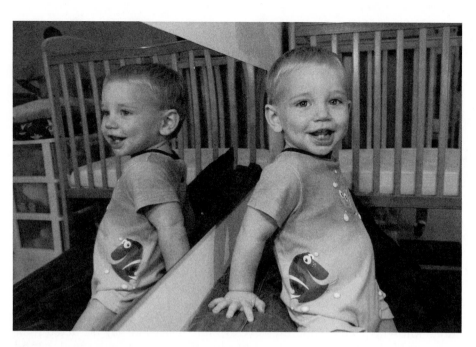

● **Figure 14-4**
This toddler sees himself as a separate individual.

Give choices only when you intend to honor them. If Johnny's mother said that her son must wear his jacket when playing outside, do not ask Johnny, "Do you want your jacket?" Instead, say "Your mom wants you to wear a jacket today." If you give a choice and the toddler tells you no, you are already in a conflict you could have avoided.

Avoid problems by being alert. Watch for signs that a child may be getting too frustrated to handle a situation, or that a fight over a toy is about to start.

Use distraction whenever possible. If you see two children insisting on the same toy, see if the children can work it out themselves. If not, try to interest one of them in something else. You might point out a toy just like it or remind them of another enjoyable activity.

If an argument does erupt, *avoid taking sides.* Help both children understand how the other child feels. *Encourage the use of words* to handle situations. Encourage the children to name things, to express happiness, sorrow, excitement, and other emotions. *Let the children talk.* Correct grammar and pronunciation will come later. Practicing verbal expression is the most important thing.

Act on your own suggestions. If you say "Time to clean up. Start putting the toys away," the children are more likely to follow your suggestions if they are accompanied by actions.

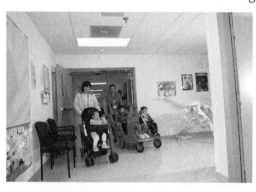

● **Figure 14-5**
Going on a long walk may require special equipment, and lots of teacher help.

Make *alternative suggestions.* If some children continually ignore safety rules or disturb others, suggest an alternate activity the child likes; suggest taking turns; suggest cooperation, or remove the child from the activity. Be firm but calm. *Do not take the children's reactions personally.* You may hear "I don't like you!" Say "I know you are angry. It's okay to be angry." Toddlers respect fairness and desperately want limits they can depend on.

Do not make promises you cannot keep. Just say that you will have to ask if you do not know if something is allowed or possible. Toddlers understand that.

GENERAL RULES AND REGULATIONS

The physical setting and philosophy of a center will determine how various routines are carried out. Centers usually have specific rules and routines regarding health and safety, medications, emergencies, feeding, diapering, and naps.

Health and Safety

- Smoking is not allowed in infant/toddler centers.
- Coffee, tea, and other beverages should only be consumed in staff areas.
- Never leave a child unattended on a changing table or in a high chair.
- Do not leave children unattended inside or outside. They can easily injure themselves.
- Ill infants should not be in the center. Infants who have bad colds, fevers, or contagious diseases are usually cared for at home.
- If you are ill, you should not be in the center. You will not be efficient if you are not feeling well. In addition, your illness may spread to the children. If you contract a contagious illness, notify the center immediately.
- Wash your hands. The most important health measure you can take is to wash your hands before and after diapering or cleaning noses and before feeding a child.
- Watch for signs that a child may not feel well. Some symptoms are digging at or pulling ears, listlessness, glassy eyes, diarrhea, and limping.
- Parents should be given the names of any facility or child care home that specializes in caring for sick children, including infants and toddlers.

Medication

Normally, only a regular staff person will be allowed to give medication. You should be aware of medication schedules for the children. You might need to remind staff when medications are due.

You also need to be aware of the effects medications may have on the children. They may become sleepy, agitated, or may even have an allergic reaction. You must be alert to changes that occur when medicine is given and you must be able to communicate these to the staff.

Emergencies

- *Stay calm.*
- Speak calmly and quietly to the child.
- Alert the staff that an emergency has occurred. They should be able to administer the appropriate first aid measures until the child can see a physician.
- Help calm the other children. They will respond to the situation the same way you do. If you are agitated and upset, they will respond to your feelings; likewise, if you remain calm, they usually will also.

Feeding

- *Wash your hands.*
- Read the child's chart to see what kind of food and/or formula to give and how much. (Remember: Do not feed a child from a baby food jar; use a dish or disposable cup (see Figure 14–6). Saliva, which contains bacteria, will get in the jar and spoil the remaining food.
- Gather all the things you need for feeding: bib, washcloth, spoons, sponges, and so on. It may be helpful to bring one spoon for you to feed the child and a spoon for the infant to "help."

  - Tell the infant what you are going to do. Let her anticipate being fed.
  - Settle the child comfortably. You may want to make sure the child has a clean, dry diaper before feeding so she will be more comfortable and attentive.
  - The child will let you know when more food is desired. When she opens her mouth, respond by feeding.
  - Talk to the child. Eating is a time to enjoy pleasant conversation and socialization, as young children like being talked to. You can talk about the food, its texture, color, temperature, and taste. Eye contact is important.
  - Encourage the child to help feed himself. It is a little messier, but it means more independence later.
  - If the child refuses to take the last ounce of a bottle or the last little bit of solid food, do not push it. Children know when they are not hungry.
  - Be sure to burp bottle-fed children when they need it. You may want to check with the child's caregiver for any special instructions.
  - When the baby is finished, wash her face and hands. Again, tell her you are going to do this and encourage the child to take part in this activity. Be gentle with the washcloth.

- Take off the bib and put the baby down to play.
- Clean up. Be sure to wipe off the high chair, the tray, the table, and the floor. Put dishes and bottles in the sink.
- Record what and how the child ate.

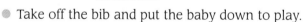

● **Figure 14-6**
In this toddler center children are encouraged to serve themselves.

Diapering

- Gather everything you need to change the baby: diapers, clean clothes, baby wipes, medicated ointment (if needed), and anything else that may be required.
- Tell the child what you are going to do. Set the child on the diaper table.
- Keep one hand on the child at all times.
- Take off the wet diaper and clean the child thoroughly with a warm, wet cloth. Apply any ointment according to the parent's instructions.

- Talk to the child about the process. Talk about being wet, dry, and clean. Describe the process of dressing and undressing; you can talk about the baby's clothes and body parts. Involve the baby in the process. Ask the child to lift the legs or give you an arm to put through the sleeve. (Note: How diapers are changed also gives children messages about their sexuality. If you are relaxed and casual about changing them and washing their genital areas, children get the message that they are okay.)
- Put the child in a safe place. Dispose of the diaper and soiled clothes according to the directions you are given.
- Clean the changing table using a germicidal solution.
- Wash your hands. Clean changing tables and clean hands help prevent the spread of disease.
- Record the diaper change. Be sure to note bowel movements. Make a note of any diarrhea, constipation, diaper rash, unusually strong urine odor, or anything else that seems out of the ordinary.

Toilet Learning

Toilet learning is too frequently treated with embarrassment in parenting books, and meager research has been done on the topic. Many parents and caretakers do not understand that although bladder and bowel control is a skill, it may not be taught; it is learned.

Infants begin life with automatic emptying of the bladder and bowel. Bladder capacity is so small that wetting may occur every hour or so. Automatic emptying is triggered by the filling of the bladder or bowel, which sets off rhythmic contractions over which the infant has no control.

It is not until the nervous system matures during the first year or two that infants and toddlers show awareness of the sensations of a full bladder or bowel. What behaviors would alert you to this?

- a look of concentration while all activity stops
- crossing the legs
- fidgeting
- holding onto the crotch with one or both hands
- less frequent wetting
- regularity you can count on
- a keener awareness of body functions
- a sudden dislike of things messy
- a more sensitive sniffer
- use of the appropriate vocabulary
- improving communication abilities
- some self-dressing skills
- an interest in the habits of others (Eisenberg & Murkoff, 1995)

Conscious holding of urine is helped by a gradually increasing bladder capacity. By the second year, capacity has usually doubled, and the frequency of wetting is about every two or three hours. Emptying is still automatic and dependent on a full bladder or bowel. When parents or caregivers boast that toddlers at 14, 18, or 21 months are toilet trained, be aware: this is more often an indication that the adult recognizes the signs of impending need and places the child on the potty than it is an indication that the child has learned how to use the toilet.

In some cultures, parents support their infants in toilet use at very young ages. This is accomplished "through close observation, physical contact, emotional support, mutual trust, and reading non-verbal cues" (Baba, 2003). When parents place their infants in an infant care center, their expectations may be that caregivers will continue to support the infants' toilet use. This can lead to misunderstandings if caregivers and parents have different perceptions about the time for toilet learning. Caregivers should be sensitive to the point of view of parents and try to honor their requests. At the same time, caregivers must be honest about their own needs and time restrictions. Open communication between caregivers and parents is essential.

By three years, most children have learned to resist the emptying of their bowels until it suits them. At this age also, most children have learned to hold urine for a considerable time when the bladder is full. This holding ability requires conscious control of the perineal muscles, which are used in the same way as the bowel sphincter. At this age, however, accidents often occur because children do not have total control over urine release. This becomes obvious when the child who has just been taken to the toilet and not urinated goes back to play and immediately wets.

During the fourth year, most children have acquired conscious control over both bowel and bladder muscles. But it is important to remember that full control is not completely accomplished until about six years of age, when starting the urine stream from a partially full bladder becomes possible.

Learning bladder and bowel control is far from simple. Think of what children must learn:

- to remove and replace pants
- to flush the toilet, eventually
- to use toilet tissue
- to wash and dry their hands upon completion

In spite of these complexities, most children acquire toileting skills with a minimum of help (see Figure 14–7).

When Should Toilet Learning Begin?

Caregivers must acknowledge that toilet learning will be most successful when the child shows clear signs of recognizing bladder or bowel tension. These signs vary from child to child; you will be able to recognize them after they have occurred several times, just before the child has wet or had a bowel movement. Look for any of the following signs, mentioned earlier: stopping what he is doing and concentrating, crossing his legs as if trying to prevent himself from wetting, beginning to fidget, pulling at you, making sounds of distress or using baby words, such as *wee-wee*, or putting his hands on his crotch as if he feels his bladder is about to empty.

◉ Figure 14-7
By repeatedly flushing the toilet, this toddler is becoming familiar with the sound of the toilet.

Sparrow (2004) cautions about being aware of when a child needs more time to learn, stating that caregivers and parents should look to see if the child:

- stands at the potty chair and urinates on the floor, or takes off his diaper and soils the chair.
- appears comfortable with, or indifferent to, a soiled diaper.
- wants to keep a diaper on and fights efforts to remove it.
- hides before soiling herself; this shows she is aware of her body functions but is not ready to involve a caregiver with them.
- withholds bowel movements.
- becomes frantic when his skin makes contact with a toilet seat, or when he hears a toilet flushing and sees a bowel movement disappear.

Sparrow (2004) provides caregivers with five training tips:

1. Parents can invite the child to pick out her own potty chair; caregivers may allow her to choose which potty to use.

2. Choose a potty that sits on the floor. She will see this as her own potty and may even want to pull it around behind her.

3. With boys, add plastic urine deflectors, which are meant to direct a boy's urine into the potty. Remember, though, children can be hurt by the deflectors when they sit on the potty.

4. If she's interested, let the child sit on the potty in her diapers or clothes. This will help her become accustomed to the routine. Be aware that a cold potty can inhibit the child.

5. As the child sits on the potty, let him sit for only as long as he chooses. If he wants to run off, let him. He may need some time to get used to what it feels like.

How Do You Handle Accidents?

The number one rule to remember is that *accidents are inevitable*. Treat accidents matter-of-factly: Wash your hands, change the child's pants, and clean him without showing any irritation. Afterwards, wash your hands again, and disinfect any surfaces contacted by soiled clothing or hands. If you miss a child's cue, or do not move fast enough to help the child urinate or defecate in the potty, compliment the child on his ability to try to get your attention. Recognize that some accidents may be your fault, not the child's.

Many people will give you advice about toilet learning. Your cooperating teacher may follow a routine of taking toddlers to a potty chair at regular intervals. Even if you know that most toddlers do not acquire complete control until four to six years of age, you can go along with the center's policy; regular toileting helps those toddlers with regular rhythmicity acquire control at an earlier age than those with an irregular rhythmicity (see Figure 14–8). If a parent complains that her child was "toilet trained" before she placed him in the child care center, and is angry because your cooperating teacher has asked her to bring in diapers, let the cooperating teacher handle the problem. If the parent tries to involve you, defer to center policy. Be patient with those parents who keep their child in diapers at age

● **Figure 14-8**
Learning to use the toilet.

three. Perhaps as busy, working parents, they find it easier than to try to learn the subtle cues the child may be providing. Or, they may not know what cues to look for.

One Final Word

Most children learn by example. As one two-year-old learns to use the toilet independently, she becomes a role model for other children. In a family-type center with a mixture of ages, older children act as role models for the younger ones. Parents also become role models for their children at home. Treat toilet learning like the natural process it is and do not worry about the three-year-old who is still having daily accidents.

Check for problems such as constipation, diarrhea, painful urination, and so on. Check for any dietary-related difficulties; a diet low in fluids and fiber will often be to blame for constipation. Above all, relax and do not make a big deal about toileting. All children will learn eventually, with or without formal teaching.

Biting

Next to toilet learning, probably no other behavior causes as many difficulties for teachers and caregivers than does biting. Carothers (1990) found that biting occurs most frequently "when children are one to two years of age" and feels that it is related to the child's social development. Biting by three-year-olds is generally related to a specific stressor in the child's life. Gillespie and Seibel (2006) assert that biting occurs when the child becomes frustrated and loses the ability to self-regulate. They suggest that caregivers can help children learn how to self-regulate by:

- observing closely.
- responding to individual needs.
- providing structure and predictability.
- arranging developmentally appropriate environments.
- defining age-appropriate limits.
- showing empathy and caring.

    Other guidelines include:

- remembering that biting, for the biter, is very effective. To persuade the child to give up the habit involves teaching the child new behaviors.
- understanding that aggression occurs most often because the toddler is unable to express wants, needs, or feelings in words.
- making a determination of what situations lead to the child's biting. Intervening and suggesting to the child that she can use words will help. Actually saying what you think the child is thinking also works, especially with a child who does not have many words in his expressive vocabulary.
- learning that redirection and distraction can be very effective with toddlers.
- responding when biting occurs by giving a firm, clear message that the behavior is not acceptable. Use the same words on each occasion: "No biting, John," or "Biting is not allowed, Mary."

- removing the biter to a short time-out after the incident.
- consoling the child who was bitten.
- noticing whether the biting appears to be related to teething; try offering the child a teething ring or a soft, pliable plastic toy to chew.
- dealing with biting immediately. Asking a parent to talk about biting at home is ineffectual. Toddlers cannot remember carry-over instructions.
- remembering that toddlers need a lot of time and repetition to learn new behaviors. You may want to keep a record of how many times a day the biting occurs and at what times of day.
- asking for the parents' help to reinforce substitute behaviors for biting when the child is at home.

What should you tell parents about biting incidents? In a student teaching assignment, defer to your cooperating teacher; she will know what to do. Carothers (1990) presents the following ideas:

- As briefly as possible, tell the parents of the child who was bitten what happened. Do not tell the parent the name of the biter.
- Ask the parents of the biter if he has bitten anyone at home. It is important to determine whether the behavior occurs only in the child care setting or if it also happens at home.
- Enlist parents' help in eliminating the behavior. Suggest that parents teach the child to use words, not teeth. Teach the parents to use the same phrases that are used at the center: "Biting is not allowed." Consistency is the key.

Using Conflict Resolution with Toddlers

When dealing with conflict between toddlers, Da Ros and Kovach (1998) suggest that, before intervening, caregivers look at what is happening (see Figure 14–9). Given toddlers' immature social development, Da Ros and Kovach feel that conflict is inevitable with toddlers and that caregivers' approaches to resolving conflict may, in actuality, exacerbate the problem. By taking time to assess where the toddlers are in the *process* of the conflict, caregivers will understand better how to react. Can the caregiver prevent whatever conflict might erupt? Once conflict has appeared, which intervention strategies work best?

Da Ros and Kovach (1998) suggest the following strategies to resolve conflict:

- Remain at the children's eye level.
- Watch and wait before interceding.
- Use *I* messages.
- Move closer to the conflict.
- Use language that tells the toddler what you see happening.
- Prevent injury by interceding quickly when necessary.
- Provide just enough help to allow toddlers to solve their own dilemmas.
- Be available to comfort each child by remaining at the child's level, squatting, with your arms open.
- Stay until toddlers disengage from the scene.
- Model gentleness to the aggressor.

Process of Conflict

	Potential Conflict	Emerging Conflict	Engaging Conflict	Struggling Conflict	(Disengaging) Resolving Conflict
Toddler Behavior	Aggressive acting Child in close proximity to other children	Two toddlers in opposition over object Dissipate/escalate	Toddlers fully involved Engage in physical contact Not at maximum level	Emotionally invested in process (crying, yelling) Actively engaged in physical contact Tug-of-war Climatic Stakes are high	Win, lose, or draw Emotional process is diffusing Anticipate Disengaging
Caregiver Strategies	Keenly observe More proximal	Assess at child's eye level Analyze Remain neutral Nonjudgmental	Watching and waiting Keep safe Allow natural consequences Remain neutral, attentive, focused	"I" messages; use singular pronouns Verbalize what is happening (sportscasting) Prevent hurting Available to each Keep own emotions in check Model gentleness	Provide help for them to problem-solve Available to each Do not leave scene until a toddler leaves Model gentleness Verbalize affect, emotions
	Least intrusive		Level of Intrusiveness Moderate		Interactive

Figure 14-9

Strategies for caregivers to use when toddlers come into conflict with each other. Reprinted by permission of D. A. Da Ros and B. A. Kaach, and ACEI. Copyright© 2001 by ACEI.

- Offer yourself, instead of objects, for comfort; offer your lap to a child seeking comfort.
- Continue to verbalize what you see going on by using active, reflective listening.

Do not try to fix the problem and do not overreact; above all, do not expect a toddler to respond in adult ways.

Nap Time

Young children may vary considerably in their nap times. You must be alert to signs of sleepiness in order to prevent a young child from becoming overtired. Toddlers usually learn very quickly to adjust to the nap schedule of the program. Watch for yawning, rubbing of eyes, pulling of hair, thumb sucking, and disinterest in toys or people. All these are signs that a young child may be ready for a nap.

Before putting a child down to nap, quickly check his schedule. Make sure he is dry and not due to be fed soon. You may want to feed a child a little ahead of schedule if he appears sleepy. Make sure you have a clean crib and blanket (see Figure 14–10). Also, check to see if the child has any special toy he likes to sleep with.

A child who is new to the center may be reluctant to take a nap. This is because the child is in an unfamiliar place that is full of strangers. Check to see if the child prefers to sleep on her back, side, or stomach but remember that most infants are placed on their backs or sides to sleep, as a precaution against SIDS. If the parent assures you that the infant prefers sleeping on his stomach, be sure that no smothering hazards exist, such as a pillow in the crib, a stuffed toy, or too soft a cover too close to the baby's face. Many older infants and toddlers enjoy sleeping on their stomachs.

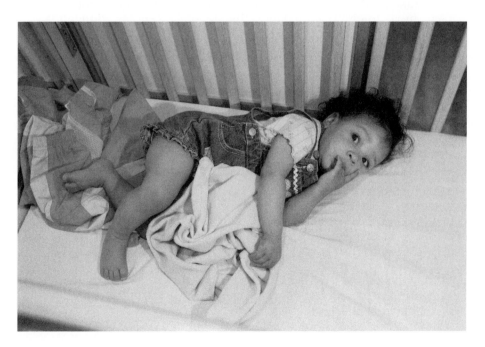

● **Figure 14-10**
Naptime is a part of the curriculum in an infant/toddler center.

You may find it helpful to sing softly, rub the infant gently on the back, or provide a rocking motion to help the child settle down to sleep. Dimming the lights may help calm the child. Many times, all the excitement of the center and the other children makes it difficult for babies to sleep. Be patient but firm.

Do not feel as though you have failed if you do not get instant success. Ask staff for suggestions. Infant center personnel are usually more than willing to answer questions, listen to concerns, or offer suggestions.

CAREGIVING AS A TEACHING ACTIVITY

Consider the following skill areas, usually included in the preschool program: motor, cognitive, language, social, sensory, self-esteem, and mathematics. All these are encountered during routine care giving activities. Bauer, Fortin, and McPartlin (2006) argue for a new model for infant curriculum development, composed of four building blocks:

- personal relationships
- classroom environment
- family connections
- care giving routines

Think about care giving routines and about what aspects of an infant curriculum are involved when you **change a diaper**:

Caregiver Action	Curriculum Area
You talk to the child, stating what is going to happen. The child is developing a sense of sequential events.	language development mathematics social development
You take off the child's diaper and let the legs move freely. The child feels the air on the body.	motor development sensory stimulation
You tell the child that the diaper is wet or contains a bowel movement.	cognitive development sensory stimulation
You wash the child with a washcloth or baby-wipe. You apply diaper rash medication if necessary. You talk about how this feels.	sensory stimulation language development cognitive development
You put a new diaper on the child and possibly, new clothes. The new diaper is dry and feels more comfortable.	sensory stimulation language development cognitive development
You talk about what is happening, encouraging the infant to help you by lifting the legs, putting out an arm, and so on.	language development motor development social development
The infant is now more comfortable and probably happier. You have had an opportunity for a special one-to-one experience with the child. For a few minutes of a busy morning, the infant has your complete attention.	self-esteem sensory stimulation social development

What about *feeding?*

- You know it is time to give a bottle or feed a child. You tell the child you are going to prepare the food. You are again helping the child develop a sense of sequence of time.

  mathematics
  language development
  social development

- The young infant may be just starting to eat or just learning to eat from a spoon; the older infant may be using fingers or learning to use a spoon. How special he feels when he succeeds!

  motor development
  language development
  self-esteem

- You sit with the child or a small group of children while they eat lunch. You talk about what they are eating, about how the food tastes, its texture, and color. A child who does not like peas may be encouraged to try three peas or two pieces of carrot.

  social development
  language development
  cognitive development
  sensory stimulation
  mathematics

- The bottle-fed child or slightly older infant has your total attention. You talk to the child. You make eye contact while feeding the infant, holding him close and safe.

  self-esteem
  language development
  sensory stimulation

- After the child has eaten, you wash his face and hands with a warm, wet cloth. First, the right hand; then the left. The older child may be able to help you.

  sensory stimulation
  language development
  cognitive development
  motor development

Diapering and feeding are just two examples of the many routines that happen in an infant center. Think of how many things are happening to a child during these routines. Think about what else is happening. What other messages is the infant receiving? Think about bathing and dressing to go outside. What about nap time? What kinds of things could you do that would make nap time smoother? What can you do to make each routine a more complete experience for each child?

A CURRICULUM FOR INFANTS AND TODDLERS

Another question often raised by people who are unfamiliar with infants and toddlers is "What do you mean when you say you *teach* them?" Many people—including parents—underestimate just how much their children learn during their first years of life. Even those who do know may feel that all children do is play. Geist (2003) looks at how infants and toddlers explore math through play activities, how children's behaviors relates to mathematics, and what you as a teacher can do to enhance these learning experiences.

Parish, Rudisill, Schilling, McOmber, Bellows, and Anderson (2006) write about how important it is to ensure that toddlers have ample opportunity for active, physical play in a safe environment. They decry the current problems of inactivity and its relationship to obesity in young children, and suggest that centers and preschools provide a variety of physical activities. Some activities take place in large groups but others occur through individual opportunities to explore attractive equipment, such as a climbing structure and tricycles, or toys, such as balloons, balls, cups, and other available materials at your center or school.

Torquati and Barber (2005) point out the benefits of planning and developing a garden for the children and allowing them to help care for it. They state:

> The natural world presents endless sensory experiences that support the observation skills underlying scientific thinking and aesthetic awareness. Toddlers readily sample fresh, nutritious foods from their own garden and demonstrate care and concern for plants, worms, and insects.

Segatti, Brown-DuPaul, and Keyes (2003) maintain that even very young children problem solve. An infant who accidentally creates a noise with a rattle may then purposefully make the sound over and over. Older infants take much joy in playing peekaboo with an adult, and may deliberately hide a toy under a scarf for the sheer excitement of finding it again and again. Through trial and error, toddlers may discover that while one child cannot push a wagon up a small incline, two can. Yet another may find out that if she spins around with a bubble wand, the bubbles rush out more rapidly than if she stands still. "In quality programs teachers stimulate development by recognizing and encouraging spontaneous problem solving" (Segatti, Brown-DuPaul, & Keyes, 2003).

Butler (2004) emphasizes the need for older infants and toddlers to be active. She urges teachers to get down on their knees and play with children, sing with them, and read with them, even if reading is not sequential, and the child continually turns to a favorite picture in the story book.

Quann and Wien (2006) write about the ability of infants and toddlers to show empathy for one another. They define *empathy* in very young children as the "capacity to observe the feelings of another and to respond with care and concern for that other." They note that in the laboratory school where Quann worked, three different forms of empathy were observed: *proximal empathy,* where a child shows concern for a classmate who is close by; *altruistic empathy,* where a child offers concern in response to another child in distress, who is not nearby; and *self-corrective empathy,* where a child offers concern in response to something he or she has done that has caused distress to another.

NAEYC's Developmentally Appropriate Practice in Infant and Toddler Programs

Editors Bredekamp and Copple's (1997) *Developmentally Appropriate Practice in Early Childhood Programs: Revised Edition* contains a section devoted to appropriate practices in infant/toddler settings. They received permission from *Zero to Three* to reprint the section on development in the first three years, which can be found in the above-named publication as Part 2: "Developmentally Appropriate Care for Children from Birth to age 3" (Lally, Griffin, Fenichel, Segal, Szanton, & Weissbourd, 1997).

This introduction is followed by an extensive list of examples of *appropriate practices*, in contrast to *inappropriate practices*. Some examples of these practices follow:

Relationships among caregivers and children

<u>Appropriate Practice</u>

Adults engage in many one-to-one, face-to-face interactions with infants. Adults talk in a pleasant, calm voice, using simple language and frequent eye contact, while being responsive to the child's cues.

<u>Inappropriate Practice</u>

Infants are left for long periods in cribs or seats, without adult attention.

Environment and experiences

<u>Appropriate Practice</u>

Pictures of infants and their family members are hung on walls at such heights that infants can see them.

<u>Inappropriate Practice</u>

Decorations are at adult eye level and do not include family photos.

Health and safety

<u>Appropriate Practice</u>

Caregivers directly supervise infants by watching and listening at all times.

<u>Inappropriate Practice</u>

Infants are left unattended, for example, at naptime.

Reciprocal relationships with families

<u>Appropriate Practice</u>

Caregivers and parents confer in making decisions about how best to support children's development and how to handle differences of opinion as they arise.

<u>Inappropriate Practice</u>

Caregivers ignore parents' concerns or they capitulate to parent demands or preferences, even when these are at odds with good practice.

There are subheadings found in some of the categories: play, for example, under *environment and experiences*. We have mentioned only one example, to give you an idea of what is appropriate and inappropriate. For more complete information, please read the section in the NAEYC publication mentioned above.

Lally (1999) identified three stages of development for infants and toddlers that educators and student teachers may find helpful. These are

- birth through eight months—*the early months,*
- eight- to 18-month-olds—*crawlers and walkers,* and
- 18-month-olds to three-year-olds—*toddlers and two-year-olds.*

(Student teachers in an infant/toddler center may find it helpful to look back at Chapter 4 and the discussion of Burton White's seven stages of development from birth to age three.)

Lowman and Ruhmann (1998) remind practitioners that toddler environments should not be scaled-down versions of preschoolers' classrooms. Classrooms that could be best described as being saturated with sensorimotor activities are more developmentally appropriate. Lowman and Ruhmann recommend a simplified arrangement, with four activity areas:

1. Large Motor Zone
2. Dramatic-Play Zone
3. Messy Zone
4. Quiet Zone

Multi-S environments, a term coined by Lowman and Ruhmann, include simplicity, seclusion, softness, sensory features, stimulation, stability, safety, and sanitation.

ACTIVITIES IN THE INFANT/TODDLER CENTER

Play can usually be divided into two types: *social play*, in which a child interacts with an adult or another child; and *object play*, in which the child interacts with an object or toy. Children of all ages engage in both types of play and the following guidelines hold true for any child.

Effective Social Play

- Activities for infants are not preschool activities that are geared down. Infants are a specific age group, and they need specific activities.
- Play *with* children, not *to* them. Try to interact, not entertain. The adult can initiate the activity but should wait for the child to respond.
- Involve different ways of communicating in your social interactions: looking, touching, holding, talking, rocking, singing, and laughing. Give infants a lot of different social responses to learn.
- Be sensitive to infants' signals. If they are interested, they will laugh, coo, look, smile, and reach. If tired or disinterested, they may fuss, turn away, or fall asleep.
- *Talk* to infants. Children learn speech from the moment they are born. The more language they hear, the more they will learn. Name actions, objects, and people.
- Offer new ways of doing things. Demonstrate how something works. Encourage persistence. Do not direct children as to the "right" way to use a toy; let them explore and experiment. Obviously, if some danger is involved, use your judgment and intervene when necessary.
- Be sensitive to variations initiated by the child, and be ready to respond to them.

A child can use play materials either alone or with an adult. Adults should use judgment in the choice of materials presented to each age group. A toy that a two-month-old might enjoy might not be appropriate for a nine-month-old. When offering materials to the children, remember:

- Toys and materials should encourage action. Materials should not just entertain but elicit some action.
- Toys should respond to the child's action. When the child pushes or pulls a toy, the toy should react. The ability to control parts of one's world, to learn cause and effect, is an important part of learning at this early age.

- Materials should be versatile. The more ways a toy can be used, the better it is.
- Whenever possible, toys should provide more than one kind of sensory output. For example, a clear rattle lets the child see, as well as hear, the action.

Play and playthings are an important part of the environment. Do not believe that constant stimulation is the aim. Even very young infants need time to be alone and to get away from it all. It is important to be sensitive to the infant's cues about feelings to help avoid overstimulation and distress.

The following are some activity ideas for infants one to 12 months old. Remember that some activities are appropriate for many ages.

- Change the infant's position for a different view.
- Use bells, rattles, and spoons to make noise.
- Exercise the infant's arms and legs.
- Rub the infant's body with different textured materials.
- Put large, clear pictures at eye level for the infant to look at.
- Imitate the sounds the infant makes.
- Record the children's sounds and play them back.
- Put toys slightly out of reach to encourage rolling over and reaching.
- Take the babies outside on warm days. Let them feel the grass and see trees and plants.
- Call the children by name.
- Play peekaboo with the children.
- Hide toys and encourage children to look for them.
- Attach a string to toys and show the children how to pull them. *Do not leave the child unattended with the string; they may get entangled.*
- Make puppets for children to look at and hold.
- Let children play with safe, unbreakable mirrors.
- Play games and sing, using parts of the body. Make up songs about feet, hands, noses, and so on.
- Show children how to bang two toys together.
- Let the child feed herself. Give peas, diced cooked carrots, or small pieces of fruit to practice with (see Figure 14–11).
- Play patty-cake and sing *Row-Row-Row Your Boat.* Encourage children to finish the songs for you.
- Listen for airplanes, trucks, cars, dogs, and the like outside, and call the children's attention to them.
- Roll a ball to the child and encourage the child to roll it back.
- Play hide-and-seek.
- Play music for the children; encourage them to clap along.
- Have hats for the children to wear. Let them see themselves in the mirror.

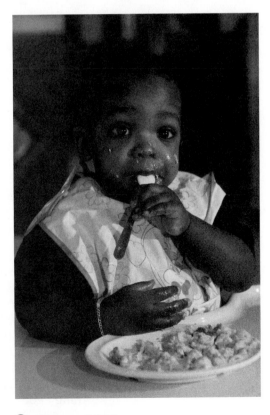

Figure 14-11
Allow toddlers to practice feeding themselves.

- Read to the children. Point out the pictures; encourage the child to point to them.
- Let the children play with different textures.
- Put toys upside down and sideways. See how the children respond to the changes.
- Play pretending games.
- Show the children how to stack blocks.
- Make obstacle courses for the children to crawl over, around, and through.
- Let children play with measuring cups and spoons in water, sand, or cornmeal.
- Play follow-the-leader.
- Make an incline for the children to roll objects down.
- Have children set the table with plastic cups and dishes.
- Hide a clock or toy under a towel and see if one of the children can find it.
- Have purses and bags for the children to carry things in.
- Give children puppets to play with. Watch how they use them.
- Let children finger paint with nontoxic paint.
- Let them go barefoot in sand and grass, so they can feel the textures (see Figure 14–12).
- Use old-fashioned clothespins for children to put around the rim of a coffee can or plastic container. (Make sure any sharp edges are filed down.)
- Encourage children to help put their toys away.
- Let them practice opening containers (e.g., plastic margarine bowls). Put a toy in the container to encourage them to open it.
- Make toys for the children; be inventive, and let your imagination go! Remember that toys should have no sharp edges and should be too large to fit in babies' mouths.

Figure 14-12
Infants and toddlers enjoy outdoor exploration.

Infant activities gradually become more and more complex as children mature. Usually, by 12 to 14 months, the child is walking and beginning to talk. An infant at this age is quite accomplished mentally. He understands that objects are separate and detached. The infant rotates, reverses, and stacks things, and places them in containers and takes them out again, to further consider their separateness.

Projects for toddlers can be more complex in response to their increased mental and physical abilities. Small-group activities can usually be tried with some success. When working with toddlers and planning activities for them, remember that the activities should be kept as simple as possible. And *plan ahead*. Anything that can go wrong will. Bring everything needed to start and finish the project with you.

Following are some ideas you might want to try with toddlers. Watch the children and see what you think they might enjoy.

- *Easel painting* (one-color paint; mix with small amount of liquid soap to make it easier to wash the paint out of clothes).
- *Waterplay.* Use measuring cups for pouring.
- *Coloring.* Use a limited number of large-size crayons and a large sheet of paper. For a change, try covering the whole table with paper.
- *Collage.* Try using starch and tissue paper with paintbrushes.
- *Finger painting.* For a change, try yogurt or pudding, but be sensitive to the feelings of parents who do not want their children to play with food.
- *Paint on cloth* pinned to the easel. It makes a great gift for parents.
- *Flannelboard stories.* Keep them short and graphic.
- *Bubble blowing.* This should be done sitting down. Emphasize blowing through a straw. Use a cup with water and soap. Collect *all* straws; they can be dangerous if a child falls on them. Note: A small slit cut near the top of the straw prevents a child from sucking up soapy water.
- *Gluing.* Use torn paper, tissue, magazine pictures, and the like. Avoid small beans, peas, and so on, which could be swallowed or put up noses.
- *Modeling dough,* made with salt, flour, and nontoxic coloring.
- *Hand and footprints.*
- *Body tracings.*
- *Paint a large cardboard box;* cut shapes in the sides. Children can climb through the sides after they paint it.
- *Go on a sock walk.* Have children remove their shoes (with parent permission) and go for a walk in the yard. Look at the seeds and other interesting items collected on the bottoms of the socks. Place any seeds collected on a wet sponge and watch them sprout in a few days. (More suitable for older toddlers.)
- *Do simple shape rubbings.* (More suitable for older toddlers.)
- *Make simple roll-out cookies,* or use frozen dough for the children to roll out and cut with cookie cutters.
- *Music.* Try drums, rhythm sticks, clapping games, and simple exercises to music.

Recent findings about music suggest that it may help the brain make connections, thus enhancing the child's ability to learn. Honig (2005) suggests that singing simple melodies is very soothing to babies; use the nonsense syllables they use. Do not be afraid to use a simple tune, like *Twinkle, Twinkle, Little Star.* *Happy Birthday* will work, too. Do not worry that you do not have a beautiful voice. Babies love all rhythmic, musical sounds. You do not even have to be able to carry a tune—infants will not care! You can also use a tape or CD player to play music softy in the background as infants and toddlers play.

Use music to announce transitions. Sing *Now We're Going out to Play* to the tune of *Mary Had a Little Lamb* and repeat it each time you go out. Soon you will find the children singing along with you (Kemple, Batey, & Hartle, 2004; Honig, 2005).

CHILD'S PHYSICAL ENVIRONMENT

As a student teacher—the new adult at your placement site—you will need to study both indoor and outdoor space. Try to answer the following questions:

- Are there as many play spaces at any one time as there are children enrolled in the program?
- Are the outdoor spaces safe?
- Are climbing structures high enough to challenge the children but low enough, and cushioned underneath, so falls will not hurt or injure any child?
- Are there enough wheeled vehicles for the number of children who want to ride them?
- Is there a "road" for the wheeled vehicles to follow? Are traffic rules made clear and enforced?
- If there is a sandbox, is there a cover?
- Are water tables set away from major play areas but close to the water supply?
- If a splashing pool is used, is it located near the water supply and sufficiently far from the rest of the play area, to prevent children from being splashed who do not want to be wet? Is the pool drained at night and stored?
- Are there outside and inside water fountains? Are these at child height?
- If cups or plastic glasses are used, are they disposable or personalized, to minimize the spread of germs?
- Are there child-sized toilets or potty chairs? Are they easily accessible to children learning to use the toilet? Are they out of the way of crawlers? Are they disinfected frequently and always after bowel movements?
- Is there a sink for washing hands by the diaper changing table? Is there a sink in the staff bathroom area for washing hands after toileting? Is there clean, dry toweling available?
- Do staff wash their hands before preparing food?
- Are children directed to wash their hands before eating (see Figure 14–13)?

Infant and Toddler Language Development

It is never too early to read to children. Just the sound of the voice, the lilting quality of speech, and the caregiver's proximity ultimately aid in language acquisition. Initially, one may just point to pictures and name objects for children. Later, explanations can be expanded and children can be asked for feedback. Although it is never too early to read, it is important to gauge reading level and length of time spent on one activity according to how the children respond.

Ability to concentrate varies dramatically among children. However, it is true that very young children generally have very short attention spans. The ability to focus on a given object or activity increases dramatically in the first three years. Studies show that the observing child is participating and learning, even while not physically involved in the activity.

Heavy cardboard books, designed for small hands, are easily handled, excellent manipulatives, and a wonderful way for children to have their

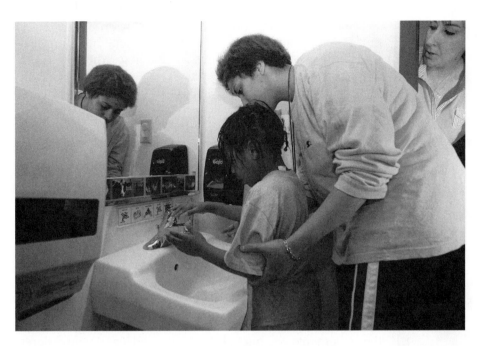

Figure 14-13
Encouraging children to develop a regular routine of hand washing is all part of the student teaching experience.

first experiences with reading. Simple board books, with brightly colored pictures, and simple, repetitive story lines are best. *Brown Bear, Brown Bear, What Do You See?* is a good book for babies and toddlers, as are *Goodnight Moon*, *The Very Hungry Caterpillar*, and *The Three Little Kittens*. Parents can point you to other good titles, as can your local children's librarian, especially newly published books or ones on special topics. The following are helpful guidelines for toddler reading activities:

- Read to a young child when you are in the mood to do so.
- Choose a book that is not only appropriate for the child but is also one you like.
- Remember that timing is important. A fussy baby or a busily playing toddler will not be interested in a book at that moment.
- Establish a special reading time.
- Position the child so that pictures can be seen easily. Many children enjoy sitting on your lap or cuddling next to you in an easy chair (see Figure 14–14).
- Allow the child to help you, and do not worry if they turn more than one page at a time, or want to start in the middle of a favorite book. One toddler, whom we both know, wanted the same book read every day, for weeks, until he had committed it to memory!
- Point to and identify things in the pictures as you read.
- React positively to the child's attempts to name objects, turn pages, and verbalize.
- Use your voice as a tool; vary pitch, speed, rhythm, even loudness. Do remember, though, that a quiet voice is often best.
- Be responsive to the children; listen to their comments.

One surefire activity of interest to children of any age is music. Simply singing can create great excitement and provides tremendous opportunities for learning. Whereas speech is unpredictable, music uses words that are the same with every repetition, even with minor variations. Children learn words to songs more easily within the pattern of melody, rhythm, and rhyme, which enhances their language development. The use of props at music time reinforces learning. There are hundreds of songs incorporating body parts and including movement components that bring forth peals of delight from children. In the context of music, even the shy child is more readily drawn out and more willingly participates.

● **Figure 14-14**
Sharing a book with a toddler.

AWARENESS OF YOUR OWN NEEDS AS A CAREGIVER

We have taken the preponderance of this chapter to discuss elements of caregiving essential to the optimal development of very young children. In reading and thinking about all these elements you might have wondered if and why children ever turn out all right. How can any caregiver provide enough essential nurturance without smothering for good outcomes? Amidst wondering all this, you might also ask "What about me as the provider? How can I take care of myself?"

The child care profession is notorious for low wages, long hours, and difficult assignments. Historically, providers have received little respect, few benefits, and not much money.

Although everyone talks about children representing the future, children can be the first to lose in times of economic hardship. Although the importance of the early years is widely acknowledged, we see poor allocation of resources to early childhood endeavors.

Fortunately, in recent years, more effort has gone into the area of early childhood development, the provision of child care, and the education of children in the early years. Also fortunately, the profession of early childhood education is increasingly espoused by informed, educated, and intelligent providers. It is essential that we view ourselves as professionals, present ourselves to the world as professionals, and that we expect to be accepted as equals in a world of professionals. To accomplish this, we must first learn to value ourselves.

In your relationships with parents and coworkers, believe in your professional status and behave accordingly. Making yourself knowledgeable, keeping yourself interested, and treating your infant charges, their parents, and your coworkers sensitively and ethically will reap great rewards for you in how all these people respond to you in turn. Continue to educate yourself, not only by participating in classes and reading but by remaining open to the different experiences of the different families in your center, the individual children, and the other staff members. A willingness to be aware of different needs and different capabilities in those around you is a hallmark of professionalism.

In the course of each day, as well as in a global sense, we as caregivers also must learn to take care of ourselves. Just as infants must be given opportunities to balance activity with periods of rest, providers must have opportunities to make choices in their activities, locations, and levels of stimulation. There are countless activities that potentially enhance any given domain of development. As the caregiver, select the one you can enjoy for that day. Children understand that the needs of their caregivers vary. They can, to a limited extent, moderate their levels of noise, activity, and curiosity if they understand that these conflict with the needs of their caregiver.

Perhaps most importantly, take your responsibilities seriously, but do not take responsibility for those elements of your job that you cannot change. Most every child care center has dysfunctional families in attendance and every center has its own challenges internally. Part of being a professional is the recognition of these challenges, the willingness to work to resolve what is in your power to change, and the ability to accept those aspects that are not changeable.

Consistent Care

For the babies themselves, consistent and responsive care is more complicated. If possible, infants should have the same caregiver for most of their time in child care. If it is absolutely necessary to have multiple caretakers, the child should be well acquainted with any secondary caregivers before her primary caregiver leaves. Any person involved with a group of children should have a thorough familiarity with the facility, its policies, and any program components.

Regular, routine care is essential for infants. Routines provide comfort and security for children, especially the very young. Learning and positive growth experiences are only possible when stress is at a minimum, and routine reduces stress for children. This does not mean that we should avoid novelty entirely. However, novel situations should occur in a context of predictability.

One of the most essential predictable elements must be that caregivers respond to the needs of the infants. Most early childhood experts agree that it is impossible to spoil a child before six months to a year of age (Bowlby, 1982; Elkind & Weiner, 1978; Spock & Rothenburg, 1992; White, 1975; Quann & Wien, 2006). White does not believe you can spoil a baby in the first seven months of life. In fact, he strongly suggests that caregivers typically respond to a baby's crying in a natural way. Elkind and Weiner (1978) cite research studies indicating

> that parents who respond to their infants' cries are likely to provide conditions of warmth and nurturance that will stop the crying, enable their children to feel secure, and make them less likely to cry or demand unreasonable attention in the future.

Elkind and Weiner (1978) go on to contrast the children of unresponsive parents; these children tended to fuss and cry a great deal later on. "Babies whose cries are heard and responded to promptly and with loving care tend to become relatively undemanding, easily satisfied, and well-behaved infants." Bowlby (1982) talks about spoiling in relation to attachment. He states

> . . . no harm comes to [the child] when [the mother] gives him as much of her presence and attention as he seems to want. Thus, in regard to mothering—as to food—a young child seems to be so made that, if from the first he is permitted to decide, he can satisfactorily regulate his own "intake."

To echo these experts, a caregiver should respond promptly to calls for attention, attempt to discover the cause of discomfort or need, and if there is no serious problem, comfort the child. Only if she clearly cannot make an effective intervention after trying the above should she allow a young infant to "cry it out" (White, 1975).

For older children, too, responsiveness can only assist in nurturing a positive developmental outcome. The basic sense of trust comes out of having one's needs taken seriously and having them responded to appropriately. Not only will responsive care create trust for the caregiver, but also the child will feel valued and validated, resulting in a positive sense of self-esteem. Elkind (2003) decries the misunderstandings about play that too many of parents seem to hold. He maintains that the best way to prepare a child to face hardship is to provide a loving, nurturing environment in which she can develop self-esteem and trust in her caregivers. He concludes:

> As teachers of young children, we need to resist the pressures to transform play into work—into academic instruction. We encourage true play by making certain that we offer materials that leave room for the imagination—blocks, paints, paper to be cut and pasted—and that children have sufficient time to innovate with these materials (Elkind, 2003).

Responsive care does not apply only to the crying infant. It is equally important for the exploring, curious, learning child. Thus, responsiveness also applies to awareness of developmental level; current level of functioning; and knowledge of appropriate tasks, objects, and expectations for given ages.

SAFETY

Probably the first element parents look for in a care situation is safety. Every parent and provider has heard countless times of the importance of childproofing their space. Gerber (1971) advocates total noninterference with infants' exploration whenever possible, and this is possible, she says, only by providing a totally safe, childproof environment geared to the developmental levels of the children.

Among the essential considerations in childproofing are:

- Dangerous objects are not present or are locked up; these objects include sharp or breakable items, chemicals (drugs, cleansers, cosmetics), plastic bags, balloons, or other items that can cause suffocation. Furniture is sturdy, and bookcases are fastened to the wall so that the children learning to walk will not pull them down on themselves when using them for support or when attempting to climb them.
- Electrical sockets are plugged with childproof inserts; electrical appliances cannot be pulled down or turned on by children.
- Heaters are safe to walk on or touch, or are covered with a safety grate.
- Windows and doors are latched with childproof latches.
- The facility is clean and well maintained; rugs are fastened down and regularly vacuumed.
- Staff members do not drink coffee or other hot liquids that can spill on children or that children can consume.
- Staff members are vigilant about activities of children, rather than conversing among themselves.

- Caregivers are aware of health hazards and infectious diseases, and take routine steps to minimize the spread of illness. It is an undervalued health fact that merely washing hands each time a diaper is changed or a nose is wiped can cut illness, or exposure to illness, by over 75 percent. Regularly wiping doorknobs, washing toys, and minimizing the use of baby bottles in the play area can likewise cut illness for both providers and children.

- Awareness of contagious illnesses and their symptoms must also be exercised by staff, with rigid attendance guidelines for children exhibiting those symptoms.

- Lists of toxic plants should be readily available, particularly if the center has either indoor or outdoor plants within a child's reach.

- Lists of parent emergency numbers, paramedics, and poison control centers should be posted in locations readily available and known to staff. Emergency treatment consent forms must be on file for each child, with guidelines about parental preferences.

- Lists of child allergies and medical conditions should also be readily available to staff.

- Food service should take into consideration potential spoilage of dairy products if left unrefrigerated or if mixed with even miniscule amounts of saliva.

SUMMARY

In this chapter, we discussed why there is a need for quality infant and toddler care. We also mentioned some of the characteristics of quality programs. The research tends to reveal more positive outcomes of early care, especially in regard to later social adjustment, and cognitive and language development.

Infant and toddler center routines and procedures depend on the philosophy and physical setting. Every center has guidelines for caregivers'

behaviors. Knowing guidelines and fitting quickly into center practice are prime student teacher goals.

Learning takes place during each child's encounter with a caregiver. Caregivers can develop many skills for the child's benefit. Many action activities and experiences planned for this age group incorporate reciprocal responses from adults and play objects. The roots of independence and verbal ability develop as do individual preferences.

HELPFUL WEB SITES

http://www.acf.hhs.gov/
U.S. Department of Health and Human Services. Search for information on Early Head Start.

http://www.zerotothree.org
Zero to Three. Investigate their journal and other publications.

http://www.naeyc.org
National Association for the Education of Young Children. Select infant and toddler readings.

http://www.whitehouse.gov
The White House. Learn about *Good Start, Grow Smart: The Bush Administration Early Childhood Initiative.*

http://www.nccic.org
National Child Care Information Center. Find the on-line library.

http://www.ehsnrc.org
Early Head Start National Resource Center. Supports high-quality services to Early Head Start and Migrant Head Start.

http://fpg.unc.edu
Frank Porter Graham Child Development Institute. A multidisciplinary institute at the University of North Carolina at Chapel Hill, whose mission is to cultivate and share the knowledge necessary to enhance child development and family well-being.

 Additional resources for this chapter can be found by visiting the Online Companion at www.earlychilded.delmar.com.

○ SUGGESTED ACTIVITIES

A. If you have not worked or done student teaching in an infant/toddler center, visit one for an hour. List all staff behaviors that protect children's health or safety. Report your findings to the group.

B. Research, through local licensing agencies, the number of infant/toddler programs that were licensed in the past year in your community.

C. In groups of three to four, discuss infant/toddler care for teenage parents. Decide what type of care would best suit the teenage parents in your community. Report your ideas to the class.

○ REVIEW

A. List three characteristics of a quality infant/toddler center.

B. Describe expected student teacher behavior during emergencies.

C. List ways a caregiver could promote learning when bathing a 15-month-old child.

D. List possible signals that indicate a child is tired.

E. Select the answer that best completes each statement.

1. The factor that may best limit the spread of infection is:
   a. periodic caregiver screening.
   b. change of room temperature.
   c. hand washing.
   d. the use of clean sponges.
   e. the use of spray disinfectants.

2. When feeding a young child:
   a. watch for signals that indicate the child is full.
   b. make sure the child finishes a small serving.
   c. expect him to try a little of everything.
   d. eat along with the child.

3. Telling infants that it is time to change their diapers is:
   a. ridiculous and silly.
   b. difficult.
   c. not important.
   d. important.

4. An important part of student teachers' work in an infant and toddler center is:
   a. recording care specifics and asking when in doubt.
   b. watching first, rather than pitching right in.
   c. letting the regular staff do most of the talking.
   d. moving quickly and efficiently.
   e. telling parents how their children are acting.

5. If an infant or toddler is using a toy incorrectly:
   a. demonstrate the proper usage.
   b. ask another toddler show how use it correctly.
   c. leave the child alone if it is not dangerous.
   d. talk about the right way to use it.

CASE SCENARIO

Setting: A family child care home. The caregiver, Robin, and her husband, Tom, recently bought a new split-level home so that the lower level could be devoted to her child care. Downstairs, there are two reasonably large rooms, a bathroom, and an ample storage area under the stairs for a lot of the children's toys.

The smaller of the two rooms is the infant room. Currently, Robin has seven children in her care: two babies (a one-month-old girl and a four-month-old boy), two four-year-old girls, and one five-year-old boy, Gordon, who attends an afternoon kindergarten program.

The infant room is furnished with a crib, a playpen, a carpeted area for crawling, a wind-up swing, and a mirror placed low on the wall, so infants can see themselves. The room for older children is well furnished, with a low table and chairs for crafts, puzzles, snacks, and so on. There is a low couch, which is perfect for Robin to sit on for reading to the older children when the infants are sleeping. Robin has decorated the walls with the letters of the alphabet and the numbers from one to ten. She also had a local artist paint a mural of teddy bears playing on the wall by the couch. The window wall

is opposite, with built-in shelves below for puzzles, small cars, and other play objects.

Outside, Robin has a large, grassy fenced area with a climbing structure, a swing set, and a paved area for wheeled toys such as tricycles, wagons, and large trucks. Tom has built a playhouse and a cave-like structure, which the children enjoy.

Gordon's mother has asked Robin whether or not Robin will be able to take care of her newborn when she arrives.

"I'm really hoping you'll be able to take the new baby. Any chance one of your current children won't be here next fall? You've been so good with Gordon so I know how good you'd be with my new baby."

"I'm not sure," Robin answers, "but Gordon will be in first grade next year so he'll not be here until after school."

"The doctor says that the baby is due in December. Hey, did you decide to follow through on applying for accreditation?" Gordon's mother queries.

"I don't think it's worth the effort for me," replies Robin. "I'm always fully enrolled. For me, taking all that time and completing all that paperwork is

continues . . .

. . . continued

almost too overwhelming to even think about!"

Questions for Discussion:

1. Would you want to place your own baby or toddler in Robin's family child care home?

2. Does Robin's family child care program seem like a quality

one? (Check the criteria listed in this chapter to guide your response.)

3. What are your state's licensing recommendations concerning adult-child ratios in family day homes?

REFERENCES

Acredolo, L., & Goodwyn, S. (2000). *Baby minds: Brain-building games your baby will love to play.* New York: Bantam Books.

Baba, S. (2003, Spring). Diversity corner: Toilet learning in different cultures. *SMAEYC Newslink* [Newletter published by the San Mateo Association for the Education of Young Children], 2.

Batshaw, M.L. (2002). *Children with disabilities,* 5th ed. Baltimore. MD: Paul H. Brookes Publishing Co.

Bauer, D., Fortin, S., & McPartlin, D. (2006, Spring). Solving the puzzle of infant curriculum: A model for infant curriculum development. *ACEI Focus on Infants and Toddlers, A Quarterly Publication for the Education Community, 18*(3), 3–8.

Bowlby, J. (1982). *Attachment and loss, 1* (2nd ed.). New York: Basic Books.

Bredekamp, S., & Copple, C. (Eds.). (1997). *Developmentally appropriate practice in early childhood programs (Rev. ed.)* . Washington, DC: National Association for the Education of Young Children.

Butler, S. (2004, November/December). Play with me, sing to me, read to me, me: fostering the development of toddlers through lots of activity. *Early Childhood News,* 28–31. Stout, WI: University of Wisconsin-Stout.

Carlson, F. M. (2005, July). Significance of touch in young children's lives. *Young Children, 60*(4), 79–85.

Carothers, L. (1990). *When young children bite: for teachers and day care workers.* [Handout]. Project Enlightenment, Wake County Public School System, Raleigh, NC.

Daniel, J. E. (1998, November). A modern mother's place is wherever her children are: Facilitating infant and toddler mothers' transitions in child care. *Young Children, 53*(6).

Da Ros, D. A., & Kovach, B. A. (1998, Fall). Assisting toddlers and caregivers during conflict resolutions: Interactions that promote socialization. *Childhood Education, 75*(1).

DeJong, L., & Cottrell, B. H. (1999, January). Designing infant child care programs to meet the needs of children born to teenage parents. *Young Children, 54*(1).

Dombro, A. L., & Lerner, C. (2006, January). Sharing the care of infants and toddlers. *Young Children, 61*(1), 29–32.

Eisenberg, A., & Murkoff, H. E. (1995, March). What to expect: Is it potty time? *Parenting.*

Elkind, D. (2003, May). Thanks for the memory: The lasting value of true play. *Young Children, 58*(3), 46–51.

Elkind, D., & Weiner, B. (1978). *Development of the child.* New York: John Wiley.

Geist, E. (2003, January). Infants and toddlers exploring mathematics. *Young Children, 58*(1), 10–12.

Gerber, M. (1971). *Resources for infant educarers.* Los Angeles: Resources for Infant Educarers.

Gillespie, L. G., & Seibel, N. L. (2006, July). Self-regulation: a cornerstone of early childhood development. *Young Children, 61*(4), 34–39.

Gonzalez-Mena, J. (2004, September). What can an orphanage teach us? Lessons from Budapest. *Young Children, 59*(5), 26–30.

Gonzalez-Mena, J., & Chahin, E. (2004, November). What's best for babies? Beyond right and wrong to different: Comparing philosophies of infant-toddler care. Paper presented at the *National Association for the Education of Young Children Conference,* November, 2004.

Greenberg, P. (1996, May). Do you take care of babies? *Young Children, 51*(4).

Honig, A. S. (2005, September). The language of lullabies. *Young Children, 60*(5), 30–36.

Kemple, K. M., Batey, J. J., & Hartle, L. C. (2004, July). Music play: musical play and exploration. *Young Children, 59*(4), 30–37.

Lally, J. R., Griffin, V., Fenichel, C., Segal, M., Szanton, E., & Weissbourd, B. (1997). Developmentally appropriate care for children from birth to age 3, Part 2 in *Developmentally appropriate practice in early childhood programs—(Rev. ed.)*, Bredekamp, S., & Copple, C. (Eds.). Washington, DC: National Association for the Education of Young Children.

Lally, J. R., & Mangione, P. (2006, July). The uniqueness of infancy demands a responsive approach. *Young Children, 61*(4), 14–20.

Lowman, L., & Ruhmann, L. (1998, May). Simply sensational spaces: A multi-S approach to toddler environments. *Young Children, 53*(3).

Meyer, D. (2005, August/September). The use of American sign language with infants and toddlers. *Early Childhood News*, 38–39. Stout, WI: University of Wisconsin-Stout.

National Institute of Child Health and Human Development. (1996). Characteristics of infant child care: Factors contributing to positive caregiving. *Early Childhood Research Quarterly, 11*(3).

Parish, L. E., Rudisill, M. E., Schilling, T., McOmber, K. A., Bellows, L., & Anderson, J. (2006, May). Healthy today and tomorrow: three strategies that work. *Young Children, 61*(3), 32–38.

Quann, V., & Wien, C. A. (2006, July). The visible empathy of infants and toddlers. *Young Children, 61*(4), 22–29.

Reinsberg, J. (1995, September). Reflections on quality infant care. *Young Children, 50*(6).

Segatti, L., Brown-DuPaul, J., & Keyes, T. L. (2003, September). Using everyday materials to promote problem solving in toddlers. *Young Children, 58*(5), 12–16, 18.

Sexton, D., Snyder, P., Sharpton, W. R., & Stricklin, S. (1993, Annual Theme Issue). Infants and toddlers with special needs and their families. *Childhood Education, 69*(5).

Sparrow, J. D. (2004, April/May). Getting ready for potty training: Let your child lead the way in learning. *Scholastic Parent & Child, 11*(5), 63–64.

Spock, B., & Rothenburg, M. (1992). *Baby and child care.* New York: Dutton.

Torquati, J., & Barber, J. L. (2005, May). Dancing with trees: Infants and toddlers in the garden. *Young Children, 60*(3), 40–46.

Watson, M. (2003, July). Attachment theory and challenging behaviors: Reconstructing the nature of relationships. *Young Children, 58*(4), 12–20.

Wingert, P., & Brandt, M. (2005, August 15). Reading your baby's mind. *Newsweek*, 33–39.

White, B. (1975). *The first three years of life.* Englewood Cliffs, NJ: Prentice-Hall.

EPILOGUE

You may be somewhat exhausted and exhilarated at this point. Finishing a student teaching training program is a tremendous accomplishment, a validation of sorts. Congratulations! The deep feelings you have experienced, the emotional highs and lows encountered in student teaching, will remain memorable. You will look back and see your student teaching as a time of growth.

The career field needs your energy, ideas, dedication, and enthusiasm. Children await the unique teacher you have become. Best wishes for your continued success.

Appendix

INTRODUCTION

The materials in the Appendix complement the materials in the chapters listed, but are auxiliary. You may find some selections more useful than others.

CHAPTER 1

When considering placement sites for student teachers, colleges and universities attempt to identify classrooms which exemplify the following ideals and principles.

1. If one exists, a demonstration preschool/child development center on campus is used for student teacher placements.
2. If the placement is in a preschool, one with accreditation by NAEYC is chosen.
3. If an elementary school, one with known excellent teachers and principal will be utilized.
4. Attempts will be made to place student teachers within a reasonable commute distance from their respective homes.
5. If placements are made in a parochial school, one that has been accredited by the appropriate accrediting agency will be chosen.

SUMMARY OF PORTFOLIO ISSUES AND QUESTIONS

The characteristics of a useful portfolio are:

A clear purpose
—To demonstrate progress toward applying competencies
—To facilitate student growth and reflection
—To provide supporting documents for articulation purposes

Integration between coursework and fieldwork
—Both processes and product are documented
—Student selected examples of applied theory are included
—Shows growth over time in the knowledge base

Multiple sources of information
—Attestations from instructors, supervisors, parents, and children may include evaluations
—Artifacts from courses and field experiences may be included
—Reproductions, including photographs, videos, and audio tapes, provide tangible evidence of skills

Authenticity: a direct link between instruction and evidence
—A road map such as a table of contents or preface is provided describing the organization of the portfolio
—Captions describing each document, its context, and the reason for including it are essential
—Course syllabi, including objectives and transcripts, detail training received

Dynamic Assessment: capturing growth and change over time
—Reproduction from each practicum, fieldwork, and student teaching experience is provided
—Selected papers over the course of study are included
—Attestations from others reveal teacher strengths

Student Ownership
—Personal statement clarifies ideals
—Philosophy of education for young children is included
—Selection of a style of organizing the portfolio and items to be included is chosen by the student, with appropriate guidance

Multiple purposes: student growth and reflection, assessment and evaluation, and program evaluation
—Identifies student strengths and weaknesses for setting goals with advisor support
—Facilitates peer support and feedback in regular portfolio sessions
—Provides feedback to instructors on the efficacy of instruction in a given course and in a program as a whole, particularly in the area of applying theoretical knowledge
—Offers tangible evidence of the degree of mastery of competencies, for purposes of articulation or transfer to more advanced study; reduces needless repetition of materials
—Shows degree of understanding of and experience with special needs, multicultural, and bilingual populations

Adapted from Turner, P. (Ed.). (2002). *La Ristra: New Mexico's comprehensive professional development system in early care, education, and family support.* Santa Fe, NM: Children, Youth and Families Department, State of New Mexico. Reprinted with permission.

CHAPTER 2

NAEYC CODE OF ETHICAL CONDUCT AND STATEMENT OF COMMITMENT

Revised April 2005

A position statement of the National Association for the Education of Young Children

Endorsed by the Association for Childhood Education International

Preamble

NAEYC recognizes that those who work with young children face many daily decisions that have moral and ethical implications. The **NAEYC Code of Ethical Conduct** offers guidelines for responsible behavior and sets forth a common basis for resolving the principal ethical dilemmas encountered in early childhood care and education. The **Statement of Commitment** is not part of the Code but is a personal acknowledgement of an individual's willingness to embrace the distinctive values and moral obligations of the field of early childhood care and education.

The primary focus of the Code is on daily practice with children and their families in programs for children from birth through 8 years of age, such as infant/toddler programs, preschool and prekindergarten programs, child care centers, hospital and child life settings, family child care homes, kindergartens, and primary classrooms. When the issues involve young children, then these provisions also apply to specialists who do not work directly with children, including program administrators, parent educators, early childhood adult educators, and officials with responsibility for program monitoring and licensing. (Note: See also the "Code of Ethical Conduct: Supplement for Early Childhood Adult Educators," online at www.naeyc.org/about/positions/pdf/ethics04.pdf.)

Core values

Standards of ethical behavior in early childhood care and education are based on commitment to the following core values that are deeply rooted in the history of the field of early childhood care and education. We have made a commitment to

• Appreciate childhood as a unique and valuable stage of the human life cycle

• Base our work on knowledge of how children develop and learn

• Appreciate and support the bond between the child and family

• Recognize that children are best understood and supported in the context of family, culture,* community, and society

• Respect the dignity, worth, and uniqueness of each individual (child, family member, and colleague)

• Respect diversity in children, families, and colleagues

• Recognize that children and adults achieve their full potential in the context of relationships that are based on trust and respect

---

* The term *culture* includes ethnicity, racial identity, economic level, family structure, language, and religious and political beliefs, which profoundly influence each child's development and relationship to the world.

Conceptual framework

The Code sets forth a framework of professional responsibilities in four sections. Each section addresses an area of professional relationships: (1) with children, (2) with families, (3) among colleagues, and (4) with the community and society. Each section includes an introduction to the primary responsibilities of the early childhood practitioner in that context. The introduction is followed by a set of ideals (I) that reflect exemplary professional practice and by a set of principles (P) describing practices that are required, prohibited, or permitted.

The **ideals** reflect the aspirations of practitioners. The **principles** guide conduct and assist practitioners in resolving ethical dilemmas.* Both ideals and principles are intended to direct practitioners to those questions which, when responsibly answered, can provide the basis for conscientious decision making. While the Code provides specific direction for addressing some ethical dilemmas, many others will require the practitioner to combine the guidance of the Code with professional judgment.

The ideals and principles in this Code present a shared framework of professional responsibility that affirms our commitment to the core values of our field. The Code publicly acknowledges the responsibilities that we in the field have assumed, and in so doing supports ethical behavior in our work. Practitioners who face situations with ethical dimensions are urged to seek guidance in the applicable parts of this Code and in the spirit that informs the whole.

Often "the right answer"—the best ethical course of action to take—is not obvious. There may be no readily apparent, positive way to handle a situation. When one important value contradicts another, we face an ethical dilemma. When we face a dilemma, it is our professional responsibility to consult the Code and all relevant parties to find the most ethical resolution.

Section I

Ethical Responsibilities to Children

Childhood is a unique and valuable stage in the human life cycle. Our paramount responsibility is to provide care and education in settings that are safe,

* There is not necessarily a corresponding principle for each ideal.

healthy, nurturing, and responsive for each child. We are committed to supporting children's development and learning; respecting individual differences; and helping children learn to live, play, and work cooperatively. We are also committed to promoting children's self-awareness, competence, self-worth, resiliency, and physical well-being.

Ideals

I-1.1—To be familiar with the knowledge base of early childhood care and education and to stay informed through continuing education and training.

I-1.2—To base program practices upon current knowledge and research in the field of early childhood education, child development, and related disciplines, as well as on particular knowledge of each child.

I-1.3—To recognize and respect the unique qualities, abilities, and potential of each child.

I-1.4—To appreciate the vulnerability of children and their dependence on adults.

I-1.5—To create and maintain safe and healthy settings that foster children's social, emotional, cognitive, and physical development and that respect their dignity and their contributions.

I-1.6—To use assessment instruments and strategies that are appropriate for the children to be assessed, that are used only for the purposes for which they were designed, and that have the potential to benefit children.

I-1.7—To use assessment information to understand and support children's development and learning, to support instruction, and to identify children who may need additional services.

I-1.8—To support the right of each child to play and learn in an inclusive environment that meets the needs of children with and without disabilities.

I-1.9—To advocate for and ensure that all children, including those with special needs, have access to the support services needed to be successful.

I-1.10—To ensure that each child's culture, language, ethnicity, and family structure are recognized and valued in the program.

I-1.11—To provide all children with experiences in a language that they know, as well as support children in maintaining the use of their home language and in learning English.

I-1.12—To work with families to provide a safe and smooth transition as children and families move from one program to the next.

Principles

P-1.1—Above all, we shall not harm children. We shall not participate in practices that are emotionally damaging, physically harmful, disrespectful, degrading, dangerous, exploitative, or intimidating to children. *This principle has precedence over all others in this Code.*

P-1.2—We shall care for and educate children in positive emotional and social environments that are cognitively stimulating and that support each child's culture, language, ethnicity, and family structure.

P-1.3—We shall not participate in practices that discriminate against children by denying benefits, giving special advantages, or excluding them from programs or activities on the basis of their sex, race, national origin, religious beliefs, medical condition, disability, or the marital status/family structure, sexual orientation, or religious beliefs or other affiliations of their families. (Aspects of this principle do not apply in programs that have a lawful mandate to provide services to a particular population of children.)

P-1.4—We shall involve all those with relevant knowledge (including families and staff) in decisions concerning a child, as appropriate, ensuring confidentiality of sensitive information.

P-1.5—We shall use appropriate assessment systems, which include multiple sources of information, to provide information on children's learning and development.

P-1.6—We shall strive to ensure that decisions such as those related to enrollment, retention, or assignment to special education services, will be based on multiple sources of information and will never be based on a single assessment, such as a test score or a single observation.

P-1.7—We shall strive to build individual relationships with each child; make individualized adaptations in teaching strategies, learning environments, and curricula; and consult with the family so that each child benefits from the program. If after such efforts have been exhausted, the current placement does not meet a child's needs, or the child is seriously jeopardizing the ability of other children to benefit from the program, we shall collaborate with the child's family and appropriate specialists to determine the additional services needed and/or the placement option(s) most likely to ensure the child's success. (Aspects of this principle may not apply in programs that have a lawful mandate to provide services to a particular population of children.)

P-1.8—We shall be familiar with the risk factors for and symptoms of child abuse and neglect, including physical, sexual, verbal, and emotional abuse and physical, emotional, educational, and medical neglect. We shall know and follow state laws and community procedures that protect children against abuse and neglect.

P-1.9—When we have reasonable cause to suspect child abuse or neglect, we shall report it to the appropriate community agency and follow up to ensure that appropriate action has been taken. When appropriate, parents or guardians will be informed that the referral will be or has been made.

P-1.10—When another person tells us of his or her suspicion that a child is being abused or neglected, we shall assist that person in taking appropriate action in order to protect the child.

P-1.11—When we become aware of a practice or situation that endangers the health, safety, or well-being of children, we have an ethical responsibility to protect children or inform parents and/or others who can.

Section II

Ethical Responsibilities to Families

Families* are of primary importance in children's development. Because the family and the early childhood practitioner have a common interest in the child's well-being, we acknowledge a primary responsibility to bring about communication, cooperation, and collaboration between the home and early childhood program in ways that enhance the child's development.

Ideals

I-2.1—To be familiar with the knowledge base related to working effectively with families and to stay informed through continuing education and training.

I-2.2—To develop relationships of mutual trust and create partnerships with the families we serve.

I-2.3—To welcome all family members and encourage them to participate in the program.

---

* The term *family* may include those adults, besides parents, with the responsibility of being involved in educating, nurturing, and advocating for the child.

I-2.4—To listen to families, acknowledge and build upon their strengths and competencies, and learn from families as we support them in their task of nurturing children.

I-2.5—To respect the dignity and preferences of each family and to make an effort to learn about its structure, culture, language, customs, and beliefs.

I-2.6—To acknowledge families' childrearing values and their right to make decisions for their children.

I-2.7—To share information about each child's education and development with families and to help them understand and appreciate the current knowledge base of the early childhood profession.

I-2.8—To help family members enhance their understanding of their children and support the continuing development of their skills as parents.

I-2.9—To participate in building support networks for families by providing them with opportunities to interact with program staff, other families, community resources, and professional services.

Principles

P-2.1—We shall not deny family members access to their child's classroom or program setting unless access is denied by court order or other legal restriction.

P-2.2—We shall inform families of program philosophy, policies, curriculum, assessment system, and personnel qualifications, and explain why we teach as we do—which should be in accordance with our ethical responsibilities to children (see Section I).

P-2.3—We shall inform families of and, when appropriate, involve them in policy decisions.

P-2.4—We shall involve the family in significant decisions affecting their child.

P-2.5—We shall make every effort to communicate effectively with all families in a language that they understand. We shall use community resources for translation and interpretation when we do not have sufficient resources in our own programs.

P-2.6—As families share information with us about their children and families, we shall consider this information to plan and implement the program.

P-2.7—We shall inform families about the nature and purpose of the program's child assessments and how data about their child will be used.

P-2.8—We shall treat child assessment information confidentially and share this information only when there is a legitimate need for it.

P-2.9—We shall inform the family of injuries and incidents involving their child, of risks such as exposures to communicable diseases that might result in infection, and of occurrences that might result in emotional stress.

P-2.10—Families shall be fully informed of any proposed research projects involving their children and shall have the opportunity to give or withhold consent without penalty. We shall not permit or participate in research that could in any way hinder the education, development, or well-being of children.

P-2.11—We shall not engage in or support exploitation of families. We shall not use our relationship with a family for private advantage or personal gain, or enter into relationships with family members that might impair our effectiveness working with their children.

P-2.12—We shall develop written policies for the protection of confidentiality and the disclosure of children's records. These policy documents shall be made available to all program personnel and families. Disclosure of children's records beyond family members, program personnel, and consultants having an obligation of confidentiality shall require familial consent (except in cases of abuse or neglect).

P-2.13—We shall maintain confidentiality and shall respect the family's right to privacy, refraining from disclosure of confidential information and intrusion into family life. However, when we have reason to believe that a child's welfare is at risk, it is permissible to share confidential information with agencies, as well as with individuals who have legal responsibility for intervening in the child's interest.

P-2.14—In cases where family members are in conflict with one another, we shall work openly, sharing our observations of the child, to help all parties involved make informed decisions. We shall refrain from becoming an advocate for one party.

P-2.15—We shall be familiar with and appropriately refer families to community resources and professional support services. After a referral has been made, we shall follow up to ensure that services have been appropriately provided.

Section III

Ethical Responsibilities to Colleagues

In a caring, cooperative workplace, human dignity is respected, professional satisfaction is promoted, and positive relationships are developed and sustained. Based upon our core values, our primary responsibility to colleagues is to establish and maintain settings and relationships that support productive work and meet professional needs. The same ideals that apply to children also apply as we interact with adults in the workplace.

A—Responsibilities to co-workers

Ideals

I-3A.1—To establish and maintain relationships of respect, trust, confidentiality, collaboration, and cooperation with co-workers.

I-3A.2—To share resources with co-workers, collaborating to ensure that the best possible early childhood care and education program is provided.

I-3A.3—To support co-workers in meeting their professional needs and in their professional development.

I-3A.4—To accord co-workers due recognition of professional achievement.

Principles

P-3A.1—We shall recognize the contributions of colleagues to our program and not participate in practices that diminish their reputations or impair their effectiveness in working with children and families.

P-3A.2—When we have concerns about the professional behavior of a co-worker, we shall first let that person know of our concern in a way that shows respect for personal dignity and for the diversity to be found among staff members, and then attempt to resolve the matter collegially and in a confidential manner.

P-3A.3—We shall exercise care in expressing views regarding the personal attributes or professional conduct of co-workers. Statements should be based on firsthand knowledge, not hearsay, and relevant to the interests of children and programs.

P-3A.4—We shall not participate in practices that discriminate against a co-worker because of sex, race, national origin, religious beliefs or other affiliations, age, marital status/family structure, disability, or sexual orientation.

B—Responsibilities to employers

Ideals

I-3B.1—To assist the program in providing the highest quality of service.

I-3B.2—To do nothing that diminishes the reputation of the program in which we work unless it is violating laws and regulations designed to protect children or is violating the provisions of this Code.

Principles

P-3B.1—We shall follow all program policies. When we do not agree with program policies, we shall attempt to effect change through constructive action within the organization.

P-3B.2—We shall speak or act on behalf of an organization only when authorized. We shall take care to acknowledge when we are speaking for the organization and when we are expressing a personal judgment.

P-3B.3—We shall not violate laws or regulations designed to protect children and shall take appropriate action consistent with this Code when aware of such violations.

P-3B.4—If we have concerns about a colleague's behavior, and children's well-being is not at risk, we may address the concern with that individual. If children are at risk or the situation does not improve after it has been brought to the colleague's attention, we shall report the colleague's unethical or incompetent behavior to an appropriate authority.

P-3B.5—When we have a concern about circumstances or conditions that impact the quality of care and education within the program, we shall inform the program's administration or, when necessary, other appropriate authorities.

C—Responsibilities to employees

Ideals

I-3C.1—To promote safe and healthy working conditions and policies that foster mutual respect, cooperation, collaboration, competence, well-being, confidentiality, and self-esteem in staff members.

I-3C.2—To create and maintain a climate of trust and candor that will enable staff to speak and act in the best interests of children, families, and the field of early childhood care and education.

I-3C.3—To strive to secure adequate and equitable compensation (salary and benefits) for those who work with or on behalf of young children.

I-3C.4—To encourage and support continual development of employees in becoming more skilled and knowledgeable practitioners.

Principles

P-3C.1—In decisions concerning children and programs, we shall draw upon the education, training, experience, and expertise of staff members.

P-3C.2—We shall provide staff members with safe and supportive working conditions that honor confidences and permit them to carry out their responsibilities through fair performance evaluation, written grievance procedures, constructive feedback, and opportunities for continuing professional development and advancement.

P-3C.3—We shall develop and maintain comprehensive written personnel policies that define program standards. These policies shall be given to new staff members and shall be available and easily accessible for review by all staff members.

P-3C.4—We shall inform employees whose performance does not meet program expectations of areas of concern and, when possible, assist in improving their performance.

P-3C.5—We shall conduct employee dismissals for just cause, in accordance with all applicable laws and regulations. We shall inform employees who are dismissed of the reasons for their termination. When a dismissal is for cause, justification must be based on evidence of inadequate or inappropriate behavior that is accurately documented, current, and available for the employee to review.

P-3C.6—In making evaluations and recommendations, we shall make judgments based on fact and relevant to the interests of children and programs.

P-3C.7—We shall make hiring, retention, termination, and promotion decisions based solely on a person's competence, record of accomplishment, ability to carry out the responsibilities of the position, and professional preparation specific to the developmental levels of children in his/her care.

P-3C.8—We shall not make hiring, retention, termination, and promotion decisions based on an individual's sex, race, national origin, religious beliefs or other affiliations, age, marital status/family structure, disability, or sexual orientation. We shall be familiar with and observe laws and regulations that pertain to employment discrimination. (Aspects of this principle do not apply to programs that have a lawful mandate to determine eligibility based on one or more of the criteria identified above.)

P-3C.9—We shall maintain confidentiality in dealing with issues related to an employee's job performance and shall respect an employee's right to privacy regarding personal issues.

Section IV

Ethical Responsibilities to Community and Society

Early childhood programs operate within the context of their immediate community made up of families and other institutions concerned with children's welfare. Our responsibilities to the community are to provide programs that meet the diverse needs of families, to cooperate with agencies and professions that share the responsibility for children, to assist families in gaining access to those agencies and allied professionals, and to assist in the development of community programs that are needed but not currently available.

As individuals, we acknowledge our responsibility to provide the best possible programs of care and education for children and to conduct ourselves with honesty and integrity. Because of our specialized expertise in early childhood development and education and because the larger society shares responsibility for the welfare and protection of young children, we acknowledge a collective obligation to advocate for the best interests of children within early childhood programs and in the larger community and to serve as a voice for young children everywhere.

The ideals and principles in this section are presented to distinguish between those that pertain to the work of the individual early childhood educator and those that more typically are engaged in collectively on behalf of the best interests of children—with the understanding that individual early childhood educators have a shared responsibility for addressing the ideals and principles that are identified as "collective."

Ideal (Individual)

I-4.1—To provide the community with high-quality early childhood care and education programs and services.

Ideals (Collective)

I-4.2—To promote cooperation among professionals and agencies and interdisciplinary collaboration among professions concerned with addressing issues in the health, education, and well-being of young children, their families, and their early childhood educators.

I-4.3—To work through education, research, and advocacy toward an environmentally safe world in which all children receive health care, food, and shelter; are nurtured; and live free from violence in their home and their communities.

I-4.4—To work through education, research, and advocacy toward a society in which all young children have access to high-quality early care and education programs.

I-4.5—To work to ensure that appropriate assessment systems, which include multiple sources of information, are used for purposes that benefit children.

I-4.6—To promote knowledge and understanding of young children and their needs. To work toward greater societal acknowledgment of children's rights and greater social acceptance of responsibility for the well-being of all children.

I-4.7—To support policies and laws that promote the well-being of children and families, and to work to change those that impair their well-being. To participate in developing policies and laws that are needed, and to cooperate with other individuals and groups in these efforts.

I-4.8—To further the professional development of the field of early childhood care and education and to strengthen its commitment to realizing its core values as reflected in this Code.

Principles (Individual)

P-4.1—We shall communicate openly and truthfully about the nature and extent of services that we provide.

P-4.2—We shall apply for, accept, and work in positions for which we are personally well-suited and professionally qualified. We shall not offer services that we do not have the competence, qualifications, or resources to provide.

P-4.3—We shall carefully check references and shall not hire or recommend for employment any person whose competence, qualifications, or character makes him or her unsuited for the position.

P-4.4—We shall be objective and accurate in reporting the knowledge upon which we base our program practices.

P-4.5—We shall be knowledgeable about the appropriate use of assessment strategies and instruments and interpret results accurately to families.

P-4.6—We shall be familiar with laws and regulations that serve to protect the children in our programs and be vigilant in ensuring that these laws and regulations are followed.

P-4.7—When we become aware of a practice or situation that endangers the health, safety, or well-being of children, we have an ethical responsibility to protect children or inform parents and/or others who can.

P-4.8—We shall not participate in practices that are in violation of laws and regulations that protect the children in our programs.

P-4.9—When we have evidence that an early childhood program is violating laws or regulations protecting children, we shall report the violation to appropriate authorities who can be expected to remedy the situation.

P-4.10—When a program violates or requires its employees to violate this Code, it is permissible, after fair assessment of the evidence, to disclose the identity of that program.

Principles (Collective)

P-4.11—When policies are enacted for purposes that do not benefit children, we have a collective responsibility to work to change these practices.

P-4.12—When we have evidence that an agency that provides services intended to ensure children's well-being is failing to meet its obligations, we acknowledge a collective ethical responsibility to report the problem to appropriate authorities or to the public. We shall be vigilant in our follow-up until the situation is resolved.

P-4.13—When a child protection agency fails to provide adequate protection for abused or neglected children, we acknowledge a collective ethical responsibility to work toward the improvement of these services.

Glossary of Terms Related to Ethics

Code of Ethics. Defines the core values of the field and provides guidance for what professionals should do when they encounter conflicting obligations or responsibilities in their work.

Values. Qualities or principles that individuals believe to be desirable or worthwhile and that they prize for themselves, for others, and for the world in which they live.

Core Values. Commitments held by a profession that are consciously and knowingly embraced by its practitioners because they make a contribution to society. There is a difference between personal values and the core values of a profession.

Morality. Peoples' views of what is good, right, and proper; their beliefs about their obligations; and their ideas about how they should behave.

Ethics. The study of right and wrong, or duty and obligation, that involves critical reflection on morality and the ability to make choices between values and the examination of the moral dimensions of relationships.

Professional Ethics. The moral commitments of a profession that involve moral reflection that extends and enhances the personal morality practitioners bring to their work, that concern actions of right and wrong in the workplace, and that help individuals resolve moral dilemmas they encounter in their work.

Ethical Responsibilities. Behaviors that one must or must not engage in. Ethical responsibilities are clear-cut and are spelled out in the Code of Ethical Conduct (for example, early childhood educators should never share confidential information about a child or family with a person who has no legitimate need for knowing).

Ethical Dilemma. A moral conflict that involves determining appropriate conduct when an individual faces conflicting professional values and responsibilities.

Sources for glossary terms and definitions

Feeney, S., & N. Freeman. 1999. *Ethics and the early childhood educator: Using the NAEYC code.* Washington, DC: NAEYC.
Kidder, R.M. 1995. *How good people make tough choices: Resolving the dilemmas of ethical living.* New York: Fireside.
Kipnis, K. 1987. How to discuss professional ethics. *Young Children* 42 (4): 26–30.

The National Association for the Education of Young Children (NAEYC) is a nonprofit corporation, tax exempt under Section 501(c)(3) of the Internal Revenue Code, dedicated to acting on behalf of the needs and interests of young children. The NAEYC Code of Ethical Conduct (Code) has been developed in furtherance of NAEYC's nonprofit and tax exempt purposes. The information contained in the Code is intended to provide early childhood educators with guidelines for working with children from birth through age 8.

An individual's or program's use, reference to, or review of the Code does not guarantee compliance with NAEYC Early Childhood Program Standards and Accreditation Performance Criteria and program accreditation procedures. It is recommended that the Code be used as guidance in connection with implementation of the NAEYC Program Standards, but such use is not a substitute for diligent review and application of the NAEYC Program Standards.

NAEYC has taken reasonable measures to develop the Code in a fair, reasonable, open, unbiased, and objective manner, based on currently available data. However, further research or developments may change the current state of knowledge. Neither NAEYC nor its officers, directors, members, employees, or agents will be liable for any loss, damage, or claim with respect to any liabilities, including direct, special, indirect, or consequential damages incurred in connection with the Code or reliance on the information presented.

NAEYC Code of Ethical Conduct Revisions Workgroup

Mary Ambery, Ruth Ann Ball, James Clay, Julie Olsen Edwards, Harriet Egertson, Anthony Fair, Stephanie Feeney, Jana Fleming, Nancy Freeman, Marla Israel, Allison McKinnon, Evelyn Wright Moore, Eva Moravcik, Christina Lopez Morgan, Sarah Mulligan, Nila Rinehart, Betty Holston Smith, and Peter Pizzolongo, *NAEYC Staff*

Statement of Commitment[*]

As an individual who works with young children, I commit myself to furthering the values of early childhood education as they are reflected in the ideals and principles of the NAEYC Code of Ethical Conduct. To the best of my ability I will

- Never harm children.
- Ensure that programs for young children are based on current knowledge and research of child development and early childhood education.
- Respect and support families in their task of nurturing children.
- Respect colleagues in early childhood care and education and support them in maintaining the NAEYC Code of Ethical Conduct.
- Serve as an advocate for children, their families, and their teachers in community and society.
- Stay informed of and maintain high standards of professional conduct.
- Engage in an ongoing process of self-reflection, realizing that personal characteristics, biases, and beliefs have an impact on children and families.
- Be open to new ideas and be willing to learn from the suggestions of others.
- Continue to learn, grow, and contribute as a professional.
- Honor the ideals and principles of the NAEYC Code of Ethical Conduct.

---

[*] This Statement of Commitment is not part of the Code but is a personal acknowledgment of the individual's willingness to embrace the distinctive values and moral obligations of the field of early childhood care and education. It is recognition of the moral obligations that lead to an individual becoming part of the profession.

Ethical Responsibilities to Practicum Sites

Some knowledge and skills needed by early childhood educators can only be acquired through direct experience in early childhood settings. Therefore, early childhood adult educators rely heavily on placements in programs at practicum sites, where students can apply what they have learned, get feedback from children and adults, and reflect on their experience.

Ideals

I–2.1 To provide practicum experiences that will positively support the professional development of adult students.

I–2.2 To foster collegial and collaborative working relationships with educators who work in practicum settings.

I–2.3 To be respectful of the responsibilities, expertise, and perspective of practitioners who work with students in practicum settings.

I–2.4 To recognize the importance and contributions of practicum staff members in the professional development of students.

Principles

P–2.1 We shall place students in settings where staff are qualified to work with young children, where mentors have experience and training in supporting adult learners, which to the greatest extent possible reflect the diverse communities in which our students will be working.

P–2.2 We shall clearly state all parties' roles and responsibilities and prepare students, mentors, and administrators for practicum experiences. We shall provide appropriate support for all parties' efforts to fulfill their roles and meet program expectations.

P–2.3 When we have concern about a program in which we place students, we shall address that concern with the classroom teacher or program administrator. If the concerns relate to the health or safety of children, see the applicable sections of the NAEYC Code: P–1.11 and P–4.9–12.

P–2.4 We shall ensure that qualified personnel conduct regular supervision of practicum experiences in order to support professional development of adult students and monitor the welfare of children.

P–2.5 We shall honor confidentiality and guard the privacy of teachers and clientele at practicum sites.

P–2.6 We shall teach adult students that they have a professional obligation to honor confidentiality and shall make every effort to ensure that they guard the privacy of the program, its teachers, and clientele.

From the National Association for the Education of Young Children, the National Association of Early Childhood Teacher Educators, and the American Associate Degree Early Childhood Teacher Educators. (2004). *Code of Ethical Conduct: Supplement for Early Childhood Adult Educators.* A joint position statement, reprinted with permission from the National Association for the Education of Young Children.

CHAPTER 3

COMPETENCIES IN DEVELOPMENTALLY APPROPRIATE PRACTICE

A. Teachers respect, value, and accept children and treat them with dignity at all times.

B. Teachers make it a priority to know each child well.

1) Teachers establish positive, personal relationships with children to foster the child's development and keep informed about the child's needs and potentials. Teachers listen to children and adapt their responses to children's differing needs, interests, styles, and abilities.

2) Teachers continually observe children's spontaneous play and interaction with the physical environment and with other children to learn about their interests, abilities, and developmental progress. On the basis of this information, teachers plan experiences that enhance children's learning and development.

3) Understanding that children develop and learn in the context of their families and communities, teachers establish relationships with families that increase their knowledge of children's lives outside the classroom and their awareness of the perspectives and priorities of those individuals most significant in the children's lives.

4) Teachers are alert to signs of undue stress and traumatic events in children's lives and aware of effective strategies to reduce stress and support the development of resilience.

5) Teachers are responsible at all times for all children under their supervision and plan for children's increasing development of self-regulation.

C. Teachers create an intellectually engaging, responsive environment to promote each child's learning and development.

1) Teachers use their knowledge about children in general and the particular children in the group as well as their familiarity with what children need to learn and develop in each curriculum area to organize the environment and plan curriculum and teaching strategies.

2) Teachers provide children with a rich variety of experiences, projects, materials, problems, and ideas to explore and investigate, ensuring that these are worthy of children's attention.

3) Teachers provide children with opportunities to make meaningful choices and time to explore through active involvement. Teachers offer children the choice to participate in a small-group or a solitary activity, assist and guide children who are not yet able to use and enjoy child-choice activity periods, and provide opportunities for practice of skills as a self-chosen activity.

4) Teachers organize the daily and weekly schedule and allocate time so as to provide children with extended blocks of time in which to engage in play, project, and/or study in integrated curriculum.

D. Teachers make plans to enable children to attain key curriculum goals across various disciplines, such as language arts, mathematics, social studies, science, art, music, physical education, and health.

1) Teachers incorporate a wide variety of experiences, materials and equipment, and teaching strategies in constructing curriculum to accommodate a broad range of children's individual differences in prior experiences, maturation rates, styles of learning, needs, and interests.

2) Teachers bring each child's home culture and language into the shared culture of the school, so that the unique contributions of each group are recognized and valued by others.

3) Teachers are prepared to meet identified special needs of individual children, including children with disabilities and those who exhibit unusual interests and skills. Teachers use all the strategies identified here, consult with appropriate specialists, and see that the child gets the specialized services she requires.

Reprinted with permission from the National Association for the Education of Young Children.

Bredekamp, S., & Copple, C. (Eds.). (1997). *Developmentally appropriate practice in early childhood programs* (rev. ed.) Washington, DC: National Association for the Education of Young Children.

NAEYC INITIAL LICENSURE (CORE) STANDARDS

(NAEYC Early Childhood Program Standards and Accreditation Criteria: The Mark of Quality in Early Childhood Education (2005). Washington, DC: National Association for the Education of Young Children.)
- Standard 1: Relationships
- Standard 2: Curriculum
- Standard 3: Teaching
- Standard 4: Assessment
- Standard 5: Health
- Standard 6: Teachers
- Standard 7: Families
- Standard 8: Community Relationships
- Standard 9: Physical Environment
- Standard 10: Leadership and Management

From Hyson, M. (Ed.). (2003). *Preparing Early Childhood Professionals: NAEYC's Standards for Programs.* Washington, DC: National Association for the Education of Young Children.

Reprinted with permission from the National Association for the Education of Young Children.

CHAPTER 4

WHAT ARE THE PREFERRED LEARNING MODALITIES OF YOUR STUDENTS?

(Appropriate for use in elementary grades)

Test for Three Types of Learners

How do you determine whether a student is a visual, auditory, or kinesthetic learner? To give the test, you need:

1. A group of not more than 15 students, because it is difficult to observe any more than that at one time.

2. A list of the students' names that you can mark as you observe their reactions.

    V—Visual learner

    A—Auditory learner

    K—Kinesthetic learner

Reactions to watch for:

Visual learners will usually close their eyes or look at the ceiling as they try to recall a visual picture.

Auditory learners will move their lips or whisper as they try to memorize.

Kinesthetic learners will use their fingers to count off items or write in the air.

The student with a photographic mind will repeat things exactly in the order they are given and will be disturbed if someone changes the order.

Giving the Test

Start by telling your students that you are going to see what kind of learners they are: visual, auditory, or kinesthetic.

This test consists of pretending that the students are going to the store to get some items for you. First you will WRITE the list on the board, allowing students to watch you, but *they must not copy it*. Next, you will give them the list ORALLY; you will not write it and *neither must they*. Then you will dictate the list orally to them, and *they will write it down*.

Note: The most predominant characteristic used is a symptom. One specific test or tests where the student has the highest recall is a reinforcement of his native way of learning. However, the symptoms are the prime indication.

First Presentation

1. Write the following list on the board while the students are watching. Do not let them write:

toothpaste	soap
Kleenex	comb
stationery	

    Note: For younger students, use the following list instead: pencil, ice cream, stamps, toy, paper.

2. Allow students to view the list for approximately one minute while you observe their reactions and mark the symptoms after the students' names.

3. Erase the list.

4. Ask, "Who would like to repeat the items for me?"

5. Observe that the visual learners will wave their hands enthusiastically.

6. Call on them to recite ORALLY, one at a time. Note that after a few students have recited, a few more timid hands will go up. These usually are auditory learners who have learned the list, not from seeing it, but from hearing the list from other students.

7. As you notice a student's symptoms, mark *V*, *A*, or *K* after her name.

Second Presentation

1. Dictate the following list orally: *no writing by either teacher or students*. Repeat the dictation a second time, pausing for a moment after each item.

binder paper		rubber bands
baby powder		notebook
nail file	or use	popcorn
cough drops		eraser
shaving cream		Band-Aids

2. Observe that the visual learners will close their eyes to try to see the items. The auditory learners will whisper each item as you dictate it. The kinesthetic learners will use their hands to mark off the number of items or will write the words in the air.

3. Ask, "Who would like to repeat the list?"

4. The auditory learners will be the most eager to respond, although other students will try to repeat the items you have dictated.

5. Make the appropriate notations of *V*, *A*, or *K* after the students' names as you observe their reactions.

Third Presentation

1. Tell students to have pencil and paper ready to write the following list as you dictate it orally. Tell them you will not count spelling. In fact, spell any words as you dictate if you see the spelling creates a problem.

lipstick		pen
Scotch tape		liquid soap
razor blades	or	candy bar
cough syrup		comb
pencil		string

2. After you have finished dictating the list, tell the students to turn their papers over and rewrite the list. Then ask them to look at the one they have written from your dictation.

3. When they have finished rewriting the list, tell them to take another piece of paper and *write the list from memory*.

4. After they have finished, check to see which students have been able to repeat the list wholly or in part.

5. Notice that students who were unsuccessful in either the first or second presentation of the test are frequently the first ones to finish. The test may be repeated, using numbers. Most students have a different form of recall for numbers than they have for words.

Evaluation of the Test

1. A teacher will have a better understanding of the individual differences of the students.

2. The teacher can encourage the students to find their natural way of learning. *Join it—don't fight it.*

3. Although all three types of learning should be developed, a student should use his natural way of learning when he is under pressure, studying for tests, and the like.

   The *visual learner* should realize that while he learns fast, he can forget equally as fast. To strengthen his recall, it is good to develop the practice of writing and outlining the subject.

   The *auditory learner* will benefit by use of a tape recorder. The more she hears a subject, the more recall is possible.

   The *kinesthetic learner* must write to recall material learned. Outlining material is a very effective method of strengthening recall.

   A photographic mind is like a polaroid camera; the picture develops fast and can fade equally as fast unless the emulsion is placed on the picture. In the learning process, the emulsion is to *write* as well as *look*. The photographic mind will often have a real problem in abstract thinking, especially in math. Seeing the picture in association with the abstraction often assists this type of learner.

   Usually, a person has more than one way to learn. He may be highly visual, fairly kinesthetic, not auditory, or any other combination. However, all three types of learning should be developed as far as possible in each student. An auditory learner should try to visualize what she hears. A visual learner should try to be more attentive in lecture programs or language laboratory work. A kinesthetic learner should try to listen and to visualize, but all three need to write.

How can a teacher cover all three types of learners in one group? By presenting material in the three ways of learning.

Visual: Ability to *hear* and *write* what is *seen.*

Auditory: Ability to *recognize visually* and *write* what is *heard.*

Kinesthetic: Ability to *hear* and *visualize* what is *written.*

The Auditory Learner

1. His attention to visual tasks may be poor.

2. He seems bored or restless during silent filmstrips.

3. He attends more to sound than to the screen during films.

4. He may have poor handwriting.

5. His drawing or other artwork is poor.

6. Work copied from the board may often turn out badly.

7. He may have reversals or inversions in writing, or he may leave out whole words or parts of words.

8. He might prefer word games, riddles, and noisy or active toys and games to more visually oriented games like checkers, board games, or puzzles.

9. He may rub his eyes or show other signs of eye problems, or complain that his eyes bother him.

10. He may do poorly on written spelling, but he may be a better speller in spelling bees.

11. He may not remember much of what he has read, and he does better on material discussed in class.

12. He may read below grade level, or below the level expected for his general ability.

13. His comprehension is probably better on oral reading than on silent reading.

14. His math errors may show consistent patterns, inattention to signs, or confusion of similar numerals.

15. He may do poorly on map activities.

16. He may not seem to observe things others comment on.

17. He may do poorly on sight words and flashcard drills.

18. He may be poor at visual word attack so that he confuses words that look similar.

19. He may do poorly on matching activities, but given the chance, will sort through a stack of photocopies for the clearest copy.

20. He probably dislikes seat work activities.

21. He may often skip words or even whole lines in reading and uses his finger as a pointer whenever possible.

22. He may enjoy memory work.

23. He may be a mumbler.

24. He may have trouble identifying *how many* without counting.

25. He seems brighter than his IQ test scores or achievement scores would lead you to believe.

26. His papers are probably poorly organized; often he writes the answers in the wrong blank on workbook pages, or can't find where the answers go.

27. He may seem lost on material requiring a separate answer sheet.

28. He has trouble locating words in the dictionary or index and has trouble telling time.

The Visual Learner

1. She may seem to ignore verbal directions.

2. Questions or instructions must often be repeated, frequently in different words.

3. She may frequently have a blank expression on her face, or may seem to daydream during classes that are primarily verbal.

4. She may substitute gestures for words, or may seem, by her gestures, to be literally groping for a word.

5. She may have poor speech, in terms of either low vocabulary, poor flexibility of vocal patterns, or articulation.

6. She may watch the teacher's lips closely and may be distressed when she cannot see her face, such as when she is talking while writing on the blackboard or discussing a filmstrip in a darkened room.

7. She often looks to see what everyone else is doing before following instructions.

8. She may play the TV, tape, or record player too loudly.

9. She may say "What?" or "Huh?" often.

10. She seems to misunderstand often.

11. She often speaks too loudly, though she may dislike speaking before the group or listening to others.

12. She prefers the *show* aspects of show-and-tell and prefers filmstrips to tapes.

13. She may have trouble discriminating similar words or sounds that she hears. *Bill*, *bell*, *bull*, and *ball* may all sound the same to her, and she certainly cannot discriminate *pin* from *pen*.

14. She may do poorly in phonics-based activities.

15. She often can't remember information given verbally.

16. She may describe things in terms of visual stimuli and omit auditory descriptive material.

17. She prefers visual games such as board games, or active games and toys to those that involve listening or speaking.

18. Her speech may be inappropriate for her age or she may not have learned the language patterns of her home, even if the home patterns are not standard American English.

19. She may have trouble associating sounds and objects.

20. She may substitute words similar in sound or meaning for one another.

21. She seems to know few words' synonyms commonly known by children at her age or ability level.

22. She may get lost in role verbalizations, even the alphabet, rote counting, or memorizing her multiplication tables.

23. She may not enjoy music as much as she enjoys artwork.

24. She may have a speech defect; if so, it is probably an articulation problem.

25. She may respond less rapidly than her peers to unusual sounds: a far-off siren, an audio source, or a musical instrument in a nearby classroom.

CHAPTER 6

BEHAVIOR MODIFICATION

In terms of behavior modification, it is important to be objective. The term has acquired a negative connotation that is unfounded. Everyone uses behavior modification, whether it is recognized or not, from turning off the lights when children are to be quiet to planning and implementing a behavior modification plan. In any plan, there are seven steps.

1. Keep a log of observations on the child. Really look at what the child is doing. Do this at least five times a day, for at least three days in a row (see Figure AP–1).

2. Read your observations; look for patterns. Is this child predictable? Does he usually have a temper tantrum around 9:30 AM? Does the child often fight with another in late afternoon?

3. Look for the reinforcers of the behavior noted in your observations. Does the child misbehave in order to get attention from the adults in the room? Do friends admire the behavior?

4. Decide on a schedule of reinforcement after finding the current reinforcer.

5. Implement the new reinforcement schedule. Give it time. Many teachers fail to use a reinforcement plan for a long enough period of time. Try a minimum of two weeks to two or three months. Behavior that has taken two or three years to develop will not change in a week.

6. Keep a second log of observations. On the basis of your study of the initial observations, analyze this second series and note whether your reinforcement schedule has worked.

7. Stop your planned reinforcement schedule. See if the child goes back to the former pattern of behavior. If so, go back to the second step and start over.

Look at the second and third steps. You have completed your observations, and now you need to find the reinforcers of the observed behavior. The behavior must bring some kind of reward to the child. As the teacher, your job is to discover what the reward is.

Many student teachers fail to understand the nature of the child's reward system. You look at what an adult perceives as negative behavior (hitting another child, for example), and you may decide to institute a schedule of reinforcement or a behavior modification plan without taking that first step: understanding why the child hits.

Study Step 4, planning a reinforcement schedule. Look at the child in the sample log in Figure AP–1. Assume that the description of behavior is typical of Maria's everyday behavior.

In your analysis of the log, what do you see? Three questions have been raised: Is Maria fairly new to the school? Does she have a hearing problem? Is she bilingual or does she have limited understanding of English? The answers to these questions come during the discussion of observations. Yes, Maria is new to the school. This is only her second week. No, she does not have a hearing problem but she is bilingual. In fact, the cooperating teacher suspects that Maria may be less bilingual than her mother claims.

What has reinforced Maria's behavior? First, she is unfamiliar with English. Second, her cultural background is different. Girls of Hispanic background are often expected to be quiet, helpful around the house, and obedient to their elders. Certainly, this explains Maria's behavior because she willingly helps with cleanup.

Student Teacher: _____

Name of School: _____ Date: _____

Identity Key (do NOT use real name)

M. – Maria
T. – Teacher
ST. – Student Teacher
J. – Janine
S. – Susie
B. – Bobby
Sv. – Stevie

Description of What Child is Doing	Time	Comments
M. arrives at school. Clings to mother's hand hand, hides behind her skirt. Thumb in mouth.	9:05	Ask T. how long M. has been coming. I bet she's new.
M. goes over to puzzle rack, chooses a puzzle, goes to table. Dumps out, and works puzzle quickly and quietly. B. & Sv. come over to work puzzles they've chosen.	9:22	Her eye/hand coordination seems good.
M. looks at them, says nothing, goes to easels, watches S. paint. S. asks M. if she wants to paint. M. doesn't answer.	9:30	I wonder why M. doesn't respond. Ask T. if M. has hearing problem.
M. comes to snack table, sits down where T. indicates she should. Does not interact with other children at table.	10:15	Is M. ever a quiet child!
M. stands outside of playhouse, watches S. & J. They don't ask her to join them.	10:47	She looks like she'd like to play.
M. goes to swings, knows how to pump.	10:55	Nothing wrong with her coordination.
During Hap Palmer record M. watches others, does not follow directions.	11:17	Hearing? Maybe limited English? (She looks of Spanish background.)

● **Figure AP-1**
Anecdotal record form

What are appropriate goals for Maria? Assume that you and your cooperating teacher decide that the most appropriate goal is to help Maria feel more comfortable in the room and that adult approval is the most logical reinforcer to use. Your reinforcement schedule might start by greeting Maria at the door every day when she arrives. Smile at her and say, "Buenas dias, Maria. It's nice to see you today." Take her by the hand and go with her to a different activity each day. If Maria seems uncomfortable changing activities so often, stay with the activities she enjoys at first.

Introduce her to the other children at the activity she chooses. Take advantage of the fact that Susie is one of the more mature, self-confident children in the room, and quietly ask her to include Maria in some of her activities. Instead of allowing Maria to watch Susie paint, go to Maria with her painting smock, put it on her, and suggest that she try the activity. When she does pick up the brush and experiment with painting, compliment her action.

Do not worry about Maria's lack of knowledge of the English language. When Maria hesitates, use pointing and naming to help her. Accept the fact that she may always be a shy child; do not push her to be outgoing if that is not her nature.

Continue these activities each day. After a few weeks, make another set of observations, though you may not need this step, as you may already see the difference; still, it is good practice to do the second observation, just to check on your feelings. It is more than likely that Maria is already greeting you with a smile as she enters, and that she is beginning to play with Susie and some of the other, more outgoing children.

Do you believe that changing Maria's behavior was easy? A more difficult example could have been chosen. However, cases like Maria's are common, and many children enjoy a period of watching and listening before joining in activities. You should become aware of these common problems in order to become sensitive about your potential power in the classroom. The word *power* is deliberately being used because, next to the parents or primary caretakers, you, as teacher, are the second most important person in the child's life. You have a tremendous potential for influencing the child.

Definitions of other child behaviors

Aggression is defined here as any intentional behavior that results in physical or mental injury to any person or animal, or in damage to or destruction of property. Aggressive actions can be accidental actions, in which there is no intentionality; instrumental actions, in which the child deliberately employs aggression in pursuit of a goal; or hostile actions, in which the child acts to cause harm to another person.

Assertion is defined here as behavior through which a child maintains and defends his or her own rights and concerns. Assertive behavior reflects the child's developing competence and autonomous functioning and represents an important form of developmental progress. Assertiveness also affords the young child a healthy form of self-defense against becoming the victim of the aggressions of others.

Cooperation is defined here as any activity that involves the willing interdependence of two or more children. It should be distinguished from compliance, which may represent obedience to rules or authority, rather than intentional cooperation. When children willingly collaborate in using materials, for example, their interactions are usually quite different than when they are told to share.

From Jewett, J. (1992). *Aggression and cooperation: Helping young children develop constructive strategies* (Report no. EDO–PS–92–10) Washington, DC: Office of Education Research and Improvement.

CHAPTER 7

DEVELOPMENTAL CHECKLIST

Name: _____ Birth date: _____

		Present	Date Observed
I. Infants			
3 Months	Motor Development		
	Neck muscles support head steadily		
	Moves arms and legs vigorously		
	May move arm and leg on one side together		
	On stomach, holds chest and head erect 10 seconds		

	Present	Date Observed
When picked up, brings body up compactly		
May bat at objects		
Reaches with both arms		
Perceptual Development		
Follows slowly moving object with eyes and head from one side of body to other		
Looks at fingers individually		
Stops sucking to listen		
Visually seeks source of sound by turning head and neck		
Hands usually held open		
Social Development		
Smiles easily and spontaneously		
Gurgles and coos in response to being spoken to		
Responds to familiar faces with smile		
Protests when left by mother		
Cries differentially when hungry, wet, or cross		
Cognitive Development		
Begins to show memory; waits for expected reward, like feeding		
Begins to recognize family members and others close to her		
Explores own face, eyes, mouth with hands		
Responds to stimulation with whole body		

6 Months

	Present	Date Observed
Motor Development		
Rolls from back to stomach		
Turns and twists in all directions		
Gets up on hands and knees, rocks		
Creeps on stomach; may go forward and backward		
Balances well when sitting, leans forward		
Sits in chair and bounces		
Grasps dangling object		
May sit unsupported for 30 minutes		
Rolls from back to stomach		
Perceptual Development		
Holds one block, reaches for a second, looks at a third		
Reaches to grab dropped object		
Coos, hums, stops crying in response to music		
Likes to play with food		
Displays interest in finger-feeding self		
Has strong taste preferences		
Rotates wrist to turn and manipulate objects		
Often reaches with one arm instead of both		
Sleeps through the night		
Social Development		
Prefers play with people		
Babbles and becomes excited during active play		
Babbles more in response to female voices		
Vocalizes pleasure/displeasure		
Gurgles when spoken to		
Tries to imitate facial expressions		
Turns in response to name		
Smiles at mirror image		
Disturbed by strangers		

	Present	Date Observed
Cognitive Development		
Remains alert two hours at a time		
Inspects objects for a long time		
Eyes direct hand for reaching		
Likes to look at objects upside down and create change of perspective		
May compare two objects		
Has abrupt mood changes; primary emotions: pleasure, complaint, temper		
9 Months Motor Development		
Crawls with one hand full		
Turns while crawling		
May crawl upstairs		
Sits well		
Gets self into sitting position easily		
Pulls to standing		
May pull self along furniture to walk		
Social Development		
Eager for approval		
Begins to evaluate people's moods		
Imitates play		
Enjoys peekaboo		
Chooses toy for play		
Sensitive to other children; may cry if they cry		
May fight for disputed toy		
Imitates cough, tongue clicks		
Cognitive Development		
Uncovers toy he has seen hidden		
Anticipates reward		
Follows simple directions		
Shows symbolic thinking/role-play		
May say *dada* and/or *mama*		
Grows bored with same stimuli		
II. Toddlers		
12 Months Motor Development		
Can stand, cruise along furniture, and may walk unassisted		
Pivots body 90 degrees when standing		
If walking, probably prefers crawling		
May add stopping, waving, backing, and carrying toys to walking		
Climbs up and down stairs, holding hand		
May climb out of crib or playpen		
Gets to standing by flexing knees, pushing from squat position		
Lowers self to sitting position with ease		
Makes swimming motions in bath		
Wants to self-feed		
May undress		
Perceptual Development		
Reaches accurately for object as she looks away		
Puts things back together as well as takes them apart		
Builds tower of two to three blocks after demonstration		

	Present	Date Observed
Uses hammer and pegboard		
Likely to put one or two objects in mouth and grasp a third		
Cares for doll or teddy bear, such as feeding, cuddling, bathing		
Enjoys water play in bath or sink		

Social Development

Expresses many emotions		
Recognizes emotions in others		
Gives affection to people		
Shows interest in what adults do		
May demand more help than needed because it is easier		
May refuse new foods		
Resists napping, may have tantrums		
Fears strange people, places		
Reacts sharply to separation from mother		
Distinguishes self from others		

Cognitive Development

Perceives objects as detached and separate, to be used in play		
Unwraps toys		
Finds hidden object, remembers where it last was		
Remembers events		
Groups a few objects by shape and color		
Identifies animals in picture books		
Responds to directions		
Understands much of what is said to him		
Experiments with spatial relationships: heights, distances		
Stops when told *no*		
Points to named body part		

18 Months   Motor Development

Walks well, seldom falls		
Sits self in small chair		
Walks up and down stairs one step at time, holding hand of adult or rail		
Enjoys push toys		
Likes to push furniture		
Enjoys pull toys		
Enjoys riding toys she can propel with feet on the ground		
Strings large beads with shoelace		
Takes off shoes and socks		
Swings rhythmically in time to music		
Follows one- or two-step directions		

Perceptual Development

Demonstrates good eye-hand coordination with small manipulatives		
Will look at picture book briefly, turns pages, but not one at a time		
Enjoys small objects she can manipulate		

Social Development

Makes distinction between *mine* and *yours*		
Makes social contact with other children		
Smiles and looks at others		
May begin to indicate what he wants by talking, pointing, grunting, and body language		

	Present	Date Observed
Cognitive Development		
Plays with blocks, can build tower of two to three blocks without model		
Can sort by colors and shapes		
Remembers where she put a toy, even the next day		

III. Two-Year-Olds

		Present	Date Observed
	Gross Motor		
2.0 Years	Runs well without falling		
	Kicks ball without overbalancing		
	Goes up and down stairs alone, two feet per step		
	Jumps from first step, one foot leading		
	Stops when running to change direction		
	Propels self on wheeled toy with feet on floor		
	Catches large ball by body trapping		
	Jumps 8 inches to 14 inches		
2 ½ Years	Walks several steps tiptoe		
	Walks several steps backwards		
	Walks up stairs alternating feet		
	Stands on balance beam without assistance		
	Throws objects and tracks visually		
	Bounces ball, catches with both hands		
	Bends at waist to pick up object from floor		
	Jumps over string two inches to eight inches high		
	Fine Motor		
2.0 Years	Turns knob on TV, toys		
	Turns doorknobs, opens door		
	Builds three- to five-block tower		
	Holds pencil in fist, scribbles, stays on paper		
	Puts ring on stick		
	Strings one-inch beads		
	Puts small objects into container		
	Paints with whole arm movement		
	Folds paper in half		
2 ½ Years	Removes jar lids		
	Builds seven- to nine-block tower		
	Completes simple inset puzzle		
	Traces circle		
	Paints with wrist action		
	Uses spoon without spilling		
	Holds glass, cup with one hand		
	Makes small cuts in paper with scissors		
	Places six pegs in pegboard		
	Language and Speech		
2 ½ Years	Receptive		
	Understands most commonly used nouns and verbs		
	Responds to two-part command		
	Enjoys simple storybooks		
	Points to common objects when they are named		
	Understands functions of objects (e.g., cups are for drinking)		
	Understands 200 to 400 words		
	Expressive		
	Verbalizes actions		

	Present	Date Observed
Uses two- to three-word phrases		
Asks what and where questions		
Makes negative statements		
Labels action in pictures		
Approximately 50-word vocabulary (at two years)		
Answers questions		
Speech Sounds		
Substitutes some consonant sounds (e.g., *w* for *r*, *d* for *th*)		
Articulates all consonants with few deviations, *p, b, m, w, h, k, g, n, t, d*		
Psychosocial Skills		
Sees self as separate person		
Conscious of possessions, understands *mine*		
Shy with strangers		
Knows gender identity		
Watches others, may join in play		
Begins to use dramatic play		
Helps put things away		
Participates in small-group activity (sings, claps, dances)		
Says *no* frequently, obeys when asked		
Understands and stays away from common dangers		
Cognitive Skills		
Responds to three-part command		
Selects and looks at picture books		
Given three items, can associate which two go together		
Recognizes self in mirror		
Uses toys symbolically		
Imitates adult actions in dramatic play		
Self-Help Skills		
Can undress		
Can partially dress		
Gains mastery over toilet needs		
Can drink from fountain		
Washes and dries hands with assistance		

IV. Three-Year-Olds

Gross Motor

3.0 Years

	Present	Date Observed
Runs smoothly		
Walks down stairs, alternating feet		
Climbs ladder on play equipment		
Throws tennis ball three feet		
Pedals tricycle		
Can execute one or two hops on dominant foot		
Can make sharp turns while running		
Balances briefly on dominant foot		

3 ½ Years

	Present	Date Observed
Stands on either foot briefly		
Hops on either foot		
Jumps over objects six inches tall		
Pedals tricycle around corners		
Walks forward on balance beam several steps		

Fine Motor

3.0 Years

	Present	Date Observed
Uses one hand consistently in most activities		
Strings ½-inch beads		

	Present	Date Observed
3 ½ Years		
Traces horizontal/vertical lines		
Copies/imitates circles		
Cuts six-inch paper into two pieces		
Makes cakes/ropes of clay		
Winds up toy		
Completes five- to seven-piece inset puzzle		
Sorts dissimilar objects		
Makes ball with clay		

Language and Speech

Receptive

	Present	Date Observed
Understands size and time concepts		
Enjoys being read to		
Understands *if, then* and *because* concepts		
Carries out two to four related directions		
Understands 800 words		
Responds to questions		

Expressive

	Present	Date Observed
Gives full name		
Knows sex and can state girl or boy		
Uses three- to four-word phrases		
Uses *s* after nouns to indicate plurals		
Uses *ed* after verbs to indicate past tense		
Repeats simple songs, finger plays		
Speech is 70 percent to 80 percent intelligible		
Vocabulary of over 500 words		

Speech Sounds

	Present	Date Observed
f, y, z, ng, wh		

Psychosocial Skills

	Present	Date Observed
Joins in interactive games		
Shares toys		
Takes turns, with assistance		
Enjoys sociodramatic play		

Cognitive Skills

	Present	Date Observed
Matches six colors		
Names one color		
Counts two blocks		
Counts by rote to 10		
Matches pictures		
Classifies objects by physical attributes, one class at a time (e.g., color, shape, size)		
Stacks blocks or rings in order of size		
Knows age		
Asks questions for information (*why* and *how*)		
Can "picture read" a story book		

Self-Help Skills

	Present	Date Observed
Pours well from small pitcher		
Spreads soft butter with knife		
Buttons and unbuttons large buttons		
Blows nose when reminded		
Uses toilet independently		

	Present	Date Observed
V. Four-Year-Olds		
Gross Motor		
4.0 Years Walks down stairs, alternating feet, holding rail		
Stands on dominant foot five seconds		
Gallops		
Jumps 10 consecutive times		
Walks sideways on balance beam		
Catches beanbag thrown from a distance of three feet		
Throws two beanbags into wastebasket, underhand, from a distance of three feet		
Hops on preferred foot for a distance of one yard		
4 ½ Years Walks forward on line, heel-toe, for a distance of two yards		
Stands on either foot for five seconds		
Walks upstairs holding object in one hand without holding the rail		
Walks to rhythm		
Attempts to keep time to simple music with hand instruments		
Turns somersault (forward roll)		
Fine Motor		
4.0 Years Builds 10- to 12-block tower		
Completes three- to five-piece puzzle, not inset		
Draws person with arms, legs, eyes, nose, mouth		
Copies a cross		
Imitates a square		
Cuts a triangle		
Creases paper with fingers		
Cuts on continuous line		
4 ½ Years Completes 6- to 10-piece puzzle, not inset		
Grasps pencil correctly		
Copies a few capital letters		
Copies triangle		
May copy square		
Cuts curved lines and circles with ¼-inch accuracy		
Language and Speech		
Receptive		
Follows three unrelated commands		
Understands sequencing		
Understands comparatives: big, bigger, biggest		
Understands approximately 1,500 words		
Expressive		
Has mastery of inflection, can change volume and rate of speech		
Uses sentences with five or more words		
Uses adjectives, adverbs, conjunctions in complex sentences		
Speech about 90 percent to 95 percent intelligible		
Speech Sounds		
s, sh, r, ch		
Psychosocial Skills		
Plays and interacts with others		
Dramatic play is closer to reality with attention paid to time and space		
Plays dress-up		

	Present	Date Observed
Shows interest in sex differences		
Plays cooperatively		
May have imaginary playmates		
Shows humor by silly words and rhymes		
Tells stories, fabricates, rationalizes		
Goes on errands outside the home		

Cognitive Skills

	Present	Date Observed
Points to and names four colors		
Draws, names, and describes picture		
Counts three or four objects with correct pointing		
Distinguishes between day and night		
Can finish opposite analogies (brother = boy; sister = girl)		
Names a penny in response to "What is this?"		
Tells which of two is bigger, slower, heavier		
Increased concepts of time; can talk about yesterday, last week, today, and tomorrow		

Self-Help Skills

	Present	Date Observed
Cuts easy food with knife		
Laces shoes, does not tie		
Buttons front buttons		
Washes and dries face without help		
Brushes teeth without help		
Toilets himself, manages clothes by himself		

VI. Five-Year-Olds

Gross Motor

	Present	Date Observed
5.0 Years		
Stands on dominant foot 10 seconds		
Walks backward, toe to heel, six steps		
Walks downstairs carrying object without holding rail		
Skips, jumps three feet		
Hops on dominant foot for a distance of two yards		
Walks backward on balance beam		
Catches ball with two hands		
Rides small bike with training wheels		
5 ½ Years		
Stands on either foot 10 seconds		
Walks backward for a distance of two yards		
Jumps rope		
Gallops, jumps, runs in rhythm to music		
Roller skates		
Rides bicycle without training wheels		

Fine Motor

	Present	Date Observed
5.0 Years		
Opens and closes large safety pin		
Sews through holes in sewing card		
Opens lock with key		
Completes 20- to 25-piece puzzle, not inset		
Draws person with head, trunk, legs, arms, hands, eyes, nose, mouth, hair, ears, fingers		
Colors within lines		
Cuts cardboard and cloth		
5 ½ Years		
Builds Tinkertoy structure		
Copies first name		
Copies rectangle		
Copies triangle		

	Present	Date Observed
Prints numerals 1 to 5		
Handedness well-established		
Pastes and glues appropriately		
Cuts out paper dolls, pictures from magazine		
Language and Speech		
Receptive		
Demonstrates preacademic skills, such as following directions and listening		
Expressive		
Few differences between child's use of language and adults'		
Can take turns in conversation		
May have some difficulty with noun-verb agreement and irregular past tenses		
Communicates well with family, friends, and strangers		
Speech Sounds		
Can correctly articulate most simple consonants and many digraphs		
Psychosocial Skills		
Chooses own friends		
Plays simple table games		
Plays competitive games		
Engages in sociodramatic play with peers, involving group decisions, role assignment, fair play		
Respects others' property		
Respects others' feelings		
Cognitive Skills		
Retells story from book with reasonable accuracy		
Names some letters and numbers		
Uses time concepts of yesterday and tomorrow accurately		
Begins to relate clock time to daily schedule		
Uses classroom tools such as scissors and paints meaningfully		
Draws recognizable pictures		
Orders a set of objects from smallest to largest		
Understands why things happen		
Classifies objects according to major characteristics (e.g., apples and bananas can both be eaten)		
Self-Help Skills		
Dresses self completely		
Ties a bow		
Brushes teeth unassisted		
Crosses the street safely		
Dries self after bathing		
Brushes hair		
Ties shoes without assistance		
VII. Six-Year-Olds		
Gross Motor Skills		
Walks with ease		
Runs easily, turns corners smoothly		
Gallops		
Skips		
Jumps rope well		
Throws overhand, shifts weight from back to front foot		

	Present	Date Observed
Walks length of balance beam:		
forward		
backward		
sideways		
Rides bicycle		
Uses all playground equipment:		
Swings herself		
Uses a merry-go-round		
Climbs on outside climber		
Swings by arms across ladder		
Other skills		
Writes name, address, phone number		
Reads *I Can Read* books		
Can count to 100		
Can retell story after having read it		
Understands concept of numbers 1–10		
Understands concept of one more, one less		
Can complete simple arithmetic problems, addition and subtraction		
Can write simple story		
Can illustrate a story appropriately		
Plays cooperatively with others		
Stands up for herself		
VIII. Seven-Year-Olds		
Performs all gross motor skills well except for mature, overhand ball throwing		
Knows when to lead and follow		
Knows what he does well		
Knows when to ask for help		
Can draw diamond		
Draws house with straight chimney		
Enjoys card games such as Rummy, Crazy 8's, Hearts, Old Maid		
Enjoys organized sports activities such as kickball, soccer, baseball, track, swimming		
Enjoys reading		
Enjoys games such as checkers, Parcheesi		
Willing to tackle new problems		
Eats well-balanced diet		
Has solid peer relations		
Is responsible		
Writes legibly		
Can articulate most speech sounds without distortion or substitution		
IX. Eight-Year-Olds		
Able to use mature, overhand ball throw		
If given opportunity for practice, can perform all gross motor skills well, including the mature overhand ball throw		
Enjoys organized sports activities, may want to play on a team, is developing a sense of industry, and an *I can do* attitude		
Knows what she can do well and when she needs help		
Enjoys reading		
Enjoys games with rules		

	Present	Date Observed
Is able to master pronunciation of all phonemes and most graphemes of the English language		
Enjoys word-play games, such as puns and double entendre		
Has solid peer relationships		
Is able to assume responsibility for his actions		
Willing to try out new activities		

X. Nine-Year-Olds

	Present	Date Observed
Masters all arithmetic operations		
Understands concepts of reversibility		
Thinks logically if provided with concrete situations and/or manipulatives		
Able to conserve mass, length, area, weight, among other operations		
Forms classification hierarchies		
Able to transfer learning from one situation to another		
May be entering a growth spurt characterized by rapid long-bone growth (especially girls)		
May develop secondary sex characteristics		
Understands negatively worded questions, such as		
"The only factor *not* in the sequence of events . . ."		
"Which one of the following is *not* . . ."		
and double-pronoun referrents, such as		
"She baked her the birthday cake."		
"He accidentally hit him with the ball."		
Enjoys the company of peers		
Groups into informal "clubs"		

CHAPTER 8

Motor Control

Definition: Ability to control the motor or physical movement made in response to a visual, auditory, or tactile stimulus.
Fine motor control: The ability to coordinate fine motor muscles such as those required in eye-hand tasks, coloring, drawing, printing, writing, and so on.
Gross motor control: The development and awareness of large muscle activity.

Most common areas of development are:

rolling	jumping
sitting	skipping
crawling	dancing
walking	self-identification
running	muscular strength
throwing	

Attention

Definition: The ability to attend to or heed the situation in which one is currently *involved*.
Characteristics of the child with an attention disability:

1. easily distracted by noise

2. hyperactive

3. gets overly excited when there is a change in daily routine

4. has difficulty making transitions from one activity to another

5. goes from one activity to another when there is free choice

6. doesn't complete work

7. is more upset by physiological distress, such as hunger or discomfort, than other children

Directionality and Spatial Relations

Definition: The ability to know right from left, up from down, forward from backward, and directional orientation.
Characteristics of the child with directionality and spatial relations disabilities:

1. does not know left from right

2. may have difficulty copying

3. has difficulty mastering concepts dependent on correct sequence: reading, writing, mathematics (place value), geography (maps), and so on

4. lack of uniformity in writing and spacing

5. letters may be placed haphazardly on paper

6. shows reversals and incorrect sequencing of letters in reading and spelling

7. may get lost easily; may often appear disoriented

8. may not know location of parts of his body; may have difficulty putting on clothes or drawing figures accurately

Verbal Expression

Definition: The ability to understand words, to express oneself verbally, and to articulate words clearly.
Characteristics of the child with a verbal expression disability:

1. shy, seldom talks in class

2. tends to respond with one-word answers

3. cannot tell what has happened in a story he has just read

4. when the child talks, he expresses few ideas

Conceptual Skills

Definition: The ability to acquire and utilize general information from education and experience.
Characteristics of the child with conceptual skills disabilities:

1. is unable to use concepts involving time

2. cannot sort pictures into categories, such as farm animals, machinery, and plants

3. cannot easily classify objects verbally (e.g., name all the animals you can)

4. is unable to use concepts relating to feelings and emotional reactions of people

5. cannot easily determine similarities and differences existing between objects (e.g., How are a pig and a cow alike? How are they different?)

Behavior

Definition: Behavior disorders include such behavior as that which is disruptive, harmful to others and to materials, or reclusive and overly quiet.
Characteristics of the child with behavioral disabilities:

1. aggressive, irritable, then remorseful

2. impulsive, lacks self-control, touches and handles things

3. withdraws to the outskirts of activities

4. easily excitable, overreacts

5. erratic behavior; quick changes of emotional response

6. hyperactive

7. hypoactive

8. short attention span compared to peers

9. easily distracted by noise, color, movement, activity, detail

10. cannot complete work independently

11. inappropriate or extreme laughter, tears, anger

12. defensiveness: denies responsibility, argumentative about obligations, rules; overreacts to demands for compliance

13. shows frequent frustration, irritation, reducing ability to cope with daily tasks

14. requires more than the usual amount of individual help and attention to learn

15. attention jumps from one thought to another

16. repeats verbally when no longer appropriate (*perseverates*)

As a student teacher you may be asked to develop a learning plan for working with only one child. This learning plan was designed for a two-and-a-half-year-old child who was overly active. The teacher's wish was that Alan would be able to sustain interest for increasingly longer periods of time. The class was studying pets, and the cooperating teacher asked the student teacher to develop the individual learning plan below.

Individual Learning Plan for Alan

Setting: preschool class for two- to three-year-olds. Alan is two-and-a-half years old.

1. Activity title: Watching a Live Bird

2. Curriculum area: Science and Language Arts (vocabulary)

3. Materials needed: Live bird in a cage. Table or counter for cage.

4. Location and setup of activity: Birdcage with parakeet will be set up in a corner of the room, where two counters come together. This will keep the cage safer than placing it on a table, and the counter is at eye level for children, so they can see easily.

5. Number of children and adults: Two; Alan and the student teacher.

6. Preparation: Talk about pets with Alan. Ask him what pet he has. I know he has a dog and two cats. Ask him if he knows what a bird is. Tell him there will be a surprise for him.

7. Specific behavioral objective: Alan will watch the parakeet for at least three minutes. He will be able to call the bird a parakeet and say its name, Ernie. (Long-range objective could be to have Alan feed the bird and give him water.)

8. Developmental skills necessary for success: Willingness to watch and listen quietly.

9. Procedure: When Alan comes to school Tuesday, greet him at the door; remind him about the surprise you promised. Take his hand and lead him to the corner where the birdcage is sitting. Ask Alan if he knows what is in the cage. Anticipate that he will know it is a bird. Tell him that this bird is called a parakeet and that the bird's name is Ernie. Ask him to repeat *parakeet* and *Ernie*. Ask him what color Ernie is. Anticipate that he knows the color green. If he doesn't say green, remind him that Ernie is green. See what else is green and remind Alan that he knows what color green is: green like the grass, for example, or green like Tony's shirt.

10. Discussion: Covered under Step 9, Procedure.

11. Apply: Later in the day, ask Alan what kind of bird Ernie is. Ask him Ernie's name. (I anticipate that Alan will be intrigued with the bird and that he will want to come back over and over to watch Ernie, if only for a minute or two. Each time, I will name the type of bird and repeat Ernie's name. I think Alan will know both *parakeet* and *Ernie* before he goes home.)

12. Cleanup: Not necessary. I will keep the birdcage cleaned.

13. Terminating statement: Probably not necessary. Otherwise, I'll remind Alan that Ernie is a parakeet and suggest that he might want to see a book about birds (I've brought several in) or play the lotto game.

14. Transition: See #13.

15. Evaluation—Activity, Teacher, Child: I am hoping, of course, that this will be a great success for all the children but especially for Alan. I'll write the evaluation after Ernie is brought in.

Glossary

A

accommodation—according to Jean Piaget, one form of adaptation, which takes place when an existing concept is modified, or a new concept is formed, to incorporate new information or a new experience.

accreditation—an official form of approval granted from a review board stating that a learning institution has met specific requirements.

active listening (with adults)—the process of putting into your own words a message you received from another based on your understanding of what you thought you heard.

active listening (with children)—Thomas Gordon's term for the technique of reflecting back to children what they have said as a way to help them find their own solutions to problems.

affective—caused by or expressing emotion or feeling.

aggression—behavior deliberately intended to hurt others.

allergies—physiological reactions to environmental or food substances that can affect or alter behavior.

anecdotal records—methods of observation involving written "word pictures" of an event or behavior; short accounts of incidents or events of an interesting nature.

assertive discipline—a form of behavior management used primarily in elementary schools. The consequences of behavior are clearly stated, understood by children, and consistently applied.

assessment—the act of appraising, judging, or evaluating another's efforts, performance, or actions.

assimilation—according to Jean Piaget, one form of adaptation, which takes place when the person tries to make new information or a new experience fit into an existing concept.

assistant teacher—also called aide, helper, auxiliary teacher, associate teacher, or small-group leader; works under the guidance of the head teacher in providing a quality program.

Association for Childhood Education International (ACEI)—professional organization that focuses on issues of children, from infancy to early adolescence, including those involving international and intercultural concerns.

at-risk children—because of adverse environmental factors, for instance, poverty or low birth weight, children are considered at risk for developmental delay and/or for doing poorly in school.

attachment—the child's bond with a teacher or caregiver, established over time through personal interactions. A child's primary attachment is usually to her parents.

attention deficit disorder (ADD)—a disorder that causes children to have difficulty sustaining attention in the classroom and concentrating on an assigned task for any length of time.

attention deficit with hyperactivity disorder (ADHD)—Like ADD, it causes attention problems and an inability to sit still and concentrate for very long. Children with ADHD are said to "bounce off the walls."

authoritarian—requiring obedience and exercising control over others.

authoritative—substantiated, supported, and accepted by most professionals in the field of early childhood education, or having an air of authority.

autonomy—the second stage of development described by Erik Erikson, occurring during the second year of life, in which toddlers assert their growing motor, language, and cognitive abilities by trying to become more independent.

balanced curriculum—a curriculum that takes into consideration and reflects a broad spectrum of cognitive, physical, socioemotional, linguistic, and creative development opportunities for young children. It attempts to neither slight nor sacrifice one developmental area for another.

behavior management—a behavioral approach to guidance, holding that the child's behavior is under the control of the environment, which includes space, objects, and people.

behavior modification—the systematic application of principles of reinforcement to modify behavior.

behaviorism—a theoretical viewpoint, espoused by theorists such as B. F. Skinner, that behavior is shaped by environmental forces, specifically in response to reward and punishment.

biases—particular tendencies or inclinations, especially ones that prevent impartial consideration; prejudices.

bibliotherapy—the use of books that deal with emotionally sensitive topics in a developmentally appropriate way to help children gain accurate information and learn coping strategies.

career lattice—a term used to recognize that the early childhood profession is composed of individuals with varied backgrounds; a lattice allows for both horizontal and vertical movement among positions, with accompanying levels of education, experience, responsibility, and pay.

checklist—a method of evaluating children or teachers that consists of a list of behaviors, skills, concepts, or attributes that the observer checks off as the child or teacher is observed to have mastered the item.

Child Development Associate (CDA)—an early childhood teacher who has been assessed and successfully proven competent through the national CDA credentialing program.

classroom management—consists of supervising, planning, and directing classroom activities and the room environment. It also involves making time-length decisions, providing appropriate direction, and guiding child behavior to enable children to live and work effectively with others.

code of ethics—agreed-upon professional standards that guide behavior and facilitate decision making in working situations.

cognitive—pertaining to the mental processes of perception, memory, judgment, and reasoning.

cognitive developmental theory—the theory formulated by Jean Piaget that focuses on how children's intelligence and thinking abilities emerge through distinct stages.

collaboration—others working together for the ultimate good of children or students. It is a process of joint decision making and involves discussion, different views and perspectives, shared goals, building new shared understandings, and perhaps the creation of a new outlook or course of action.

communication—giving or receiving information, signals, and/or messages.

competencies—the knowledge and skills desired in education professionals in various staffing positions in early childhood care.

computer literacy—familiarity with and knowledge about computers.

confidentiality—the requirement that results of evaluations and assessments be shared with only the parents and appropriate school personnel.

conflict resolution—a process to resolve disputes between people with different interests. This resolution process can have constructive consequences if the parties air their different interests, make trade-offs or compromises, and reach a settlement that satisfies the essential needs of each.

congruent—refers to the similarity between what a person (the *sender*) is thinking and feeling and what that person communicates; behaving in agreement with or as a reflection of inner feelings and values.

conservation—the ability, usually acquired during the concrete operational phase, to recognize that objects remain the same in terms of size, volume, and area despite perceptual changes.

constructivist theory—a theory, such as that of Jean Piaget, based on the belief that children construct knowledge for themselves rather than having it conveyed to them by some external source.

curriculum—overall master plan of the early childhood program, reflecting its philosophy, into which specific activities are fit.

Developmentally Appropriate Practice in Early Childhood Programs (DAP)—guidelines developed by the National Association for the Education of Young Children, as a response to the growing trend toward more formal, academic instruction of young children. The primary position of the guidelines is that programs designed for young children should be based on what is known about their development. DAP also reflects a clear commitment regarding the rights of young children, to respectful and supportive learning environments and to education preparing them for participation in a free and democratic society.

didactic—often applied to teaching materials, indicating a built-in intent to provide specific instruction.

discipline—generally considered a response to children's misbehavior.

dispositions—the values, commitments, and professional attitudes that influence behaviors toward children, families, colleagues, and communities, and affect child's motivation and development as well as the educator's own personal growth.

emergent model—a program of instruction, based on child, parent, teacher, or community interests or concerns, in which there is a logical sequence of study using interconnected activities and experiences.

empowering—helping parents and children gain a sense of control over events in their lives.

equilibration—according to Jean Piaget, the state of balance each person seeks between existing mental structures and new experiences.

feedback—information given and deemed to be a true and accurate account of what happened. May be evaluated as positive, negative, or otherwise by the informant or listener.

field independent—a child who works independent of distractions in the surrounding environment; a child who is self-motivated and self-monitoring.

field sensitive—a child who needs encouragement from the teacher and peers for motivation, does not trust himself, and looks for reassurance from others.

flexible—willing to yield, modify, or adapt; change or create in a positive, productive manner.

formative evaluation—ongoing assessment to ensure that planned activities and methods accomplish what the teacher intended.

gifted children—children who perform significantly above average in intellectual and creative areas.

goals—overall, general overviews of what student teachers expect to gain from the program. The term goals is frequently used to refer to curriculum goals or to concepts children are to learn.

group times—also called *circle* or *story* times; time blocks during the day when all of the children and teachers join together in a common activity.

guidance—ongoing process of directing children's behavior based on the types of adults children are expected to become.

***I* messages**—Thomas Gordon's term for a response to a child's behavior that focuses on how the adult feels rather than on the child's character.

identity formation—the way in which young children separate from their parents and establish their own character traits and personality.

idiosyncratic—a characteristic peculiar to an individual.

ignoring—a principle of behavior management that involves removing all reinforcement for a given behavior to eliminate that behavior.

inclusion—a term that has widely replaced the term "mainstreaming" and that emphasizes placement of the child with special needs in the regular classroom with, perhaps, greater assistance from special education services. There is still controversy as to whether total inclusion is best for every child with special needs.

Individual Education Program (IEP)—with children with special needs, an individual education program that states the short-term and long-term learning objectives, how they will be accomplished and by whom, and applicable dates. It must be approved by both parents and school.

Individualized Family Service Plan (IFSP)—required by the 1986 Education of the Handicapped Act Amendments for handicapped children under the age of three and their families; the IFSP, often developed by a transdisciplinary team that includes the family, determines goals and objectives that build on the strengths of the child and family.

industry—the fourth stage of development described by Erik Erikson, starting at the end of the preschool years and lasting until puberty, in which the child focuses on the development of competence.

initiative—identified as the third developmental stage of three- to five-year-old children by Erik Erikson and involves their desire to do something by themselves.

integrated curriculum—a curriculum in which concurrent learning is possible by focusing on more than one ability, developmental skill, or subject matter area at the same time in the same activity. It is believed to promote children's problem solving and aid the children's ability to see relationships among a variety of ideas or events. Also called a holistic curriculum.

instructional objectives—aims or goals, usually set for an individual child, that describe in very specific and observable terms what the child is expected to master.

interactionists—those who adhere to the theory that language develops through a combination of inborn factors and environmental influences.

journal—a written, pictorial, audio, or computerized record of experiences, occurrences, observations, feelings, questions, work actions, reflective thoughts, and other happenings during student teaching.

Kinesthetic sense—provides information from the body's system that gives knowledge about where the body is in space, what body parts are doing, and movement.

latchkey children—school-aged children who, after school, return to an empty home because their parents are at work.

learning disability—a condition thought to be associated with neurological dysfunction and characterized by difficulty in mastering a skill such as reading or numerical calculation.

least restrictive environment—a provision of Public Law 94–142, and reaffirmed in PL 101-476, that children with disabilities be placed in a program as close as possible to a setting designed for children without disabilities, while being able to meet each child's special needs.

lesson plans—the working documents from which the daily program is run, specifying directions for activities.

licensed home care—child care for young children in a private, licensed home.

logical consequences—Rudolf Dreikurs's technique of specific outcomes that follow certain behaviors and are mutually agreed upon by teacher and children/students.

manipulatives—toys and materials that require the use of the fingers and hands, for instance, puzzles, beads, and pegboards.

Maslow's Hierarchy of Needs—a theoretical position which attempts to identify human needs and motivations. It describes the consequences of need fulfillment and the consequences of unmet needs on growth.

mentoring—guidance by an experienced and trusted teacher who is frequently paired with a new and inexperienced teacher or aide, and who assists the new teacher with ideas and advice.

modeling—in social learning theory, the process of imitating a model.

Montessori equipment—early childhood learning materials derived from and part of the Montessori approach.

National Association for the Education of Young Children (NAEYC)—largest American early childhood professional organization, which deals with issues of children from birth to age eight and those who work with young children.

National Council for Accreditation of Teacher Education (NCATE)—an organization that accredits colleges, schools, or departments of education in higher education programs at the baccalaureate and advanced degree levels in the United States.

nativist—one who adheres to the theory that children are born with biological dispositions for learning that unfold or mature in a natural way.

nurturist—one who adheres to the theory that the minds of children are blank or unformed and need educational input or direct instruction in order to develop knowledge and appropriate behavior.

objectives—aims; specific interpretations of general goals, providing practical and directive tools for day-to-day program planning.

observable behavior—actions that can be seen rather than those that are inferred.

observation—the process of learning that comes from watching, noting the behavior of, and imitating models.

one-day wonders—preplanned and often prepackaged collections of materials that student teachers can easily set up or use on the spur of the moment to engage young children.

parent cooperatives—programs staffed by one professional teacher and a rotating staff of parents.

practitioner—person engaged in the practice of a profession or occupation, in this case, early childhood education. Other terms used: educator, teacher, assistant teacher, aide, student teacher.

professional portfolio—a representative collection of your student teacher accomplishments.

project approach—an instructional method that encourages children to investigate a topic. It can be undertaken by a small group, whole class, or an individual child. A key feature of a project is using research to find answers to questions.

psychosocial theory—the branch of psychology founded by Erik Erikson in which development is described in terms of eight stages that span childhood and adulthood, each offering opportunities for personality growth and development.

rating scale—a checklist that assesses specific skills or concepts that are rated on some qualitative dimension of excellence or accomplishment.

reflective teaching—a serious effort to thoughtfully question teaching practices, perceptions, actions, feelings, values, cultural biases, and other features associated with the care and education of young children.

reinforcement—in behavioral theory, any response that follows a behavior that encourages repetition or elimination of that behavior.

reliability—a measure indicating that a test is stable and consistent, to ensure that scoring variations are due to the person tested, and not the test.

role model—a person whose behavior is imitated by others.

scaffolding—a teaching technique helpful in promoting language, understanding, and child solutions that may include supportive and responsive teacher conversation and actions following child-initiated behavior.

schedule—a planned series of happenings for a specific time period to accommodate needs and goals.

self-concepts—perceptions and feelings children may have about themselves, gathered largely from how the important people in their world respond to them.

self-control—restraint exercised over one's own impulses, emotions, or desires.

self-esteem—children's evaluation of their worth in positive or negative terms.

separation anxiety—emotional difficulty experienced by some young children when leaving their parents or other primary caregivers.

skill-based model—refers to a curriculum model that identifies specific physical, social, or intellectual knowledge, skills, goals, or objectives, and then plans learning activities that promote the attainment of expected child behavior, information, or action.

specific behavioral objectives—clearly describes observable behavior, the situation in which it will occur, and the exact outcome or the criteria of successful performance.

Stanford-Binet intelligence scale—a widely used test that yields an intelligence quotient (IQ).

stereotype—a simplified conception or image of a person or group based on race, ethnicity, religion, gender, or sexual orientation.

stress—internal or external demand on a person's ability to adapt.

sudden infant death syndrome (SIDS)—where death of an infant occurs without warning, generally during the first three months of life, and for which there is no known cause.

summative evaluation—an assessment that follows a specific lesson or unit to evaluate whether the children have met the objectives.

syntax—involves the grammatical rules that govern the structure of sentences.

team teaching—an approach that involves co-teaching, in which status and responsibility are equal rather than having a pyramid structure of authority, with one person in charge and others subordinate.

temperaments—children's inborn characteristics, such as regularity, adaptability, and other dispositions that affect behavior.

terminating statement—a summary or recap of what has been discovered, discussed, experienced, enjoyed, and so on, after a learning activity.

thematic teaching and instruction—a theme approach to child program planning, including theme identification, environmental needs, activities, presentation, and evaluation, usually designed for a selected period of study. It can encompass a wide range of curriculum areas including art, music, mathematics, language, science, motor, social, and other development opportunities. This may also be called the project approach.

theme approach—a popular child program planning approach that involves a course of study with identified child activities focused on one subject, idea, or skill such as butterflies, friendship, biking, or a picture book.

time-out—a brief social isolation and temporary suspension of usual activity, used at times by some educators to decrease young children's undesirable behavior.

time sampling—a quantitative measure or count of how often a specific behavior occurs within a given amount of time.

transition statement—planned verbalization that moves young children from one activity to another.

trust—the first stage of development described by Erik Erikson, occurring during infancy, in which the child's needs should be met consistently and predictably.

Wechsler Intelligence scale for children (WISC III)—another widely used test that yields an intelligence quotient (IQ).

Wechsler Preschool Primary intelligence scale–Revised (WPPIS-R)—a test sometimes used with young children to determine their ability to learn and which yields an intelligence quotient (IQ).

***you* message**—Thomas Gordon's term for a response to a child's behavior that focuses on the child's character (usually in negative terms) rather than on how the adult feels.

zone of proximal development (ZPD)—in Vygotsky's theory, this zone represents tasks a child cannot yet do by herself but that she can accomplish with support of an older child or adult.

Index

Note: Page numbers followed by f denote figures.

A

Acceptance, 52, 191, 192
ACCESS. *See* American Associate Degree Early Childhood Education
Accidents, infant/toddler center, 455–456
Accommodation, 104, 105
Accountability, 419
Accreditation, relationship to quality, 13, 374
   in elementary school programs, 374–376
   NAEYC accreditation, 376–379, 397–398
Accrediting Commission for Schools, 374–377
ACEI. *See* Association for Childhood Education International
Active learning development, 135
Active listening, 310
Active vocabulary, 360
Activity planning
   and language instruction, 147–149
      diversity and citizenship, 150–151
      non-English-speaking children, 149
      working with Hispanic families, 150
      written activity/lesson plans, 151–158
   guide, 152f
   need for, 301–303
   other areas, 162
      unforeseen distractions, 162–163
   outdoor activities, 177
Activity resources, 140
ADD. *See* Attention deficit disorder
Adding It Up: Helping Children Learn Mathematics, 140
Adequate Yearly Progress (AYP), 363
ADHD. *See* Attention deficit disorder/attention deficit with hyperactivity disorder
Administrator, meeting with, 20–21
Administrative planning for professional growth, 401
Adult intervention in conflicts, 190, 236
Advocacy, for professionalism, 392–393, 393f
   becoming aware, 394–395
   effect of past advocacy, 394
Affective, defined, 45
African American children
   advocacy for, 395
   demographics, 414
After-school programs, 197, 241, 421–423
After-session conferencing, 25
Age of child and empowerment, 196
Aggression, 205, 496
Agricultural Extensive Service, 379
Allergies, 23, 271
Altruistic empathy, 462
American Associate Degree Early Childhood Education (ACCESS), 5, 48
American Federation of Teachers, 390
American Montessori Society (AMS), 367

AMI. *See* Associatione Montessori International
Anecdotal records, 247–248, 248f, 495f
Anger, 308–309
Anti-bias curriculum, 246
Anxiety, 393–297, 391
Apprenticing, demonstrating, and exchange teaching, 404
Articulation agreements, 402
Asian students, 414, 425
Assertive behavior, 496
Assertive discipline, 216–217
Assessment, 66
Assimilation, 104, 105
Assistant teacher, 235
Associatione Montessori Internationale (AMI), 367
Association for Childhood Education International (ACEI), 131, 405
Associative play, 253
Asperger's syndrome, 269, 278
Asthma, 271
At-risk children, 143, 282, 373
Attachment
   common student teacher problem, 299–300
   issues in infant/toddler care, 444
Attention, 507–508
Attention deficit disorder (ADD)/attention deficit with hyperactivity disorder (ADHD), 270, 277–278
Attention-getting behavior, 200
Attention span, 113
Attitude
   communication and, 335
   cutoff, 311
Auditory learner, 109, 491, 493
Authenticity, 308–309
Authoritarian, defined, 56–57, 441
Authoritative, defined, 56
Autism spectrum disorders, 266, 269, 278
Autonomy
   learning as a stage of psychosocial development, 228–230
   meeting children's needs, 358
AYP. *See* Adequate Yearly Progress

B

Balanced curriculum, 138, 360–361
Barbour, Haley, 373
Beginning Teacher Support and Assessment (BTSA), 380
Behavior. *See also* Self-control
   anticipating — (with-it-ness), 205
   call child on, 233
   case studies and, 225–226, 246–247
      cultural differences, 245–246
      Erikson's psychosocial development theory, 226–235
      observation forms, 247–254
      Maslow's hierarchy of needs, 242–245

   student teacher, roles of, 254—255
      White and self-control, 235–242
   conflict resolution, 205–207
   disorders, 266, 273–274, 508–509
   labeling, 199–200
   logical consequences, 200–205
   managing routine problems, 190–192
   managing serious problems, 214–215
   misbehavior, 202
   mistaken, 194, 202–203, 203f, 204f
   modification, 198, 280, 494–496, 495f
   out-of-control children, 212–213
   professional
      advocacy, 392–393, 393f
      becoming aware, 394–395
      effect of past advocacy, 394
      how to begin advocacy, 393
   same behavior, different strategy, 208
   setting limits, 198–199
   socially influenced mistaken behavior, 202
   staff, 28–29
   survival behavior, 202
Behavioral skills, 240
Behaviorism, 104
Behavior management, 197. *See also* Behavior
Belonging, sense of, 359
Benchmarks
   accountability and, 419
   clarification of term, 400
Biases
   defined, 76
   reacting to, 306
Bibliotherapy, 193
Bilingual program, 149–150
Biting, 456–457
Blank slate, 104
Blind children. *See* Visually impaired children
Bloodborne pathogens, exposure to, 15–16
Bodily-kinesthetic intelligence, 110, 491
Body talk, 336
Books, for toddlers, 468–469
Brain-based learning, 116–117
Brain development, research on, 114–116
Brain injuries, 266
BTSA. *See* Beginning Teacher Support and Assessment

C

California Association for the Education of Young Children (CAEYC), 377
CAEYC. *See* California Association for the Education of Young Children
Call on behavior, 233
Calming-down periods, 211
Candor in managing behavior, 191
CARE
   conflict resolution, 206
   ethnic, racial, family differences, 197
   initiative and, 232, 233

H

I

Unit planning, 108
Universal pre-K, 418, 419–420
University of North Carolina, 378
University supervisor. *See* College/University
    supervisor
Unobtrusive observation, 69
Unwritten rules, 195
Urban schools, quality issues of, 421–432
U.S. Bureau of Labor Statistics, 429, 430
U.S. Department of Education
    ethnicity and gender of educators, 430
    standards of quality, 361
U.S. Department of Justice, 270

Values, 40–50
    acquiring, 42–45
    knowing yourself and your values, 41–42
    personal values and activities, 46–47
    professional ethics, 47–49
    when values clash, 49–50
    your values, 45–46
Verbal communication, 508
    basic types of, 310
Videotaping, observation, 76
Violence, in society and curriculum develop-
    ment, 427
Violent play, 213
Visits and travel, 405–406
Visual learner, 109, 491, 493–494
Visually impaired children, 266, 272–273
Volunteers, 27, 329, 331–332, 343, 347
Vulnerable children, 281
    attributes of teachers working with, 281f
Vygotsky, A., 120

Walking the Walk, 378
Webbing, 172, 173f, 174f
Web sites for standards, 131
Wechsler Intelligence Scale for Children (WISC-
    III), 283
Wechsler Preschool/Primary Intelligence Scale-
    Revised (WPPIS-R), 283
Weekly activity sheet, 25
Week of the Young Child, 393
White, Burton, 235–242, 245, 250, 252
Whittle, Chris, 420
Whole teacher, 89
    personal abilities and characteristics, 89–90
Windows (sensitive periods), 115
WISC-III. *See* Wechsler Intelligence Scale for
    Children
Work ethic activities, 177
Working memory, 107
Workshops, meetings, and skill and study ses-
    sions, professional, 406
Worry, common student teacher problem, 297
WPPIS-R. *See* Wechsler Preschool/Primary
    Intelligence Scale-Revised
Written activity/lesson plans, 151–158
Written communications, 343

"You" messages, 199, 310

ZDP. *See* Zone of proximal development
Zone of proximal development (ZPD), 120